I0818897

The Dog's Gaze

The Dog's Gaze

A Visual History

THOMAS W. LAQUEUR

Penguin Press
New York
2026

PENGUIN PRESS

An imprint of Penguin Random House LLC
1745 Broadway, New York, NY 10019
penguinrandomhouse.com

Illustration and photo credits appear on pages 379–389.

ISBN 9780593652794 (hardcover)
ISBN 9780593652800 (ebook)

First published in the United States of America by Penguin Press, an imprint of Penguin Random House LLC, 2026
Published simultaneously in Great Britain by Allen Lane, an imprint of Penguin Random House UK, 2026

Printed in Latvia
10 9 8 7 6 5 4 3 2 1

Contents

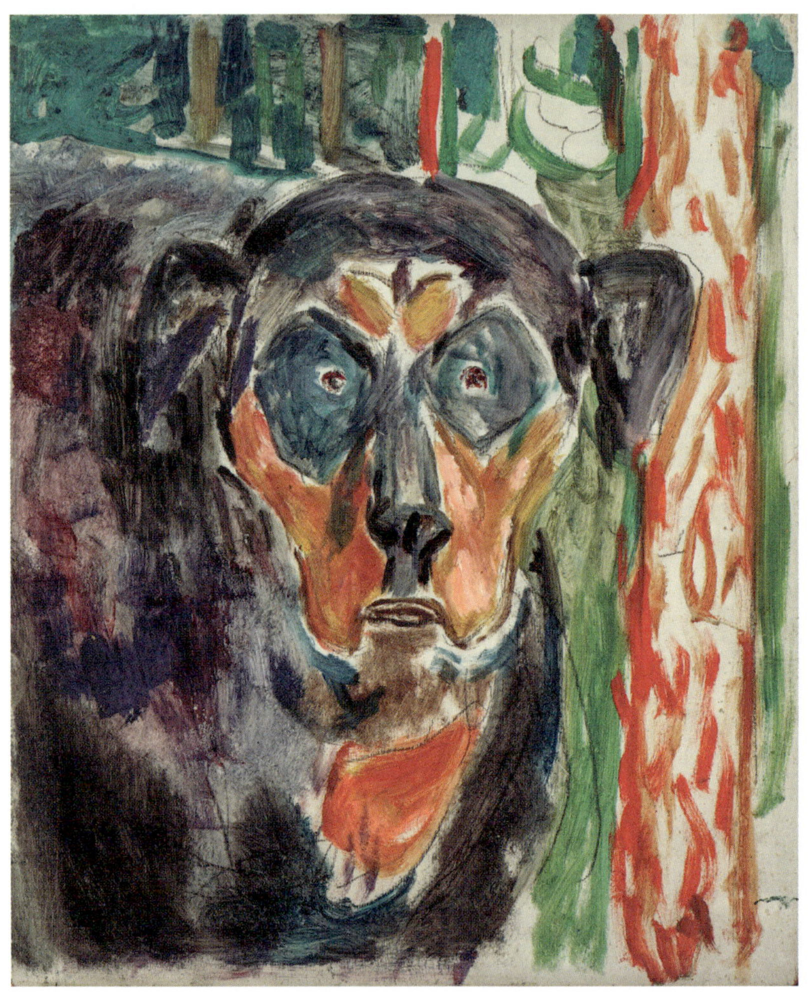

1 The dog's gaze: Edvard Munch's *Hundehode* (Dog's Head) (1942).

. . . my dog used to gaze at me,
paying me the attention I need,
the attention required
to make a vain person like me understand
that, being a dog, he was wasting time,
but, with those eyes so much purer than mine,
he'd keep on gazing at me
with a look that reserved for me alone
all his sweet and shaggy life,
always near me, never troubling me,
and asking nothing.

Pablo Neruda, 'A Dog Has Died'

PREFACE

Dogs and Me

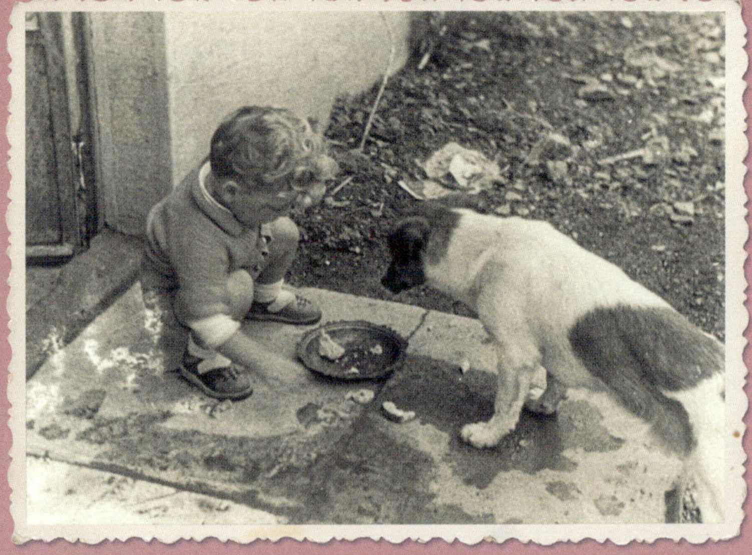

2 'Thomas and Job as the dog feeds'. A photograph taken by my father in Turkey.

I DID NOT COME to this book from a lifelong love of dogs. My first pet, acquired in my late twenties, was a cat named Lydgate, after Tertius Lydgate, the doctor-reformer in George Eliot's *Middlemarch*. In my teens and all through graduate school I was passionate about horses. Dogs entered my life late. Or at least as I remember them because there is a picture of me when I was three or four taken by my father in Kuzguncuk on the Bosporus straits with a dog in whose dinner I seem interested. He labelled it, 'Thomas und Job beim Hundefressen' ('Thomas and Job as the dog feeds') [**2**]. We are both looking intensely at his bowl. My parents were in Turkey as refugees from Nazi Germany.

My family had dogs when I was growing up but my relationship to them was shallow and vicarious. They were my mother's, and I remember her through them. I don't know what dogs meant to her; what childhood memories she had of them. She grew up in a large house with land around it in Holzminden an der Weser, a small town in the northwest of Germany, the daughter of a Jewish grain and animal merchant. I suspect her family had dogs but have no evidence for this.

I know that very soon after we arrived in Bluefield, West Virginia, from Istanbul in 1950 my mother acquired a dog – a boxer. She named her Heidi, the first of a succession of boxers with that name. I have a stuffed boxer, whose leg was broken and splinted at some point, that I retrieved from my mother's house after she died. I don't remember how it originally came into my life or how it was injured, and I don't remember it ever meaning much to me. I keep it now because she kept it.

After the Heidis came a succession of cocker spaniels: Sapphos, a name suggested by my best friend from college – and ever after – a Greek who was visiting over the Christmas break. In the last decades of my

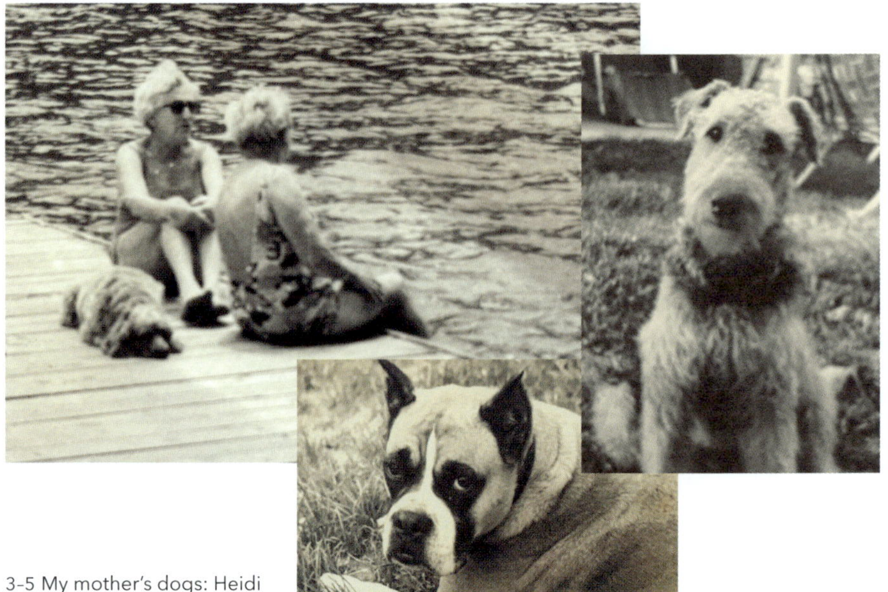

3–5 My mother's dogs: Heidi (*below*), Sappho (*above left*) and Druže (*above right*).

mother's life came Airedales, two of them in succession both named Druže – Serbian for 'comrade'. My mother did not speak Serbian. Tante Elli gave my mother the first of this line and he came with the name; she had escaped the Nazis by going to Yugoslavia and had Airedales after she got to America. Dogs as gifts between rulers, friends, lovers, and family, as if they carried with them a declaration of intimacy, will appear often in this book [**3-5**].

My mother in her eighties made heroic efforts to care for Druže II; she broke her hip carrying a twenty-pound bag of kibble on slippery ice but recovered from that. When he died, she lost interest in living; the dog's death seemed to signal that it was her time to die too.

Before starting to write this book I had never noticed the dog in a photograph of my father, mother, and little brother on the porch of our house that I must have taken when I was eleven or twelve. (In fact, I never noticed the dogs in so many of my early family pictures.) In **6**, Heidi I is coming into our world, that is, entering the frame of the picture as dogs do in a great deal of the art in this book. Maybe my mother had called her, although I don't remember her calling her dogs very often. I do remember her sending them away. 'Go to your place' in heavily

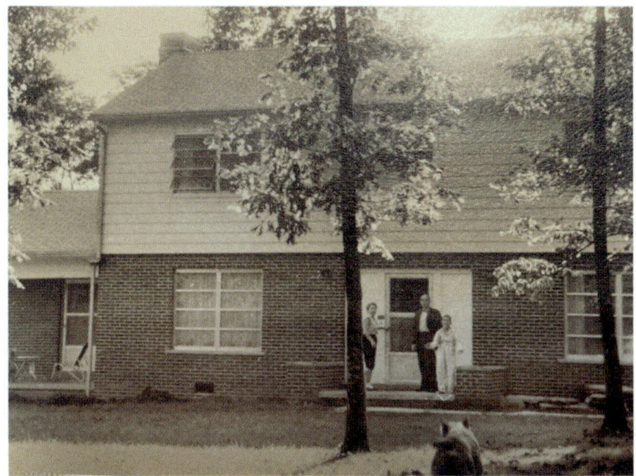

6 Heidi entering the frame of the picture. We will encounter this motif many times.

German-accented English sent generations of Heidis, Sapphos and Družes obediently to their beds.

My father had little interest in my mother's dogs or dogs in general. I did not know his father, my paternal grandfather Walther Laqueur, who died in 1927. But I know he had a dog who was important enough to him to have commissioned a professional photographer to take a formal portrait of the two of them in the early 1920s on the steps of a large brownstone at 106 Hochallee in Hamburg [7]. My grandmother took the photograph with her when she narrowly escaped Germany in December 1939, aged almost seventy. My father learned that she been ordered to report to the Gestapo and managed very late in the day to persuade her to secure a Turkish visa and transit to Istanbul where he and my mother lived. (Her eldest daughter, my Tante Toni, who had emigrated to Holland and was subsequently murdered at Sobibor, had been urging her to come to Amsterdam.) The dual portrait of her husband and his dog sat in a silver frame on my grandmother's desk in West Virginia from 1950 until five years before she died at age 100 in 1973. It is now, in the same silver frame, on my desk.

My grandfather Walther and his dog are poised in mid-action. The dog is coatless; his master fashionably bundled up against the cold – there is snow on the steps – and ready for a walk. I can imagine my grandfather as the narrator in Thomas Mann's 'Herr und Hund' (A Man and His Dog), the longest of his short stories and clearly an autobiographical account of his life with a pointer-mix named Bashan. I do not know the name of Walther's dog. I think the two of them are heading out

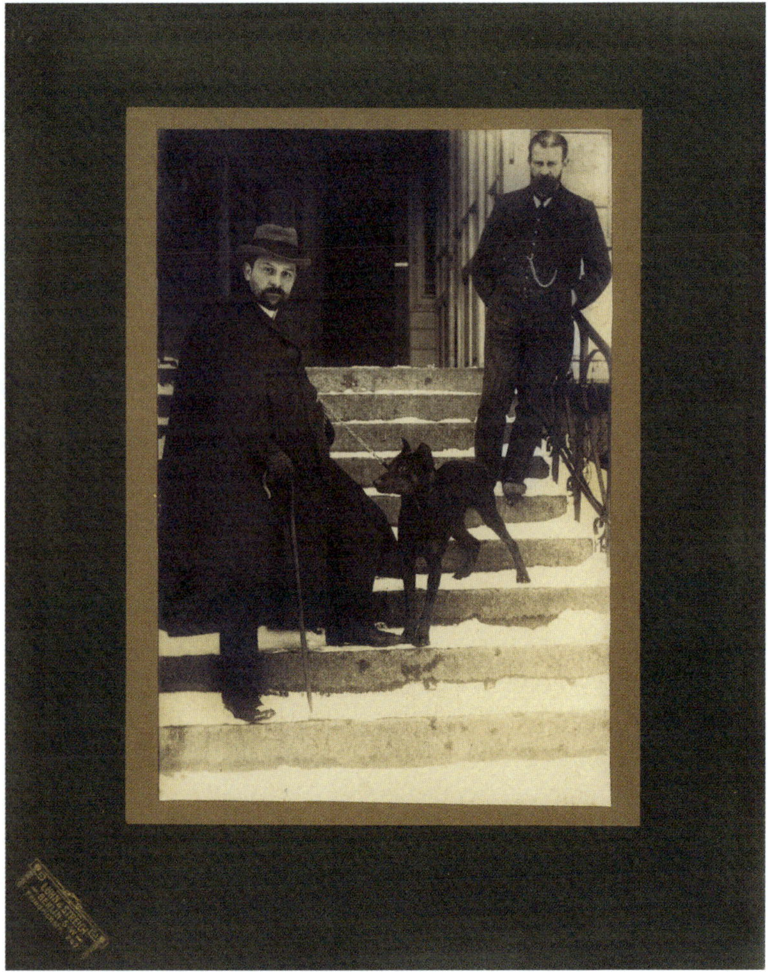

7 A very German image: my grandfather Walther posing with his Doberman in front of 106 Hochallee in Hamburg around 1924, about to go on a walk.

rather than coming back from a walk. The lead is in my grandfather's left hand; if he were turning to go up the stairs, he would have tripped over it or over the dog. The dog's eyes, so clearly visible along the vertical axis of the photograph, are directed to the right, away from the stairs, and toward grandfather's cane in his right hand and the street. My sense is that this dog, unlike Thomas Mann's on many occasions, would not be disappointed when his master headed for city streets.

An image like this invites questions about both the immediate circumstances in which it was made – exactly what is going on between this *Herr* and this *Hund*? – and about its broader social and cultural context. We know that they are posed together and professionally photographed in an artfully arranged tableau: a diagonal line runs from the main character sharply in focus on the lower left to the unknown well-dressed, coatless, man with the fob watch highlighting his waistcoat, who is more of a blur on the upper right. The dog is indispensable to the architecture of the image. We know the photograph was important to the subject's widow, my grandmother.

We know also that it stands in a long tradition of man and dog portraiture that continues into the present, great hound and prince, formal and majestic, in the paintings of Titian, Velázquez, Van Dyck, Goya and, by the eighteenth century of a broader social range of sitters, in a variety of poses, in paintings and later photographs by hundreds of artists. There are far fewer paintings from the earlier period of women with dogs anywhere near the size of those featuring men: those we have are mostly of women with lapdogs who are almost, but not quite, lap cats. They are more attentive to both the subject and the viewer than a curled-up cat would be. Images of the hunter goddess Diana and of aristocratic women represented as Diana for the hunt are exceptions until the late eighteenth century, when portraits of women with sizeable dogs started being painted; by the 1880s the new woman with a large dog in the country, on city streets, and in the home had become almost a cliché.

Like all portraits, that of my grandfather is about the private world of its sitters as well as their social position and setting. It is a good likeness when I compare it to other pictures of him: a representation of this appropriately dressed man in a conventionally gendered pose at a particular time and place in a particular relationship. But what my familial 'Herr und Hund' might mean in a more general sense, and specifically what the dog means or represents, is harder to say.

Iconography – enquiries about what an element in a painting might symbolize or stand for – is often the place where people begin when thinking about why there is a dog in the picture. The claim that it represents faithfulness or fidelity is a starting point and at the most abstract level that is probably true in art and in life. As the first animal to be domesticated and the first animal that could, and indeed wanted to, live intimately with humans, it has become a way for us to imagine that all is well between us and nature and between each of us and the social world we live in. In the face of famine, disease, ecological disasters, death, war, betrayal, and all the ills of civilization, dogs are a sort of intellectual, or in this context, visual comfort food. They have their lapses, but they seem resigned to living with what we have wrought and, despite our many sins and weaknesses, remain faithful to the relationship that evolution wrought tens of thousands of years ago.

But there are many other possibilities for what a dog might represent other than faithfulness: the art historian Simona Cohen, for example, argues that it stands for heresy in one version of a Tintoretto *Last Supper*, and 'wise perception' in another where it seems to identify the traitor. Erwin Panofsky, one of the most influential art historians of the twentieth century, interprets the dog in Albrecht Dürer's *Knight, Death, and the Devil* as standing for 'lesser virtues . . . untiring zeal, learning, and truthful reasoning' (*see* 146). That dogs can be interpreted to mean so many things is evidence for how deeply they are implicated in the ways that artists create a visually coherent world through representing our relationship with them.[1]

In specific instances iconography is helpful in understanding that imagined world. Renaissance scholars and artists, for example, thought that Egyptian hieroglyphics represented an almost Adamic language. So, when a fifth-century CE text discovered in the early fifteenth century claimed that when the Egyptians wanted to represent a scholar:

> . . . they draw a dog . . . since he who wishes to become an accomplished scribe must study many things and must bark continually and be fierce and show favours to none, just like dogs.

They therefore had new grounds for the meaning of a dog in an image. Dürer was among the first to take up the idea. But there are lots of images of dogs in studies before the discovery and printing of this text, and also lots of images after, which owe nothing to the ancient associations.[2]

Decoding iconographical associations is seldom a sufficient interpretive strategy. The two dogs playing near a man and woman kneeling on a wing of an altarpiece are without doubt symbols of faithfulness [8]. But why, we might ask, would a couple kneeling at an altarpiece that they paid for need dogs to attest to their faith? What do the dogs add? The answer starts with thinking about what living creatures of another

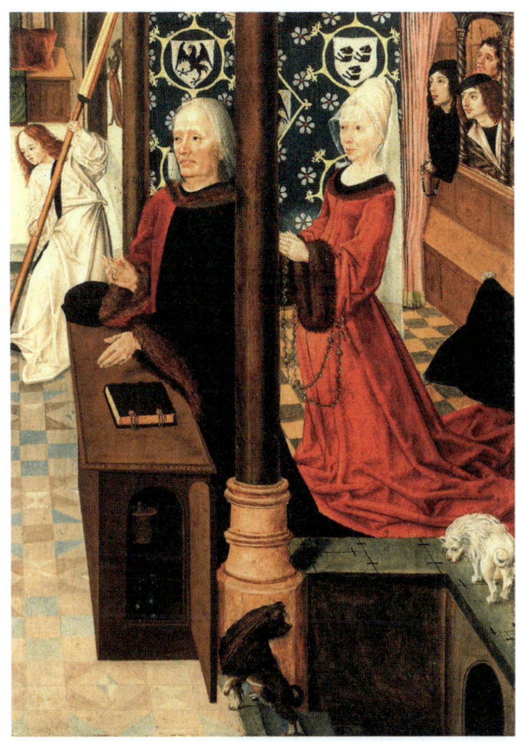

8 Detail from the *Crucifixion Altarpiece* (1492–5) by the anonymous Master of the Aachen Altarpiece. The two dogs are depicted at play amidst an otherwise still scene.

species sharing a space with us, looking at one another, at us, or at something else, add to an image. The humans are still; the dogs are in action, playing. They draw us into the picture.

More generally, looking at pictures iconographically can become something of a fool's errand. The history of how art historians have struggled to interpret Jan van Eyck's so-called *Arnolfini Portrait* – one of the world's most famous paintings with one of the most famous dogs in Western art – offers a warning [9]. It got the label largely because in 1934 Panofsky argued that the signature in the background – '*Johannes de Eyck fuit hic*' ['Jan van Eyck was here'] – meant that the artist was a witness to what he thought was the wedding of Giovanni de Arrigo Arnolfini and Jeanne de Cename.[3] (It had before been thought that the couple was van Eyck himself and his wife.) The painting thus became, in Panofsky's account, a visual, symbolic marriage contract. Subsequently, a great deal of learning and ingenuity went into identifying each element in the picture in support of this interpretation. The burning candle, for example, symbolized the matrimonial oath and the little

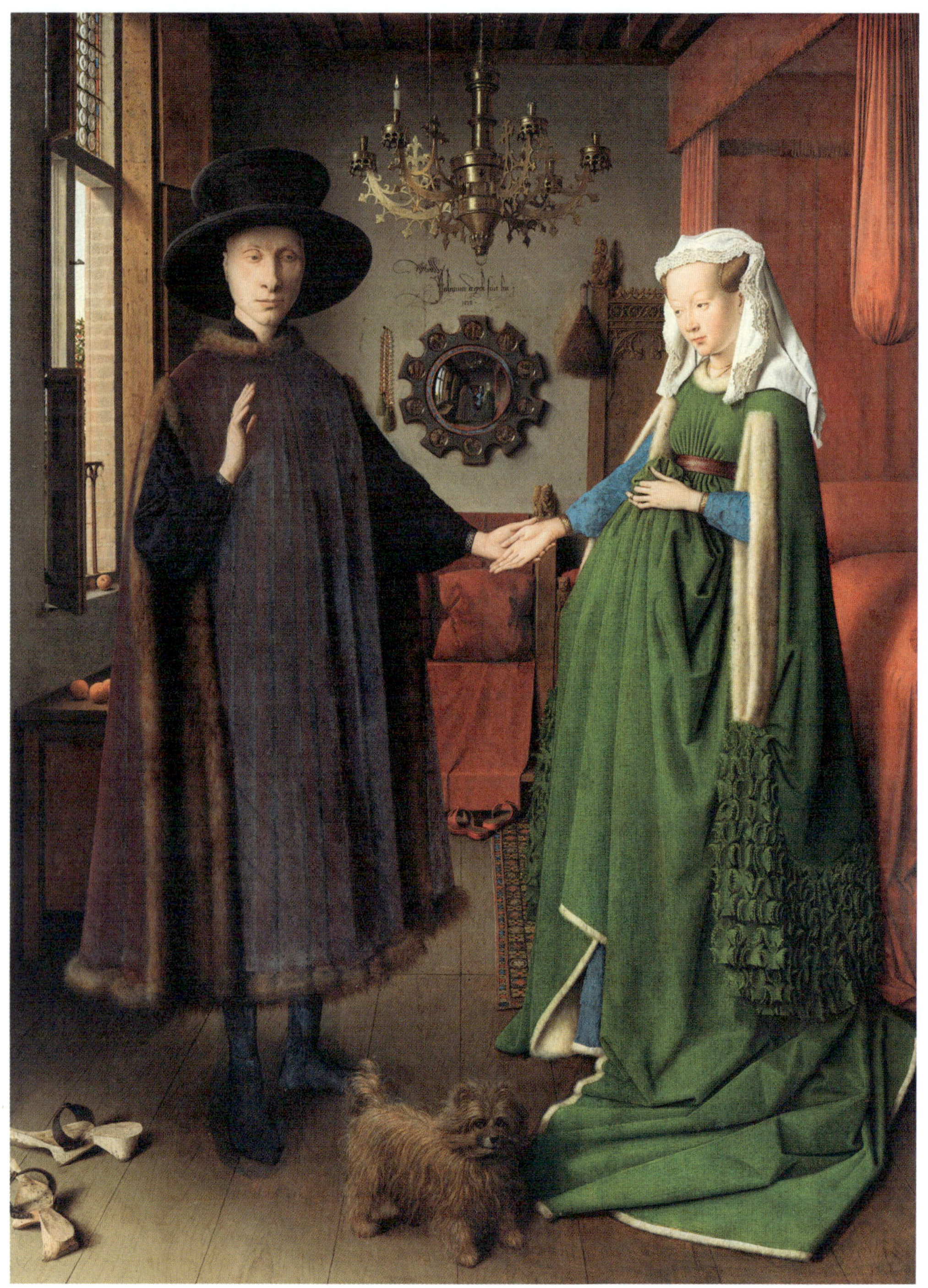

9 Jan van Eyck's *Arnolfini Portrait* (1434) portrays one of the most famous dogs in art history.

terrier symbolized fidelity. Or, others argued, the dog represented lust in the interest of procreation.

In the decades since 1934 art historians have been revising Panofsky's analysis. They discovered, for example, that the man and the woman he identified as the subjects of the painting didn't marry until thirteen years after their purported wedding picture was painted. And the supposed bride of the Arnolfini who is in the picture might be Arnolfini's first wife who died a year before it was painted. It could therefore be a memorial painting, and the dog an allusion to similar dogs on tomb sculptures: still a symbol of faithfulness but now not in marriage but in death: a memento mori.

A century of scholarship has not exhausted an iconographical interpretation of what is now called 'the Arnolfini Portrait' in part because the identities of the subjects remain unresolved but more generally because a symbol-by-symbol excavation has proven to be futile. 'There is no substantive evidence from the fifteenth century that any of these things were understood symbolically,' concludes the author of a book-length study of the painting. Its meaning is not restricted to being a one-stop emblem book. It is rather an invitation to ever more looking and thinking with the aim of understanding how the parts of the painting make it a beautiful and coherent whole, how they come to give us pleasure.[4]

Start with the dog, perhaps a progenitor of today's Brussels griffon. In the Arnolfini picture it emerges from a welter of luxurious, richly painted cloth, standing on a bare floor at the absolute front and centre of the image closest to where we and the artist are perceived to be standing. It is the only creature in the painting that is looking out through the fourth wall, inviting us to look in, holding a space between inside and outside the frame, reminding us, the viewers, that this is a picture. (The eyes of the two humans are lowered and directed at one another.) Unlike many of the dogs we will see, it is not looking at the perspective vanishing point – at the mirror and its infinite regress of images – but at some position outside of the painting from which the painter and the viewer see it. Like the writing on the wall above the mirror, the animal opens the seemingly closed world of the couple. This dog is also a creature of the home, a representative of dogs making any room a more human space and connecting the people in it to each other: an avatar of the family dog.

It is the couple's dog. The question we might ask in looking at this famous painting is less what the dog means than what it does and how it does it, that is, how it makes us understand the world created by the artist.

Like 'the Arnolfini Portrait', an interpretation of the photograph of my grandfather is not a cypher to which there is a key. We need to look at it both from a formal perspective – how the elements of the image are placed and how its living subjects, especially the dog, seem to see and move, as well as how the artist wants us to see – and historically from the perspective of the deep history of dogs as a species and the more bounded history of an image's context. I want to approach my grandfather's portrait with what the art historian Michael Baxandall called a 'period eye', that is, a historically and culturally grounded way of seeing, attuned to representational conventions like perspective and joined with particular interpretative skills and knowledge drawn from general experience.[5] I take this to mean both the ways in which our brains and eyes today, as well as those of the artist's time, allow us to see, give meaning to, and be moved by an image: how the facts of the image emerge from and become facts of culture. The photograph of my grandfather and his dog demands such an eye in both temporalities. Perhaps all interpretation demands that, but understanding what the dog does in so great a swathe of Western art certainly does. In most of the images in this chapter, dogs humanize the human as well as helping organize the space in which we see them.

We could begin seeing with a 'period eye' by focusing on the social status of the dog in joint portraits as if they were there to bear witness to the status of the human sitter: a luxurious and costly accessory in the way that gold jewellery or a gorgeous dress might be. The Borzoi breed works this way in late nineteenth-century and early twentieth-century advertisements and in photographs of their famous owners [**10**]. Kathleen Florence May Pelham-Clinton, sixth Duchess of Newcastle, was said to have paid almost £15,000 in today's money for two Borzois that she bought from Tsar Nicholas II's Kennel and often had herself photographed with them. (She also founded the women's branch of the Kennel Club, which did not admit women to full membership until 1979.)

The same sort of case – dog as expensive accessory – might be made for the dog in Bronzino's 1533 *Portrait of a Lady in Red* [**11**]. But that does not begin to exhaust its meaning. The human sitter's status, from her

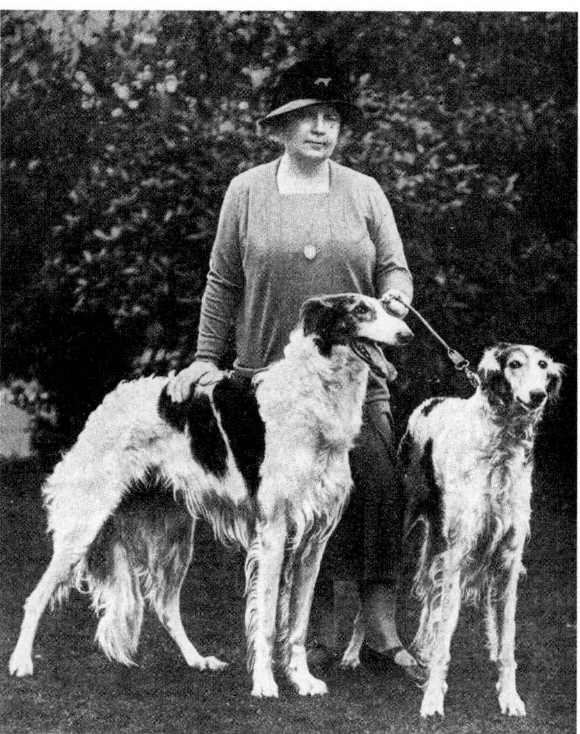

10 The sixth Duchess of Newcastle with her Borzois (1935).

Overleaf:
11 (*left*) Bronzino's *Portrait of a Lady in Red* (c. 1533);
12 (*right*) Titian's *Federico II Gonzaga, Duke of Mantua* (1525).

distant regal pose to her overwhelmingly sumptuous dress, gold jewellery, and the chair she is sitting on, is unmissable. The well-coiffed and undoubtedly expensive spaniel is certainly appropriate to her status; a mutt would be jarring. But it cost pennies compared to her other accessories. Bronzino's other portraits of aristocratic women, *Woman in Green* or *Eleanora of Toledo*, for example, unmistakably convey their sitter's status without their holding a dog. In the *Portrait of a Lady in Red* the dog is supernumerary as a sign of social standing.

The question becomes why the lady – the woman in red – wanted it in her portrait and why Bronzino represents the two of them as he does. To start with, perhaps because she cares about the dog, perhaps even loves it. She might have thought that it humanizes her and reflects her sensibilities. Although she might not have had it in mind, it also transforms the image. She looks calmly, almost haughtily, out and past us; the dog too looks at us, a little to the side, with a certain 'keep your distance' look. It mediates between his mistress and the world and emphasizes the distance between her and us although it also makes her

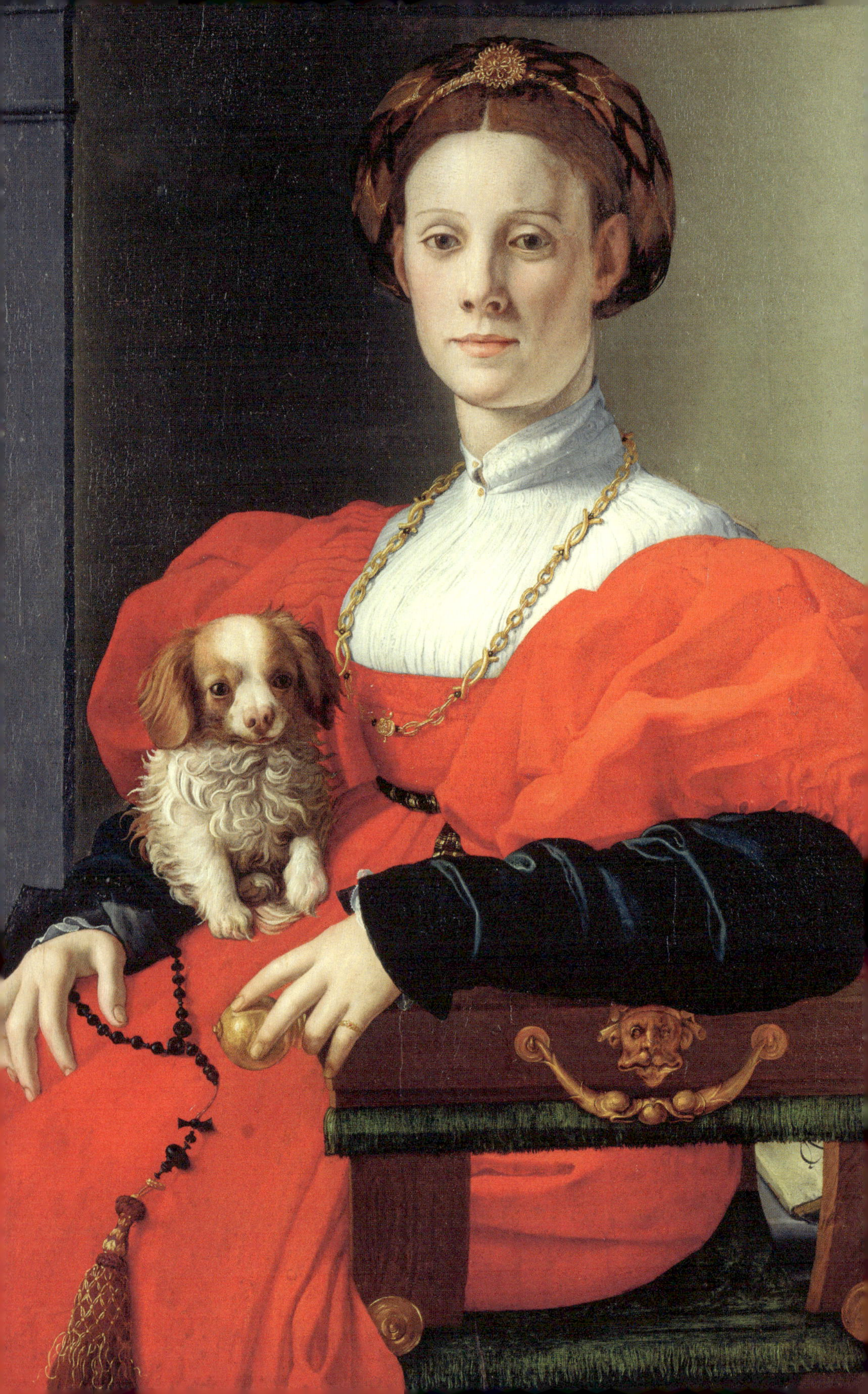

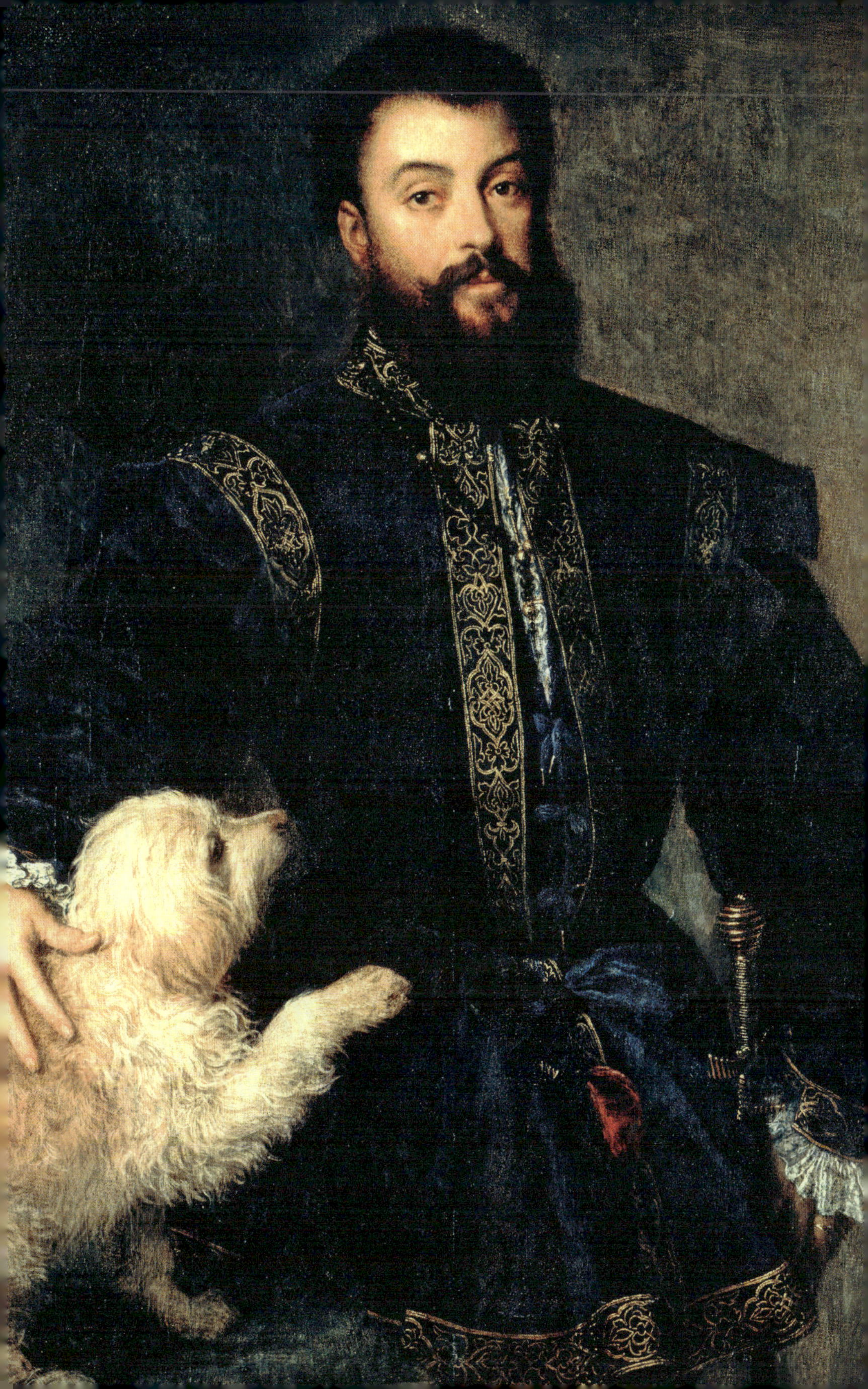

look a little less haughty. The dog is also painted with great attention, its nose glistening, its fur given as much attention as her white bodice, its eyes fixed with a glint of impasto. We see the *Lady in Red* with eyes accustomed to four centuries of such portraits. It is part of a long and multi-layered history of cross-species relationships and their role in the making of art.

In the case of Titian's portrait of *Federico II Gonzaga, Duke of Mantua*, we can say more about why the sitter might have wanted to be painted with a particular dog [**12**]. He certainly does not need it as a status symbol. The light on his face shines on the brocaded doublet of precious cloth; he wears a gold and deep blue coloured lapis lazuli paternoster around his neck; there are two jewelled rings on his right hand. But it would have been no surprise to contemporaries as to why he might have wanted to be painted with a friendly dog. Federico was known to be a great dog lover who came from a family of dog lovers. (His great-grandfather Ludovico III appears in the Mantegna fresco with his favourite, Rubino; *see* 19.) But why this gender-inappropriate dog, a 'Maltese', a category of small, spoiled lapdogs associated with women since classical antiquity?

Art historians have pointed out that Titian painted this portrait at a time when Federico was negotiating a second marriage and therefore wanted to have himself represented as domesticated and even uxorious.[6] His so-called private life up to then had been less than exemplary: he managed to have his marriage to his first wife annulled and, while still married, carried on a very public affair with a woman who was subsequently poisoned. In the Titian portrait, his left hand is resting on his sword, an allusion to his military career, now seemingly a thing of the past. But his right hand softly touches the beautifully painted fine-haired little dog who looks up at him with devoted affection. Anyone who is this nice to a small dog who loves him can't be the monster he might appear to be. There is in fact no documentation that this is the reason for why Federico chose this pose with this dog. Yet, the beauty of this work and the seriousness with which the relationship between dog and master is represented should invite us to think about how the facts of an image, formal and figurative, become facts about culture and human relations. The dog's devotion suggests his master is worthy of our love.

If I were trying to develop a chronologically specific 'period eye' for the picture of my grandfather and his dog I would begin by saying it is a photograph of modern life. My grandfather is pictured as a man of the city taking the air on Hamburg's streets with a dog that has been demanding a walk. It is less likely that the dog would have had an urban walk a century earlier – although possible – and unlikely that if it had, it would be on-lead.

It is also a very German image. I wonder whether my grandfather read Thomas Mann's *Herr und Hund: Ein Idyll* (*A Man and His Dog: An Idyll*), which first appeared in 1919 and, in a new edition, with pictures in 1925. Mann's most popular book, it elevated walking one's dog as an event worthy of the attention of the giant of twentieth-century German literature. I suspect that my grandfather, and more likely the photographer, had seen reproductions of Impressionist paintings of men on walks with their dogs.

The Doberman breed was barely twenty-five years old when these photographs were taken: a blend of older German lines – the Rottweiler, the Pincher, and the short-haired Pointer – first bred by the eponymous Karl Friedrich Louis Doberman from the late 1870s but not recognized as an official breed by the German Kennel Club until 1897. It caught on quickly and was by far the most common German military service dog during the Great War. Perhaps my grandfather's choice of breed and his decision to pose for this picture reflect his pride at being a decorated soldier who served as a doctor in a typhus hospital on the Eastern Front. It is certainly a breed he would have known. It is inconceivable that he would own, or represent himself with, for example, a poodle – too French. He was suspicious of France because of what he understood to be the distinction between Gallic *civilisation* – superficial – and German *Kultur* – deep – and because he came to hate it, according to my father, because of its occupation of the Ruhr from 1923 to 1925. A Dachshund would have been too funny and close to the ground I imagine.

He might have chosen a mastiff, *der deutsche Dogge* (the German Mastiff), more like a Great Dane than Renaissance mastiffs like Philip IV's Spanish mastiff, who will enter our story later. The German mastiff was Otto von Bismarck's favourite breed and had a large public following. There are many photographs of the Iron Chancellor with a succession of them: perhaps most

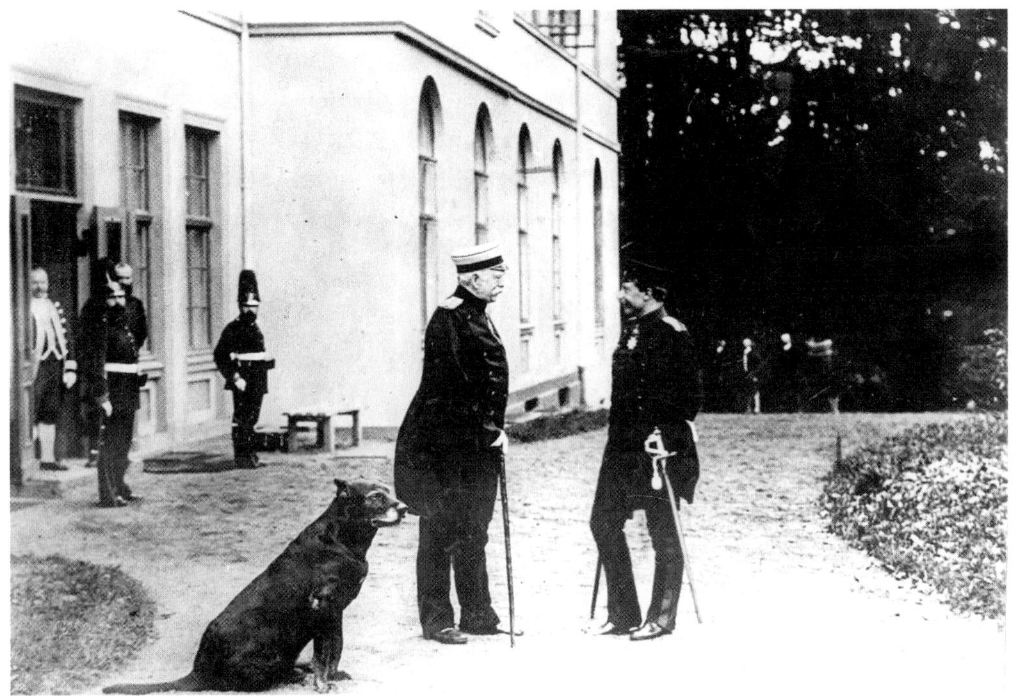

13 Otto von Bismarck meeting the Kaiser in 1888, accompanied by his *deutsche Dogge*.

famous is the one who came with him to see the Kaiser when Bismarck was forced to resign as Chancellor in 1890 [13], but there are many others – on walks, or in his study, or sitting by a park bench. One of his dogs, in a well-publicized encounter, bit the Russian ambassador at the Congress of Berlin in 1878. But a *deutsche Dogge* might have been too Prussian and perhaps too aristocratic for my grandfather. Or maybe too big for a city dog even in a large apartment. In any case, he chose a Doberman.

Finally, this is not only a distinctly German but a German-Jewish picture, a picture of a certain sort of German Jew for whom taking walks with a large and very German dog sent a message to himself and his world. My grandfather was an active member of the *Centralverein deutscher Staatsbürger jüdischen Glaubens* (The Association of German Citizens of Jewish Belief), founded in 1893 to advocate for cultural assimilation and full political participation as citizens of the Reich and to combat anti-Semitism that threatened, but in its view, did not belie that hope. He, unlike his brother Ernst, refused Christian baptism. Being Jewish was 'something he never denied, indeed something that he was proud of,' said Ernst in his eulogy in 1927. Moreover, 'He never allowed the fact that some, even a good many, so-called Germans believed it to be their duty to take a stand against, yes to revile and disdain those of Jewish belief, to make him love Germany any the less.'[7]

To me the dog humanizes and softens my grandfather. There is something about how he is poised with his cane that reminds me, despite the very different setting, of man in the great German Romantic painting *Wanderer above the Sea of Fog* (1818) by Caspar David Friedrich. My grandfather appears in the family archive as an austere and forbiddingly serious figure. Loving Germany for him meant living for the ideal of 'Bildung', that hard-to-translate German word denoting a kind of cultivation and education that lay at the heart of humanism, the belief in the possibility of human brotherhood. Germany, or more specifically the tradition of Bach, Beethoven, Goethe and Schiller, as his brother said at his funeral, gave meaning to his life. My grandfather kept diaries of books he read and of books he read with my father and of concerts he and my grandmother attended. As a young couple they heard Brahms conduct. He died before 1933. That he was also a man who walked his dog makes him more ordinary in my eyes, more human.

He was a German Jew in another sense too, or to put it negatively, not the stereotype of the Ostjude, the eastern European Jew. There is a Yiddish saying, 'If you see a Jew with a dog, either the Jew isn't a Jew, or the dog isn't a dog.' The founders of the State of Israel understood that these alternatives would not do. The Haganah – the Jewish defence forces – asked Rudolphina Menzel, an Austrian cynologist and expert on police dogs and who, during the Weimar Republic, had been a frequent consultant to the Reichswehr's military dog-training programme in Berlin, to breed a guard dog for use in the new Zion. (She had made Aliyah to Mandate Palestine in 1938 after the *Anschluss*.) Menzel began on this project with the herding dogs of the Bedouin, supposedly descendants of the ancient breed that had guarded the flocks and houses of Abraham and his descendants. The so-called Canaan dog became the future Israeli national dog. How this happened is a story, like that of the Irish wolfhound, bound up with nationalist myth-making, although far better documented as an exercise in breeding and self-conscious nation-building. The Canaan dog was Menzel's contribution to Zionism. 'Here in Eretz [The Land of Israel],' she writes:

> . . . our people found their way back to the earth and it is time we found our way back to the dog . . . He who has not overcome the fear of the dog from the ghetto is not a renewed Jew . . .

My grandfather had no interest in Zion; but he was a 'renewed Jew', an undeniably German Jew with an unmistakably German dog.[8]

I was in my early forties when I first had an affective relationship with a dog – a boxer who came into our household as a puppy. Perhaps I chose the breed in memory of my mother. My daughter named her Curious because she – the dog – seemed endlessly interested in looking at, under, and over the people, objects, and spaces of her new surroundings. (Maybe the children's book about Curious George the monkey prompted her.) I would not, and could not, have written this book had I not lived with Curious and a succession of dogs and enjoyed the intimacy of a dog's gaze over the next four decades: that is, had dogs not become a part of the story of my life, keeping company, and had I not begun to watch them watching.

Curious overlapped for a year with a new dog, one of a litter of puppies born to a 'yard dog' who escaped her chains under a porch in deep rural south-western Virginia. We were feeding the lactating mother for weeks. While we were away on an errand one day her purported owners called the animal control authorities who took the lot of them to a nearby kill shelter. We could rescue only one – the white-nosed one – whom Curious is looking at with especial interest [**14**]. We named him Newbern after the nearest village. We had both dogs until Curious died suddenly the next summer of a heart attack. ('You know,' writes Dimitri Shostakovich, 'I have a theory that dogs lead such short lives because they take everything so much to heart.')[9]

Newbern died eight years later, fearless, gored by a deer that had got into our yard in Berkeley, California. A generic hunting dog, had he been in the pack of the sort that one sees in seventeenth-century hunting scenes he might have fared better. I am not sure that I would have noticed the great abundance of dogs in art had I not developed an affection for Curious, and then Newbern. My history with dogs as companions in life and work allowed me to recognize that something beyond the personal, something more general, about dogs in art was worth exploring.

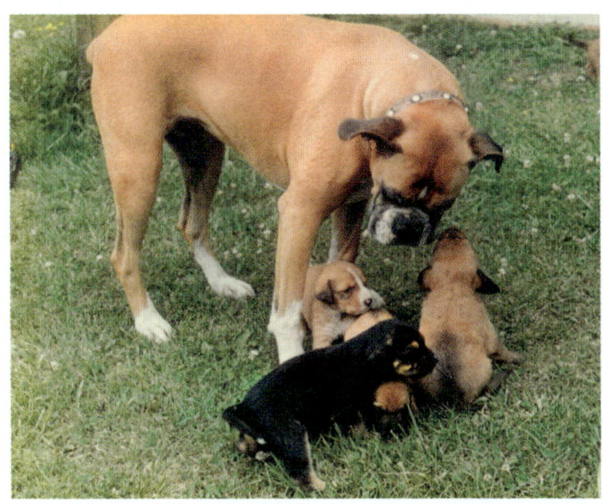

14 Curious the boxer, the first dog I loved.

None of us, however, can escape how our own histories affect what and how we see, which raises for me the question whether my intimacy with dogs and relative lack of intimacy with other animals over the last thirty years – the likely candidates would be cats and horses – distort my ability to see them as they are in art. As I learned from my cat Lydgate, cats seem to us the most inscrutable of the animals we live with on an intimate basis – 'when I am playing with my cat how do I know my cat is not playing with me?' Montaigne famously asked. Dogs are the opposite. A 'Cheshire Dog' in Wonderland would be absurd. Horses gain our intimacy through the body, through the sensation of touch rather than sight. This book is about dogs – and not cats, horses, or cattle – because it is about an aesthetics of sociability rather than alterity and it is about sociability rather than utility as represented in art. Dogs pay attention to us; they see us; they join us in a great number of things we do. The book is about an animal that, because it sees with us, is uniquely gifted at breaching the bounds of species in art and perhaps also in life.

CHAPTER 1

The Dog's Gaze

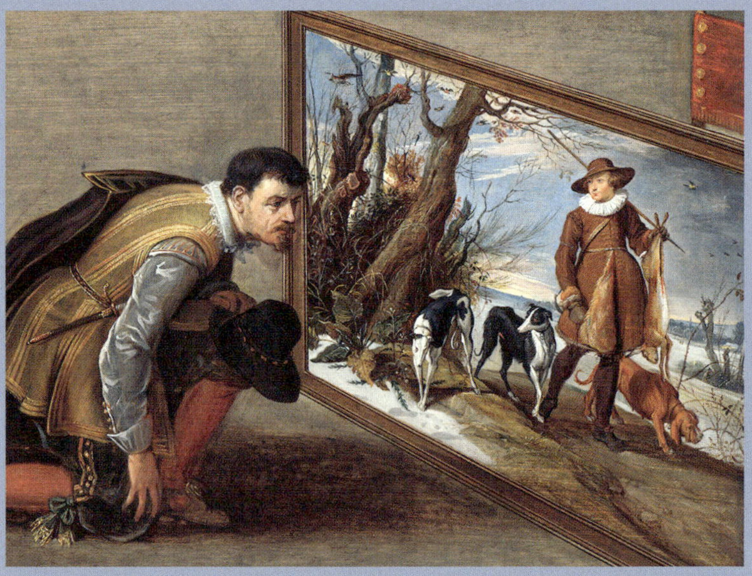

Detail from 15. A painting (*Hunter in a Winter Landscape with Dogs*, 16) within a painting (*Gallery of Cornelius van der Gheest*).

THERE IS ONLY ONE dog in the space of Cornelius van der Gheest's *Wunderkammer* (wonder cabinet) that Willem van Haecht painted in 1628 for his patron to commemorate the visit of Archduke Albert, Governor General of the Hapsburg Netherlands, and his wife Isabella Clara Eugenia, to his magnificent art collection [**15**]. That dog is looking up at her, a well-known dog lover, sitting on the lower left of the picture. But if we were to count the dogs in the image we would find at least three more in one of the paintings within the paintings. On the lower right side on the plane nearest the viewer is a man in red garters kneeling to look intently at a picture that rests on the floor. Two sighthounds – ancestors of the modern greyhound – are looking back at him from the canvas: a cascade of looking within looking within looking. If we were to stand in front of Jan Wildens' 1624 *Hunter in a Winter Landscape with Dogs* ourselves, in Dresden's Gemäldegalerie, the two principal dogs would be looking at us at eye level from the wall [**16**]. We would also be seeing the third dog, a scenthound, with its nose to the ground but its head and eyes looking, almost at a right angle to everyone else, past the hunter and his two canine companions and past the painting's border into the world beyond.[1]

It is light that first demands our attention and directs our gaze to the outdoors in Pieter de Hooch's *Man Handing a Woman a Letter in the Entrance Hall of a House* (1670) [**17**]. But almost at the same time we see the dog, a studio dog who makes regular appearances in de Hooch's work. It looks as if it were heading out into the light. Our eye might at first be inclined to follow it to the open archway; its white nose is in a direct line to the girl who is standing between shadow and light and pointing the way out. It could be looking at her as if nothing were happening. But it isn't. It is looking over its shoulder at the shadowed space where the

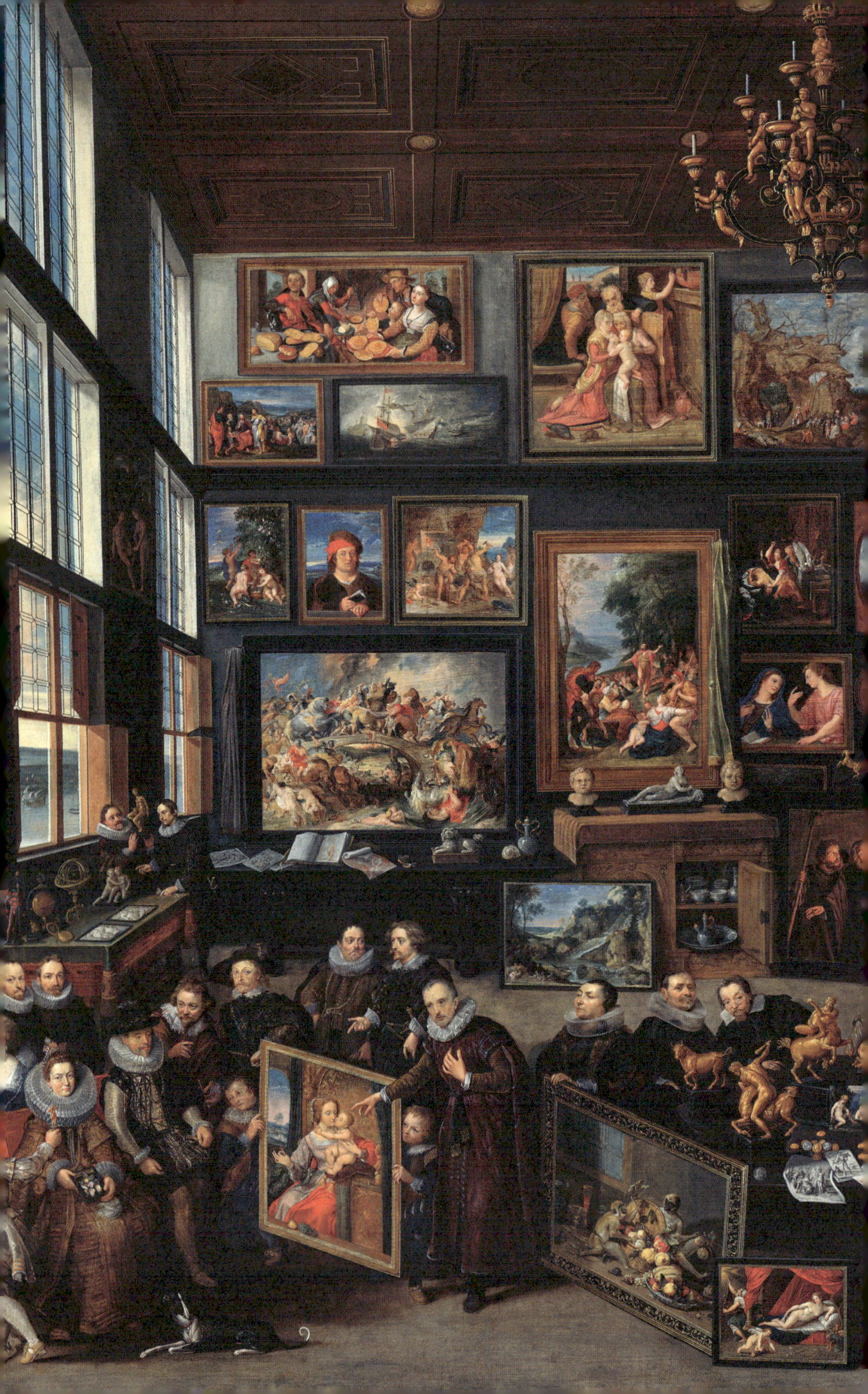

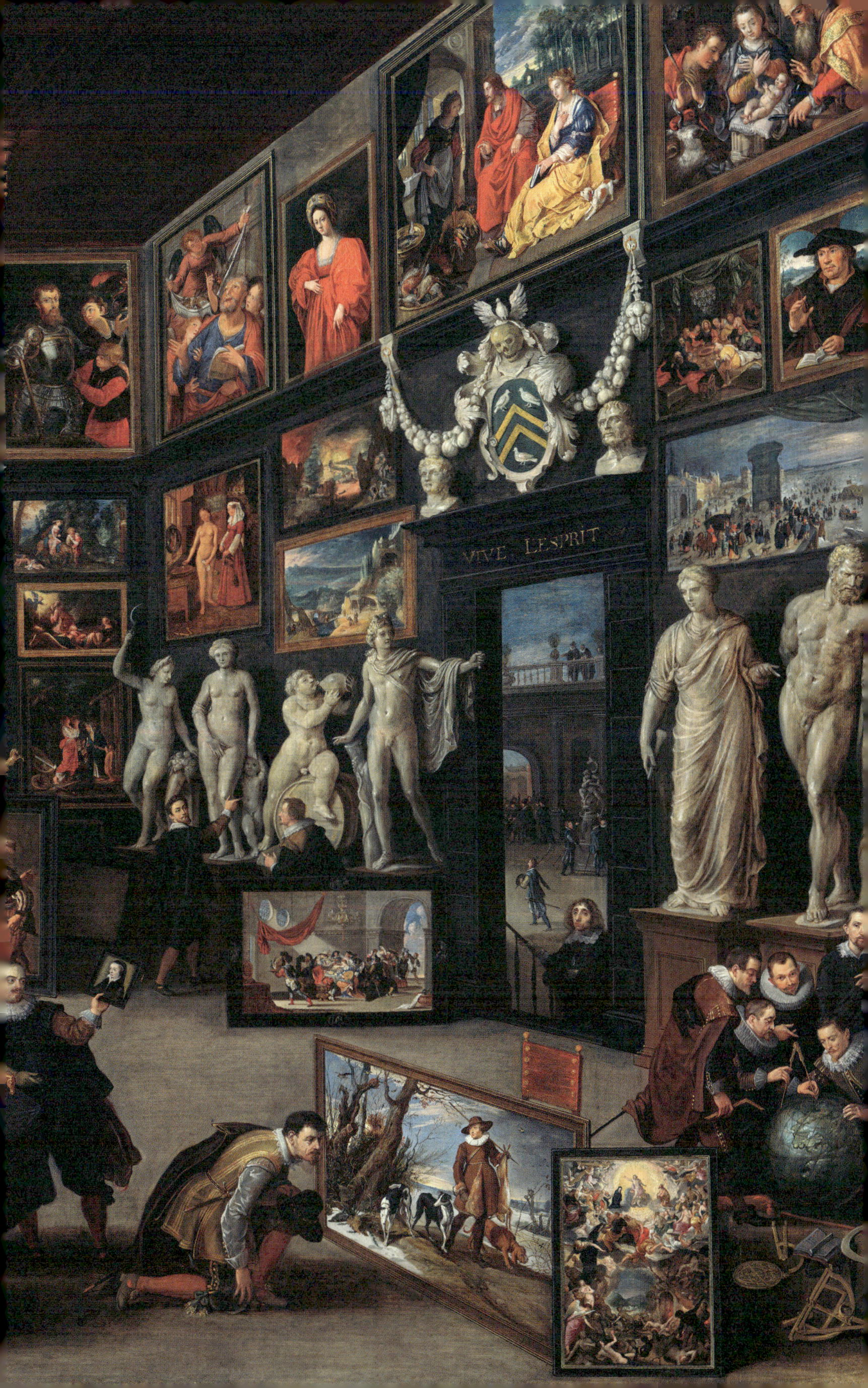
VIVE LESPRIT

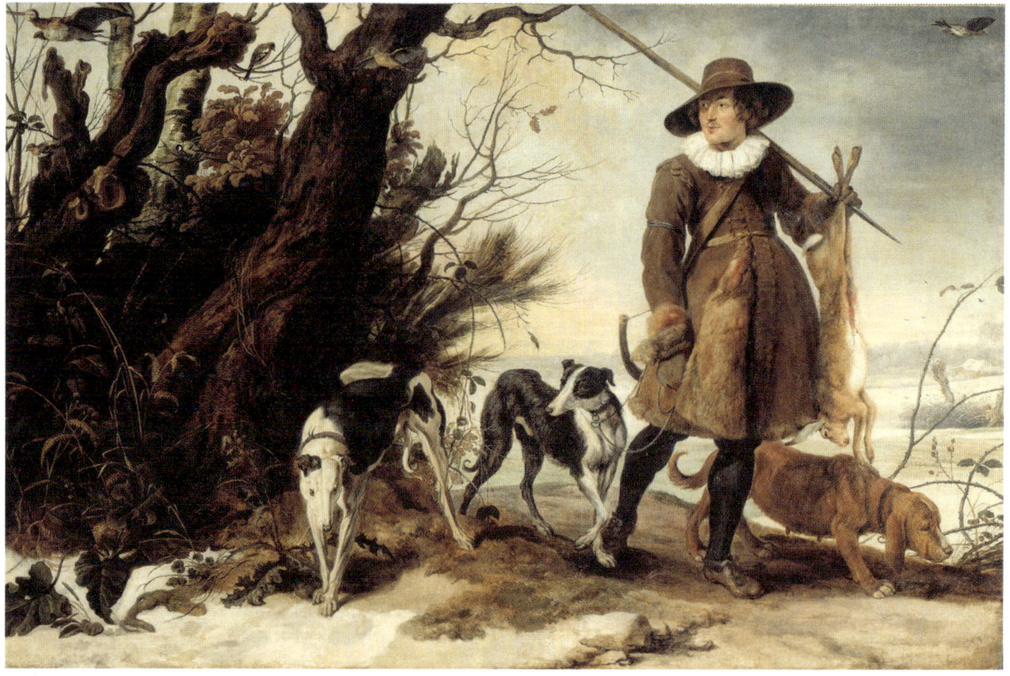

16 The original *Hunter in a Winter Landscape with Dogs* (1624) by Jans Wildens. Previous page: 15 Willem van Haecht's *Gallery of Cornelius van der Gheest* (1628).

painter is standing and from which we too are looking through the room to the threshold of the brightly lit courtyard. Poised in the middle, the dog stops the action. It looks at us as if to demand 'are you paying attention to what is happening?' Meanwhile, as the girl and the dog are starting to respond to the entrance of the messenger, the little dog on the woman's lap has already noticed him, looking directly at him even before its mistress does.

Perhaps these dogs are to be expected. The great Flemish painter Pieter Bruegel the Elder laid the foundation of genre art in the sixteenth century – there are scores of dogs in his work and many more in the art of those who came after him.[2] But great numbers of dogs in art are not limited to one tradition or period. The former curator of the Whitney Biennial, Lawrence Rinder, asked the Belgian abstract painter Raoul de Keyser why there was what seemed like an almost accidental and incongruous dog in one of his paintings. 'Every painting must have a black dog,' he replied; the one in question was inspired by the dog in Picasso's

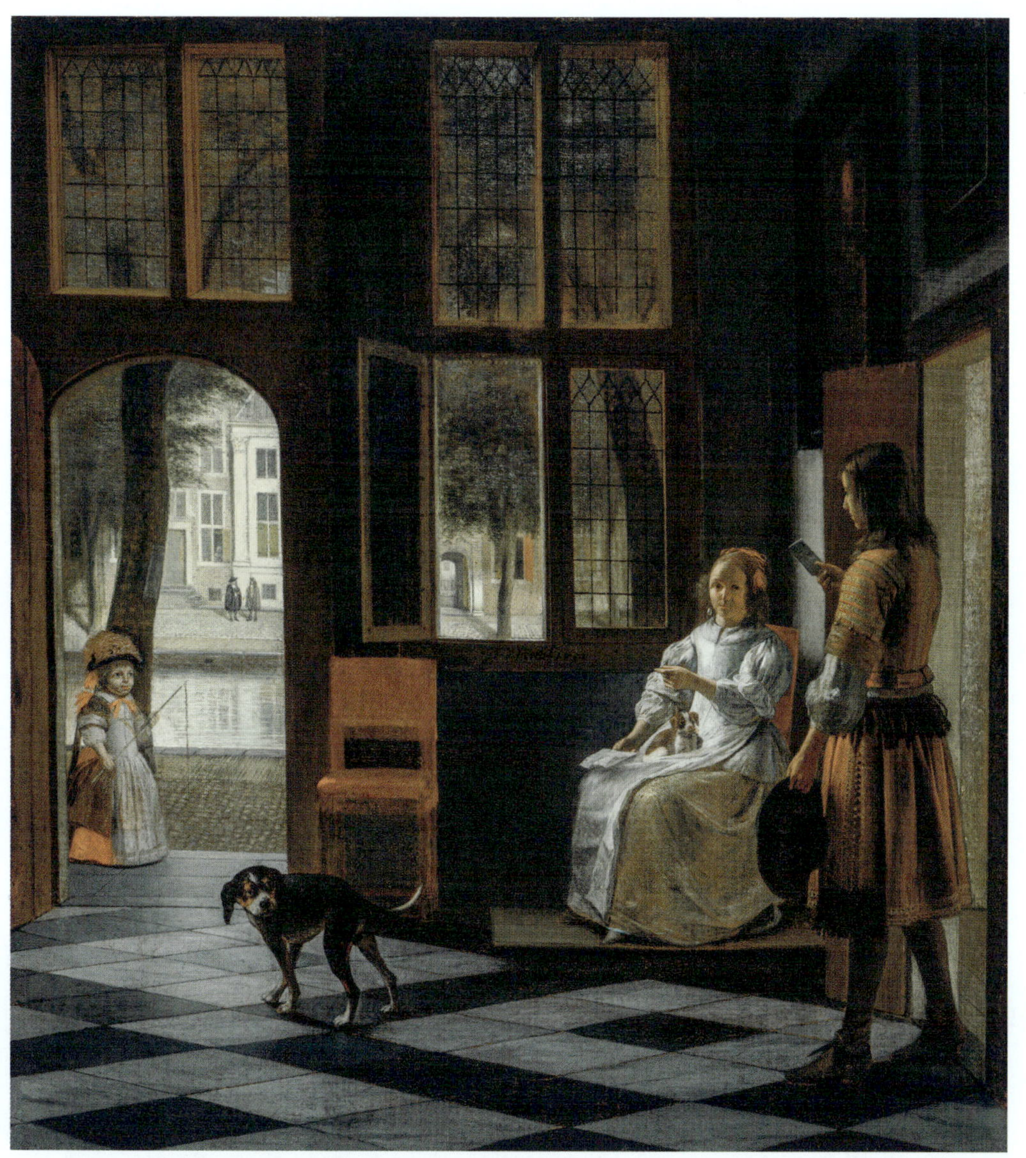

17 *Man Handing a Letter to a Woman in the Entrance Hall of a House* (1670) by Pieter de Hooch.

Three Musicians.[3] That one we might track back to Velázquez and from there down a historical escalator.

In galleries large and small there are tens of thousands of dogs in Western art, from Greek antiquity to the present, doing some of the things that the dogs in 2–5 are doing and much else besides. They are dogs in religious, historical, and mythological art, and in the art of everyday life. And soon after the rise of human portraiture and cross-species portraits there appeared portraits of dogs on their own, dogs who look out at us, as the humans who sit for portraits do, with eyes that promise both familiarity and distance. We are looking at them; they are looking back at us. These are individualized dogs, albeit in the early days anonymous. It may be too much to assume that the two hounds Jacopo Bassano painted around 1575 belonged to him, but he painted them in many of his other masterpieces with the same anatomical and emotional precision as in the dual portrait [**18**]; he must have known them well. There is a sort of intimacy about them born of the eyes of the one dog looking with bowed head out at us and those of the other looking into the distance. Paintings of dogs whose names we know with their masters are there already in the Renaissance.

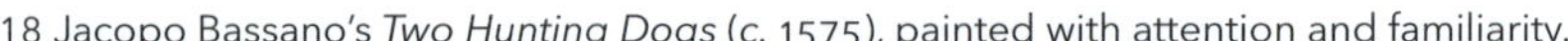

18 Jacopo Bassano's *Two Hunting Dogs* (*c.* 1575), painted with attention and familiarity.

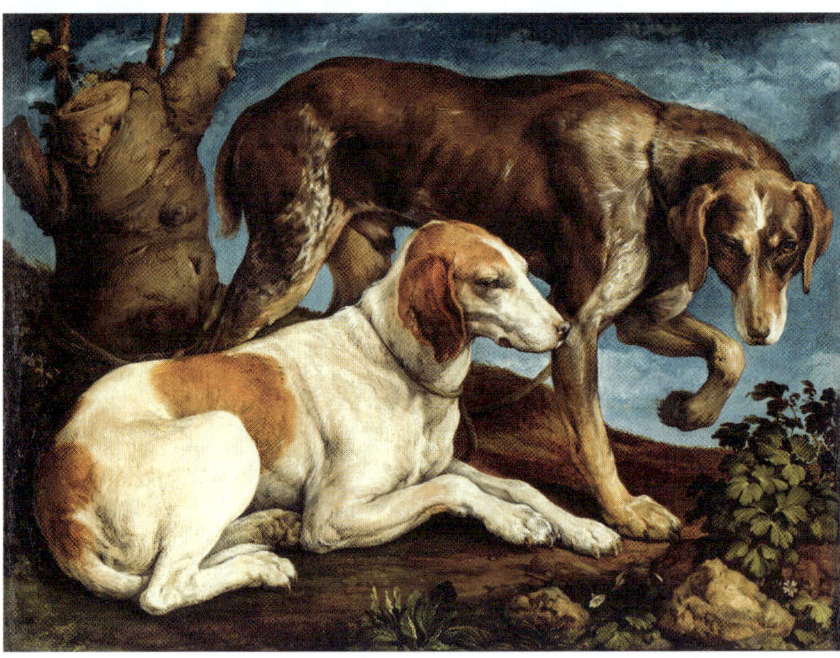

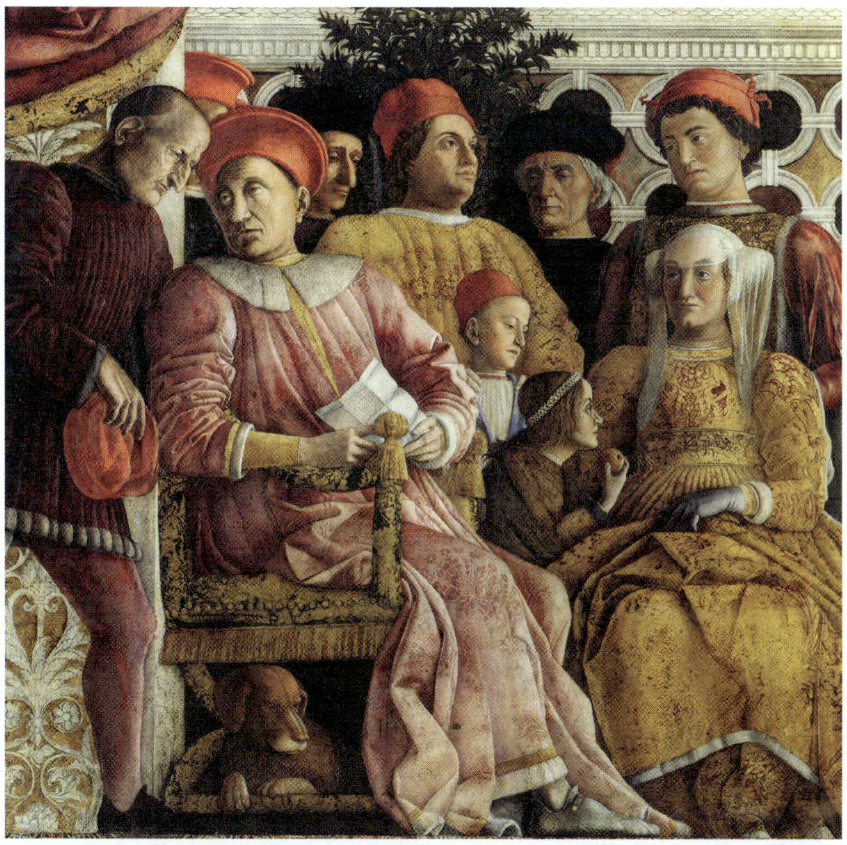

19 Detail from Andrea Mantegna's *Family and Court of Ludovico III Gonzaga* (1465–74).

Rubino, the favourite of Marchese Ludovico III Gonzaga of Mantua, is one of the first. There he lies under the family patriarch's chair in one of Mantegna's frescoes *c.* 1465 in the Camera degli Sposi of the Ducal Palace [**19**]. Rubino's final illness caused a great deal of anxiety; he was buried in a specially designed tomb with an appropriate epitaph.

Portraits of dogs whose names we know become commonplace in the eighteenth century. William Hogarth's pug Trump, a celebrity in his own right, is among the most famous of a long line (for more on him see chapter 5). The nineteenth-century dogs of Rosa Bonheur, one of the greatest animal painters in the Western tradition, are no longer the anonymous descendants of Bassano's hounds. Barbaro's tired and demanding eyes – he has just been bathed after the hunt – speak of the gaze that captured Neruda's imagination in the lines at the beginning of this book [**20**].

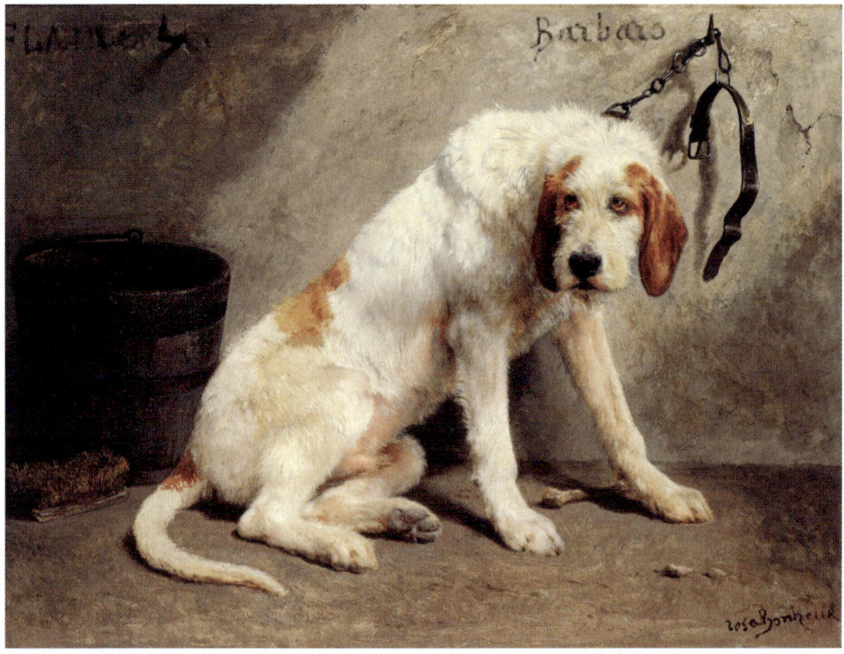

20 A named hunting dog stars in Rosa Bonheur's *Barbaro After the Hunt* (*c.* 1858).

There is also a vast corpus of generic dog images that bear testimony to the attraction that the dog and the dog's gaze holds for artists as a creature so near humans, intimate and yet distant, a creature that looks back in a very real if mysterious way. The painting of an unknown plebeian dog lying on a ledge draws us in first by the streaks of bright white, then the impasto on the nose and the red paint for the tongue, and finally the glint in its eyes. They are perhaps the dog's eyes that the American novelist Edith Wharton wrote about. She said she was afraid of all animals except dogs. 'Is it because,' she asks, 'of the *us*ness in their eyes, with the underlying *not-us*ness which belies it, and is so tragic a reminder of the lost age when we human beings branched off and left them?'[4] [**21**]. The gaze of the scruffy but magnificent plebeian wolfhound dominates a canvas by Paulus Potter [**22**]; we are of course looking at him, but it is impossible not to think of his poignant lonely gaze out at the flat Dutch landscape which it sees much as we see it, and as artists of the Dutch Golden Age saw it, extending, map-like, to the horizon.[5]

Finally, there is art of a very high order such as Gerrit Berchheyde's *The Town Hall on Dam Square, Amsterdam* of 1672, in which a dog might

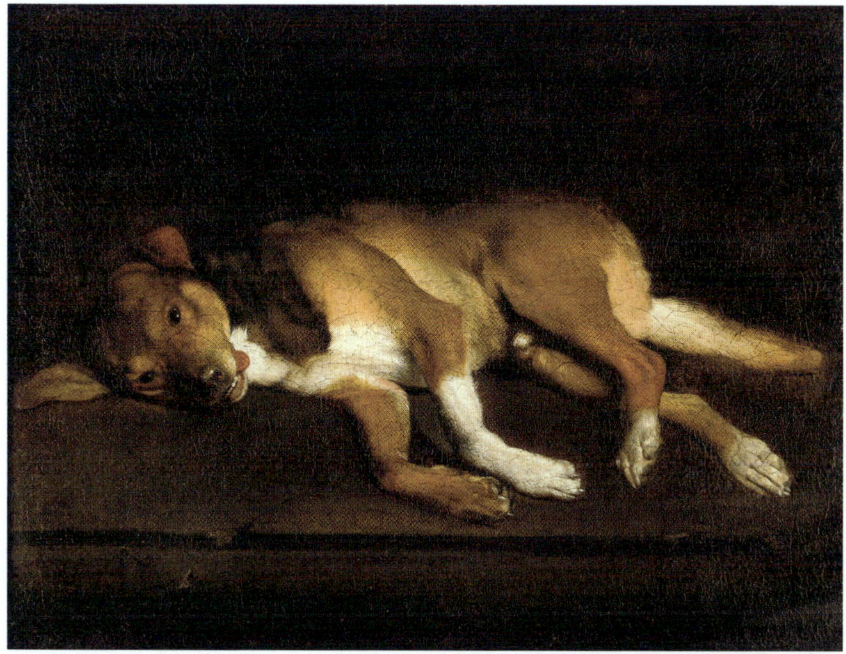

21 *A Dog Lying on a Ledge* (Anon., late seventeenth century) with an impasto glint in its eyes.

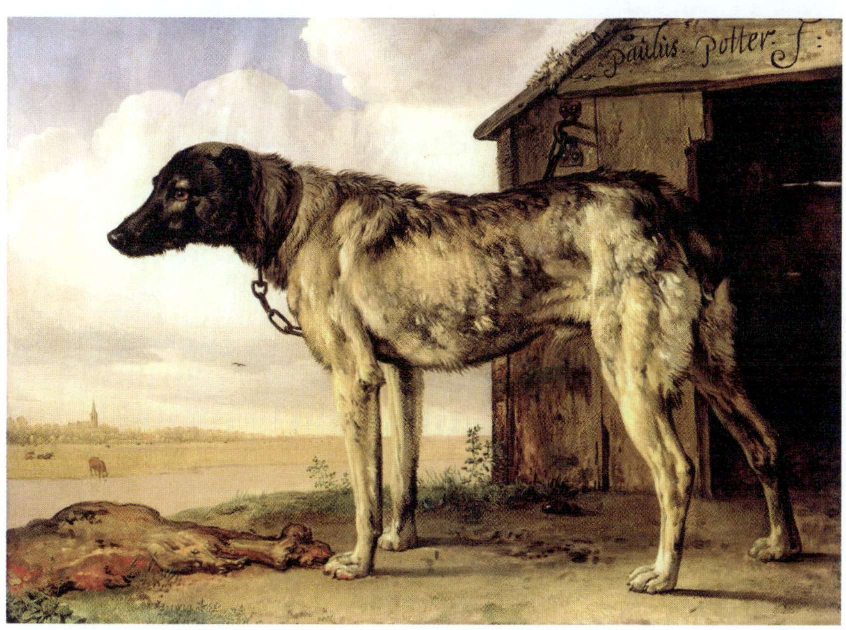

22 *Wolf Hound* (*c.* 1653–54) by Paulus Potter. The dog's gaze suggests the Golden Age Dutch landscape beyond the frame.

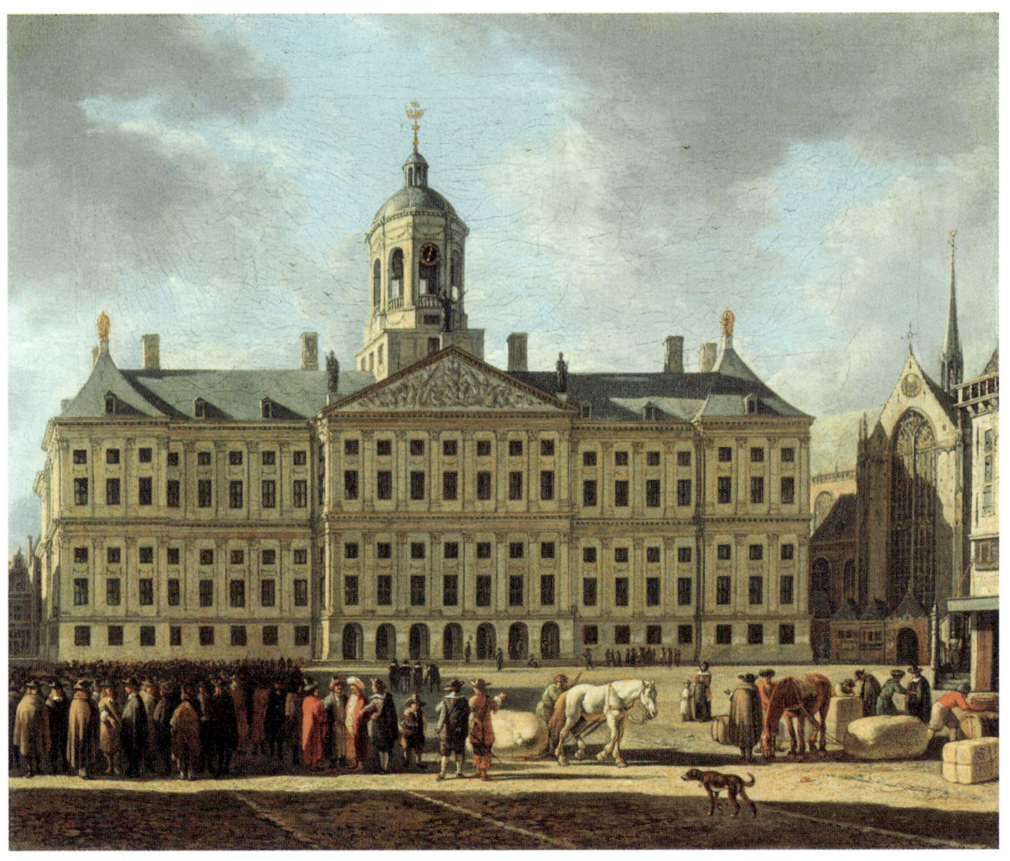

23 A dog leads us into Gerrit Berchheyde's *The Town Hall on Dam Square, Amsterdam* (1672).

seem like only a bit player but one who plays an outside role [**23**]. It is crossing a line between darkness and light; half its body is brightly lit and half in shadow. With its head cocked attentively and its tail raised it stands in for us coming into the world of the image. These sorts of dogs are everywhere; they are not needed for the narrative but are employed by artists to create their visual worlds.

What are all those dogs – far more than any other animal – doing in thousands of years of Western art? Why are they there in such numbers and in so many different kinds of images? This book is my answer to that question.

I am writing about dogs in the Western tradition, but they are there well beyond the boundaries of the so-called 'West' and in contexts where the term is not applicable. There are lots of dogs in Neolithic and even Palaeolithic art. They are there in the art of the ancient Middle East and of Shang China. Dogs figure prominently in other modern traditions as well: in Intuit art, for example. 'The West' is also not a culturally hermetic geographic category: plenty of Italian and northern Renaissance images make their way into Persian and Moghul art, while contact with the West in the second half of the nineteenth century made dogs more prominent in Japanese art than they had been in previous centuries.

There are also cycles in the history of the dog in art. The colourful sculptures of playful laughing dogs by prominent twentieth-century Japanese artists owe a great deal to sixth- and seventh-century Haniwa dogs – earthenware funerary effigies – that in turn look very much like pre-Columbian dog effigies that accompanied the dead.[6] All sorts of formal and historical considerations underlie these continuities and discontinuities. But there is only so much one can take in, so the weight of this book is on the art of Europe and later North America from classical antiquity to the present with only relatively brief looks back and further afield.

In the Chauvet cave on the Pont d'Arc along a river gorge in the Ardèche region of France, Palaeolithic artists around 35,000 years ago began painting a visually spectacular world of animals. Why we do not know. John Berger gives us a speculative, general sort of answer: 'With their parallel lives,' animals 'offer man a companionship which is different from any offered by human exchange. Different because it is a companionship offered to the loneliness of man as a species.' Dogs are a special intimate case of this sort of companionship. They play a part, more than any other animal, in the stories we tell about ourselves and our world.[7]

Maybe humans walked hundreds of metres into the darkness of the cave to paint animals so as not to be lonely. Maybe they came to understand, as Proust said somewhere in *Time Regained*, that 'through art alone are we able to emerge from ourselves, to know what another person sees of a universe which is not the same as our own'. The art of the dog perhaps represents to us over the millennia the seeing and being seen in the closest cross-species relationship we have. A new era in the cultural evolution of humans, a revolution in naturalistic representation of our relationship to the world of animals of which we were – and were not – a part comes into being in the art of the walls of the Chauvet cave. Extraordinary amounts of time, energy, and skill were lavished on this project at the dawn of art.

There are no images of dogs on the walls. But there are traces of canid pawprints next to a human's footprints made as they stood together c. 25,000 BCE and looked at the art from c. 10,000 years earlier. Palaeo-archaeologists and anthropologists can reconstruct this moment from footprints and pawprints on the limestone floor and smudges on the ceiling of the cave: the first evidence we have of a dog-like creature doing something with a human: looking together at the image of a horse drawn with one or two fingers in a soft rock face in what is now called the Gallery of Crosshatching. The human was not alone but with an animal to keep it company.[8]

The human left a seventy-metre-long broken track of footprints near the left arm of a Y-shaped chamber deep in the cave; next to some of them are the footprints of a canid. The tracks of this single human visitor fit into one another; no other human tracks have been found here, although similar ones can be seen through binoculars nearby in an area that is now inaccessible. The canid footprints are more numerous and go from near the entrance and into the right arm of the chamber. Radiocarbon dating of the soot left on the ceiling by a torch allows archaeologists to date the visit to c. 25,000 BCE.

If one accepts, as the team studying this cave does, that the anatomical structure of the feet of Cro-Magnons are roughly those of modern Europeans, the prints were left by a young person, someone about 1.3 metres (4.25 feet) tall. Their length-to-width ratio suggests that they were left by a boy. And as for the canid who appears to have been with him, it would seem awfully early to assume that it was a dog. It could have been a tame proto-grey wolf or a proto-dog. It *could* even have been a dog. 'The digital pads of the second and third digits are clearly positioned between the laterals, which is the rule for dogs including the largest specimens,' the experts conclude.

Whatever creature in the canid evolutionary lineage left the pawprints might, of course, have been in the chamber on its own, before or after the human. But their paths in the areas where there are human footprints are congruent. The palaeontologist Philippe Fosse, who oversees research at the Grotte Chauvet, tells me: 'we can identify only canid footprints close to the ornamented panels and not randomly', that is, only where there is art to be seen. Would a dog alone, much less a wolf, have been so discriminating in the deep dark of a cave?

We might, therefore, well imagine a boy and a doggish creature together looking at the image of a horse very near the beginning of our recorded relationship with animals and with representational art. We cannot know how the human understood his relationship to the dog although all the evidence points to a far more intimate relationship to the animal world than would become the norm in later times. We also cannot know whether they looked at each other as they stood there in the cave, but it is likely that they did. No animal lives more easily in the visual field of humans than the dog; none is so uncannily attuned to our gestures; none is better at consistently reading our wishes and emotions. The proto-dog must have been well on the way to all these social skills of dogdom. Its descendants are interested in us, in the spaces that we inhabit, and in doing with us what we do there: as a practical matter hunting, guarding, herding, and, less instrumentally, hanging around, keeping company, and pretty much everything else.

Dogs are, by many thousands of years, the first domesticated animal, quite likely the prototype – the proof of concept – for Palaeolithic humans that domestication is possible. They are the first animals that could comfortably share our living spaces. They participate in a far greater variety of human interactions than any other domesticated animal, not wholly attributable to their gaze but also to their other attributes – their sense of smell, their evolutionary grounded sociability – which allow them to master specific skills that allow them to relate to us and vice versa. All this is mobilized in a narrative artistic tradition predicated on the belief that dogs see us and our spaces in a mutually intelligible way. And in our desire to feel 'less lonely as a species'. It is therefore not surprising that there should be so many of them in the visual arts engaged, as they are, with seeing, being seen, and interpreting what is seen.

They see us in a way we think we understand at the same time as we recognize that they are another kind of being. We take there to be meaning in the dog's gaze. It invites figuration both in the visual arts and in literature as a 'fact of culture' even as we know that it is also a fact of nature, or at the most, a fact of an animal culture to which we can have very limited access. 'One was disquieted,' writes Proust about the eyes of a devoted servant, 'as one is by the frank, intelligent eyes of a dog, to which, nevertheless, one knows that all our human concepts must be alien'. She, like dogs, knew nothing 'save the rare truths to which the heart is capable of directly attaining'. Theirs are 'eyes deprived of enlightenment and yet more naturally, more essentially akin to the chosen spirits than most educated people'.[9] Artists understood that the eyes of a dog in a painting are meaningful in ways that demand and will sustain interpretation well beyond the facts of mere looking.

If we ask why, we need to go back tens of thousands of years – maybe 50,000–70,000 years – to when the now extinct ancestors of the grey wolf, which looks into the eyes of its fellow wolves as they hunt, began slowly to evolve into *Canis familiaris*, which looks into ours. And we into theirs. In other words, the dog's gaze – and the fact that we find meaning in it – is part of the joint cognitive evolution and social history of our two species. Art, and especially the visual arts, are the media that translate this cognitive co-evolution into culture. The way in which the dog is represented as being engaged with what it sees and does in a painting is both determined by, and constitutive of, the social world represented in the image.

Through its gaze and, more generally, through its gestures of attention to what humans do and to where we do it, the regard of the dog is foundational to sociability – and most centrally the shared act of seeing – in the visual arts. It is an animal version of how regarding others works for us in life; the dog invites us to see our human world from a place outside it. It stands in for both the painter and the viewer – we recognize our gaze in theirs.

Adam Smith argued that the moral bonds between individual self-interested humans were possible because we act in a way that others, seeing us, would approve of what we do. As a species, he thought we wish 'to be observed, to be attended to, to be taken notice of with sympathy, complacency, and approbation'.[10] Perhaps dogs act as they do toward humans because they feel the same way as us. We cannot know whether dogs empathize and judge, although we can be sure that their gift for seeing is essential to their ability to live with us. The dog's gaze as represented in Western visual art enacts this Smithian moral recognition, the need to be seen, to be regarded, to have someone bear witness to our lives. They are doing what we so deeply want from them and from living creatures more generally.

Dogs are the friend of last resort of the forsaken, the creature who seems to care when no one else does, when through poverty, or old age, or other misfortune, we have lost the regard of others. It is an old theme that we see evidence of every day on the streets of our cities and in the image-making that it provokes: the bereft and homeless in photographs with their dogs; the lonely and elderly during Covid. We see it in the imagination of painters: dogs with the impoverished blind, with beggars, with Irish peasants as they bury their dead or bewail another failed crop.

If to be less alone is to be the object of the attention of someone who we think understands and accepts us, the dog is the creature above all others that saves us as individuals and as a species from loneliness. The unrelieved and sometimes intrusive thereness of dogs that people who prefer cats find so annoying – dogs will not leave us alone even if we would like them to – is built into their DNA. Cats are in general creatures of the moment which is why they are so popular in the thirty-second videos of the internet. Dogs are long-form creatures. Cats live on what seems to be their own terms; dogs – that is those who live intimately with us and not in packs around villages – live in the rhythms of human time and in tune with what we are doing. Even in the village dogs live in the rhythms of their human communities.

What any animal thinks or feels when it engages with us is a mystery. (The same might of course be said about our encounters with fellow humans.) I want to pause for a moment and ask why this book is not about how other domesticated animals constitute sociability through art or about the cat's or the horse's gaze. 'Am I making too much of the dogs?' I ask myself. Is my subject the result of selection bias? My answer is less in the form of self-reflection than a response to a less personal question: 'Why are cats and horses not like dogs for the purposes of world making in art?'

If I were writing about the first 40,000 (+/– 5,000) years of visual representation the question would be irrelevant. Language was our first entry into symbolic representation. No one knows when that happened. Maybe 250,000 years ago. But we can speak about a second great leap into symbolic thought: the moment we started to make representational art, to say things which we could not yet – or perhaps ever – say in writing. Animals, and to a lesser extent animal/human hybrids – therianthropes (the Greek '*thērion*', 'beast', + '*anthrōpos*, 'human') – were our first subjects: tiny animal-headed humans chasing pigs and dwarf bovids in a 44,000-year-old Sulawesi cave stand at ground zero of pictorial narrative. Present at the birth of visual storytelling is the animal in a world in which the borders between animal and human were porous. The people who made this art, one might speculate, understood themselves for a very long time as the near kin of their prey: themselves, part beast. Theirs was an animistic world.[11]

There are 900 paintings of animals dating from c. 35,000–33,000 years ago that stretch over 200 metres within the Chauvet cave. Most are relatively small and unprepossessing, but the herds of horses and of Palaeolithic lions with almost, but not quite, human faces, are spectacular, individually and as compositions made over time. We know that men and women who were highly skilled at representational art entered the darkness with torches and the tools of their trade to paint animals. Jean Clottes, one of the greatest palaeoanthropologists of his generation, thought that with this art *homo spiritualis* was born.[12]

There are no paintings of dogs; and no cats either, at least none that were smaller than a prehistoric lion, standing 1.2 metres high at the shoulder and more than two metres long without the tail. Of all the creatures that Palaeolithic artists painted, only the horse might give me pause about my claims for the special status of the dog in art. But the horses of Chauvet and Lascaux, and the other great cave galleries of Palaeolithic art, are not the horses we have known in the last 6,000 years or so. They were prey: hunted and eaten, not ridden or yoked to chariots or ploughs. The earliest evidence for a horse that was not food is from circa 3500 BCE, at least 10,000 years after the dog was domesticated and almost as long after the dog first appeared in art.[13]

But by around 8000 BCE the answer to the question of why this is a book about dogs and not, or not also, about cats or horses in art, becomes clearer. To begin with, there is the matter of demography. There were lots of cats in Pharaonic Egyptian art; and lots of dogs – or in any case jackals – too. But with this exception there are relatively few cats to be seen in art. Almost fifty years ago Kenneth Clark, former director of the National Gallery in London and a popular broadcaster in his day, asked in his survey of animals and humans in art from prehistory to the present why this was the case; why could he find so few cats? The art historian James Rubin's equal-opportunity *Impressionist Cats and Dogs* has almost twice as many pictures of dogs as cats (seventy-five to forty-one) and twice as many index entries, not even counting those under sub-headings, e.g., 'loyalty, dogs as symbols'. The National Portrait Gallery's book about animals in its portraits managed to find only twelve in which the sitters were with cats compared to fifty with dogs. A book on Dürer's animals – paintings, woodcuts, and etchings – has only one domestic cat in a menagerie of hundreds ranging from insects, crustacea, birds of all sorts, horses by the score, and even more dogs.[14]

A non-starter explanation for this demographic imbalance is that a disproportionate number of artists and art historians writing about them have been dog people. There is no evidence for this. We know, for example, that Dürer loved and admired cats, with an especial fondness for grey ones, and yet showed no interest in representing them in his art. Nor can it be the case that the portrait-commissioning classes were disproportionally favourable to dogs although the preponderance of men in portrait art and in narrative art generally may skew the sample. And we have no reason to believe that there have been fewer cats than dogs around through the ages.

The reason for why cats aren't dogs – at least in art – is that artists understood dogs as witnesses to us as a species doing what we do and had the opposite understanding of cats. Dogs can't help being there, being social – sometimes excessively social – and paying close attention with their eyes to our every move. Cats, on the other hand, come and go, look at what interests them, socialize or not, all as they please. They are socially competent; they live happily with us, at least house cats do. But it is on their terms: one moment resting their head on one's pillow or sitting on a desk; the next off somewhere.

The fluffy white Angora in Courbet's 1855 *The Studio of the Painter: A Real Allegory Determining Seven Years of the Artist's Life* – along with the cat in Manet's *Olympia*, one of the two most famous cats in art history – will have to stand for a great deal of further evidence for why the cat's gaze and feline sociability would not sustain this book [**24**]. What exactly is *The Studio of the Painter* an allegory of? Almost everything one might want to say about it is open to question. Courbet himself wrote that it was 'pretty mysterious' and wished 'good luck' to anyone who can figure it out. Every inch of this painting has been scrutinized and heatedly debated for more than a hundred years. In 1983 the cat entered the interpretive fray.[15]

It is odd that it took so long. The Angora cat is front and centre at the base of the vertical axis which divides dog people from well-known

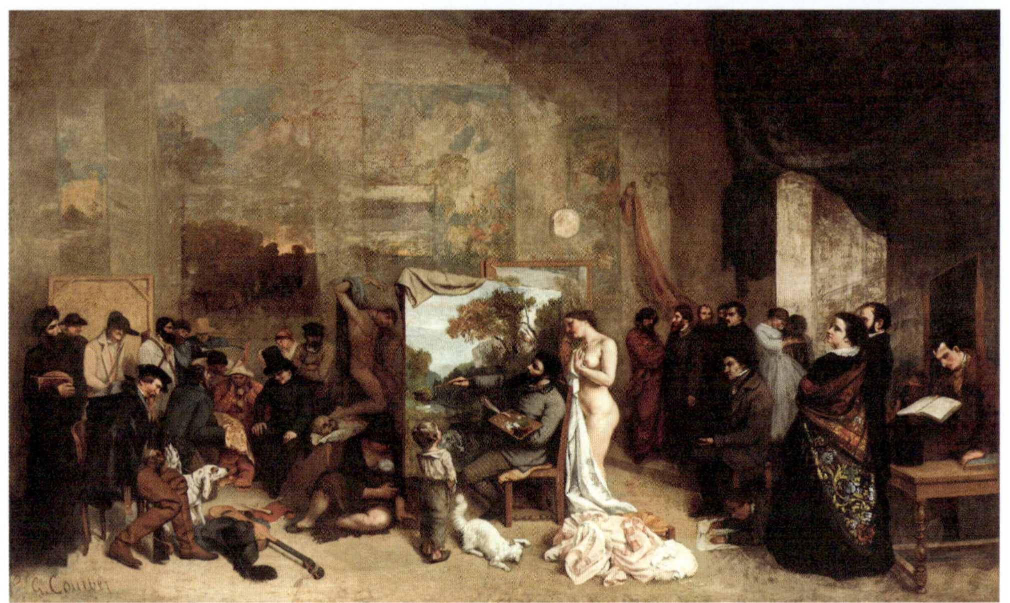

24 Dog people versus cat people: Gustave Courbet's *The Studio of the Painter* (1855).

cat people. On the left side facing the painting is 'the world of commonplace life' according to Courbet. Dog people: chief among them Courbet's bête noire, the emperor Napoleon III, and two dogs who make him look like a poacher with the accomplices of his shady trade. One of the dogs is looking up into his master's eyes. The other one is like the innocent boy who is looking intently at the painter and his muse. Both dogs are doing the sort of looking and gesturing that dogs do – being sociable, being engaged with their human, scoundrel though he is in this case.

On the right are Courbet's friends and supporters, all famously, indisputably cat people. There is the poet Charles Baudelaire, who, in his collection *Les Fleurs du Mal*, wrote the most famous cat poem of the century: 'Le Chat'. 'A voluptuous wheedling cat, with velvety manners,' a friend said of him. Erebus, the primordial deity of darkness, born of chaos, he writes, 'would have used them to draw his funeral carts/If their pride could let them stoop to bondage'. One over toward the back is Jules François Felix Fleury-Husson, one of Courbet's best friends and most important supporters who, under the pen name 'Champfleury', would a few years later publish one of the century's most famous books about cats: *Les Chats, histoire, moeurs, observations, anecdotes* (*The Cat: history, behaviour, observations, anecdotes*). 'The origin of the cat as a symbol of independence is of remote antiquity,' Champfleury writes. More than any other domestic animal, 'it preserves the independence of its tastes'. 'It lives alone, has no need of society.' 'It does not obey except when it likes, pretends to sleep that it may see more clearly . . .' 'Les chats c'est moi,' Courbet might have said, declaring his artistic independence in this instance although not in his work more generally. His first, and at the time controversial, self-portrait is with his large dog by his side (*see* 127).[16]

Courbet is drawing upon a long line of depictions of cats not paying attention to anything but what interests them: the cat in Veronese's *Wedding Feast at Cana* (*see* 88), which he knew well, is clawing playfully at the nose of the satyr bas-relief on the urn while the five dogs are variously engaged with the human scene; the one in Velázquez's *The Spinners* is playing with scraps while the women work. In Goya's *Clothed Maya* it is playing with what seems to be an all-time feline favourite toy: a skein of wool. In some Dutch genre paintings, cats happily slurp milk, ignoring whatever else is going on.

They sit on the laps of humans, almost entirely women and mostly young girls. But there is a certain temporal fragility in these poses; the cat is liable to leap off as it pleases. In the 1470s Leonardo da Vinci did a series for a never-to-be completed Madonna and Child painting. A cat is represented as desperate to get away from the Christ Child who tries to hang on to it [**25**]. Its progeny in art over the next half millennium,

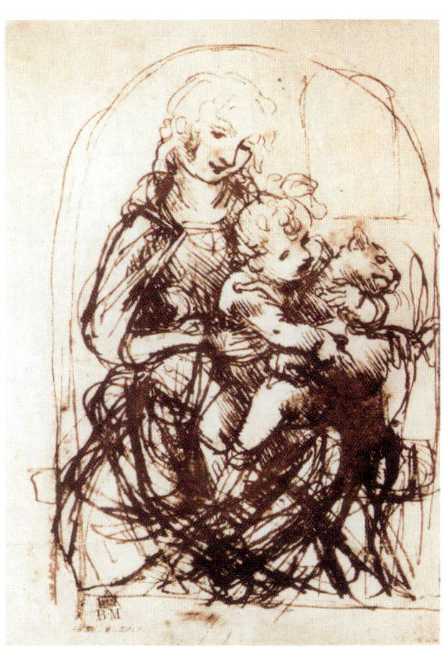

25 The cat in this study by Leonardo da Vinci tries to escape the grasp of the Christ Child (1478).

unhappy with being groomed or held or teased, or even played with, are often anxious to leave. By virtue of their relative wildness, a cat, like a human, comes and goes as it pleases. The deep domestication of the dog, on the other hand, makes our lives irresistible to them. A dog almost forces its way into the picture; at least painters make it seem as if its presence were part of the order of things. A cat is hard to pin down.

Sex is the one arena in which we might expect artists to imagine the engagement of the human – women in particular – and the feline worlds. A great deal has been made about cats and sexuality, especially female cats who were said to mirror women – deceptive, seductive, inconstant – and, perhaps less so, the tom cat – aggressive, prowling, promiscuous. The black cat in Manet's *Olympia* has been the locus classicus of such a sexualized cat in modern art history ever since it was first displayed in 1862: supposedly a lubricious female doppelgänger with the brazen gaze of the prostitute but at the same time with its raised tail like a male predator. But the overtly sexualized cat in the Western canon is rare and fraught, strange, and hard to interpret. It is often homoerotic and not engaged with female sexuality at all.

The answer to Kenneth Clark's question about the relative scarcity of cats in art and the reason this book is not about them is that the ways in which artists have been able to imagine cats in relation to us is limited and limiting. And that is because the cat remains an animal still very much in nature, only precariously and, only of its own volition, in culture. The cat stalking birds or mice or prowling for food is a creature in its own space and not ours. The sleeping cat is in its own world. If the dog and the dog's gaze are evidence of the closeness of the animal and human worlds – their imbrication – the cat is evidence of the fragility of that relationship. A dog among humans comes to seem commonplace: dogged, settled in our company, a creature comfortably in culture. The thereness of the cat in art as in life is fleeting and uncertain.

Horses are an entirely different matter. Their absence from this book is not a consequence of demography; there are almost, though not quite, as many of them as dogs in the Western pictorial record. And on occasion in some art of the nineteenth and twentieth centuries the horse becomes almost a dog. The horse in Frederick George Cotman's *One of the Family* (1880), chosen for its broad popular appeal as the first painting

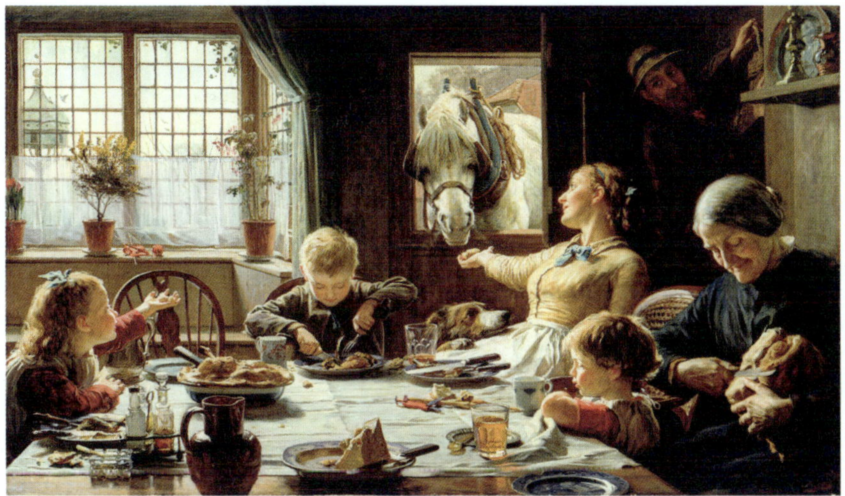

26 A horse joins the table in Frederick George Cotman's *One of the Family* (1880).

acquired by Liverpool's Walker Art Gallery, makes the equivalence explicit: both horse and dog are at the table [**26**].[17]

A great deal is made in myth and the visual arts of the remarkable fact that humans ride on the backs of these magnificent creatures, large enough to crush a rider, wild until broken, and yet at the command of our physically inferior selves. Ruling a horse is figured as a primal act of mastery over an animal but also, by extension, over the animal nature in us. 'To rule is to ride', as the political philosopher Carl Schmitt put it.[18] A comparison of the two portraits by Titian of Charles V from 1533 and 1548 makes the point in relation to the dog [**27-28**]. The earlier one is a dull likeness of the emperor; but it is a very good and affective painting of his dog. It enters the space of the emperor; it looks lovingly up at him, a little white impasto glint in its eye; its head snuggling against his leg, white and light brown against the burnt gold of the human's doublet. Charles's thumb and index finger are crooked around the dog's collar, his other fingers rest on the fur. This is an image of easy intimacy conveyed by the gaze and the soft touch of the hand. The dog humanizes the emperor.[19]

Charles V on his horse features also in battle scenes. Titian's 1548 enormous state portrait, more than three metres on its long edge, figures power. The emperor is in full armour, the same that he had worn in battle. He carries a spear and sits easily on the back of a beautiful,

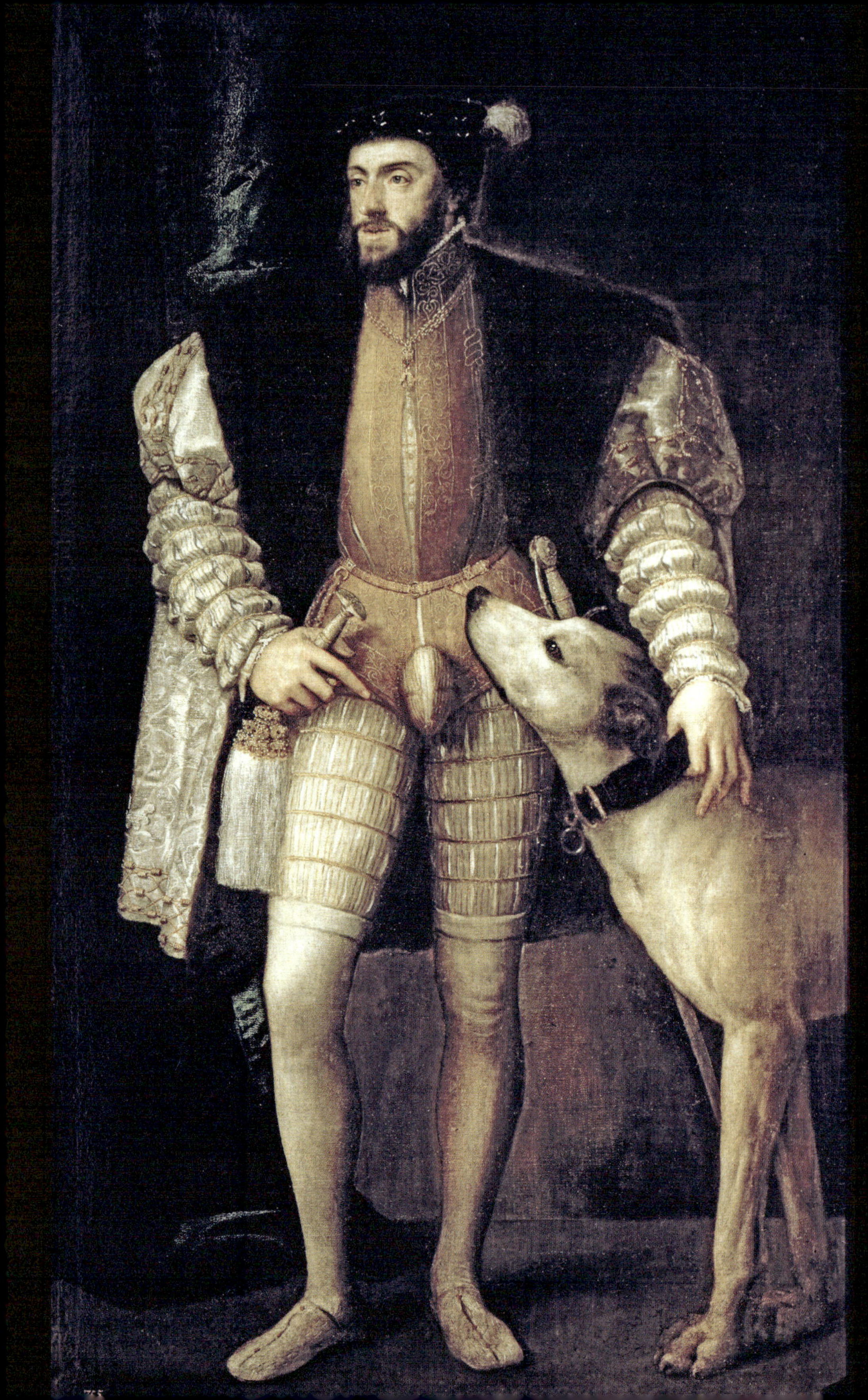

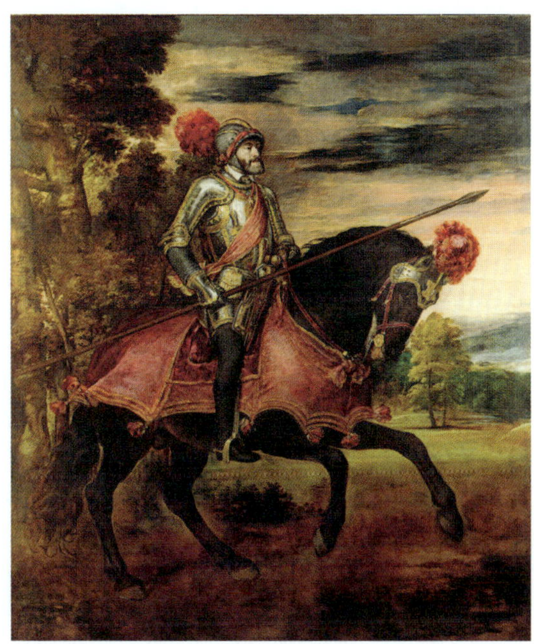

27 (*left*) Titian paints Charles V with his dog (1533) . . .

28 (*right*) . . . and then, fifteen years later, on his horse (1548).

plumed, black war horse; both are bedecked in the Burgundian colours. We know that Titian had seen in Rome the great bronze equestrian statue soon to be identified as that of the Emperor Marcus Aurelius. His equestrian portrait of Charles V stands in a lineage stretching back to Lissipos' fourth-century BCE equestrian statue of Alexander the Great and to statues on the triumphal arches of Rome and their Renaissance revivals – Donatello's *Equestrian Statue of Gattamelata* (c. 1447) is the first. The lineage continues through the ruler-portraits of Velázquez, Rubens, van Dyck, and El Greco, to David's *Napoleon Crossing the Alps* and beyond. A ruler on a smartly striding or rearing horse, often lavishly dressed in a painting, is one of the longest-lived tropes in political imagery. In this art and in the thousands of equestrian statues that dot the cities of the West and its former empires the horse is a prop for the man, and very occasionally also for a woman.[20]

Finally, and most importantly, the horse's gaze figures scarcely at all in art. Even though its eyes are the largest of any land mammal and are strikingly expressive, the eye contact that is so central to our relationship to dogs is missing. The relentless focus of the dog's eyes would have been evolutionarily disastrous for a horse, a prey animal whose eyes evolved to scan its surroundings. There is terror in their eyes in paintings of battle and benign indifference in landscapes and paintings of farmyards and inns. This is a book about intimate cross-species seeing and being seen.

Cows and sheep are seldom represented as having any subjectivity when we see them seeing us or returning our gaze. Only in Nativity scenes – the adoration of the shepherds or the visit of Magi – are they paying attention. They gaze on the Christ Child, witnesses to a miraculous birth. There are a few exceptions when these creatures pierce the veil of mere existence: the bull in Titian's *Rape of Europa*; one of the poor oxen – its ribs are showing – pulling the wagon in Courbet's 1850 *Peasants of Flagey Returning from the Fair* turns its head and looks out at the world, at us. It is the only creature in the painting that is not entirely absorbed in its own thoughts. The eyes of the middle pair of oxen in Rosa Bonheur's 1849 *Ploughing in the Nivernais* also look out at us, especially the brilliantly coloured white one in which the dark eyes reveal just a touch of its sclera matching its coat. These paintings stand out because they are exceptions and come late in the history of Western art. If Europeans had the sort of intimate relations with tamed wild animals that so surprised them when they encountered them among the indigenous people of Central and South America, the visual arts have left no record.[21]

The repertoire of the visual intimacy of the dog with our species is at the heart of this book because it is unique. Dogs have long occupied a position at the boundary where the human animal meets the rest of creation. The great Victorian critic John Ruskin thought that the artists of Renaissance Venice – Titian, Veronese, Tintoretto – painted dogs 'to give the fullest contrast to the highest tones of human thought and feeling'. They attracted these painters not because they are 'the basest of animals, but the highest – the connecting link between man and animals'. This is not a claim about their position on an imagined evolutionary tree or even a Great Chain of Being, but a status conferred on them by artists who thought of dogs on a social and moral continuum with humans, as a kind of double in another register.

This idea has a long history. Diogenes the Cynic, a younger contemporary of Plato's, was known as the dog philosopher – from the Greek word for dog, *Kynikós* – because he lived a life at the borderlands of culture: like a dog. Diogenes was a liminal creature; he lived on the street, close to nature; he did in public what civilized humans did only in private. And why not? he argued. He was ever unmasking the natural man who resides within the civilized one. Plato is reported to have thought of him as a mad version of Socrates in his challenges to civic convention. Diogenes the dog philosopher was not – could not have been – the cat, or the horse, or the donkey, or the bird philosopher; there is no equivalent thinker for other species.

If we were to translate Diogenes' real-life effort to live on the same scale as a dog – 'like a dog' – into a continuum of the visual and literary figuration of animals more generally, we might put birds at one end. They stand in a metaphorical relationship to us – a parallel world on another level – that takes on various meanings. Think of doves in paintings of the Annunciation or dead pheasants in Dutch still-life paintings. Dogs would be at the other end of the scale, metonymic creatures that stand in for us – and did for Diogenes – by virtue of their cultural proximity. They are 'almost human'. They go with us as a double, a step or two ahead or a step behind or a step at our side; looking at us; looking at what we are looking at or in a direction we might look to next; or showing us where to look; or looking as if from the position of the artist or in the direction he or she wants us to look; or looking with a central human figure in an image; or sometimes dogs are just being there in a great variety of spaces and places represented in the visual arts, doing their part to create an imaginary world.

Winslow Homer's *The Morning Bell* (originally *The Old Mill*) [**29**] is illustrative of this distinction in art. The dog on the raised walkway and the bird in the sky above the girl entering the mill make us think in an altogether different register about the painting. That is, they are details that get our attention, that make us focus. Like the punctum of a photograph, they visually and emotionally grab us. The bird is such a detail: a metaphorical creature from a parallel world, from the light-blue sky that stands in contrast to the more sombrely painted earth. It could mean the 'naturalized image of the soul's ascent', as one critic suggests, or the freedom of flight as opposed to the oppression of long days in the factory, or the possibility of escape. But whatever it means it captures our attention and it is not in the girl's world, a different, hence metaphorical creature.[22]

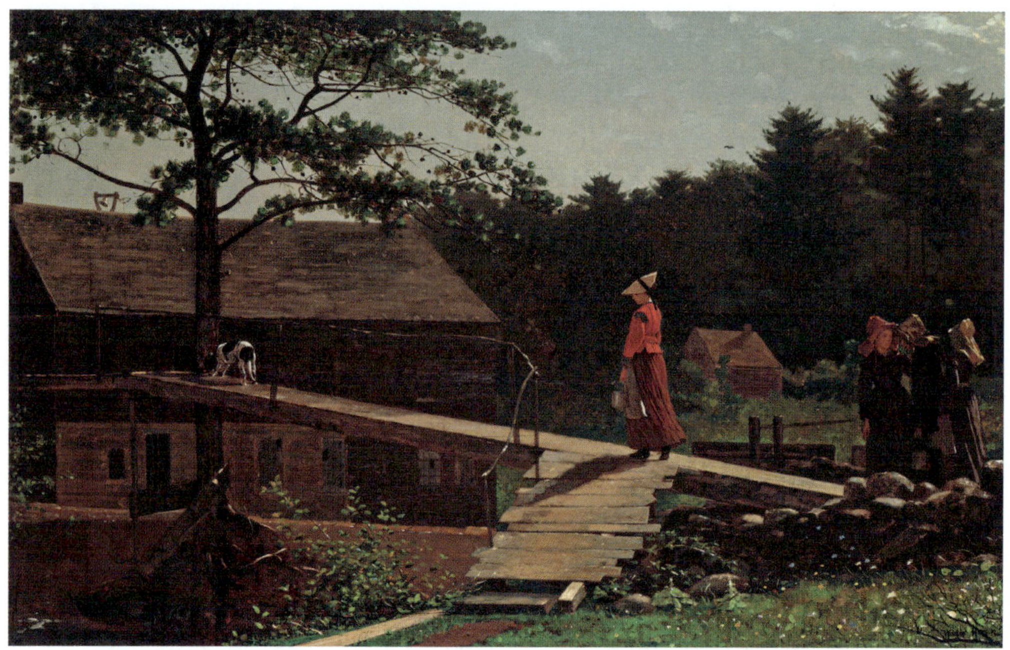

29 The dog as the girl's double in Winslow Homer's *The Morning Bell* (1871).

The dog is an altogether different matter. It is a metonymic creature in this painting: very much a part of her, a double, a few steps ahead. The two are painted as a pair formally and in any narrative account we might give of the painting. Their images divide the diagonal axis almost exactly into thirds. Unlike thousands of hunting pictures, including those by Homer, where dogs belong, there is no such reason for the dog to be here; workers did not take dogs into the factory. And indeed, it is not clear in the painting where the girl and dog are going; the walkway seems to end in shadows, in a dead end. The dog is ahead and has stopped by the tree that bisects the diagonal; the girl with the bright red coat who seems to be paused behind him. They are in synch, emotionally and visually bound together (but for how long?), poignant and hopeless together on a bridge from somewhere to somewhere. They – together – make us focus; they make demands on how we see the painting. This is what I mean by dogs as doppelgängers.[23]

Or close relatives. From the Neolithic rock art of what is now Libya to ancient Egypt, China and India, to medieval and Renaissance Europe, creatures at borderlands of what was taken to be civilization were represented as cynocephalic, that is, humans with dog heads. These are not like the bird-headed therianthropes of Palaeolithic and later rock art, which are evidence of cultures that understand the boundaries of the human and the animal to be porous as part of themselves and the world they inhabit: animism. They are visual claims about purportedly dog-headed creatures in the natural world. St Christopher is represented as dog-headed, for example, in icons of the Armenian and Byzantine churches because he was said to have been from a strange savage tribe in north Africa before his conversion, or more generally because he was a foreigner who might also be interpreted as a protector of Christ and his people. He is doing one of the things that dogs do: protect humans. There are humans with a dog's head in John de Mandeville's account of Ethiopia, his fourteenth-century *Book of Marvels and Travels*, which became one of the most popular travel books ever; they are there from very near the beginning of the age of print in books, like the widely circulated illustrated encyclopedia, the *Nuremberg Chronicle* [**30-31**].[24]

30-31 (*below*) Woodcut of a cynocephalic creature by Hartmann Schedel in the *Nuremberg Chronicle* (1493); (*right*) an icon of St Christopher depicted with the head of a dog, made in seventeenth-century Cappadocia.

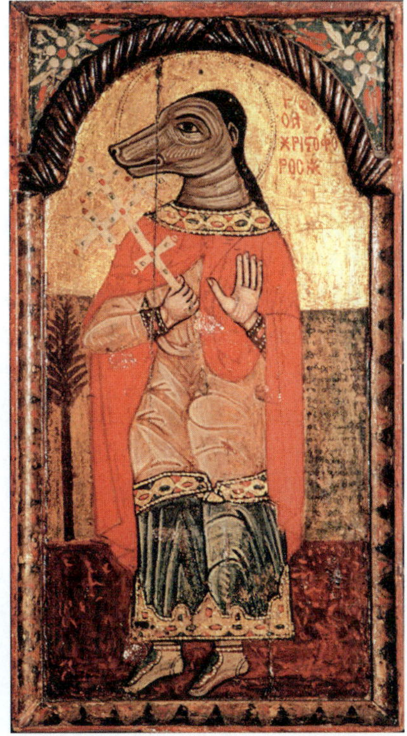

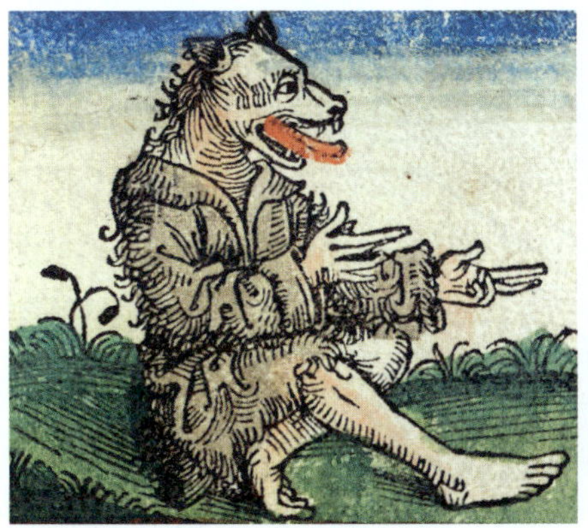

St Augustine was sceptical that these strange creatures existed on the other side of the world, which may not exist either: 'what am I to say of those dog-headed men whose dog's heads and actual barking show they are more beasts than men'. But he concludes that if there were such a place and if dog-headed people lived there, and no matter how unusual they might be, they 'derive from the original and first-created man'.[25] That is from Adam, just over the border of the fully human from the very beginning. In the visual arts that I engage with in this book there are no paintings of cynocephalic humans. But these images as well as those from other cultures are evidence of how deeply the dog is lodged in folk consciousness as an imaginary animal alter ego. We not only see them but we understand that they see us and our environment in a mutually intelligible way, gazing and not just being gazed at.

Readers might think that from the perspective of the dog my engagement with its gaze is naively anthropocentric. If a dog were writing this book, it might be called 'What the Dog Smells', because we know that it is the dog's prodigious olfactory powers that determine much of how it experiences the world it inhabits and presumably its relationship specifically with us.[26]

But such a book is not possible. First, of course, because a dog would not be writing a book; but also because smell is so hard to represent. Proust in speaking of his aunt's apartments in Combray writes about 'the countless odours springing from their own special virtues, wisdom, habits, a whole secret system of life, invisible, superabundant and profoundly moral, which their atmosphere holds in solution'; smells 'coloured by circumstances as are those of the neighbouring countryside, but already humanized, domesticated, confined, an exquisite, skilful, limpid jelly . . .' Proust has no equal in conjuring the culturally and physiologically dense human experience of smell. But no human can begin to describe the granularity of the world present to the dog's refined sense of smell as it takes a walk or runs in a field.

Visual artists are severely limited in how they might represent the sense of smell in humans. There is a small genre of works that tries in the context of paintings of 'the five senses', which either represent people happy and contented smelling something that we take to smell good – flowers for example – or scrunching up their noses when confronted by

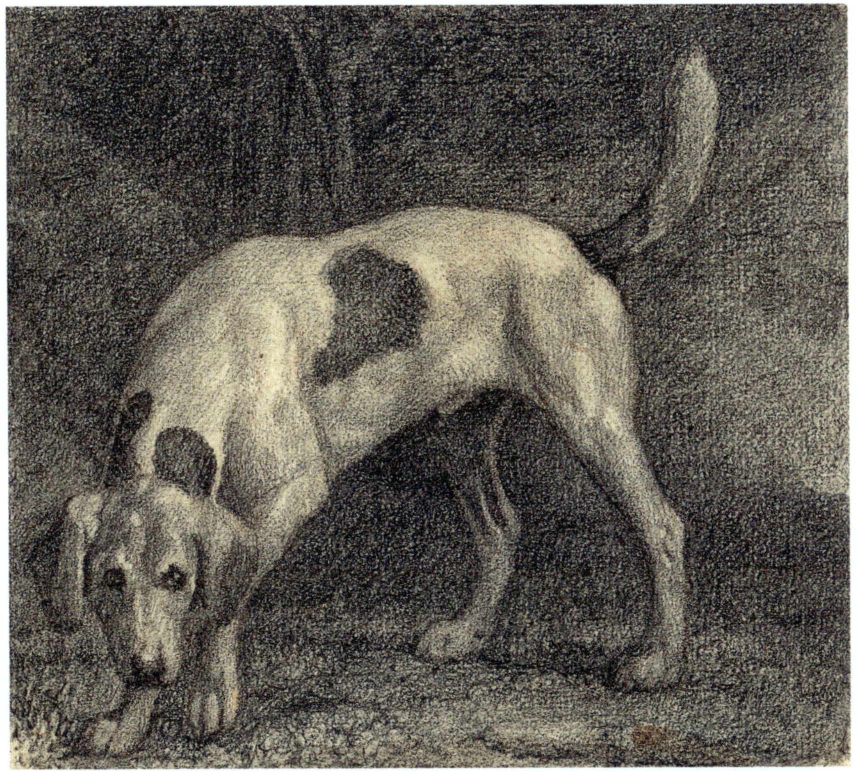

32 *A Foxhound on the Scent* (1788) by George Stubbs, in which smelling looks like looking.

something we understand as smelling bad – a rotten egg or a decomposing body for example – or in some other way responding to something under their noses; Rembrandt in his study of the five senses paints a woman being revived from a faint by smelling salts. None of these strategies would work to represent a dog smelling. Their faces cannot express how they think about a smell and they are not very discriminating. As Darwin pointed out, dogs seem to delight in pretty much anything. We have far fewer common references with them than we have with other humans.

And there is another problem. Even when artists represent dogs doing what they do best, their long, dolichocephalic heads with their long noses make it seem that they are simultaneously making a visual gesture. Even when they aren't, their noses are like a pointing index finger in the direction of their eyes. They appear to be looking and pointing even if, as in a Stubbs' drawing, the artist tells us explicitly that the dog is smelling [**32**]. In countless pictures of dogs with hunters holding game or in the presence of well-perfumed humans we can infer that they are smelling something of interest but that is not what we see. Neither word nor image is adequate to the task of representing the dog's sensorium. This is inevitably a book by a human about how humans – the makers of art and its viewers – understand the dog seeing in relation to our species.

And yet, even from the dog's perspective, its sight is essential to its ability to live with us and join in what we do. A dog's responses to visual cues from humans is the foundation of its social competence generally and in particular contexts. So-called sighthounds, for example – greyhounds, whippets and their kin – are disproportionally represented in the Western visual arts from Giotto to the nineteenth century because of their skill in coursing, a favourite subject for artists. This is a special case. The pervasive cross-species relationship we have with dogs is grounded in their gaze which, in turn, makes possible their wide social competence and the ease with which they live with us so comfortably and in such numbers.

But this reality itself does not account for their place in the artistic imagination. Artists are free to choose to include them or not. There are two dogs, for example, in Bartholomeus van Bassen's painting of an imagined church interior with the tomb of William the Silent [**33**]. The same holds true for dogs in fields, and taverns and studios and all the other places where they might have been or not. Their outsize presence in mythological paintings is of course not a question of reality – of naturalism – at all. The stories need them but this is the case because dogs figure so powerfully in how literature and the visual arts imagine human interactions among themselves and with the gods who themselves have dogs. In all these cases their presence thus represents not so much reality as the reality effect, the sense that this is how a world is made to seem as it is.

In one important way the dog in art does not reflect reality, in the real world, or in the imagination, the reality effect. There are very few hints in art of dogs being dirty, vicious or rabid. Nothing about the frequency of dog bites. Nothing that reflects the sheer abjection of the murderous dog pounds of the nineteenth and twentieth centuries or the many individual cruelties visited upon dogs. Nothing in art about their being polluting.

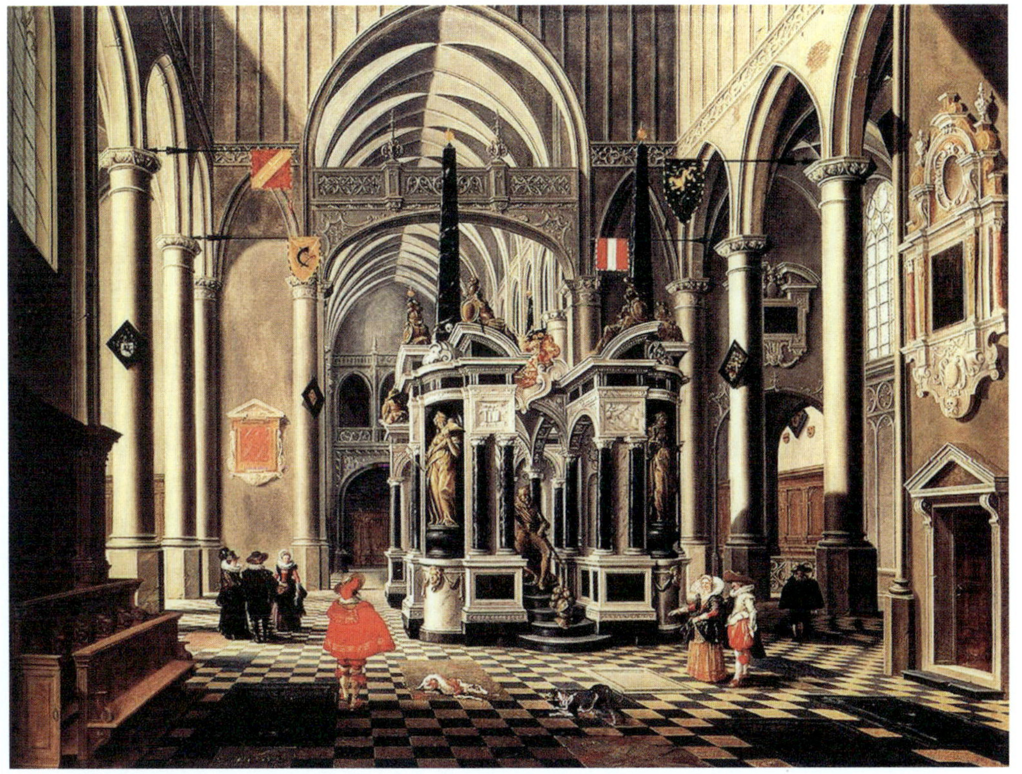

33 Two dogs give an impression of reality in van Bassen's imagined church interior (1620).

The reason for this absence is that dogs appear in art as part of a social contract; they see us, and we see them; and we engage with the world together. On occasion, artists represent dogs gently breaking out of the comforting premises of good order (*see* chapter 6, pages 295–6). The dogs in paintings of the story of Diana and Actaeon who attack their master after the goddess has turned him into a deer bear witness to the fragility of our mastery of nature and the compact we have with some animals. It touches the boundaries of what it is to be human; Actaeon becomes a man in a deer's body (*see* chapter 2, pages 97–104). Generally the vicious or rabid dog or the cruelly treated dog or the dog who acts out of character in art is a sign of something morally amiss.

If paintings were like unedited photographs in the all-seeing eye of God – a record of human attitudes toward, and treatment of, the dog's ubiquitous presence in life – then reality might explain why there are so many of them in art. But neither painting nor photography imitates nature.

If anything, it's often the other way around. The story is told that Sir Peter Lely, the most important portrait painter of the British Restoration period, claimed that for want of a dog he could not finish a portrait of the well-known artist Mary Beale. A friend searched the vicinity of Covent Garden to find one: 'I hunted about ye towne from one end to the other after a dogg,' he reports, and finally found one that he dragged back – kidnapped – to Lely's studio. The painting was completed and 'dispatched to Allbrook' where the Beales were living.[27] Three centuries later Richard Avedon, one of the twentieth century's great portrait photographers, writes that when he was a child his parents used to borrow a dog for their family portraits. Such social conventions dictate how nature is imagined and represented in art, not the other way around.[28]

The philosopher Nelson Goodman goes a step further. He argues 'that nature imitates art is too timid a dictum'; 'nature is a product of art and discourse'. We make the world we live in as creatures in culture through symbols and signs, and dogs in art constitute part of that symbolic system. They bring their world into ours, which is perhaps how they make us feel less lonely as a species. This is the abstract answer to the question of why there are so many dogs in Western art and what they are doing there.

A less abstract one would be: Formally, dogs are there in art because they organize the visual space of an image and the ways we are asked to respond to it. They point to things, they tell us where to look, they make connections both between things in the image and gesture to us as observers of the image. They don't all do it in the same way. Sometimes it is perspective that they help create; sometimes looking out at a great expanse; sometimes intimate close looking and pointing.

Dogs are also there because of the emotional work they do: they humanize humans. They have done this since the earliest days of Western literature, since Homer. When Odysseus returns to Ithaca he sees the dog with whom he had 'hunted down wild goats and roe deer and hares . . .', missed by no one since his master had gone away:

> So there lay Argos – 'Flash' – riddled with vermin, that plague of dogs.
> Now, though, as soon as he sensed Odysseus was close by,
> Look! – he wagged his tail and both his ears went flat.

> But after he hadn't the strength to come closer to his master,
> Who looked in the other direction and brushed away a tear.[29]

The formal and the social and psychological work of dogs in art are both consequences of their gaze. The rest of this book explores these themes.

CHAPTER 2

The Deep Time of the Dog

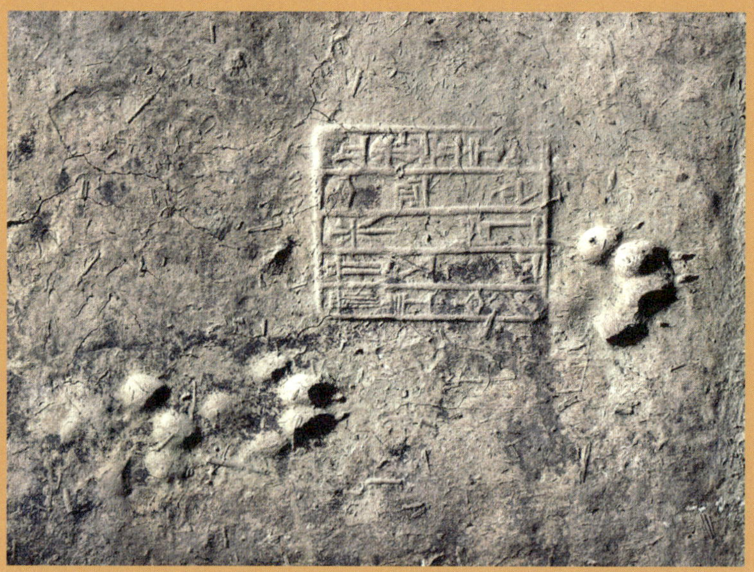

34 Pawprints on a Mesopotamian pavement brick alongside cuneiform text (c. 1900–1600 BCE.).

IN THE BEGINNING THERE was a dog. It is there in origin stories from around the world. Maybe, as the indigenous Chato Indians of California thought, the creator had one as a companion, or as the Plains Shawnee would have it, the creatress was followed by a dog along with her grandson. Or perhaps the dog was part of a new beginning: the story the Tehuelche people of Chile and Patagonia tell is that after a deluge in which all mankind was destroyed, 'the sun god decided to create new people. First he made a man, then a woman, and finally a dog to keep them company.' This sense of the dog as the primal companion has a very long life.[1]

Next to a boy's footprints deep in the south-western French cave of Chauvet that he left 25,000 years ago are a dog's pawprints. It may not have looked quite like the dogs that we know but the marks it left in mud now turned to limestone were made by a canid friendly enough to walk next to a human. By 4,000 years ago the pawprints of dogs we would recognize are commonplace. Those left in the wet clay of ancient Mesopotamian brickyards, by workmen's or village dogs, are eerily familiar. The dog's pawprint on a brick in the Hearst Museum of the University of California, Berkeley, is almost as large as the cuneiform text [**34**], which says that whoever commissioned the building for which it was destined was 'beloved of the god Tishpak'.[2] (Tishpak was the patron god of the city of Eshnunna, in central Mesopotamia, now Iraq, dating back to the third millennium BCE.) These sorts of dogged bricks are not rare.

From Mesopotamia there is a continuous trail of pawprints to relatively new and un-eroded pavement at the start of the Yorkshire Dales Walk near Ilkley, in northern England [**35**]. Thousands of dog generations have left their marks in cement, mud and clay. Like the footprint that

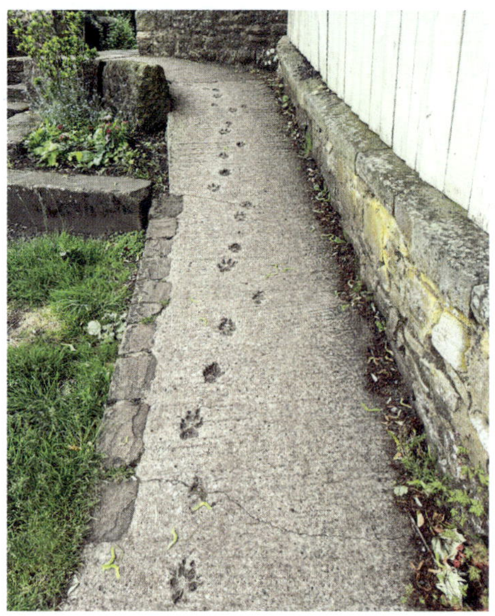

35 We are not alone: pawprints at the start of the Yorkshire Dales Walk.

Robinson Crusoe found in the sand that told him he had human company, pawprints are evidence that we as a species have not been alone. In Defoe's novel, the protagonist was not alone either before Friday appeared. A dog swam to shore with the eponymous hero: there was, he says, 'no company that he could not make up to me; I only wanted to have him talk to me, but that he would not do'.[3]

Dogs, like us born of evolution a very long time ago, became part of the social and cultural history of our species through the lives we have shared with them over the millennia. How they then came to be part of our visual culture is a further step in this deep co-evolutionary history: we joined them in myth; we thought about how they think and the meanings of their gestures – their paws raised, their heads turned, their bodies pressed on ours, their eyes fixed on us; we selectively bred them for specific social roles; and we represented all this to ourselves in art.

Before Art

The foundation of the story of the dog in art was laid in deep evolutionary time. Genetic evidence would push it back to 70,000–90,000 years ago; statistical sampling of masses of bones suggests that the proto-dog had already separated from its ancestor 40,000–50,000 years ago. By 20,000–25,000 years ago it had happened, and dogs have walked the earth with and among us ever since. Recognition emerged of its 'human likeness', its 'human specific skills', its 'evolutionary social competence', that is, its species-specific ability to live with us where we live.[4] It was the first domestication, a momentous event in the relation of humans to the rest of living creation. There was no going back.

First there is the genetic story. We gape at the endless variations that evolution has created: flesh-eating plants; spiders with eyes in the front and back of their heads; platypuses that detect the electric fields of their prey using electro receptors in their bills; millions upon millions of wonders among which is *canis familiaris*. 'Natural selection,' said R. K. Fisher, one of the greatest of Darwin's successors, 'is a mechanism for generating an exceedingly high degree of improbability.'

The dog is improbable. Pigs have an extraordinary capacity for empathy and respond easily to human gestures; crows have spectacular memories and like dogs can follow a point; whales and porpoises have far more developed language than a dog's bark; cats have a vast repertoire of meows; and octopuses during their short underwater lives seem to have undreamed of emotional gifts.[5] None have the communicative skills for dealing with us on terra firma in the sustained way that the dog has. That the dog is distinct from the wolf is even more improbable. The modern wolf is genetically almost identical to the modern dog – they produce fertile offspring and are considered by some taxonomists as a single species.[6] Yet wolves aren't dogs; even those that are hand-raised entirely by humans from birth are far less socially competent in their interactions with us than puppies are within weeks of coming out of the womb.

Subtle as is the genomic difference between wolves and dogs, the chasm between humans and our animal doppelgänger, the dog, is vast. The order Carnivore (that includes cats and dogs) broke off from our lineage, the Hominidae, some 60 million years ago. Seven million years ago we and chimps, on the one hand, and gorillas, on the other, parted ways. Then a million years later we split off from chimpanzees. But even after six million years we still share at least 96 per cent DNA of our base pairs with the chimp.[7] And yet, the chimp is not even in the running to be our best friend. It isn't close to having the social competence of the dog, with whom we share roughly the same percentage of our genomes that we do with cows, 82–84 per cent. And we share more DNA with cats (about 90 per cent).

'It would be hard if not impossible,' writes Jane Goodall, the most important student of chimpanzee behaviour of her generation, 'to produce a chimpanzee who could live with humans and have anything like as good a relationship as we have with our dogs.' This is not a matter of 'intelligence', however understood, but of the capacity 'to help, to be obedient, and to gain our approval'. She reports that she learned from her dog Rusty that 'animals have minds, personalities and feelings', which gave strength to the convictions that informed her life's work. Ninety dogs attended her ninetieth birthday party in 2024 at Carmel Beach in California; no chimps were invited, she said, because they would have caused chaos.[8]

How the dog, so genomically distant from us, found the evolutionary niche in which to become socially and culturally close to us remains a just-so story although by no means unique. (How the zebra got its stripes is still a controversial question.) When, where, and how it happened are unanswerable and probably ill-posed, if often asked, questions. 'In a land far away, in a time long ago . . .' is the answer I got from the molecular geneticist who led the mapping of the dog genome.[9]

Ill posed because in general the search for an originary moment always ends up with one more question, one more set of antecedent connections to be explored. And ill posed specifically in the case of the dog because the more data we have on genomic divergence the more difficult the question has become and because it is hard to say exactly what we mean by a 'dog'. Its early ancestors may have looked more like the ancestral wolf but acted something like the modern dog. Even today, the indigenous dogs of Siberia, for example, are closer genetically to their modern wolf relatives than are more recent western breeds, but they still act like dogs. How do we differentiate? There have been efforts to characterize the differences between dogs and wolves by matching specific genetic mutations to social behaviours: the dog's friendliness, for example, some have speculated, may be due to a specific mutation which in humans results in abnormal friendliness.[10] But this is a stretch.

Where the now extinct ancestor of the modern grey wolf evolved into dogs is clearer: after humans left Africa it happened in at least two distinct regions – in what is now Siberia and Mesopotamia. Both humans and wolves were faced with new ecological and hence evolutionary challenges – intermittent periods of intense dry cold – that changed their relationship.

Ethology and historical anthropology permit us to develop this story further. The wolf was the alpha predator of Early Ice Age Eurasia, a social animal that hunted in packs, worked co-operatively, communicated through its eyes, and lived in a hierarchical social order organized around a senior male and his mate – a family of wolves we might say. They started sharing an environment with our similarly situated and socially organized ancestors. Wolves were poised to connect with humans and vice versa. If the behaviour of the modern grey wolf can stand in for its ancient and extinct ancestor, the potential to become our best friend was there at the beginning.[11]

From a human perspective this is one version of how it might have happened: during the Eurasian Ice Ages the least afraid among wolves wandered into one of our camps in search of food and dined on our leftovers. We took them in – or simply allowed them to hang around our garbage heaps – and gradually they lost their wolfish standoffishness. Humans came to have more and more of a role in controlling their reproduction – this is what defines domestication – and gradually over the generations these relatively friendly wolves lost their standoffishness and became dogs.

The most satisfying proof-of-concept for this view comes from a remarkable longitudinal series of breeding experiments, using foxes as a model, begun by the Russian geneticist Dmitri Belyaev in the 1950s and continued for almost sixty years by his student Lyudmila Trut at the Institute for Cytology and Genetics in Novosibirsk, Siberia.[12] Belyaev reasoned that the wolf became a dog through a process of natural – and/ or artificial – selection for tameness: survival of the friendliest.[13] In ten generations he produced a dog-like fox.

This story is not without its problems. There is considerable evidence that wolves and humans did not have the sort of adversarial relationship in which the dangerous wolf had to be tamed and ultimately domesticated by us. To the contrary, indigenous people in Siberia, North America, and in early modern Japan lived in harmony with wolves and there is no reason to believe that it was otherwise for Palaeolithic humans. They did not bite our heads off.

There is a co-evolutionary, less anthropocentric, and more compelling co-operative version of the story of how the lives of dogs and humans became joined and eventually became the subject of art. Wolves as the experienced alpha predators of Eurasia were far better at taking down large game than the newly arrived migrants and at least as good at hunting deer and other small game; they ate first and then humans took what was left. Or they ate at the same time but separately. The process of domestication was a two-way street: sometime in the last Ice Ages some humans 'teamed up with pastoralist wolves'. As the evolutionary behaviouralists Wolfgang Schleidt and Michael Shalter imagine it, humans 'adopted the wolves' lifestyle as herd followers and herders of reindeer and other hoofed animals'. The teamwork was mutually advantageous; teamwork with dogs still offers significant advantages to hunter-gatherer peoples today. 'Subsequent changes in both wolves and humans [must therefore],' they conclude, 'be understood as co-evolution.'[14]

Further elaborations of this story tie the evolution of the dog even closer to the social and cultural evolution of humans and hence to art. In addition to tool-making, symbolic behaviour, language, and the domestication of plants and animals, certain animals came to be incorporated into our social, cultural, and symbolic lives.[15] Wolves, and eventually dogs, became deeply connected to humans in our symbolic systems. Visual communication was at its core.

There is a relatively well-established 'co-operative eye hypothesis' developed by some researchers: humans are the only primates, it holds, with white sclerae (the white of the eyes). We know that these appear occasionally in chimps for whom it offered no particular advantage to their way of hunting, but in humans this variation offered an evolutionary adaptation that made it easier to detect the gaze of a fellow human, to predict their actions, and to act co-operatively. It also made it easier for the dog to co-operate with humans in hunting. And, more speculatively still, it gave *homo sapiens* an advantage over Neanderthals in whom the whites of the eye had not evolved.[16]

Except for the footprints in the Chauvet cave, archaeological evidence for modern dogs living with modern humans so far dates to less than 20,000 years ago, although earlier and earlier finds are being reported. A humerus of a dog discovered in a cave in the Basque country is firmly dated to 17,000 years old and seems really to be that of our kind of dog.[17] Three thousand years later we know that a dog had become part of how we care for our dead. A three-month-old disabled puppy's body was buried with its humans and grave goods 14,000 BCE in what is now Oberkassel, a suburb of Bonn. The dog could have had no utility to its people beyond the bonds of affection, the utility of emotional connection. Two thousand years later there is the skeleton of a woman with her hand under the head of a puppy curled up beside her among the burials of humans with dogs from the Natufian culture in what is now Israel. The aboriginal people of Australia have been burying their dead with dingoes for at least 3,500 years.[18]

Genetic evidence suggests that dogs were by the sides of their humans as they migrated to the far corners of the earth, from Siberia around 16,000 BCE to the Americas, north and then south, then back to Africa with humans around 7000 BCE and everywhere else – except Amazonia, where they did not arrive until the twentieth century – over the next millennia. In other words, when we have moved, dogs have moved with us.[19]

Gradually the dog developed the specifically visual abilities that would tie its evolutionary history to its place in the cultural history of humans and animals. When exactly the unique capacity of dogs to communicate with humans through their gaze – interspecies social bonding through eye contact – evolved is hard to establish with precision. It happened gradually. Dingoes (*canis dingo*), a sort of evolutionary middle point in canine domestication between the modern dog and extinct grey wolf, initiate eye contact far better than the modern wolf but not for as long as the modern dog. This suggests that the motivation to make eye contact with humans that is a foundation of our unique bonding with the dog – and of the art in this book – began before the dog/dingo divergence and has become stronger since.[20]

Interaction with humans sharpened the dog's visual social competence. They follow a point, for example, much better if preceded by the human looking in its direction, i.e. following our gaze. They develop cross-attention looking, that is, looking back and forth to be sure the cues we give them are correct. They focus on our faces and more specifically our eyes. If a wolf and a dog are both given the impossible task of getting food out of a closed container the wolf will keep trying to get it open; the dog will look back at the human to ask for help rather as we might look toward a friend to open a door when our arms are full. And there is some experimental evidence that humans shift attention based on cues from the gaze of a dog.[21]

Moreover, as the dog's gaze evolved so did its face musculature in ways that made its eyes more expressive. Dogs acquired small muscles around the eye socket – the *levator anguli oculi medialis* – that allow them to raise their eyebrows in a gesture of interest that we recognize. This muscle also tended to expose the whites of their eyes, which made them seem more like ours. It is not present in the wolf or in the most wolf-like dogs – the Siberian Husky, for example – but is there in other domestic breeds. Evolution on a scale of 10,000 years made it seem to us that the dog's eyes and facial expressions worked by the same emotional economy as ours.[22] From a human perspective, this long evolutionary history anthropomorphizes the dog; from a dog's perspective, it 'canispomorphizes' the human. Seeing together and seeing one another is the basis of our co-evolution, and joint social lives. It is the deep biological and evolutionary beginning to the story of the dog's gaze in art.

From Evolution to Culture

The dog has long been poised on the porous border between the wild and civilization. For thousands of years before anyone thought of evolution, humans have been puzzled by how the wolf morphed into our closest animal companion. One version of how it came over to our side is that in fact it had always been there: the she-wolf that suckled Romulus and Remus, children of Mars and founders of Rome, and the wolf that suckled Cormac, the mythic high king of Ireland, are examples. This benign version of the wolf who lived peacefully with humans, and humans and their dogs, is also found in Siberian and North American indigenous accounts.

Aesop, c. 600 BCE, himself purportedly a slave but possibly a fictitious figure, tells a sadder version of the story. One day a thin, hungry and bedraggled wolf meets a well-fed house dog. He contemplates eating him but thinks that maybe the buff dog would put up too much of a fight. The two start talking instead. The dog tells the wolf that he doesn't need to live in the wild and fight for every bite of food. He himself lived in a warm house, was fed all sorts of good things, and enjoyed caresses and kind words in return for which he had to do very little: bark at strangers mostly.

The wolf was in tears of envy until he noted some chafing around the dog's neck and asked what had caused it. Nothing much, the dog protested. After some probing the wolf got his answer: it was a collar, which kept the dog from going where he pleased. 'No thank you,' said the wolf; 'I will forgo all those goodies and comforts. Nothing is worth so much as liberty.' The dog in this old story is a wolf who sold his lineage into permanent servitude – domestication is slavery.[23] Aesop also has a reversed version of this story in which a hunting dog, tired of risking his life in pursuit of dangerous animals in return for food, walks away and lives as a beggar: a return to nature, an escape from slavery.[24]

Fifteen hundred years after Aesop, St Francis of Assisi's negotiations with the Wolf of Gubbio offer a cheerier, co-operative story. It seems that a particularly ferocious wolf was threatening the lives and livestock of

36 Detail from *St Francis of Assisi Speaking with the Wolf of Gubbio* (1437–44), painted by Sassetta for the high altar of San Francesco in Borgo San Sepolcro, Italy.

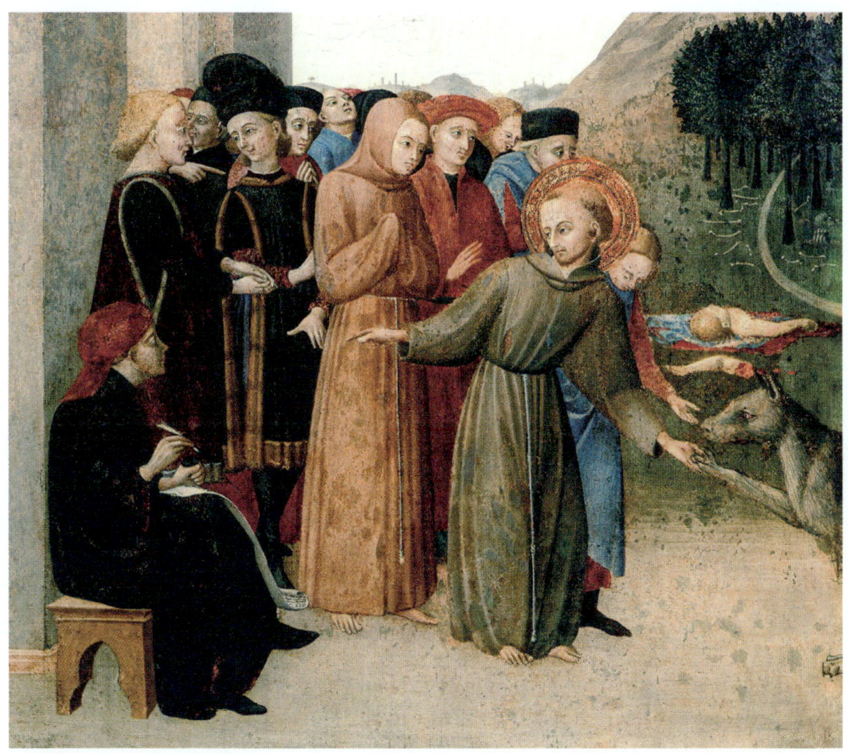

the city. St Francis went out beyond the gates to meet with the creature, who lay down quietly to listen to the deal he offered:

> Friar wolf, inasmuch as it seemeth good unto thee to make and keep this peace, I promise thee that, so long as thou shalt live, I will cause thy food to be given thee continually by the men of this city, so that thou shalt no more suffer hunger . . . I desire, friar wolf, that thou shouldst promise me that never from henceforward wilt thou injure any human being or any animal. Dost thou promise me this?

Regular food in return for peace. The wolf took the deal. 'St Francis held forth his hand to receive his fealty, and the wolf lifted up his right forefoot and put it with friendly confidence in the hand of St Francis.' The wolf, now dog-like, makes an intentional act of mutual trust and reciprocal obligations, a cross-species re-enactment of an idealized feudal order. The painting of St Francis and the wolf also shares a common formal feature of a great deal of the art in this book: a dog coming into the world of the humans from the world beyond the edge of the picture, its eyes and more clearly its paw in this case, creating a visual axis that takes the view that the dog initiates from our right to left through the picture along a trail of hands [**36**].[25]

The raised paw added to an attentive gaze will have a long life in art. In **37** it mirrors the eyes of the dog on the title page of the cartographer Gerard Mercator's famous atlas printed by the Flemish engraver Jodocus Hondius. Potential buyers are assured by Hondius' motto on the platform where the dog stands that the work was 'executed under the watchful eyes of a dog'. One might want to translate 'excusum sub cane vigilanti' as 'printed at the sign of the watchful dog' because a dog is so visually prominent, holding up an armillary sphere, over the firm's business on Amsterdam's dog-friendly Dam Square. Of course, these interpretations of the dog's gestures – mine and those of the makers of the image – are based on treating them as if they were a human's. Human gestures too demand interpretation. This sort of cognitive equivalence is what domestication made possible; a dog is, among other things, a readily intelligible wolf.

Five hundred years after St Francis negotiated with the wolf to act like a dog, the greatest naturalist of the eighteenth century,

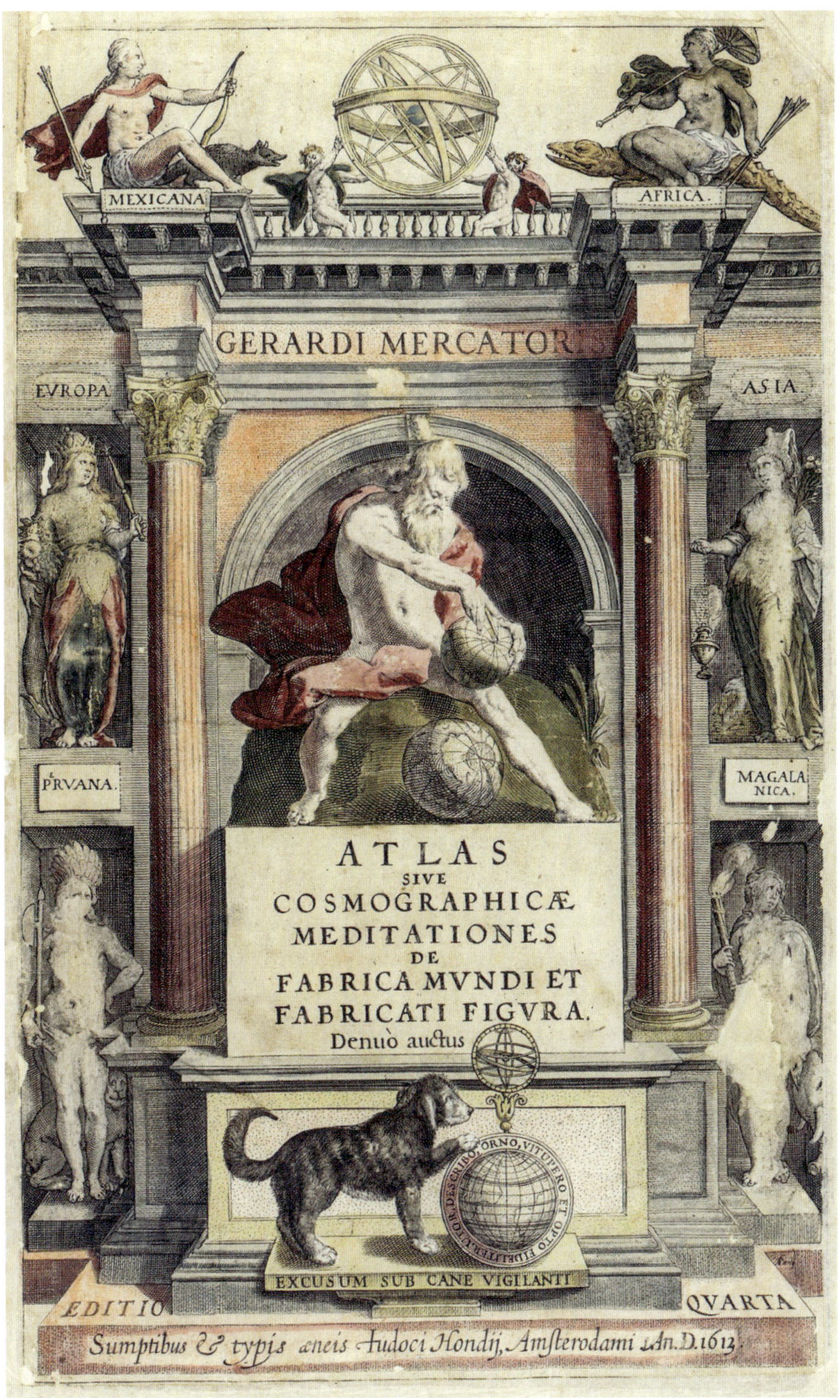

37 Hondius the engraver assures us his work is 'executed under the watchful eyes of a dog'.

Georges-Louis Leclerc, Comte de Buffon, in his best-selling book *Histoire Naturelle* (1749) had this to say about the world-historical importance of the consequences of the first domestication, that of dogs:

> To conceive the importance of [the dog] in the order of Nature, let us suppose that it never existed. Without the assistance of the dog, how could man have conquered, tamed, and reduced the other animals into slavery?

'The training of the dog,' he continues, 'seems to have been the first art invented by man.' Perhaps he exaggerates; perhaps this was not the very first art but still a very early one. A man of the Age of Enlightenment, Buffon invites us to look for the success of our species not in divine ordinances but in human history. He also unintentionally points to the sadness of it all, to a kind of secular Fall: we came to believe in an unsustainable story that we could dominate the natural world through a series of victorious battles. Horses, Buffon thought, were with the dogs' assistance man's first animal conquest.[26]

The association of humans and dogs as a marker of the entry of humans into culture itself has a history stretching back thousands of years, and continuously informing the visual record. An early nineteenth-century French author tells young readers that it should come as no surprise to them that the ancients would think of dogs as a species of divinity – he gives as examples Annubis among the Egyptians, and Sirius who, with his master Orion, the greatest hunter among the Greeks, became the dog star, the brightest in the constellation Canis Major. (In one version of the story, Gaia, the earth goddess, sent a scorpion to kill Orion, after which he was transported by Artemis, goddess of the hunt, to the heavens accompanied by his dog. *See* chapter 4, note 36, for another version.) In literature, too, dogs came to the fore very long ago:

> One knows Argus, Ulysses' dog, through the beautiful verses of Homer. Other poets have immortalized the dog of Cephalus [the magic hound Laelaps]; of Diana; of Adonis . . .[27]

The English engravers Thomas Bewick and Ralph Beilby, in their popular late eighteenth-century classic *General History of Quadrupeds*, begin the long section on dogs – the longest in the book – by telling

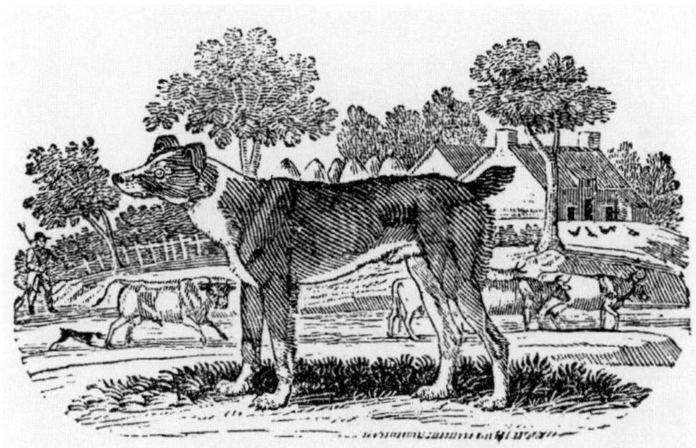

38 *The Cur Dog* (1800), a woodcut by Thomas Bewick.

readers why it was not even longer: 'to give the history of the dog would be little less than to trace mankind back to their original state of simplicity' [**38**]. Six centuries earlier the learned twelfth-century abbess Hildegard von Bingen writes in her book on the properties of the natural world that the dog:

> . . . is very hot and has a common and natural affinity with human ways. It senses and understands the human being, loves him, willingly dwells with him and is faithful.

'Satan,' she thought, 'hates the dog more than all other animals because he is so close to man.'

Five hundred years before Hildegard the seventh-century encyclopedist St Isidore of Seville writes that dogs are smarter than other animals, by which he means that dogs are more sociable and more socially responsible than other animals. Only dogs, he writes:

> . . . recognize their own names, know their masters, and will protect their master's house, die for their master, hunt with their master, and refuse to leave the dead body of their master. Dogs do not live separately from men.

The historical escalator could keep going. Six hundred years before Isidore, Pliny the Elder wrote in his vast *Natural History*, a work that would influence writers for almost two millennia, that dogs are 'the only animals that are sure to know their masters'; the only animals that 'will answer to their names and recognize the voices of the families; the only

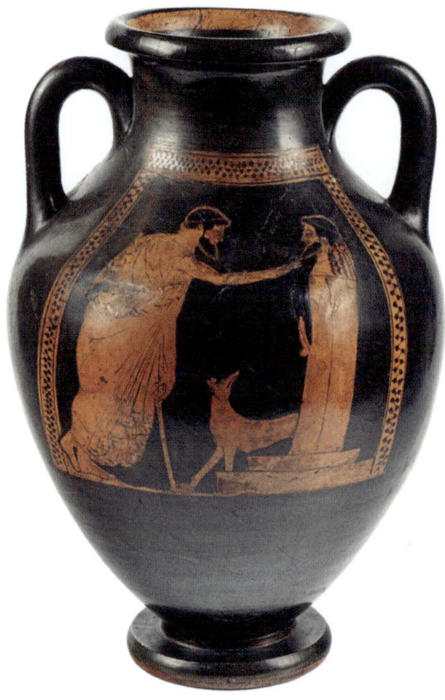

39 Man and dog look together at a monument's erect phallus on an ancient Greek vase (*c.* 500–450 BCE).

'living creature whose memory is so retentive'. And a thousand years before that there were the dogs of the Sumerians of Mesopotamia.[28]

In 1962 the most influential French anthropologist of his generation, Claude Lévi-Strauss, said that 'animals are not just good to eat, they are good to think' ('*Les animaux sont bons à penser*') – usually translated as 'good to think with'.[29] Dogs beginning in Western antiquity, through the work of Charles Darwin in the nineteenth century, and well into the most abstruse twentieth-century debates about humanism and post-humanism, have been good to think with about the nature and boundaries of human reason and intention. Still today, evolutionary cognition studies are dominated, rightly or wrongly, by research on dogs because of the belief that the specific skills of the dog mirror in their development these skills in human infants.

We humans have long thought that we could understand dog gestural language and they ours. Greek kraters of the fifth and sixth centuries BCE already show a sophisticated appropriation by artists of canine ways of expressing themselves in relation to human gestures and non-verbal communications.[30] The dog on the vase in **39**, for example, has passed the ithyphallic herm – a flat statue with head, perhaps torso and genitals, in this case four sided and sacred to the god Hermes; it looks back over its shoulder, a common canine visual gesture, at the erect phallus; his master looks with him. It is for both an arresting sight. If this were a short video, he would then look back at his master.

The question whether, and in what respects, a dog's ability to reason is human-like and culturally developed rather than pure instinct was posed by Stoic philosophers in the third century BCE very near the beginning of the debate about the nature of reason generally, and it is still around today. Recently of course the intelligence of whales, porpoises, octopuses, birds, and lots of other animals and even plants have come into focus as the nature of intelligence itself has come under scrutiny and the naturalistic tradition dedicated to setting human intelligence and culture apart from that of animals has lost much of its urgency. But for a very long time the dog was the limit case. When Wittgenstein, for example, is thinking about the human capacity to dissemble – to pretend – which requires reason, he asks 'Why can't a dog simulate pain? Is he too honest? Could one teach a dog to simulate pain?' In this meditation another animal name could not possibly be substituted for *canis familiaris*.[31]

It was the Greek Stoic philosopher Chrysippus (279–c. 206 BCE) who first proposed what he regarded as a telling thought experiment. Imagine, Chrysippus says, as he assumes any educated gentleman could, that a hunting dog comes to a three-way junction. It sniffs the first path, finds no scent of rabbit, and moves on quickly to the second. There it again sniffs, finds no scent and moves to the third. But once there it runs down that path without stopping to sniff. The dog seems to have solved what is known as Aristotle's fifth disjunctive syllogism, which would be formally described as 'if not p, and not q, then r; not p, not q, therefore r.' (Everyone who commented on this thought experiment over the next two thousand years assumed that the dog would do as it claimed. I have no evidence that this was ever tested.)[32]

In the context of the Stoic doctrine that only humans have *logos* – the capacity to make an argument, to reason – the story is usually interpreted as a sort of *reductio ad absurdum*: of course, dogs can't do logic. But if not by logic, then how are they doing it? The question was asked repeatedly over the ages. Fifteen hundred years after Chrysippus, St Thomas Aquinas, for example, acknowledged that the dog finds the rabbit through cognition of a sort but not through rational inference.

A strong counter-tradition holds that what dogs are doing is, in fact, roughly equivalent to what humans would do at the crossroads of a hunt, and hence intelligible to hunters and to humans more generally. The second-century CE philosopher Sextus Empiricus, in the tradition of philosophical scepticism that goes back to Pyrrho in the third century BCE which questioned the rationality of belief itself, turned the Stoic example on its head: humans had no special claim on reason, in any case on reason that can give definitive answers to problems of importance. In many cases animals are better than we are at solving problems. (It is through Sextus's refutation that we have Chrysippus's argument.)

The Christian father of the Church St Basil the Great (329–379 CE) appropriates Chrysippus's dog to make a case for the ethical treatment of animals and argues that while humans and dogs may have different ways of solving problems, they are mutually intelligible:

> Whereas the wise of our world may spend a lifetime of laborious meditation on the making of syllogisms, dogs manage to clear up such problems naturally. Pursuing his quarry and finding that the tracks part in different directions, the dog examines the tracks, and with little trouble he works out his syllogistic reasoning.[33]

When the great essayist and sceptical philosopher Michel de Montaigne (1533–92) thinks about what mental worlds we have in common with animals he puzzles over his cat. 'When I am playing with my cat, how do I know she is not playing with me?' he asks: a case of epistemological alterity. But when he thinks he knows what animals think, he turns to the dog. He describes the purposive behaviour of dogs and how we can interpret their inner states in relation to ours. And again, he invokes the philosopher's favourite canine: Chrysippus's dog. Having not found his scent on either of two possible paths he 'infallibly' takes the third, assured by 'inference and reasoning' and having no reason therefore to 'any longer use his sense of smell'.[34]

Montaigne gives an example from real life of canine inference. He reports that he has seen a dog leading a blind man 'along a town ditch leave a smooth path and take a worse one to keep his master away from the ditch'. Other dogs he had observed with the blind nudging their masters to 'avoid being hit by coaches and carts, even when for their part they have enough room to pass'. How, he asks, could a dog know that he is responsible for his sightless master and ignore his own comfort? And how, Montaigne asks, could he know a road is broad enough for him to pass but not broad enough for a blind man without 'reasoning and understanding'?

Montaigne's swerve from writing about the logical abilities of Chrysippus's dog to writing about a dog seeing for the blind is an example of the most literal account of the dog's gaze, one that is mirrored in a long visual tradition of dogs leading the blind (chapter 4). It is a tradition based on the belief that a dog sees and judges more or less as we do; that the dog is making its way through a world that is intelligible to it, as it is to us, by sight.[35]

In 1615, James I ordered a disputation at Cambridge about Chrysippus's dog. Lots of classical references were traded back and forth in a spirited and good-humoured debate. At one point the king himself intervened, based, as were Montaigne's views, on personal observation. He sided with the team that maintained that dogs think and judge more or less as humans do. The report of His Majesty's views is as follows:

> I had myself (said he [the king]) a dog that, straggling far from all his fellows, had light upon a very fresh scent, but considering he was all alone, and had none to second and assist him in it, observes the place and goes away to his fellows, and by such yelling arguments as they best understand, prevailed, with a party of them to goe along with him, and, bringing them to the place, pursued it to an open view.

How, James asked, could the dogs have done that without 'the exercise of understanding'? The moderator could not have done better himself and therefore should think more highly of his dogs. Or less of himself.[36] The other side retorted that the king's dogs were special but lost the disputation anyway.

David Hume, the eighteenth-century sceptical philosopher, takes ancient arguments one step further. He is committed to the claim that humans and animals basically share an epistemology: central to cognition is not language but mental images. Again, with the dog as the prime example, he concludes that:

> ... no truth appears to me more evident, than that beasts are endow'd with thought and reason as well as men. The arguments are in this case so obvious, that they never escape the most stupid and ignorant.[37]

Hume's near contemporary philosophical adversary Immanuel Kant makes a sharp distinction between human and animal rationality: animals have no self-consciousness, no capacity to make judgements, and in general no concepts, i.e. they lack 'the higher cognitive faculties'. But even for him the dog is the liminal case: dogs, he says, 'seem to be the most perfect animal, and to manifest most strongly the analogue of rationality'.[38] We do not have to engage in the long debate about what constitutes thought or the relative importance of images and language in cognition. The important point is that the dog – and specifically the dog hunting – is its protagonist: the metonymic thinker whose thinking is a version of ours.

The visual arts illustrate the point in influential and widely translated books. Some editions of Cesare Ripa's *Iconologia* (1555–62) explain one of the ways a dog can be allegorically significant by citing Sextus Empiricus as his authority for the claim that an artist wanting to represent 'investigation' should have 'a dog nosing around for prey'. Others suggest that

40-41 Ripa's *Investigatione* (*left*) and *Spia* (*right*); both are accompanied by a sniffing dog (1618).

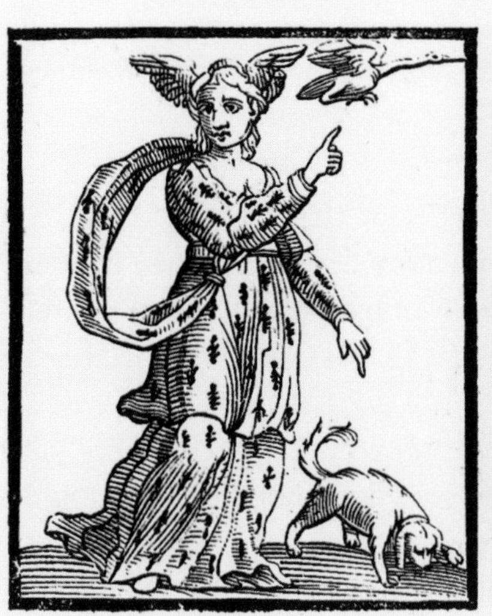

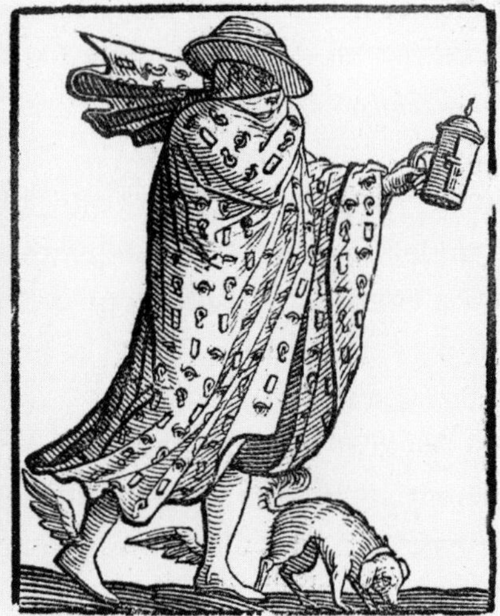

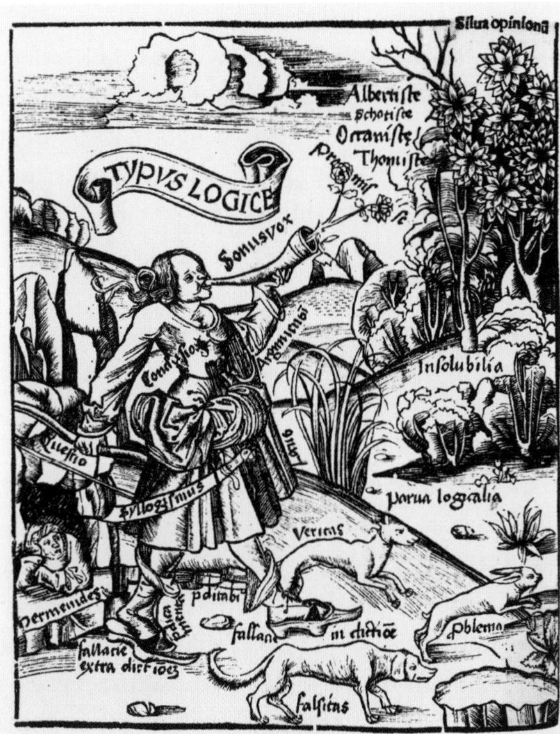

42 Gregor Reisch's engraving of Logic as a hunter (1503).

a spy, cloaked by a cape decorated with eyes and ears and tongue, might do well with a dog when in pursuit of information [**40-41**]. Ripa was appropriating an older tradition in which the hunt is an allegory for the search for truth and for knowledge more generally. Dogs – allegorical dogs – figure by leading the hunter in his pursuit. Medieval Christian images show Gabriel, for example, as a hunter with her horn and spear following four dogs with Truth closest to the viewer in the foreground.[39] The monk Gregor Reisch's *Margarita Philosophica* (*Philosophical Pearl*), published in 1503, reprinted at least eleven times in the sixteenth century, was one of the first great Renaissance compendia of knowledge and a standard university textbook [**42**]. Reisch represents 'Types of Logic' as a hunter whose dog 'Truth' ('Veritas') is in full chase of the rabbit 'problem' who is about to go off on a path on the far right. The dog 'falseness' is clueless. David Hume thought that 'there cannot be two passions more nearly resembling each other, than those of hunting and philosophy, whatever disproportion may at first appear betwixt them'.[40]

But of course, artists did not need this sort of philosophical guidance. They are thinkers too and, like Chrysippus's dog, think in images. They think about formal, affective, and philosophical questions: how to narrate a story, how to connect the elements of a picture, how to direct a viewer's attention, how to shape emotional responses, how to render arguments into pictures, how to think like – or minimally with – a dog as well.

The Primal Scene

Why, 40,000–50,000 years ago, did humans begin to make art? Or why did we as a species need to make visual representations in the first place? No one has a coherent theory of how to interpret Palaeolithic or Neolithic art. But we do know that more than 9,000 years ago – maybe even longer ago than that – early Holocene people carved the very first images we have of our species doing something in co-operation with, rather than to, another animal on massive rock panels around Shuwaymis, in the Ha'il region of north-west Saudi Arabia: representations of the primal scene of the hunt, the joint activity in which our relationship with dogs began tens of thousands of years before [**43**]. Across many square metres of rock are tableaus of cross-species social engagement, of the shared project of dogs and humans hunting an equid (a mammal of the horse family).[41] They seem almost to illustrate Buffon's claim that the first domesticated animal helped us subjugate the rest of nature (*see* page 74). There are a great many dogs in these images: 156 of them together with 64 humans on 52 of 273 recorded panels. They offer an astonishing window into the life of Arabian desert people before the hunt ceased being an existential pursuit and became, for the rulers of settled Neolithic communities, a ritual display of power.

They also bear testimony to a sort of Big Bang of the human imagination, a trace of the stories, lost in air, that our ancestors might have told each other by the campfire about the hunt and that now were recorded in stone. At the cost of a great deal of labour, hunters took time from gaining subsistence to represent their relationship with dogs on a hunt. There are images of ancestors of salukis, sighthounds adept at chasing small game and one of the oldest breeds, on Iranian pottery from just a little later, circa 8,000 years ago, but no humans with them. But

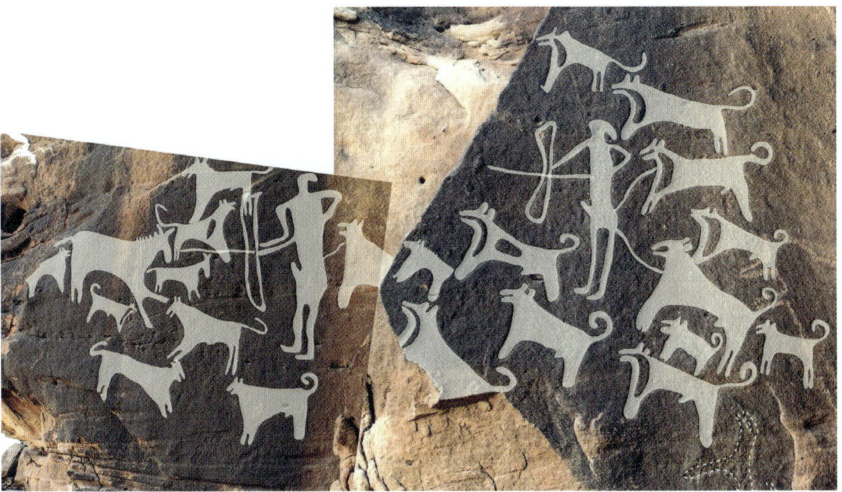

43 Petroglyphs in Saudia Arabia depicting dogs and humans hunting together c. 9000 BCE: The first images of our species doing something in co-operation with another animal.

the fact that so specialized a dog is there at all is evidence of the attention humans have given over the millennia to creating specialized hunting partners.[42]

Our interest in representing the hunt itself was far from new at the time the Arabian rock art was made. We as a species have been hunting for as long as we have existed and our ancestors have been telling stories about it in pictures beginning at least 45,000 years ago when they painted tiny bird-headed therianthropes hunting a large pig-like creature on the walls of a Sulawesi cave.[43] There is a bird-headed man being charged by a wounded bison in Lascaux from 17,000–20,000 years ago; 12,000 years ago someone painted strangely fluid figures that seem almost human (despite their cinched torsos and small round circles for heads) hunting deer-like creatures with bows and arrows in the Cova dels Cavalls (Horses Cave) between Valencia and Barcelona.

But while the examples of Arabian rock art have none of the dramatic, naturalistic detail of the paintings in the Chauvet or Lascaux caves, or the strangeness of the Sulawesi or Spanish rock art, they also lack their irresolvable mystery. The hunters are unmistakably human, the dogs are unmistakably modern dogs – curly tails, relatively short noses that comes with domestication, and resemblance to the modern Canaan dog – and it is perfectly clear what they are doing. These panels constitute a short

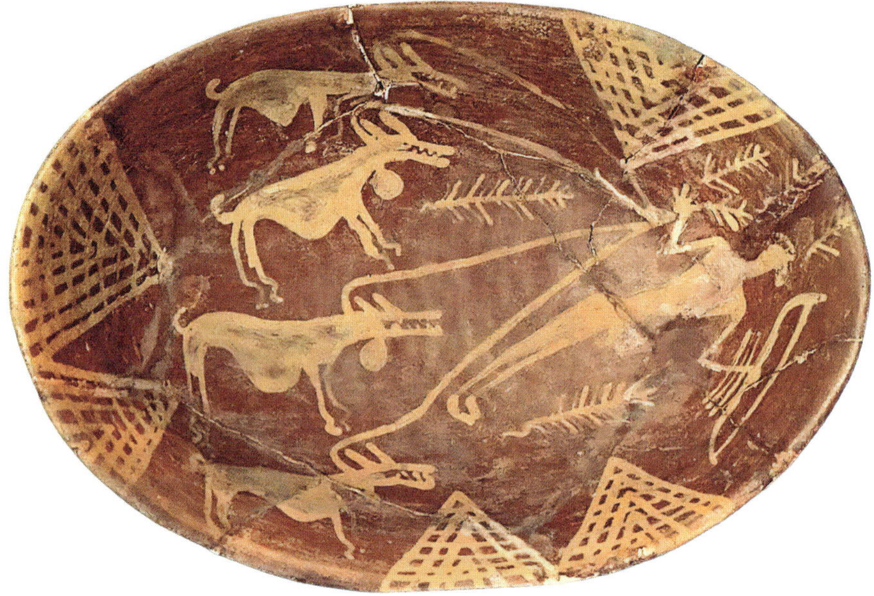

44 This Egyptian dish shows we have been training dogs on leads for at least six thousand years.

answer as to how the dog got into art with us: this is how one might react pointing at them. The dog and the human on the hunt stand at the beginning of an extraordinarily generative representational tradition.

We don't know if the lines between the man and some of the dogs represent leads or a way of suggesting a more abstract connection. Two thousand years later a pre-dynastic Egyptian pottery dish suggests that by then at least dogs were being trained to hunt on-lead [**44**]. But the dogs depicted in the Shuwaymis' hunting party already knew what they were doing. Most are pointing in the same direction as the hunter, but four or five are working on their own corralling what is probably a wild ass: proto-herding for the purpose of hunting. On another panel the dogs seem to be making eye contact with one another as their wolf ancestors might have done on the hunt and as they would do with humans in life and art for the next 10,000 years. The dogs on the lower left edge may even be looking at their master, the first example of the dog's gaze in art history.

For a very long time dogs were not only the first domesticated animal but also the only one whose engagement with our species seemed to capture the visual imagination. Horses were domesticated around 5500 BCE, initially for meat and milk; people may have started riding them by 3000 BCE. But the earliest representation of a man on a horse was not until a thousand years later, circa 2000 BCE.[44] There is even more of a gap between the earliest possible date for the domestication of cats. Possibly, based on genetic evidence that happened as long ago as 10,000 BCE, but it left no morphological evidence for another 3,000 years. Not until around 2000 BCE did anyone notice them in art.[45]

A naturalistic artistic tradition represents what is out there in the world. But more importantly it represents what makers of images take to be important to render into art. There were of course other forms of joint activities, of sociability between humans and dogs: guarding; herding; walking together; hanging out where we live; doing with us what we do. There are other imagined relationships: dogs as guardians of the dead and as psychopomps, guides for the souls of the departed. All these relationships are ancient, born of the deep time of the dog, and we can find ancient visual representations of all of them. They also found their way into mythology, which was one of the major sources of Western art until the eighteenth century.

But hunting and its place in mythology has a special status. It was always the primal techne, a skill of existential importance. After the Neolithic revolution, hunting in western Asia and Europe became less important for subsistence and more important as a ritual – an almost entirely male elite ritual of mythic proportions upon which an extravagant amount of knowledge, resources, and energy were expended. Of course, hunting continued into modern times as a source of food for those below the elite. But it became for them, as the Italian writer Roberto Calasso suggests, an 'art for art's sake'. They did not need the meat. At the boundary between the wild and the civilized and between the human and the non-human, hunting became a religious rite, a re-enactment of the existential struggle that the hunt had once been (and would remain in hunter-gatherer societies and frontier regions). Here again, dog and human mark together the border between nature and culture through a shared pursuit.

We could trace a continuous tradition from Arabian rock art through Assyrian ritual lion hunts to the art of classical antiquity and on to the traditions grounded in it. Start circa 1000 BCE with a violent goddess: Artemis, the Roman Diana, older twin sister of Apollo, born of Leto, one of the Titans, and one of the most important gods of the ancient pantheon. (There were versions of her in other mythic traditions – Celtic,

Norse, as well as Mesopotamian from which the Greek stories sprang.) She was most famous as the goddess of the hunt, but Artemis more generally was 'the goddess of transitions', the 'goddess who presides over changes of being', who 'mediates between the savage world of wild animals and the tool-making world of humans'; between wildness and civilization more generally. Childbirth, understood by the Greeks as existing firmly in the sphere of nature, was one of her purviews. Wild herself; a hunter of stags; a vengeful destroyer of humans. (One might think of how much of Greek tragedy is about taming the wildness of women.) At the same time Artemis was the most chaste of the goddesses and spent a great deal of time lounging about naked, out of sight of gods and man, with her nymphs and her dogs.[46]

It is as the goddess of the in-between, of transitions, that Artemis comes to be the most prominent goddess of the art of the hunt. With her come her dogs, liminal creatures joined with her time out of mind and in many places and guises. 'Hunting and dogs were contrived by Apollo and Artemis,' wrote the late fifth-century general and philosopher Xenophon (c. 430–355 BCE) at the beginning of his book *Hunting with Dogs – Cynegeticus (Κυνηγετικός)*. (The verb 'contrived', *Εὕρημα/ heúrema* – as in Archimedes' *'Eurēka'* – has the sense of 'discovered not by chance but by thought'.) The twin gods in turn 'gave them [the dogs] to Chiron as a reward for his virtue'. Xenophon goes on to explain that Chiron was the brother of Zeus and that his list of pupils includes a whole cast of mythic figures in whose stories dogs figure prominently: Cephalus, whose magic hunting dog Laelaps always caught his prey and who would end up killing his wife Procris in a hunting accident; Asklepios, the demi-god of medicine often portrayed with his dog; Meleager of Calydonian boar-hunt fame who is almost always represented with his hunting dogs; Odysseus wept when his once swift hunting dog Argos, who had waited for him until he was so old he could scarcely move, was the only creature to recognize him when he returned to Ithaca; Aeneas and Achilles, both of whom were favoured by the gods in their time and who had begun their education in learning about dogs and the hunt. (Xenophon does not mention that the great hunter, the ill-fated Actaeon, was also a pupil of Chiron's but was not favoured by the gods.)[47] Artemis was the goddess who caused the death of Orion, a figure who dates back to Hesiod and Homer, and who

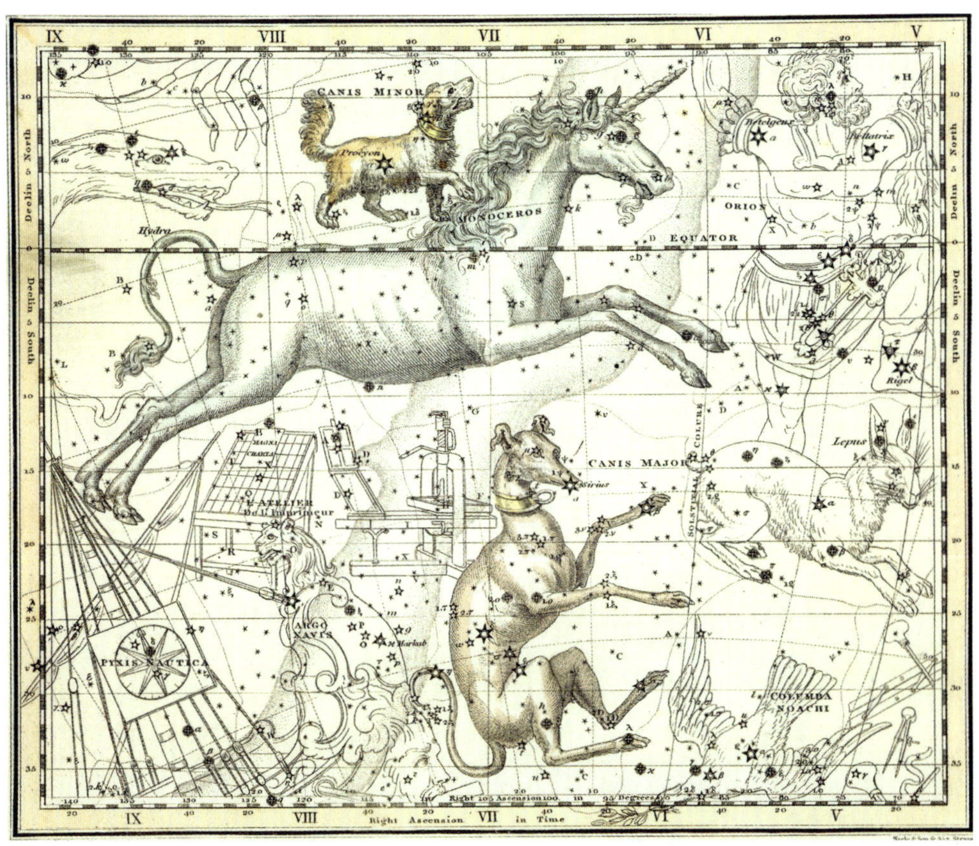

45 Orion, Canis major, Canis minor and Monoceros in Alexander Jamieson's *A Celestial Atlas* (1822).

ended up as a constellation in the heavens with his dogs, Canis major and Canis minor [**45**]. We know many of the dogs' names; Procyon is the brightest star in Canis minor.

On the Hunt

Out of this mythic history evolved a museum's worth of paintings, engravings, and statues of Artemis/Diana and one or more of her dogs. The dog's role in her representations is both pictorial as well as iconographical. In a Roman copy of a Greek statue [**46**], one of many possible examples that also find echoes of related goddesses in other pagan traditions, we would probably recognize Artemis in her accustomed tunic (although it is covered by a gown here); she is armed for the hunt with a bow and arrow (sometimes it's a spear); a crescent moon emphasizes her syncretism with Luna and

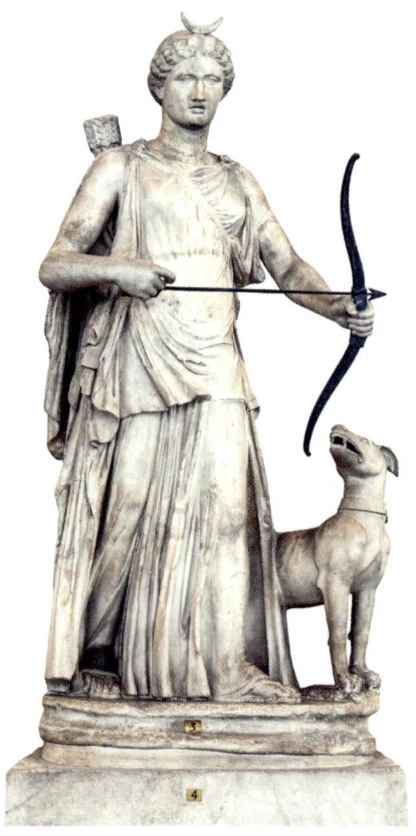

46 A tunic, bow and arrow, crescent moon and hunting dog: the symbols of Artemis represented in a Roman copy of a fourth-century BCE Greek statue.

hence women's cycles of fertility. A dog is almost always with her, and in this statue it is almost supernumerary as an identifying sign. But it is doing the formal work of looking up at her as she looks out at the world; they are joined. In an engraving after Parmigianino [**47**] she bears a spear and she holds her dogs on-lead as they surge forward in the chase, a primal conjunction of hunter and dog, an emotional as well as formal nexus. A dog off-lead seems almost to block her way as it looks back at a rustic shelter; perhaps the quarry has hidden there.

In a painting by Rubens and Jan Bruegel the Elder [**48**], Artemis, preparing for the hunt in her red tunic and crowned by the crescent moon, is surrounded by her nymphs on the left and balanced on the right by a finely differentiated pack of dogs. Bruegel had done preliminary dog studies to achieve the desired effect. The dog in the middle of the painting is looking up at her, and in the opposite direction of the nymph next to him blowing a hunting horn and the other nymph pointing in the

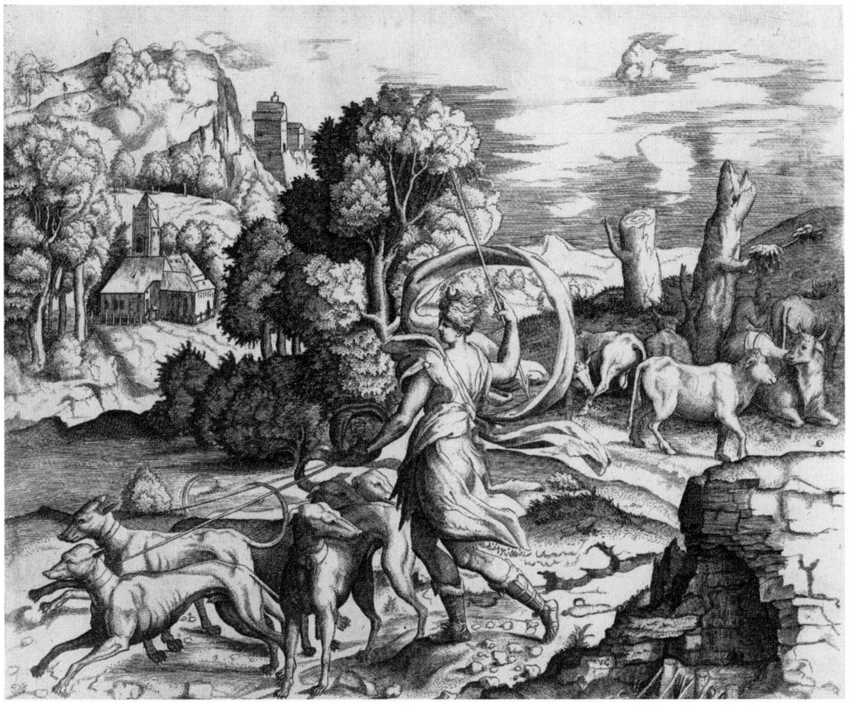

47 An emotional and formal nexus of hunter and dog in an engraving of *Diana the Huntress* (1530–42) by Vincenzo Caccianemici after Parmigianino.

direction of the chase. It is a 'can't we get going' look. (Diana will be a prototype for the art of women and hunting in the modern period.)

The classical mythological image of Artemis/Diana and her dogs was appropriated in the Renaissance for, among other things, a particular political aesthetic: she became closely associated with representations of Renaissance French kingship in the sixteenth century. The French royal house had already for centuries been associated with Diana and the hunt. Fontainebleau, the site of a medieval hunting lodge where Francis I built his magnificent palace, took its name, so it was said, from a lost hunting dog named Bleau who came upon a nymph, a Diana stand-in, resting by a clear stream: Bleau's fountain [**49**]. The brown dog is drinking from its waters while the white one nuzzles her. The three nude figures on each pedestal are allusions to the many-breasted ancient Diana of Ephesus, goddess of the hunt, of plenty, and of fertility.[48]

Diana became the alter ego – perhaps allegorical representation is a better term – for Diane de Poitiers, the mistress of Francis I's successor,

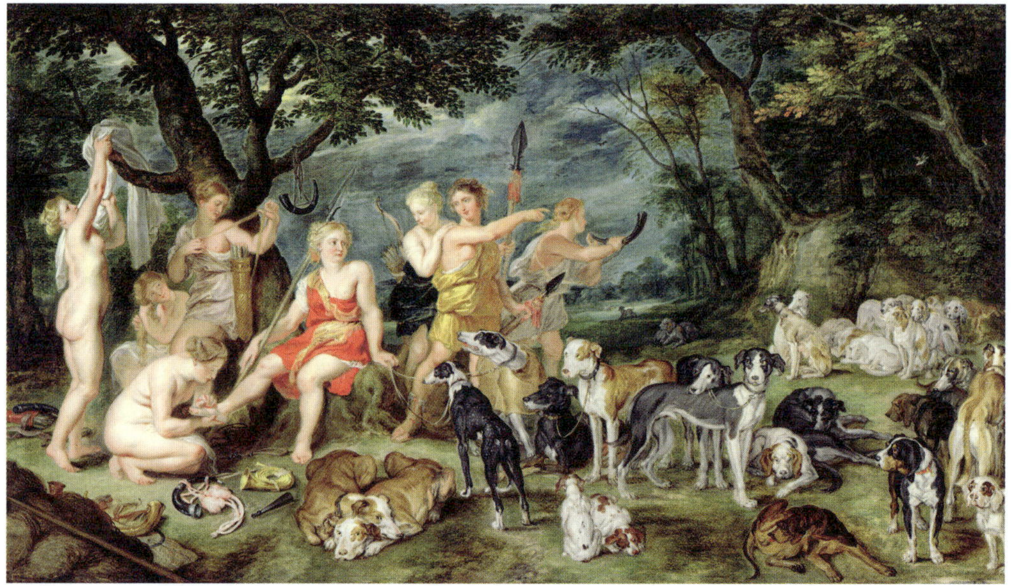

48 'Can't we get going': *Diana and her Nymphs Leaving for the Hunt* (1623–4) by Rubens and Jan Bruegel the Elder.

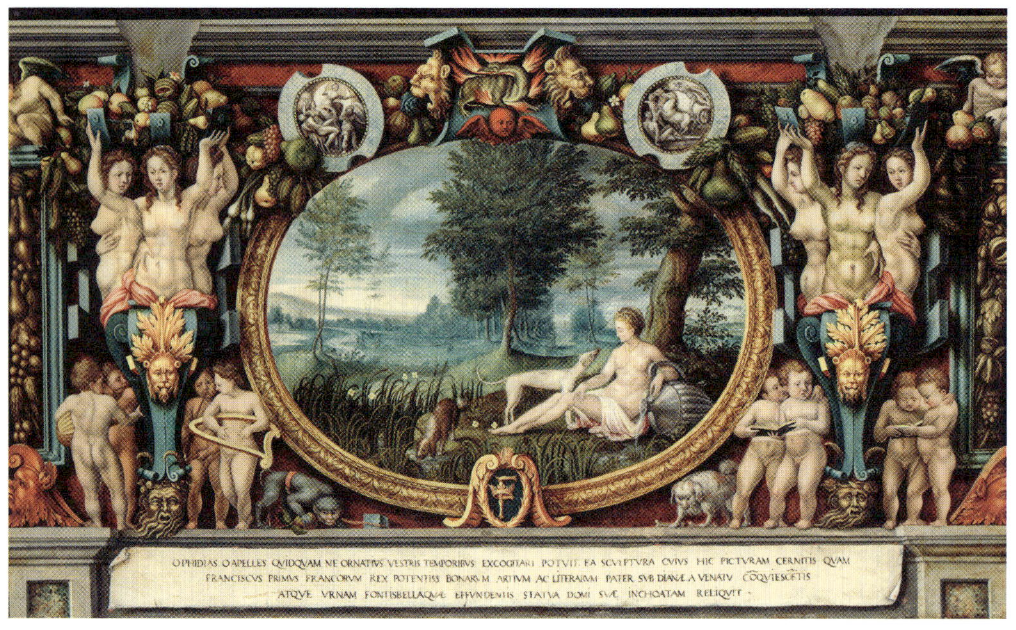

49 *The Nymph of Fontainebleau* (Anon., late sixteenth century). Fontainebleau is named after Bleau, a lost hunting dog, who chanced upon a nymph resting by a clear stream.

Henry II. She and her dogs are everywhere in the palace and its gardens as well as in widely circulated images: paintings and plates and statues. Gone to the Louvre is the most famous of the Fontainebleau paintings: Diane the Mistress as Diana the Huntress and her dog [**50**]. He bounds forward in the direction they are headed, sweeping us off the image, looking toward the chase. She, an arrow in one hand, a bow in the other, and a full quiver over her shoulder, looks back coyly, lingers and beckons us along. Gone to the Louvre as well is Benvenuto Cellini's famous bronze relief, *Nymph of Fontainebleau*, with boars on the left and a stag in the middle looking over Diane as she bends her head to her left and looks over at the dogs, her companions and work mates, in the right corner.[49]

Artemis/Diana also figures in three mythological hunts that have engaged artists from antiquity to modern times. First, the gender-bending story of the alliance of Meleager and Atalanta, joined by a reunion of some of Jason's other Argonauts in the successful hunt for Calydonian Boar. Second, the story of the beautiful but ill-fated hunter Adonis who, urged on by his dogs, left Venus' embraces to hunt boar and died in the chase. In paintings of these two subjects Artemis is at work indirectly, in the narrative background that viewers will have known. Her direct violent encounter with the hunter Actaeon, whom she turned into a deer and who was then attacked and torn apart by his own dogs, was the subject of art – and a great deal of literature as well – in antiquity and in the millennia that followed. It inspired some of the most celebrated paintings of the Renaissance.

Atalanta and Meleager: King Oeneus, who had learned how to make wine from Dionysus, failed to honour Artemis with an invitation to a feast to which he had invited the other gods. The wild, chaste, and vengeful goddess made known her displeasure by sending a giant boar, one of the great monsters of Greek mythology, who uprooted vines and generally terrorized the countryside around Calydon. Meleager, the king's son, gathered a crowd of male heroes to hunt down the monster: the Argonauts – and one female hero, Atalanta (from the Greek word '*atalantos*' = equal in weight, equivalent). She was a mortal Artemis, abandoned by her father, suckled by a bear, found by hunters who had raised her. Atalanta became a great hunter herself, a virgin sworn to chastity who at the goddess' behest killed with her bow two centaurs – Roescus and Hylaios – who had tried to rape her. The so-called Calydonian hunt for the giant boar was

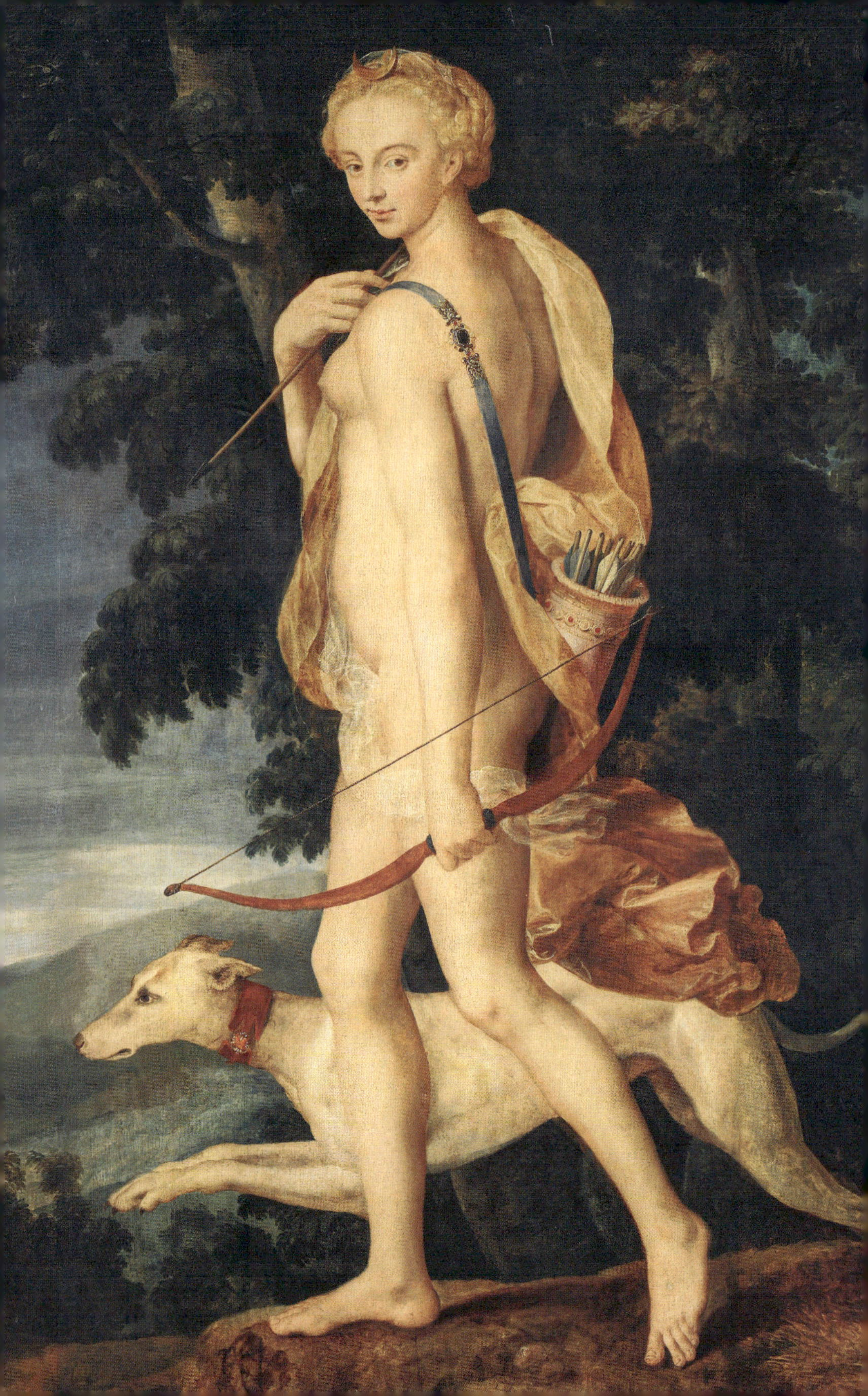

one of the most famous gatherings of heroes in Greek mythology. Atalanta's arrow was said to have inflicted the mortal wound to the boar; Meleager gave her the beast's hide as reward; his uncles were jealous and stole it; he killed them; and then his mother contrived his death for having killed her brothers. Atalanta went on to other adventures.

The hunt story and the relationship between the two main protagonists and their dogs have been a subject of art since at least the sixth century BCE. In the oldest of these from one of the most important kraters of early Greek art, parallel dogs alternate with the heroes [**51**]. One walks beside Atalanta, her dog; a second, next to Meleager, lies defeated on its back with his head just under that of her dog's nose. They are inverse images of one another. Both are named – Òrmenos (*ὄρμενος* or ὅρμενος = to stalk) wounded on the ground, and Méthepon (from the imperfect of the verb *μεθέπω* = to pursue). (A third dog, along with another hero, attacks from the rear but isn't shown.) Five hundred years later, Atalanta, Meleager, and their dogs were represented on a fresco in Pompeii; two centuries later their story is carved on a magnificent sarcophagus.

There are scores of versions by the artists of the Renaissance and their successors: Jacopo Archangelo in the fifteenth century; Battista Dossi in the sixteenth century; Poussin painted a spectacular version in the seventeenth century, among many more artists including painters of the Dutch Golden Age. Rubens especially was fascinated by the story of Atalanta and Meleager and painted many versions. In the one shown here [**52**], dogs thrust forward parallel to the heroes at the level of the ground: one surges onto the scene from the left, his snout touching Atalanta's tunic; a second is behind Meleager; ahead are two others attacking the boar; on the other side another has sunk his teeth into his prey. One is dead at the left foot of the boar mirroring the dead hero. The terrified horses bear witness to the violence of the scene but play no part. The dogs, on the other hand, are creatures of the primal hunt, descendants of those who first made league with our species thousands of generations ago. It is a picture not only of canine gaze and of the transformation of myth into art but exemplary also of a whole genre of pictures of the hunt that pits the human's animal – the domesticated animal – against animals

50 Diane de Poitiers, the mistress of Henry II, here rendered as *Diana the Huntress* (c. 1550) by Charles Carmoy.

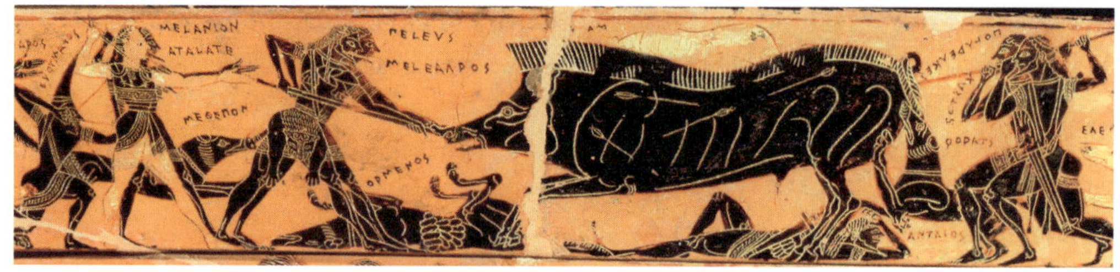

51 Detail from the François Vase (*c.* 570 BCE) by Kleitias, showing Atalanta and Meleager hunting the Calydonian Boar. The heroes alternate with their dogs in the composition.

in the wild. They are joined in an existential battle, a reprise of how it was in the beginning.

A second mythic hunt that involves Artemis, although again indirectly, brought dogs into art: the hunt of Adonis, who leaves the arms of Venus/Aphrodite to go in fatal pursuit of a boar. The goddess of the hunt managed to have him killed either because he had claimed to be as great a hunter as she or as a way of getting back at Aphrodite, who had killed Hippolytus because he had rejected her in favour of chastity. The story begins innocently enough. Having been wounded by Cupid and fallen in love with the beautiful Adonis, Venus in Ovid's account 'holds him, and is his companion . . . she roams mountain ridges, and forests, and thorny cliff-sides, her clothing caught up to the knee, like Diana and she cheers on the hounds, chasing things safe to hunt, hares flying headlong, stags with deep horns'.[50]

But Adonis and his hounds will give chase to more dangerous prey. Titian represents the lovers on the cusp of disaster [**53**] in one of his so-called 'Poésie Series' for Philip II of Spain, six completed canvases in addition to the one unfinished one, which in their emotional and expressive appeal were meant to be the visual equivalent of poetry. Venus' breathtakingly painted back is visual poetry of the highest order. The pioneer of abstract expressionism Willem de Kooning once said that 'flesh was the reason why oil painting was invented'. He might have had this Venus in mind when he added 'Never before in history had it taken such a place in painting.'[51] It is an emotionally charged pose. Her left foot is pushing her around – clockwise – so that her head might end up pressed on Adonis' right shoulder, turning around to embrace him and keep him with her. She fears what she knows is his fate. Her back glows

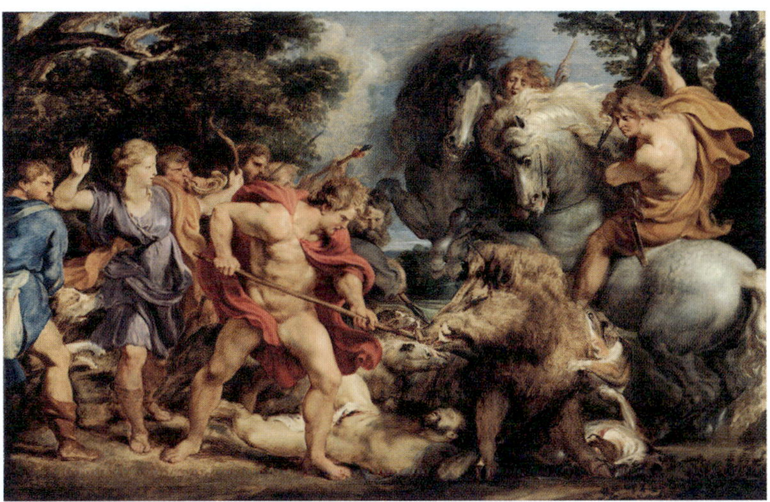

52 The dog's gaze bisects Rubens' *The Calydonian Boar Hunt* (1615) on the diagonal axis: there is calm on one side, terror on the other.

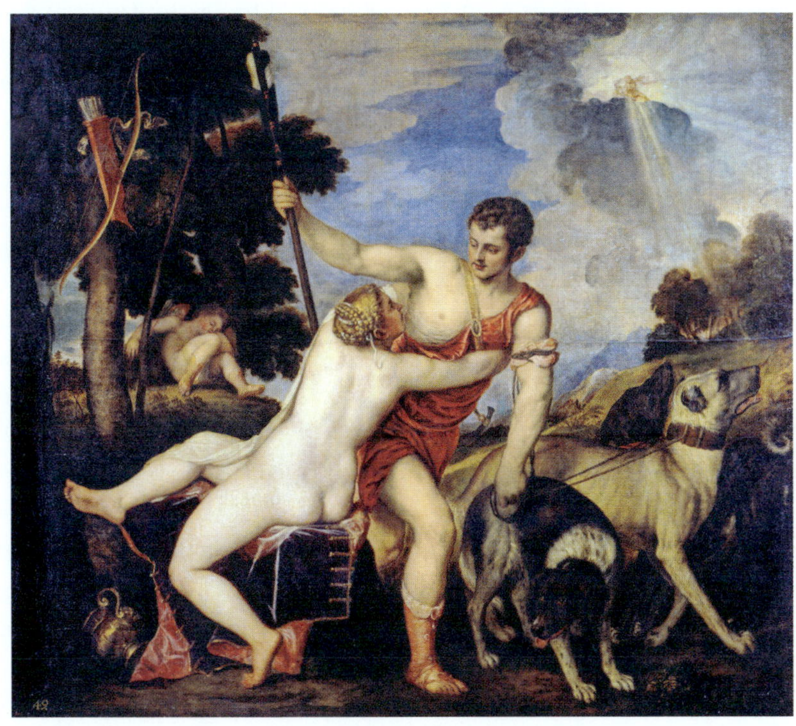

53 Adonis' dogs pull him towards his fate in Titian's *Venus and Adonis* (1554).

in the morning light. Cupid, having done his work, is asleep. The lovers have awakened; Adonis with an intense poignant look back into her eyes is leaving. It is the morning after; he has other things on his mind.

If we can take our eyes off Venus, the miraculously painted dogs direct our eyes to other matters: to the hunt and Adonis' fate. The hue of the painting moves from the glowing flesh of Venus' back to the darker hindquarters of the black dog, one of a staged pack of three painted with almost ostentatious virtuosity. One of the dogs, the one whose lead Adonis holds in his left hand, is anxious to pull him on to the hunt as if to fulfil Artemis' plan to have him killed by a boar; light falls on the exquisitely fine brushwork of hair around his collar. The dog's eyes, glistening, look to the light. The whitish tail of the dog furthest from the plane of the painting defines its right edge as if he has already left the frame but is coming back in to urge the others on to their master's fate. Almost in the middle is a dog with white-ruffled neck; we will see that dog – a studio dog – again in another of Titian's paintings. It is looking not in the direction of the hunt and the fatal denouement but out: at the painter and at us. A white spot of paint makes its nose glisten; tiny white impasto and a thin edge of red draws our attention to its eyes. The dogs' gazes are rivals for our attention as much as those of the hero and goddess; they – and their intricately intertwined bodies – translate the deep time of the hunt into the poetry of visual art.

Of course, Titian's painting and the centuries-long tradition of Venus and Adonis have at their core the passion of the goddess and her ill-fated lover. But the countervailing force is his intimacy with his dogs and their common pursuit in the hunt: an alternative passion. In Cornelis Cornelisz van Haarlem's *Venus and Adonis* [**54**] he does not seem ready to chase boar, but his affections are divided: one arm around Venus; his cupped hand, mirroring that of Venus, on the dog whose nose is delicately resting on his naked thigh. As the couple gaze into one another's eyes, the dog looks wistfully at a thirty-degree angle from theirs. His hand is nuzzling the dog's neck, a common trope of intimacy. Below is a second dog whose ear must just be touching Adonis' leg. Its eyes are unambiguously looking away from lovemaking, and directed, along with its white snout, out of the frame of the painting at us and at the artist.

Finally, there is a version of an Artemis/Diana myth in art that represents her not offstage in revenge plots or on the hunt with her own

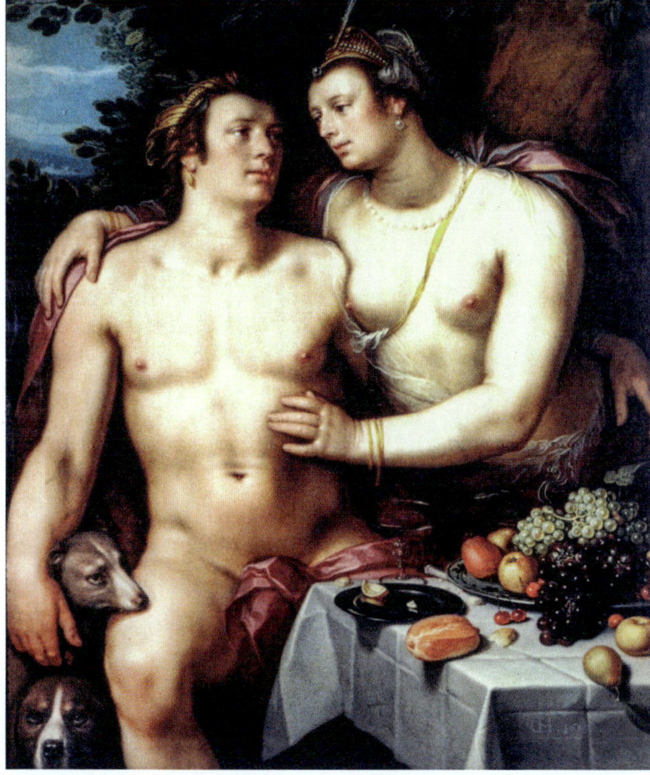

54 Cornelis Cornelisz van Haarlem's gentler version of *Venus and Adonis* (1619).

generally well-behaved hunting hounds, but in the middle of an elaborately staged punishment of a human – the hunter Actaeon – who had seen her in her nakedness. She turned him into a stag – or more precisely a human in a stag's body – which his own dogs then chased and killed. Their story has generated a library of interpretations and a gallery's worth of images that go back to archaic Greece, blossom in the Renaissance, and continue to engage artists into the modern period.[52]

The goddess turned the world upside down, a reversal of a relationship born in deep time between humans and dogs. The earliest version of the story from the sixth century BCE avoids the issue of motivation and casts Artemis, known for her violent wild streak, as Zeus' hit woman. He was angry with Actaeon for having tried to seduce Semele, Princess of Thebes, before he himself succeeded. Artemis had nothing against Actaeon personally.

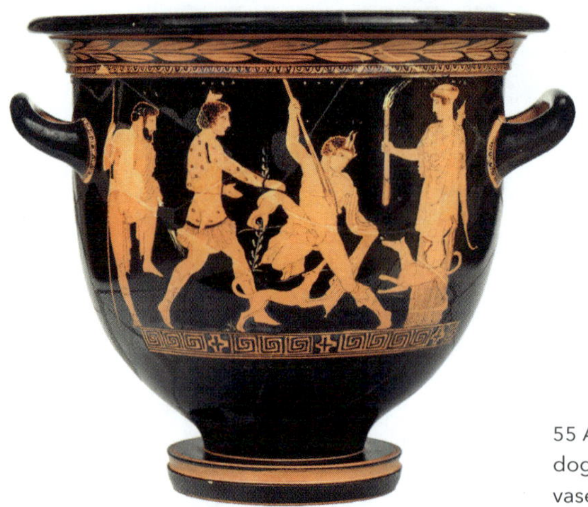

55 Actaeon mid-transformation as his dogs begin to turn on him (Greek vase, *c.* 440 BCE).

Pausanias (c. 110–c. 180 CE), the Greek traveller and geographer, weighs two versions of the story he had heard. In one Artemis cast a deer skin around Actaeon to make sure his hounds would kill him so that he could not take Semele as his wife. In the other, more common one, she, the most chaste in the godly pantheon, punished him for looking upon her in her nakedness when he stumbled upon the pool where she was bathing with her nymphs. Pausanius proposes a third interpretation. He blames the dogs indirectly although they were not really at fault. 'The hounds of Actaeon,' he thinks, 'were smitten with madness and so they were sure to tear to pieces without distinction everybody they chanced upon.' It is a version of the world-turned-upside-down story; the dogs' reason had abandoned them.[53]

Pausanias is unusual in the attention he pays specifically to the dogs, but his interpretation of their behaviour is not new. The so-called Lykoan Painter represented the madness version seven centuries earlier [**55**]. Actaeon on this red-figure krater has just begun his metamorphosis into a stag and is poised between three of his dogs, vainly trying to defend himself with his spear as his dogs move in for the kill. The scene is framed by Zeus looking on from the left and Artemis from the right. It would seem there would be no need to explain what is happening in this narrative tableau of madness; the dogs are doing what hunting dogs are supposed to do except that they do not recognize that the stag is almost entirely human; only tiny horns have begun to grow out of his head.

The key figure for the interpretation that the dogs were mad is standing in front of Zeus: the figure of 'Lussa' (*Λύσσα*) in ancient Greek, alternatively 'Lyssa', the goddess of rage – of frenzy. A rabid dog is emerging from her head; perhaps, we are led to think, the others had been figuratively born from her brain earlier. (The rabies pathogen is today classified in the genus *lyssavirus*.) But this was not a random outbreak of disease; Artemis, known for unpredictable wildness, had, through Lyssa, returned the dogs to their wild selves, back into their wolf ancestors before the primal scene of civilization.

The interpretive crux of the story has more commonly focused not on the dogs but on the human, on what Actaeon had done to so enrage the goddess: either he looked, however haplessly, upon holiness – a religious transgression – or he was a voyeur, in some versions climbing a tree to spy on the naked goddess; or he was an upstart predator who boasted of his superior prowess as a hunter and thought himself worthy of marrying the goddess; or he was a figure of unmanaged desire. Or, as an allegory, it is about what it means to be human, specifically what it means for a human to retain consciousness as a human, 'his mind has remained unchanged', in a body that was turned into 'a dumb animal'. Trapped. Speechless. In a sense, Actaeon was not turned into a deer but into a human with the body of a deer. (The French psychoanalyst Jacques Lacan makes much of Actaeon's trying to keep his dogs at bay with the words 'Actaeon ego sum' ['I am Actaeon'] that they could not hear because 'alas no voice came'. Lacan takes it as a metaphor for Freud in search of truth.)

Ovid's version of the story in *Metamorphoses* is by far the most influential of the ancient retellings of the story and offers support for all of these interpretations. (More generally Ovid was the most important source for mythological painting from the Renaissance on and this was the most painted of his stories.) The Diana and Actaeon myth, as the literary critic Leonard Barkan points out, is about 'sexuality, holiness, mirror images, and the mysteries of human identity'. Ovid spends considerable time on the dogs in relation to human identity:

> In his prosperity a grandson first [the hunter Aktaion] was source of Cadmus' [founder of Thebes and Europa's brother] sorrow, whose young brow sprouted outlandish antlers and the hounds, his hounds, were sated with their master's blood.

'His hounds', he says by way of emphasis. It is an emphasis with a long history of horror. 'The dogs destroyed their master utterly' says a fragment from Aeschylus.[54]

At the start of the tale Ovid is agnostic on the question of blame. Like Oedipus, his fellow Theban, Actaeon stumbled into tragedy:

> Though, if you ponder wisely, you will find the fault was fortune's and no guilt that day, for what guilt can it be to lose one's way?

And Ovid is open to all sorts of interpretations by way of conclusion:

> As the tale spread views varied; some believed Diana's violence unjust; some praised it, as proper to her chaste virginity. Both sides found reason for their point of view.[55]

What sets Ovid apart, in addition to his vivid description of the setting in which Actaeon found Artemis, is his extensive account of the hunt and the collapse of the ancient order of dog and man that is central to it. The setting could not be more beautiful and peaceful: the 'living limestone' into which 'she had carved a natural arch'; the 'limpid spring' that flowed lightly babbling there into a wide pool; the grassy sward where next to the pool Artemis and her nymphs were bathed by 'the water's balm', the pool from which came the water that Artemis splashed onto Actaeon to turn him into a silenced stag.

The solitary young hunter, tired and hot, has left his friends and wandered into this idyllic scene. It was there that his hounds would turn on him. Over fifty dogs are named one by one, intimate, known companions, each with a personality: Ladon (shepherd), an ancient breed of guardians of sheep; Melampus (Blackfoot) and Ichnobates (Tracker) first 'gave tongue', that is, barked; wise Ichnobates; Cnosius (Tracker, a Cretan hound); Melampus (Blackfoot) of Spartan breed . . . ; Lycisce (Wolf) and his nimble brother Cyprius (Cyprian) . . . moody Laelaps (Storm) . . . and many more too long to tell'. Some had names of mythic fame, for example, Laelaps, the dog that Zeus gave to Europa which always gets its prey. Some had names that bespeak of ancestry; Lycisce (*Λύκος* = *Lýkos* = wolf); bold Hylaeus (Woodman), a centaur who died either at the hand of either a boar or a mythic hunter.

Ovid's account of the pursuit and killing of Actaeon is terrifying: surrounded by his dogs he gave a scream, 'a sound that no stag would make' but no human either:

> Now they are all around him, tearing deep their master's flesh, the stag that is no stag; and not until so many countless wounds had drained away his lifeblood was the wrath of Artemis satisfied.

Ovid does not say what happens to the dogs, what responsibility they might share in Actaeon's horrible death and how they might feel after the encounter. A second-century compiler of myths who clearly knew Ovid's account does. They had been driven mad and knew not what they had done:

> They say that the goddess changed him on the spot into a deer and drove his fifty hunting dogs into a frenzy so that they unintentionally ate him. When he was no more, they looked for their master with great howls and bays, coming in the course of their search to Chiron's cave. He made a likeness of Aktaion, which assuaged their grief.[56]

That is, they became dogs again – Hamlet-like dogs wracked by grief and conscience – who recognized their dead master in a portrait. Order was restored between man and dog after madness had wrought death and havoc, a regression to a time before dog and human formed their alliance. (Chiron, the wise Centaur, had been one of Actaeon's teachers.)

This cascade from the hunt in the deep time of evolution to the time of myth comes to rest in two great and exemplary paintings: Titian's *Diana and Actaeon* [**56**] and his unfinished *Death of Actaeon*. His interpretation of the Diana and Actaeon myth is quite possibly unique in that it represents the human – and his perfectly agreeable dog – before anything has happened except that they had haplessly come upon the forest pool of the goddess and her nymphs. Actaeon has entered into what looks like a stage set with a deep, illusionistic background; his hand does not quite reach the deep rich red curtain – a prop in Titian's studio that appears in other of his paintings. It seems like a stage curtain has been pulled back. Actaeon is taken aback by what he sees; he drops his bow. A tiny figure to the right of the plinth and left of the tree in the deep background suggests that Actaeon's hunting companions are safely in the world beyond, safely

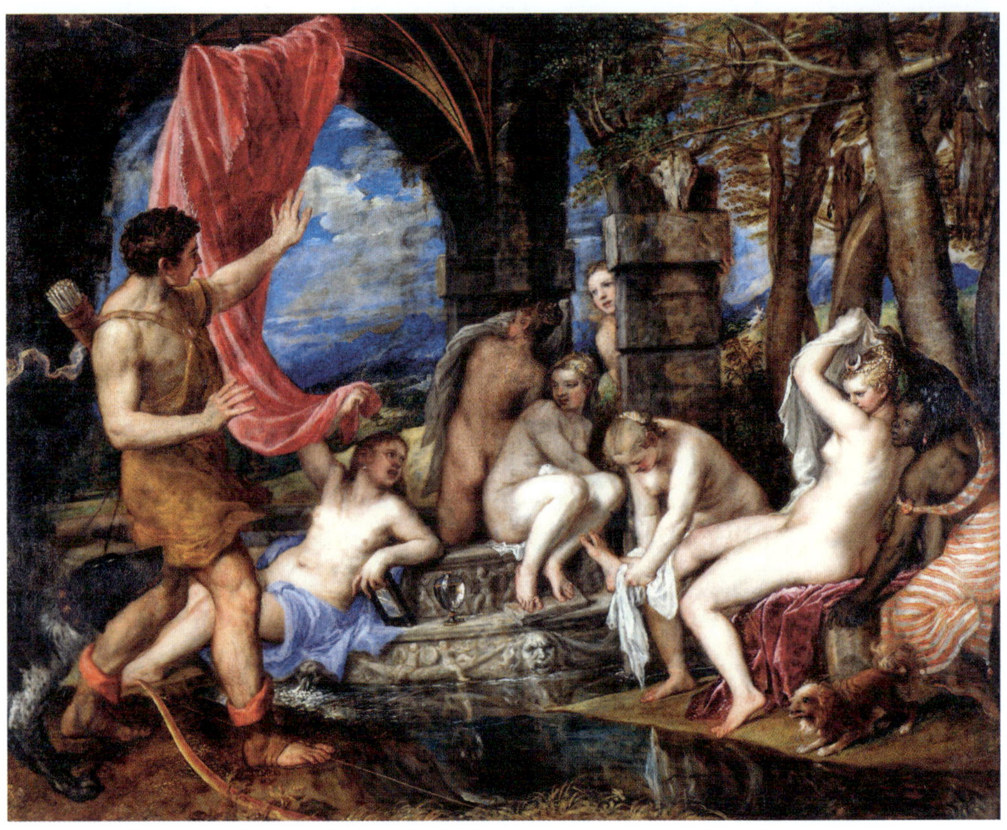

56 Actaeon stumbles upon the naked goddess in Titian's *Diana and Actaeon* (1556–9).

outside the goddess' grotto. It is not clear whether Actaeon has even seen the goddess; his eyes engage the nymph hiding modestly behind the column. Only the deer skull on the column foretells Actaeon's fate.

Nearest the bottom edge of the frame of the painting, defining its left edge and the beginning of the action, is the dog entering the frame; just one paw in. Two leads – Actaeon has dropped them – suggest there is a companion following. The dog seems to know it has stumbled into the wrong place, as much or as little the voyeur as its master: 'Sorry . . . sorry' or 'Who are you?' It has caught sight of something unfamiliar. Actaeon has already stepped onto the fateful stage; the dog is *in media res*, the creature to whom the scene unfolds almost cinematically. If anyone sees Diana it is the dog. Its head is raised in a gesture of attention, perhaps in response to the barks of Diana's lapdog, yapping at the opposite edge of the painting, who seems to be the first creature to notice the intrusion.

Rembrandt's *Diana Bathing with her Nymphs with Actaeon and Callisto* has two subjects linked by a Diana who reacts violently to a lapse of chastity in two quite different cases [**57**]. The first is represented by the brightly lit group of nymphs cascading diagonally down from where the goddess has just discovered Callisto's state – she had become pregnant through sex with Zeus in disguise – and is about to banish her for breaking her vow of chastity. Further down, halfway across the horizontal axis and near the end of the cascade of nymphs begins the Actaeon part of the story among a second group of nymphs. A dog in their midst crouching down recognizes the intruder who has already begun his transformation into a deer. Two of the dogs – those in shadows above the last of the brightly lit nymphs – are playfully fighting with each other. The five around the hunter are caught just seconds before the recognition that their master the hunter is a deer. Two are still wrestling with each other, but the one with its jaws open and Actaeon with eyes lit in terror: this is the moment in the story where Titian's *Death of Actaeon* begins.

The seventh, unfinished, painting of the 'Poésie Series' – *The Death of Actaeon* [**58**] – that Titian had promised to Philip II was found in his studio after he died. He used canvas from the same bolt as the other six delivered pictures and may or may not have worked on it at the same time. It is as terrifying as the finished *Diana and Actaeon* is mysterious.[57] There are patches of light in the clouds and, rendered in white impasto, light reflecting off the churning waters of the stream. The same bright light illuminates the face of the central figure – Diana – and her right foot as

57 Detail from Rembrandt's *Diana Bathing with her Nymphs with Actaeon and Callisto* (1634).

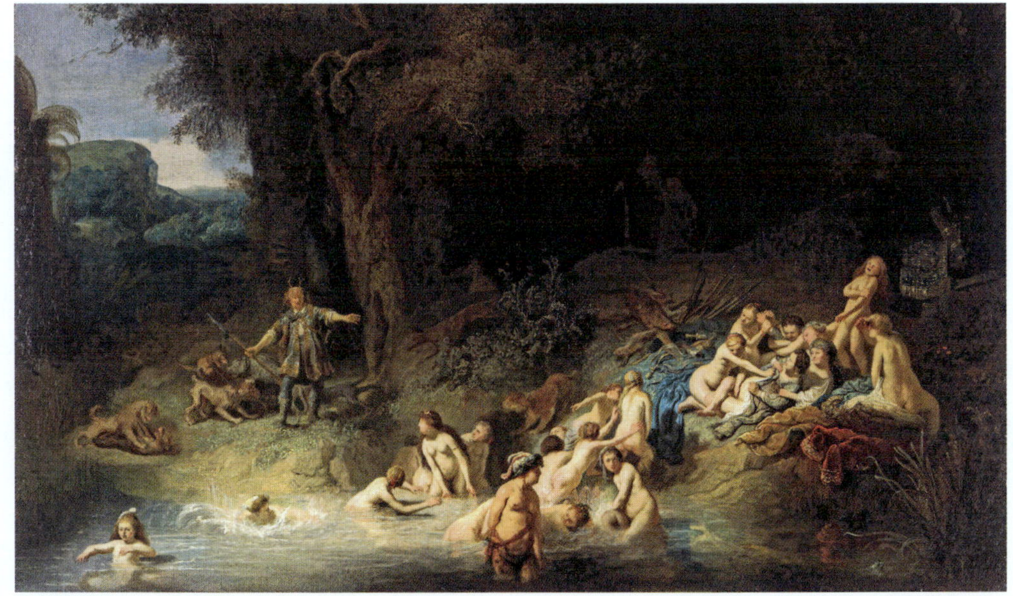

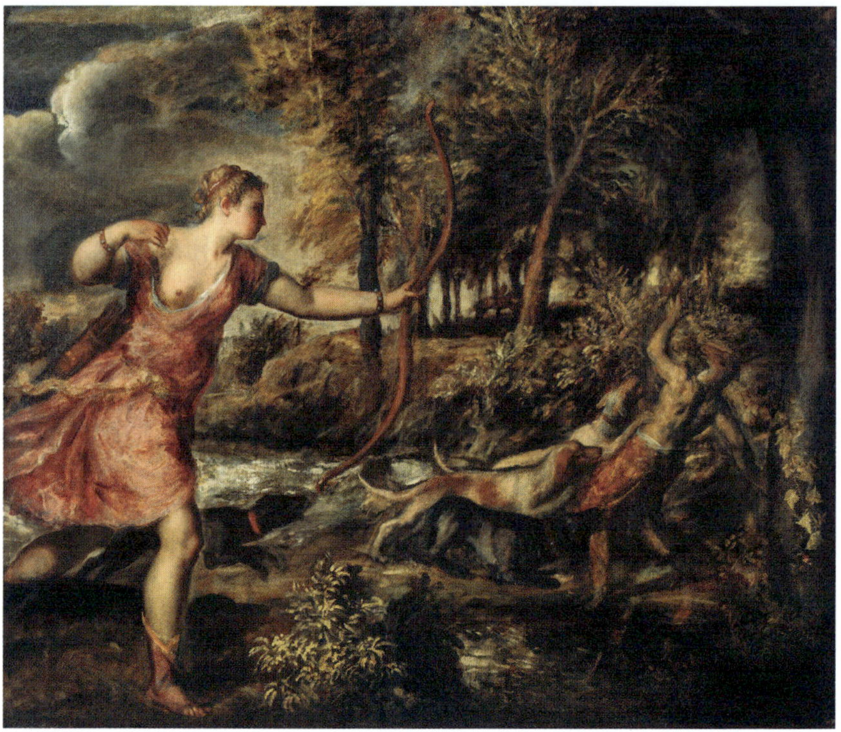

58 Tearing the flesh: *The Death of Actaeon* (1559–75), found unfinished in Titian's studio.

she balances to shoot an arrow from her stringless bow. Two light- and two dark-coloured dogs sweep across the painting as if they were the missing arrow. Streaks of black on the dog coming from under Diana's red tunic are punctuated by the red of its collar – the red of the collar of the dog entering the scene at the beginning of the story.

It leads our eyes to the black crouched dog with its teeth in Actaeon's leg and to the two brown and white hounds, the one nearest to the head of the human-deer, its paw raised and mirroring Actaeon's raised arm, futilely trying to ward them off but exposing his breast to the dog's bite. They are poised against the red of what scraps are left covering their master's body, the instrument of the goddess' steel fury hurling across the painting in great streaks of paint from one side to the other. The dogs are almost larger than Actaeon; he falls back, and they overpower him: a primal scene of violence as if the evolutionary civilizing process were reversed. In the background is a darkly sketched rider, one of Actaeon's clueless companions, from the quotidian world.

Beyond Myth

The history of humans and dogs hunting from not long after its evolutionary beginnings in the Palaeolithic has generated an almost endless range of narratives. We do not know what stories were being told in the rock art of Arabia from the eighth, ninth, or tenth millennium BCE or the pottery of pre-dynastic Egypt from 6,000 years ago. They are lost in the air. But they were representing the oldest relationship humans had with other animals beyond hunting them for food: a relationship created in evolutionary times and recast through the ages. The domestication of the dog represents the beginning of our seeing and being seen by another creature. Dogs, the hunt, and the gods of the hunt entered Eurasian mythology very early, which in turn became the subject of art in antiquity, inspired Renaissance artists, and continued to engage the visual arts until our day.

The dog and humans on the hunt remain embedded in deep time in vernacular settings where there is no explicitly mythological theme. They are joined from the very beginning of vernacular art. Think first of Pieter Bruegel the Elder's 1565 *Hunters in the Snow* [**59**]. There is no hint of ritualized royal hunts or of the gentlemanly pursuit of game by men in classical antiquity, the real-life Adonises and Actaeons for whom the hunt was part of their education. It is not mythologized.

But still it is in the tradition of a primal pursuit, of what brought dogs and humans together. Tired villagers are emerging from a forest or from uncultivated land just out of the picture; their hunt has been only minimally successful: only a fox. Their dogs, black and brown – the most vivid colours in the painting – look as tired as the men as they make their way through the darkly painted trees. Hunter and hound are as one. Below them is the civilized world of agriculture and wintertime leisure; people are skating on the ponds. Almost like a map, that world stands in contrast to the group on the hill. As a painting in the tradition of 'seasons of the year' it speaks to the eternal cycles of human life. It is also a successor to the Arabian rock art of 8,000 years earlier. But in no prior image was the visual tradition of the ancient alliance of hunter and dog so centrally and emotionally joined.[58]

Winslow Homer's 1891 *A Huntsman and Dogs* is a modern version of the relationship born so long ago [**60**]. Like the Bruegel and so many other vernacular pictures of the hunt, it is mythological only in the sense that

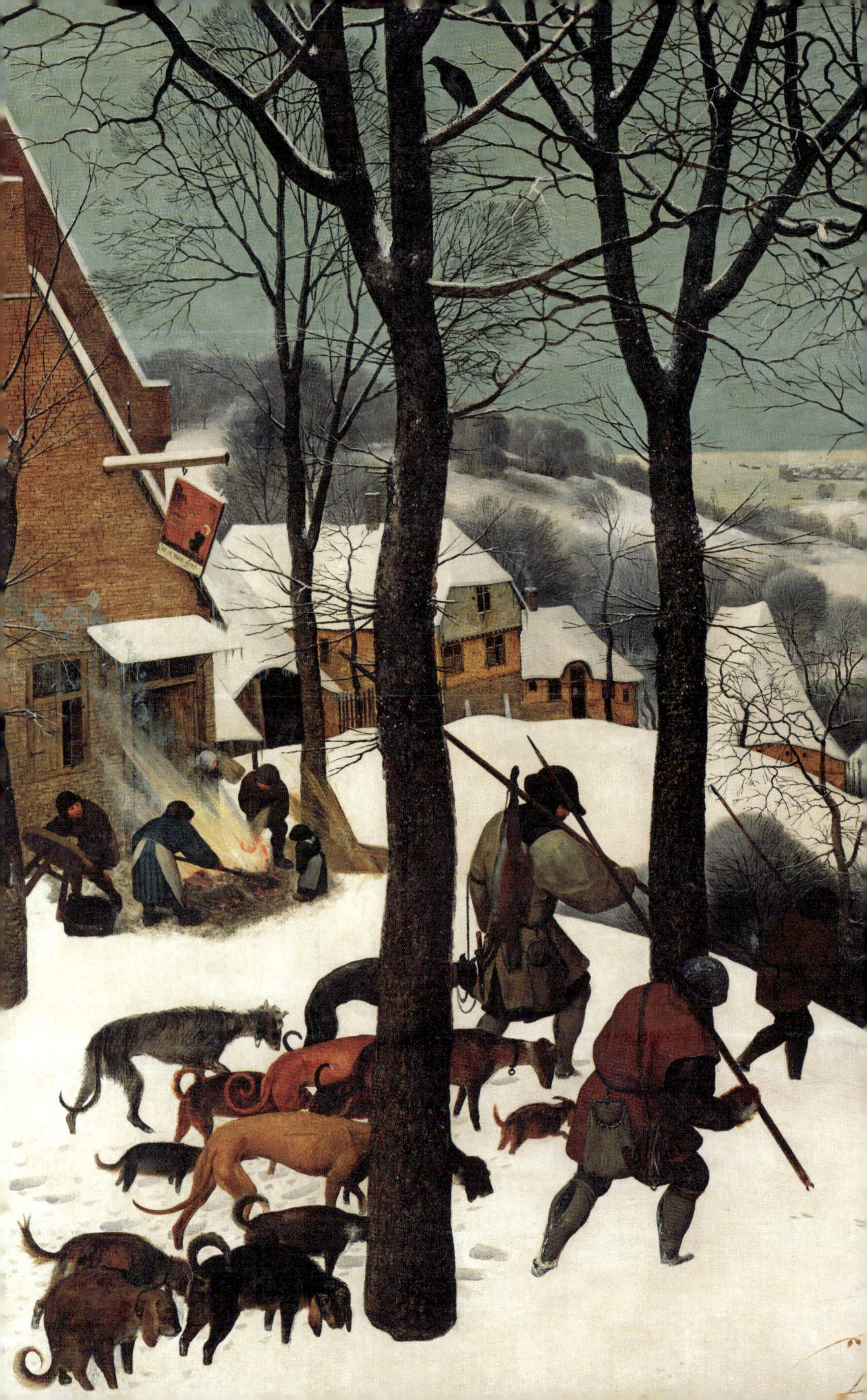

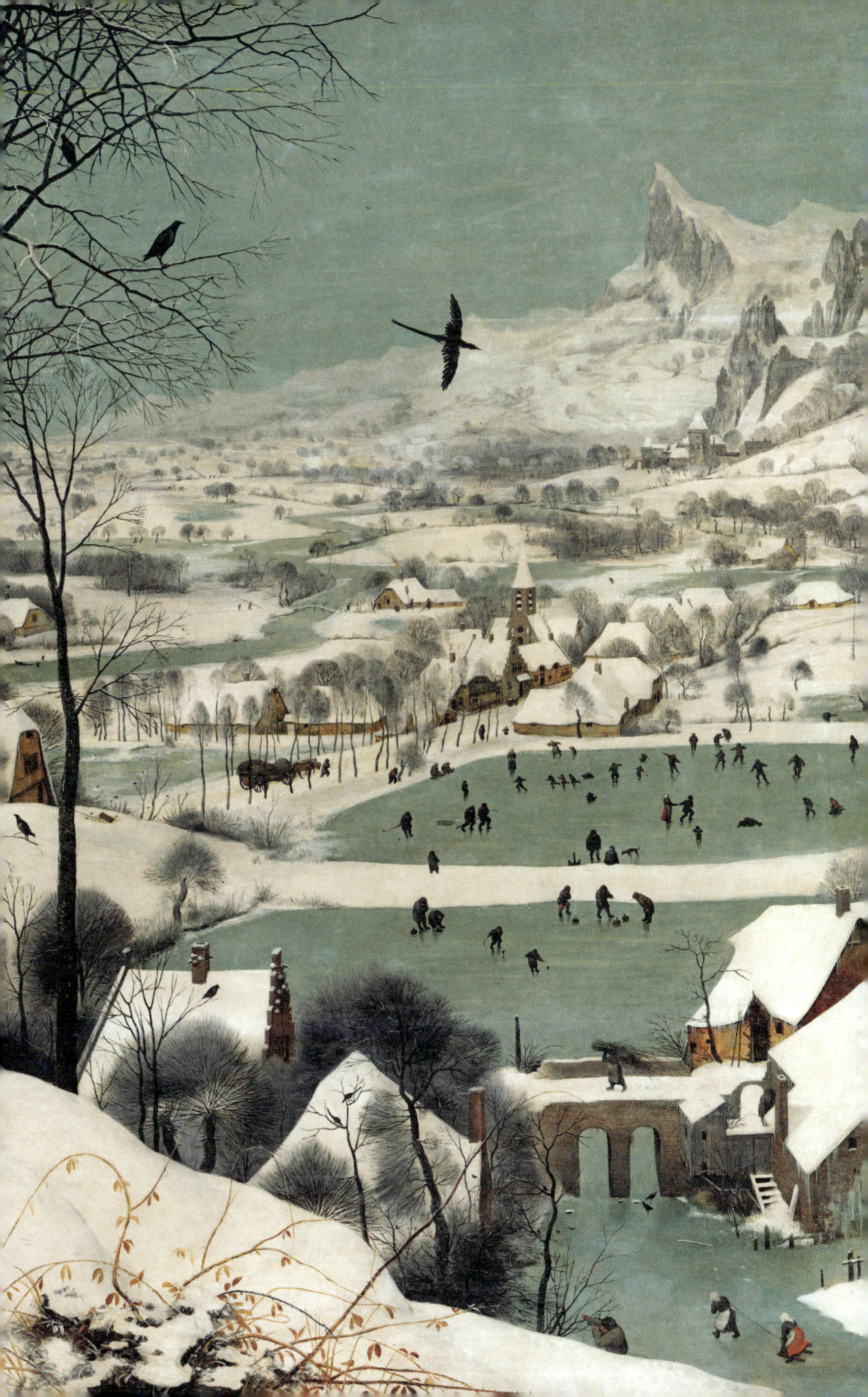

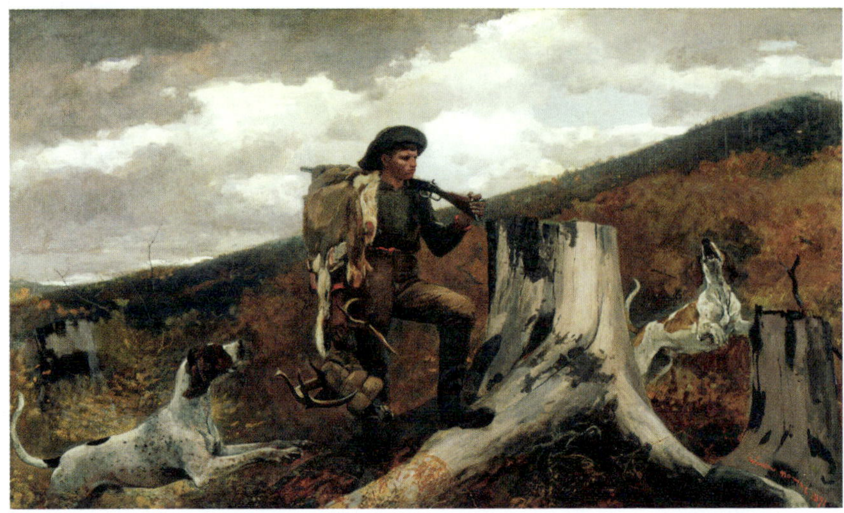

60 Winslow Homer's vision of an age-old partnership in *A Huntsman and Dogs* (1891). Previous page: 59 The ancient alliance of hunter and dog in Pieter Bruegel the Elder's *Hunters in the Snow* (1655).

the hunt itself, shrouded in the moist ancient history of our species, can almost not be in some sense mythic. The painting shows an Adirondacks trapper or guide taking a pelt and meat home, a modern sport or occupation and a modern human with recognizably modern hunting dogs. The man is poised between sky and earth that seems to absorb most of his body. Two bounding dogs frame him; the one between the two dead trees seems almost wild as it rears up, mouth agape, trying to speak perhaps. Leave out the gun and the clothes and this could be seen as Homer's way of imagining mankind's first art and alliance with the first domesticated creature, the first out of the gate of co-evolution.

Paul Gauguin's *Arearea* [**61**] links the deep time of the dog with a modern artist's connection to this primal past. In the background are women performing some ancient, perhaps Hindu, rite in front of a stone statue; in the middle ground, two women, one playing a wooden flute, the other looking out and toward us, her head tilted, curious, questioning as if to ask what we are doing looking at her. She is seated in the lotus position, but her hands are not in the usual place on her thighs. Her left one is on the ground behind her and the other pointing to the ground in front. One critic identifies the gesture as 'calling the earth to witness', a reference to the mythic triumph of the Buddha over

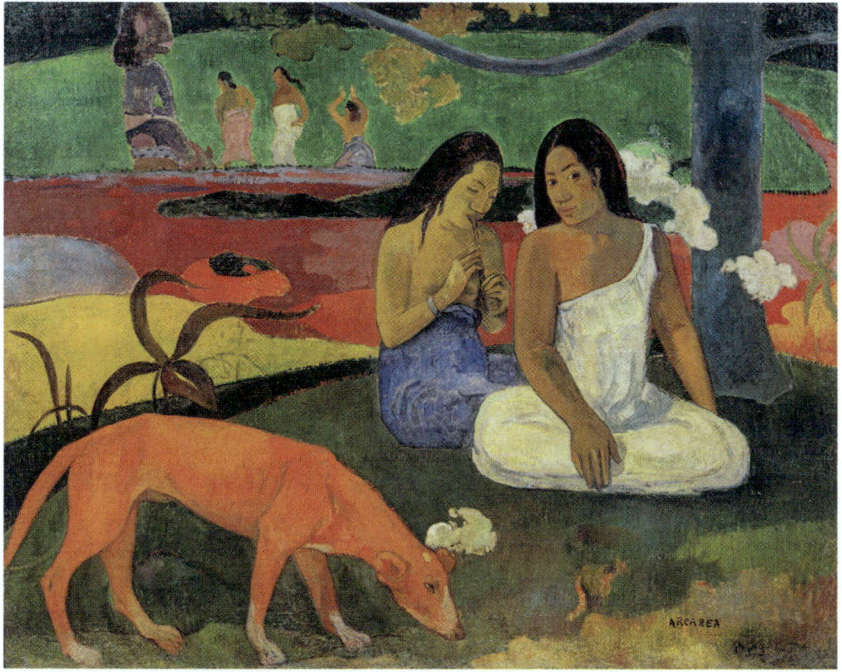

61 Paul Gauguin foregrounds the deep time of the dog in *Arearea* (1892).

the demon Mara. Prominently in the foreground is a large orange collarless dog entering the frame; all but the tip of its tail is in. Its nose is to the ground.[59]

Most of Gauguin's oeuvre after the late 1880s is of course connected to his search for a primitive world in Polynesia. But at stake here are not his colonial fantasies but his long identification with dogs in his art. We know that Gauguin himself, like van Gogh, identified as a 'rough, shaggy, dog' who in Tahiti sniffed the ground liberated from civilization: savage, primitive and free from the sexual constraints as dogs had been before their reproduction came to be controlled by humans. In 1896 he acquired a dog named Pego, a version of the name Pgo with which he signed some works (but also slang for penis) and that he regarded as an alter ego for his savage self.

Gauguin more than any other artist imaginatively absorbed what he understood about the dog. It was, for him, the representative of a lost world. But he was far from unique in translating the heritage of a remarkable evolutionary history into culture.

CHAPTER 3

The Art of the Dog

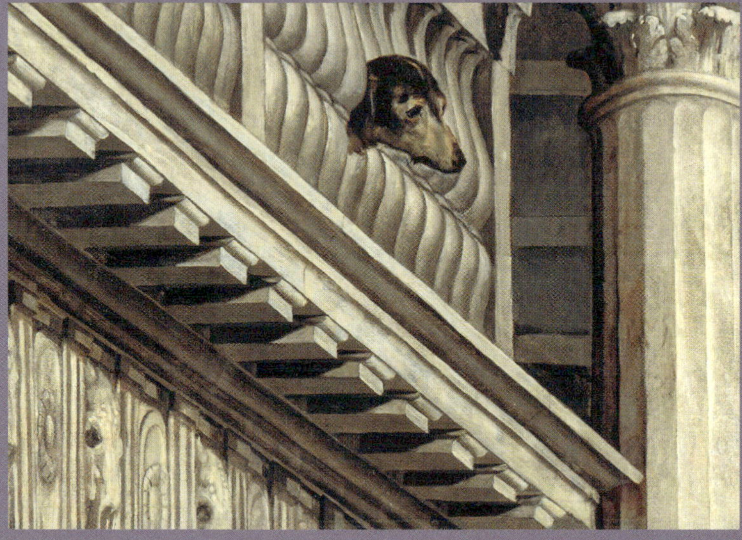

Detail from 88, *The Wedding Feast at Cana* (1562–63) by Veronese. A dog gazes from the balcony and directs ours.

IT IS IMPOSSIBLE TO disentangle the 'how' of a painting, its formal features – the shapes, colours, shadows, the light and the dark in which painters think and the representational techniques an artist employs – from its 'what' – from what it is ostensibly about, its content, its social, moral, and more generally cultural meaning. The ways that the elements come together in a configuration that makes sense to us cannot be decoupled from how a picture comes to mean what it does to viewers at the time it was made, or to us, or to the artist as the primal viewer. The little dog in Carpaccio's *St Augustine in his Study* (*see* 76) as it sits on the diagonal of the painting, for example, plays a critical role in making the elements of the image come together; it makes us look at the miraculous light streaming in; and it connects us to the artist both through a sign next to it and as representing the act of seeing itself. It is part of a story. And it is beautiful. I do not want to claim that I can, or want to, decouple the formal configuration of a picture from its meanings and aesthetic qualities. But still, I will try in this chapter to keep my attention on the 'how' part, that is on the formal work that a dog does for an artist. The two chapters that follow will put more emphasis on the 'what' question, on the content and cultural meaning of the work of art.[1]

By form I mean, in the first place, what people usually mean by form, that is structure: the dog as the base of a pyramid, or the midpoint of a painting, or a point on its diagonal, or a way of creating its edge. Think about how the dog in the de Hooch interior (*see* 17) divides inside from outside or how in Joshua Reynolds' painting of the family of the Fourth Duke of Marlborough the bodies of the dogs are the base of a pyramid and their eyes look toward its apex (*see* 189).

But I also mean the ways in which viewers are invited by dogs in art to see parts of a painting; the ways in which they look out and invite us in; the ways in which they see as the artist sees; the ways in which we are led by them to believe what the artist sees, that is, how they define an artist's position in the dance of looking; the ways in which they generate visual narrative by how they look; and the ways their look creates visual pleasure. These senses of 'form' are of course not independent of each other.

I have not been rigorous distinguishing 'the dog's gaze' from 'the dog's looking' or occasionally even from 'the dog's seeing', although I never mean simply the dog's use of the faculty of sight. Whether a look is intense or sustained enough to qualify for a gaze is contextual. I mean throughout that the visual attention of a dog – however much it might be a false front for olfactory attention – is a central element in the formal workings of an image.

The Eye of the Dog

> Tiepolo relieves dogs of all social responsibility . . . They concentrate visual interest as strongly as the people they appear with, while diverting us from human affairs. A good dog registers pictorial problems engaged . . .[2]

Svetlana Alpers and Michael Baxandall support their claim about the formal work of the dog in the work of Tiepolo in their discussions of two paintings. 'The brilliantly white hound left of center in the Edinburgh "Finding of Moses", echoing the white background and adjacent white breeches, head and tail alert, is a diversionary link between the figures of discovery and response to either side' [**62**].[3] 'Diversionary' in the sense that it is not focusing our attention on the primary narrative. It is not a character in the Biblical story of the finding of Moses; no other literary source mentions a dog. It has nothing to do with the main action or with the humans in the picture except that it formally connects the two groups; it mediates between them. As the Renaissance polymath Leon Battista Alberti might put it, 'It points out to us what is happening there', without having any specific views on the subject.

But it is, as its evolutionary history makes possible, a socially competent dog. It is doing what members of its species do: it is looking back

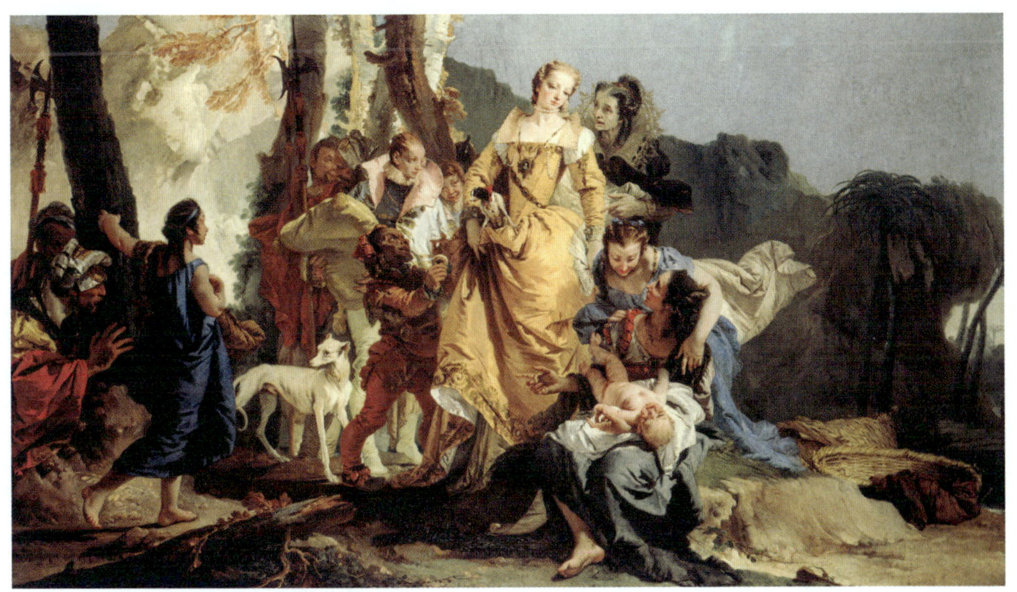

62 A white dog holds together Tiepolo's *The Finding of Moses* (early 1730s).

in the direction of the point of Moses' sister, who is gesturing out of the frame of the painting to the world beyond the frame where the narrative will unfold further. It is pointing to where she says she can find a 'Hebrew woman' – her mother – who will nurse the baby that the Pharaoh's daughter has saved. The dog has its eye on the future beyond this slice of narrative that viewers will know.

Alpers and Baxandall offer a second example [**63**]:

> . . . [The] tawny dappled dog seated behind Antony in the Painting of 'The Banquet of Antony and Cleopatra' . . . Taken from Veronese's 'Esther before Erasures [Ahasuerus]' at San Sebastian – all tensed, head turned against the direction of its long back, a figure of alertness color keyed to Cleopatra, registers Antony's part again in a diversionary way.[4]

Here again, the narrative does not need a dog, and especially in this context, not a hunting dog. It is 'diversionary'. Antony is dressed for battle, not for the chase. And there are enough markings of gender to make the distinction between the feminine lapdog and the masculine, independent coursing hound superfluous. But now that the hound is there it's hard to imagine the painting without it. The torsion of its body makes us look counter-clockwise along the curve from its tail, which echoes the curve of Antony's chair and of the amphora, to its nose and

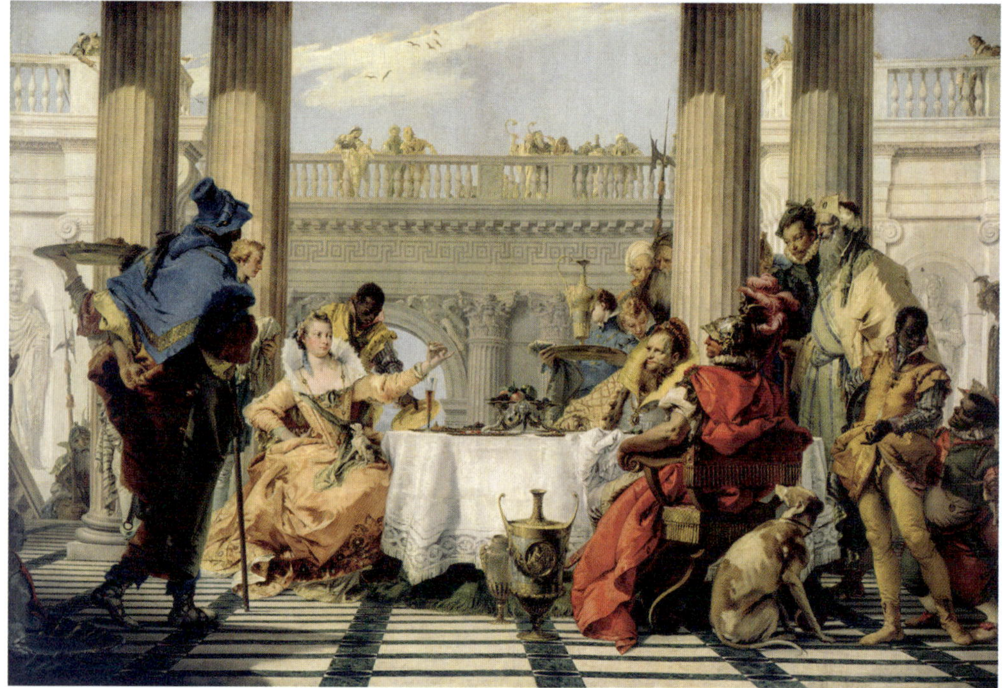

63 *The Banquet of Cleopatra* (1743-4) by Tiepolo. The dog is borrowed from Veronese.

just a hint of its eyes focused on Antony who is looking over the table and toward Cleopatra. The gesture of the black servant toward the dog invites us to pay attention to where it is pointing. Far more than the figure of the servant dressed in blue on the left, the dog is doing the serious looking and registering of Antony's gaze. Maybe it is Cleopatra's hand gesture that is catching this hound's eyes. It is in any case paying more attention to what is happening at this dinner than anyone else except perhaps the artist himself.

Tiepolo's dog was, as Alpers and Baxandall say, borrowed from Veronese where it had lived almost two centuries earlier. (They make the more general argument about the extent to which Tiepolo took up a certain style from Veronese.) And Veronese's brown and white dog was, in turn, borrowed from his fellow Venetian Jacopo Bassano's *Two Hunting Dogs* (*see* 18). Dog memes time-travelled within an artist's work and between generations of artists because dog gestures are, and have been, recognizable since Greek antiquity and very quickly entered the artistic imagination in the centuries after Bassano. Dogs 'concentrate visual interest' because viewers believe in their social competence, that their looks and gestures are consequential and meaningful. At least so we believe:

Like a dog
Cézanne says
That's how a painter
Must see, the eye
Fixed & almost averted.[5]

I am not sure that we should take literally the claim W. G. Sebald's poem makes in Cézanne's name. A good case might be made on the basis of one of his early paintings, the 1873 *A Modern Olympia*, in which a stylishly dressed artist – 'the painter' of Sebald's poem – is looking intently at a luminously painted oil sketch of Manet's infamous 1862 nude *Olympia* on a bed of clouds. 'Like a voluptuous vision,' a critic of the time called it. No modern painting engages the male gaze more than the original *Olympia* and here, in bright colours, Cézanne almost parodies it.[6] With him – seeing like, or at least with, a painter – in this erotic reverie is his bouncy dog with its red collar [**64**].

I don't think this is what Sebald had in mind. His poem is based on a quotation he took from a letter the poet Rainer Maria Rilke wrote from Paris in the autumn of 1907 to his wife, the sculptor Clara Westhoff, at a time when he was besotted by Cézanne's work and fascinated by the philosophical implications of how the painter saw. He and a broader philosophical community came to regard Cézanne as a kind of prophet.

'Imagine my surprise,' Rilke writes, 'when Miss Vollmoeller with her painterly training eye, said: "He [Cézanne] sat there in front of it like a dog, just looking, without any nervousness, without any ulterior motive."' Rilke understood the painter to be phenomenology in action, that is, he was working with the idea that objects get their meaning through perception in someone's, the painter's, consciousness. (He was not the first to have that interpretation – the founder of phenomenology, Maurice Merleau-Ponty, wrote a famous essay called 'Cézanne's Doubt' – nor was he the last.)[7] Cézanne, Rilke writes, is painting a part of an apple as 'something he knew'; and next to it there is an empty space 'because there was something he did not know yet'. Rilke considered Cézanne's way of seeing and his struggle with representing reality as exemplary of

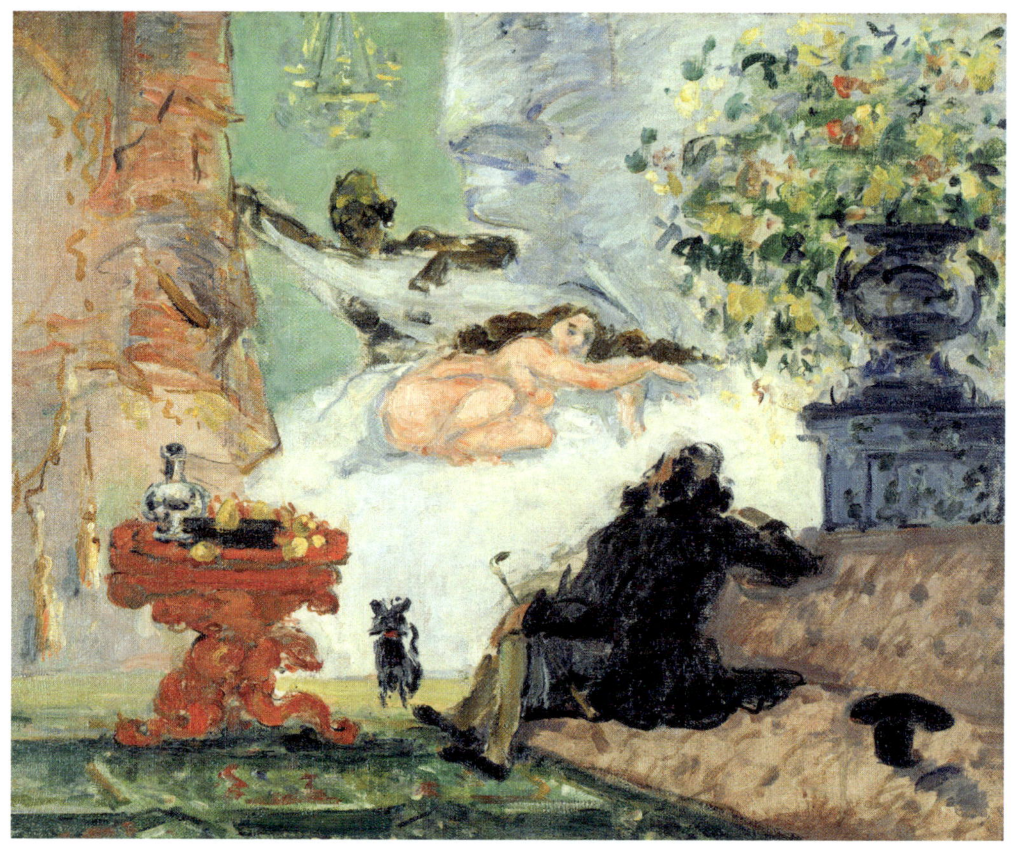

64 The painter 'seeing like a dog' in Paul Cézanne's *A Modern Olympia* (1873).

the protracted gaze in its efforts to get beyond nature and naturalism. To know. He called it a 'conflagration of clarity'.

Art was not about imitating reality but about rendering some deeper underlying truth that emerged into consciousness. This was possible, according to Rilke's interpretation of Cézanne, only through an innocent and purified vision untainted by civilizational overlays. Without 'partiality and conscious intention', as one commentator put it; there was no intentional symbolism in Cézanne's work, no prior intention to mean something. It was based in that sense on seeing like a dog: the human alter ego; an epistemological doppelgänger. Not mindless staring; somewhat averted.[8]

Anyone who has ever taken a dog for a walk at a familiar spot knows there is not merely seeing or smelling, and knows that its head is filled with history, with the sights and particularly smells of past walks. There must be meaning prior to consciousness even for a dog. I also think that what might be said about Cézanne may be less the case for other artists, that is, they do not all paint so self-consciously what is in their minds rather than what is out there in the world. But I cite Sebald's poem for two reasons: because dog cognition and visual perception are again a crux, and because dogs like artists do seem to look more intently than the rest of us. And one more reason: because in a great deal of visual art they see with the freshness and wonder of the artist's gaze.

*

> In an *istoria* [the narrative structure of a work] I like to see someone who admonishes and points out to us what is happening there; or beckons with his hand to see; or menaces with an angry face and with flashing eyes, so that no one should come near; or shows some danger or marvellous thing there; or invites us to weep or to laugh together with them. Thus, whatever the painted persons do among themselves or with the beholder, all is pointed toward ornamenting or teaching the *istoria*.
> Alberti, *On Painting* [9]

Alberti says nothing here about dogs although he did have a pet dog of no specified type and wrote a Latin encomium, *Canis*, that praised a dog's humanist-like qualities: a good memory, a devotion to scholarship, and the ability to tell good from bad, or at least friend from foe.[10] He is in this quotation offering advice about the formal structure of a painting, advice on composition: the 'rule of painting by which the parts of the things seem to fit together', specifically on how a good *istoria* makes for an effective composition. Alberti means this much-controverted term not in its eighteenth-century sense of a history or novel but, as his modern editor notes, in the sense of how 'figures are to be so ordered that their emotion will be projected to the observer'. Although the first work of art that Alberti alludes to does not, in his description, mention dogs, it might as well for the case in point:

> An *istoria* is praised in Rome in which Meleager, a dead man, weighs down those who carry him. In every one of his members he appears completely dead – everything hangs, hands, fingers and head; everything falls heavily.

I suspect that Alberti is thinking here of a third-century Roman sarcophagus that depicts the death of the hero of the Calydonian boar hunt whose body is lying limply in a shroud. There is no dog; but there are in many similar sarcophagi, in which a dog looks up in mourning for its master lying dead on a bier.

Alberti's description fits as well a sixteenth-century engraving of the same subject by Girolamo Faccioli. Meleager's dog is just coming upon the horrible scene. Its paw, not quite in the picture yet, breaks the fourth wall as if to let the world in. Its tensed muscular body, raised head as if in full cry and upward gaze from the lower left, is the image of emotion 'projected to the observer' that demands that we pay attention to his 'completely dead' master, his body falling heavily onto a shroud [**65**].

There are further cases that extend their reach of the opening epigrams. First, the case of paintings in which the dog's gaze is less in the service of the '*istoria*' or of resolving a pictorial problem or of being a surrogate for how a painter sees or wants us to see, but straightforwardly about a dog seeing and being seen and about the social connections born of the mutual gaze. Seeing as form becomes seeing as content, in other words the subject of the painting. Bartolomé Esteban Murillo's circa 1655 *Boy with Dog* [**66**] could be interpreted in the context of Spanish genre painting, or of the artist's well-documented engagement with religious obligations toward the poor, or in relation to his other genre paintings,

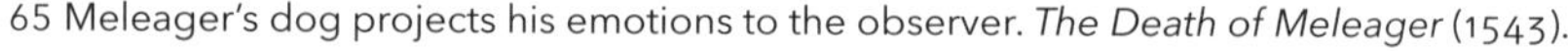

65 Meleager's dog projects his emotions to the observer. *The Death of Meleager* (1543).

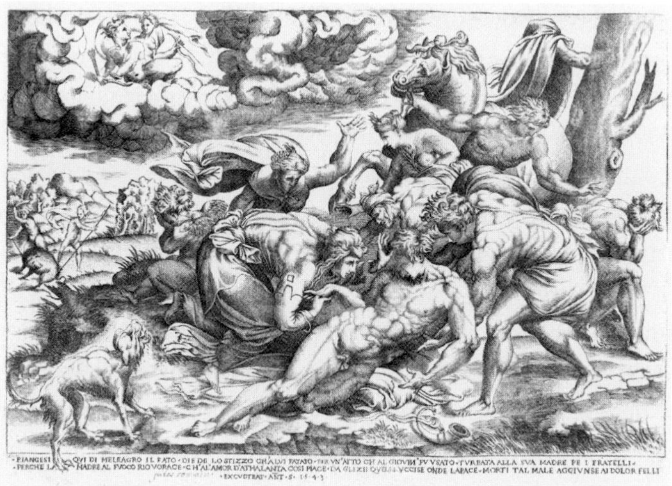

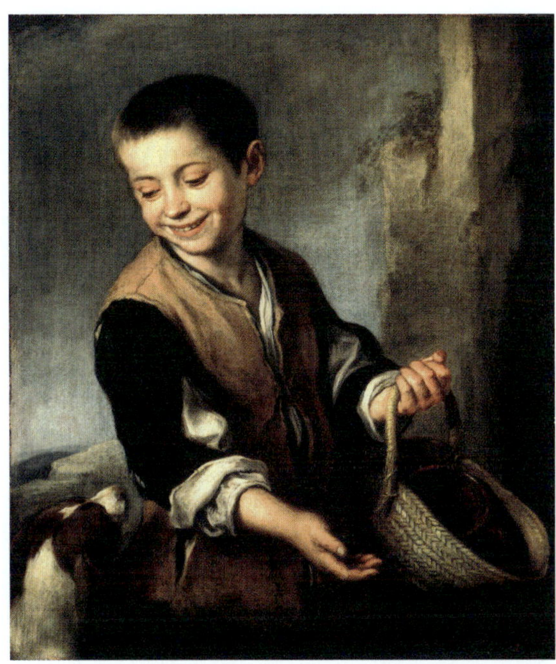

66 Cross-species seeing in Bartolomé Esteban Murillo's *Boy with Dog* (*c.* 1655).

many of which also have dogs in them. We could take it as social historical evidence for the fact that the poor too had and loved pets well before the purported age of widespread pet-keeping in the nineteenth century. But most immediately *Boy with Dog* is about a dog's and a human's gaze, which creates the formal axis of the painting and is its manifest content. The painting is about cross-species seeing.[11]

The Bolognese portrait painter Bartolomeo Passerotti's *Man with Dog* (*c.* 1585), on the cover of this book, makes the same claim [**67**]. Again, there are many other things to be said about it: about interspecies tenderness, for example. The dog and the human are hugging each other, his hands, fingers spread – flesh on fur – holding tightly the dog's shoulder, the dog's white paws on his doublet. But the most striking aspect is the centrality of the act of seeing itself. The dog looks intently into the face of the man who is holding him. The man is looking out at us as if he were suddenly disturbed by someone coming in, as if moments before he had been looking at the dog. His look demands that viewers take notice of what the dog is doing: seeing him. It is almost a schematic of a face-to-face gaze interrupted, the two subjects are now seeing at right angles, the dog laterally, the man turned 90 degrees straight out.

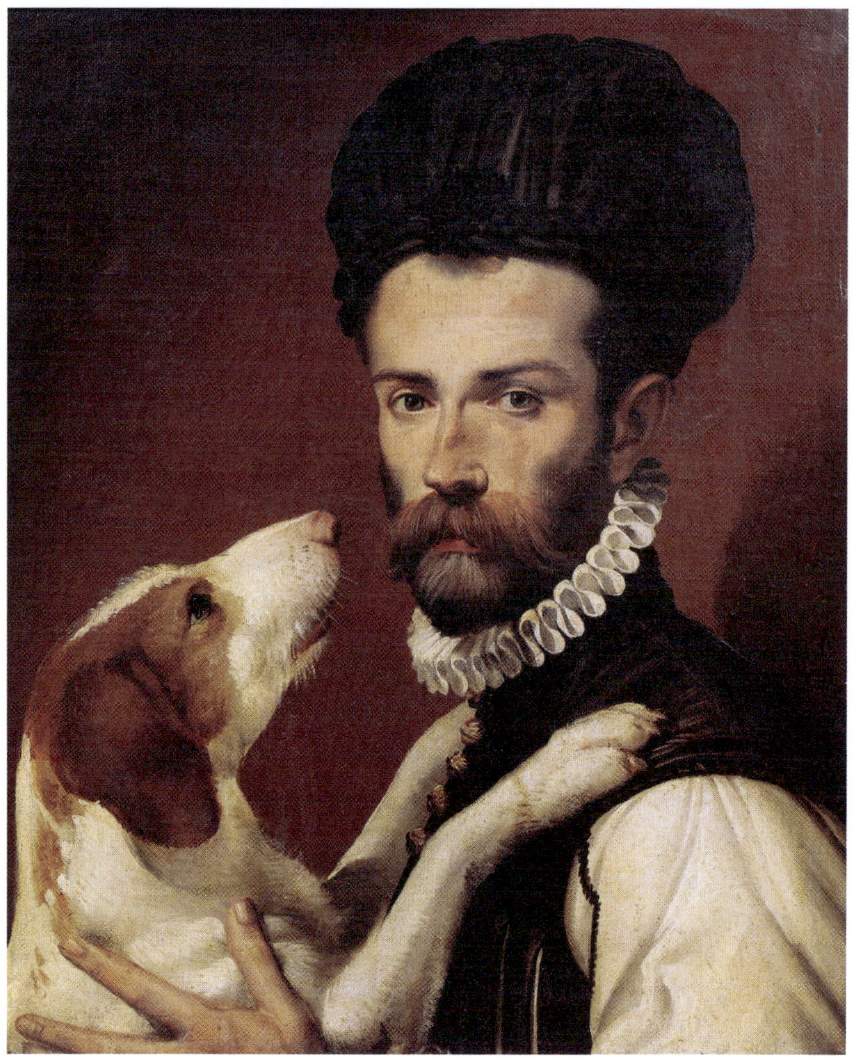

67 The act of seeing: *Man with Dog* (*c.* 1585) by Bartolomeo Passerotti.

Angelica Kauffman, one of the most celebrated eighteenth-century artists, used the same device for a different purpose in *The Return of Telemachus Greeted by Penelope* [**68**]. The gazes of the two dogs poised in the space between the human protagonists are paradigmatic examples of what Alberti might want in an *istoria*, beckoning with their eyes and directional gazes to make the narrative clear to viewers. 'Look right' says the one in the shadows, directing our attention to Eurycleia, the faithful nurse, beside herself with excitement, who welcomes her former charge with open

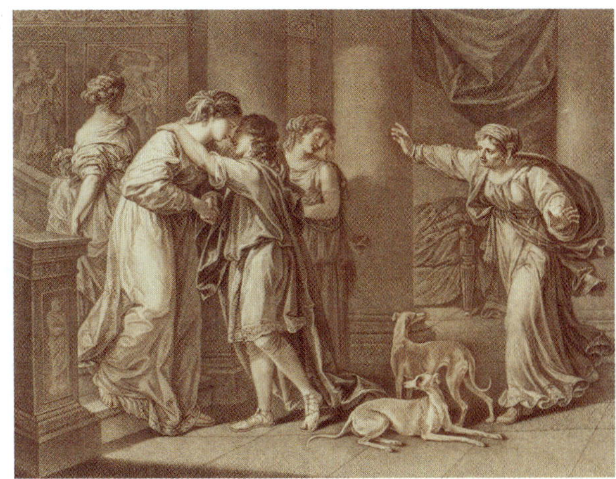

68 Beckoning with their eyes: print after Angelica Kauffman's *The Returning Telemachus Greeted by Penelope* (1777).

arms. 'Look left' says the brightly lit brown dog nearest the front plane of the image, inviting us to look at the main action as Penelope descends the stairs and is about to kiss her son who had long been in search of his father Odysseus. Neither of these dogs looks like how we might imagine the aged Argos, the only creature who recognizes his master dressed as a beggar.[12]

There are also images in which the dog stands in for the artist, a kind of alter ego without whom the scene could not exist, like a tree falling in the forest when no one is listening. In Johannes and Lucas Van Doetechum's *Landscape with the Baptism of Christ* (circa 1562), it is as if the dog's being there is a necessary condition for John baptizing Jesus [**69**]. There are humans going about their business but they are paying no attention to what is happening centre stage; they are not really seeing it. The dog is. Its front paws are on the parapet of the bridge that crosses the winding river gully. It is leaning forward from the exact middle of the image, watching the action, intent on looking at the picture within a picture, the ostensible subject of the etching and the painting from which it was made: John baptizing Jesus.

We'd be watching too if we were in the dog's place. The artist was. Maybe it is a joke; or maybe the message is that the dog, ever faithful, is watching and we are being told that we should. There is no question that the dog is paying attention. And so, in a different way, is the beggar's dog in the lower right corner although less centrally and less ostentatiously. It is doing what dogs do in so much art and in life: looking back at its person as if to move him along and be sure he is still there.

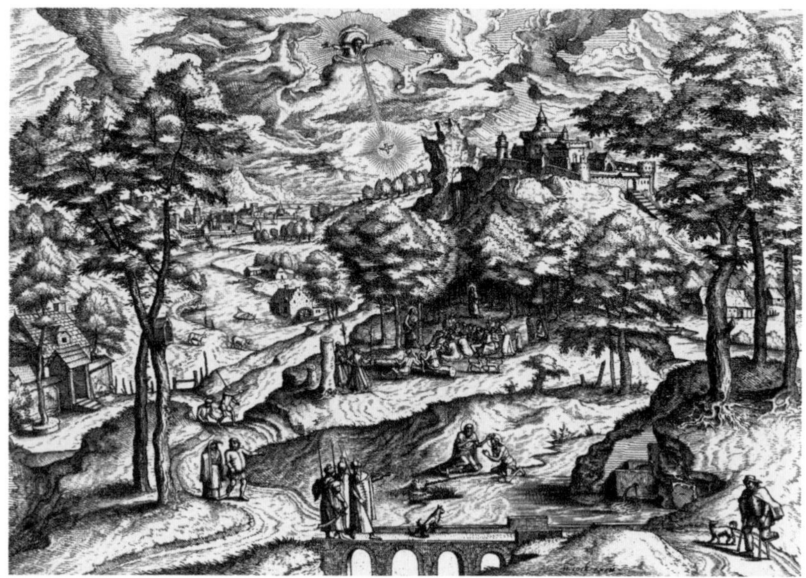

69 A dog as the central witness in *Landscape with the Baptism of Christ* (c. 1562).

In J. M. W. Turner's *Mortlake Terrace* (1827) the dog is not quite the only one looking over the river; there are humans peering over the wall further along [70]. But Turner clearly thought he needed it there; at the last minute he cut out a figure of a dog on brown paper, stuck it on the canvas, and painted it black because, as Tom Taylor, the nineteenth-century writer, art critic, and editor of *Punch*, says, 'it suddenly struck the artist that a dark object here would throw back the distance and increase the aerial effect'. The absence of a dog in the previous year's painting of Mortlake Terrace looking east makes the point [71]. Turner did not add just any dark object; he added a dark living creature – specifically a dog; a cat looking out at the landscape would not have had the same effect.[13]

There are paintings in which the dog looks at the artist, not outside the painting doing his job, but inside as part of the staging of a self-portrait within the narrative. In Cranach the Elder's 1531 *Judith Dining with Holofernes* [72], for example, a large white greyhound, its head raised, is looking along the diagonal axis past the cup-bearer to the man in a fur coat who is pointing at Holofernes and whose face is just visible in the upper left-hand corner. That man is Cranach himself: a self-portrait. The eyes of the artist and the eyes of the dog search for each other. No one else in the picture is looking so directly except perhaps Landgrave Philip of Hesse, the

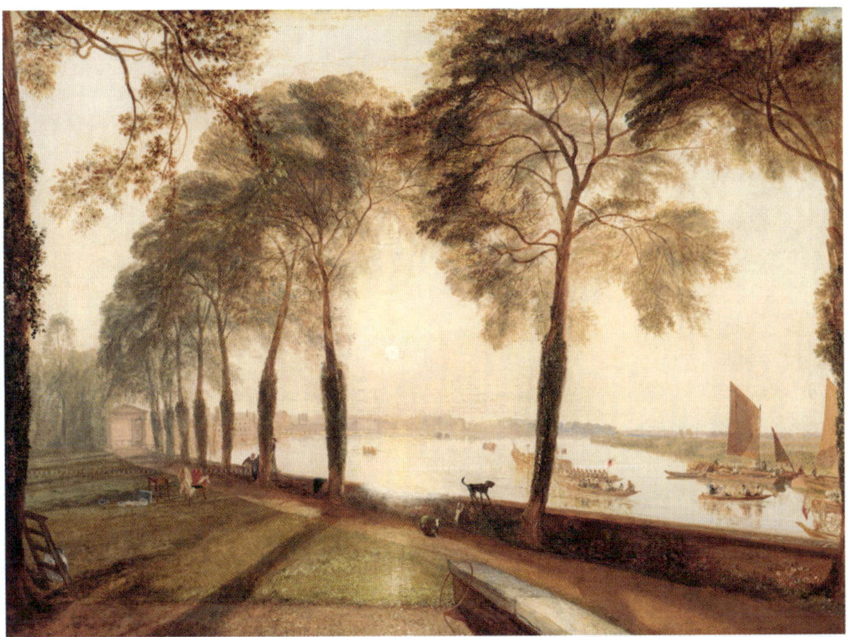

70 J. M. W. Turner's *Mortlake Terrace* (1827), with the last-minute addition of a dog.

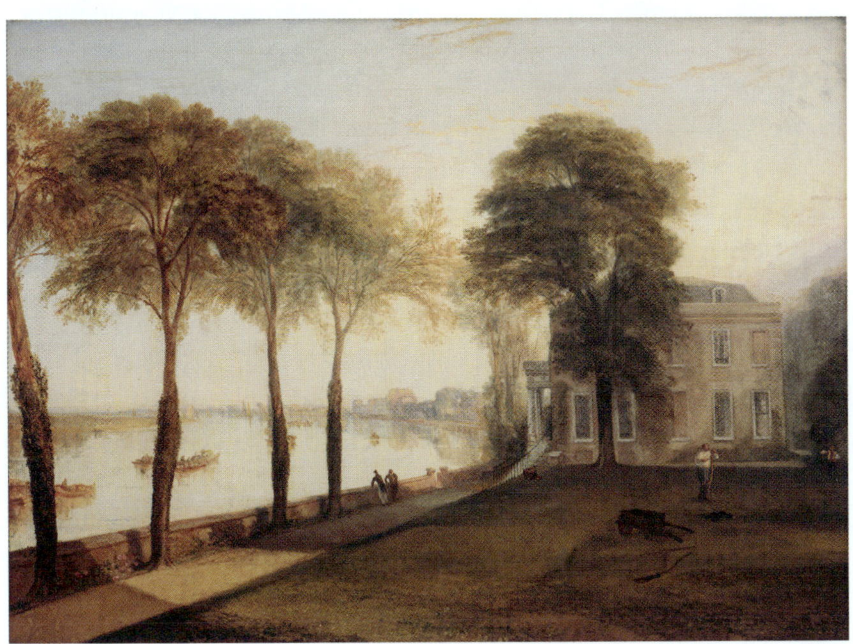

71 An earlier view of Mortlake Terrace (1826) without the anchoring dog.

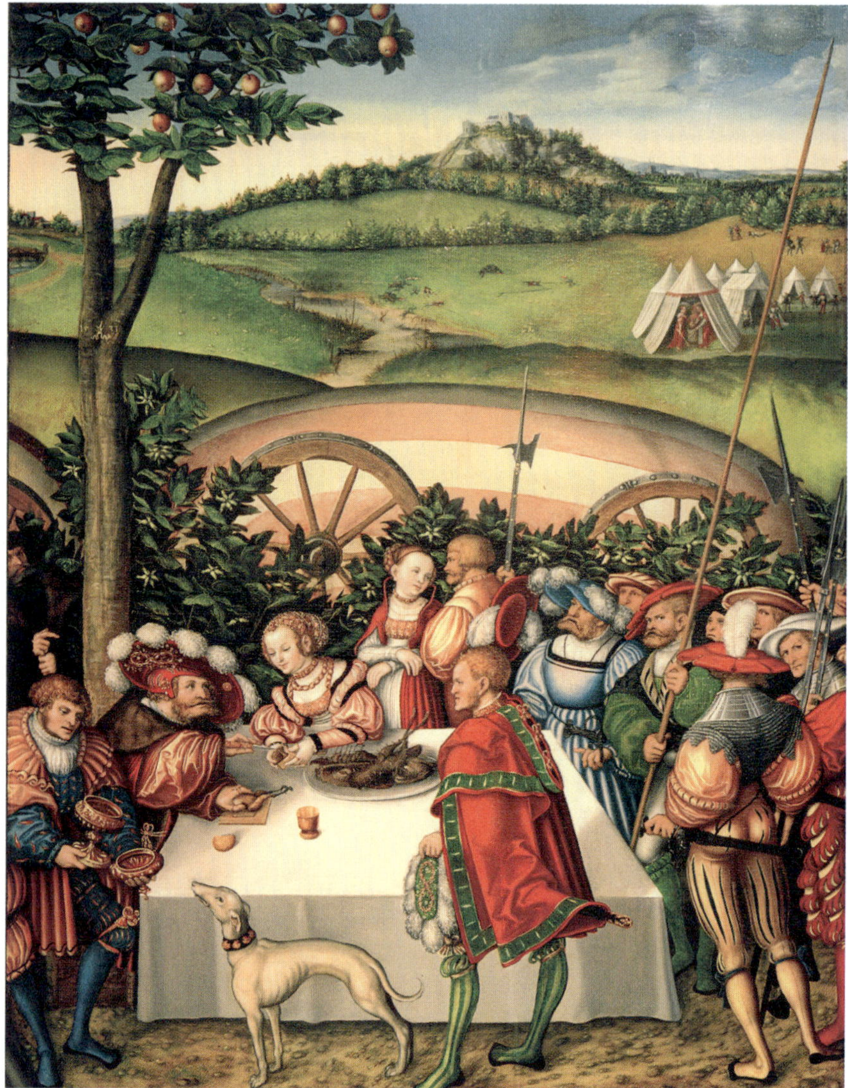

72 Cranach the Elder stages a self-portrait within *Judith Dining with Holofernes* (1531) along the axis of the dog's gaze.

Magnanimous, to the right of the hound, glaring at the doomed Holofernes, a stand-in with the characteristic protruding Hapsburg chin for his real-life enemy, Charles V, sitting at the head of the table.[14]

There is a kind of cascade of the dog seeing within seeing, of the observer observed, in all of these images. It is an explicit theme in a painting by Sebald's friend Jan Peter Tripp that the novelist writes about

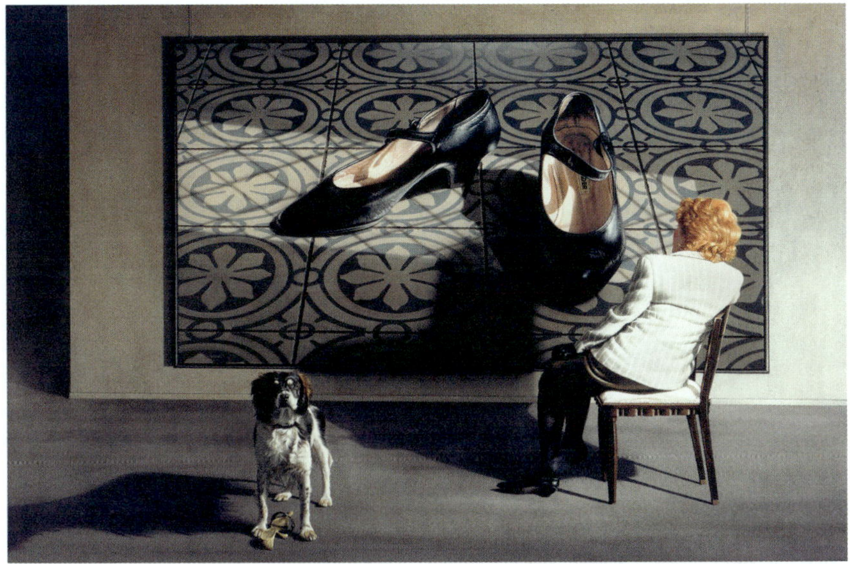

73 The dog in Jan Peter Tripp's *Déjà vu or the Incident* (1992) 'runs over the abysses of time'.

[**73**]. A woman, tired and with one of her shoes off, is looking at a painting by Tripp of the shoes she is wearing: a painting of an observer observed. A different shoe – a clog – is next to a dog who is casting a shadow in parallel to hers: a dog who is keeping her company – she is not alone in her solitude – a 'knowing dog':

> Attentively his left (domesticated) eye is fixed on us; the right (wild) one has a trace less light, strikes us as averted and alien. And yet it is precisely by this over-shadowed eye that we feel ourselves seen through.[15]

We are being seen by a dog while we are seeing the woman who is seeing. The clog is a citation to other clogs and the dog to another dog: to the clogs and the dog in Van Eyck's *Arnolfini Portrait* (*see* 9). 'With ease,' comments Sebald, the dog 'runs over the abysses of time, because for him there is no difference between the thirteenth and the twentieth centuries'. It might be a dog of faithfulness in both cases, as Sebald speculates; it is a dog of companionship; it is without question a dog of the outward gaze – a dog of recognition who insists we are being observed from inside the work of art, from another world; a dog whom we will encounter again over the ages. Timeless, but also in time.[16]

In the Beginning was Giotto

There are inflection points where deep structures – the biology and the historical anthropology of the dog – become grounded in history, when older traditions of representation take a new turn, and when, what and how the dog sees, notices, and attends to something becomes an important feature of Western art. One such inflection point was 1300, the year when Giotto began his 'Life of the Virgin' cycle in the Scrovegni Chapel in Padua. He was the master, as T. J. Clark recently wrote – the Shakespeare – of Western art who told us what 'job of exemplification was called upon to perform'. Giorgio Vasari claimed in his *Lives of the Most Excellent Painters, Sculptors, and Architects* that Giotto alone had 'revived through God's grace what had fallen into an evil state and brought it back to such a form as it could be called good'. He meant that in his view Giotto began the exploration of how to visually create space and more generally how to translate ways of seeing as a physiological attribute into culture, into art. The invention – or reinvention – of perspective played an important part but was by no means the whole story. Present at that creation of the regime of vision was a dog.[17]

The first six panels of the cycle are a sort of prequel to, or elaboration on, the birth of Jesus in the Gospels of Matthew and Luke. Based on the second-century apocryphal *Protoevangelium of James* (*First Gospel of James*), Anne or Anna, wife of Joachim and the mother-to-be of the Virgin Mary, was childless after twenty years of marriage. Joachim goes to the temple on a feast day to offer a sacrifice, which the priests refuse because, in their view, Anne's barrenness was a sign of God's displeasure. (The temple story is entirely from the *Protoevangelium.*) Joachim in his shame retreats to the desert to pray while Anne remains at home and promises God in prayer that she will dedicate a child, should she conceive, to his service. An angel appears and announces that Anne would conceive; the couple honour Anne's promise and at age three they take their child Mary to the Temple where the more commonly told story of the life of the Virgin begins.

The first image of Giotto's cycle illustrates the 'Expulsion of Joachim', an emotionally fraught moment when the priests of the temple refuse his sacrifice. Humiliated, he looks at them over his shoulder in abject disbelief; the priest's eyes speak of rejection; his hand pushes Joachim

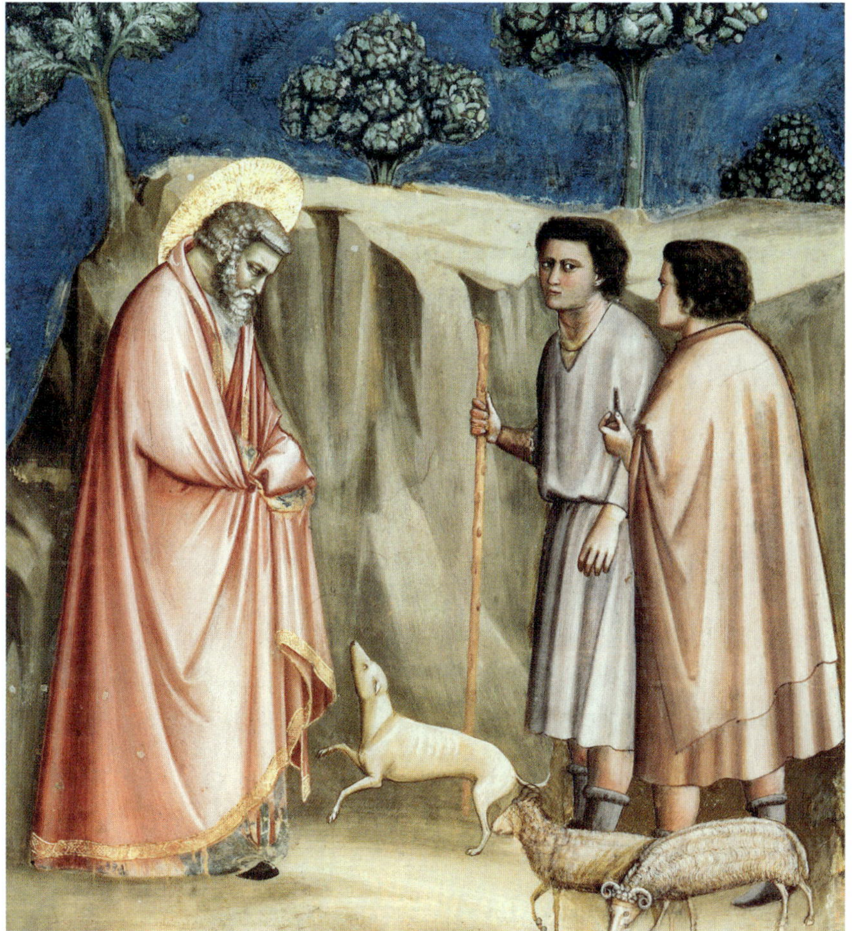

74 A dog doing what dogs do at a foundational moment in Western art: Giotto's *Joachim among the Shepherds* (c. 1305).

away. There are no dogs. In the second image Joachim has fled into the desert where he meets his shepherds; uncertain why their master is there, surprised at the presence of so august and distraught a figure, so far from the city, they give no sign of greeting [**74**]. The shepherd nearest Joachim looks out of the corner of his eyes at the other; perhaps also quizzically at us. The second shepherd looks sideways and back at the first; both ostentatiously avert their eyes from Joachim as if not quite knowing what to do or say.

For the very first time in Giotto's Scrovegni Chapel representation of the story there is a dog in the picture; there are none in earlier

Italo-Byzantine versions: a friendly almost funny dog; a theatrical dog who as one art historian notes turns a religious narrative into a play.[18] It stands between, and visually and affectively connects, the clueless, puzzled shepherds and the distraught Joachim. Their coloured robes stand in contrast to the dog's white fur. The dog is not quite in the geometric centre of the image, but it controls the space between the human protagonists: it is formally central in a way that transforms the painting and sympathetically engages Joachim in a way that promises a brighter future.

The dog is painted in mid-motion getting up on its hind legs; both front paws are off the ground as if in the next moment they will come to rest, or pull, on Joachim's cloak. *In media res*. It is the only movement in the image: a canine gesture of greeting recognized already by artists in ancient Greece. The dog raises its head, wags its tail, and looks Joachim straight in the eyes. He returns the look. Utterly banal gestures; canine and human commonplaces. But also, in this context the recognition of humanity, of caring, energy, and joy: the dog's eyes meet the saint's, from which the shepherds had averted theirs. When Joachim looks up, he will see the dog's co-workers – the shepherds. In the way a dog's attention mediates between strangers in a park, so this dog mediates between the man with a halo and the ordinary men.

This image in Giotto makes me think of an encounter described six centuries later by the philosopher Emmanuel Levinas. He writes about a dog named Bobby who recognized him and his fellow prisoners in a German prisoner-of-war camp as human beings by greeting them – by 'barking with delight' – as they returned to their barracks. 'The last Kantian in Germany,' he says of Bobby, contrasting him to the prison guards. He cannot really mean this. If Levinas were reflecting in his study on the moral capacities of a dog he would not have said it. In fact, he hedges: 'The last Kantian in Germany without the brain needed to universalize maxims and drives', which it would need to make moral judgements in Kant's view.[19]

But Levinas is not writing from the perspective of a philosopher in his study. He is writing about a friendly dog in a prison camp named Bobby who, as a witness to the violence of human crimes, stands in a millennia-old succession of dogs. He is writing from the perspective of a prisoner. Bobby in this context is 'a descendant of the dogs of Egypt', who did not bark as the Children of Israel fled. He is capable of – exemplary of – acting as if he could act ethically, could bear witness with

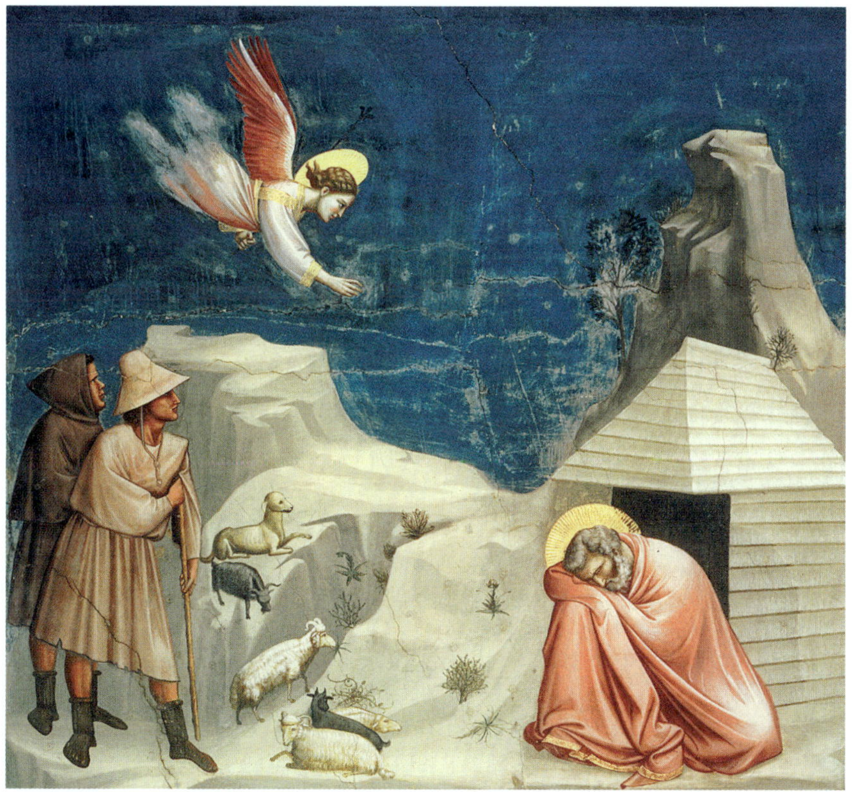

75 A dog looks over the sleeping saint in Giotto's *The Dream of Joachim* (c. 1305).

understanding to the humanity of bedraggled captives. And that is what the dog in this panel of Giotto's cycle also exemplifies. It is the power of the image to make us believe that which, under other circumstances, we might question: that a dog can recognize a human's sadness and act on that recognition to cheer him up. It is what psychoanalysts might call the power of transference.[20]

The third and fourth images in the Scrovegni Chapel – Anne praying at home and Joachim in the desert offering a sacrifice – have no dogs. But in the fifth image there is the dog again [**75**]. Joachim has fallen into a deep sleep. An angel comes out of the deep-blue heavens, a heaven that touches the earth like one of two giant geotechnic plates meeting the other. It reaches toward him from on high as the dog had earlier reached to him from below. The angel announces to Joachim in his dream that Anne has conceived. Directly below the angel is the white dog, now lying solidly on the brownish white rock of this world that separates the two continents of the picture. Giotto does not need the dog to tell the story. It is there to draw us in. Its nose is in line with the sleeping face; its eyes on Joachim while the shepherds are looking at the rock above. At a foundational moment of modern Western art and its interest in how we see, there is the dog doing what dogs do.[21]

The Allure of Venice

I am not sure that the great Venetian painters, Veronese, Titian, and Tintoretto, were more engaged with dogs – or to be more precise, with the use of dogs as formal elements in their art – than other Italian or Northern Renaissance artists, although it is hard not to think that they were. A character in Orhan Pamuk's novel *The Colour Red* makes a good point when he says that 'The infidel masters have committed an unforgivable sin by daring to draw from the perspective of a mangy dog.' He is speaking of 'the Venetian masters', of the 'undeniable alure [of] the paintings they make by these new methods. They depict what the eye sees just as the eye sees it . . . they paint what they see while we [artists in the Ottoman court] paint what we look at.'[22]

John Ruskin argued that the Venetians had a particularly morally edifying view of dogs. They put them in their paintings not because they were 'the basest of animals, but the highest – the connecting link between man and animals'. They exemplify not the worst in humanity – gluttony and indolence – but the best – love, patience, loyalty. The Dutch on the other hand, thought Ruskin, perpetuated through art the baser side of both man and beast. David Teniers – I think he meant David Teniers the Younger – and 'other Hollanders' used dogs 'merely to obtain unclean jest'; more serious painters – Rembrandt and Rubens – painted them 'only in savage chase, or butchered agony', 'signs of disgrace all the deeper because the powers desecrated are so great'. This is not a fair assessment of Rembrandt and Rubens and only slightly less unfair about Teniers, but it suggests that such an astute critic thought there was something distinctive about the art of dogs of Venice. He is right.

The dog's gaze and the dog's body come into their own first in the work of the Venetians. No longer just an occasional figure in a great religious cycle, a new naturalism, the surge of interest in classical subjects and more importantly, the revolution wrought by Giotto in what it meant to exemplify, brought a whole kennels of dogs. Titian, Veronese and Tintoretto worked in the same place at roughly the same time; their rivalry is reflected in their art. They share a certain theatricality. No group of artists ever did more with dogs than they did.[23]

The Storyteller

Vittore Carpaccio in the generation before Veronese, Titian, and Tintoretto could not resist a dog doing the work of world-making. One of the great narrative painters of the Renaissance, he mobilized dogs – a lot of them emerged from his imagination – in his visual stories even though none of their literary sources mentioned them.

The most famous and funniest one is the small white dog – critics have variously described it as a spitz (Ruskin), a spaniel, a Maltese, and a mongrel (Jan Morris) – in *St Augustine in his Study* (1502) commissioned by the Scuola di San Giorgio degli Sciavoni in Venice [**76**].[24] It steals the show. Augustine is writing to St Jerome with whom he had previously exchanged almost a dozen letters. He looks up to see 'an indescribable light, not seen in our times, and hardly to be described in our poor language' that suddenly floods his study; the room is bathed in it. It mystically bears the news that Jerome has died. 'Naturalistic Supernaturalism,' one art historian calls the broader Venetian interest in representing otherworldly events through the ways in which light falls on the physical world. The late medieval account on which this interpretation of the painting is based also says that the light came with an 'ineffable and unknown fragrance, of all odours'. There is no hint that the dog notices those smells. But it, along with its master, sees the 'indescribable light'. Maybe Carpaccio meant for us to think that the dog even saw it first because, as Erwin Panofsky suggested, animals 'were credited during the period with superior awareness of the supernatural'. But there is no question, and without any reference to the painter's intention, that the saint and his dog were seeing it together.[25]

In a preparatory sketch Carpaccio had put an ermine, a species of weasel, where the dog is in the finished painting; infrared reflectography

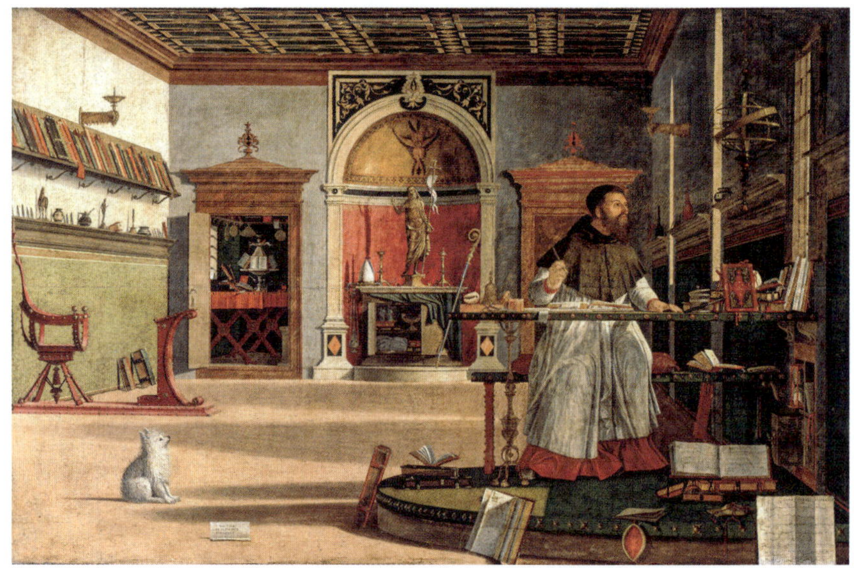

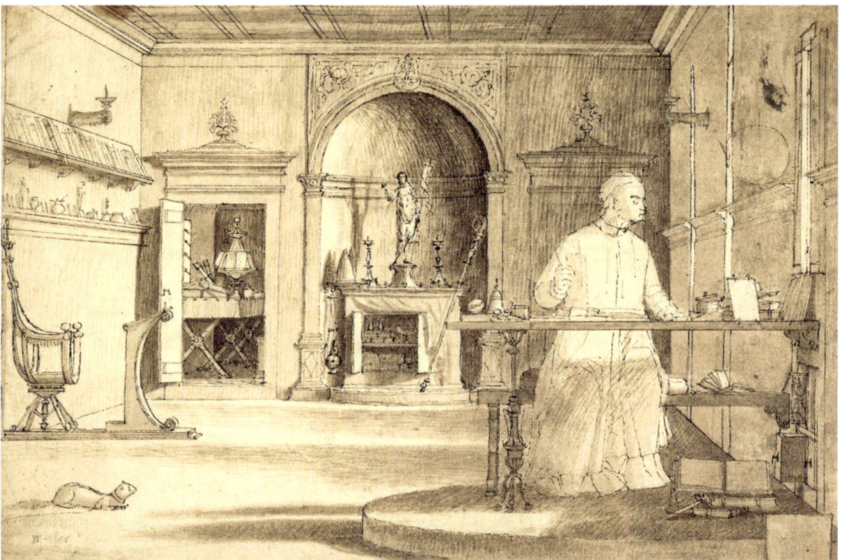

76–77 The little white dog steals the show in Vittore Carpaccio's *St Augustine in his Study* (1501–5), but a preparatory sketch tells us that the artist had first considered painting an ermine.

reveals that it was still there in the painting until he thought better of it. Had the ermine remained we would be seeing an entirely different final picture [**77**]. Legend had it that weasels would sooner die than have their white fur bloodied by a dog and hunter. A weasel in the painting, had not Carpaccio changed his mind, would have been an iconographic sign identifying Augustine with purity. There would be no naturalistic interpretation for its being there: weasels – unlike dogs – do not frequent the studies of saints and scholars. But more importantly, we would have been forced to see differently had Carpaccio stayed with the low-slung weasel.[26] Without the dog's upward gaze the painting would have lost its diagonal axis; we'd be looking at St Augustine's feet and not up to the light and to the human figure 'admonish[ing] and point[ing] out to us', in Alberti's words, 'what is happening'. The dog is essential to the painting's *istoria*.

It guides the gaze to what it needs to see and understand; the shadows on the floor do some of the same structural work, but only the dog directs us to its meaning. The lower-left to upper-right diagonal axis passes right through it. It is sitting in a field of geometrically organized light and shadow. A small white patch catches the glint in its eyes and is reflected on its wet nose. Its face is as captivating as the human's; the saint and his dog are in this together, witnesses to the revelation of Jerome's death. Next to the white dog is a sign that says 'VICTOR CARPATHIUS FINGEBAT' (Fashioned [or imagined] by Vittore Carpaccio). Carpaccio puts his mark where our eyes go first as if he too were seeing like – or at least with – a dog. (It would be abandoning the period eye to suggest that the dog may also be asking for a walk, although Carpaccio himself in his *Arrival of the English Ambassadors* represents three dogs on-lead walking out in the piazza.)

The dogs in his strange and mysterious *Young Knight in a Landscape* (*c.* 1510) are not as prominent or central as the one in the St Augustine painting. It is the young knight in armour who first commands our attention; the snow-white ermine on the lower left and white lily on the right are probably next; or perhaps the knight in heraldic garb on horseback in the upper left. But if we look again we will notice the white dog with brown around its ears and eyes coming into the scene from the left; unlike the horse it surveys the scene. On the right side is a brown dog with a white snout and white paw climbing out of a dream-like landscape onto the main plane of the picture. The knight's sword leads our eye to it. These two are innocent dogs, intent on being dogs, and not getting mixed up with all the erudite symbolism in the painting [**78**]. They seem to be interested only in seeing what is going on.

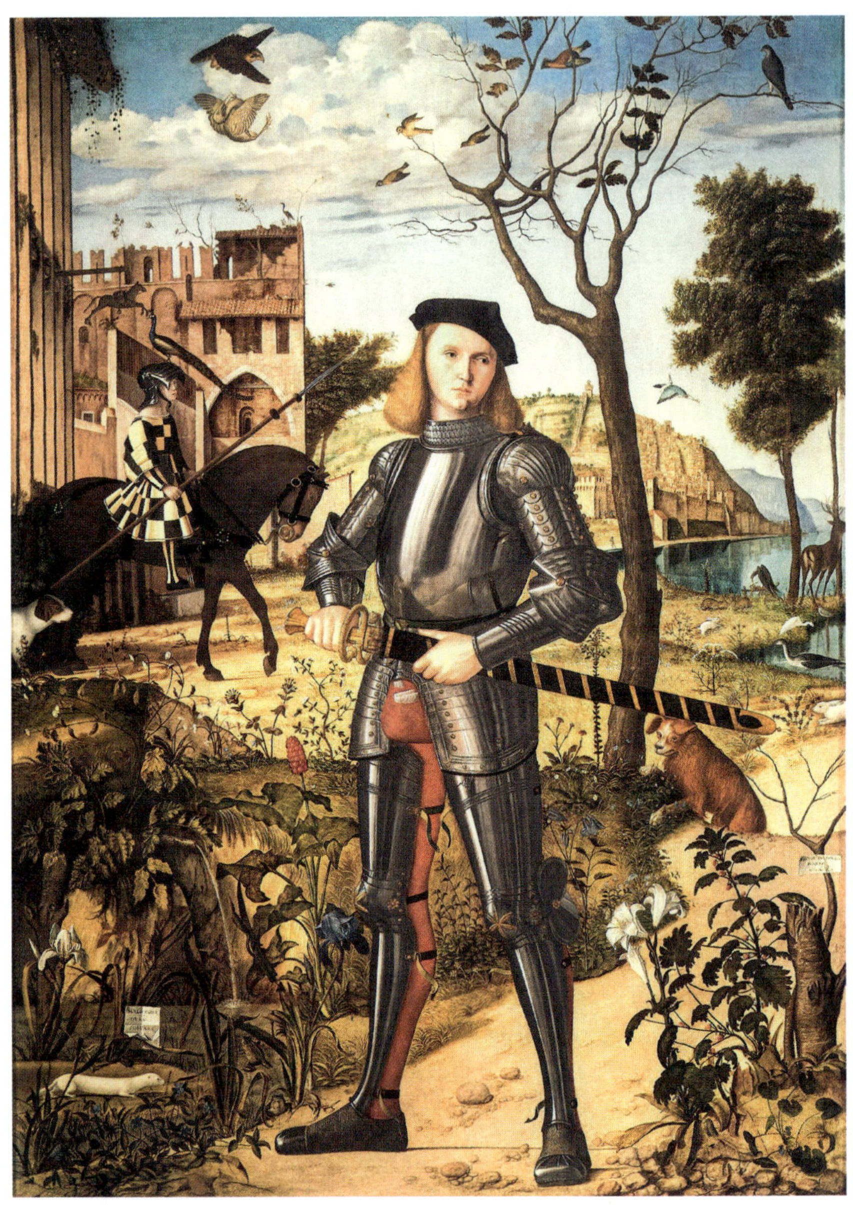

78 Carpaccio's *Young Knight in a Landscape* (c. 1505), with the ermine and two dogs.

No one knows the identity of the knight or even whether he is anyone in particular. (If he were, it would make this the first Renaissance full-length portrait.) The figure is almost a mannikin for the virtuosically painted armour that, thanks to oil paint, can be rendered so shiny that it reflects the inside of the elbow. And because no one knows who the sitter is, no one seems to know what the painting is about. It is full of heraldic and other sorts of signs that must have iconographical significance: lilies, a weasel/ermine, a deer with horns, a rabbit, a cut tree. But a great deal of effort has not come closer to decoding what this configuration of elements means.[27]

Paying attention to the dogs offers a different approach to seeing this painting. They are come into its world much like naïve human viewers might with no sense that they need to decode anything. If I were the poet Rilke, I'd say this is as close as art gets to representing innocent seeing, although there probably isn't such a thing; that is, the dogs are seeing things for themselves in the way that so impressed Rilke about the way Cézanne saw. The dog on the right is on its hind legs, half in and half out of the plane of where the knight and the horse stand, climbing out of a still more mysterious world, scrambling up to the main action, looking past the foreground and out at us and at the knight in a sly sort of way. In a painting suffused by shades of brown, its reddish clay colour calls attention to itself; its face is a real face, the face of a creature who is anxious to see what is going on.

Carpaccio did not invent the dog on the right; it is based on a drawing by Pisanello [**79**].[28] He elaborates in great detail down to the space between its toes, the tiny dab of paint representing the whites of its eye, and the fine hair on its ear. And he invented its place in the *istoria* that organizes this image; that is, he took a one-off sketch from one of Pisanello's notebooks and mobilized it for his purposes, a visual cue to look.

The second dog, the one on the left, is wandering in, looking straight ahead to see what is to be seen; it represents us as we first come upon this strange tableau. The colours of its body are the inverse of the other dog's brown ears on white. Carpaccio seems to have invented this particular dog, but its formal role, half in and half out, had been a formal commonplace for at least a hundred years. Together these dogs frame the central figure of the knight almost like theatregoers straining to see the action on stage.[29]

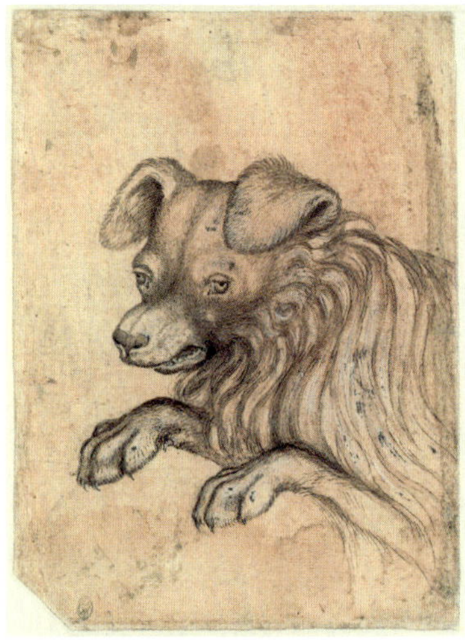

79 Pisanello's *Head of a Dog* (fifteenth century) is the model for one of Carpaccio's dogs.

The dog in the seventh of Carpaccio's nine-part narrative series, *The Legend of St Ursula: The Arrival of St Ursula during the Siege of Cologne*, plays a central role in the composition but, unlike the dogs in other paintings of the series – walking on the piazza in *The Arrival of the Ambassadors* or guarding her bed in *The Dream of St Ursula* – it plays no part in the narrative or in setting the scene [**80**]. Ursula has gone to Rome where she convinces the pope to join her on a pilgrimage. The Pope, Ursula, and 11,000 virgins have arrived in Cologne that is being besieged, by the Huns in the Roman martyrology from which the story comes, by the Ottoman Mehmet II, Venice's great enemy, in Carpaccio's modernized version. There Ursula will be shot through the heart with an arrow by the Hun leader and her 11,000 virgins slaughtered; this is the subject of the next, the eighth, painting of the series. In *The Arrival of St Ursula during the Siege of Cologne* Carpaccio seems only marginally interested in representing the arrival of the protagonist and her companions; the pope and St Ursula are tiny figures leaning over the ship's railing and the crowd of virgins on the deck are easy to miss. The stage of their coming martyrdom – the city – fills the image; there is not much evidence of a siege except for the Ottoman flags and little to suggest what is to come except for the presence of armed men.

But the dog with its red collar, painted with great care and detail, is unmissable. It sits on the edge of the dock that is at the end of a path that wends down from between buildings in the distant city. The path, seeming to narrow as it rises, is part of Carpaccio's creation of a sense

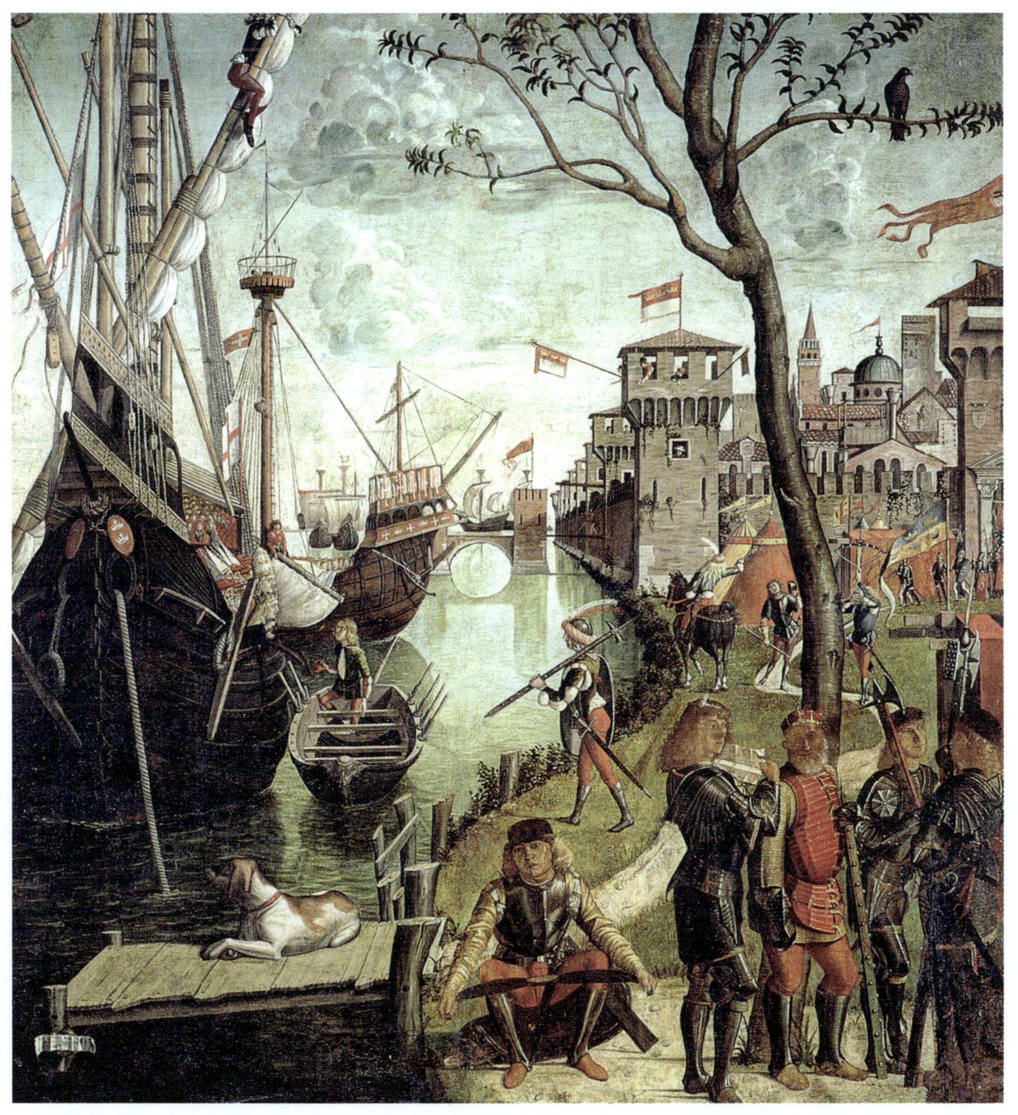

80 *The Arrival of St Ursula during the Siege of Cologne* (*c.* 1490), the seventh painting in Carpaccio's nine-part narrative series describing the legend of the saint.

of depth. The dog has wandered down to the harbour and looks dreamily across the bow of the ship at a right angle to the longitudinal perspective that guides our eyes along the shimmering waters of the river to the architectural vista that fills the background and the ships seen hazily beyond the bridge. It is interested in what is going on outside the frame. Its brown and white dappled coat demands attention. It is part of a triangle with the five men grouped to its right; like the anchor rope mooring the ship, it moors the painting at its apex.

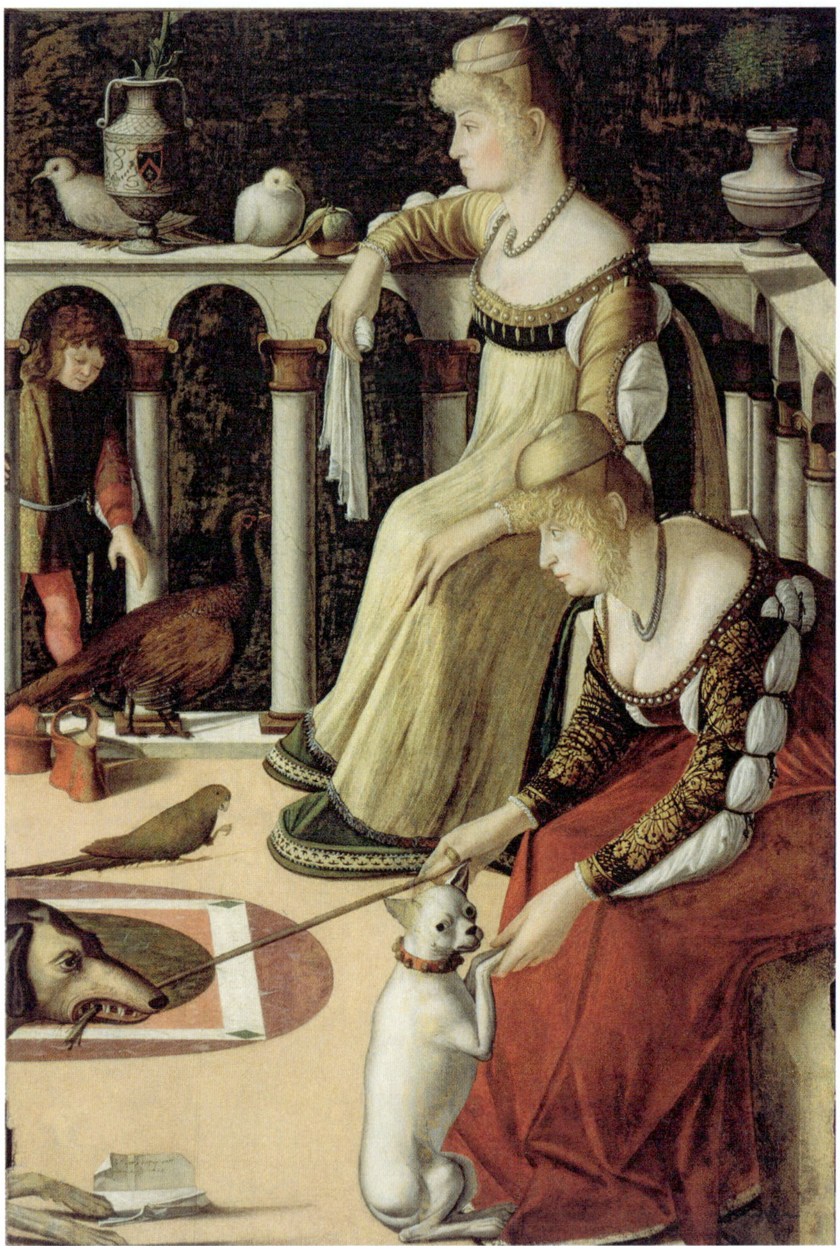

81 Carpaccio's *Two Venetian Ladies* (*c.* 1490), one of four wooden panels that constitute a larger work. As the adjacent panel of the painting is lost, we do not know what, if anything, the women fixate upon.

The dog's gaze suggests perhaps the painter's attention to worlds beyond that of the immediate story. Maybe it is dreamily looking toward Ursula's martyrdom, the dog with a premonition of what is to come. Maybe it is just looking, being engaged with an almost religious devotion. It is the strongest gesture in the painting while at the same time it has no place in saints' hagiographical tradition. But imagine this image without the dog's strong lateral gaze, without its brilliant white colouration, without its anchoring the dock and just looking. Without its weighty presence. One can't miss the dog; the arriving pilgrims take a little more looking.

Dogs in Carpaccio are worth our attention because they are formally so prominent in making the configuration of his paintings cohere – visually and emotionally – and at the same time largely irrelevant to their narrative content or meaning in a larger sense. They are not needed, as we saw in chapter 2, in the way they are in many hunting pictures. They are not mythical or even traditional in their settings. Dogs do less pointing out what is happening in Carpaccio than they do in the work of some other artists, although they do that as well; in fact, they often, like the dog on the dock here, look at what is ostensibly not happening. Perhaps all they are doing is seeing, which is what our relationship to the visual arts entails. They are us.

We know something of the women in Carpaccio's *Two Venetian Ladies* [**81**]. They are members of a Venetian elite; they wear expensive clothes; there is a family crest although it has not been identified. But that does not get us very far. We don't know who they are – nineteenth-century critics thought they were courtesans.[30] What we see are dogs that are ostentatiously seeing; the woman in the red dress is only vaguely looking toward the dog to whom she is joined by a stick; the dog is not looking at her; and the white dog is far more interested in where the painter would be than in the women. All that gazing seems to do little for the purposes of narrative while at the same time it is doing a great deal formally and affectively: the brown dog establishes the horizontal axis of the painting; it looks resigned; the white one, forming a vertical axis, turns it head to give us – and the painter – a worried almost unbelieving look, to be sure we are looking. Carpaccio, over and over again, allies himself and his viewers with a dog seeing.

The Grand Master

Boy with Dogs in a Landscape [**82**] deserves special attention because of its place in the new order of dog portraiture that Titian and his colleagues started – Veronese's *Cupid with Two Dogs* and Bassano's *Two Hunting Dogs*, for example; because one would have to have a heart of stone not to be touched by it; and, in the context of this chapter, because of the formal features of the painting. It was painted in the 1570s when Titian was over eighty. The boy, the nursing dog, and the background are rendered in broad strokes suggestive of his 'late style', much like the dynamic swerves of the *Death of Actaeon* (*see* 58); less so the large lab-like creature who dominates the right side of the painting, perhaps because it is borrowed from his 1550s *Portrait of a Soldier*.

No one has been able to say who the boy represents or what either he or the dogs framing him mean, each of them taking up more space on the canvas than its human – or mythical – putative subject. (Two more dogs are puppies nursing while their mother watches.) The gaze of the dog that the boy clutches is focused intently on a point just outside the frame of the painting where, if we were to reconstruct the geometry of the picture, the gaze of the nursing dog – her teats brightly lit – meets his as if to close a circle around the pups. And the brightly lit white of the puppies' heads pointing to the right is also part of a visual rhythm in a painting structured by the bodies and the eyes of the dogs.

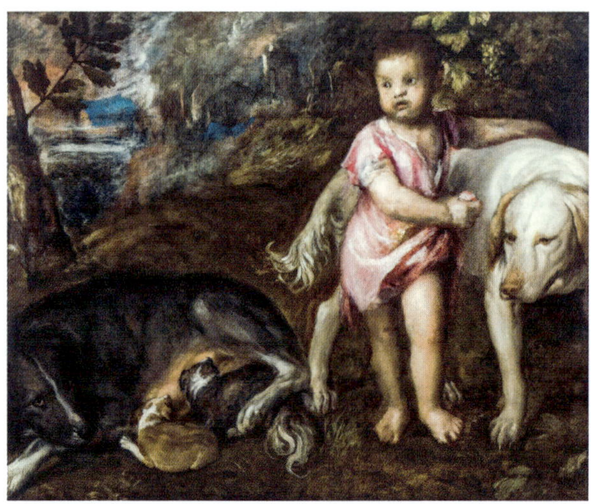

82 Titian's *Boy with Dogs in a Landscape* (1565–76).

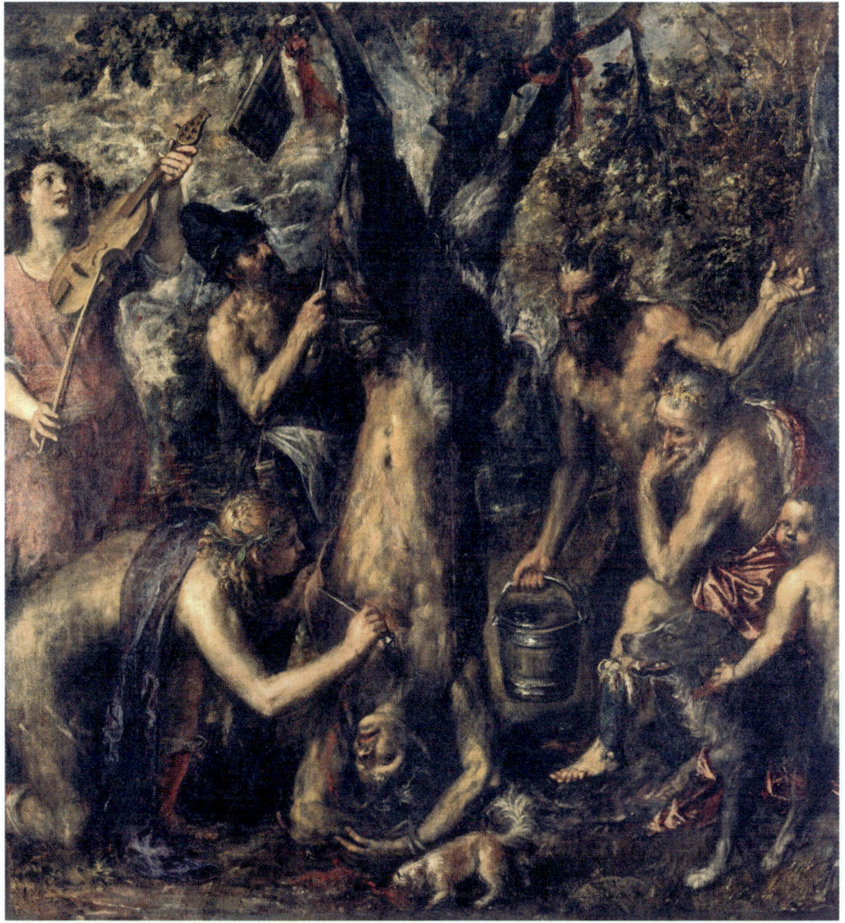

83 A mythological mash-up: Titian's *The Flaying of Marsyas* (c. 1570–76).

A vulnerable boy rendered in broad strokes is clutching a finely painted dog as a refuge from loneliness; its body, right rear leg, and bushy tail embrace him. They are bound together; their intimacy is mirrored in the dog with its puppies. We do not know if Titian loved dogs, but we know that like Carpaccio and Veronese he understood the power of their gaze.[31]

The boy in this painting gets a reprise in another of Titian's last works: *The Flaying of Marsyas* [**83**]. It is a bit of a mythological mash-up conflating the story in Ovid's *Metamorphoses* Book 6, in which the satyr Marsyas has foolishly challenged Apollo to a musical contest – pipes versus lyre – loses, and is flayed as punishment, with another story from Book XI in which King Midas – far right – judges Pan to be a better musician than Apollo and has his ears turned into those of an ass. (In the painting Titian interprets the lyre mentioned in Ovid as a *lira da braccio*, which was used in the Renaissance to accompany sung poetry as the ancient lyre had been.) A great deal of scholarship has gone into interpreting this painting with no consensus in sight. But there is no argument about the suffering of the satyr as the laurel-crowned god delicately carves skin from the flesh around his heart and a rough Phrygian satyr butchers his leg. Another Apollo figure – or maybe it is Orpheus – plays the lyre as he looks heavenward.

And then there are the dogs, one with the boy entering the scene, the other small one lapping blood. That one is not there because of its gaze but because of its intense concentration on blood – real blood. It is the same lapdog that appears in Titian's *Venus of Urbino* in the Uffizi but closer in spirit to the dogs in crucifixion paintings who attest to the reality of the bones and blood on Golgotha. The other dog, restrained perhaps by the boy, ever so lightly looks directly at the hand of Apollo. It bounds onto the scene while the strange and mysterious boy looks out at us. Together they do not so much help create the *istoria* of the painting as remind us that it is a narrative world – a horrible and gruesome one created by Titian that they have come upon and which they invite us to view.

The Greatest Dog Lover of the Renaissance

Kenneth Clark thought that Veronese was 'the greatest dog lover of the Renaissance', which accounted for why there are so many in his paintings. We have absolutely no biographical evidence to support this explanation.[32] Clark is right that there are a great number of dogs in Veronese's work but also, at least in Ruskin's eyes, these are dogs of a distinctive moral and social quality. While 'hard as he [Veronese] is on lap dogs', he also painted, Ruskin thought, 'one great heroic poem': *Cupid with Two Dogs*. In that painting two of them are shown with the 'highest, or spiritual view' of their nature: two magnificent mastiffs: 'wildest of beasts perhaps they would have been by nature' [**84**]. Between them is a beautiful boy, 'golden quivered', who represents, Ruskin thought, human love and is holding the great beasts by a chain in his hands.

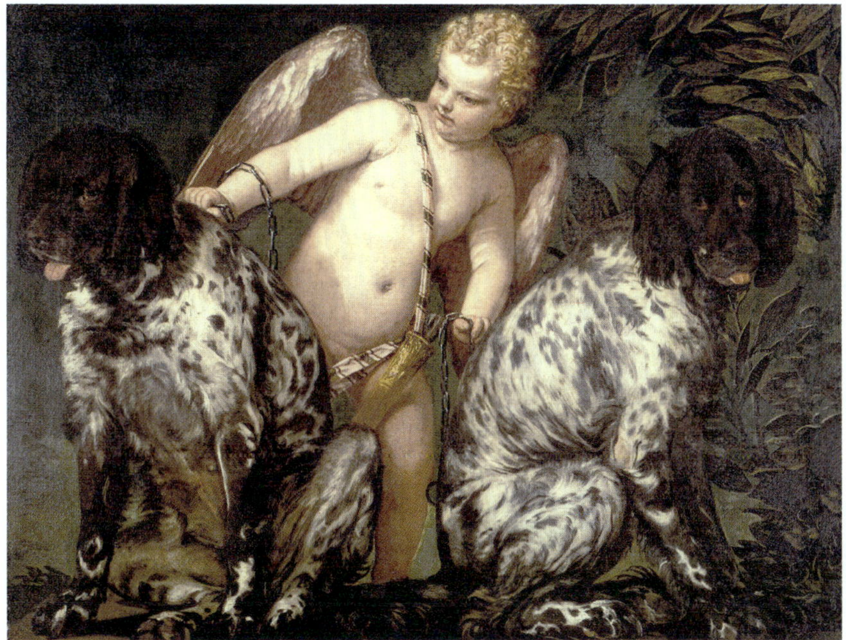

84 Veronese's *Cupid with Two Dogs* (1580), a 'great heroic poem'.

Love conquers savagery is how Ruskin would interpret the painting. But perhaps, the boy between these spectacular dogs becomes less a stand-in for human love – unpredictable – than the caretaker for dogs whose love is known for its steadfastness: amorous union as faithful as that of dogs. Their allegorical meaning, whatever it is, seems to me less important in looking at this painting than the sweet intimacy with which the dogs are painted, grounded in their gaze and their sheer benign weightiness. That is, if we forsake the 'period eye' – the way engaged Renaissance viewers might look for allegorical significance – and instead we see two minutely observed dogs. The one on the right looks quizzically and seductively out at us; the other, the more relaxed one on the left, looks with Cupid toward the painter outside the frame. Perhaps contemporary viewers would have seen them as having been once the 'wildest of beasts' but they seem very far from that now.

Visually they are the stars of the show in their almost psychedelically painted black on white spotted fur, their red tongues and glistening eyes like points of light. The curves of their backs frame the bathed, soft flesh of the Cupid figure; the leg of the dog on the left is intertwined with his

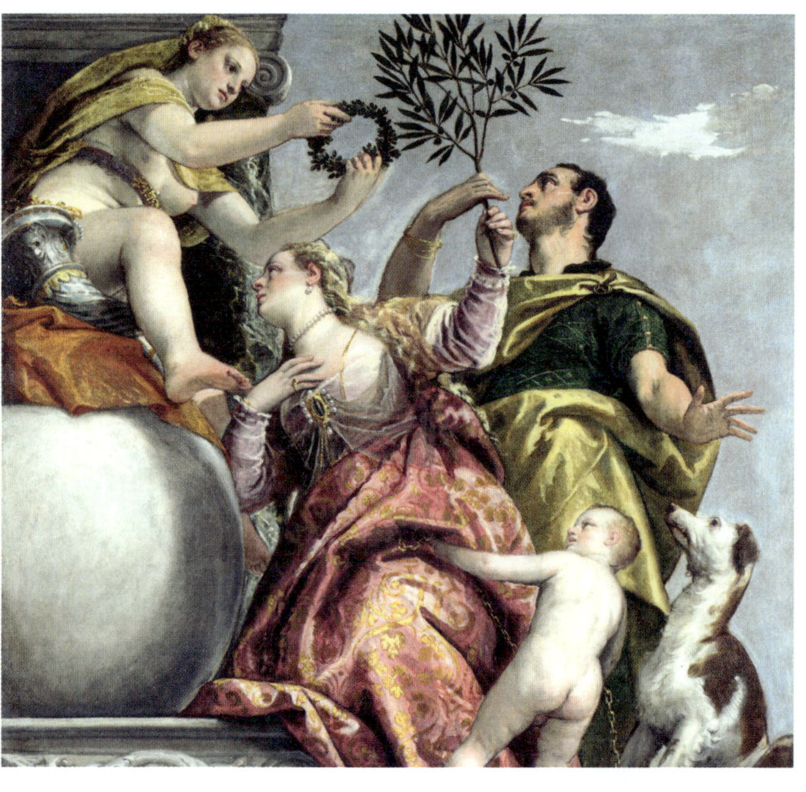

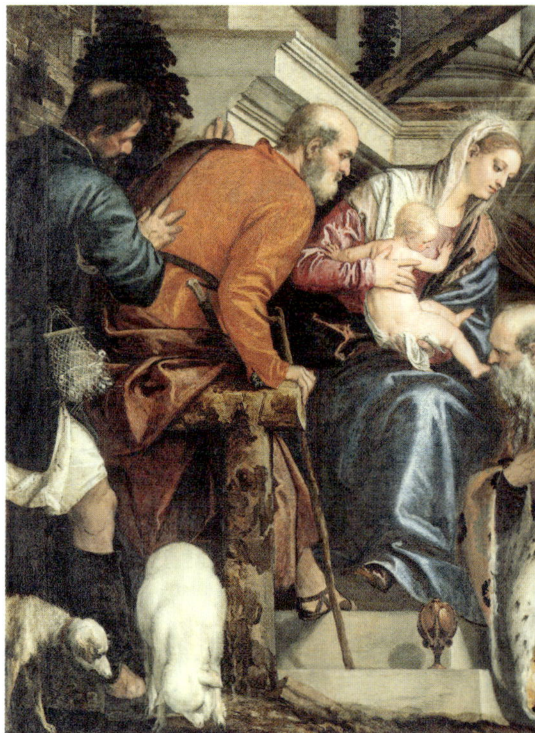

85 (*above*) An engaged dog is witness to the crowning of love in Veronese's *Happy Union* (*c.* 1575).

86 (*right*) The sombre dogs in *The Adoration of the Magi* (1571) are more typical of Veronese.

leg – he is astride of it – and touches the left paw of the other dog. All this in a severely constrained space, a vignette, that stands at the opposite end of a scale, with Veronese's great theatrical scenes with their dogs at the other. This is a formally virtuosic painting, whatever else it is about or means, about dogs, doggishness, and the gaze. T. J. Clark gets us closer to how dogs figure more generally in Veronese's thinking. His 'attitude to earthly existence', Clark suggests, '. . . make[s] for a special kind of sympathy and tenderness where four-footed animals were concerned'. His case in point, the fluffy furred white and brown dog in the *Happy Union* of the fourth of the 'Allegories of Love', firmly grounded in the lower corner looking with big wide-open eyes at Love herself, is a good but perhaps not a typical example. A dog in a great allegorical ceiling painting where it does not belong is funny in ways that dogs usually aren't [**85**].[33]

The dogs in the Dresden version of *The Adoration of the Magi* are more typical of Veronese [**86**]. The one on the lower left is 'in thoughtful dialogue with the marvelous wooly lamb', both absorbed in the ground they stand on, the lamb nosing around for food perhaps, the dog intrigued by whatever is going on if not talking to the shepherd's lamb. Yet there are two other dogs in the painting that Clark does not mention but that

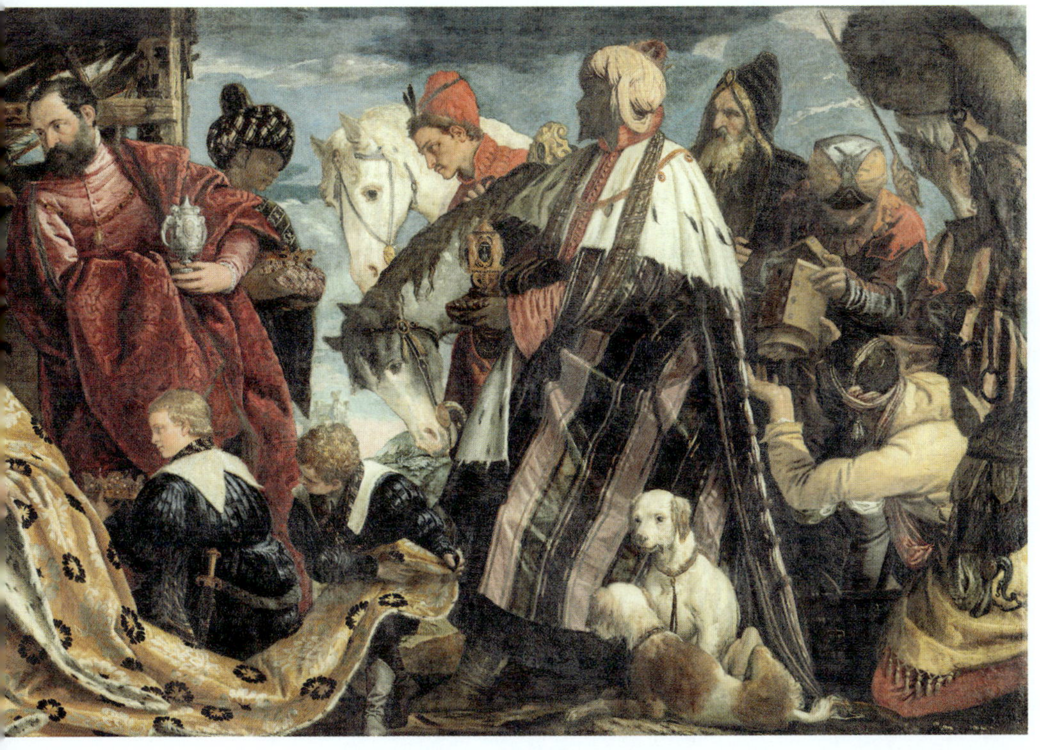

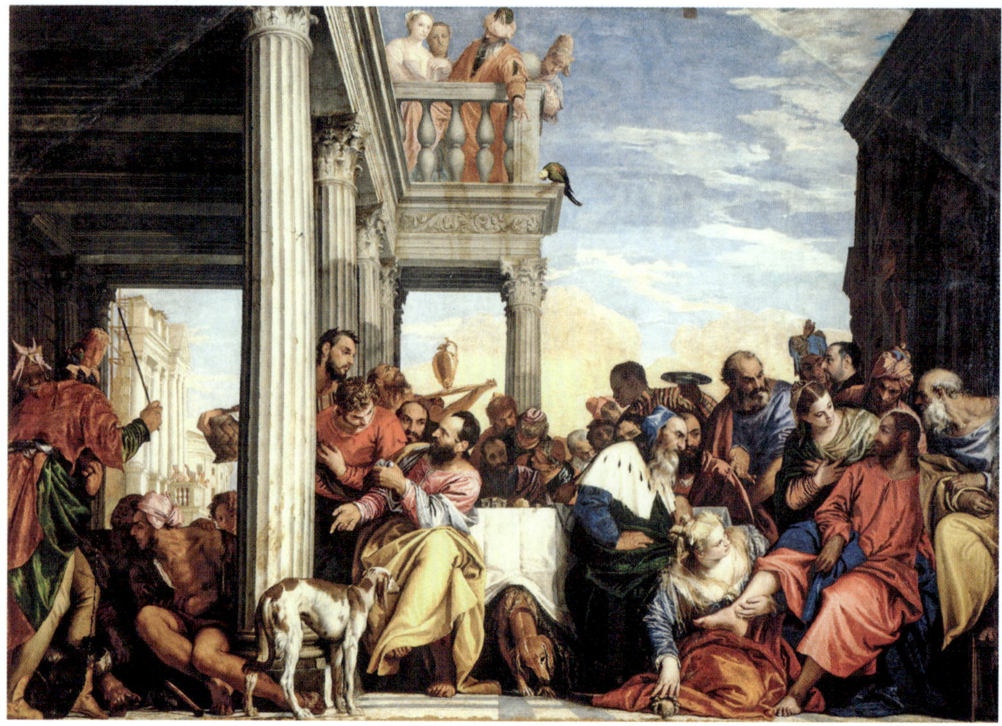

87 The Turin version of Veronese's *Christ in the House of Simon the Pharisee* (c. 1556).

are worthy of our attention: the brilliantly painted white one enveloped in the magenta cloak of one of the Magi, gazing out, as modest and humble as his master is grand. A down-to-earth creature. And just in front of this dog at the front edge of the painting is a third one, shaggy, brown and white, looking in the painting. These two dogs are a pair, an intimate encounter in a great spectacle: formally important in the structure of the painting but also – and because of that – loci of emotion. The white dog looks out patiently at us, resigned to waiting, quizzical and unknowing about the great event that the Magi and we are witnessing. It seems to stop or at least to slow time.

T. J. Clark asks his readers finally to look at the Turin version of *Christ in the House of Simon the Pharisee* as an example of the 'kind of exchange between animal and human that goes on repeatedly in Veronese' [**87**]. Luke 7:36–50 tells the story of Simon inviting Christ to his house. 'A woman in the city, which was a sinner', in other words a prostitute – often identified as Mary Magdalene – learns that Christ is there and comes to him weeping. She kisses and washes his feet and anoints him with ointment. Simon is appalled that Jesus allows this, and Jesus replies by saying that the woman – a sinner – treated him with respect while Simon failed to offer any of the signs of hospitality: 'thou gavest me no kiss: but this woman since the time I came in hath not ceased to kiss my feet'. To her Jesus says, 'Thy faith hath saved thee; go in peace.' (Veronese added Mary and Martha from St John's version of the Feast at the House of Lazarus and perhaps also, in the Turin version, the figure in yellow, who may be Judas protesting the waste of ointment.)

The dogs' world mirrors that of the humans: as the Magdalene is washing Christ's feet a dog is attending to its paws nearby. It emerges from under the tablecloth as if from behind a stage curtain, looking at the hand of Mary which is touching the fragrant ointment in the jar. Its brown fur emerges from the linen's whiteness. Its right paw is but one tile's distance from the shoeless left foot of the human. The other dog – the brown and white one – is 'dignity itself, four legs planted firmly, its colour as the column behind it'. Its rear feet overlap the feet of the beggar and visually balance Mary on the same plane on the right. It looks over at the brown dog with a side glance at the anointing of the feet of Jesus.

That lower rectangle of the painting – the feet of the beggar, the dog looking past the intensely yellow cloak and at the Magdalene – is a virtuosic example of Veronese's theatrical gifts, of how in even the grandest tableaus (this one is 4.1 x 4.7 metres) dogs humanize humans. Formally, they constitute the visual centre of a storm of action and look where we are meant to look. Two brightly painted humans are of course looking intensely at the main action – at Jesus – in the tableau to the right of the painting. But the white and brown dogs on the left are taking it all in as if Veronese were seeing like – or with – them, connecting the human with the animal world.

Veronese's sympathy and tenderness toward dogs and his insistence on having them help us see through their eyes are most prodigally on display in *The Wedding Feast at Cana*, painted for the refectory of the monastery San Giorgio Maggiore [**88**]. It is the only one of his feast pictures in which Jesus is performing a miracle – turning water into red wine – and not just dining: the divine immanent in the world. It is also the most wildly profane, operatic of Veronese's feast paintings: a festival of eating

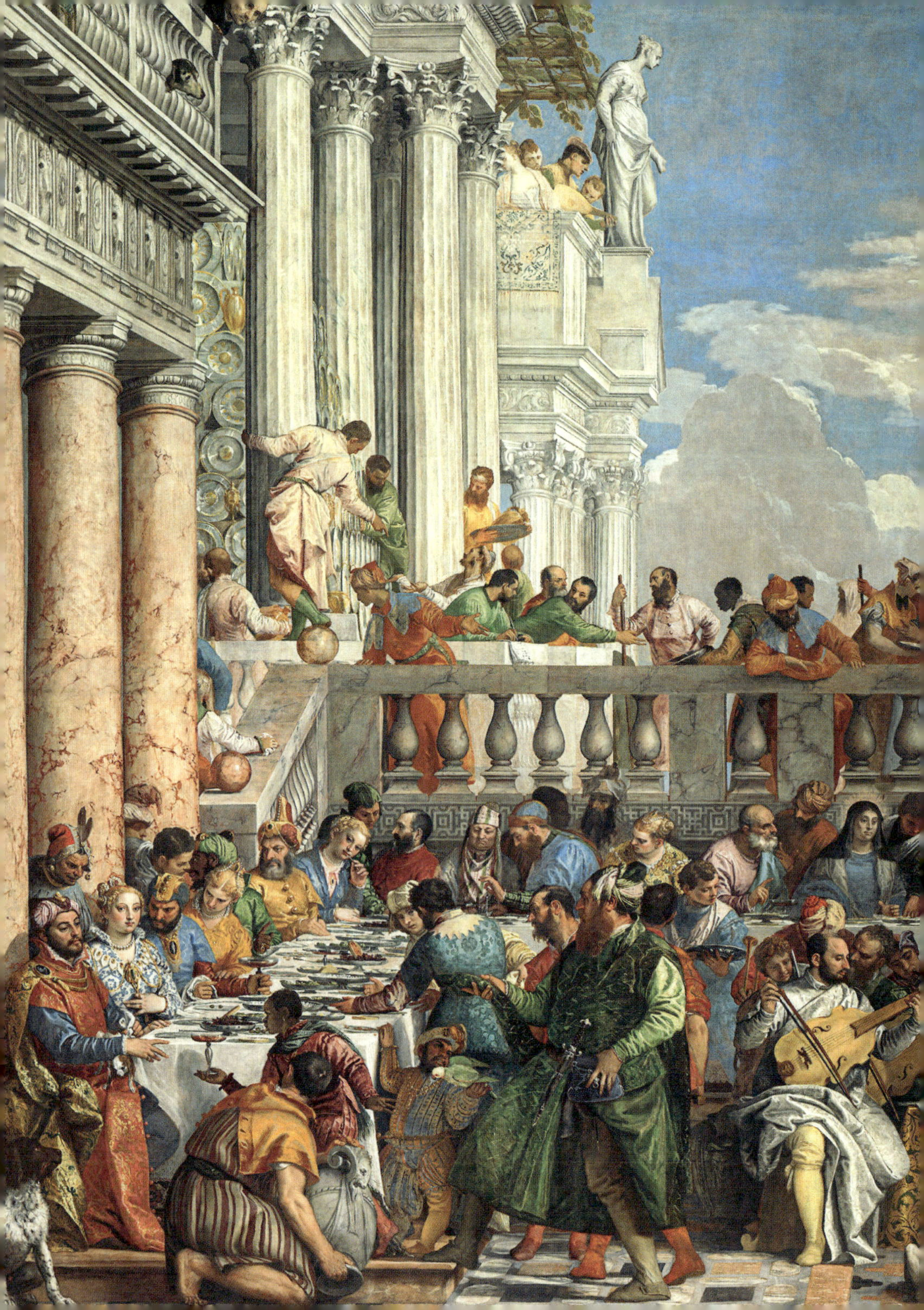

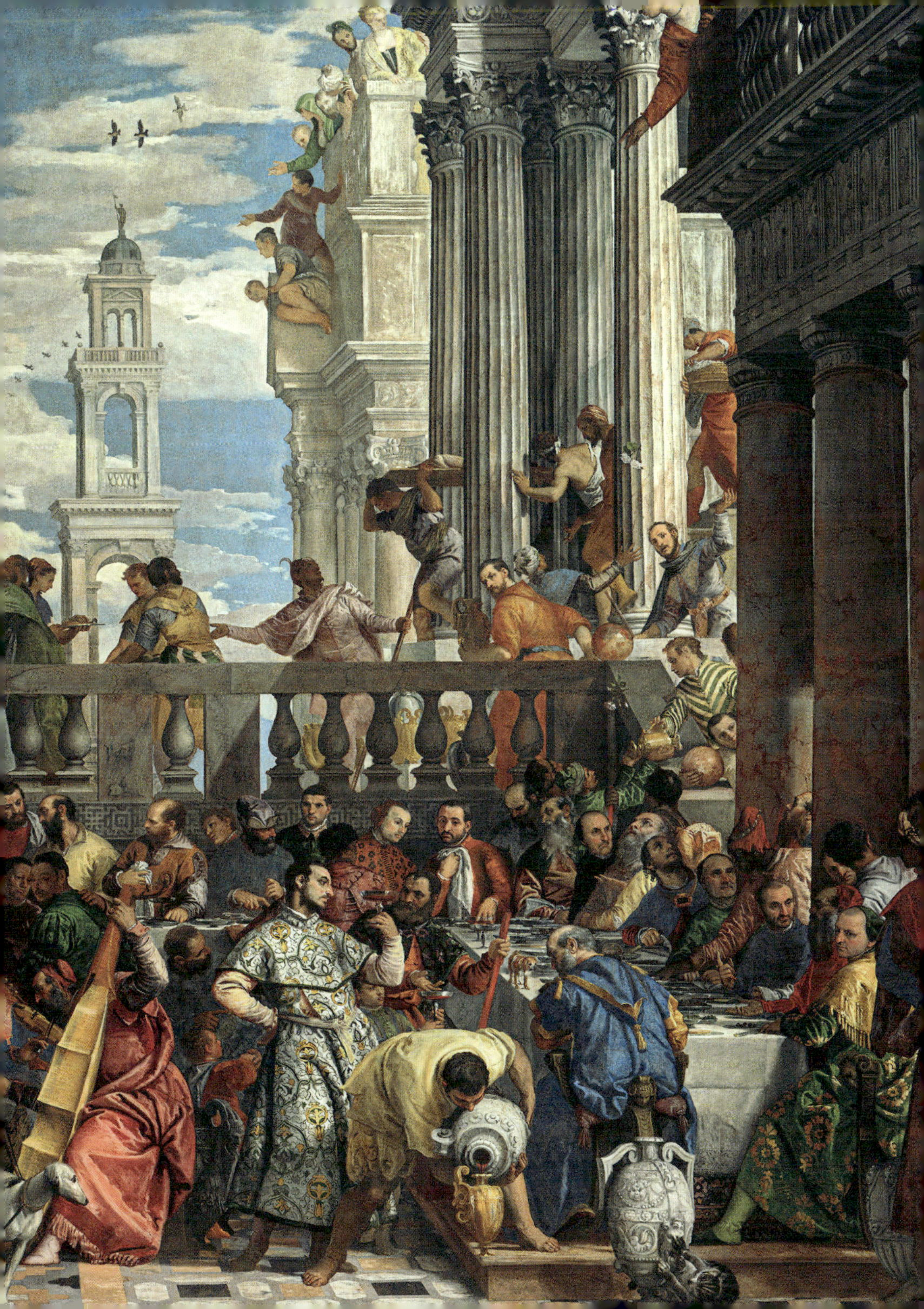

and drinking and music-making luxuriantly set in sixteenth-century Cana. Dogs as formal elements in the structure bring the miracle down to earth; sweet, innocent, puzzled in their gaze, absorbed in the here and now. Grounded. Or to be more precise, they are grounded in the here and now of the human drama. Only the small one on the right arm of the table as we look at the painting is probably only interested in the food.[34]

It is Veronese's best-known and at 6.8 x 9.75 metres the largest of his paintings. The young General Napoleon showed ruthless good taste in art when, after his troops conquered Venice in 1797, he ordered it ripped from the walls of San Giorgio Maggiore and taken to Paris as war plunder, wrapped in a Titian, a Tintoretto, and two other Veroneses. It now hangs in the largest room of the Louvre, easy to view in a leisurely way because it is on a wall opposite the *Mona Lisa*, almost 200 times smaller, which draws the crowds to its side of the room.

A Cecil B. DeMille epic of a painting, it fills 75 square metres of canvas with 135 human characters, five dogs, and one cat, who may be playing with one mouse in a spectacular Roman classical setting. (In real life, before it was stolen, the painting had hung in a famous neo-classical building designed by Palladio.) It is vast also in reputation and influence: the Venetian painter and seventeenth-century engraver Marco Boschini said it was not just a painting but magic on canvas. It was studied and copied by generations of painters. Jacques-Louis David, the French Revolutionary painter, who saw the loot after it was installed in the Louvre, thought it 'the greatest known picture in the world' and said that it inspired his *Coronation of Napoleon*.

Multiple dogs' gazes frame the painting and look at the party from more angles than we can. Amid all the festivities and the halo on Christ they are its humble observers; self-contained; keeping company; witnessing. At the top left nearest the front plane of the painting is dog no. 1 looking down through the balustrade directly at Jesus; the humans further along are looking elsewhere except for a woman paired with the dog looking down from the other side. At the bottom left is dog no. 2: its head brown, its delicately painted chest white with brown spots; Veronese's dog fur is a virtuoso performance. That dog is coming upon

Previous page: 88 *The Wedding Feast at Cana* (1562–3), Veronese's epic painting.

the scene just as we, its viewers, are. It is half in and half out and seems to be looking both up at the black serving boy and over to the rest of the action, curious perhaps at what the hubbub is about. The bright white paint of its fur begins the swathe of white cloth a third of the way up that will take our eyes to the central figure. It is looking up at Jesus' white shining face and invites us to join it.

Down-stage centre are two more dogs – large greyhounds – nos. 3 and 4. They are at the viewer's eye level and form the horizontal base of the painting as well as of its vertical axis. Together they hold down the floor. The nose of dog no. 3, the contemplative one, lying on the ground, resigned as dogs are to waiting patiently as its humans do what they do, is at the front edge of the canvas. Its nose is about to poke out. It is at the exact midpoint of the painting looking dreamily along the floor. Maybe it is glancing over at dog no. 2 entering, but really it has a look of being there, near asleep but still watchful, a quiet pose like that of the more famous dog in Dürer's *Melancholia I* (*see* 102).

Its companion, dog no. 4, stands and looks to stage left. In contrast to that of its partner, it leans, straining on its lead, in that direction and invites us to move our eyes there. It may be looking over at the cat which, like most cats in Western art, is paying no attention to what humans are doing. Perhaps it is looking at the last dog in the painting as we scan left to right: the small one on the table intent on food. 'Oh, if I could only pray,' Luther says of his dog Tölpel, 'the way this dog watches the meat.' A dog in art is so often about attentiveness. There is also a vertical connection between that dog and the rest of the painting. The bow of the bass viol players looks almost like a lead; when our eyes follow it upwards, they come to Christ, who is seated directly above the space between the two dogs.[35]

We in fact have almost no documentary evidence why any painter, and Veronese in particular, was interested in thinking with dogs. But we do in his case have a tantalizing small hint because on 18 July 1573 he was called before the Inquisition to answer questions about one of his paintings, specifically about a dog that figures prominently, front and centre [**89**].[36]

The Inquisitor asked if he had any idea why he had been summoned. Veronese replied that he did not although he speculated it might have been because the Inquisitors had summoned the Prior of San Giovani e

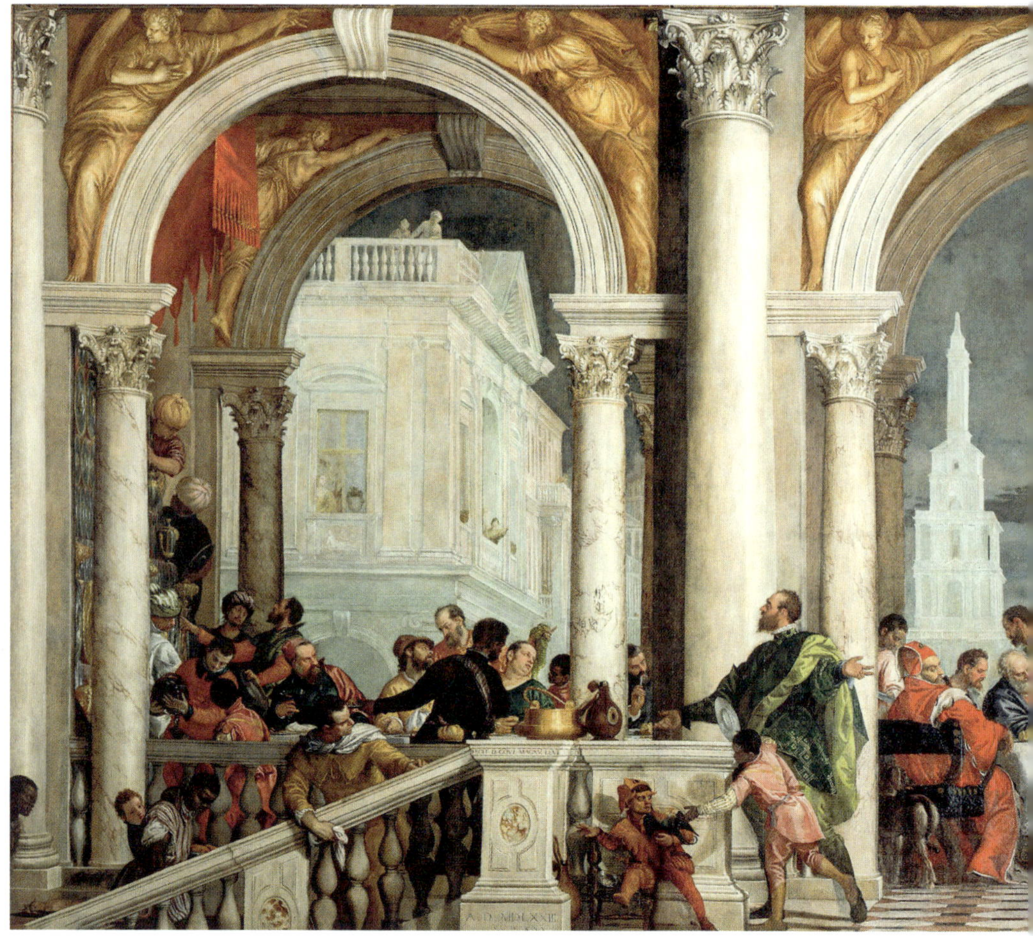

89 Veronese was challenged by the Inquisition for his inclusion of a dog in what was to have been a Last Supper, so he changed the title to *The Feast in the House of Levi* (1573).

Paulo who had commissioned a 'Last Supper' from him as a replacement for a Titian on the same subject and 'ordered him to have painted [in the picture] a Magdalen in place of a dog'. It had been more than three months since the painting had been finished; the dog was still there; no penitent prostitute had been added. Veronese confessed, that he had not done what they had ordered the Prior to order him to do. He told the Inquisitor that he would gladly do 'everything necessary for my honour and for that of my painting', but that he did 'not understand how a figure of Magdalen would be suitable there . . .'

He had every reason not to understand. It is generally accepted that the painting in question was intended to be, as requested by the monastery, a Last Supper; we can identify it from all the detailed questions the

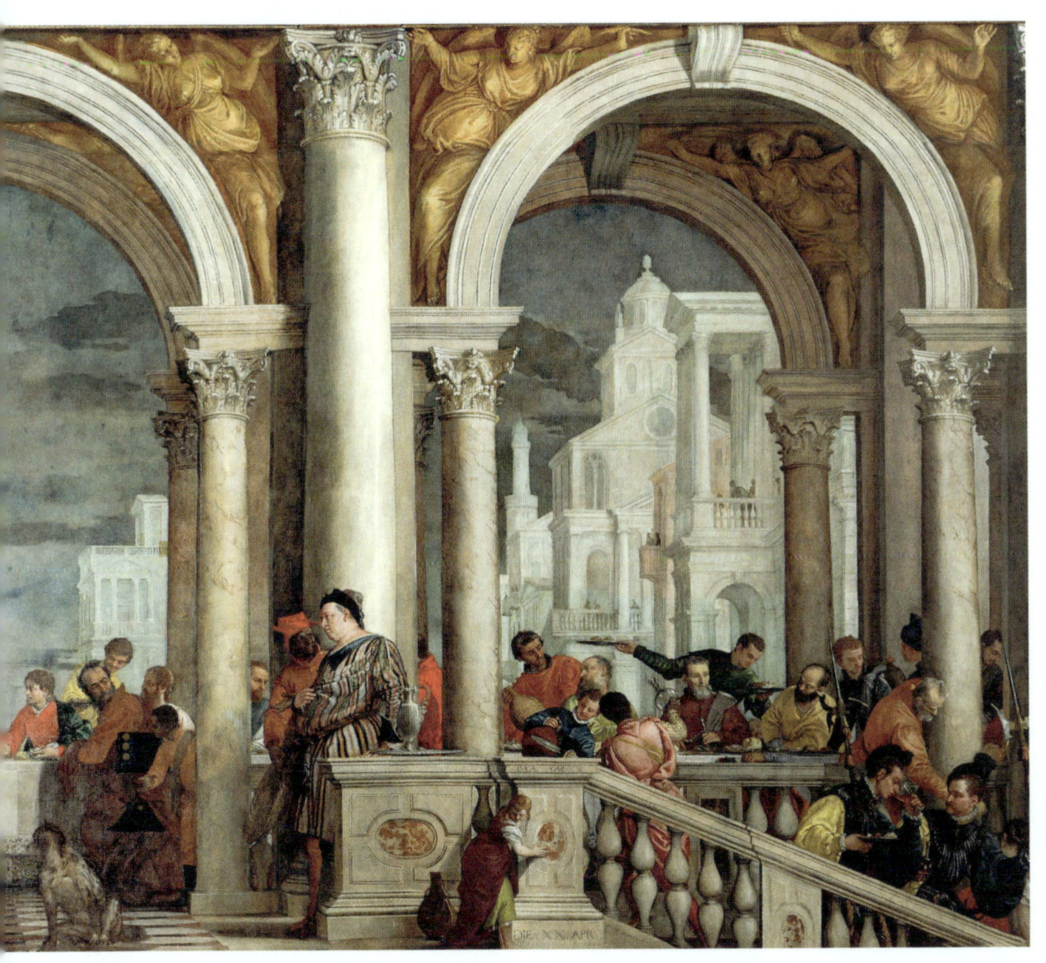

Inquisitors asked and from its subsequent history. He might himself have caused some confusion by saying the painting was of the 'Last Supper that Jesus Christ took with His Apostles in the House of Simon . . .' when the Inquisitor asked what picture he was speaking about, although the Last Supper was neither at the house of Simon the Pharisee where the Magdalen story took place (Luke 7:36–50) nor of Simon the Leper (Mark 14:3–9 and Matthew 26:6–13) where Mary anointed Jesus. Veronese made no pretence in any of his feast scenes or other religious painting of faithfully illustrating a text. He was not unusual in this regard.

This was also not a Galileo moment: dogs in religious paintings did not threaten the teachings of the Church; there are plenty of them in paintings of The Last Supper. And they would be particularly appropriate in a commission from a Dominican monastery because of their well-known association with the order's founder, St Dominic de Guzman.

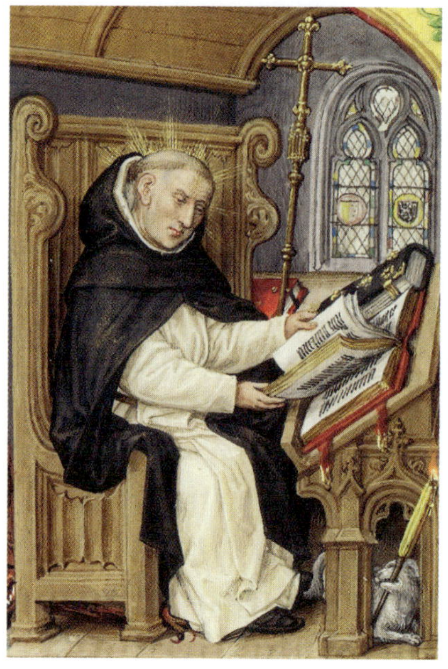

90 St Dominic reading with his trademark torch-carrying dog. Detail of a miniature from the *Spinola Hours* (c. 1510–20).

91 (*right*) Dogs as doppelgängers: detail from the *Allegory of the Active and Triumphant Church* (c. 1365–8).

A black dog had announced to the saint's mother 'that she would bear in her womb a dog who, with a burning torch in his mouth and leaping from her womb, seemed to set the whole earth on fire'.[37] She named her son after St Dominic of Silo, who had interceded on her behalf when she had failed to conceive. A dog with a torch in its mouth had already become in the late Middle Ages an iconographical sign for her son, the saint, in painting and sculpture for the order named after him and a logo until this day also for parishes named after the order's founder [**90**]. Everyone would know this. And, either in response to this story or independently much was made already in the Middle Ages of how the name of the order in Latin – '*Dominicanus*' – could easily be repurposed as *Domini canis* ('Dogs of the Lord'): dogs as the doppelgängers of the monks themselves, scurrying around corralling souls as in Andrea di Bonaiuto's 1365 fresco *Allegory of the Active and Triumphant Church* [**91**].

But the problem was not, as Veronese first guessed, the presence of a dog instead of a Magdalen. In fact, he was not summoned in front of the Venetian Inquisition for heresy or even dubious iconography, although that charge was the ostensible subject of his trial. Veronese was collateral damage of local ecclesiastical politics, caught up in a struggle between Rome and Venice. The Inquisitor needed to prove himself to a new papal

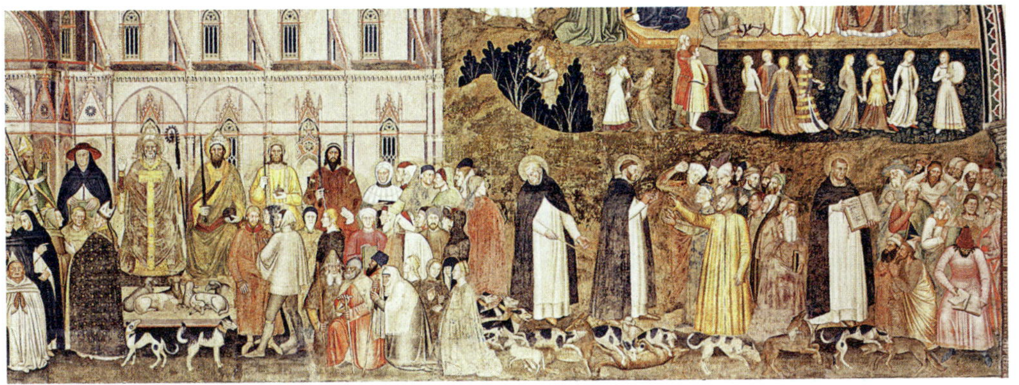

nuncio.[38] In the context of the Counter-Reformation this painting could be construed as suspicious because of its indisputable theatrical extravagance; the Council of Trent had charged bishops with making sure that religious paintings were appropriately decorous and true to text.

Veronese's only defence against this sort of attack – in addition to trying to claim he was no worse than Michelangelo in allowing his imagination full play – was a version of art for art's sake: 'We painters take the same licence the poets and the jesters take . . .' He filled the vast space of the canvas appropriately as his imagination dictated: his job was 'to create the painting as I thought fit, it was large and could accommodate numerous figures': 'figures as ornaments, of my own invention'. The Inquisitor would have none of this. Everything in appropriate religious art, he was told, everything 'befits the spiritual – there are no jesters, no dogs, no weapons, or any such silliness [as in yours]'. Veronese was ordered to 'correct the painting' within three months.

In fact, all he did was put in a label where before there had been none. It read in the Latin of the Vulgate '*Et fecit ei convivium magnum Levi in domo sua*' ('Levi made the Lord a Great Feast', Luke 5:29). A new name transformed Veronese's *Last Supper*, in which soldiers and dogs and jesters might be regarded as sacrilegious and disrespectful, into a painting of a relatively obscure dinner with tax collectors and a great company of publicans at a rich man's house to which Jesus had been invited.[39] *The Feast in the House of Levi*, as the painting was now called, remained in the refectory of the priory for which it had been painted, watching over the monks as they ate, until it was moved to the Gallerie dell'Accademia in Venice in the nineteenth century.

The Many Lives of *Las Meninas*

Las Meninas has been an icon of Western art history for centuries [**92**]. Already in the eighteenth century the critic Anton Raphael Mengs confessed that 'as this work is so well known on account of its excellence, I have nothing to add but that it stands as proof that the effects caused by the imitation of the Natural is already so well known on account of its excellence'. The painting was canonized by nineteenth-century artists and critics as Velázquez's masterpiece and one of the greatest paintings in the Western tradition. Its influence has been vast.

Consequently, it has also generated a range of readings: emblematic readings that see the painting as being about the education of a princess; readings that emphasize Velázquez's technical learning, his standing at court, his refined taste – note paintings based on oil sketches on classical themes by Peter Paul Rubens – and his claims for painting as a liberal art and for the nobility of the art of painting itself. And in the last half-century *Las Meninas* has come under theoretical and philosophical scrutiny as a painting about representing representation itself, as a painting about the intentionality of art, that is, as a painting that asks how pictures come to mean something. 'Few paintings in the history of art,' writes Jonathan Brown, 'have generated so many and varied interpretations as this, Velázquez's culminating work.'[40]

It is not hard to see why: Its miraculous naturalism – illusionism is a better term; its representational elusiveness that invites efforts to figure it out. It is impossible to settle on where we stand as viewers. Philip IV and his queen, Mariana of Austria, reflected in the confounding mirror, are where we ought to be standing and looking and where the painter is standing painting himself in his studio. Unlike Courbet's self-portrait in *The Studio of the Painter* (*see* 24) in which we can see the landscape he is working on – he is painting himself painting – we have no clue what is on Velázquez's canvas. Possibly it is a fictive portrait of the king and queen seen reflected in the mirror in a position where they might have stood while posing, although no such portrait exists. There is no clear account of how they got there; only a door in the back is open.

I think Velázquez is painting this painting, a visual self-reference in the sense that Proust ends *Remembrance of Things Past* with the intention of writing the book we have just read. I say this because we know from

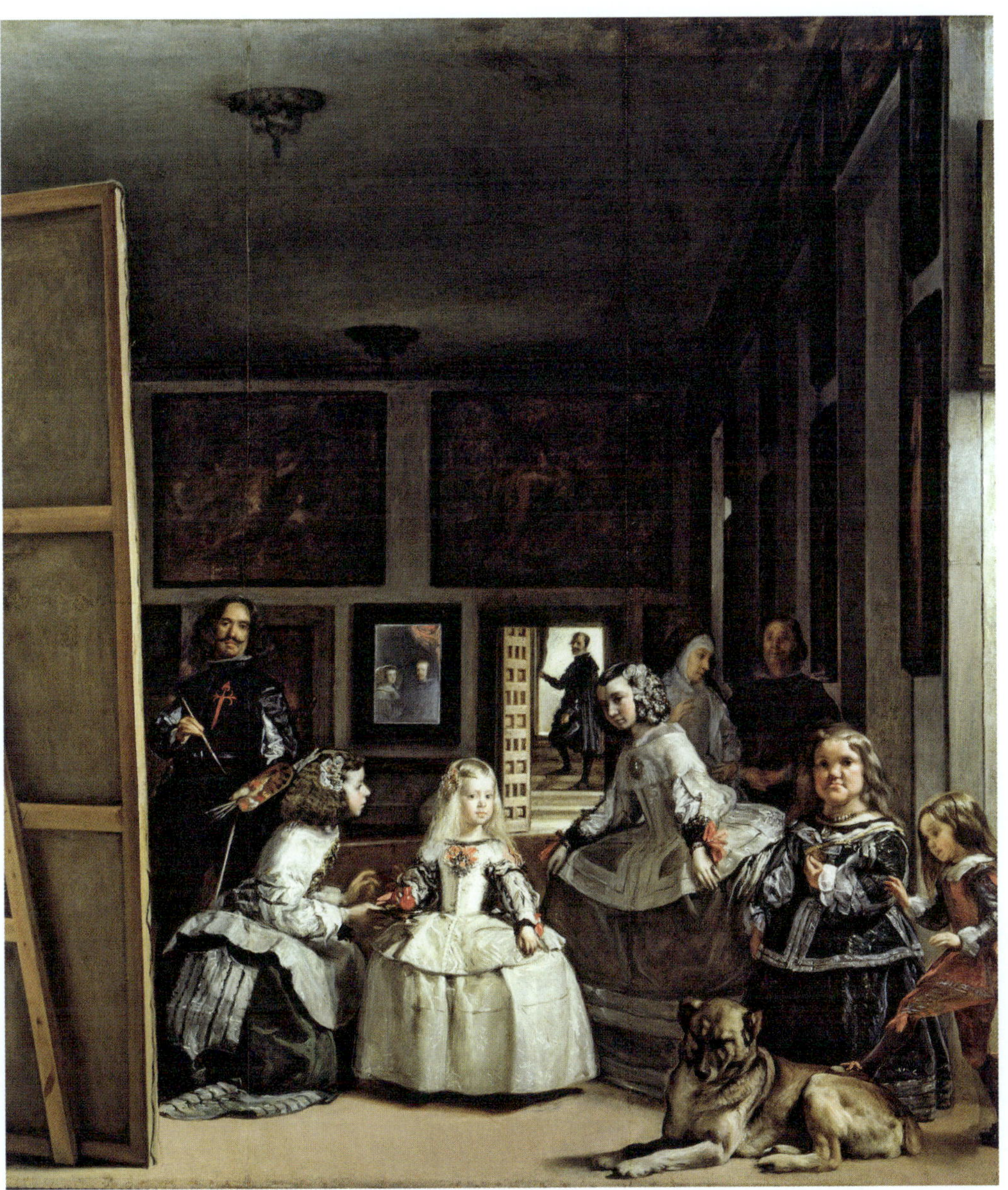

92 The Spanish mastiff in Diego Velázquez's *Las Meninas* (*c.* 1656) is a fixed and steady point in the restless scene.

the painter Antonio Palomino (1655–1726), Velázquez's first biographer who had access to reliable witnesses, that Philip IV often visited the studio to see how the painting was coming along:

> This painting was highly esteemed by his Majesty, and while it was being executed he went frequently to see it being painted. So did our lady Doña Mariana of Austria [intended bride of the dead Baltasar Carlos whom Philip IV married when his son died] and the Infantas and ladies, who came down often . . .

Proust makes me think '*this* painting' refers to the painting on the easel which is the one we see: *Las Meninas*, the antecedent to '*it*'. Velázquez captures the moment when a royal entry or exit attracts everyone's attention. Finally, his bravura pose itself demands attention and calls attention to the painting as painting. It seems to speak of his enjoyment in his wizardry that makes the painting so compelling. It is hard to look away and yet impossible to encompass.

One review of the vast literature it has generated ends in a sigh of resignation: 'at the beginning of the twenty-first century, despite all the analysis of it, *Las Meninas* somehow still eludes us'. Critics have turned metaphysicians: Velázquez 'invents a reality . . . within a culture and historical moment in which it was incessantly repeated life is an illusion'. Or John Berger's take: 'truth is found *behind* appearances. And what is behind appearances is a great darkness.'[41]

I do not propose any new interpretations to add to the hundreds already proffered but instead to think specifically about the Spanish mastiff and what it is doing for this artist in this painting. It has been largely unseen by art historians, but I am not the first to notice it. Felix da Costa, a late seventeenth-century Portuguese painter and writer on art, invites his readers in what is the first substantive description of *Las Meninas* to notice it: nearby to the princess and the ladies-in-waiting, he says, 'is a large dog belonging to the palace, lying down obediently among the ladies'.[42]

Whatever else it might be, it is a family dog. The actual subject of this deeply studied painting is banal: 'an informal group portrait in an artist's studio' in a room of the Royal Alcázar of Madrid that was once part of the suite of the recently deceased Baltasar Carlos.[43] Specifically it is a portrait of the king's family in the old-fashioned sense of close members of his household: his daughter, the Infanta Margarita; her 'las Meninas', 'ladies-in-waiting'; a court dwarf and a 'midget'; a nun who is the Infanta's chaperone; a bodyguard; the royal chamberlain caught in the act of opening the door; reflected in the mirror, the royal couple themselves – Palomino thinks it is a reflection of what is on the canvas; and the much esteemed court painter himself, Diego Rodríguez de Silva y Velázquez, a trusted and honoured advisor to the king on artistic matters that were more and more preoccupying him in his old age. And the family dog.

We know, thanks to Palomino, the name of every figure in the painting except those of the dog and of the guard standing next to the nun, Doña Marcela de Ulloa, the Infanta's chaperone. But we have reason to think that it was the king's dog; family dogs are often the dog of one member of the family or the other. It is the same breed with which the king had himself painted in the 1632 *Philip IV in Hunting Clothes* and was known to be his favourite. If it is the king's dog, then its seeming to take notice of his master either coming or going out – one cannot be sure, and I don't think it makes a difference from the dog's perspective – is a sort of parallel gesture to Velázquez's stepping away from his easel and looking toward the royal couple himself. Painter and dog each respond to the intrusion. The dog's attention is clear whether or not the dwarf got his attention by kicking him. The fact that *Las Meninas* was placed in the king's private apartments suggests it was regarded not as a public work. But that has changed. Today we see it hanging in a place of honour in a great museum as – whatever else it is – an informal family portrait with a beloved dog.

Again, thanks to Palomino we have a near contemporaneous description of the dog that gets us closer to its formal role. Here it is in full:

> In the foreground is a dog lying down, and next to it the midget Nicolasito Pertusato, who treads on it to show – together with the ferocity of its appearance – its tameness and its gentleness when tried; for when it was being painted it remained motionless in whatever attitude it was placed. ['Lying down obediently', as da Costa noted earlier.] *This figure is dark and prominent and gives great harmony to the composition.*[44] [italics added]

What exactly does he mean? The description is accurate. While the dog is not as dark as his predecessor in the portrait of Philip IV in hunting costume, it is of a dramatically different hue from the figures that surround it. The deep-set eyes, the black of its downturned snout, the shadows and charcoal hairs amid the brown, all give it a sombre countenance. 'This figure is dark'. This is a serious dog.

And it is, as Palomino says, 'prominent'. It defines the bottom limits of the painting, the floor on which the easel sits. Its body is meticulously painted, the only unclothed body in the painting. Velázquez lavishes great attention on it. The fur is finely drawn; the muscles show through folds of flesh; the nose glistens with a touch of white impasto; the eyes are darkly hooded; its limbs and their anatomy – unlike the hands of the human figures for example – are clearly articulated, especially its left front and rear haunches where the light falls. It is a weighty dog, a fleshly dog. Our eyes move from it upwards diagonally to the Infanta and her maids and on to the painter. Maybe that is part of what Palomino means by it giving great harmony to the picture.

But there is more. The dog is fixed and steady – 'motionless in whatever attitude it was placed' – in a tableau that is both narratively and formally unsettled. Narratively because the rest of the protagonists are caught mid-action in the moment when the royal company either enters or leaves; formally, because of all the illusionistic tricks, strange perspective, and visual legerdemain that constitute this image. The dog is unmoved. It is the only creature at rest in the painting, the only one not caught in action looking this way or that.

Of course, the dog might get up to greet its master. But not yet. In the instant, its steady, attentive, slightly downturned eyes gaze somewhere out of the studio tableau and intersect with Velázquez's eyes as he looks at and past his canvas. A pure gaze, rather like how Rilke imagined Cézanne's. A gaze that connects us and the cascade of worlds of the painting. Imagine it without the dog; it would be suspended with no connection to the world beyond, with the floor like the surface of an infinity pool drifting off. The lady-in-waiting, dwarf and midget would be unanchored. Perhaps this too is what Palomino meant by the dog giving great harmony to the picture.

Almost three centuries later another Spanish painter – Pablo Picasso – engaged with *Las Meninas* [**93**] and specifically with the dog, not in words but in images. Between the middle of August and the end of December 1957, working in near isolation in his villa 'La Californie' near Cannes, he produced forty-five paintings on the subject. *Mano a mano* with his great predecessor: 'la Bataille des Ménines', his friend and political ally, the journalist and art critic Hélène Parmelin, called it. The series is an important element in the art-historical assessment of Picasso. His 'dialog with *Las Meninas*,' writes one critic, 'provided [him] the opportunity, even the challenge, to further amplify [his] counter classicism'. It was not an entirely happy moment. 'Picasso frankly acknowledges the modern artist's loss of belief in the power of painting to represent the world fully . . .' writes Susan Galassi, 'and mourns his own period of producing masterpieces.' But I call him as a witness to the work of the dog in Velázquez: to seeing like an artist.[45]

The first painting in the series, made on 17 August 1957, is a recognizable version of the original, obviously different in its stylistically layered cubism – but substantively similar except in two respects: the image of Velázquez looms large here, larger than in the original. (It is either absent or diminished in the rest of the series; he appears in only three studies.) And, right in front, in place of the Spanish mastiff of the original is Picasso's beloved dachshund, Lump. He appears in fifteen of the studies: a funny not a sombre dog, light not dark. (The painting itself is large [1.94 x 2.60 metres], the biggest Picasso had painted since *Guernica* and almost on the scale of Velázquez's original [3.18 x 2.76 metres].)

Lump came into Picasso's life on 19 April 1957. He had been rescued the year before in Stuttgart by the photojournalist David Douglas Duncan, best known at the time for his war coverage, who brought the dachshund with him when he visited La Californie, where he spent months photographing the artist at work and with his family. He and Douglas became great friends. Lump quickly changed allegiances and joined the boxer Jan and the goat Esmerelda in the Cannes household. Picasso almost immediately painted a plate for him and became besotted: 'he's not a dog, he's not a little man, he's somebody else'. Lump stayed for six years until he developed back problems and returned to Douglas. He died a week before Picasso. Picasso's passion for this dog and for dogs in general

Overleaf: 93 Picasso's *Las Meninas, No. 1* (1957), with Lump in place of Velázquez's mastiff.

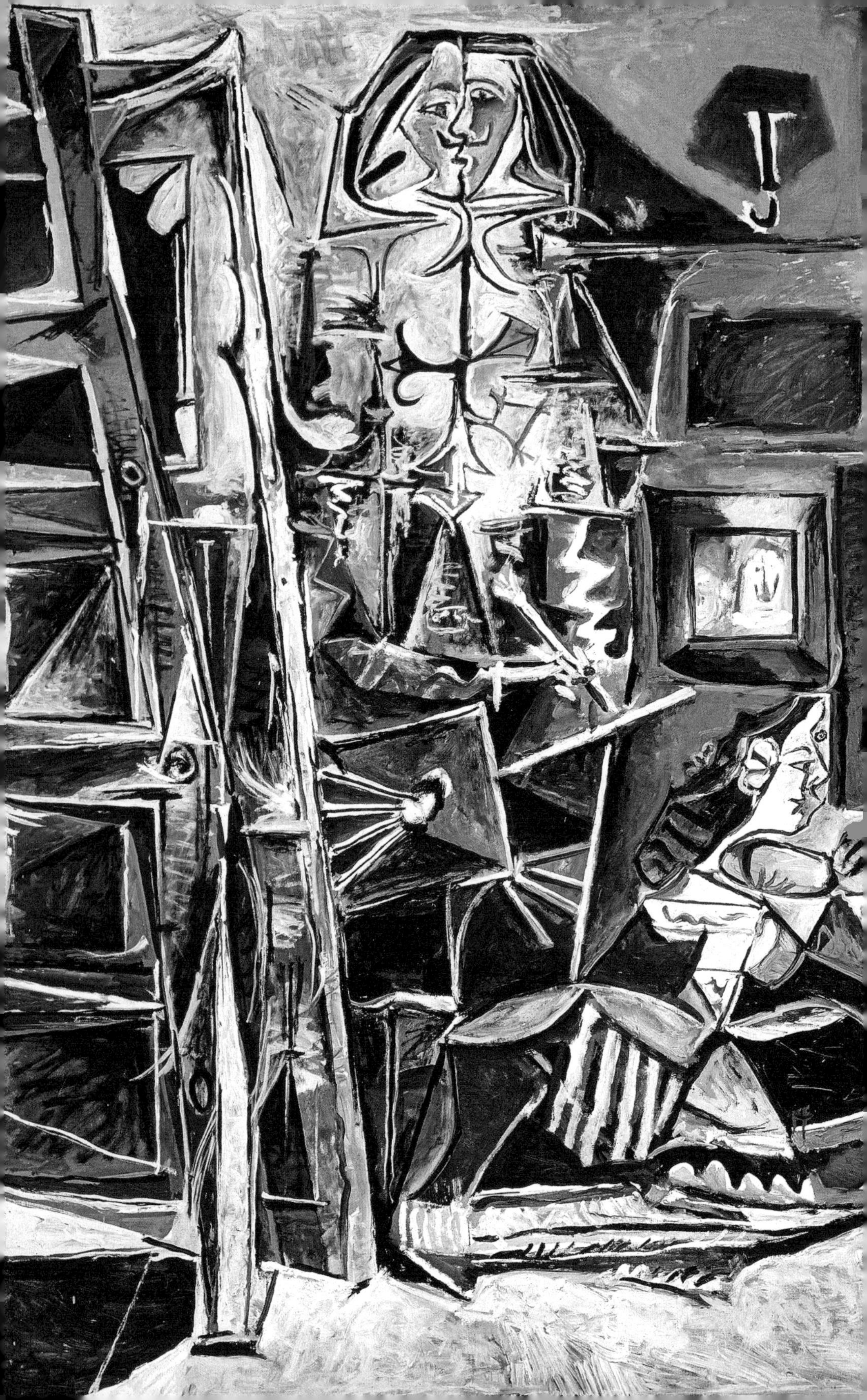

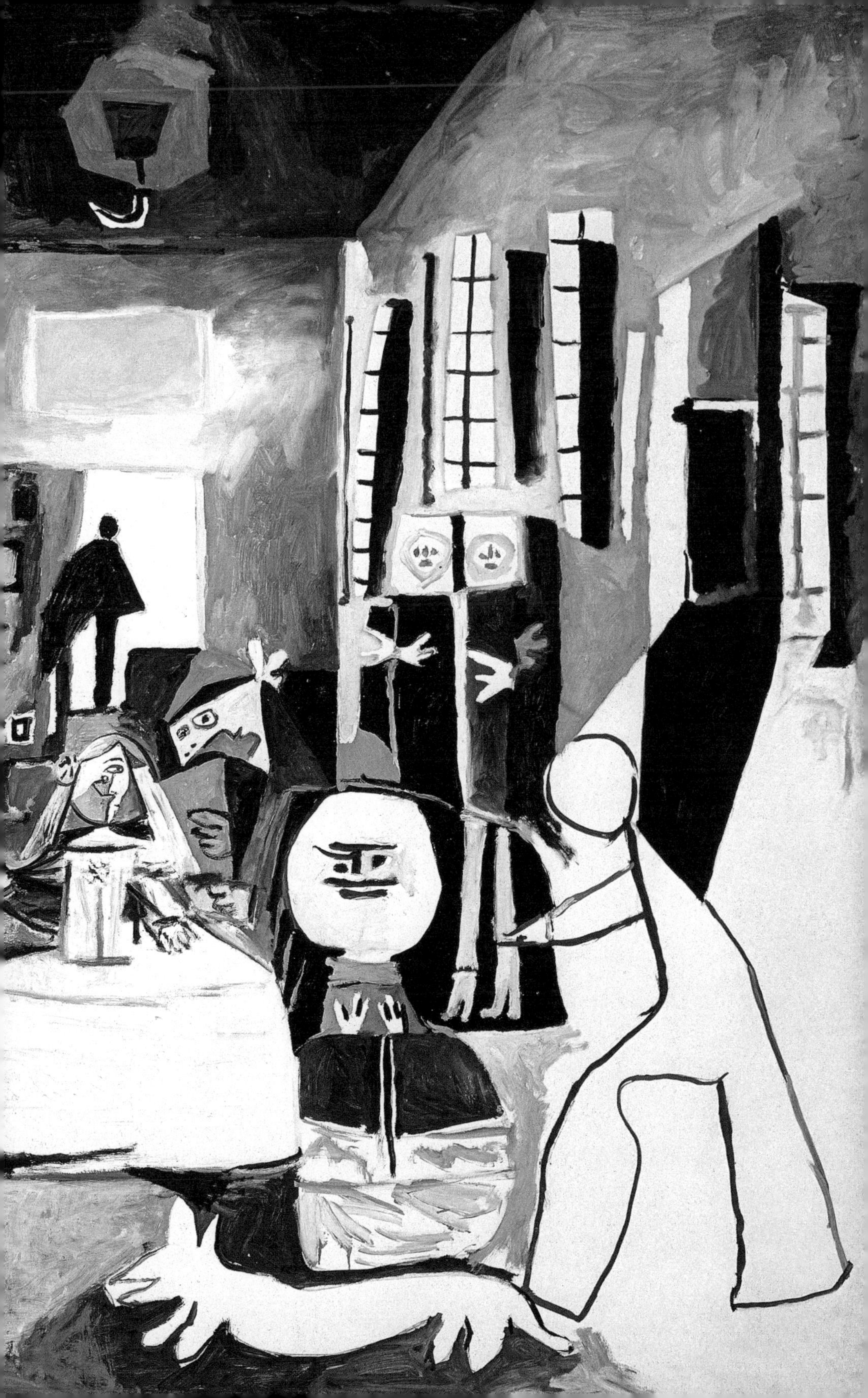

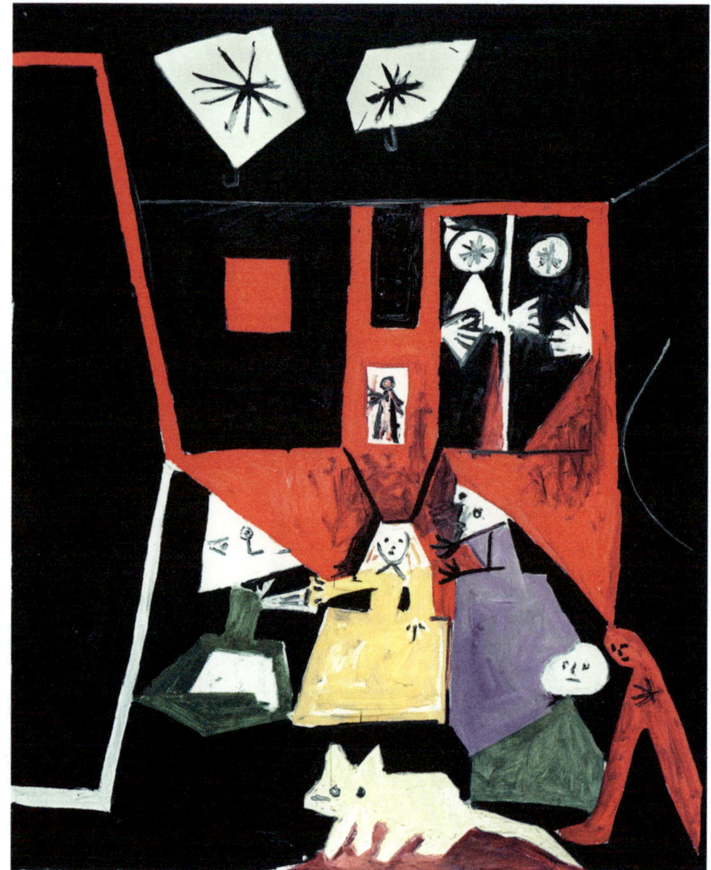

94 A brazen outward gaze: One of Picasso's forty-five *Las Meninas* studies (1957).

does not, however, explain why Lump figures so prominently in his studies of *Las Meninas*. I take his presence as testimony to Picasso's recognition of the importance of the mastiff in the original.[46]

Like the dog in *Las Meninas* described by Palomino, Lump in Picasso's studies is 'prominent', the foundation for the fifteen images in which he appears – elongated or curled up. And he adds 'great harmony' to the paintings through his gaze, the brazen outward gaze, the bright eyes even when the eyes of the human characters are like coals, the head white in a field of blue [**94**].

The eyes stand out in all the studies but perhaps most in *The Piano*, the most distant from the original and something of a joke [**95**]. Picasso imagined that the midget Nicolasito Pertusato, who in *Las Meninas* seems

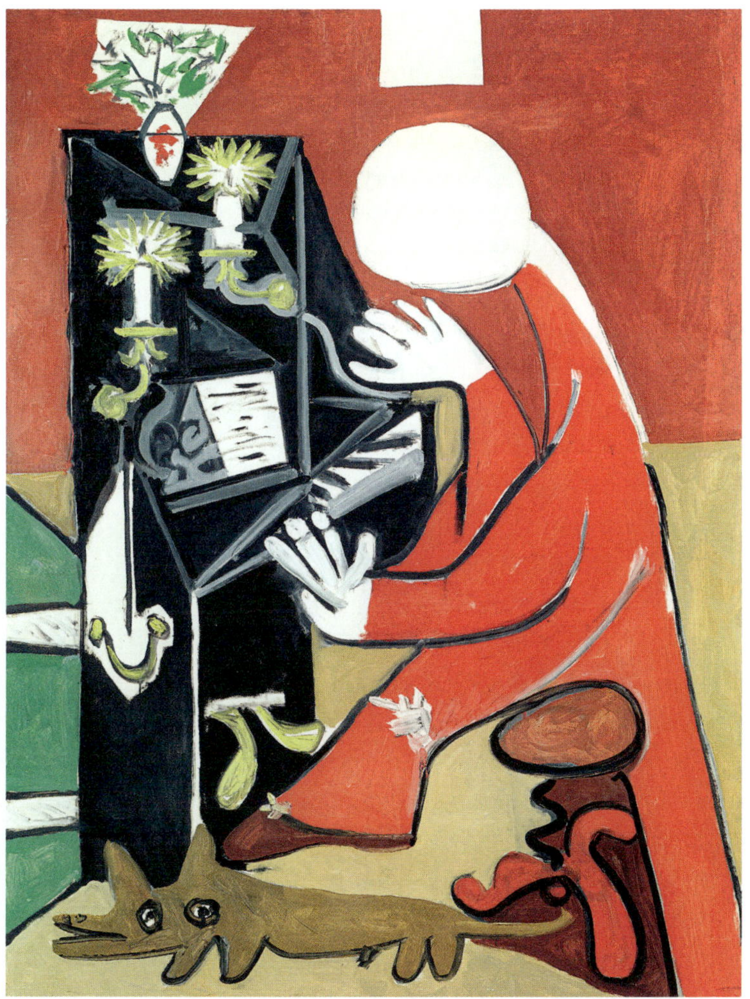

95 Lump makes a playful appearance in *The Piano* (1957).

to be nudging the dog, might be playing the piano. The human in Picasso's *jeu d'esprit* of a painting has no eyes; Lump like the mastiff in Velázquez is dark and its eyes see. David Douglas Duncan wrote:

> Fantasia: Picasso painted Velázquezes
> Velázquez painted Picassos
> Lump searched wildly for Jacqueline and Home
> Claude! Paloma! . . . Where are you?[47]

The Flâneur

I jump almost two centuries to demonstrate that, in the late nineteenth century, dogs are still seeing for and like the artist and for the viewer, but they are seeing in a world very different from that inhabited by Velázquez when he finished *Las Meninas* in 1656. An almost timeless formalism – perspectival seeing – connects that world to earlier art – while at the same time it makes sense of an altogether new world. In all the paintings from Giotto on the sociology has been clear; we can place the humans in relation to one another and to the spaces they inhabit even if we cannot quite be sure what all the allegorical details of their fanciful and symbol-laden landscapes mean.

Gustave Caillebotte's *Le Pont de l'Europe*, first shown in the Impressionist exhibition of 1878 along with Monet's study of the St Lazare railway yards, which the bridge crosses, is an exemplary case of formal continuity in the representation of a modern scene difficult for contemporary viewers to understand [**96**]. It is a painting of, and a commentary on, everyday life in a city: Paris, capital of the world.[48]

The defining feature of this painting is the giant iron double girder and the roadway it supports seen from the Rue de Vienne, one of six avenues named after a European capital in the newly modernized Paris, which converge on a bridge over a railway to form a huge plaza. It was less than a decade old when Caillebotte painted it. No previous art had been so engaged with urban infrastructure. But formally it is familiar. The girder takes us into the distance where a horse stands in front of a carriage looking still further on. Another carriage takes our eye on toward the rue de St Peterbourg. That much is clear.

It is also clear that the working man is looking over the bridge toward St Lazare; or perhaps not looking; his hands might be shielding his eyes as if in contemplation. We have no idea if he is despondent or idly thoughtful. The bourgeois man in the top hat may be looking at the working man; perhaps to start a conversation. Art historians interested in 'queering' Caillebotte could read him as a representation of the artist eyeing a working class man. Or, more likely, he may be leaning forward, turning his head, to address the overdressed woman who may or may not be a prostitute. But it is broad daylight and this is not a red light district, and she may not be alone but rather with him. What is

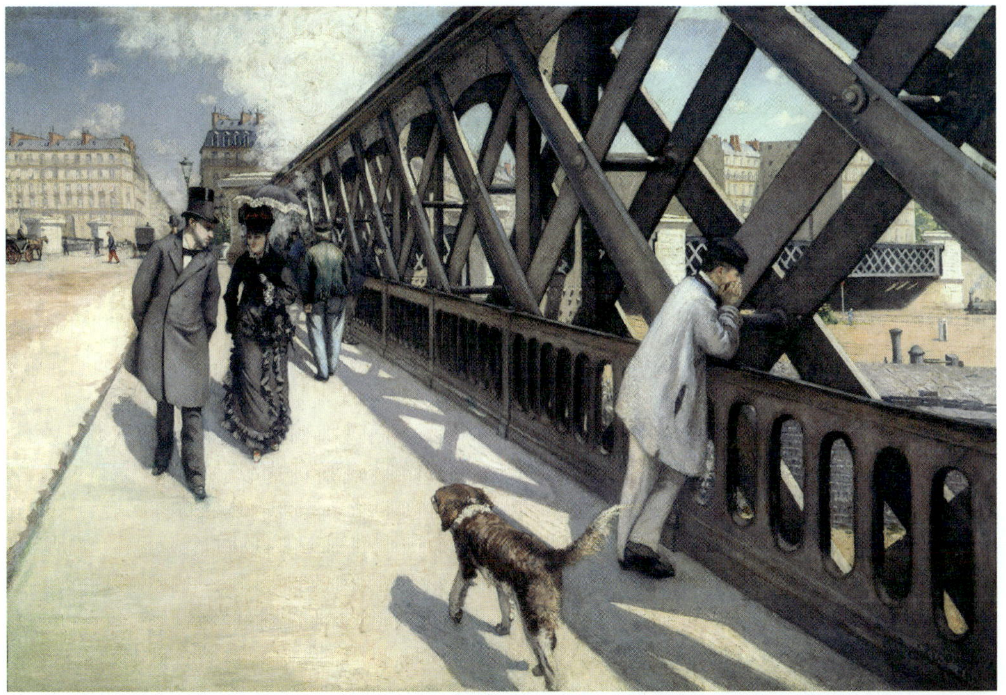

96 A newly modernized Paris in Gustave Caillebotte's *Le Pont de l'Europe* (1876).

happening and what all this looking means is much debated. Caillebotte's work is often used in history textbooks to suggest the unreadability of modern life and the modern city.

But the dog knows exactly where it is, where it is going and what it sees. Its owner is, we can guess, six feet back, just a little in front of the spot from which the painter is seeing the scene and its perspective. The dog is from the painter about as far as is the dog from its master in another Caillebotte painting: in *Richard Gallo and his Dog Dick at Petit Gennevilliers* (*see* 166), Gallo's dog too knows resolutely where it is going: it is the principle of motion. Its gaze and prancing steps are straight ahead.

In a formal sense the dog's gaze in *Le Pont de l'Europe* is crucial to how painting works; its resolute sight line takes our eye into the distance toward a vanishing point. But the dog is also a *flâneur*, the surrogate in this case of the painter and the doppelgänger of the man in the top hat – the other *flâneur* in the painting. The dog is doing the most serious looking, for the painter, for the painting, and for us.

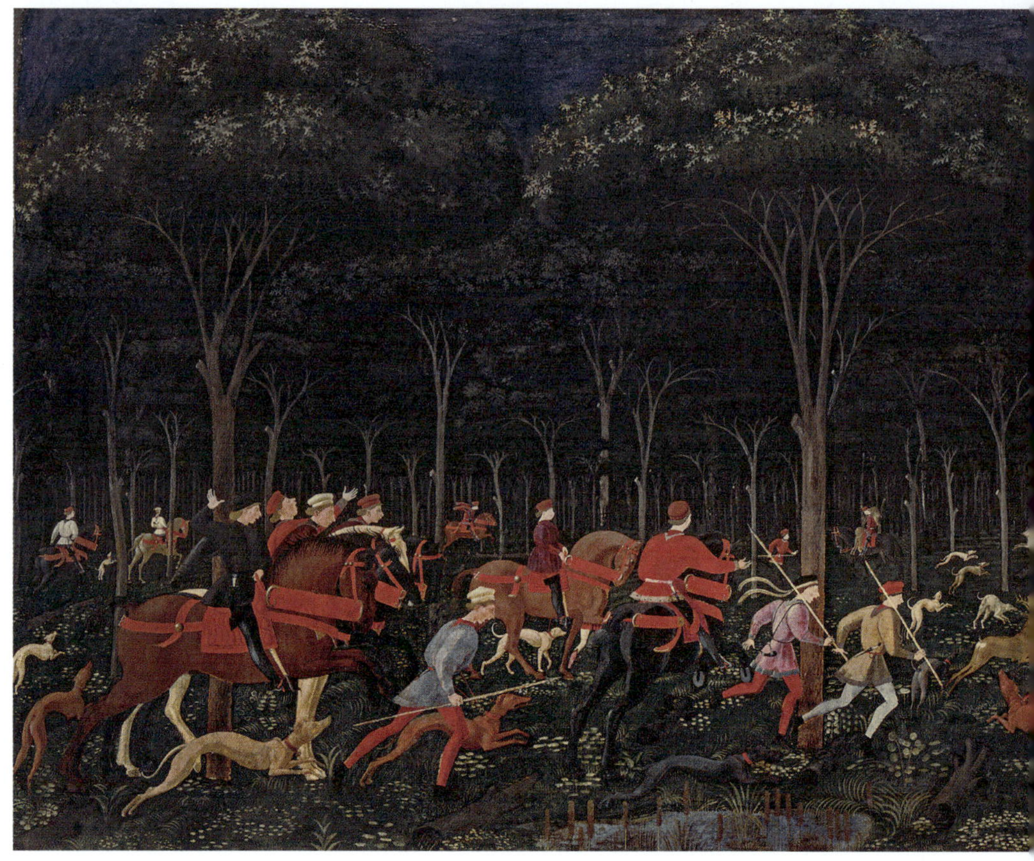

The Dog Vanishes

Paolo Uccello's *The Hunt in the Forest* (c. 1470) takes us back to the formal question that engaged Giotto: the creation of space [97]. It is neither a generic aristocratic hunt scene nor a reworking of a mythological one, although the horses' seats bear the signs of the goddess Diana. The hunt is taking place at night; the foreground, lit as if by floodlights, recedes mysteriously into a dark and endless background. Few paintings have this variety of hues, light to almost black. It came from a marriage chest on which it may have been meant, as an allegory of the hunt, as the pursuit of love or sexual desire. In that sense it represents the ways in which the oldest of the human arts is figured in painting. Dogs have been part of that art from the beginning.

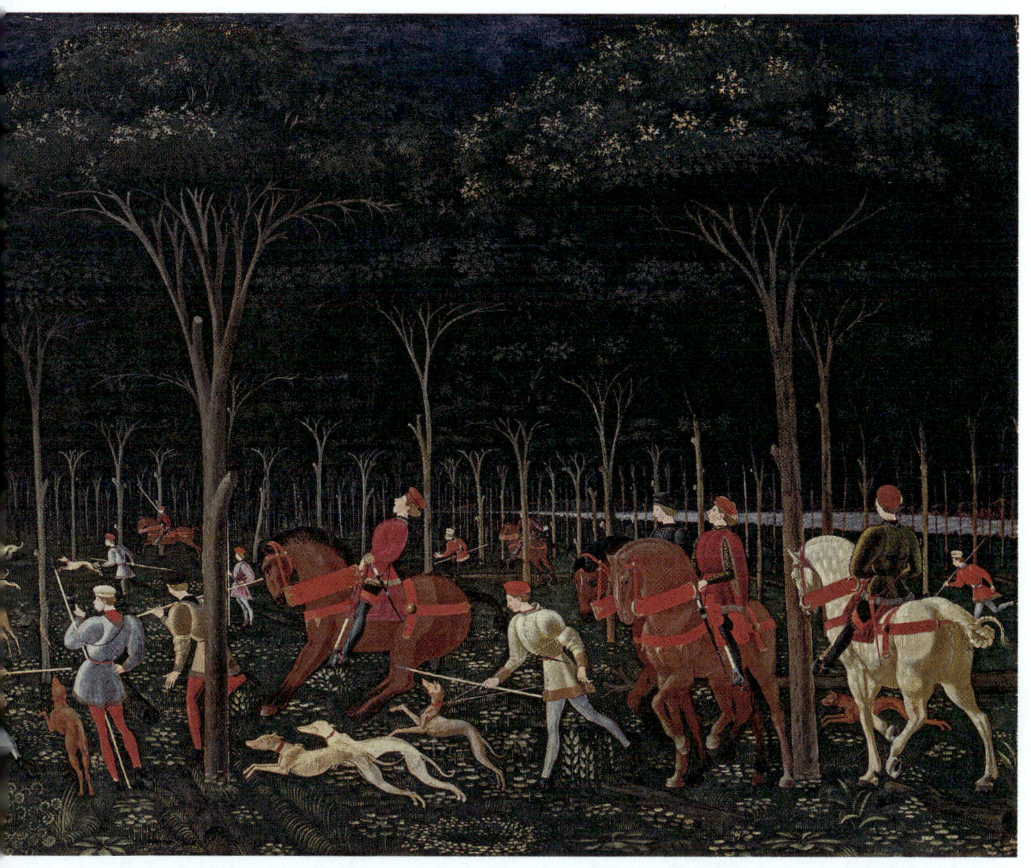

97 What dogs do for artists: Paolo Uccello's *The Hunt in the Forest* (c. 1470).

The logs on the forest floor in this painting, like the spears in his *Battle of San Romano*, are laid along receding lines, but the dogs do far more than create the deep space of the images. (Uccello is famous as an early master of perspective.) While the horses and the hunters, as if hanging back, are almost all in the foreground, the dogs are bounding forward. At the start, dead centre between two humans is a large brown dog starting the chase. His companions fill the space from the light of the foreground where he stands into the darkness of the forest. Running in pursuit, they propel our view like a volley of canine arrows flying to a vanishing point. They are doing the serious formal work of the dog, doing what dogs do for artists.

CHAPTER 4

Dogs and the Human Condition

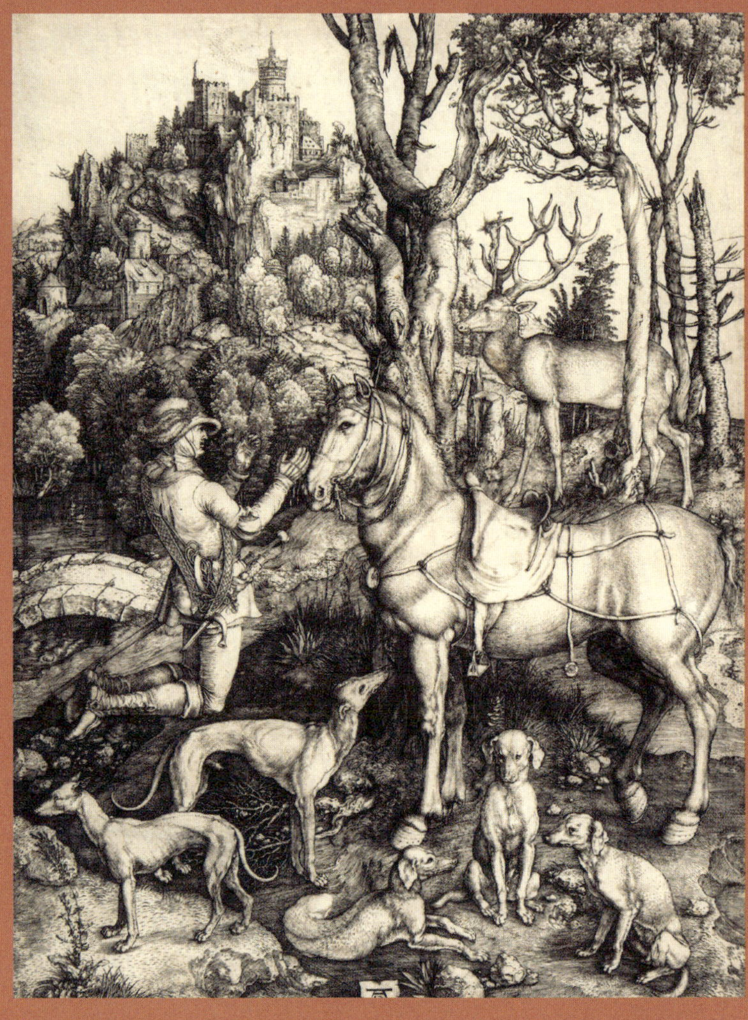

98 Albrecht Dürer's *St Eustace* (1501), the dream of salvation, with attending dogs.

SINCE THE BEGINNING, DOGS have played a central part in representations of the human condition: mourning the dead; companions in solitude or as part of the human pack; seeing for the blind; friends in good times; friends of last resort. I mean friendship here not in Aristotle's sense of true or virtue friendship, the relationship between two men of equal status and virtue: clearly an impossibility. Dogs are perhaps what he calls 'pleasure friends', those who are dear to us; those who share affections and spaces; those who bring joy to our lives; those who live, however asymmetrically, for us and we for them. They are certainly 'use friends' who help us in one way or another.

Montaigne concluded, after enumerating the virtues of his best friend Étienne de La Boétie, that even his long list could not explain their friendship. It came down to who they each were: 'because he was he and I am I'. Alexander Nehamas writes about why he and I are friends not by adducing my virtue or his, but by narrating the things we have done together, the conversations we have had, the things we have shared. It is not a ranked order of qualities – virtues – that each of us finds in the other or even a list of pleasures we have shared but a cascade of stories; many stories of things done together.

This is a version of what the philosopher Stanley Cavell says about a particular friendship between the characters of Clark Gable and Claudette Colbert in the 1934 romantic comedy *It Happened One Night*:

> What this pair does together is less important than the fact that they do whatever it is together, that they know how to spend time together, even that they would rather waste time together than do anything else – except that no time they are together could be wasted.[1]

That is, it is not what we do with our friends that matters but that what we do, we do with them. On this criterion a dog would qualify as friend, indeed it might well rank high. Being there is their strong suit; in art they are a chosen witness to the great moral and affective dimensions of the human condition – our universal friend.

Dürer's *St Eustace* [**98**] is a window into how art represents this shared social universe. It is his largest and, in his lifetime, most popular etching. The eponymous subject is an early second-century Roman general who was out hunting deer when the 'more fair and greater than the others' among them left the herd and ran into the deepest part of the forest. Placidus followed, and seeing the deer now high on a hill, beheld in its antlers the crucified Christ. He became a Christian, changed his name to Eustachious and was ultimately martyred for his faith.[2]

In this version of the St Eustace story (1501) the hunt is over, unlike, for example, in Pisanello's painting (*c.* 1438–42) where one of the dogs can't resist going after a rabbit, two are still sniffing the ground, and

99 *The Vision of St Eustachius* (*c.* 1438-42) by Pisanello.

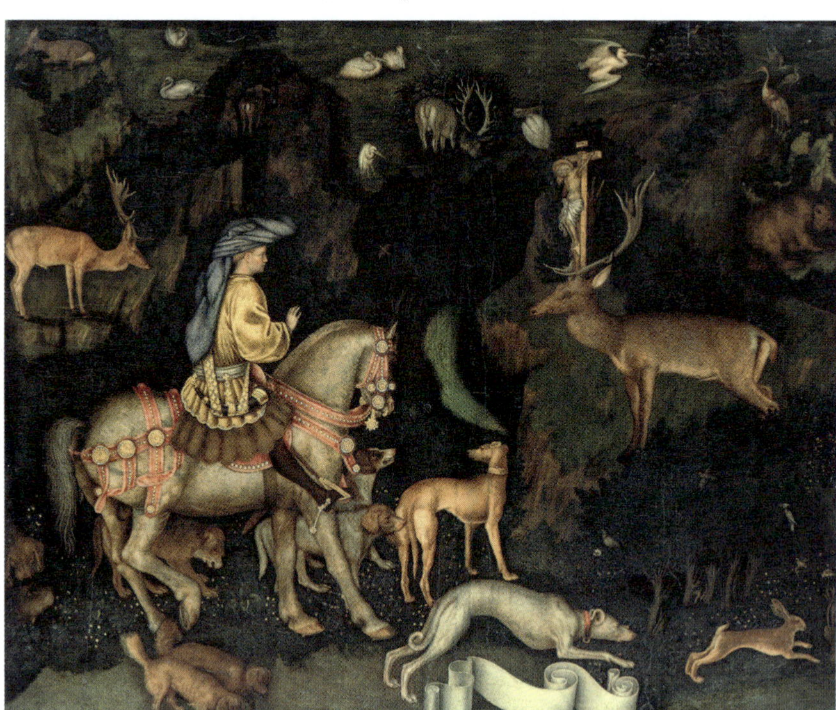

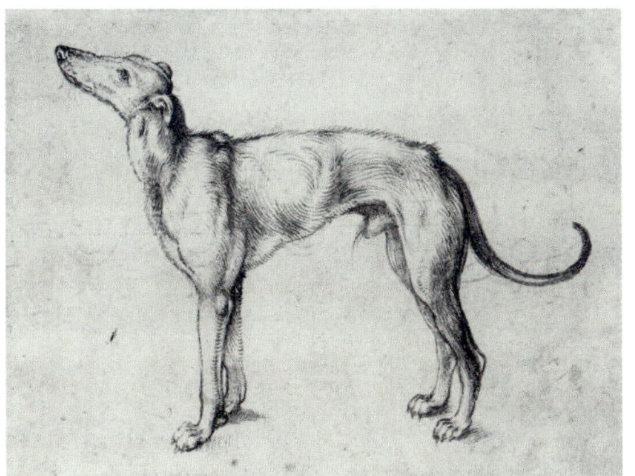

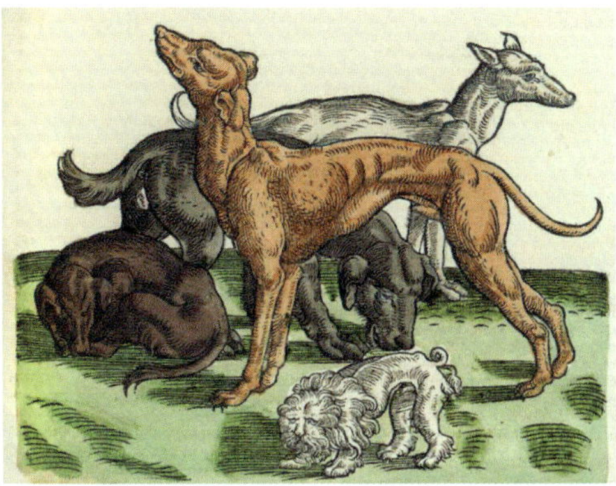

100–101 (*left*) Albrecht Dürer, *Study of a Dog for St Eustace*; (*right*) Illustration from Conrad Gessner's much pirated *Historia Animalium* (1551–8), with dogs borrowed from Dürer.

only one – the brown one in front of the horse – is looking with its master [**99**].

The most striking aspect about Dürer's image are the five exquisitely individuated dogs that are the foundation of the picture, a scene of spiritual calm against the busy background. They are beautifully solidly present. We have Dürer's drawing – the only extant study for this etching – of the tallest of the dogs looking up to where the deer stands [**100**]. (It is reversed in the etching.) Alone he is more plangent, more engaged, than the others. But each of these dogs is looking patiently; one might almost believe knowingly. The cluster of dogs demand our attention not only because they are so ostentatiously there, spread out over the base of the image, but also because their bodies and faces, hair and musculature are so attentively rendered. Each pose is a masterpiece unto itself. Dürer's dogs – not just the ones from the St Eustace etching but others of his as well – will be the model for dogness of different sorts for centuries to come. The tall one in Conrad Gessner's huge, encyclopedic, much copied and pirated *Historia Animalium* (*History of Animals*, after Aristotle) [**101**] is based on the St Eustace print; the curled-up one is from Dürer's *Melancholia I* [**102**].

We might ask what each one is doing: 'To what is it attentive?' 'What is it thinking?' Almost all the art of dogs assumes an anthropocentric eye, an assumption that there is something intentional in their relationship to us, something humanly social. But they don't need to be thinking about anything to be socially engaged. The whole diagonal left half of the Dürer etching is an image of man and dogs being together as a psychological and sociological fact: a unit. And in being there the image is not only about their being social; it is also representing 'sociability'; that is, it 'shew[s] forth an evident sociability and likelihood, that he will be very well to be lived withal' (as the *Oxford English Dictionary*'s first, 1581, example of 'sociability' has it). The dogs are witnesses to a solitary act of spiritual conversion. It is precisely because the most important thing in the scene – the conversion – cannot be represented that the dog is there to bear witness.

Melancholy

Since its creation in 1514, Dürer's *Melancholia I* has become 'virtually an icon, [which] succeeds like no other in embracing pictorially, on a few square centimeters, the boundless cosmos of melancholy'.[3]

Erwin Panofsky, in what is still the most influential interpretation of the engraving, combines two iconographical traditions: on the one hand, images of the figure of Melancholy herself – in the shadows, swarthy, dejected, sluggish, frozen in inaction. She is a figure who resembles a late medieval and Renaissance tradition of the personification of a sort of madness that has been the domain of doctors and philosophers since antiquity. On the other hand, she is set among the tools and symbols of Geometries – 'abstract personifications of a noble science', but 'devoid of human emotions and quite incapable of suffering'.

Her chaotic surroundings are filled with objects that are allusions to what Melancholia is failing to engage. The perfect sphere, the rhomboid, the 4 x 4 number table, and the straight edge allude to mathematics and geometry that are particularly useful for the mechanical arts. Bellows, hammer, pincers, and nails are tools that she is not capable of using creatively. In other words, a marriage of madness and a creative imagination on the edge. This conjuncture would be felt for centuries, especially, but not exclusively, in German thought.

The intellectual revolution that made it possible was wrought largely by the Florentine Neo-Platonists, most importantly Marsilio Ficino, who joined 'melancholy' with creativity through a reading of Aristotle and a major reinterpretation of astrology, a central interest of Renaissance humanism. The planets and stars brought affairs on earth into an

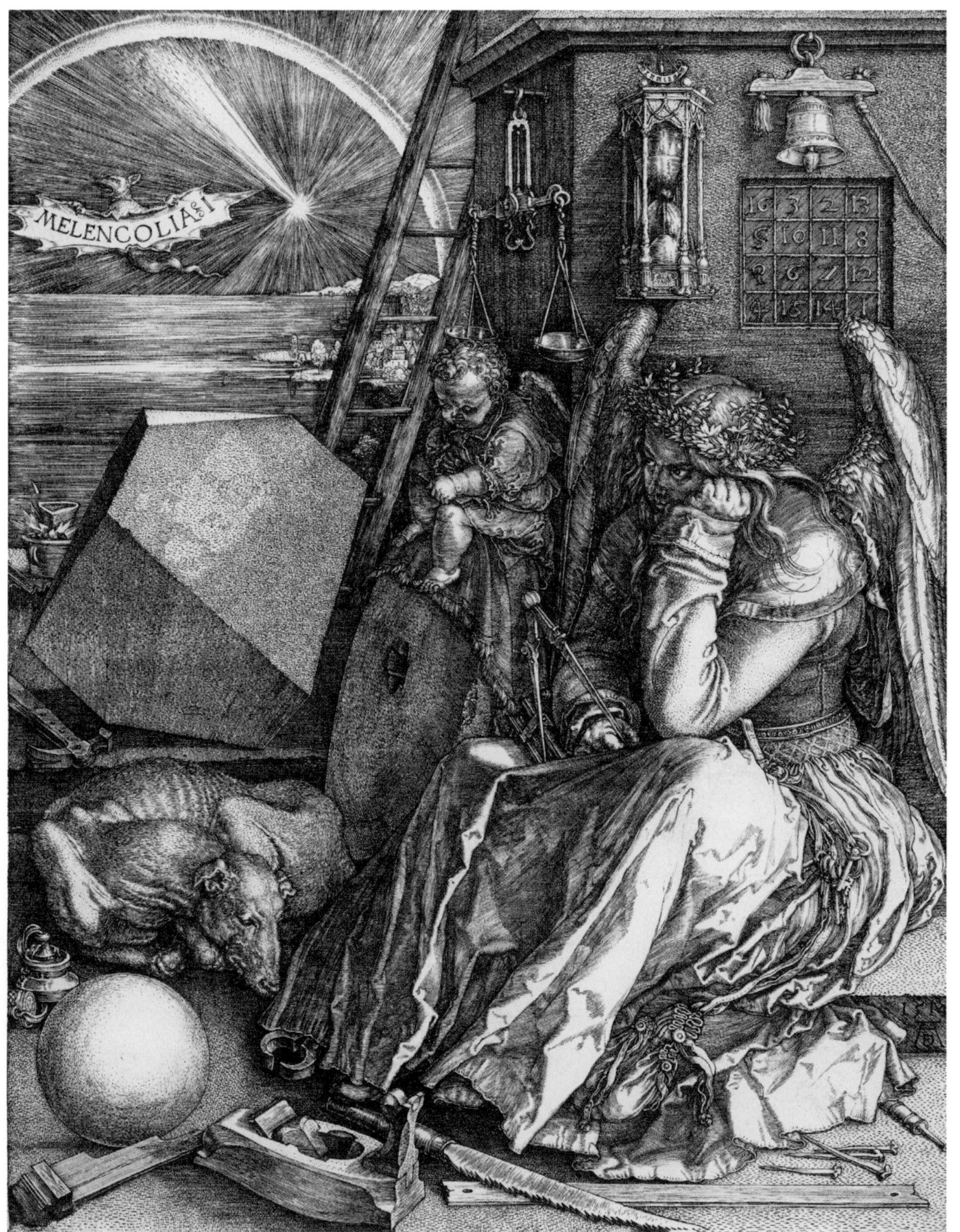

102 Dürer's *Melancholia I* (1514), the first time a dog appears in a depiction of Melancholy.

analogical relationship with the heavens. The genius of melancholy was in the stars. 'Divine contemplation . . . is signified by Saturn,' as Ficino puts it. Panofsky elaborates the point: 'The humanistic glorification of melancholy entailed, and even implied, another phenomenon: the humanistic ennoblement of the planet Saturn.'[4] Dürer knew all this – he was friends with Willibald Pirckheimer, one of Germany's foremost humanists – and created an image of the 'artist's melancholy' and, more generally, of the aspirations of the artist and thinker in the Renaissance. It became an icon for the ages.

Enter for the first time in history a dog in representations of Melancholy. There are iconographical reasons for its being there. Dogs have since antiquity been associated with spleen and black bile, the humours of madness (think rabies) and with dejection. They are also creatures associated with earth, the Saturnine element, the element of earthliness, as well as with creatureliness: the root of all human misery since the Fall and the coming of death. But when I see the image of the dog at Melancholy's side, I do not in the first instance turn to a decoding of what dogs mean based on esoteric knowledge. I see a dog keeping a dejected figure company.

These ways of seeing are not incompatible. Panofsky translates doggy iconography into the realm of the emotions by reminding us that the dog – this dog – is a living creature that is 'shrivelled up with general misery', a mirror of artistic torpor and atrophied imagination, a creature who resembles Melancholia and amplifies her heaviness and torpor: a 'drowsy idle dog is emblematic of the melancholy temperament' according to one museum label. The dog is her double.

Walter Benjamin, the German Jewish philosopher and critic, makes a more general argument about Melancholy. He starts with a long excursus on the history of the Saturnine dog but ends up not depending on it. Melancholia, he suggests, is 'the most truly creaturely of the contemplative impulses, and one has always noticed that its power need be no less in the gaze of a dog than in the attitude of a brooding genius'. Anyone who has ever been depressed understands the creaturely qualities of that state of mind and the feeling of looking dejectedly into emptiness. It is not hard to see how one can read empathic mirroring into a sad dog's gaze. The novelist Edith Wharton writes about the '*us*ness in their eyes', and at the same time their underlying '*not-us*ness'. The gaze of the dog and of Melancholia mirror each other in a sense of loss.

Dogs 'dream as men do, and through violence of melancholy run mad,' wrote Richard Burton in *Anatomy of Melancholy*. The curators of the 'Melancholie: Sinn un Wahnsinn' exhibition in Berlin argue that the dog 'above all other animals is given to dejection [*Niedergeschlagenheit*] and even madness', which makes it, as it is in the Dürer engraving, a suitable companion for the despondent human. At least the human, if not loved – though that too is implied – is not alone in her despair.[5]

But there is another way to look at the dog of *Melancholia I*: as a creature who is, and remains, company whatever its human might be feeling or doing. The 'thereness' of the dog is less a mirror of its human or another emblem of melancholy than a comfort: a sociable dog; a dog sharing a room with a human. One piece of evidence for this reading comes from a closer look at the dog. Its eyes are not so sad; they are not really closed. The flickering eyelids of the dog in *Melancholia I* might just be a sign of doggy dreaming and contemplation rather than dejection. Dogs dream with half-open eyes. My perfectly happy dog sleeping doesn't look so different from that of *Melancholia I* [**103**]. Neither do Matisse's dogs [**104**]. Franz Marc's peacefully sleeping dog in the snow is at peace with the world [**105**].

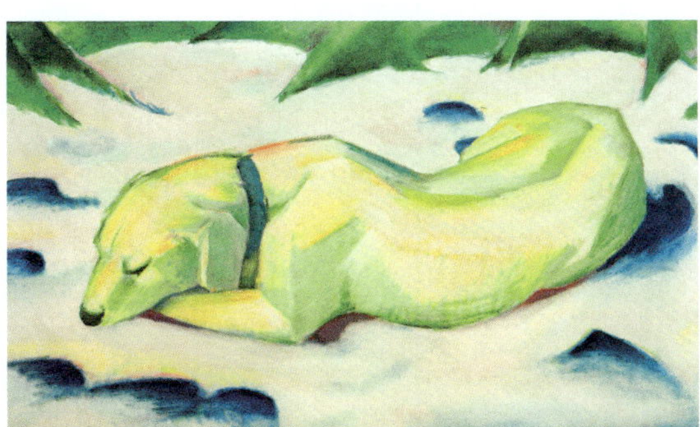

103–105 A dreaming dog is comforting company: My dog Rudi sleeping peacefully in my study (*below right*); detail from Henri Matisse's *Interior with Dog* (1934, *below left*); detail from *Dog Lying in the Snow* (1910/1911) by Franz Marc (*left*).

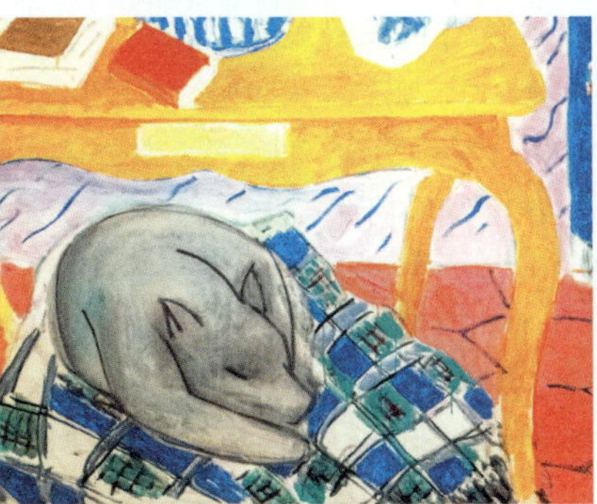

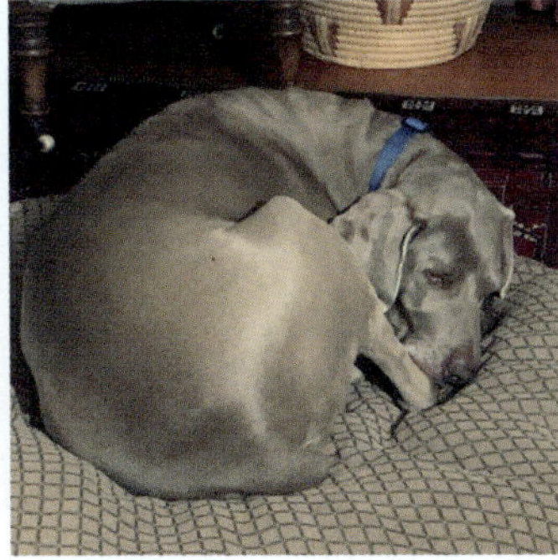

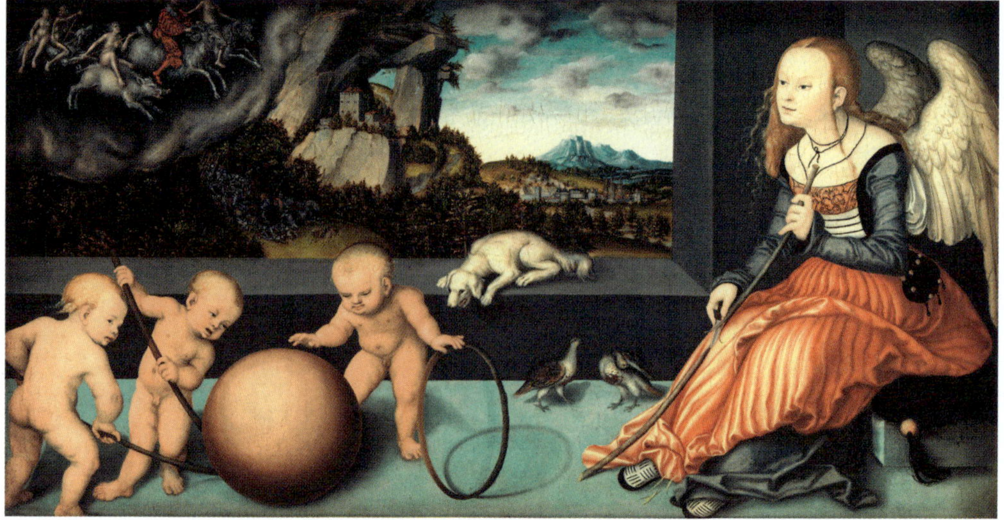

106 The dog looks on with interest in *Melancholia* (1532) by Lucas Cranach the Elder.

A dreaming dog is comforting company.[6] So is my dog, now dead but who was in my study all the years I was working on this book.

Because of the power of Dürer's image Melancholia has had a dog since the sixteenth century – from Lucas Cranach the Elder, struggling as he was to differentiate himself from Dürer's almost instantly iconic engraving, to painters in the Moghul court who found the dog in Maarten de Vos's *Dolor* with Dürer's dog at his side, to the Baroque painters Domenico Fetti and Giovanni Benedetto Castiglione to the moderns – Lucian Freud and George Grosz. All belie the claim that Melancholia's dog stands only for 'animalistic heaviness' and rather takes a variety of attitudes toward its master's condition

Cranach painted at least three 'Allegories of Melancholy', all with dogs, all different but none dejected. All three share some of the iconographical elements of the Dürer but are even more difficult to figure out. No one has a clue, for example, what the putti are doing as they try to put the perfect sphere through a hoop in the Copenhagen version [**106**]. Cranach, however, adds something important to all three that absolves the dog: the devil and his minions in the upper left-hand corner from our vantage suggest that Cranach's vision is of a very different, non-canine, melancholy: Martin Luther's melancholy. 'All sadness, plagues, and dejection come from Satan.' There are no dogs among his minions. Melancholia's dog peering over the ledge is curious, however, as is its mistress, about what the putti are doing.[7]

Melancholia's later dogs are an even more mixed lot. The version of Dürer's dog by the Moghul court painter Farrukh Beg is a self-portrait of the artist in his old age [**107**]. The dog comes in part from Dürer's Melancholia and from a tradition of representing the aged St Jerome. It is not about the melancholia of impotent creativity but of the sadness of old age at the end of a long and successful career; Beg died at seventy-four in 1619, four years after this picture was painted.[8]

107 Farrukh Beg's *A Sufi Sage* (1615).

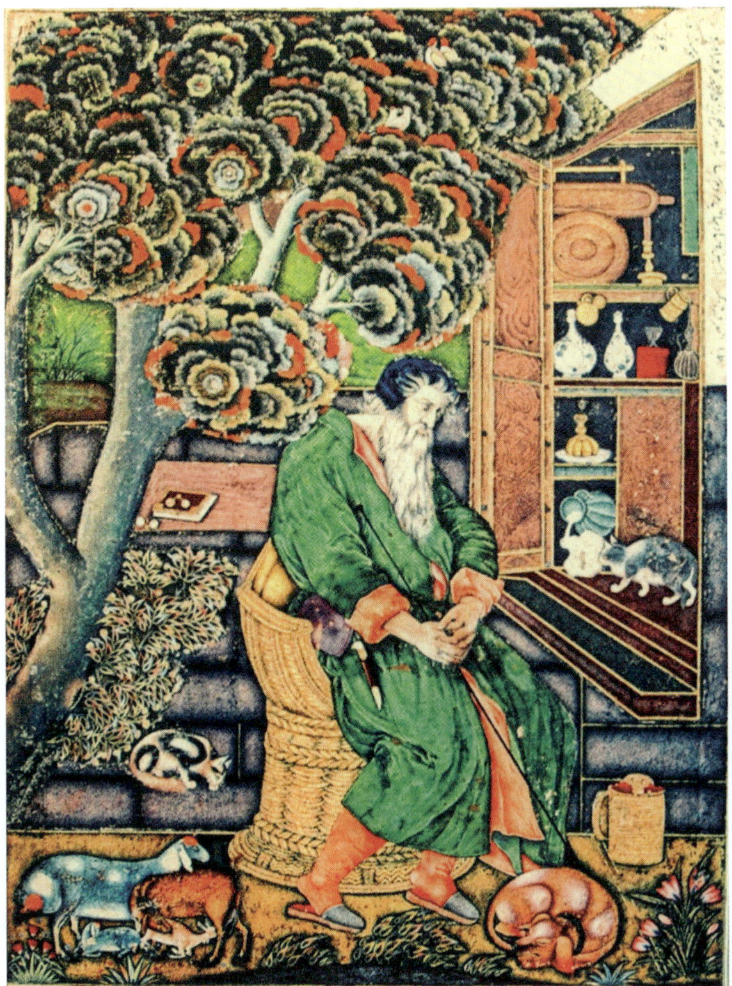

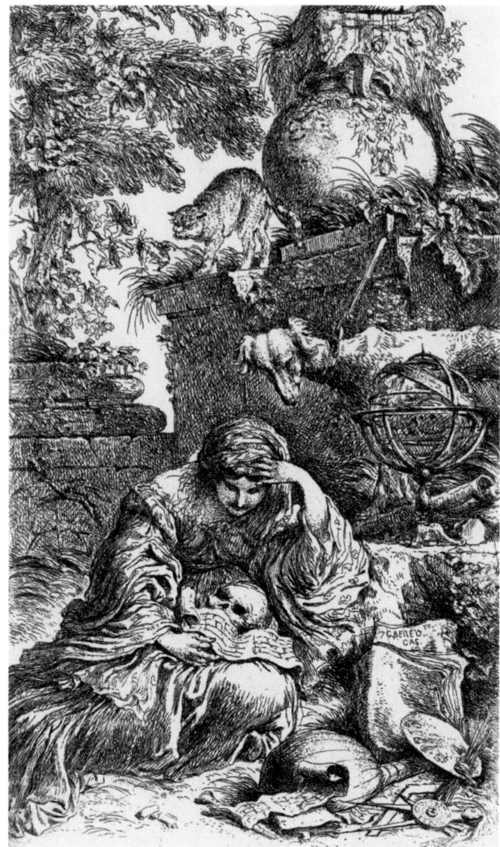

108–109 Contemplating mortality: Castiglione's *Melancholia* (before 1647, *left*); Domenico Fetti's *Melancholy* (1616, *right*).

Castiglione's etching (c. 1640s) is of a figure very much in the spirit of Dürer's, surrounded by the tools of her trade and seemingly impotent to mobilize them [**108**]. She is contemplating mortality: all human achievements are meaningless in the face of death. The thin dog whose body divides the image into a top and a bottom half knows none of this: it gazes sympathetically and with a certain air of puzzlement down at the musical instrument, palette, score, and other detritus, trying to figure out the relationship between all this stuff and its mistress's anxiety. The cat is completely absorbed, as cats are wont to be in art, with something in the tree. It might be her cat, but it has no interest in her mental state. Her dog on the other hand is worried about why she is so distressed.

Domenico Fetti's *Melancholy* (1616) is not winged or swarthy like *Melancholia I* but, like her, she is in a study surrounded by paraphernalia of scholarship and the tools of art-making: books, a globe, sculpture,

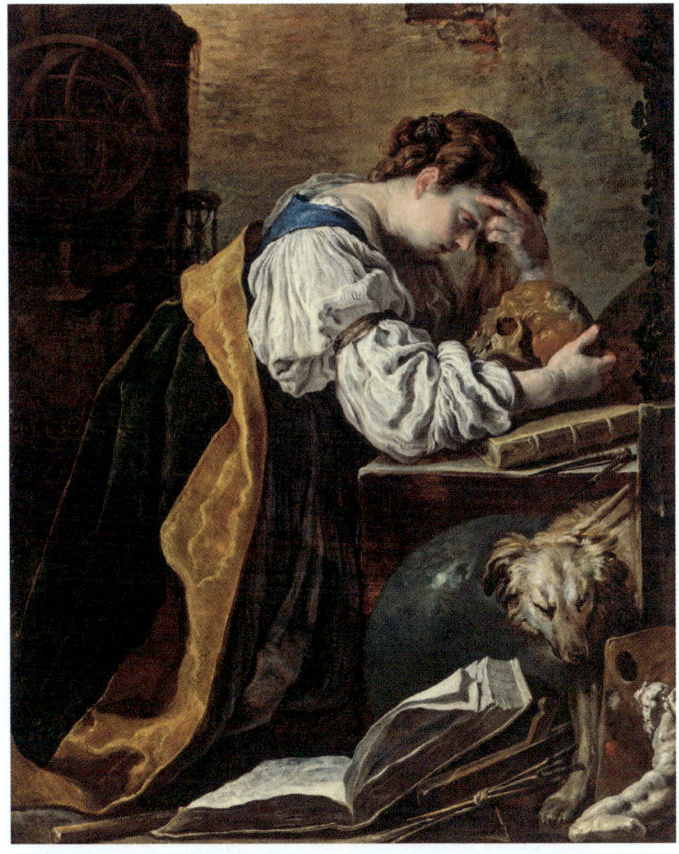

paint brushes, a palette, a compass, a carpenter's plane [**109**]. It all matters nothing to her as she, skull in hand, contemplates mortality. The dog, as so many dogs in art do, comes out from under the table and is interested in what it sees: the marble model on the floor in this case. Its right paw seems to reach out from behind the palette. As Melancholy looks inward, the dog looks out and knows nothing of mortality and the meaninglessness of life.

The dog of *Melancholia I* still finds echoes in the twentieth century, in Lucian Freud, for example, who, like Dürer, was a great animal painter. He even more than Dürer could not resist dogs in his art. It was their 'lack of arrogance, their ready eagerness, their animal pragmatism'. It was because, he said, he was interested in 'people as animals', creatures who shared their physicality with animals in his art. Dogs populated his portraits from the beginning, weighty creatures like the white bull terrier that rests its head on the lap of his first wife, Kitty Garman, the model for *Girl with a White Dog*. The intensity of her gaze is matched by the dog's easy resignation, eyes half-open [**110**].

'Perhaps no one has brought more feeling to the scrutiny of dogs since Landseer,' the most famous of Victorian painters in his day, writes art critic Robert Hughes. 'Freud,' he was sure, 'would doubtless prefer a comparison to Stubbs.' He certainly would not have wanted to be compared to Landseer. Freud's dogs are unsentimentally painted dogs; Landseer's are almost humans in fur. Freud's objectivity is much closer to something like the early twentieth-century German art movement, the *Neue Sachlichkeit*, than to Victorian sentimentality. Dogs and humans in Freud's paintings are ostentatiously seeing together.

There are two ways to see Freud's work in the tradition of *Melancholia I*. The representation of canine joined to human melancholy in Freud does not depend on the viewer's ability to read a complex of signs as it did in Dürer but on a shared affect. The model in *Triple Portrait* [**111**] shares a great deal with *Melancholia I*. She stares vacantly into space; again, her arm rests heavily on one of the two whippets that frame her at right

110 Modern melancholy: *Girl with a White Dog* (1951–2) by Lucian Freud.

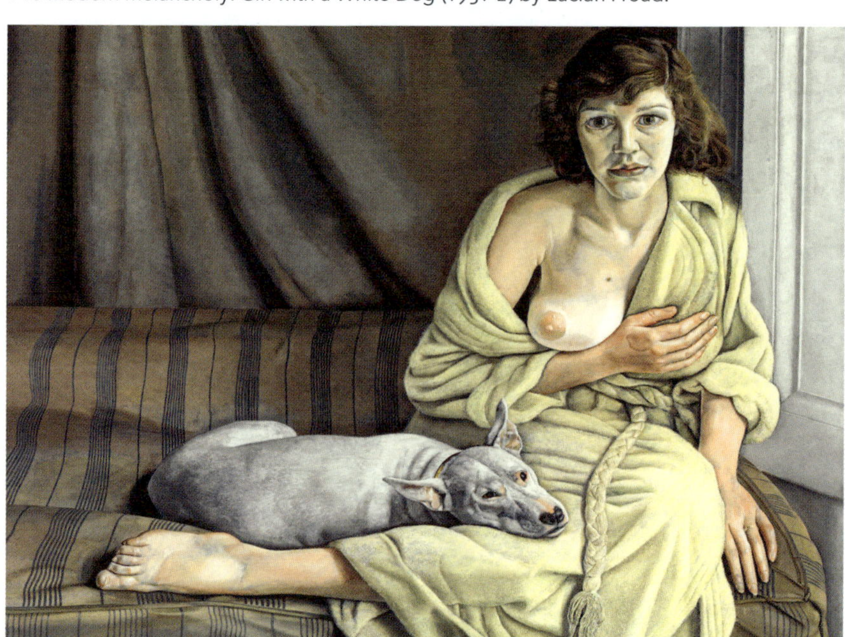

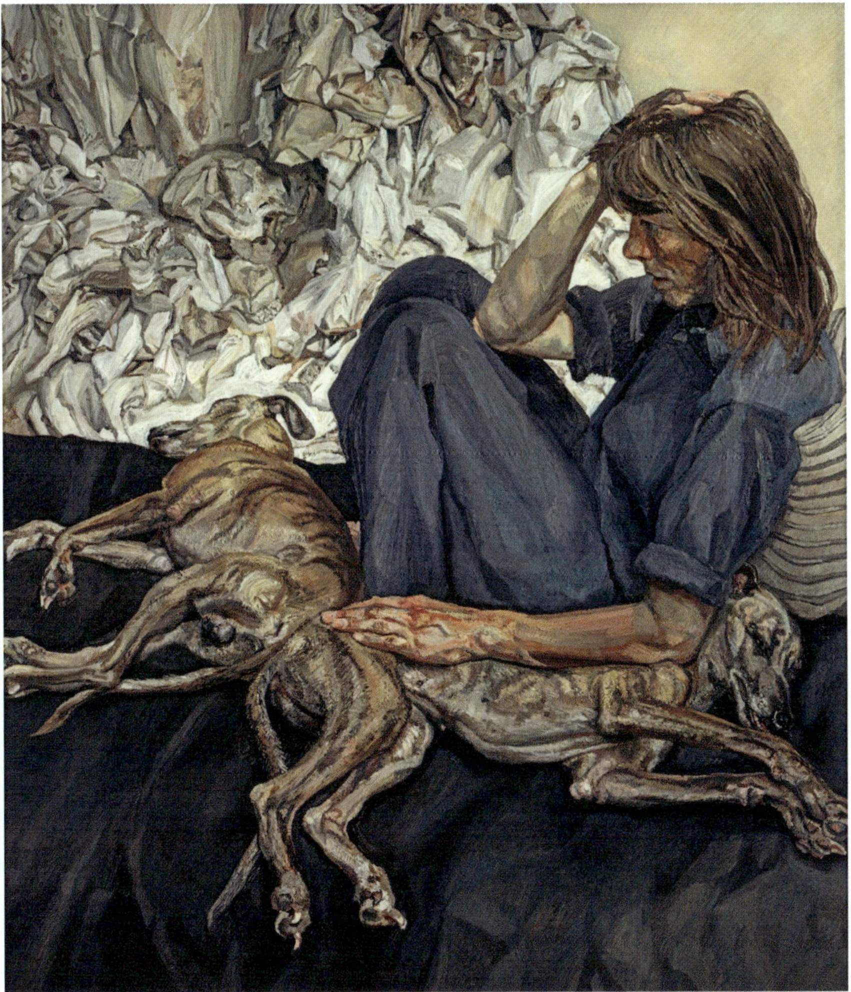

111 Lucian Freud's *Triple Portrait* (1986–7) with the whippets Pluto and Joshua.

angles to each other. They are withdrawn from the world together; speechless. They evoke solitude. If weightiness had since antiquity been associated with melancholia and as Dürer represented it, then these portraits are in that tradition. Dog and human are joined in a common finitude, the dog a doppelgänger of human loneliness in a supposedly disenchanted world. But it is also a creature without hope, bereft of longing; or longing for something beyond reach.

There is another, very different, way to see the sleeping dogs and humans in Lucian Freud. He noted that Pluto, one of the dogs in *Triple*

Portrait, 'sleeps well' and is 'an excellent sitter'; the other dog in the painting is the whippet Joshua who is solo in another of his paintings – *Double Portrait* – and was also said to sleep well. We sleep peacefully when in familiar, comfortable circumstances and in intimate ones; sleeping is beyond anxiety. '"Being there", in Walt Whitman's phrase, "so placid and self-centered", a model of animal behaviour', is how Freud described dogs.[9] He denied fellow feeling – they like habit, he did not – but acknowledged that Pluto often acted and reacted as he wished he himself would, an aspirational doppelgänger. (Pluto is on the label that Freud sketched for his daughter's design studio.) The sleeping dog is not sad or solitary in Freud's painting but, as his biographer William Feaver suggests, is trusting, unselfconscious, and complicit with its human. There is an ease of being together.

The human subject in *Triple Portrait* is not asleep but she is also not about to move. Framed at right angles by the two whippets, raising a foot would wake one; moving her left arm would wake the other. They are in this together. And even when neither dog nor human seems comfortably settled in sleep, they are intimately joined in Freud's work.

The second important candidate for a twentieth-century melancholy dog, which argues for the continuity with earlier ways of thinking about canine sociability, is George Grosz: his 1916 *Der Liebeskranke* ('The Lovesick') [**112**]. It is a self-portrait, the artist dressed as an aristocrat, one of the roles he played as a habitué of cafés frequented by fellow artists and writers. A man in a dark suit sits at a table in a café which is usually a place of conviviality but is here a place of isolation. There is a skeleton in the upper right corner – a *memento mori* as in a Renaissance *vanitas* picture – except that the bones of fish on the table and the dog's bones on the floor seem to mock it. A house is burning in the background. Death seems everywhere in this picture. The heart on the man's chest speaks less to the pains of the heart or for love lost than for worlds lost: a cosmic sense of loss.

And on the floor next to the artist in drag is Dürer's dog, almost literally quoted except for its colour, a sickly blue, with light red-rimmed eyes and a bright red tongue. It seems a suitably dejected double for the modern man as Melancholia. But that is too limiting a role for a dog, so garishly painted, and so central to this painting.[10] It is perhaps a dog for the end of time, one of the central themes of German expressionism in the shadow of the Great War. Grosz served on the western front; its

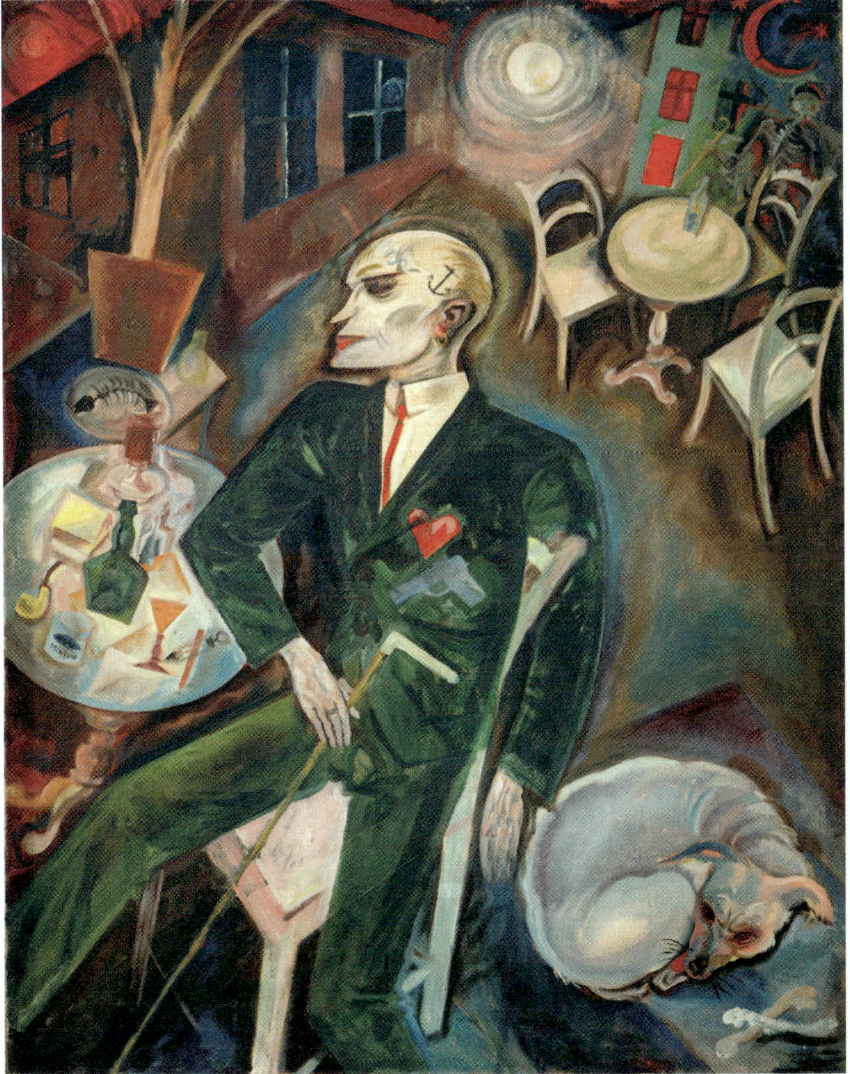

112 George Grosz quoting Dürer's dog in his self-portrait *Der Liebeskranke* (1916).

grotesque consequences inform his art. The painters of the expressionist school understood animals, and dogs in particular, as representatives of a freer, more primitive world. They are appropriated in an artistic tradition struggling with how to represent an apocalypse and a mythical other world on the other side. Grosz's dog is formally close to Dürer's but a distant cousin in its meaning: a dog that speaks less to an individual heaviness or the burdens of genius than to a cosmic condition.

Companions in Solitude: Dogs in the Study

The dog in *Melancholia I* has cousins in art history: dogs in studies and workplaces more generally, keeping humans' company just like the one, for example, in another of Dürer's three so-called 'Masterprints' – *St Jerome in his Study* [**113**]. Jerome's dog is a little plumper than the one in *Melancholia I* and a little smaller. It is sleeping, in the comfortable, brightly lit study of a relaxed saint in his slippers, hard at work, guarded by his iconic lion: '*Gemutlich*' – snug and cozy – as Panofsky points out. The surroundings and the feel of the space – tightly drawn, intimate – are radically different from *Melancholia I*. The dogs, however, are not so different. While the lion is the sign of the saint – Jerome once took a thorn

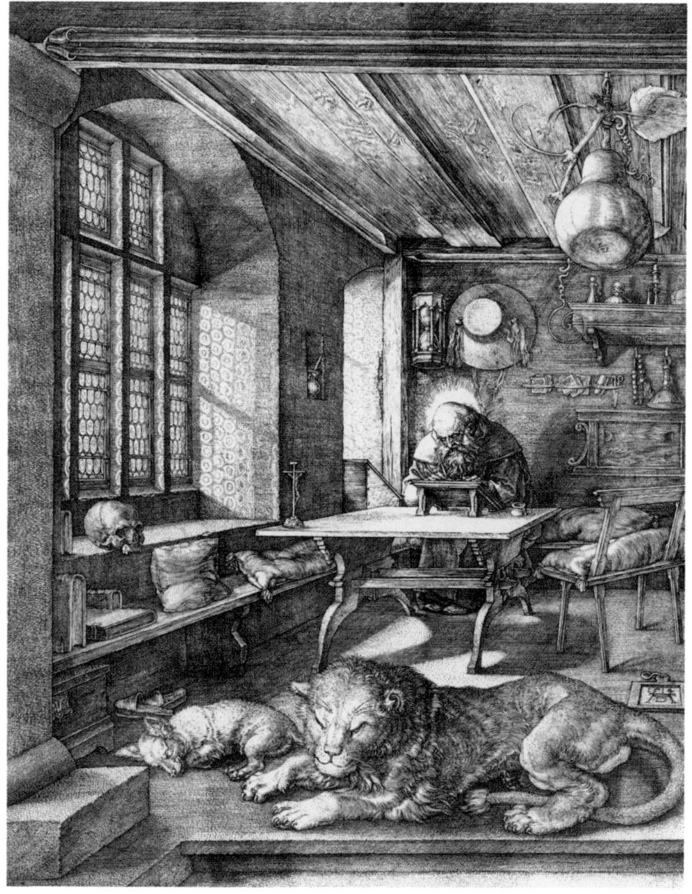

out of his paw – there is little to be said about the iconographical meaning of Jerome's dog beyond the generic 'faithfulness' or its being 'a living symbol of the contemplative life'.[11] It contributes to what Panofsky identified as the 'impression of peace and remoteness' of the room as a place of 'enchanted beatitude'.[12] The saint is alone but not quite alone. A dog is keeping him company in his intellectual labours.

St Jerome in his Study had little of the extended influence or critical attention that *Melancholia I* exerted, but it did introduce a dog to representations of the saint at work. Lucas Cranach the Elder's 1525 version of *Cardinal Albrecht of Brandenburg as Jerome* [**114**] represents its subject in the guise of the saint and includes a small white dog with brown ears, its head cocked, watching his master at his labours, or nudging him for

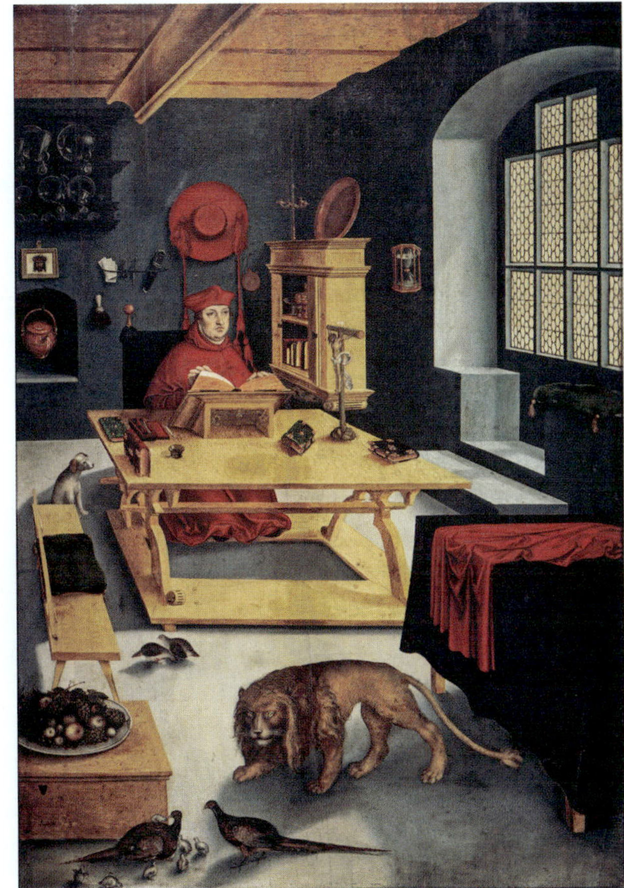

113 (*left*) A plumper dog features in Dürer's *St Jerome in his Study* (1514), another of his three 'Masterprints'.

114 (*right*) Lucas Cranach the Elder's *Cardinal Albrecht of Brandenburg as Jerome* (1525).

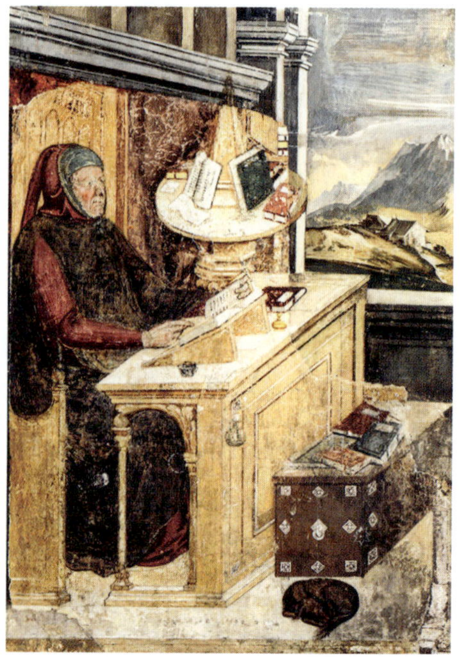

115 A portrait of Petrarch (1370s) introduces the visual trope of a dog in the study of scholars, writers and artists.

a walk. Domestic company. It is clearly painted in the shadow of Dürer. In a second, almost identical 1526 version, Cranach replaces the dog with a rabbit so that knowledgeable viewers could not but think of resurrection; rabbits do not generally keep humans company and especially not inside studies. The funny companionable dog in the 1525 version is emblematic of nothing; unlike the rabbit, it is there as a witness to the scene on the painter's behalf. And it is the representative of sociability. The cardinal is doing something in company when a dog is in the painting, which is not the case when it is replaced by a rabbit.[13]

Dürer's peaceful dog in the study of the scholar-saint Jerome fits into an older tradition of representing scholars at work in canine company. Shortly after Petrarch, the poet and early humanist, died in 1374, he appears in a putative portrait on the walls of the Palazzo della Ragione, the most important civic building in fourteenth-century Padua, where its citizens were invited to imagine one of their most illustrious compatriots. He is in his study with a dog at his feet [**115**].[14] It began a visual trope with scholars, writers, poets and painters in their studies, studios and other workplaces with their dogs, one that continues to the present.[15]

Its origins can to some extent be explained biographically. Petrarch had, and was known in his lifetime to have had, dogs who kept him company. 'I live in it [his house] with a dog and two servants,' he writes in a letter in the summer of 1352, when for over a decade he lived in Fontaine-de-Vaucluse, east of Avignon in France. We know the dog's name: Zabot, from the Arabic 'strong, stable'. The next year he wrote to another correspondent about how contented he was with his quiet life: sufficient food and drink, shoes for his feet and clothes for his body, and 'a dog to keep me company'. And, in a long and lyrical letter-in-poem form Petrarch calls the dog 'my companion constantly', who 'continuously gives amusement'.[16] We know that Petrarch's dogs were large and consequently do not correspond precisely to the relatively small dogs we see in pictures of him. That is, this is not art that slavishly imitates nature. The dog represented dogdom.

The German poet and *Der Erzhumanist* – 'arch-humanist' – Conrad Celtis (1459–1508) had a small dog who was his constant companion, who barked when people entered his study, and with whom he went to bed and even to the privy. He commissioned Dürer's assistant to create a woodcut depicting him with 'my dog' for inclusion in his *Amores* of 1502, and insisted that it should go top centre of the page facing his master's image of Lady Philosophy [**116**]. The dog's name – Lachne – is on the image, the name of one of Actaeon's dogs. It means 'shaggy' or 'woolly' in Greek. We do not have independent evidence that Celtis's Lachne really was shaggy, although we know that the Renaissance

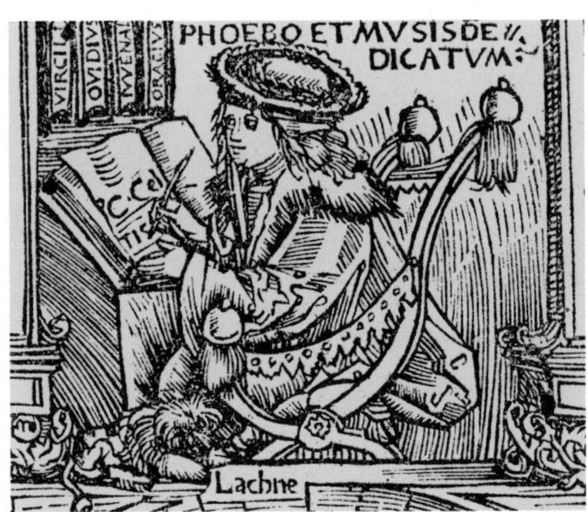

116 Conrad Celtis and his dog Lachne in a woodcut by Hans Süss von Kulmbach (1502).

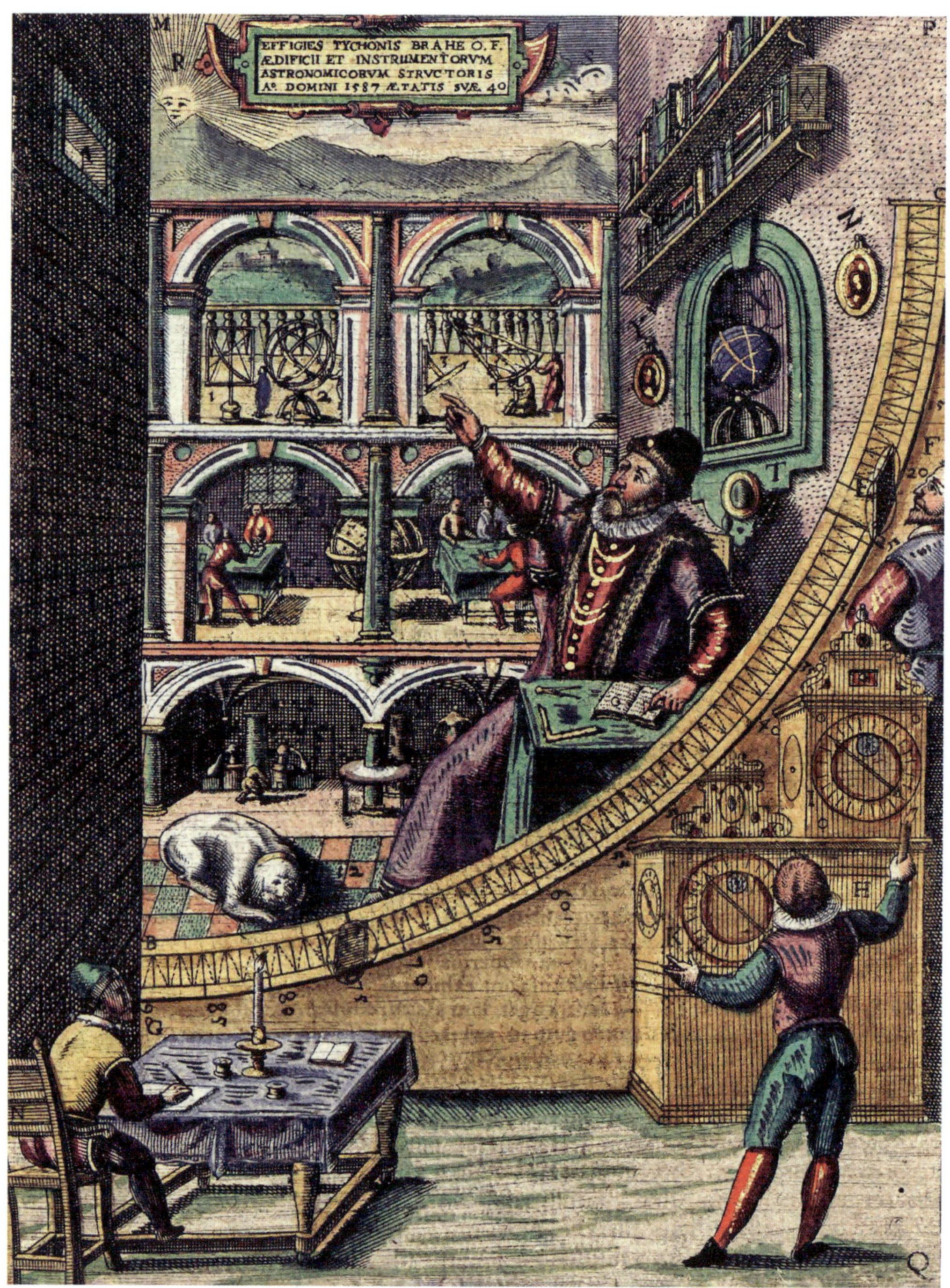

117 'This dog was exceptionally faithful and sagacious': an engraving from the Danish astronomer Tycho Brahe's *Astronomiae instauratae mechanica* (1598).

physician and writer Michelangelo Bondi argued that a *canis sodalist* – a companion dog – ought to be 'shaggy or hairy', and that is how Dürer and many others generally represented the scholar's dog-in-the-study. (The poet Emily Dickinson referred to her beloved dog as 'my shaggy ally'. He was not shaggy and was named Carlo.)[17]

We know that Tycho Brahe – the astronomer whose measurements in his observatory in Denmark made possible Johannes Kepler's calculation of his famous three laws of planetary motion – had a dog, that it was large, and that he insisted that its image be prominently included and identified in a full-page engraving that illustrated one of his most important works. Brahe is sitting in his observatory in front of his giant instrument painted on the wall of his Uraniborg observatory: 'At the number 12,' the legend reads:

> . . . is one of my hounds lying at my feet. This dog was exceptionally faithful and sagacious and is shown in shape and size much as he was in life, a symbol not only of his noble race but also of his sagacity.[18]

It is comfortably curled up, not so differently from Melancholia's and St Jerome's dogs [**117**].

The most extensively documented relationship between a scholar and dogs in early modern Europe is that of the great Flemish humanist and scholar Justus Lipsius, whose voluminous writings on Stoicism brought its moral philosophy into dialogue with Christianity. Everyone knew about his dogs. He took them with him to lectures. A dog is there with him in various portraits and frontispieces: specifically, Saphyrus, who died a tragic death in 1601 by falling into a pan of boiling water. In the portrait of Lipsius by Isaac van Swanenburg, his left hand is resting as tenderly on the dog's head as his other hand holds one of his books [**118**]. Versions of this painting were engraved as frontispieces for his works. Lipsius wrote about dogs extensively in private correspondence and published work and thought they were exceptionally appropriate companions for men like him: 'If this doggy partnership suits any mortals, these are the scholars, and people who are dedicated to eloquence and learning.'[19]

Lipsius argues by analogy: like scholars who work long hours at their desk, dogs are alert, strong, indefatigable, intelligent, and loyal to their studies. Perhaps there is also a bit of Stoic ethics in this claim: man ought

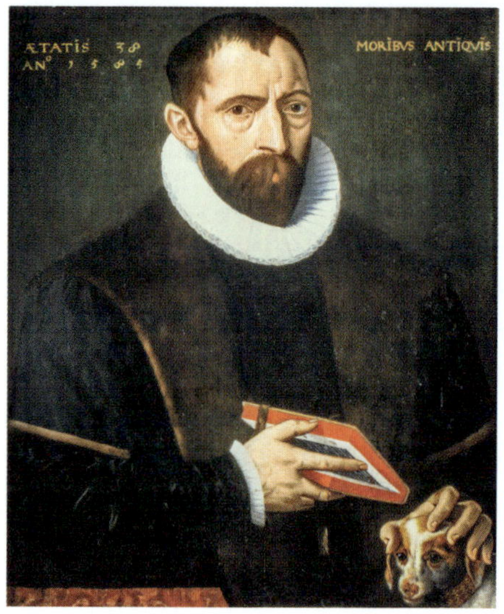

118 Isaac van Swanenburg's portrait of *Justus Lipsius* (1585) with the ill-fated Saphyrus.

to live according to nature, which he shares with dogs. Intimate friendship, which Lipsius understood through the metaphor of the *contubernium* – literally, those who shared a tent – was a central concept for his study of Stoicism, for his relationship to his students and with dogs who lived with him in his house.[20]

Lipsius was heartbroken when Saphyrus died and wrote a long letter about his grief to one of his students, Philip Rubens, brother of the painter. He recounted in detail the dog's agonized death and the Latin epitaph he had written for its tomb. Lipsius died in 1606; Philip in 1611. Early the next year Peter Paul painted a tribute to his brother, to Lipsius and to neo-stoicism: *The Four Philosophers* [**119**]. It was often reproduced in etchings in which the dog's presence is even more pronounced.[21]

The painting is a post-mortem portrait of a small friendship circle – a *contubernium*. To the right of centre is the teacher, Lipsius, in a fur wrap, the great modern exponent of Stoic ethics; seated to his right is the painter's beloved brother Philip, one of Lipsius's favourite and most promising students, who died young; above and behind is a self-portrait of Rubens, who was closely connected to the circle but is here as a mourner. To Lipsius's left – closest to the viewer – is his friend, former student and literary executor, Johannes Woverius, who, like Philip, lived in his teacher's household while studying with him in Leuven. To a learned and informed viewer there are a great number of biographically resonant references in this painting: the bust which belonged to Lipsius was believed since the late sixteenth century to be of Seneca and alludes to Lipsius's engagement with Stoic ethics; it is today in the Rubens House in Antwerp. The books on the table allude to Lipsius's well-known admiration of Tacitus's account of Seneca's death and to his editions of the historian.[22] There is, through Tacitus, a link between the death of Seneca and of Socrates.

Entering from outside the frame of the picture is a dog who had lived with his deceased master and his students. For a long time, it was

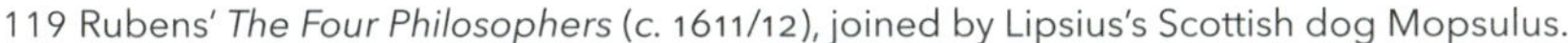

119 Rubens' *The Four Philosophers* (c. 1611/12), joined by Lipsius's Scottish dog Mopsulus.

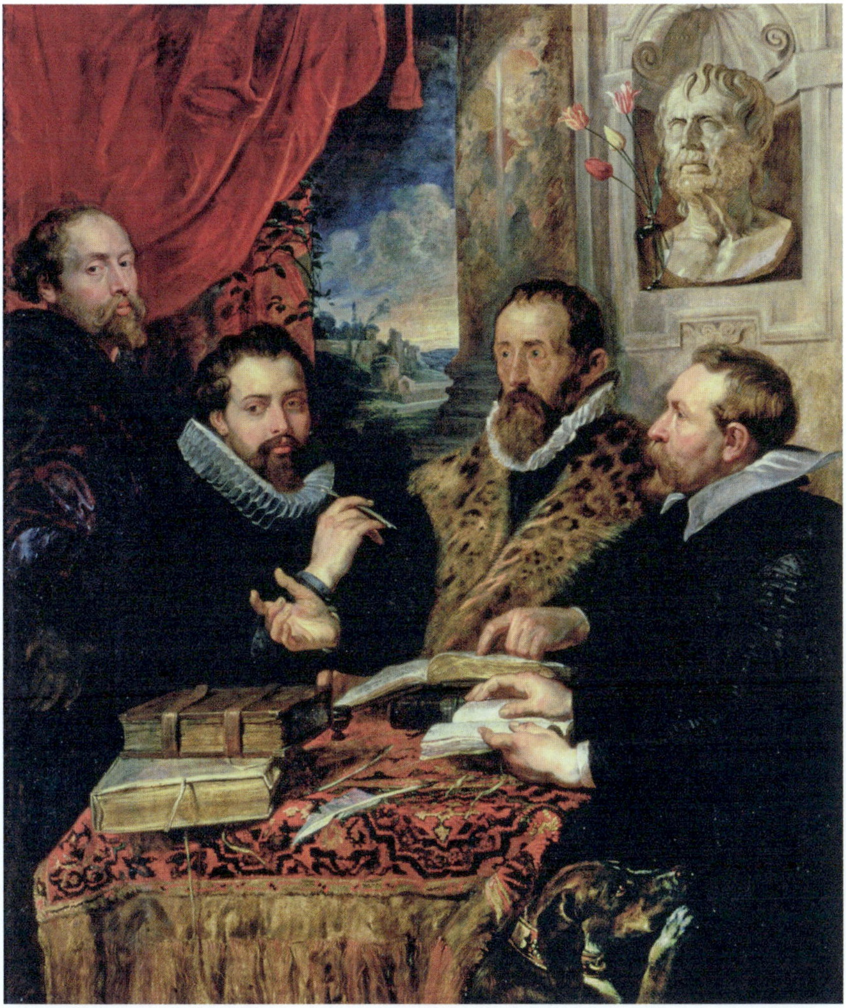

thought that he was Mopsulus, one of Lipsius's two surviving dogs. Lipsius in his long letter on the virtue of dogs described Mopsulus 'as white on the body and the head', which does not describe the dog in the painting. It therefore has to be Lipsius's Scottish dog Mopsius, 'brown on the ears, round the mouth a little yellow, over each eye two yellow spots'. The very fact that we know so much about these creatures testifies to their intimate connection with their humans. The dog is nestling on the leg of his new master, Johannes Woverius, whom Lipsius before he died had asked to take care of him. Mopsius is insisting on being in the picture as he had been, and in some degree still was, part of his old master's circle in real life. Formally, the dog is doing what so many dogs do in painting: mediating, like the painter standing half in and half out, between the inside and outside world, drawing attention to the fact that this is a painting. It is insisting on being social; on connecting with a particular human – the man on whose leg his head rests – whom he knew when Woverius was Lipsius's student living in his house.

A biographical and historical account of canines-in-the study will get us only so far in understanding this niche of representing sociability in art. It is silly to ask whether either St Augustine or St Jerome had a dog. And we have no idea whether people whose pet preferences we might be able to know about – for example, Christine de Pisan (1364–*c.* 1430), the poet and writer in the court of the French king Charles VI – had a dog or not. The dog's presence is generic, although in this image of her [**120**], unlike in others where it is just curled up at her feet, he is next to her chair, waiting patiently for his mistress to finish what she is working on and to pay attention to whatever is happening outside the frame. The image says nothing about her feelings about dogs; at least we have no evidence on that subject. Nor does the dog have a specific symbolic meaning. It is an image about life in a study with a dog keeping one company.

In the absence of a biographical explanation and the more general one I have just offered for the presence of a dog, we might turn to an iconographical one: a dog in the study is an emblem that says the portrait is of someone – a scholar – who is attentive like a dog in the way that a white lily in a painting of the Virgin is a sign of her purity. Reasons why artists might make this connection have ancient sources. Pliny the Elder notes dogs' *sagacitas exempla* – their exemplary mental acuteness – and their *sollertia* – their cleverness, their skill. Lucretius writes about their

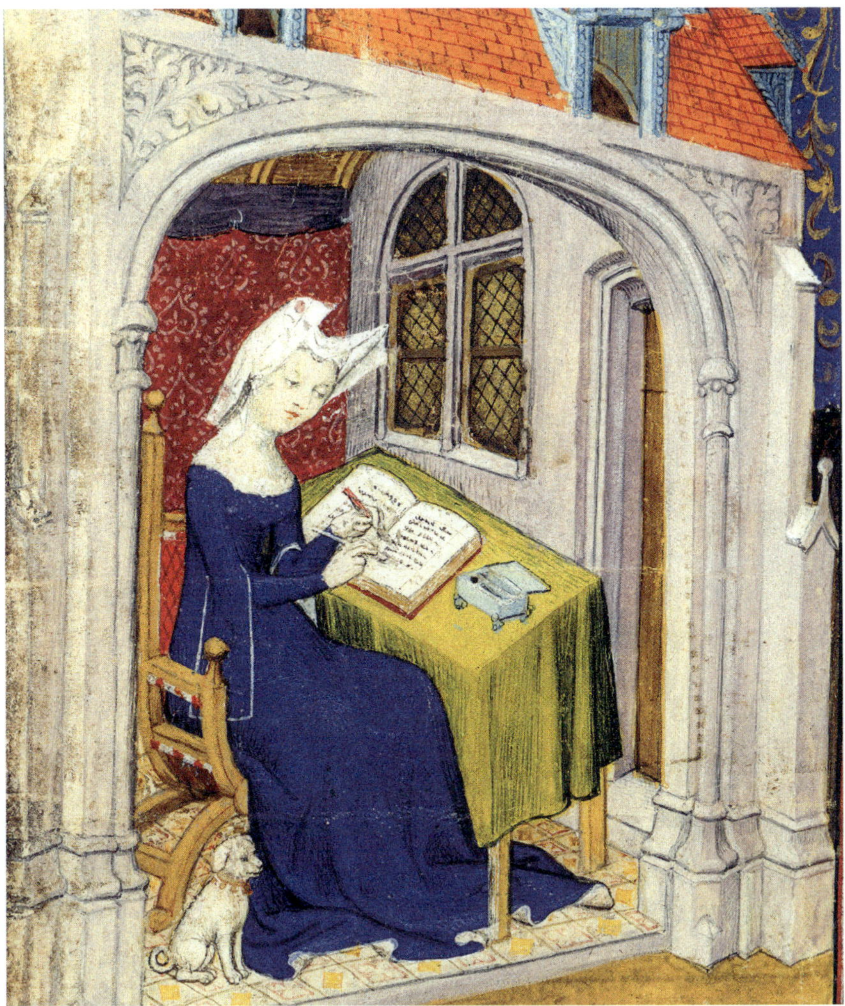

120 *Christine de Pisan in her Study Writing 'Cent Ballades',* an illustration by the Master of the Cité des Dames in the *Book of the Queen* (1410–11).

sagacitas as proven by their capacity to follow scents on the hunt and decide which ones are relevant to the task at hand.[23] It is a common trait that they share with scholars, and is ascribed to dogs well into the nineteenth century.

In addition to the biographical associations and iconography born of the reception by Renaissance readers of what they took to be ancient Egyptian wisdom (*see* page 14), there is a deeper connection between the dog and the writer or scholar that is suggested by a photograph of Franz

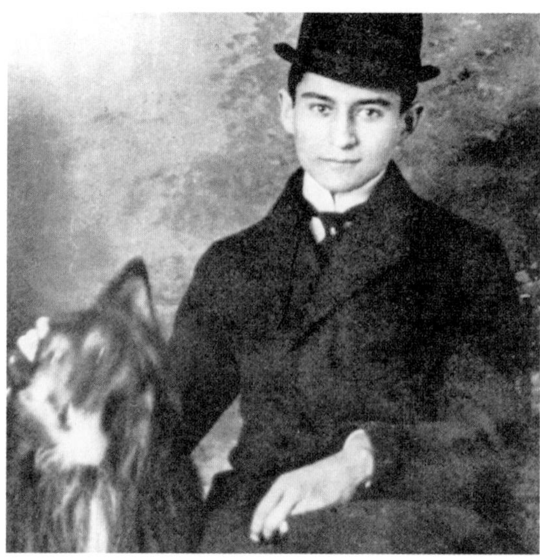

121 The student Franz Kafka with his hand affectionately on his dog's head (1910).

Kafka as a university student with a German shepherd [**121**]. It was taken while he was writing one of his posthumously published stories in which a non-human animal – a dog – declares himself to be 'very different from the rest of my species' and tries to make sense of the relationship between the world of animals and that of humans. 'What is there actually except our own species?' asks the canine narrator of his short story, 'Investigations of a Dog'. 'To whom but it can one appeal in the wide and empty world? All knowledge, the totality of all questions and all answers, is contained in the dog.' The context is the dog's struggle to get past the limits of his species-being, his doggedness. But this is also something with which Kafka struggles. In this and, of course, other stories, he stands on the threshold of the divide. It is the dog-philosopher who stands as Kafka's surrogate in exploring a question that occupied him all his life: What are the origins of music? What is music about?[24]

The French writer and poet Jean-Christophe Bailly thinks that Kafka's hand on the dog's ear is something of a bridge between it and its human: 'This portrait,' he writes, 'conveys a power held in reserve, as if an inexhaustible battery of presence were being endlessly recharged.' That power is born of the intimate sociability of touch. Their eyes – Kafka's and the dog's – are seeing the same world. We can of course not know this, but all the art in this book is grounded in the belief in cross-species sociability and intelligibility.[25]

Companions in Solitude: Dogs in the Studio

No iconographical tradition connects dogs with visual artists. And visual artists are not often alone in their studios with only a dog for company. But dogs do speak and see for artists at work and are represented as company in a joint enterprise.

The historian Carlo Ginzburg makes the case for the young Parmigianino's sixteenth-century self-portrait that shows the artist holding up a very pregnant bitch [**122**]. He was a superb draftsman who painted and drew many beautiful, thoughtful dogs: a red-chalk dog's head; a dog in the Diana and Actaeon story. But in this case the dog looking out with the artist is making a claim in the context of a Renaissance debate on the long-vexed subject of the souls of brutes. Ginzburg interprets Parmigianino's holding up the dog, its eyes like his looking intently to his left, as an ironic rebuttal to the claim in Ovid's *Metamorphoses*, echoed through the centuries, that God gave man an upturned visage, in other words the ability to look heavenward and behold the cosmos, as a sign of his preeminence in his creation. It is also a reprisal of the rebuttal by Diogenes the Cynic (the dog philosopher, founder of scepticism) to Plato's definition of the human as a featherless biped: behold a plucked chicken. Parmigianino's drawing is for Ginzburg a visual argument for the intimate and close relationship between humans – this artist – and an animal – this pregnant dog – in the context of an age-old debate about the soul of brutes. Yes, they have souls.[26]

No such claim is made by Rembrandt's 1631 self-portrait with a dog with whom he shares a space [**123**]. It is the only self-portrait that shows the artist standing up. The dog, some speculate, may have been added to an earlier version, of which there is a copy by one of his students, because Rembrandt was unhappy with how his legs looked [**124**]. The copy of the original and the repainted version are very different paintings less because of how the legs appear – there were other solutions to that compositional problem – than because of the dog. The painter represents himself as being in company with a dog in the studio; the poodle's winsome gaze to the right invites us to look in and mirrors Rembrandt's *contrapposto* pose. Even if the dog was not there when Rembrandt looked at himself in the mirror in 1631, it is there in the painting now. As in many of Rembrandt's paintings and etchings – *The Visitation* is one

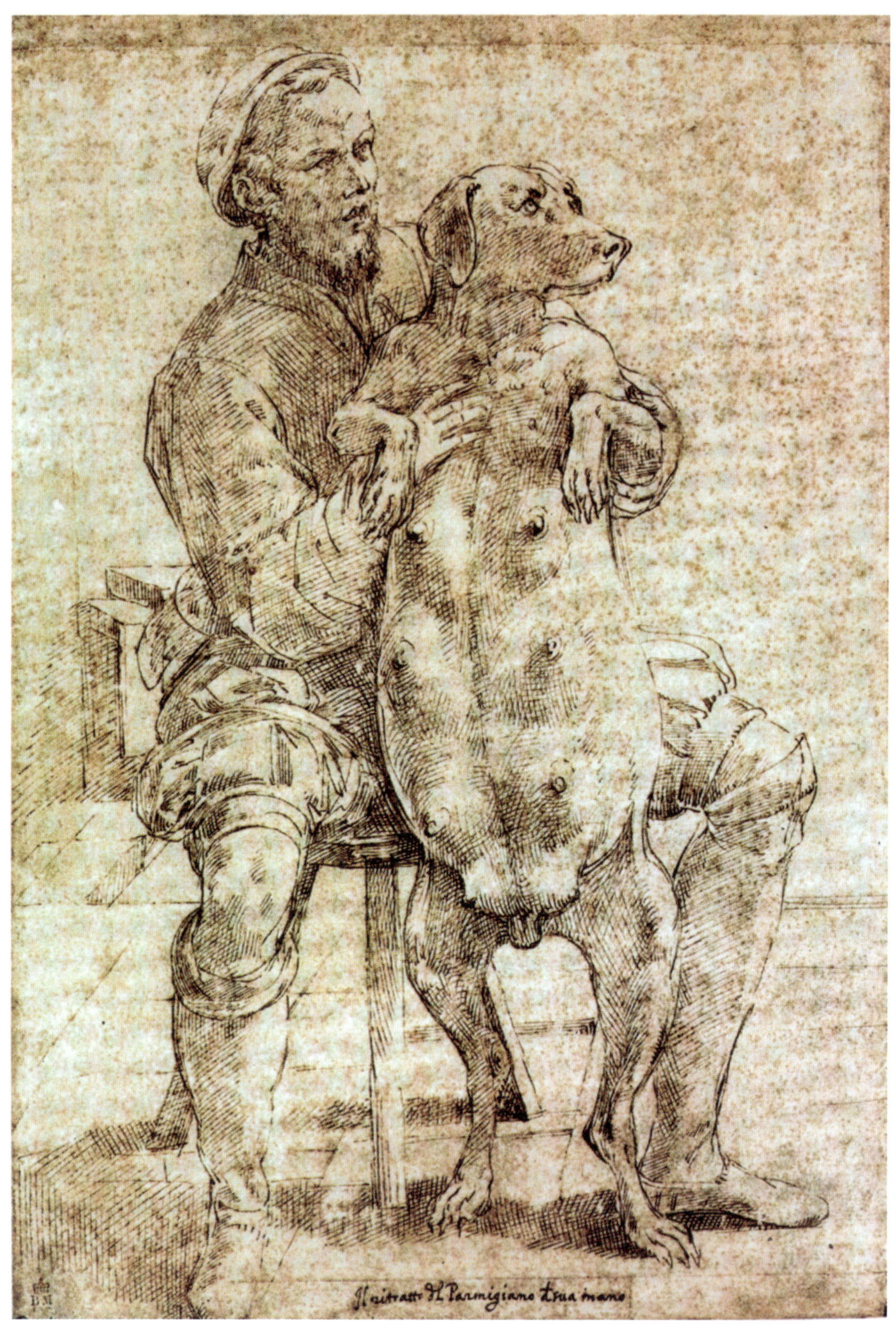

122 The soul of a dog: *A Man Sitting on a Stool, Holding up a Pregnant Bitch* (1518–40) by Parmigianino.

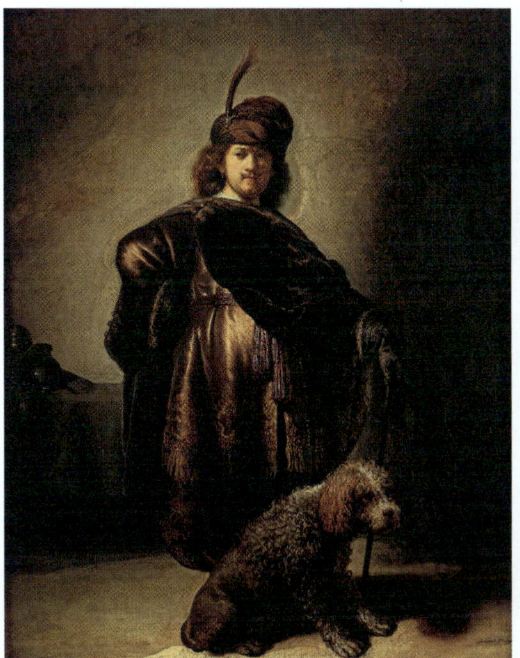

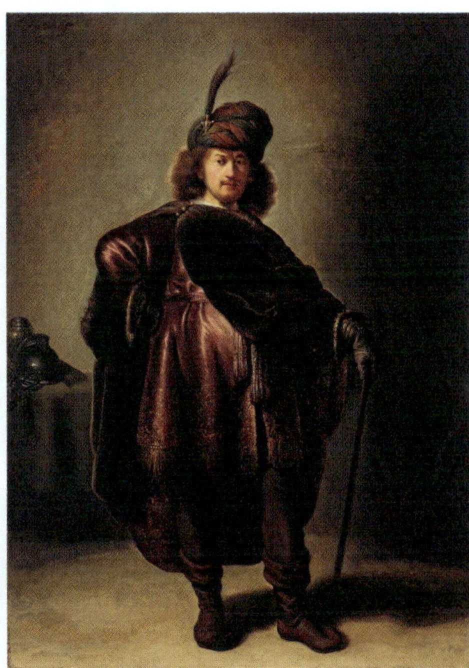

123–124 (*left*) Rembrandt's *Self-Portrait in Oriental Dress*; (*right*) Isaac Jouderville's copy. Rembrandt added the dog to the original because he was unhappy with how his legs looked.

example; the *Good Samaritan* (*see* 210–211) is another – it would be a different, emptier world without the dog.

The same sort of thing might be said about Hubert Robert's self-portrait c. 1763–5. Dog and master share more than a common space [**125**]. They are each in their own way absorbed in what they are seeing: he on the sculpture he is drawing that seems to be looking back at him; the dog on the slippers that it may, or may not, eat. The artist's bare leg painted in flesh colours forms one side of a parallelogram with the dog, painted in the same hues, forming the other side. They are together, absorbed each in their own world. Parallel play we might say if they were two-year-olds: parallel seeing.

Each self-portrait with dog tells a story about companionship as well as about self-presentation. In the self-portrait by the eighteenth-century Austrian artist Martin Quadal the dog is putting his right paw over the hand in which the artist holds a brush as if to stop him working and attending to it instead [**126**]. Its eye is painted with more attention than the human's, gazing on the artist's face; its paw next to his hand; four

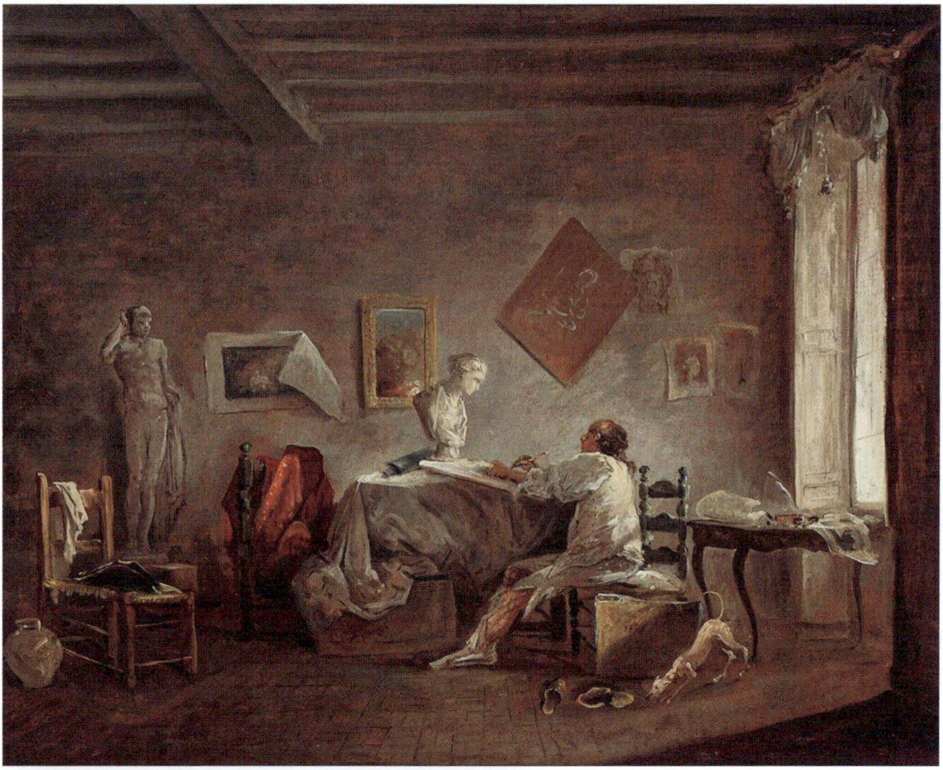

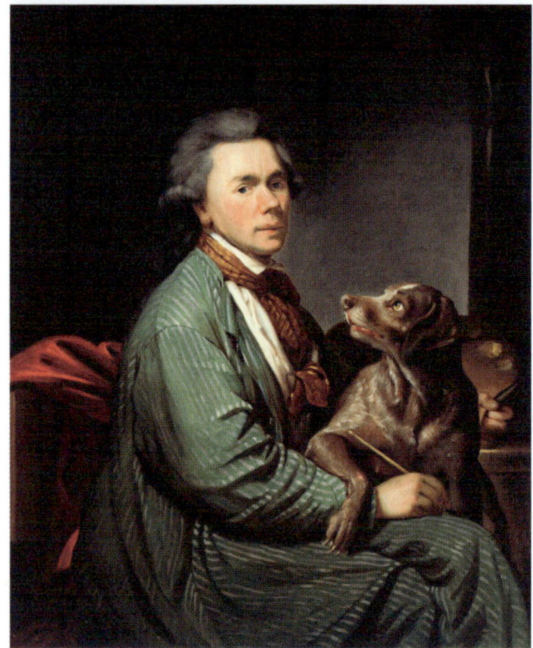

125 (*above*) Parallel seeing in Hubert Robert's self-portrait *The Artist in his Studio* (*c*. 1763–5).

126 (*left*) Holding hands: *Self-Portrait* (1788) by Martin Quadal.

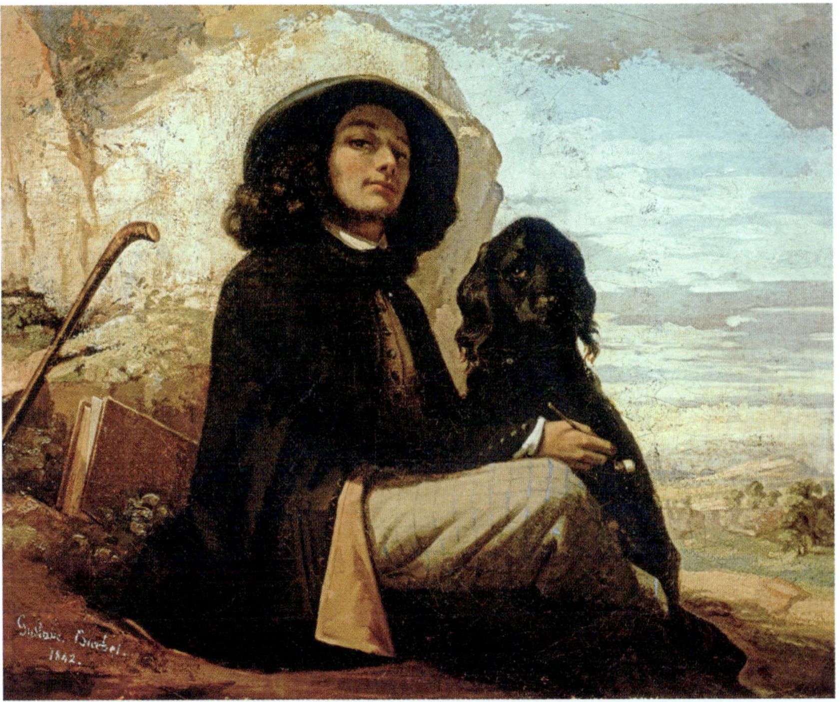

127 Artist and dog appear almost as one in Courbet's *Self-Portrait with Black Dog* (1842–4).

digits showing on each. Almost holding hands. Or does the dog want to grab the brush and work in the studio?

Self-portraits with dogs are almost by definition about the dog's presence in the studio or, if represented *en plein air*, outside but painted – reimagined – inside. Courbet's *Self-Portrait with Black Dog* – called *Portrait of the Author* in the 1844 Salon – is a good example [**127**]. A young man in bohemian fashion poses ostentatiously on a rock out in nature, alone, except for his carefully posed spaniel in shiny dark fur, the same colour as his master's cloak. He has put down his sketching pencil and holds a pipe in his right hand. The art historian James Rubin notes that smoking suggests the sort of quiet contemplation associated with the artistic imagination, but his more trenchant observation is that the dog is sitting patiently sharing a quiet smoke. Among the qualities that make a dog a good candidate on the 'and then, and then' model of friendship is that it is very good at waiting. At least outdoors.[27] The painter touches the dog who seems almost a part of him. He is looking up, his face brightly lit with a knowing smile; the dog, backlit by the sky, is looking straight ahead at us. A curl on its left ear matches the whiff of hair sticking out from Courbet's hat above his right ear.

In Edwin Landseer's much-reproduced self-portrait the two dogs are keenly interested in what the great animal painter is doing [**128**]. He is painting them. If the dogs were human, we might tell a story of two people stopping by a famous artist's studio to watch him work and perhaps offering their advice: social call of interested parties. In Manet's *Marcellin Desboutin*, a portrait of his friend the painter Desboutin, the dog is in the studio as a simple canine presence, but also perhaps as a double for the painter of the portrait himself [**129**]. It is a painterly dog that commands our attention with its beautiful tufts of fur that seem like brush hairs. White strokes of paint outline its body, which is lit as brightly as the human subject's face.[28]

The case of Alberto Giacometti is both a more indirect, and a more immediate, case of the dog with the artist in his studio. *Dog* is one of his most famous and personal works [**130**]. In an interview in preparation

128–129 (*left*) Landseer's *The Connoisseurs* (after 1865); (*right*) Manet's *Marcellin Desboutin* (1875).

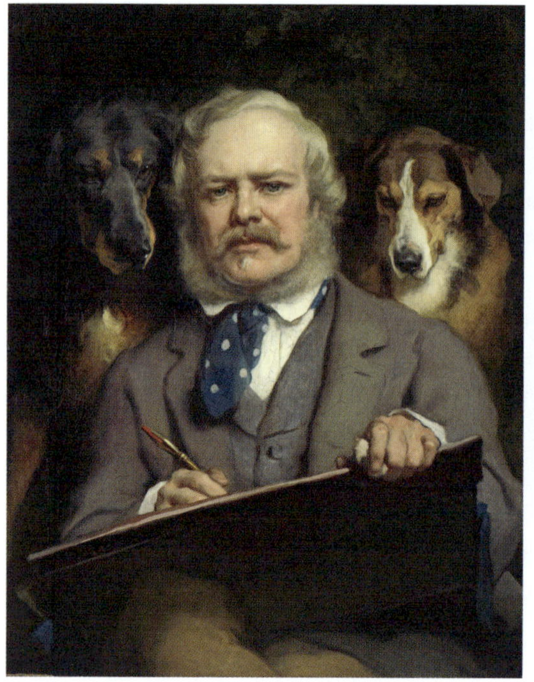

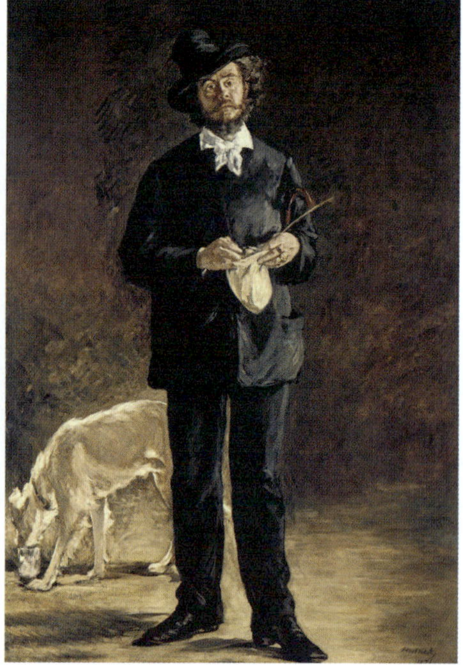

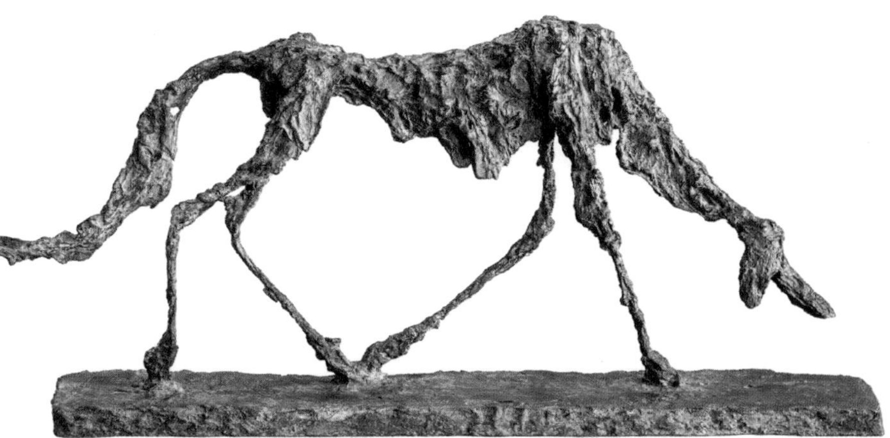

130 Alberto Giacometti's *Dog* (1951), a self-portrait of sorts.

for an exhibition at the Guggenheim Museum in New York featuring this work, he said that:

> For a long time, I'd had in my mind the memory of a Chinese dog I'd seen somewhere. And then one day I was walking [. . .] in the rain, close to the walls of the buildings, with my head down, feeling a little sad, perhaps, and I felt like a dog just then. So, I made that sculpture.

Giacometti confessed to the interviewer that this was a self-portrait of sorts. The only problem in art, he continued, was 'to express oneself' not in any space or time but as oneself.[29] It would be a fool's errand to try to translate what Giacometti said he felt – 'sad', 'perhaps like a dog' – into the sculpture before us. A sense of weightiness; looking down; a creature who is with its human, even if in solitude.

Few artists' relationship to their dogs is more important or better documented in word and image than that of Giacometti's contemporary Constantin Brancusi with his Samoyed Polaire. 'The power and effectiveness of Polaire as a device through which [he] could communicate his preoccupations and artistic identity was not limited to the studio,' writes the critic Jon Wood. She was with him when he worked and accompanied him to cafés and on visits to his friends. He was bereft when Polaire was struck by a car and died and he buried her in the pet cemetery at Asnières-sur-Seine on the north-west outskirts of Paris. A small album's

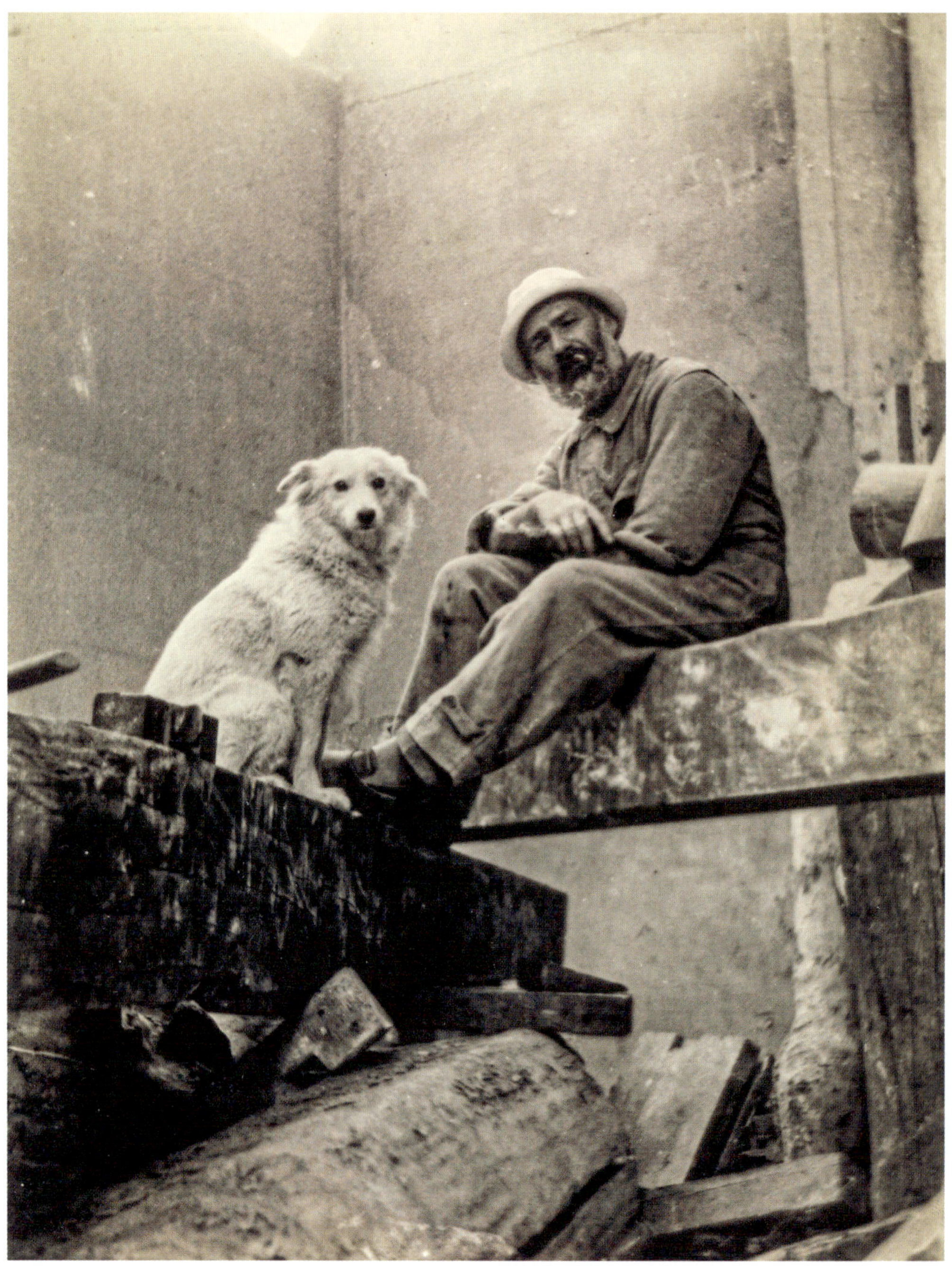

131 A 'souvenir of the two of us': Brancusi with his Samoyed Polaire.

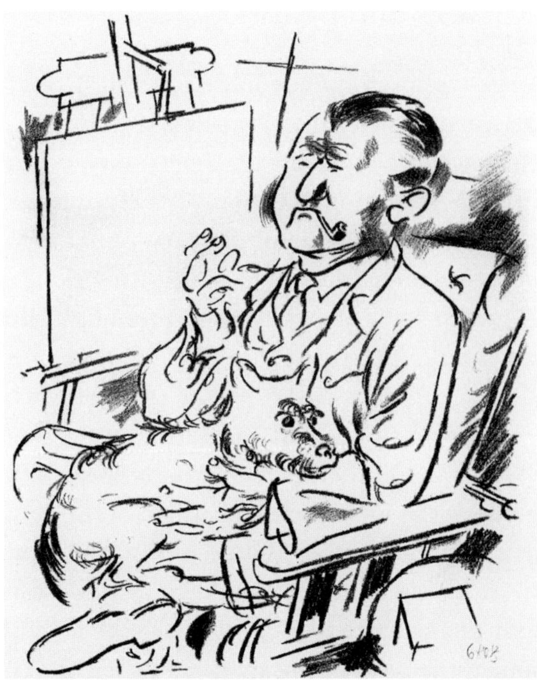

132 *Self-Portrait with Dog* (1926) by George Grosz.

worth of 'selfies' of the two of them in the studio bear witness to the importance of her as a companion in art-making. Polaire sits on a column looking with interest at Brancusi in a photograph that he sent to Ethel Moorhead – suffragist, artist, and editor of an arts journal for which he wrote – as a 'souvenir of the two of us'. In another photograph they are posed together on two beams looking down at the camera and us [**131**]. Brancusi's friend Man Ray took a triple portrait of Polaire draped over her master in his studio with the photographer Edward Steichen's dog at his feet. The dogs look out at us. These dogs, and in many more images of artists, are manifestly in the social world of their art-world masters.[30]

At a minimum at least this art documents reality – dogs in the studio and in the artists' lives. George Grosz painted himself in 1917 with the dog of Dürer's *Melancholia I*, and almost ten years later in a lithograph in front of his easel with a terrier (his own) in his lap [**132**]. But of course they were not compelled to document this reality. The dog in the studio comes to create a reality and our consciousness of it. It is generative of the artistic process of representing sociability.

Dogs and Death

Dogs and eschatology have a global history. They guard the borders between this world and the next as they guarded the boundaries in life; they accompany souls on their journey: Cerberus of the Greeks with origins in older civilizations; the hounds of Yama from the Vedas; the two dogs in the Avasten texts of ancient Persia. Sagnid – 'dog seeing' – in ancient Zoroastrian texts guards the bridge to heaven. The gaze of the dog with spots above its eyes in funerary rituals – the 'four-eyed' dog – was said to purify the dead and help them along their way. To this day they accompany bodies to the platforms where they will be eaten by vultures in traditional Zoroastrian funerals.[31] But their eschatological work is not limited to the Indo-European world. The Egyptian Anubis – guide to the underworld, guardian of the grave, witness to the weighing of souls – was either represented as a dog or as a human with a dog's head. In Mesoamerican myth the hairless Xoloitzcuintili guards the dead as it carries them over the water to the next life; clay figures of dogs that joined the dead in the shaft graves of the Colima culture of north-west Mexico 2,000 years ago are still there in the art of Central America today. Dogs are present too in the folklore of death: the ghost dogs who can see both heaven and earth; dogs who can see ghosts that humans cannot see; ghosts that appear as dogs with glowing tongues.[32]

These widely disparate and dispersed cultural associations put the dog in the realm of the dead through its many roles in the lives of humans: as guardians of sheep already in Neolithic Iranian pottery and by extension guardians of humans and their souls. They are creatures who know the way. Who more than the dead need protection, attention, and guidance? There is also a structural analogy between the liminal standing of the dog as a species (between nature and culture) and its mythic status as an intermediary creature, between life and death. All of this is part of the deep time of cross-species intimacy refracted as a way of representing our recognition of the horrible fact of death. The dog grieves; it mourns. It bides with the dead as it does with the living. There are dogs buried in human graves on all the inhabited continents.[33] And there are dogs figuratively with the dead in Western tomb sculpture. On the fourth-century BCE stele over the grave of a boy – Moschion – a dog jumps up waiting to be petted [**133**]. A dog looks up at its mistress

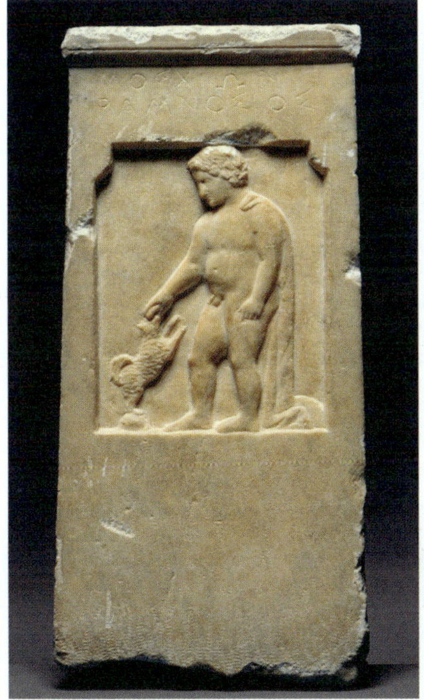

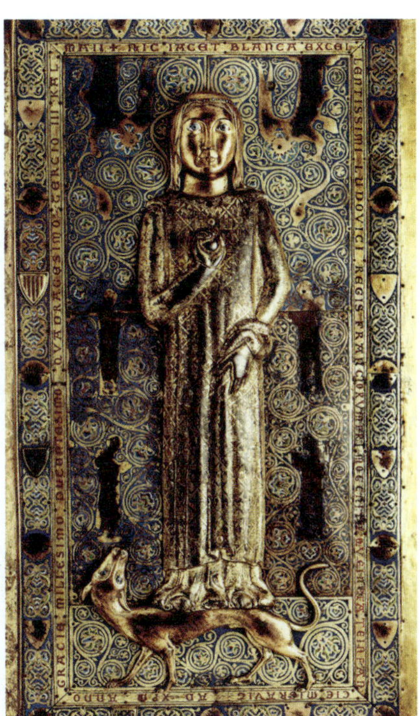

133–134 (*left*) An ancient Greek grave stele (*c.* 375 BCE); (*right*) recumbent effigy of Blanche de France, daughter of the king Saint Louis (late thirteenth century).

on the thirteenth-century brass plate that guards the grave of Blanche of France, daughter of Saint Louis, as if urging her to come for a walk [**134**].

The modern visual representation of the human belief that we might live in a dog's knowing recognition of death begins with Piero di Cosimo's *Satyr Mourning Over a Nymph* (1495) [**135**].[34] The landscape is hazy, dreamy, sad, unbounded; the flowers by the dog are drooping and the plant that follows the curve of its back is bowed. It is an 'empathic landscape', a visual version of the ancient trope that nature too mourns: 'for we know that the whole creation groanest and travaileth in pain together,' writes St Paul. The trope is still there in an apostrophe in Milton's 'Lycidas':

> Now thou art gone, and never must return!
> Thee Shepherd, thee the woods and desert caves,
> With wild thyme and gadding vines o'ergrown,
> And all their echoes mourn.

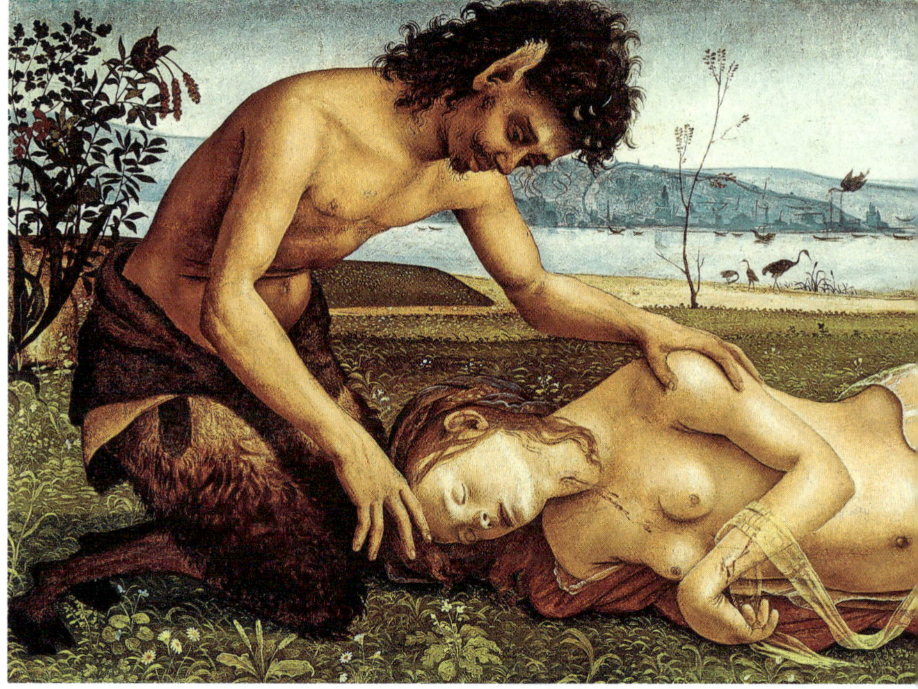

135 Piero di Cosimo's *Satyr Mourning Over a Nymph* (1495). The dogs see and recognize the satyr's grief.

Nature is the *mise en scène* for mourning and itself a mourner in this painting. Not just the mourning dog, but Nature 'seemingly [responds] to the emotional state of its human or half human inhabitant'.[35]

How the nymph came to be dead followed upon Piero's interpretation of a story in Ovid's *Metamorphoses* VII. Through a series of misunderstandings and jealousies in a troubled marriage, Cephalus the great hunter-husband killed his wife, the nymph Procris. After one spat, she had given him as a gift of reconciliation a magic javelin that never misses its mark, and a hunting dog named Laelaps who always catches his prey that Artemis had given her. That's how the dog enters the picture.[36] Soon Cephalus is off hunting again and malicious gossip makes Procris mistrust him. She goes into the forest to spy on him and overhears Cephalus 'wooing the breeze' – that is, Aura, a minor goddess whose name means breeze – asking her to refresh him. Procris thinks he is calling to another lover and makes a sound; he, thinking the noise is coming from an animal, throws the magic javelin and kills her. She dies in his arms.

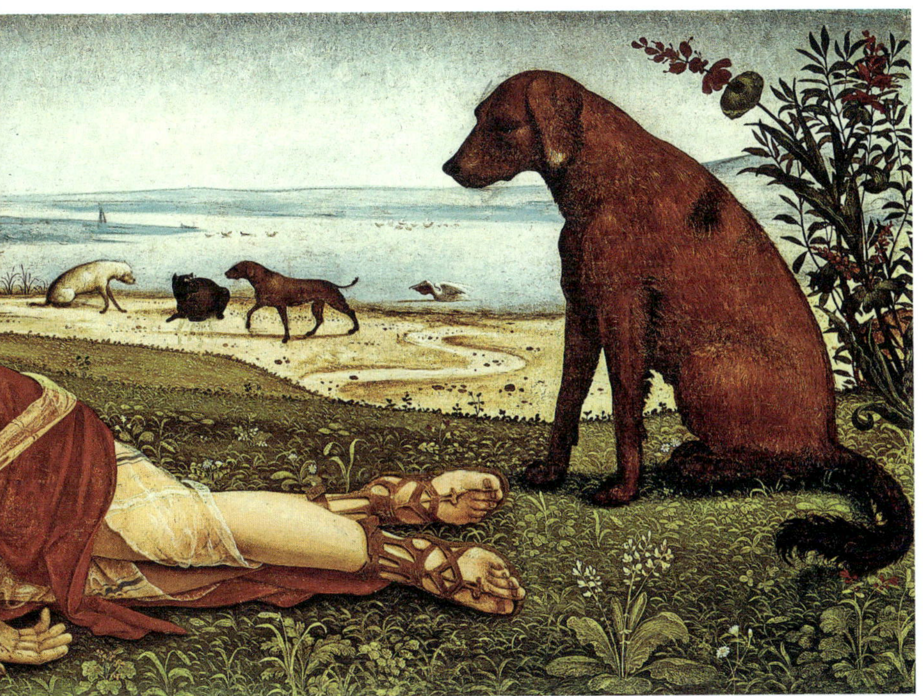

In the face of the many details that don't fit, a great deal of scholarly effort has gone into reconciling Piero's painting with its putative source.[37] But people have generally given up trying to make sense of the painting based on multiple sources and iconographical details. Best to leave it that Piero is 'conjuring a mourning scene from his own mythopoetic imagination', as the art historian Dennis Geronimus suggests. Of course, there are two creatures mourning the dead nymph Procris: a dog and a faun. But fauns/satyrs have no relationship to our lives; we have no sense of what it would mean for a satyr to mourn. The large brown dog is another matter. 'Could any viewer have ever wished for a more soulful expression of a dog's gift of human sentience?'[38] It had once been hers. Framed by the flowers that follow the curve of its back, it looks with a superordinate gaze over the whole mournful scene. Its sheer size and solidity on the ground, its exquisitely detailed fur with a white patch on its ear and black spot on its haunches, and its doleful eye, together constitute a visually irresistible presence.

Vasari says of Piero that 'he had led the life of a brute rather than of a man', who believed that in the pre-lapsarian world humans and other animals understood each other. In this painting he saw through the eyes and felt through the body of the large brown dog the heaviness of grief and the timelessness of death. This beautifully painted creature who, like the dog in Carpaccio's *St Augustine in his Study*, sees the light announcing St Jerome's death, is intently engaged and is formally essential to the painting. This soulful dog is represented as a sentient, feeling being who is mourning the death of an all too human Procris.[39]

There are three more dogs in the painting – a white, a black and a brown one – next to the path on the shores of a lake. The standing brown one is a double of the mourning dog; the crouching black one looks at him imploringly with conspicuously open eyes; the white one is quizzically looking at the one in the middle. If these were three deer, creatures of the wild, grazing by the water we would be thinking about them, if at all, as a naturalistic convention. But here they are socially embedded creatures in a scene of mourning: dogs at the borderland of earth and water perhaps dividing the realms of the dead and the living. The fact that they are paying no attention to the dead nymph makes the attention of the large brown dog in the foreground seem still more powerful.[40] Whether naturalistic realism or allegory, that dog is the emotional centre of this figuration of loss.

Less than a century after Piero a new image of a dog mourning enters the visual imagination, not exactly mourning the dead but saddened by a final farewell. Michelangelo and his contemporary Correggio are the starting points for this history of canine emotions. The philosopher Hagi Kenaan became interested in welcoming and in bidding farewell, that is, 'negotiating the dimensions of transience and finitude'. One dimension of this human condition is the aloneness of the one left behind and the comfort that one might feel at the prospect of being missed. It is about imagining that someone, if not the cosmos, cares.[41] Kenaan reports that she asked the Renaissance art historian Giancarla Periti whether she could think of any interesting farewell gestures in art and Periti suggested Correggio's *Ganymede Abducted by the Eagle* (1531–2): 'Listen to the barking in the painting', 'The dog is the one saying goodbye' [**136**]. His eyes look up toward the eyes of his master, who looks down at him in turn; the dog is reaching up as if to keep Ganymede present.

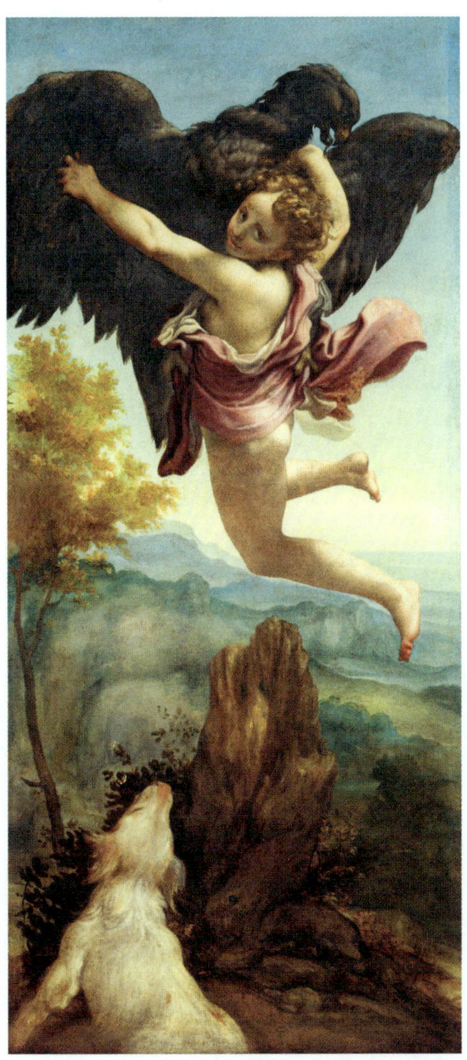

136 'Listen to the barking in the painting': Correggio's *Ganymede Abducted by the Eagle* (1531–2).

Correggio in this painting was the first to include a dog in a representation of the myth. There is no dog in any previous image of the eagle abducting the beautiful young shepherd with whom Zeus had fallen in love. Likewise, there is no dog in any of the many ancient textual versions of the story – those of the lyric poet Theognis of Megara, or Plato, or Virgil, among many others. The crux of the story is not about farewell but desire. No dog is needed. And it is not needed as an iconographical sign: the boy in Correggio's painting is too young and soft to be a hunter, or a shepherd in need of a dog.

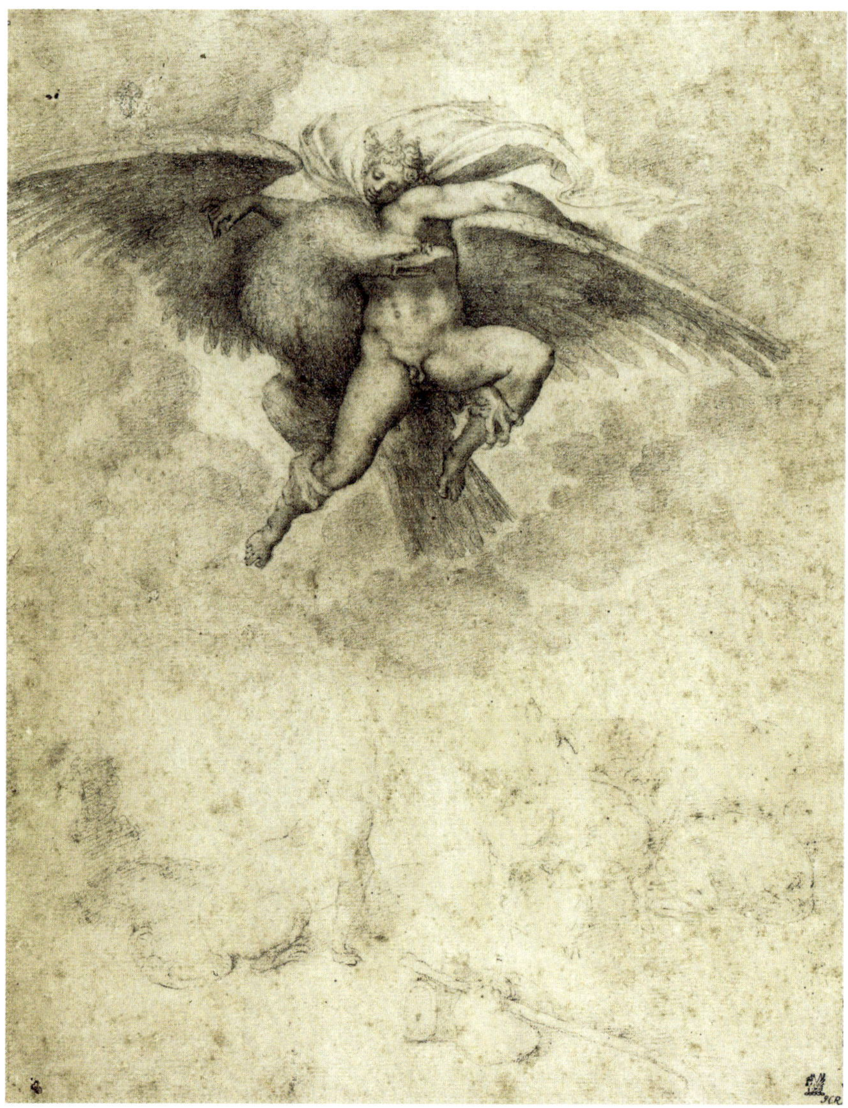

137 A beautiful sixteenth-century copy of Michelangelo's lost *Rape of Ganymede*, the dogs faintly visible in the foreground.

At about the same time as Correggio's *Abduction of Ganymede* there appeared another version of the abducted shepherd boy and of his dog saying farewell, Michelangelo's *Rape of Ganymede*. (The historical relationship between the two images is unclear.) In 1532 the fifty-seven-year-old artist fell in love with the beautiful young nobleman Tommaso dei Cavalieri, and gave him as a gift a series of drawings on classical themes,

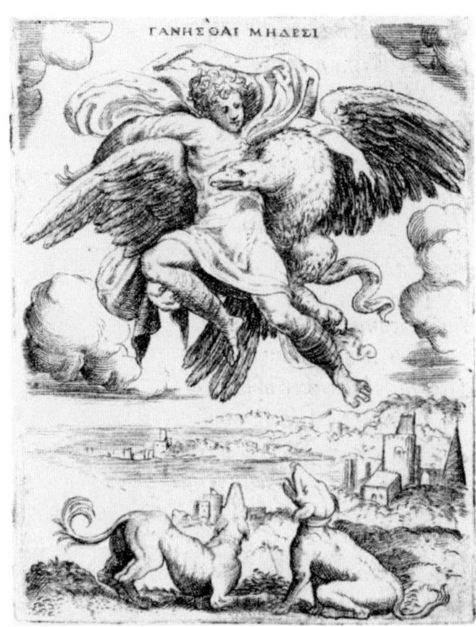

138 Howling dogs appear again in Achille Bocchi's depiction of the Ganymede story in his popular *Symbolicarum Quaestionum* (1574).

among them one about Zeus's passion for the young shepherd whom he abducted to be his cup-bearer on Olympus. Art historians have written a great deal about the next three centuries of representations of Ganymede and homoeroticism, but not about the dog.[42] The original of the Michelangelo drawing has disappeared. We know it from a very early – and very beautiful – copy that is today in the Fogg Museum at Harvard University [**137**]. In the left foreground is a lightly drawn and difficult-to-see dog; centre and right are a shepherd's crook and further right and up are the sheep he has abandoned. One moment the dog and the solitary shepherd are guarding sheep together. The next moment the shepherd is gone, his cloak and crook left on the ground with his dog and his sheep. The dog barks farewell and looks forlorn: a dog – this dog – the dog whom we imagine to be howling over its loss.

Once in place, this scene takes on a pictorial life of its own through the proliferation of print. It appears with one dog gazing upward in various editions of Andrea Alciato's *Emblemata*, the most popular and widely translated emblem book of its kind in Europe, under 'Ganymede', which, it tells readers, means 'Joy is to be found in God', and in Achille Bocchi's often reprinted *Symbolicarum Quaestionum* (here it is said to mean 'Know God with all your heart and mind') [**138**]. We do not need to go into the history of interpretations of the abducted boy shepherd to notice that there are two howling dogs looking up as their master is borne away.[43]

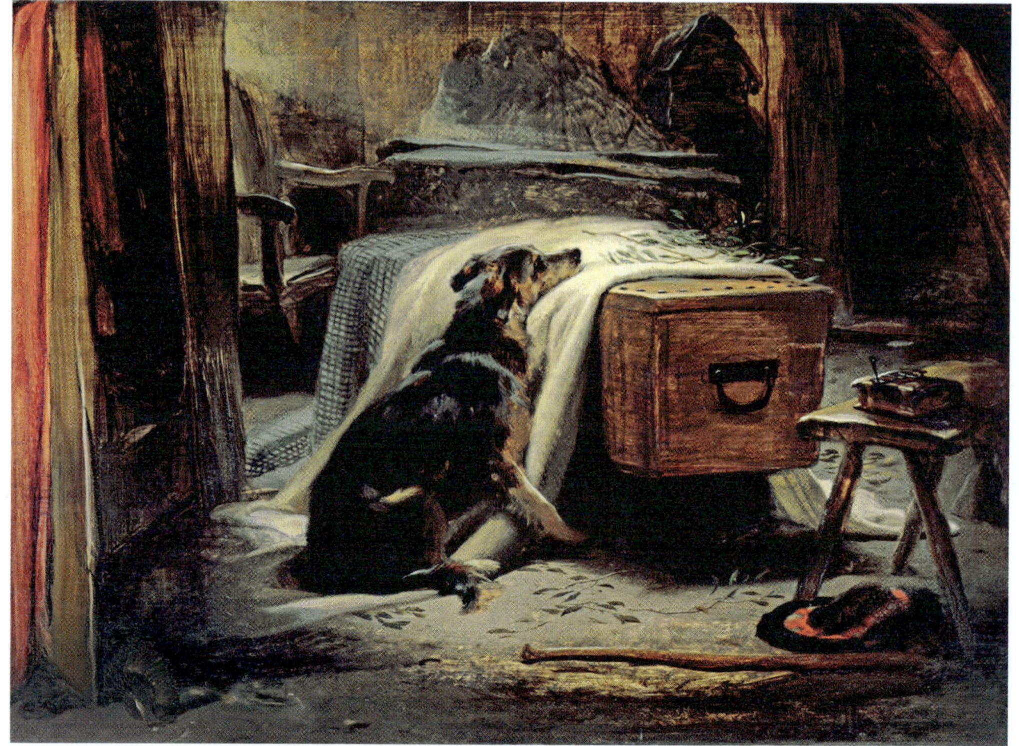

139 Landseer's staggeringly popular *The Old Shepherd's Chief Mourner* (1837).

Centuries after the mourning, longing, bereft dogs of Piero di Cosimo, Rubens, and Correggio, they still appear in modern art, overly sentimentalized perhaps, but given a new life in a new age. Edwin Landseer's 1837 *The Old Shepherd's Chief Mourner* [**139**] was one of the most internationally reproduced and popular works of nineteenth-century English art. It was so resonant because it appeared at a time when to die friendless, to die a pauper whom no one mourns, had become a fate to be feared. The dog becomes not only a non-human animal that mourns a human but the mourner of last resort, the only friend, the guard at the abyss of worthlessness and oblivion. This may explain the descent into bathos from the purer heights of its more august predecessors.[44]

Ruskin thought it was 'one of the most perfect poems or pictures (I use the words as synonymous) which modern times have seen'. He points to both the painterly qualities of the painting – 'the exquisite execution of the crisp and glossy hair of the dog, the bright sharp touch of the green bough beside it' – and specific affective features of the dog – 'the fixed and tearful fall of the eye in its utter hopelessness, the rigidity of repose which marks that there has been no motion nor change in the trance of agony since the last blow was struck on the coffin-lid'. It may be excessive to impute so human a range of feelings to a dog but perhaps not to its sociability. Something living remains as company of the dead.[45]

The trope of the dog waiting inconsolably for its dead master has subsequently gone global: from Edinburgh to Tokyo. The most famous European case, among many others, is that of Greyfriars Bobby, a terrier of some sort who purportedly waited for fourteen years beside the grave of his owner, John Gray – either the farmer John Gray or the nightwatchman John Grey – in the churchyard of Greyfriars in Edinburgh [**140**]. Bobby's story generated a whole gallery of popular art: pictures of him in the arms of a family that fed him; *cartes de visite*; a statue; a Disney movie; illustrated children's books; engravings in the popular press.[46]

At the opposite end of the scale of art-historical importance from Landseer's *The Old Shepherd's Chief Mourner* and the many images of the

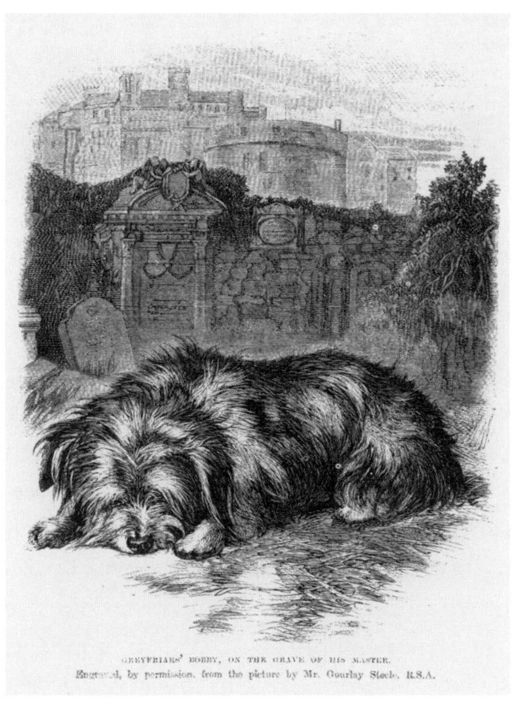

140 Greyfriars Bobby in *The British Workman* (1 January 1868)

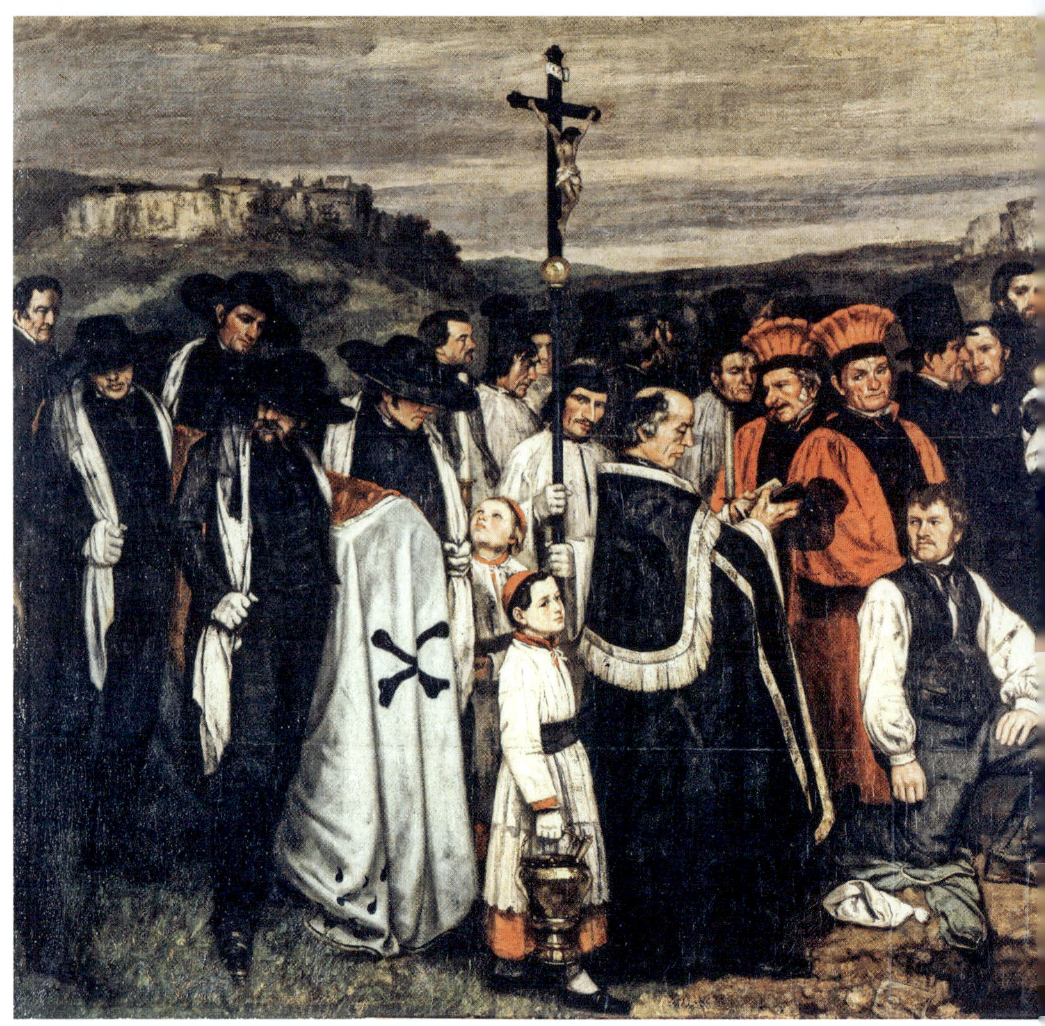

141 *A Burial at Ornans* (1849–50) by Gustave Courbet, in which an ordinary scene is provocatively rendered on a gigantic scale.

Scottish Bobby is another dog by another grave: the dog in Courbet's 1849–50 *A Burial at Ornans* [**141**]. It is as radical as Landseer's painting is conventional, as controversial in its day as Landseer's work was widely praised. Critics at the 1850–51 Salon thought the people in Courbet's painting were ugly and that the whole scene was far too ordinary for a canvas of that size – 3.1 x 6.6 metres – a scale usually reserved for history paintings. It was, and it was meant by Courbet to be, a genre-busting provocation. And it remains what one critic in 1851 predicted: one of 'the Herculean pillars of realism in modern history'. There, almost life-size on the front plane of this epochal painting is a dog.

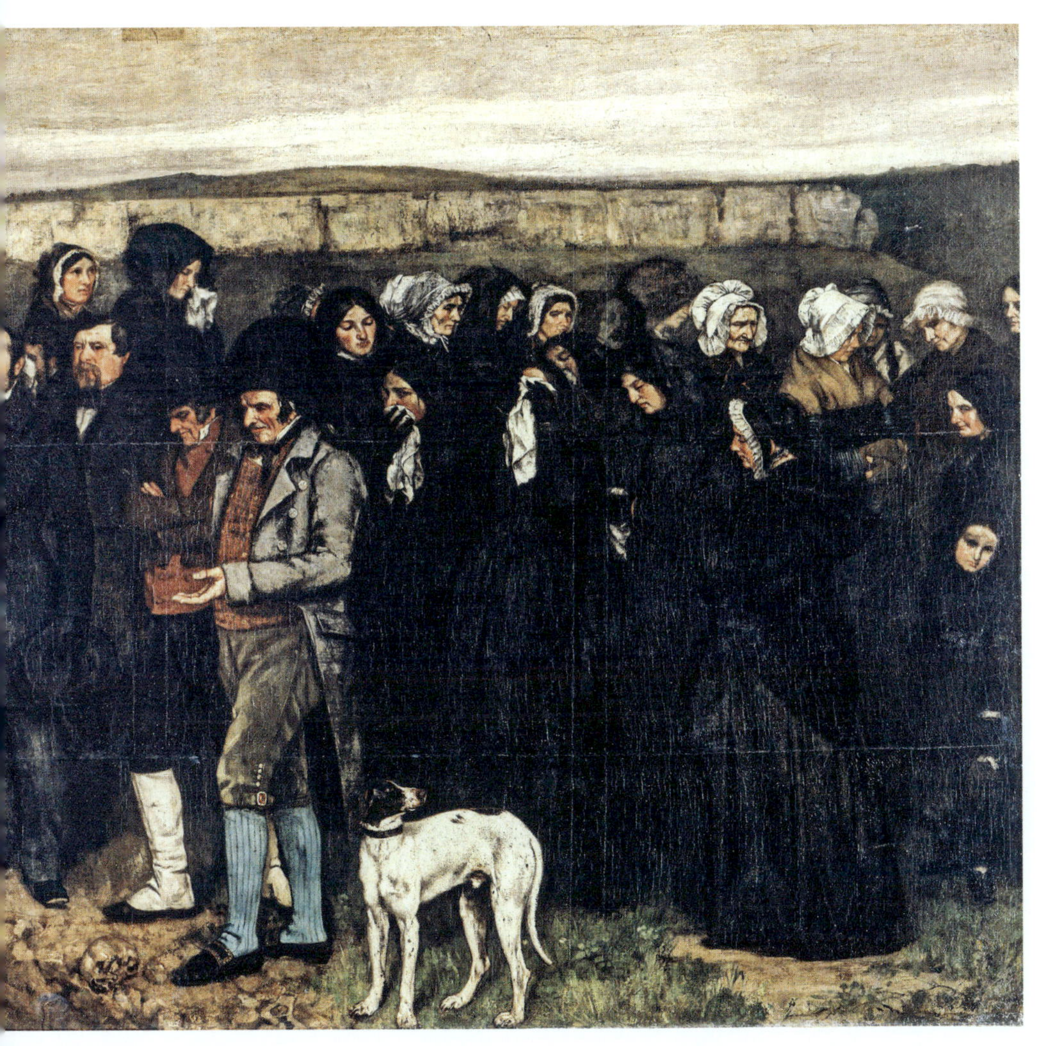

How we are to understand the painting remains controversial. *A Burial at Ornans* is, at its most literal, a representation of a funeral in the new cemetery at the outskirts of the commune in the Jura mountains of eastern France where Courbet was born. Questions about its formal sources – a range of seventeenth-century Dutch group paintings as well as contemporary popular prints have been proposed – are still debated. But the *Burial* is sociologically spot on: women are separated from men as was the custom of the day; class-appropriate dress distinguishes peasants from the bourgeoisie; there is function-appropriate dress – pallbearers with white scarves; and age-appropriate dress – two old men in old-fashioned breeches.[47]

T. J. Clark's interpretation of its social and political message remains the most subtle: 'between smock and dress-coat', between peasant and bourgeois, 'the picture does not take sides'. It is not a political polemic.[48]

But the difficulty of arriving at an interpretation of the painting as a comment on socio-political history is less exigent than how we are to interpret its affect. Clark's observation that the picture 'deliberately avoids emotional organization', that it is difficult to come to terms with 'the burial's affective atmosphere', is spot on. The participants offer few clues: 'only the inquisitive, upturned face of the serving boy seems definitely to be looking at something; the rest are averted, impassive, the eyes seemingly focused on the air'.[49] But this is not true of the dog. Its gaze is not impassive; it is looking at something just outside the frame of the image; maybe at people leaving or coming, mediating between the open grave and the world beyond. It suggests that movement into and out of the painting has been from the direction in which it looks.

This dog is without precedent. There are no dogs in Dutch group portraits that have been proposed as formal models for Courbet's *Burial*, although there are many in group pictures to which this one has been compared, Rembrandt's *Night Watch* for example. Nor are there dogs in the putative popular print antecedents of the *Burial*. Although there is one in Courbet's preliminary study, it is not nearly as prominent as in the final version where it stands out, differentiated in its whiteness from a mass of people in their dark clothes and the blackness of much of the painting besides. The dog in the finished painting of *A Burial at Ornans* represents a serious artistic choice.

The funeral is a closely observed scene. Thirty-seven of the fifty-one people in the painting can be identified thanks to information provided by Courbet, his friend Champfleury, and later sources. From the precise topography of the painting and other evidence we know whose funeral it was – Courbet's maternal great-uncle, a friend of his recently deceased grandfather, and the first person buried in the new cemetery. Courbet knew these people. Maybe he knew the dog. He was interested enough in it to paint a substantial copy of it in 1856: *Le Chien d'Ornans* ('The Ornans Dog'), even larger (65.1 x 81.3 cm) than the one in the original, standing alone in a valley of the Jura [**141a**].

What is this dog doing in the *Burial* as he stands a few feet from the graveside, framing the central image from one side as the priest does

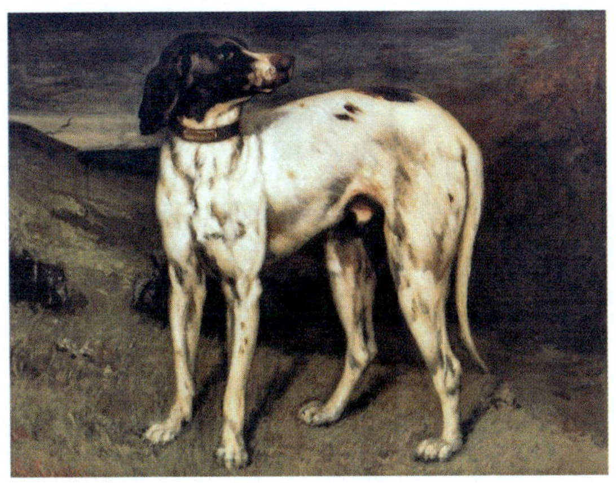

141a In *Le Chien d'Ornans* (1856), Courbet made an even larger copy of the *Burial* dog.

from the other? Something caught its attention. Just to the right of the grave is a skull and a bone – a femur – on the ground. Such detritus of the dead would be commonplace in old cemeteries and churchyards but not in the brand-new one captured at the moment of its inauguration. Perhaps these are a lapse in realism for some old-fashioned symbolism: the common fate of all humans. But this dog, unlike so many dogs in paintings set in Golgotha – the skull-shaped Jerusalem hill where Christ and many others were crucified – is not there to gnaw on bones or to help with the reality effect.

The dog of Ornans is there to attend the burial. Maybe his attention has been commanded by the rustling of the women shuffling on the upper right; maybe whatever it is that has caught the attention of the little girl looking out at the far-right margin. Like the little choirboy looking up at one of the pallbearers, the dog is looking at something. It will turn back to the grave. It is in fellowship with the other mourners and the officiants. It is not there for allegorical or mythological reasons but as part of a world that had never before been given the attention Courbet lavishes on it: a burial in a small provincial cemetery.

The dog is also the only creature who suggests by his gaze beyond the frame that this is a painting – a fiction – and the one who lets us – the spectators – know that there is a world beyond, spatially and temporally. The burial will end; the mourners will go home. The dog will go somewhere. The tiny white impasto of its eye is like a tear in the fabric of this tableau; it looks out; after the grave is filled another story will begin. Sociability with humans goes on.

Friends of the Blind and the Beggar

As if it were a commonplace, the eleventh-century notary and teacher in Constantinople, Nikephoros Basilakes, makes essentially the same claim as Montaigne would make five centuries later (*see* pages 78–9) about dogs and the blind:

> Why do I not mention the most unusual characteristic of all, that he [the dog] leads the blind and becomes another eye for them, and that he leads them around everywhere to beg for bread at people's doors, and then leads them back again to their lodging?[50]

Thomas Bewick's immensely popular late eighteenth-century *History of Quadrupeds* says it again: everyone will have seen a dog lead a blind beggar through a busy street to the place where he commonly sits and then back home again.[51] At issue is not, as it had been for Montaigne, a dog's cognitive capacity but a specific variety of canine sociability: the dog's assistance to a vulnerable human, to the blind. The dog seeing for another, not for an artist, but the unsighted: social seeing. The term 'seeing-eye dog' is less than a century old, first used in 1929 by an American association – The Seeing Eye – founded that year to train puppies rigorously to guide the blind; its British equivalent, 'Guide Dogs for the Blind', started in 1932. Similarly named regional or national organizations were founded all over Europe before the Second World War and somewhat later in Asia and Latin America.

There is a certain strange magic about these dogs, about the intensity of their eyes. The actor Al Pacino reports that in one particular performance of the play *Scent of a Woman* he found himself 'relating to a pair of eyes in the audience' and began 'gearing [his] performance to that section of the audience'. At the curtain call he was determined to see who it was: 'sitting there, of course, was a seeing-eye dog'. Pacino admitted that the story, though 'poignant, provocative', and a little eerie', had no point except that he learned something from that dog that he could not quite put his finger on.[52]

The history of dogs seeing for the blind before the early twentieth century has not been written. Visual record and literary evidence, however, go back a long way. Johann Wilhelm Klein's *Lehrbuch zum Unterrichten*

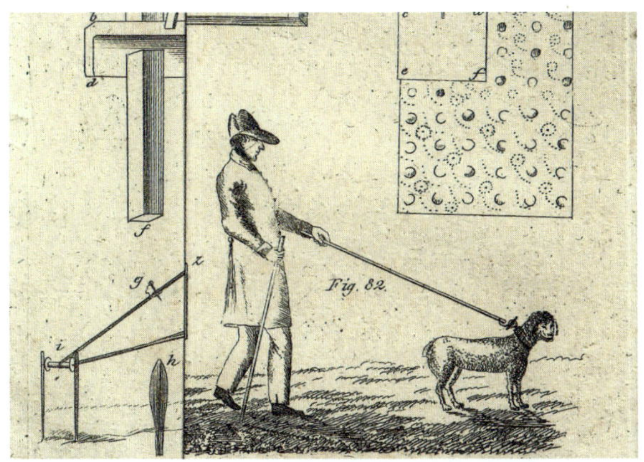

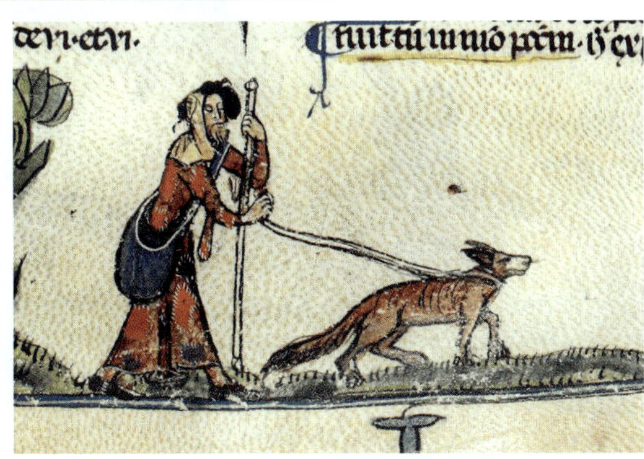

142–143 Leading the blind: (*above*) a rigid guide-dog lead in Johann Wilhelm Klein's *Textbook for Teaching the Blind* (1819); (*right*) marginalia in a twelfth-century manuscript.

der Blinden offers the first image of a blind person led by a dog on a rigid lead – the standard in the twentieth century – that allows the dog to signal not only 'go' but 'stop' [**142**]. (Invariably this is a blind man; blind women are invisible until the nineteenth century.) Images with a loose lead go back to the Middle Ages and possibly to a fresco of a beggar with a dog from Pompeii.[53] Most blind people, except the well-born, were reduced to begging and to a daily life of impoverished wandering before the advent of more systematic training and education in the nineteenth century, so the categories overlap: the key concept is sociability – dogs as friends for the otherwise friendless blind.[54]

Almost all the images of the blind with their dogs in medieval manuscripts are of beggars. In one illumination a man is dressed in rags; in another, a dog, his lead tied to his master's waist, is guiding his master while also carrying his – or perhaps his own – begging bowl; the two of them are in this together [**143**]. In Pieter Bruegel the Younger's version,

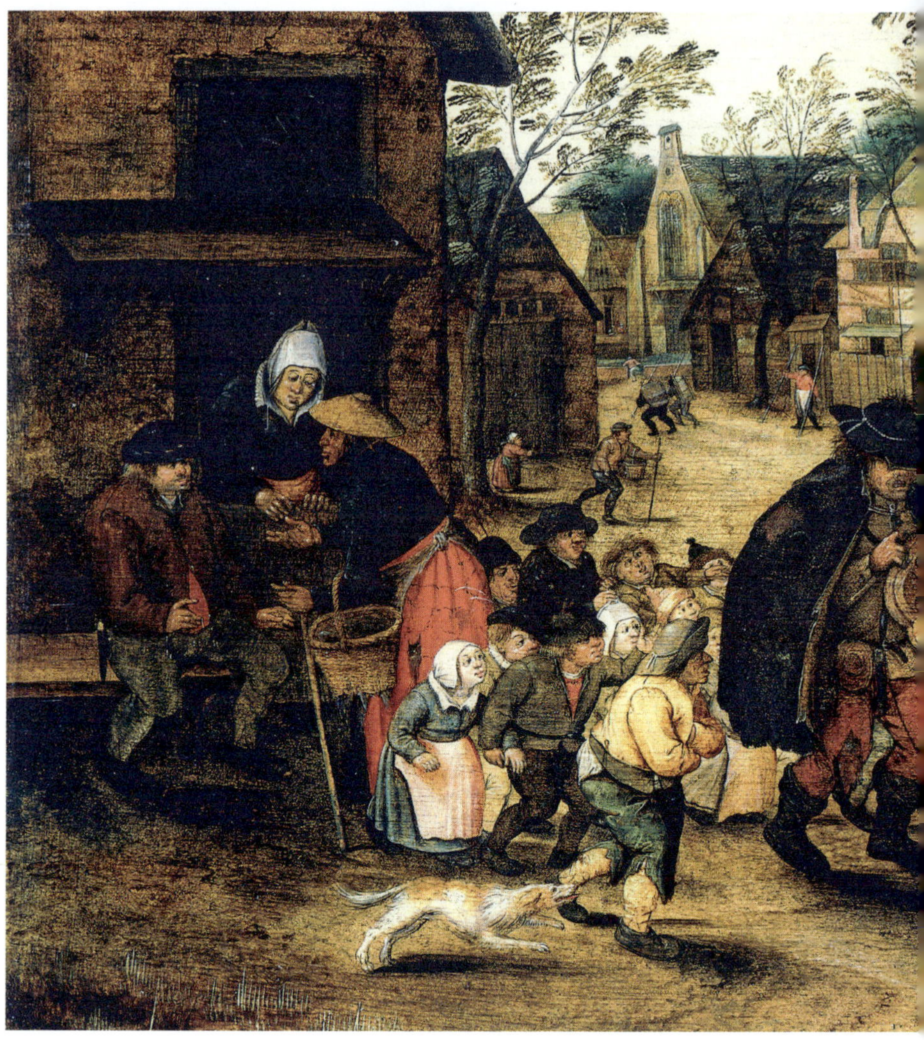

144 Pieter Bruegel the Younger's *A Blind Hurdy-Gurdy Man* (1610) guided by his dog.

A Blind Hurdy-Gurdy Man, the man's brown dog with a steady head-to-the-ground look is trying to get his blind master through a crowd of children as the village dog is chasing them [**144**]. The dog and blind musician will live on as a visual trope well into the nineteenth century.[55]

Again and again, the affective power of the image arises from the interdependence – the connectedness of the human condition and the dog. In the 1649 edition of the widely known and reprinted *Totentanze* ('Dance of Death') by Matthäus Merian, the blind person is described as a beggar – he cannot, he says, earn his own bread – but the emotional heart of the picture is born of his aloneness and dependence [**145**].

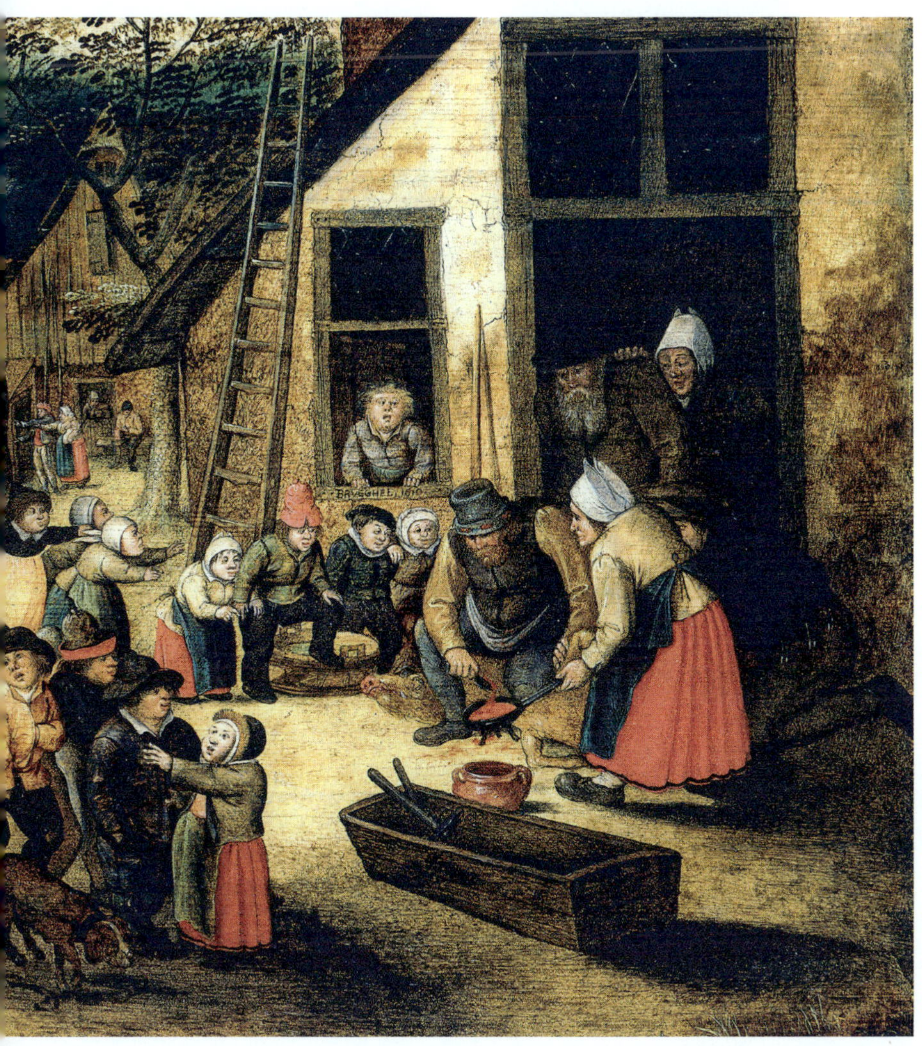

'I cannot take a step without my dog,' he says to Death, who, scissors in hand, tells him 'Your guide I will cut off.' The blind too die alone without their only intimate companion. Unlike other figures in the dance of death who figuratively do not want to see that the grave that awaits them awaits us all, the blind beggar literally cannot see it. Unseeable terror: the dog looking back in a characteristic gesture that does not recognize Death but wants to know what is holding up its master.

In the first of Dürer's three so-called 'Masterprints' – *Knight, Death and the Devil* – the horseman is not literally blind as he sits on his exquisitely etched horse as if on an equestrian statue, static, modelled perhaps on one that Dürer saw in Venice [**146**]. Its rear feet are poised above a lizard, a

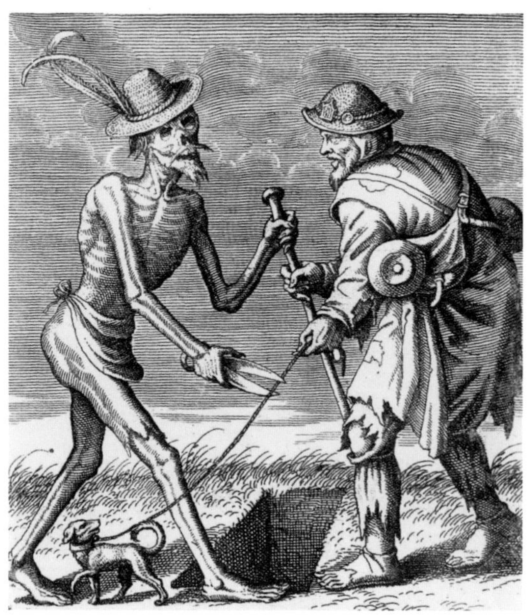

145 'I cannot take a step without my dog': Matthäus Merian's *Totentanze* (1649).

symbol of death; its raised left foot might come down on a skull if it were not rendered so sculpturally. The knight is blind – frozen as he stands in front of death holding an hourglass, static in the pilgrimage of life. Blind to what is in store. The wild-looking shaggy dog, unlike the horse, is entirely Dürer's invention. Like the beggar's dog it is also blind in one sense; it does not, cannot, know Death. Neither in life nor in art do dogs know things in the abstract. The dog – the only creature in motion – is bounding forward, its fur flowing back as if it were in flight. His half-opened eye, its pupil shaded by its eyelids, has a resigned look, a look that catches our eyes in contrast to the lizard's that looks in the opposite direction away from us. The dog's nose points the way forward. It is the most – indeed almost the only – visually dynamic creature in the etching.

The rider perhaps 'personifies Christian faith', while the dog 'denotes three less fundamental virtues: untiring zeal, learning, and truthful reasoning' (*see* Preface, page 14). But this is also an image of an unshakeable being together of man and dog amid the perils of life. Or put differently, if this print, like Dürer's *Melancholia I*, 'pictures a relation of the self to the self . . . enacted always against the temporalizing horizon of death', as the art historian Joseph Koerner puts it, then the dog mediates that relationship.[56]

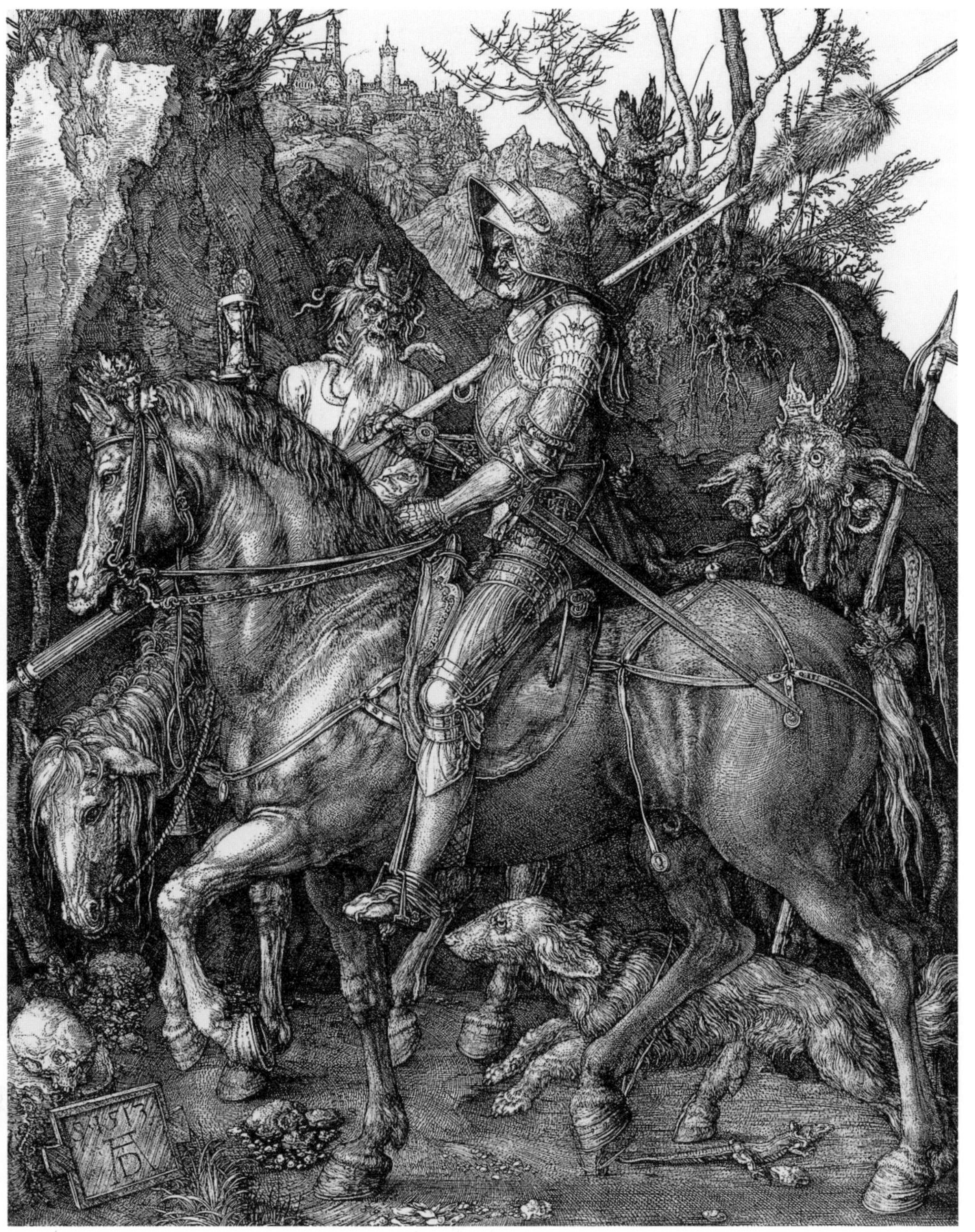

146 The first of Dürer's three 'Masterprints', *Knight, Death and the Devil* (1513).

The dog and the blind in art is a genre about trust. Rembrandt was interested in one version, a particular blind man and his intimate relationship with a particular dog: in Tobit, the eponymous main character of the Book of Tobit, a canonical book in Catholic and Orthodox scripture and in the Apocrypha of the Protestant Bible. Rembrandt and his students returned to his story almost sixty times, perhaps as Simon Schama suggests, because it was the master's favourite 'parable of inward and outward illumination'. He illustrated it more often than any other Biblical story; the dog is there in almost every episode as Rembrandt and his students imagined them.[57]

The Book of Tobit is about two completely unrelated and equally strange misfortunes that God decided to deal with together. The first is about the man himself, Tobit, a pious Jew living in Nineveh during the Babylonian Captivity, who performs many acts of kindness including burying a corpse. This makes him feel polluted; he falls asleep by a wall under a swallow's nest; a bird defecates in his eye, and he becomes blind. He is now impoverished and wholly dependent on his wife Anna, whom he falsely accuses of having stolen a kid goat. He immediately repents his outburst and prays for death.

The second story is about a distant relative, Sarah, in a distant city, who is accused of demonic possession because all her suitors are struck dead. Tobit remembers that a far-away friend owes him money and sends his son Tobias, along with a companion – introduced as a well-born stranger who reveals himself at the end to be the archangel Raphael – to collect it. As they are crossing a river Tobias is attacked by a large fish, which he manages to kill. The angel in disguise advises him to save the gall, namely the bile, because it is a medicine for blindness, and the heart and liver, because when burnt their smoke drives away demons. They reach their goal, the debt is collected, Sarah's demon is exorcised by heart-and-liver smoke, and she marries Tobias. They prosper. They then return home to Tobit and his wife, Tobias cures his father's blindness, and the companion (Raphael) reveals his identity and flies away. (Rembrandt and others in fact always painted him with wings so there cannot be much of a secret about who the stranger was.)

In Rembrandt's 1651 etching the aged Tobit is stumbling toward what he takes to be the door to greet his returning son [**147**]. His eyes are narrowed and hollow; he has knocked over his wife's spinning wheel

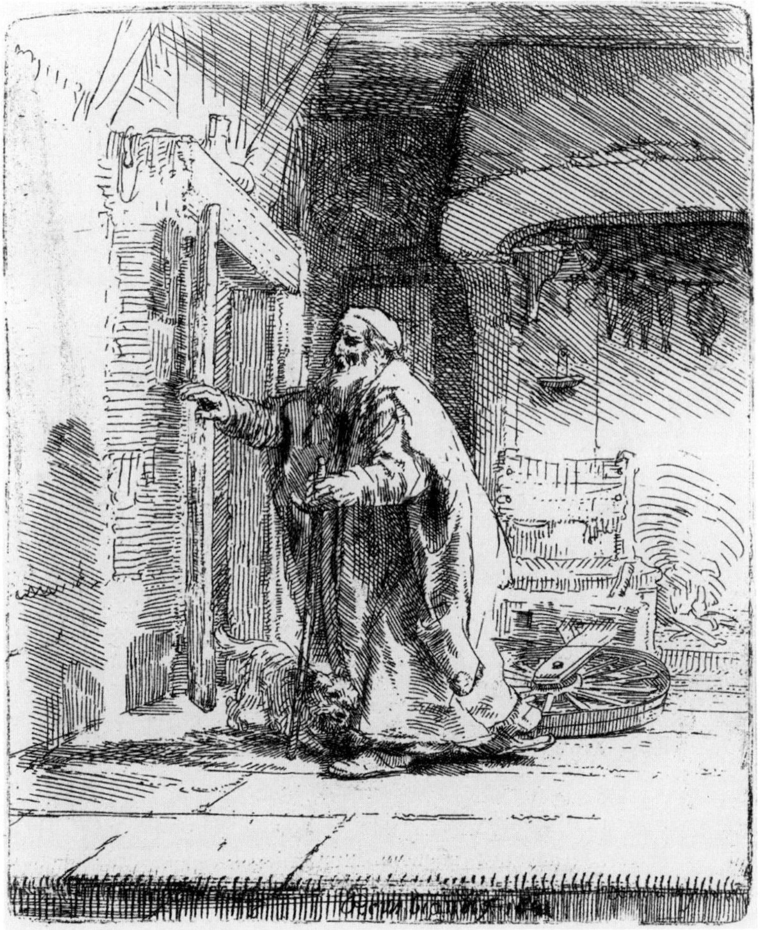

147 *The Blindness of Tobit* (1651) by Rembrandt, who returned to this subject many times throughout his career.

and crashed into a chair. He stumbles, arm outstretched to feel his way and reaches for a shadow that is not the door. A small dog, its head purposefully down, pushes against his leg and nudges him in the right direction to the actual opening. The blind man Tobit and his dog is a subject that seems to have stayed with Rembrandt from the very beginning of his career.[58]

In Jan Matsys' telling of the end of the story, namely when Tobias brings home the cure, the dog's brightly red tongue is licking Anna's left hand, a comforting gesture as if in sympathy with the relief and gratitude one can see in her face as she watches her son putting the salve – the

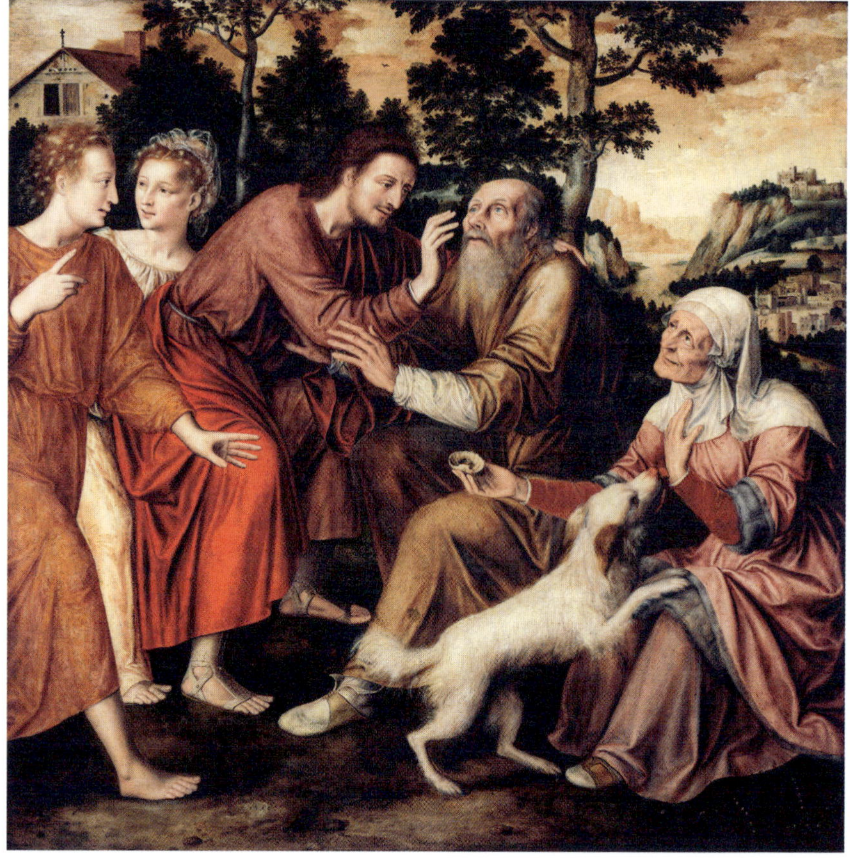

148 Jan Matsys' *The Healing of Tobit* (*c.* 1540), with a well-socialized blind man's dog.

magic fish gall – into her blind husband's eyes [**148**]. Her head is inclined toward him; her left hand is over her heart: a socially competent blind man's dog attentive to his master.

Until the eighteenth century the art of the blind and the dog offered little about the psychological relationship or shared experience of the sort one sees between dog and human in images of the melancholy dog in Jean-Baptiste-Siméon Chardin's *Blind Beggar* [**149**]. The man is not looking downward or eliciting pity as are the blind in many earlier images. He is not a social type but a man whose uniform identifies him as a resident of the Quinze-Vingts, a Parisian hospice for the blind whose members were licensed to beg. He and his dog are quietly at rest; the dog's long lead hangs loosely from the man's arm. Its eyes are deep set

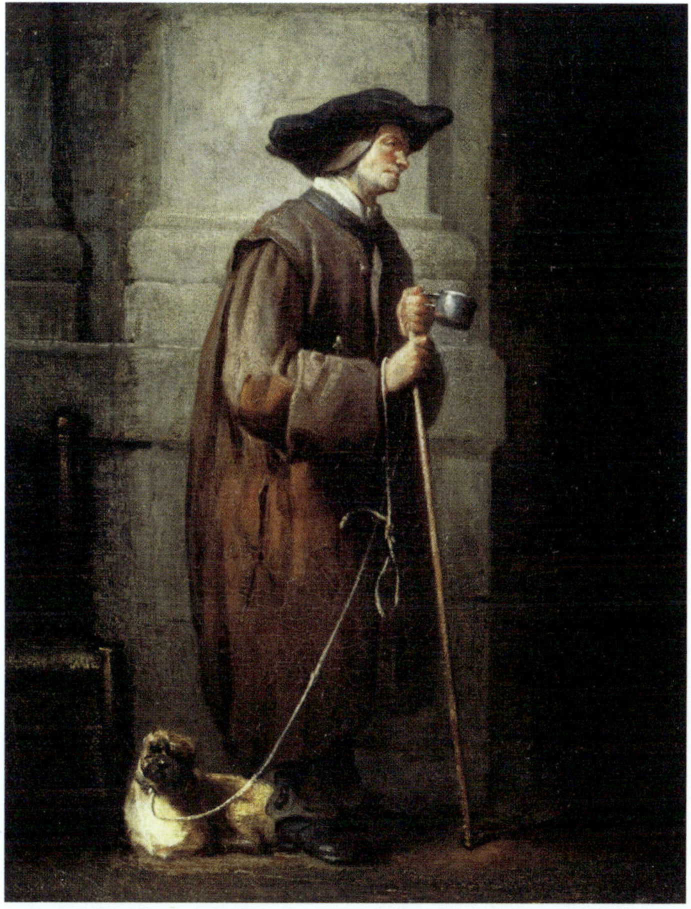

149 Chardin's *Blind Beggar* (1774) and his brightly painted dog at rest.

and dark in a head tilted in the same direction as its master's. Its chest is a brilliant, almost iridescent white, the brightest spot in the painting in contrast to its dark face and the man's body. It demands the attention of the viewer almost as intensely as his master's rosy face. Neither of their eyes are blank; the dog's eyes are on us; the man's eyes seem focused on something far away. Seeing something in his mind. The two stand together in a shaft of light between shadow. An almost contemporary print – *L'Aveugle* – by the prolific and well-known engraver Louis Surugue has the dog with dark irises surrounded by just a little sclera in them, which make its eyes look more like the blind man's; their faces seem aligned.[59]

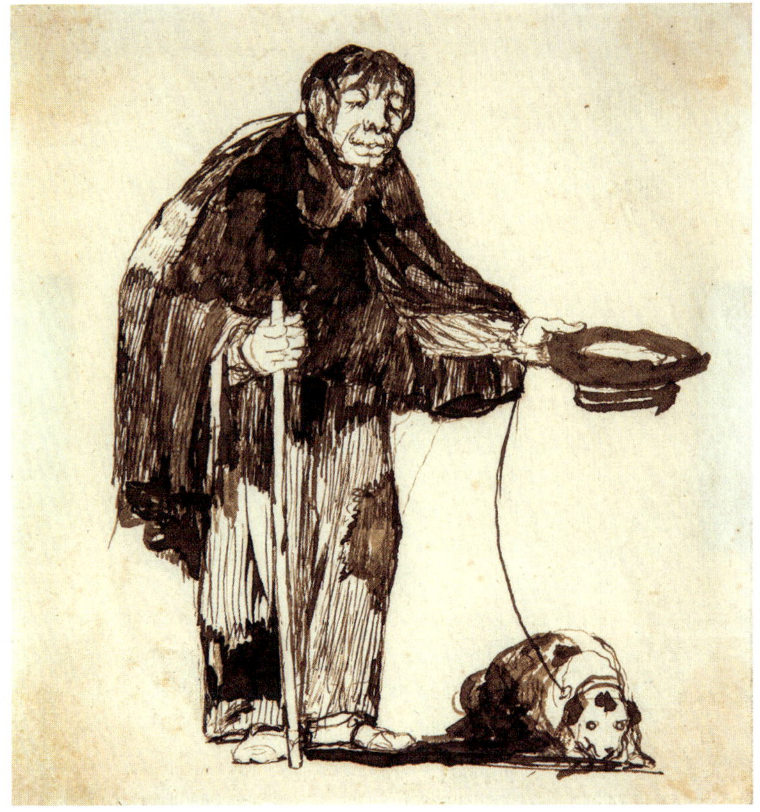

150 Goya's *Blind Beggar with Dog* (c. 1801–25), who fixes us with its gaze.

Goya's *Blind Beggar with Dog* shares a great deal with Chardin [**150**]. He is not abject, pitiful, or in disarray; he is dignified in his poverty and debility. This is a compassionate image. The striking difference from the Chardin is in the eyes of both the man and dog. Rather than looking inward they are looking outward – he of course with unseeing eyes but still eyes that confront us through heavy eyelids. And the dog, its face, continuous with its back, made prominent by the white shading topped by a black patch and framed by a dark ear, is looking straight out at us – seeing us for the blind man, demanding that we pay attention to his master. The beggar holds his outstretched hat insistently; the dog's nose and eyes are breaking the fourth wall. The image is as theatrical as the Chardin is absorptive, but either way the two are in it together. Beggars and dogs are bound together in art as friends: what they do they do together and as representatives of the deep interspecies bond we have with them.

Companions in the Journey of Life

The story in the Book of Tobit generated a great deal of distinguished art representing the sociability of the dog apart from its engagement with the blind: the dog on the journey of life. In Florence, where young men were routinely sent out on long commercial missions, this theme was especially resonant although it was by no means restricted to the art of the city. In the gallery of work that deals with the Tobit story dogs are there not because the family dog plays an important part in the account of the mission of the son Tobias to collect the debt and find a cure for his father's blindness; in fact, the dog plays almost no part in that. Near the beginning, after readers have learned of the old man's misfortunes and the preparations for Tobias's trip, we are told that 'The boy left with the angel, *and the dog followed behind* [italics added]' (Tobit 6:2). A lot happens and then, heading home after their adventures, Raphael suggests that he and Tobias leave Sarah and their party and hurry ahead to announce their return to Tobit and his wife Anna. 'So both went on ahead together, and Raphael said to him, "Take the gall in your hand!" *And the dog ran along behind them* [italics added].'

Artists could easily have ignored the dog because in the Biblical story it does nothing except for starting on, and finishing, the trip: 'following behind'. But that is exactly why it is there, a quotidian companion on a trip that does not need to earn its keep by being useful other than just being there. It is a small but visually compelling part of a story of a journey together.[60] In Andrea del Verrocchio's *Tobias and the Angel* the ghost dog, almost translucent, a swirl of delicate curls, is leading the way just in front of Raphael – a protector of travellers. It is looking back to be sure that the others are following, afraid of being left behind, a common dog gesture; or maybe it is also being careful not to be stepped on [**151**]. Perhaps it is, in its ethereal whiteness, a second angel. Dark eyes with just a glint of reflection and a black nose whose bit of white impasto makes it glisten, it and the many-hued gutted fish whose scales are as scrupulously painted as the dog's fur. These details may both be the first works we have of the young Leonardo, painted while he was an apprentice in the master's workshop.[61]

Dog, angel, and Tobias, starting out, returning, and on their journey, were a popular subject for at least six centuries. In a thirteenth-century

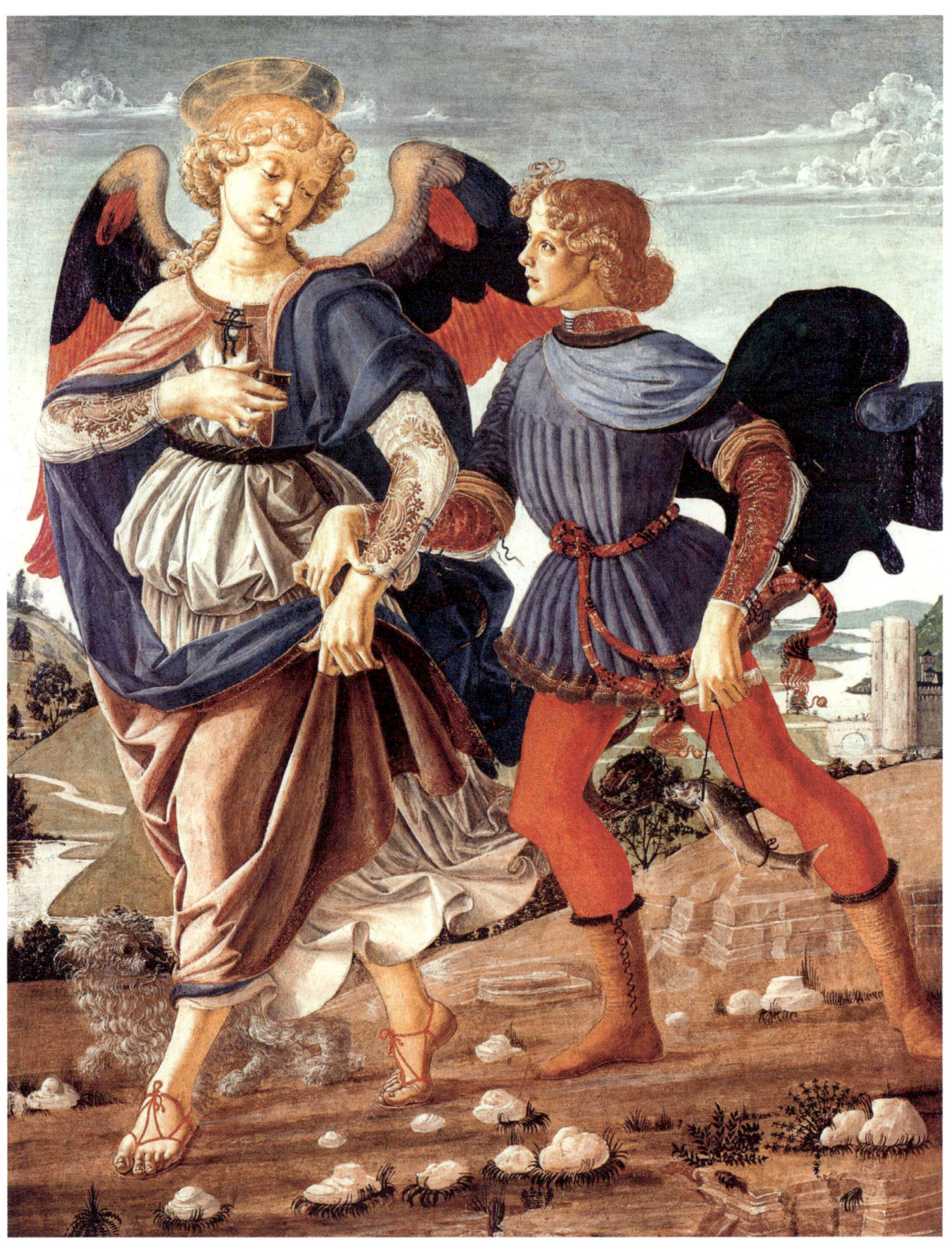

151 The translucent dog leads the way in Verrocchio's *Tobias and the Angel* (1470–75).

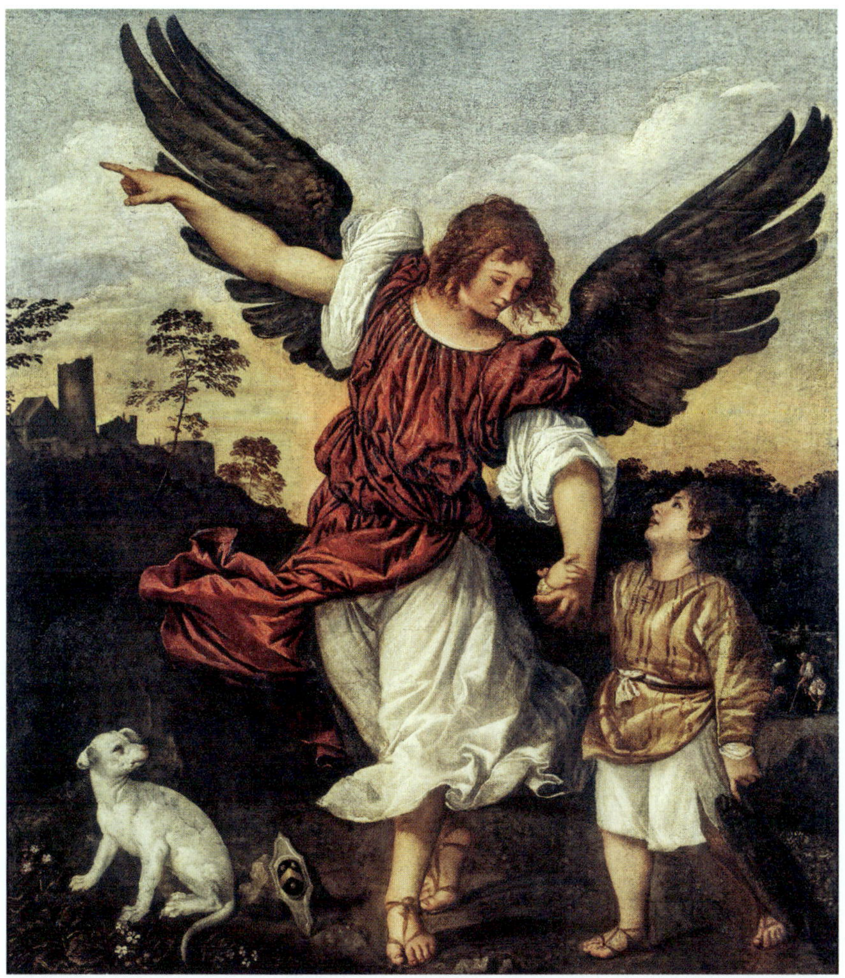

152 *The Archangel Raphael and Tobias* (c. 1512–14) included Titian's first animal portrait.

illuminated manuscript version the dog rushes ahead to meet Anna as Tobias and Raphael walk slowly behind (*see* 155). Titian painted the three travellers twice, once in circa 1512 and again in circa 1545 [**152**]. The dog in the earlier one is his first animal portrait. It is looking back at the boy and the angel, a classic dog gesture, wondering perhaps when they will set off in the direction in which the angel is pointing. A 'let's get on with it' look.[62] In a print by Claes Jansz Visscher II from the 1620s, it is running home to Anna with no companions in sight [**153**].

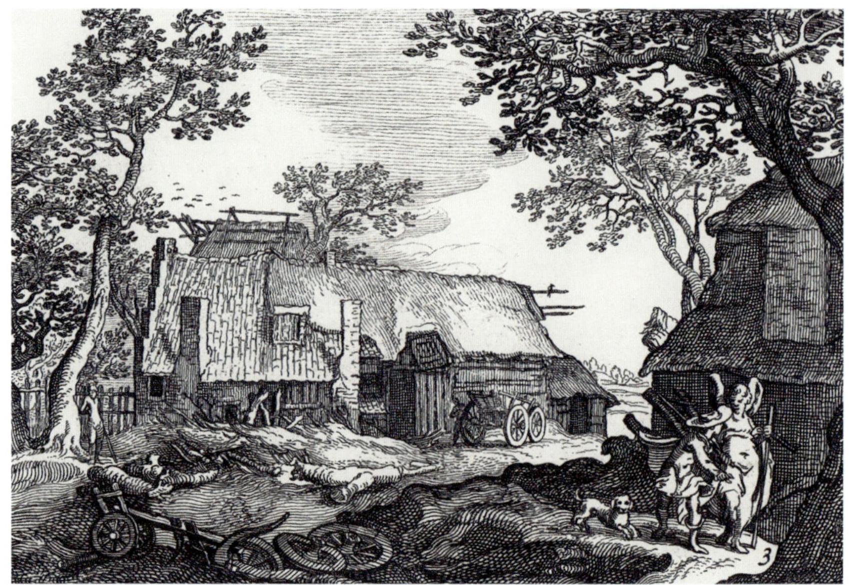

153 The joy of return: *Tobias and the Angel* (1620) by Claes Jansz Visscher II.

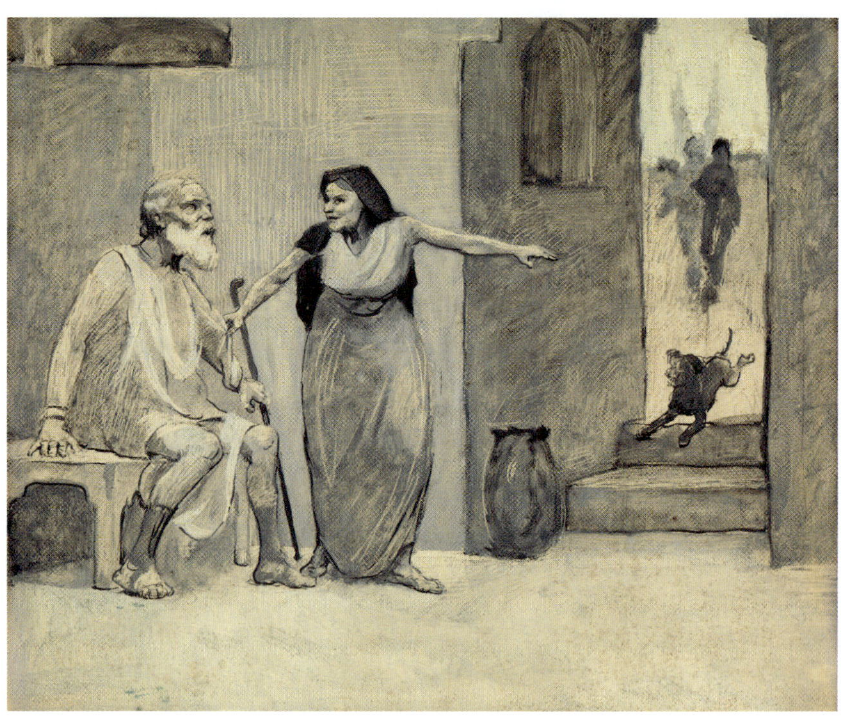

154 Cecilia Beaux's *Tobias Returning to his Family* (*c.* 1888). The story of Anna, Tobit, Tobias and their dog was still a popular theme in the late 19th century.

And in *Tobias Returning to his Family*, a grisaille from the 1880s by Cecilia Beaux, an American artist of the Gilded Age (1865–1902), the human and angelic figures are sketchily suggested in the doorway while the dog is bounding into the room toward the outstretched hand of Anna [**154**]. It is the principle of movement; of the joy of return. 'The Dog Returning to his Family' would be a more apt title if one did not know the story of how it had come to leave in the first place.

Going along on Tobias's travels, the dog is a token of a more general type: the dog in the human journey through life. While this tale will lose its purchase as a specific story, it will reappear in other forms and venues down into our own times: new kinds of sociability in the circumstances of modern life.

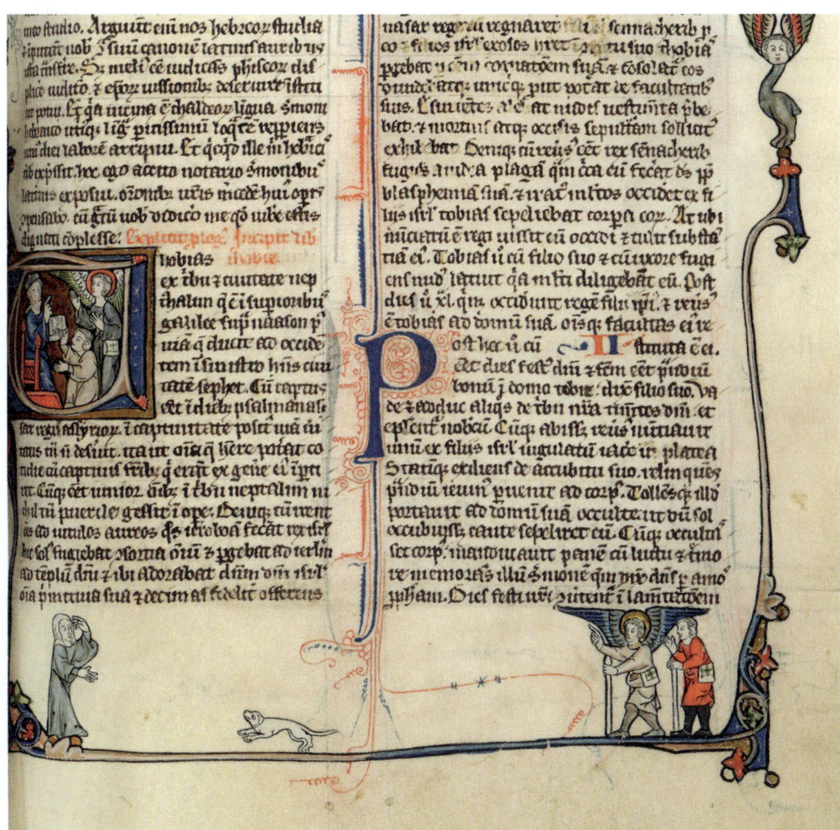

155 Anna's dog rushes home to greet her in a thirteenth-century French illuminated Bible.

CHAPTER 5

Dogs in the Art of Modern Life

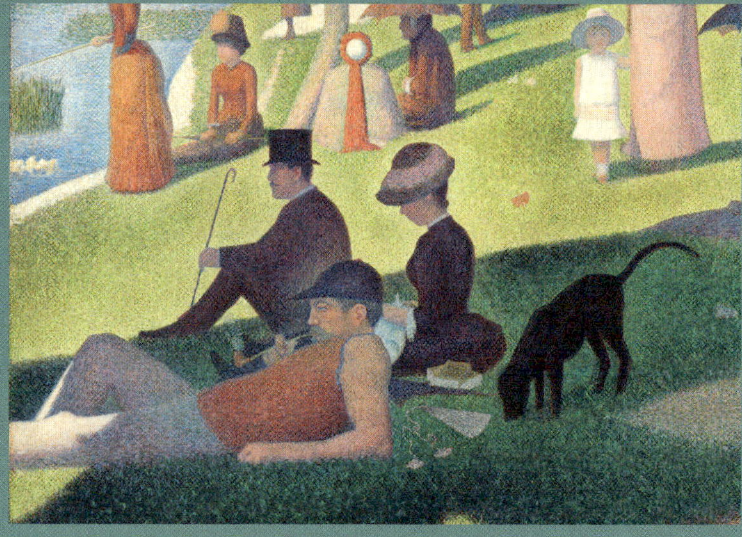

Detail from 208, George Seurat's *A Sunday Afternoon on the Island of La Grande Jatte* (1884–6).

THE GREAT EIGHTEENTH-CENTURY revolutions – intellectual, political, and economic – led artists to imagine dogs in new ways. They used them to make visual sense of changes in relationships of class, gender, and family; they reimagined solitude and loneliness and modern forms of sociability. The art of the dog's gaze in turn led modern viewers to interpret the world anew. Paradoxically, as the Impressionists show so well, the consciousness of change demands a new kind of effort to capture the specificity of the moment. The dog came to play a special role in this effort.

The dog in the midst of life is of course not new and many of the places in which they appear are not novel either. With the rise of genre painting in the seventeenth century there are already very few places where dogs do not appear and very few things that they do not share with their humans. They are in taverns and farmhouses: 'those homes with their tin pans, their brown pitchers, their rough curs and their clusters of onions', as George Eliot put it.

A dog barks at the drummer in Rembrandt's great painting *The Night Watch* (1642), another barks at a cat in a tavern. There are at least three of them ice-skating with a socially diverse group of burghers in Hendrik Avercamp's *Winter Scene on a Frozen Canal* from c. 1620 [**156**]. They are on the sand with their humans in Adriaen van de Velde's *The Beach at Scheveningen* from 1670 [**157**], and walking with the well-dressed couple in Eugène Boudin's *On the Beach at Trouville* from 1863. A dog is interested in her mistress wringing out her wet dress on a beach near Boston in Winslow Homer's *Eagle Head* from 1870 [**158**]. Dogs are still there a century later in five of Eric Fischl's early beach paintings [**159**]. Of course, being at the beach in the late nineteenth century was not what it had

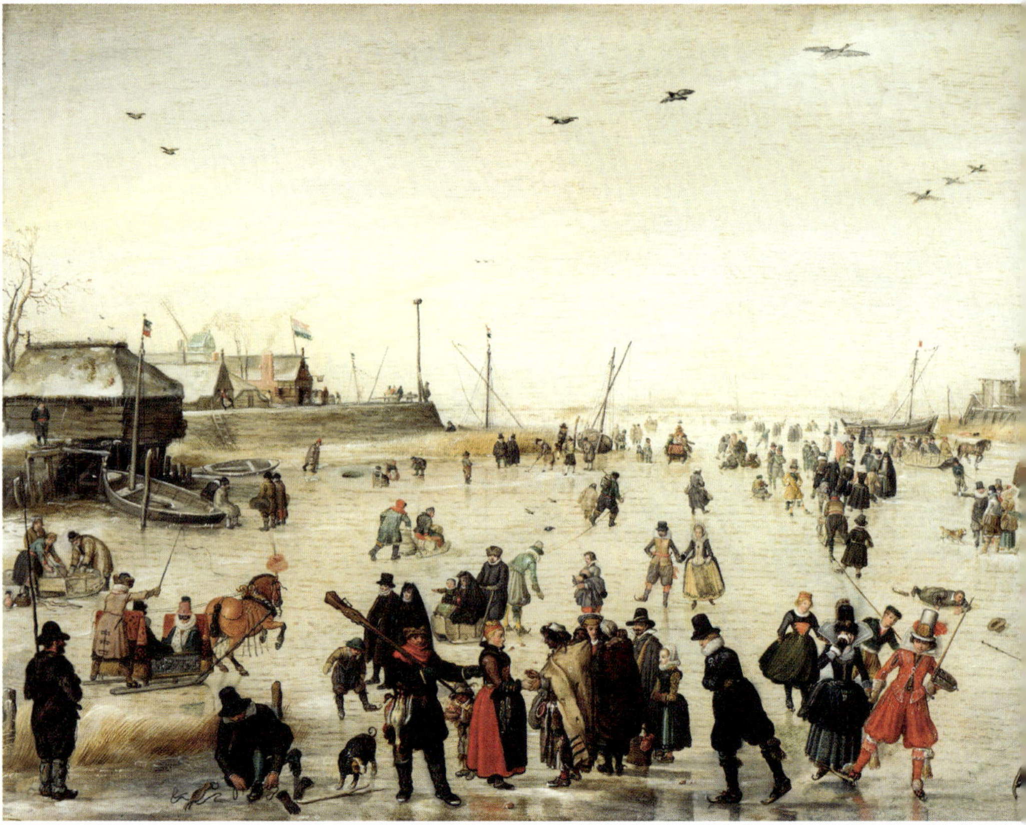

156–157 (*above*) Hendrick Avercamp's *Winter Scene on a Frozen Canal* (*c.* 1620); (*below*) Adriaen van de Velde's *The Beach at Scheveningen* (1670).

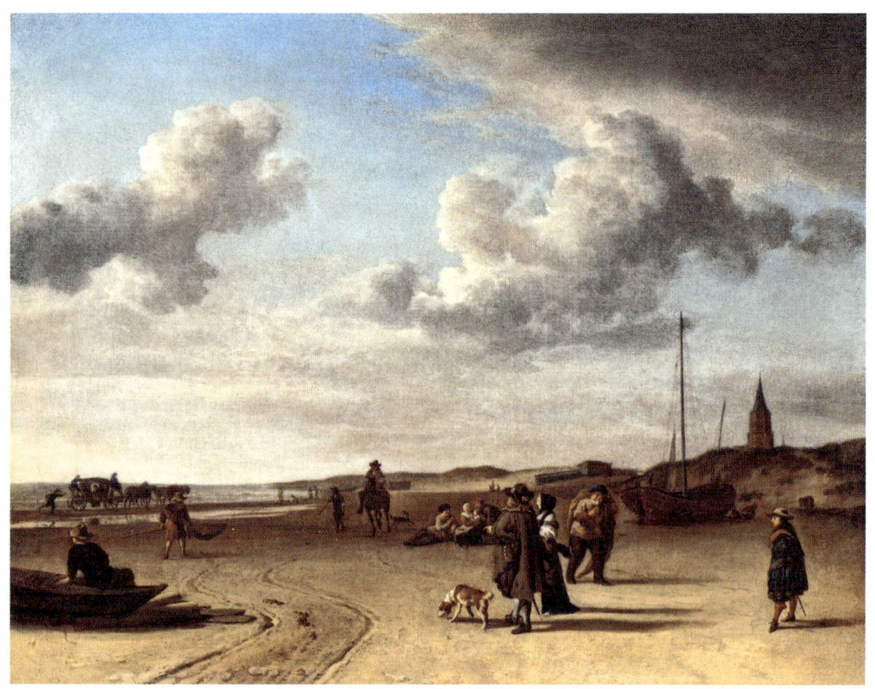

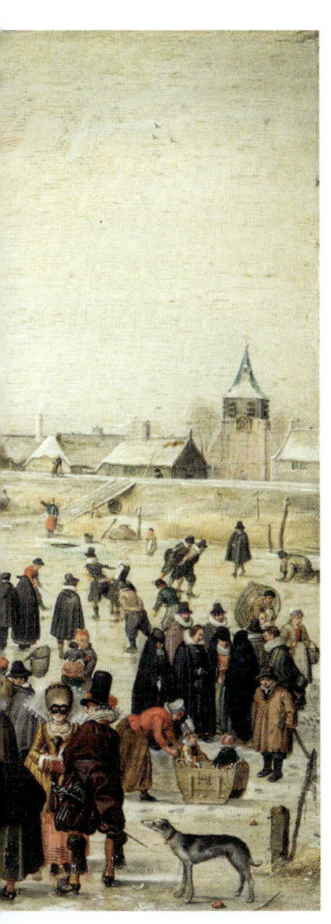

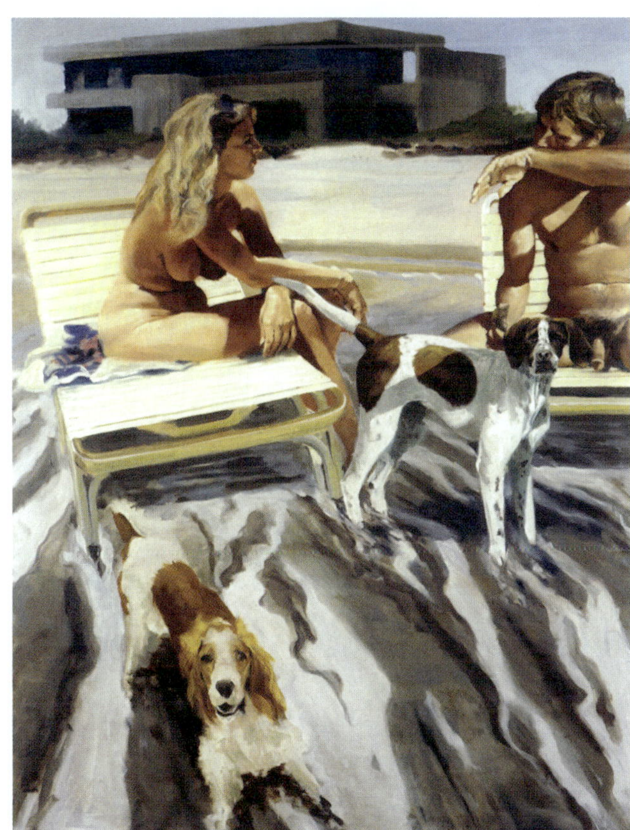

158–159 (*above*) Eric Fischl's *A View from the Shallows* (1993); (*below*) Winslow Homer's *Eagle Head, Manchester, Massachusetts* (1870).

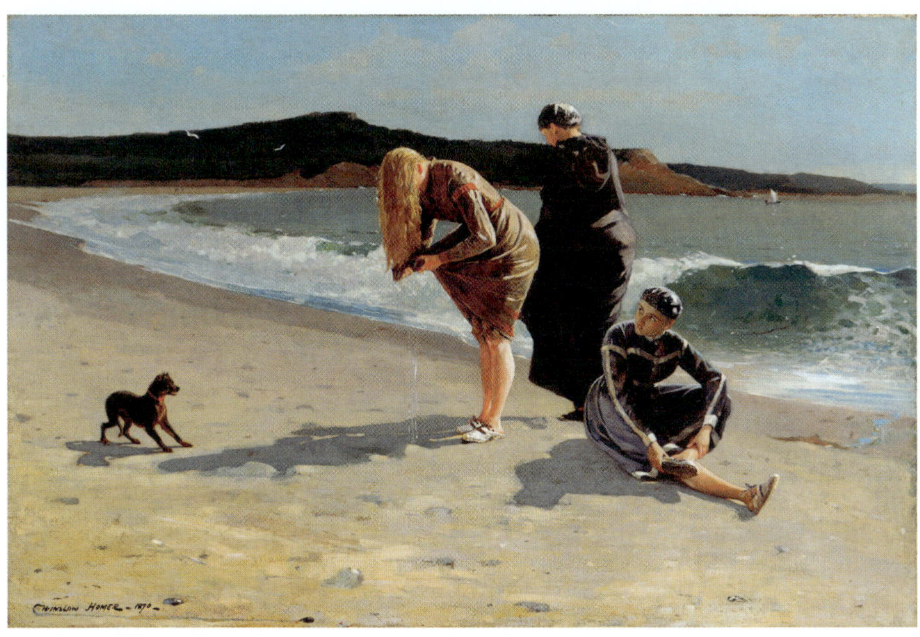

been two centuries earlier or would be a century later in the sexually charged beach encounters that Fischl imagines. Being in a Berlin café (*see* 112) is not the same as being in a modest Dutch tavern. But dogs in these radically different social contexts on the sand – or the tavern or wherever – mediate the new social relations of humans and attest to the fact that they share, albeit from their distinct perceptual viewpoint, their world.

They are also with their mistresses and masters as they listen to or play music, write and receive letters, read books; they sometimes exhibit less than chaste intimacy with their mistresses.[1] They are with families, and with revolutionaries, and on their own in their loneliness. Dogs are everywhere in the art of the last two hundred years and they help define how we imagine various new forms of sociability and live in new kinds of spaces. (We have already seen an example of how they navigate a bridge over a Paris railway yard in 96.)

Walking the Dog

Walking is the world in motion. In chapter 1, I used an account of a photograph of my grandfather about to set off for a walk with his Doberman from the steps of his home on Hamburg's Hochallee – an assimilated Jew walking his dog in Weimar Germany sometime around 1924.

Although there are mythological references to dog walks and a small number of paintings based on them – Hercules's dog on a walk with its master on the beaches of Tyre bit into a mollusc and thereby discovered the dye for royal purple – the dog walk as a sub-genre in Western art begins in earnest in British art of the eighteenth century with paintings of the gentry class at leisure on their country estate.[2]

There is earlier not a single other painting remotely like Francis Wheatley's *Man with Dog* (1775) as they are about to get into a rowing boat [**160**], or George Romney's Sir Christopher and Lady Sykes out for an evening walk, dressed in their finery, accompanied by their dog [**161**]. The Wheatley painting is more plausibly a painting of a man of the minor gentry out on a walk with his dog. He is using his staff to pull a rowing boat to the sandy beach where the two of them can board. The dog is not very happy about it. The Romney painting is more incongruous. (It was

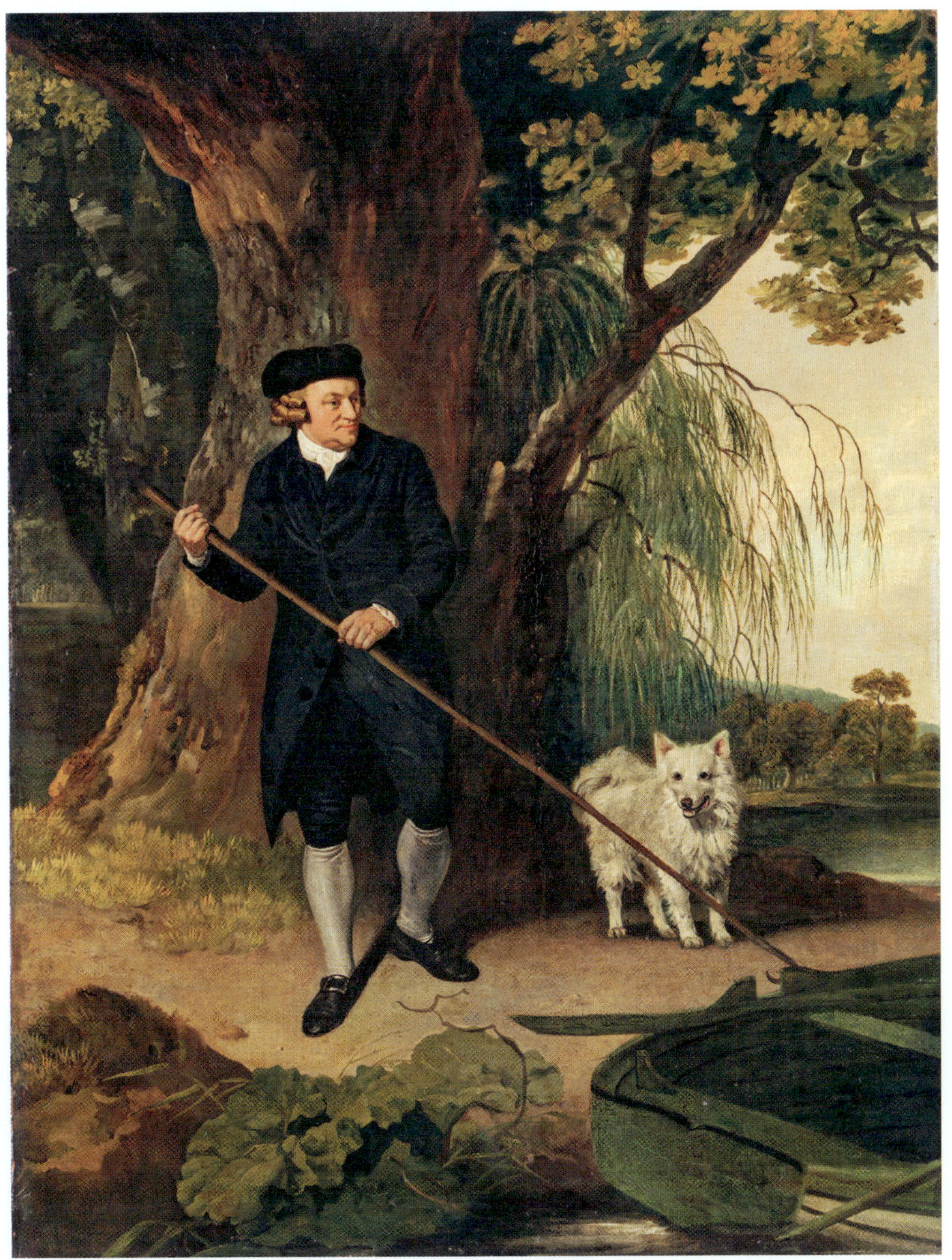

160 Francis Wheatley's *Man with Dog* (1775) was one of the first paintings to show a strikingly modern activity: walking the dog for leisure.

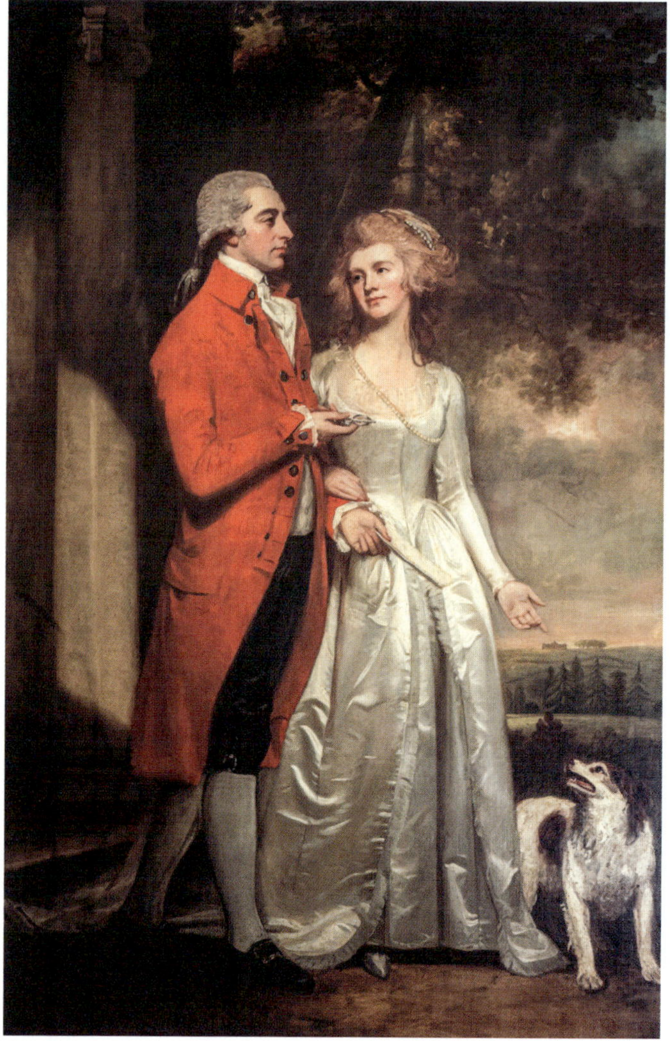

161 Promenade with dog: Romney's *The Evening Walk of Sir Christopher and Lady Sykes* (1786).

inspired by the equally incongruous famous 1785 portrait by Thomas Gainsborough, *Mr. and Mrs. Hallett*, a couple out on a walk dressed in their wedding clothes, with their – probably her – spitz, off-lead and looking up at her beside them.) Even in eighteenth-century England the gentry did not go on dog walks dressed as these couples are. In these paintings walking with one's dog is a record of a culturally resonant form of canine sociability, which becomes more and more integrated into the vernacular art of the next two centuries.

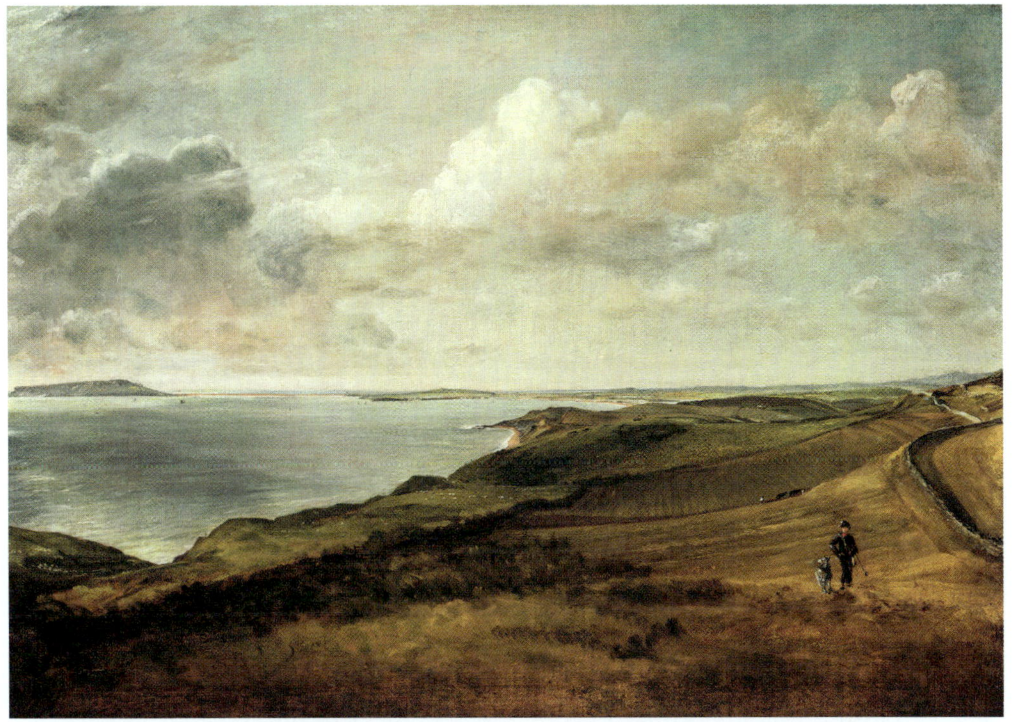

162 Good company: Constable's *Weymouth Bay from the Downs above Osmington Mills* (1816).

Two paintings make that point. John Constable's *Weymouth Bay from the Downs above Osmington Mills* is primarily a landscape painting of the bluffs above the village of Osmington Mills in Dorset with Weymouth Bay in the background [**162**]. But there is a human in the picture, not alone but walking with a dog at his side, maybe back to Osmington or to one of the nearby villages, Ringstead or Upton. The painting becomes a more socially grounded scene; they are together keeping each other company in the countryside. Unlike the dog in Rubens' painting of the story of Hercules on the beach at Tyre, Constable's landscape does not need a dog. It has one because it is about contemporary not mythic life, about a modern sensibility. It would be a very different painting were the man alone.

Courbet's 1852 *Young Ladies of the Village*, modelled by his three sisters, is set in a small meadow amid the outcropping rocks of his native village of Ornans [**163**]. The sisters are giving alms to the young girl cowherd. Critics hated the picture when it was shown at the Salon: its perspective was incompetent; it seemed unfinished; the strangely fashionable quality

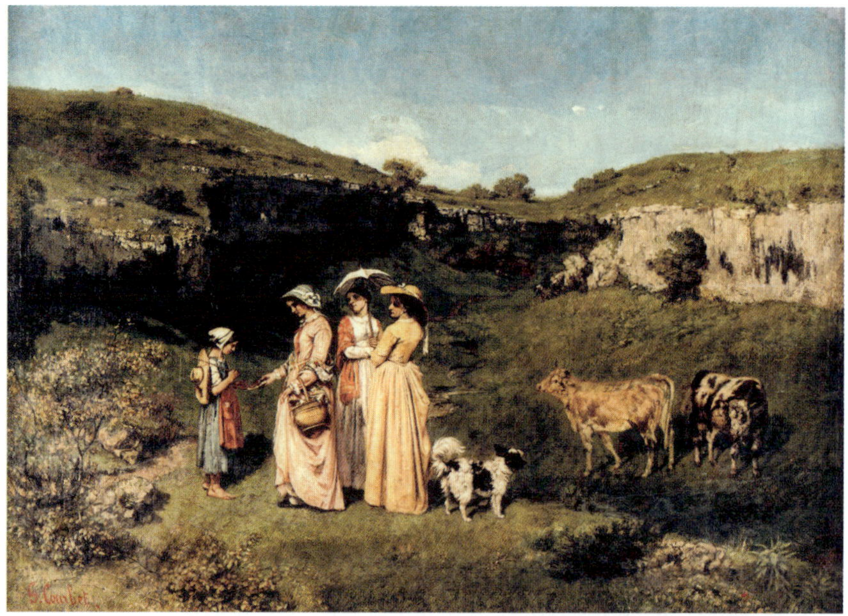

163 The dog in Courbet's *Young Ladies of the Village* (1852) was criticized as 'ridiculous'.

of the clothes on supposed country ladies was thought to be inappropriate or politically provocative; it made a mockery of an older tradition of paintings of almsgiving and much more.

And specifically, they noted the 'ridiculous' dog eyeing one of the cattle. It is hard to see what about the dog is ridiculous. Perhaps it is the painterly attention given to it, not just the bright light that it shares with the humans but the attention given to every bit of fur and fluff from the tip of its nose to the fluttering tail. In a small way, like the *A Burial at Ornans*, the dog broke generic conventions. And perhaps, by extension, what the critics thought was ridiculous was a painting on this scale – 2.13 x 2.74 metres – of young city ladies on a country walk with their dog. Taking a dog along on a walk was not a subject that the traditionalist at the Parisian Salon expected to see in 1852.

In *Le Rencontre* or *Bonjour Monsieur Courbet* (1854) the dog walk comes into its own [**164**]. On the right is a self-portrait of the artist setting off to paint *en plein air* near Montpellier in southern France. The light is Mediterranean. Facing him is Alfred Bruyas, the son of a wealthy banker, a friend, patron, and a major collector of nineteenth-century art who commissioned the painting. He stops to greet Courbet. As does his dog.

Like *The Artist in his Studio* (see 125), it is a painting that proclaims the artist's independence and standing; he is the dominant figure. Bruyas was happy enough with it until almost all critics at the 1855 Universal Exposition in Paris mocked his subordinate standing and made much of Courbet's hubris. Their relationship was strained for a time but recovered; Bruyas made the painting into the centrepiece of the collection that he gifted to the Montpellier Museum where it has hung ever since.[3]

Next to Bruyas is his valet Calas looking deferential; Courbet is at his ease. And in the centre of the painting between the two parties is Bruyas' dog looking up at Courbet. It is out for a walk with its master but knows the social drill. All four feet firmly on the ground, no hint of wanting to move on, waiting patiently as the humans have their conversations. The dog has stopped as if to fix the encounter in time and space. 'Monsieur et chien' out for a walk. The dog is outside the social and class context in which critics first saw the painting; it knows nothing of such matters and they said nothing about its role in the painting. They missed something. The dog mediates formally between the two halves of the painting; its

164 The dog understands the signals in Courbet's *Le Rencontre* (1854).

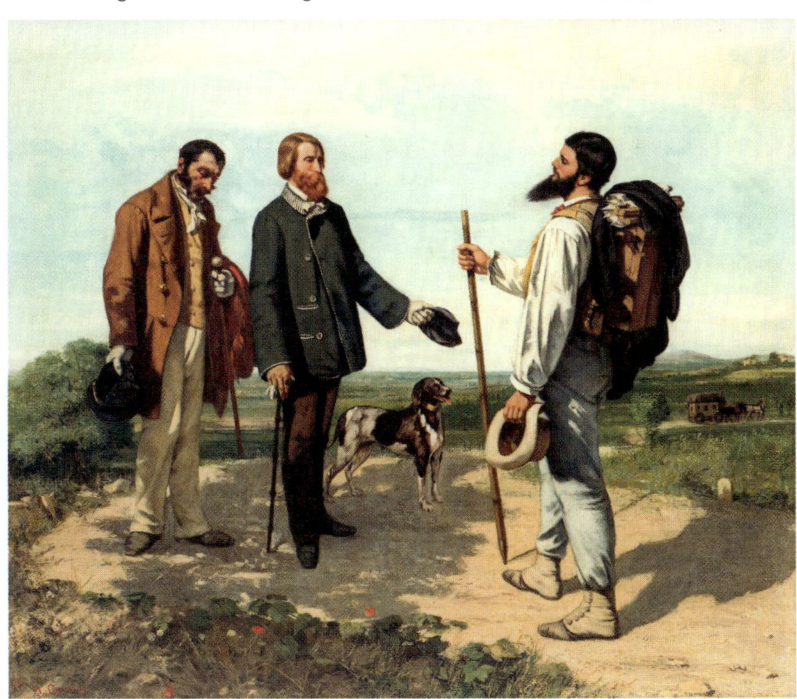

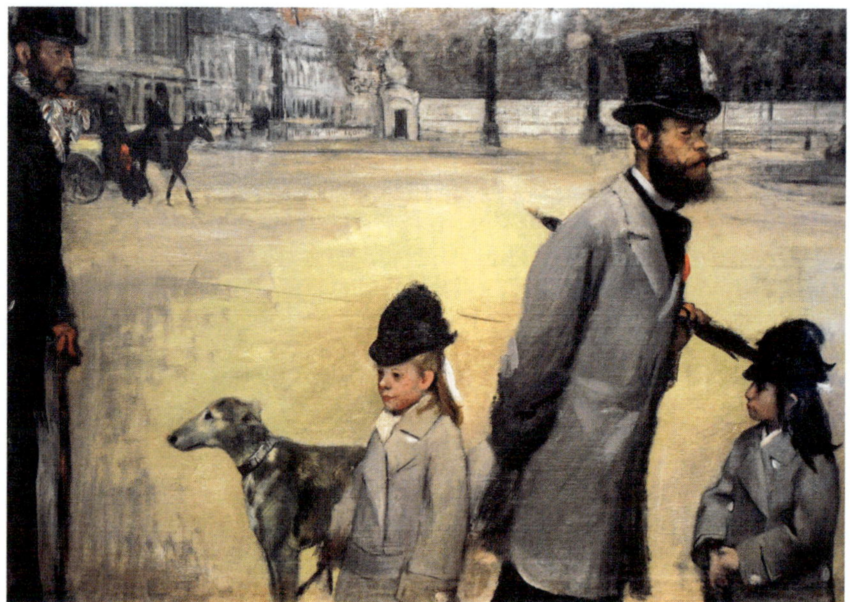

165 Degas' *Viscount Lepic and his Daughters Crossing the Place de la Concorde* (1875).

black and white fur echoes the shadows in Courbet's shirt and trousers. It also provides a narrative context for why the two main characters are out in the countryside: Courbet to paint and the patron on a walk with a well-behaved dog. This social mediation is needed because the tensions and status ambiguity sensed by critics haunt this encounter in which the dog holds the social moment together – both enabling it and disarming it. The dog has mastered the 'stay' command.

Baudelaire in *The Painter of Modern Life* defined the *flâneur* as an urban 'psycho-geographer'. Dogs, and their masters, out for a walk qualify. In Caillebotte's *Le Pont de l'Europe* (*see* 96) it is the dog who is taking a measure of the urban landscape. We do not know what is in its psyche, but we know that he is a 'geographer' locating himself in urban space. In that sense he is allied with the bourgeois gentleman on the bridge and perhaps also with his invisible master – the artist – six feet behind him just outside the frame.

Edgar Degas' *Viscount Lepic and his Daughters Crossing the Place de la Concorde* is an even clearer example of dogs taking the measure of social space and human relations [**165**]. Lepic, who was one of Degas' best friends until they broke up over the artist's virulently anti-Semitic position during the Dreyfus Affair, appears in at least eleven of his paintings.

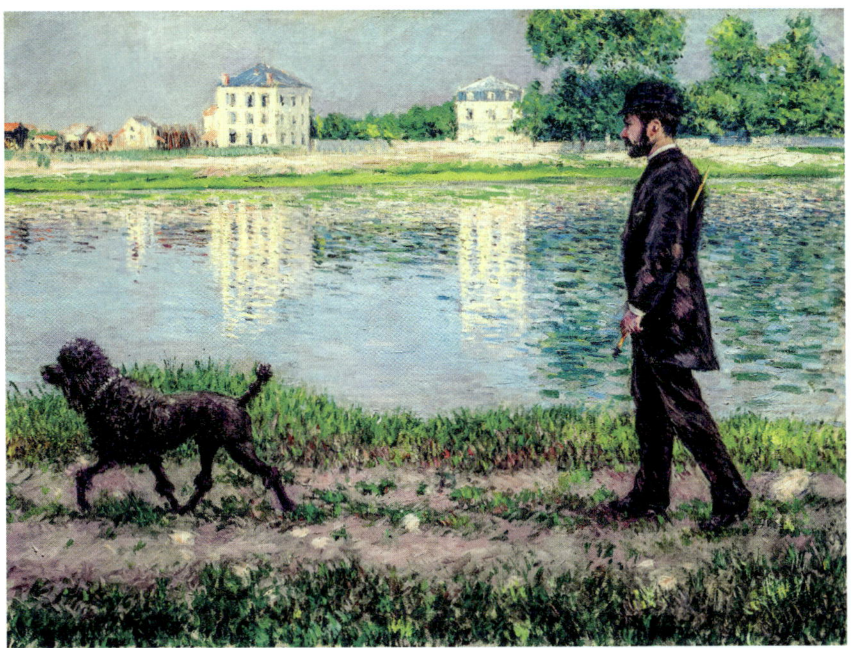

166 The mediator: Caillebotte's *Richard Gallo and his Dog Dick at Petit Gennevilliers* (1884).

The fashionably dressed *viscomte*, cigar and umbrella at jaunty angles like the sides of an isosceles triangle – a *flâneur* type – is leaning forward as he leaves the great, flatly painted, empty space of the Place de la Concorde. The portrait is cropped at the knees which makes the urban space behind him seem even more vast. To the left is Lepic's greyhound Albrecht looking resolutely out of the frame; Degas probably painted him from a photograph. Cropped in half is another man, said to be the playwright Ludovic Halévy, whom the dog might have noticed although it looks like he is taking a longer view. That is what was there – a dog on a walk between two men – in a vast empty urban space – before the viscount's beautifully painted two daughters were added. All four humans are looking in a different direction, none with eyes as fixed as Albrecht's. What we see is a man taking the air in central Paris with his family including his dog.[4] It is a world of social disconnection, with a dog at its centre.

In Caillebotte's *Richard Gallo and his Dog Dick at Petit Gennevilliers* [**166**], we see the journalist Richard Gallo, dressed in his city clothes, walking his dog in the countryside along the Seine in a village across the river from Argenteuil, a favourite spot just outside Paris for the Impressionists. Both poodle and master are in black, and they get equal painterly attention against the glimmering blue of the river.[5] In these paintings, and in many more like them, the dog is no mere extra, as it was in some early modern painting. It is not a street or neighbourhood dog, captured, as if incidentally, in the human scene. The modern dog walking is there with a purpose to guide and mediate human sociability in an age of rapid change – the bridges, the rivers, the depictions of vast openness, all focus the eye on the painting's anchor – the dog. There would be no picture without it. And once one starts looking for them, man and dog on a walk are everywhere in casual sketches and posed photographs of representative figures. Picasso sent his friend the poet Apollinaire – who, among other things, coined the terms cubism and surrealism – a postcard in 1905 complaining that he hadn't seen him for a while [**167**]. The poet is walking by the bourse – he worked as a clerk in his twenties – with his dog on-lead looking at the urban scene beyond the frame.

In a photographic archive of various 'types' of people – from artists, women, and professionals to skilled workers and 'the last people, the homeless' – which would cumulatively mirror the social world of his age, the German documentary photographer August Sander produced over 600 images. *Der Notar* ('The Notary') is there with his dog, a Doberman like my grandfather's, out on a walk like the one he was beginning from the snow-covered steps of his house. The images are generic: a bourgeois gentleman on a walk with his dog [**168**].

There are very few women of any social class walking their dogs in high art before the late nineteenth century, in part because at the advent of modern urbanism women walking alone in public was morally suspect. But as urban space became domesticated and socially tamed, photographs and commercial art all over Europe and North America began to represent women of the respectable classes about town with their dogs. Van Gogh's woman walking her dog is not one of these ladies [**169**]. She is hard to place socially: not of the lowest class because she is wearing shoes rather than clogs and thus is hovering in the middle-ground of a newly stratified urban social order. The canine/human intimacy is palpable; another dog, running free, is not with her. She carries a short lead and looks down at the untethered and yet completely attached dog and at their common path. It is a joint portrait of a stable relationship in an unstable world.

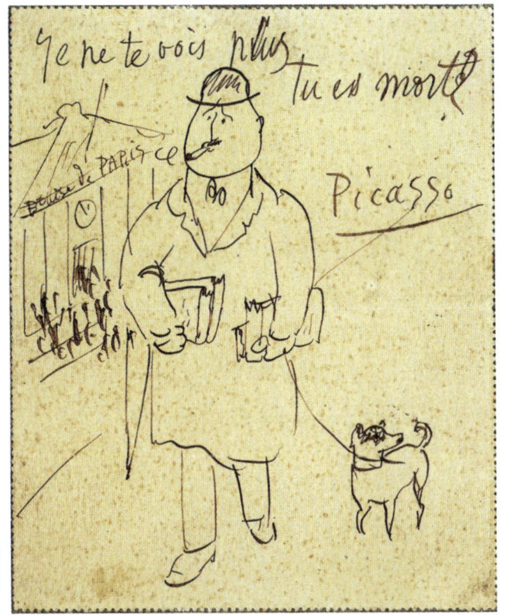

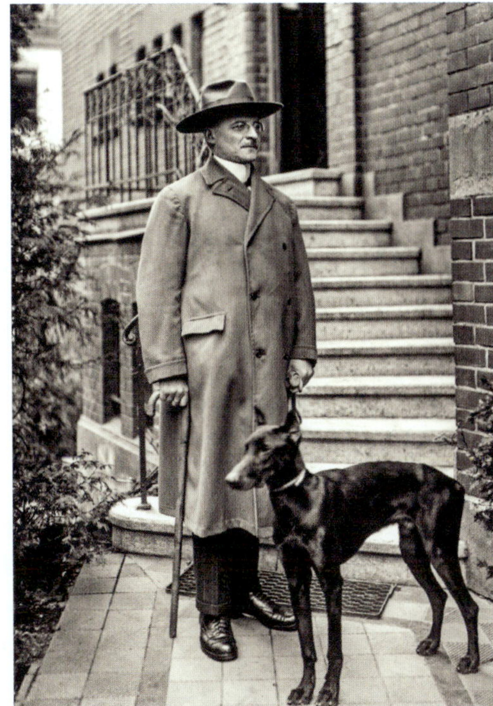

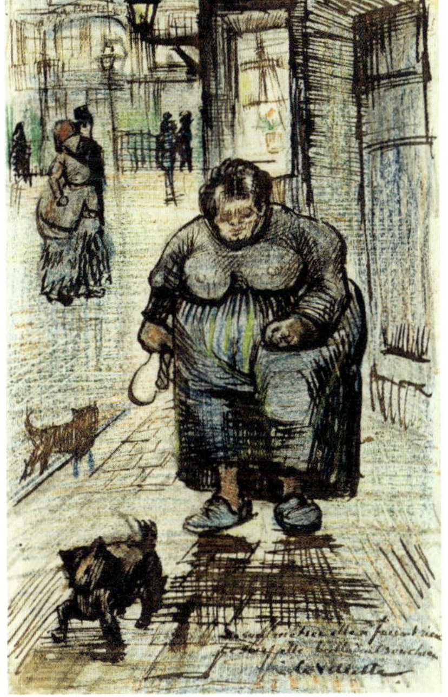

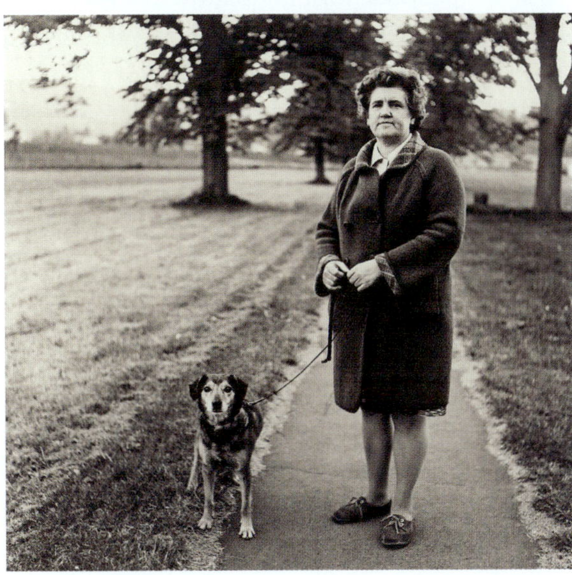

167–170 Dog walking is everywhere in the visual culture of modernity: Picasso's postcard to Apollinaire (1905, *above left*); August Sander's *Der Notar* (1924, *above right*); Van Gogh's *Woman Walking her Dog* (1888, *below left*); a photograph from Keith Arnatt's *Walking the Dog* series (1976–9, *below right*).

The dog walk found its modern master in the work of the conceptual artist Keith Arnatt. He made tightly focused, head-on images of the delicate relationship between dogs and humans his subject [**170**]. The surroundings were of no interest. If a whistle or the calling of the dog's name did not get it to look his way, he barked. From over 200 photographs – an unrivalled effort to document this genre of dog/human sociability in a wide range of settings – he chose fifty for a book. Others were in exhibitions at Tate Modern and other major museums. These photographs take us back to the photograph of my grandfather and of August Sander's *Der Notar* with their similar dogs, and to the art earlier in this chapter. A visual reminder of Thomas Mann's *Herr und Hund*. In all of these images the attachment to the dog gives the person their standing and their stature.

The sociology of Arnatt's photographs is of secondary and indeterminate importance: some dogs look like their owners, others do not; in some, the class of the owner matches what a fancy breed might signify and in others not; gender and dog size do not align. But they all have in common the intimacy of two creatures doing something together, something routine, something like what is happening in pictures of hunting together, which gives them a sense of purpose and pride.

They are different from hunting pictures because in them the dog and its master are focused on something – their prey. In his photographs Arnatt's people are not on a mission. They stop to say something to a passer-by because the dog notices them, or they notice the dog. The dog walk is a public as well as a private engagement. George Melly, the editor of the published collection of these photographs who was himself a distinguished musician and art critic, suggests a broader connotation of these images. Because the life span of a dog is so much shorter than a human's, death, he suggests, haunts their relationship with us. There is a case to be made. The 'last walk' has become a minor genre of pet memoirs.[6] Perhaps 'the dog is a reminder of mortality', as Melly suggests, 'a barking *memento mori*', although I find life is enough of its own *memento mori*. But photographs in the hundreds of millions remind us that we have lived with generations of pets whose passing marks the decades. I think of the pictures of my mother in the Preface. As Roland Barthes and Susan Sontag remind us, there is a proleptic quality to all photographs, frozen in the flow of time that in fact does not stop. The dog walk is a metonym – a capture in miniature – of this modern preoccupation with evanescence.[7]

Naming the Dog

Three social historical, or more broadly cultural, developments influenced how dogs are represented in the painting of modern life after the great expansion of their presence in the genre art of the seventeenth century. The first is the reification of breed – the creation of fixed categories of dog – that for the first time in the nineteenth century resulted in a standard for each of an ever-increasing number of dog sub-species. Each came to have named progenitors and named successors.

There have of course been kinds of dogs since the Palaeolithic. A – arguably *the* – defining characteristic of a domestic animal is that humans control much of its reproductive life. Our species has used this power for its own purposes over tens of thousands of years to create dogs for specific purposes, including just keeping us company. Aristotle writes about several 'breeds' of dogs and notes that 'certain critics' think Homer 'did well in representing the dog of Ulysses as having died in its twentieth year', because he was a Laconian (a swift dog from Sparta) who, while living in general for only ten to twelve years, can live to twenty, the age of Argos when his master returned.[8] Diogenes the Cynic, the dog philosopher, was supposedly asked what sort of hound he was and, according to Diogenes Laertius, said that when he was hungry, he was a Melitan (a dog from Malta of ancient lineage), the ancient world's favourite kind of lapdog; when satisfied, a Molossus, a fierce hunting and guard dog, bred first by an eponymous ancient Greek tribe living in the rugged region of Epirus, and best left undisturbed.

The numbers of different kinds of dogs from which recognized breeds emerged in the nineteenth century grew over the millennia. Edward Topsell in his *History of Four-Footed Beasts and Serpents* (1658) lists twenty-two: the greyhound, the bloodhound, the village dog or housekeeper, various terriers and spaniels, the Meletian-dogs of gentlewomen in addition to the cur or mongrel, and the strange 'outlandish dog'. We have only the most general sense of what any of these looked like. The eighteenth-century French naturalist the Comte de Buffon lists over thirty types of dog. By the late eighteenth century, artists came to represent general categories of dogs but without the fixed standards and genealogical details of images created after the breed revolution in the nineteenth century. (See an example from the naturalist and engraver

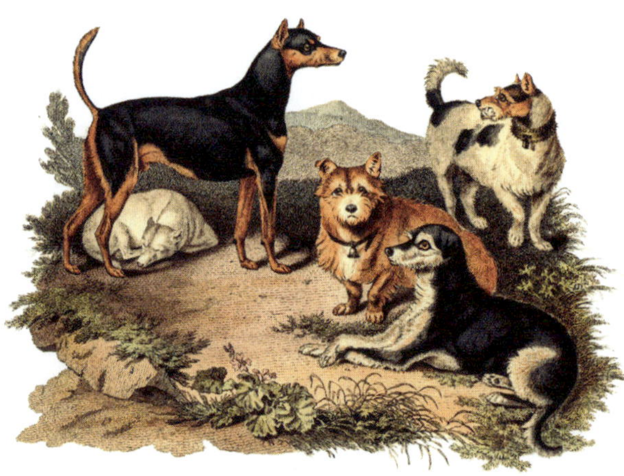

171 Sydenham Edwards illustrates different breeds of terrier (1800).

Thomas Bewick's early nineteenth-century illustrations of kinds of dogs, 38.) 'Terrier', for example, was a broad category, and in the naturalist painter Sydenham Edwards' 1800 book they are posed in the tradition of art-historical models and not engaged in breed-specific activities [**171**].

So-called breeds defined by their functions did not disappear as a way of classifying dogs. But the reification of breed – or pure breed – came to entail adherence to a particular standard of beauty and appearance, and membership in a lineage from a progenitor who represented these standards in the way a 'type standard' represents a species of plants in botany. Starting in the 1870s and 1880s national clubs – the Kennel Club of Great Britain in 1873; the US Westminster Kennel Club of 1877; the French Société Centrale Canine in 1881; Ente Nazionale della Cinofilia Italiana of 1882 – subsumed earlier regional and speciality breed clubs and became the arbiters of what counted as this or that kind of dog. All those dogs that were excluded were just dogs – 'mixed Breed or mongrels'.

There is an obvious parallel to this story with the rise of scientific racism.[9] But the origins of these clubs are less important here than the fact that every formally recognized breed demanded – or rather their owners demanded – images, or copies of images, of a creature who fully met the standard. Every breed had its founder: its ideal token of a type. A portrait of Adonis, an Irish setter, born in 1875, the first dog registered by the Westminster Club, hangs in its New York headquarters.[10] The naming and proliferation of breeds produced little canonical high art – the dog portraits of Rosa Bonheur and Edwin Landseer are exceptions – but it created a huge new market for individualized breed portraits, which was met by a cadre of artists among whom women were prominent. (Eighty-three 'female [dog] artists' are represented in the collections of the Kennel Club, its website announces, whereas the National Gallery in London has works by only seventeen women.)

Maud Earl, 'whose name is virtually synonymous with portraits of purebred dogs', the daughter of the animal artist George Earl, is among the best known of these.[11] Her portraits of dogs are eerily like human portraits, individualized, posed, engaging. These black labs are not holotypes but named, knowable fellow creatures [172]. Collectively an army of animal painters made the dog's gaze a resonant image in popular culture that would, in turn, affect how the dog's ethical and moral standing would be represented and understood. Dogs look out intensely, curiously, engagingly, imploringly, happily, and sadly in this mountain of commercial art that addressed a broad public. It is also an art about dogs doing with humans

172 Maud Earl's portrait of Peter of Faskally and his mate, Dungavel Jet (1912).

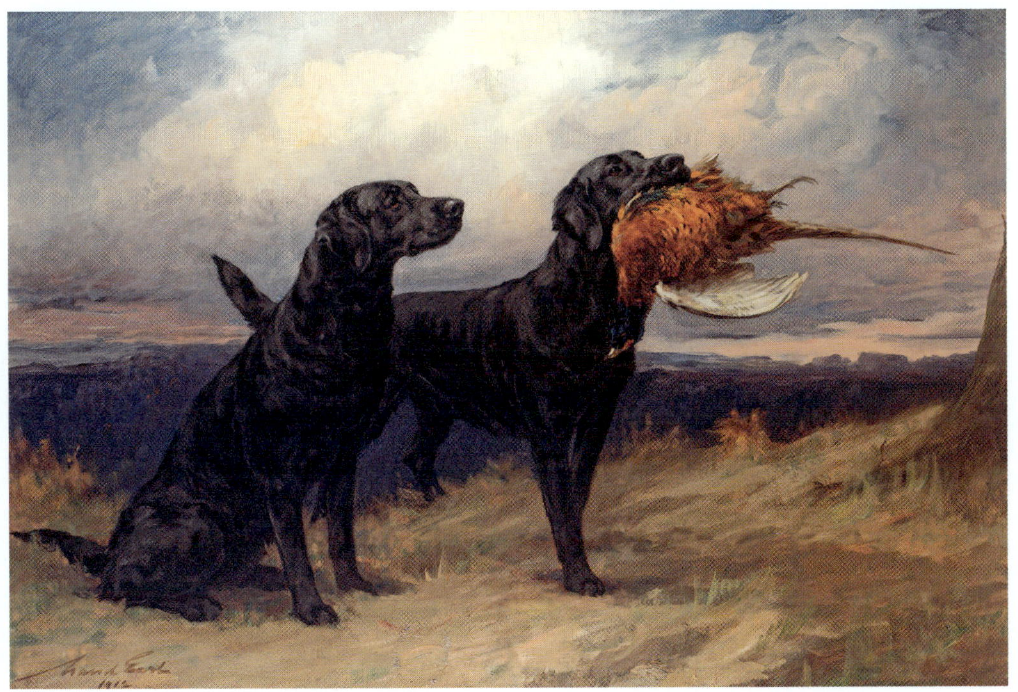

what each breed was said to do best, and in a sense of how each breed of dog fits into the world of humans: specialized forms of hunting, guarding, rescuing – walls full of St Bernards with their brandy casks around their neck – cuddling and doing all the other things dogs do. There are thousands and thousands of engravings of so-called pure-breed dogs in the popular press. *Harper's Weekly* magazine published a long article on the first Westminster Dog Show; the engraving that accompanied it names each dog; from its two bottom corners dogs' eyes reach out to readers [**173**].

The second development that massively affected the representation of dogs is the rise of pet-keeping in the nineteenth century as part of what the French sociologist Pierre Bourdieu might call the 'habitus' – the norms and values – of the middle and upper classes. Keeping pets was not in itself new and we do not know if, in fact, there were more dogs or cats per human in the nineteenth century than there were before. Dogs have been 'kept for pleasure or companionship' – the definition of a pet – since the Palaeolithic era – and have been represented in art as part of the lives of a broad range of social classes. But in the nineteenth century the

173 The first Westminster Dog Show, illustrated in *Harper's Weekly* (26 May 1877).

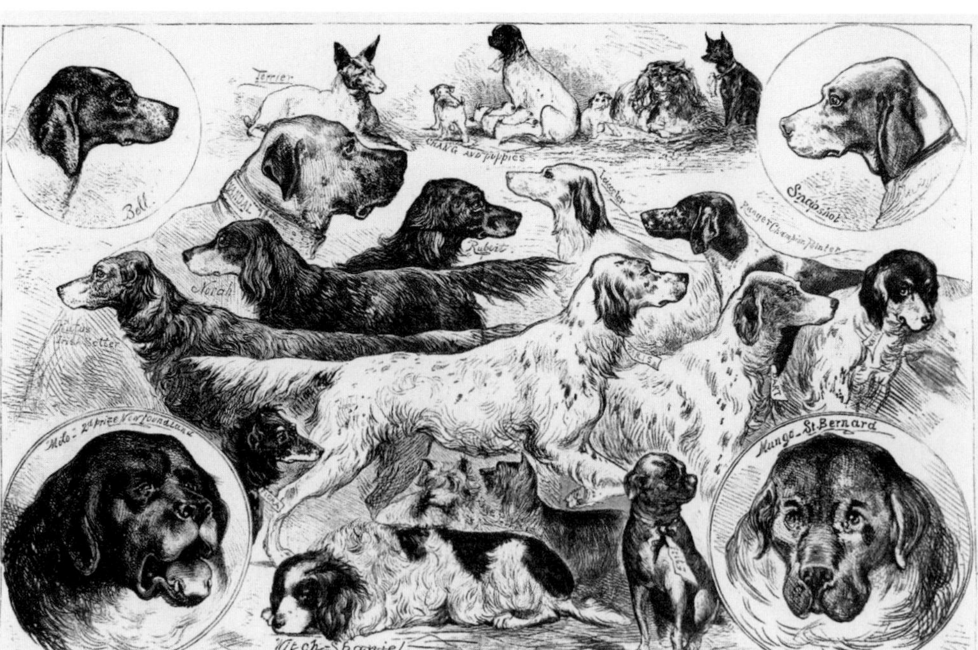

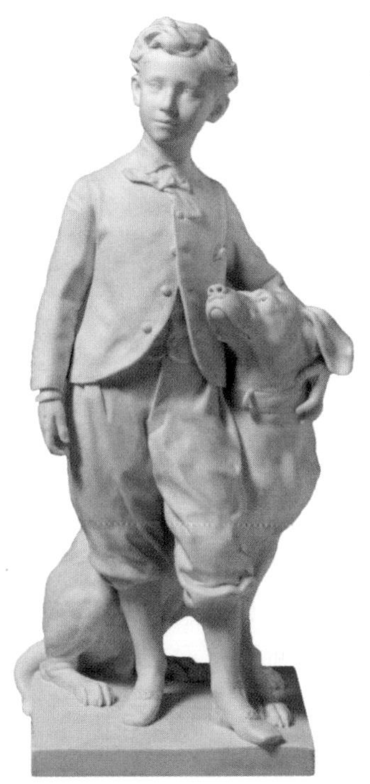

174 A copy of Carpeaux's 1866 statue of the Prince Imperial, son of Napoleon III, and his dog, Nero, produced by Sèvres (1912).

keeping of pets became self-consciously part of a way of bourgeois family life that was supported by a whole new world of goods and services.[12]

Among the most striking visual representations of the new status of the pet is that by Jean-Baptiste Carpeaux, one of the greatest French sculptures of the nineteenth century: *The Prince Imperial [the son of Napoleon III] and his Dog Nero* [**174**]. He is represented as an ordinary lad – nothing imperial here – with undistinguished baggy trousers and an admiring dog. (Carpeaux also made beautiful images of the so-called races of man which are now at the centre of political controversy for having put a gloss on slavery and colonial oppression.) The Napoleon piece was first done in plaster and then marble for the Salon of 1866. It followed the imperial family into exile and found a place on the prince's tomb in Hampshire before being returned to France and finally added to the French national collection in 1930. It is now in the Musée d'Orsay. The statue was reproduced in various media from high-end biscuit porcelain Sèvres pieces of various sizes that mimic marble to cheaper bronzes and tiny doll's-house versions in addition to endless postcards. Representing the prince as a middle-class boy made the 'boy and his dog' into an archetype.

More generally, advances in lithography during the late 1860s – steam-driven presses and the offset process most importantly – made possible a seemingly endless supply of the art of children and dogs. There is probably not an antique shop in North America or Europe where one can't find examples for very little money. Some are updated versions of Old Masters, others are examples of new Victorian ideals – of charity, of little girls as mothers [**175**], and more generally of family life. And all of these are once again multiplied in advertising images – a little girl lying by a boat protected by a Newfie on a calendar that hangs in my house [**176**]. Sociable dogs are ubiquitous in the visual world of modernity.

Finally, a third story influenced how the dog is seen – and sees – in art: that is in how it was written about in the burgeoning popular genre engaged in everyday life. In the novel and its allied popular genres animals begin to find a voice as speakers and as characters. Frances Coventry's immensely popular *Pompey the Little* (1751) giving voice to a pug is an early example. Anna Sewell's *Black Beauty*, one of the best-selling books of all time, gave voice to a horse. By the nineteenth century, animals join the great traditions of literature. One thinks of the horse Malek Adel in Turgenev's *Sportsman's Sketches*. Successors to Pompey and Black Beauty include the unnamed ape in Kafka's 'Report from the Academy', and the dog in the 'Investigation of a Dog'. Dogs who don't speak – and there are those too – but are every bit as much characters with names and personalities, are everywhere: Emma Bovary's 'Djali' is a canine

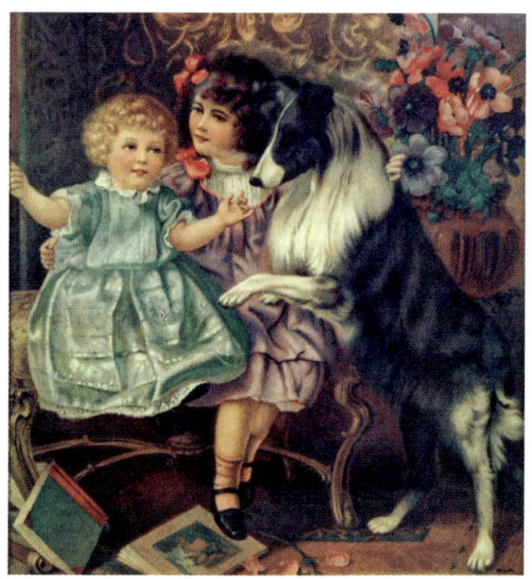

175 One of innumerable nineteenth-century lithographs of children with dogs. This one, *Two Sisters and a Collie* (c. 1900), is from Germany.

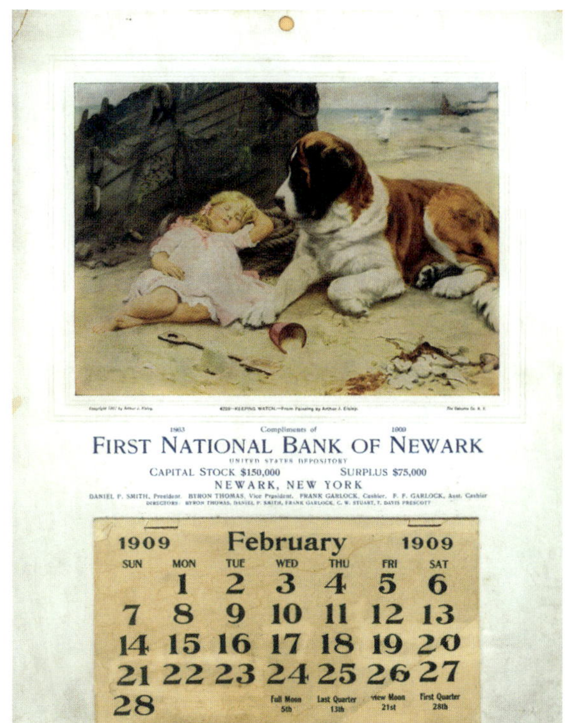

176 This calendar, with a lithograph based on Arthur J. Elsley's painting *Keeping Watch*, hangs in my house.

doppelgänger if ever there was one. There are five named dogs in George Eliot's *Middlemarch* plus the unnamed Maltese whom Dorothea rejects when she is being courted by Sir James Chatham. Bill Sikes' dog Bull's Eye in *Oliver Twist*, the circus dog Merry Legs in *Hard Times*, and Jip in *David Copperfield* are just some from Dickens.[13]

One of the most vivid examples of literary companionship is the dog Laska with the human Levin in Tolstoy's *Anna Karenina*. It fills a whole chapter. They are out hunting. 'Laska stopped, looking ironically at the horses and inquiringly at Levin. Levin patted Laska and whistled as a sign that she might begin. She obeyed him, pretending she was looking, so as to please him,' when he gave an incoherent demand. He saw from his horse that she smelled something:

> 'Fetch it, fetch it!' shouted Levin, giving Laska a shove from behind.
> 'But I can't go,' thought Laska. He gives her a nudge . . . 'Well, if that's what he wishes, I'll do it, but I can't answer for myself now,' she thought, and darted forward as fast as her legs would carry her between the thick bushes.

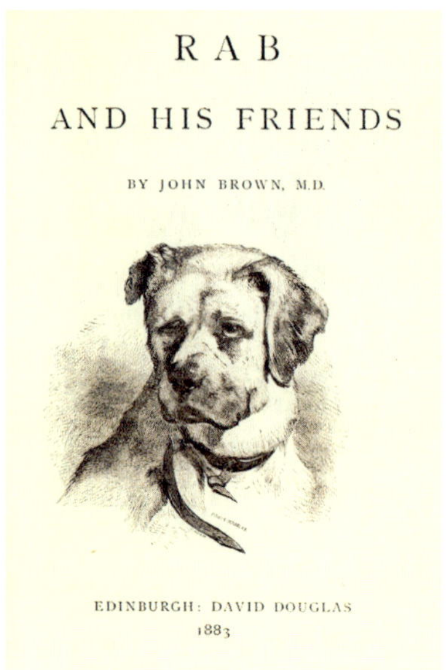

177 The frontispiece to the 1883 edition of *Rab and his Friends*.

To some extent this literary menagerie reflects the biographies of their authors and how they are represented in portraits. Dickens was famous as a dog lover: the small white spaniel Timber in the early days followed by large St Bernards and bloodhounds – Turk, Sultan and Don. Everyone knew that Pug was an important member of the household of George Eliot and her husband George Henry Lewes. Elizabeth Barrett Browning had Flush; the Brontë sisters had Grasper, Keeper, and Flossy, a black and white Cavalier King Charles Spaniel that belonged to Anne, who was devoted to her. The eponymous mastiff Rab belonging to a carter in Dr John Brown's *Rab and his Friends* (1859) is one of the most famous literary dogs of the century and a prime example of how fiction about dogs generated what Lewes characterized figuratively as a 'charming bit of sympathetic painting'. Rab and dog stories more generally generated galleries of illustrative art for more than half a century [**177**].[14] No one had to explain why in Dickens' *Pickwick Papers* – and in its illustrations – there is a 'sagacious' dog nor indeed why fictional dogs figure so prominently in the moral economy of his novels and in the illustrations that accompany them.

New, lower-cost technologies democratized the representation of dogs, and, at the same time perhaps paradoxically, gave them greater individuation, as breeds, and then as unique characters with names and roles in the everyday life of the industrial world.

Top Dogs

'Celebrity', 'a characteristic of modern societies', and specifically of a driven public life emerging around 1750, came to include dogs along with their well-known and celebrated humans. The key to celebrity was that it depended less on what a person was known for having done than for being known by strangers for being famous or associated with someone famous. William Hogarth's pug Trump, who appeared with him in his 1745 self-portrait and on his own in cheap prints and both high art and mass-produced pottery, is probably the first celebrity dog.

There is a sense in which one of Hogarth's dogs was for a moment an explicit stand-in for the painter himself. In a moment of none too subtle nationalistic and artistic self-assertion, another dog – Trump's successor – was originally peeing on a pile of Old Master prints in his 1757–8 self-portrait. Hogarth thought better of the idea and painted it over. The 1745 Trump, however, is more than what his successor might have been. He is engaged with the artist and the viewer, formally and affectively. In Hogarth's self-portrait there is a dual gaze: the artist's and the dog's [**178**]. Trump is standing entirely outside of the frame within a frame as if more a part of our world than its master's; its eyes are large, slightly protruding as is characteristic of brachiocephalic breeds, and painted with exquisite care. Tiny bits of white impasto catch the light as reflections on its pupil; the vitreous iris is a shiny transparent green. The dog's eyes follow the eyes of his master, looking to the right from its liminal perch between the self-portrait – the canvas stitched on an oval frame – and the world beyond, that is, at the world where his master would be standing painting himself. He is joined in his looking with the artist paying attention to us.

Trump almost immediately became a celebrity independent of his master. Louis-François Roubiliac, who made statues of Shakespeare, Handel, and Pope, and was one of the best-known sculptors of the eighteenth century, created a terracotta statue of Trump. Josiah Wedgwood mass produced stand-alone black basalt figurines of him. There are high-end Chelsea Pottery versions in porcelain, an example of which sold recently at Christie's for more than £40,000, and cheap knock-offs that sells today for pennies. Engravings of the dual portrait are available by the thousands. The age of the celebrity dog had begun.

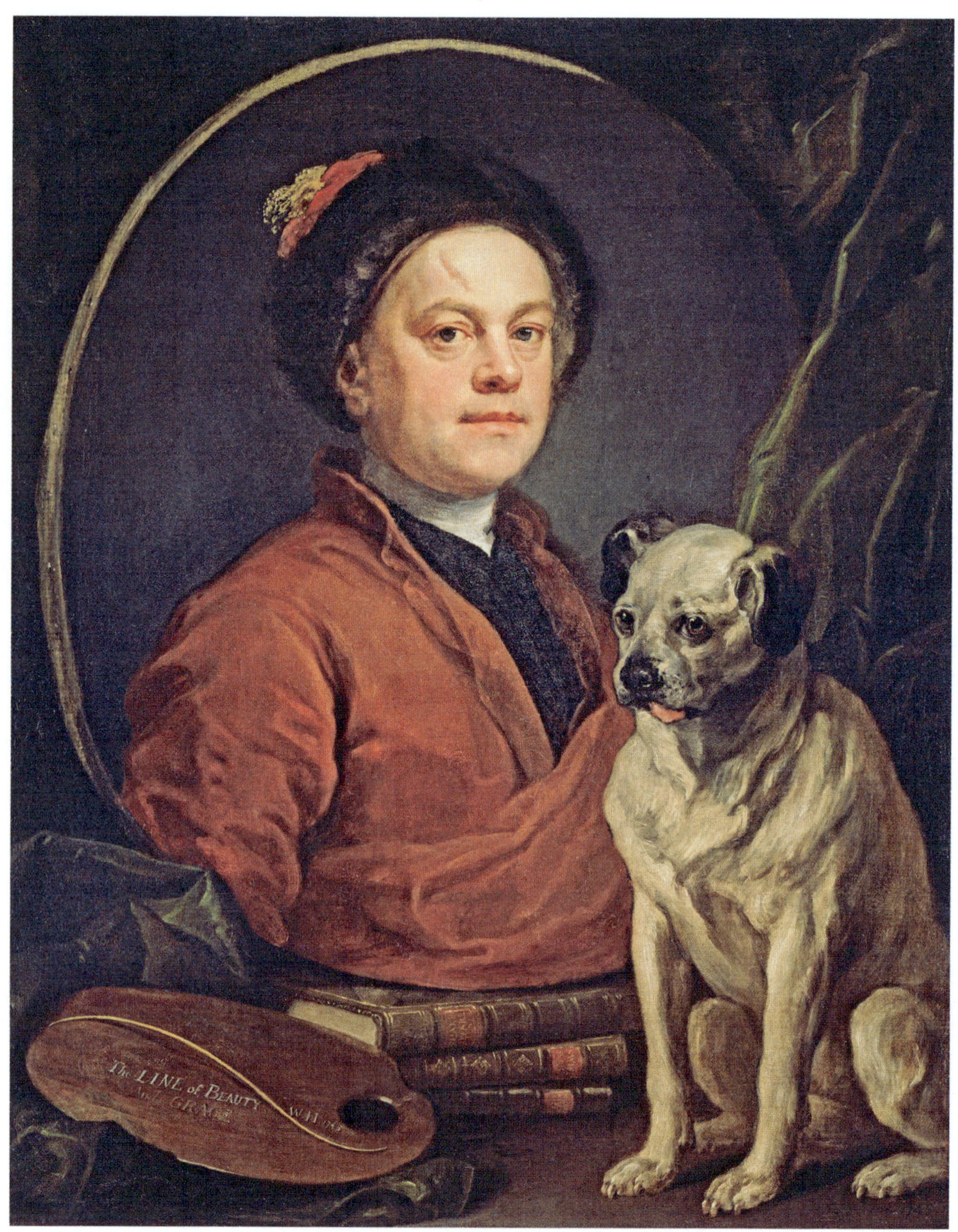

178 William Hogarth's *The Painter and his Pug* (1745). With Trump, the age of the celebrity dog had begun.

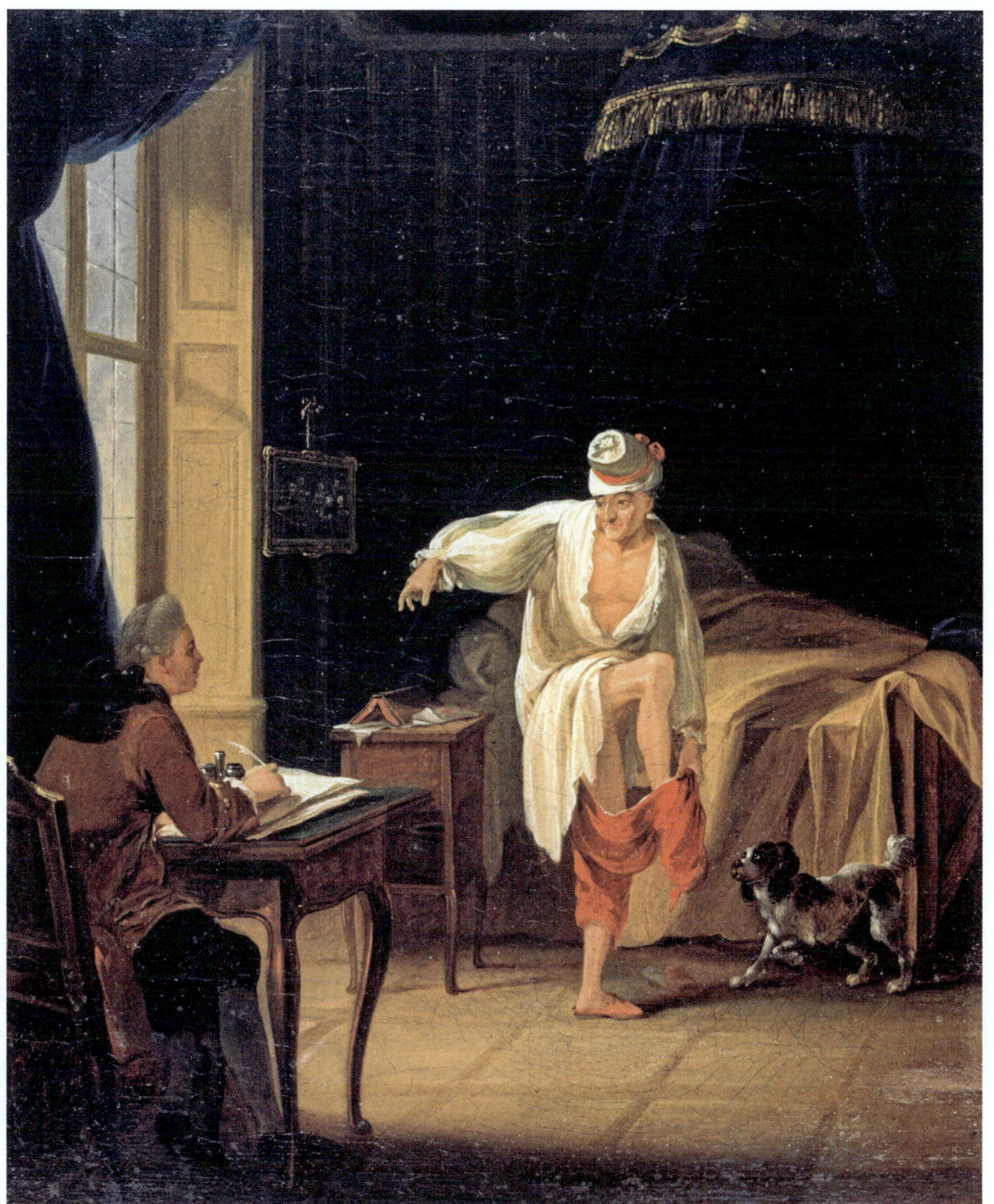

179 Voltaire's dog stands in for a public hungry to look behind the scenes of celebrity life in Jean Huber's *Voltaire Getting Up at Ferney* (after 1759).

The dog who is intently watching one of Europe's first great human celebrities – Voltaire – get out of bed is another early candidate. The dog here is standing in for a new public that demands to know more about this intimate, private moment in the celebrity's daily life [**179**]. Voltaire's secretary is taking dictation; the dog is looking and has the sort of inside access that thousands crave. Intriguingly, the dog is missing from what seems to be the original, but once added transforms the picture by inviting the viewer into this intimate corner of the great man's life. We do not know the name of the dog or anything about Voltaire's view of dogs except perhaps that he was the one who suggested to Frederick the Great that a dog was a man's best friend and that he thought Jean-Jacques Rousseau was 'a bastard of Diogenes' dog'.[15]

Rousseau's decorous dog was known in his own right because his famous master was known as a great dog lover. The dog is represented sitting quietly in nature with his master contemplating a waterfall [**180**]. This image, by an anonymous artist, appeared in an engraving for a famous, widely circulated and translated book on solitude. The philosopher could be making a point to which the dog is listening attentively. The dog is probably Sultan, the dog of Rousseau's period of loneliness whom he took with him into exile in England. David Hume said that Rousseau loved this dog 'above all expression and conception'. It was very hard for Rousseau to love humans in that way; Hume tried but failed to be his friend.[16]

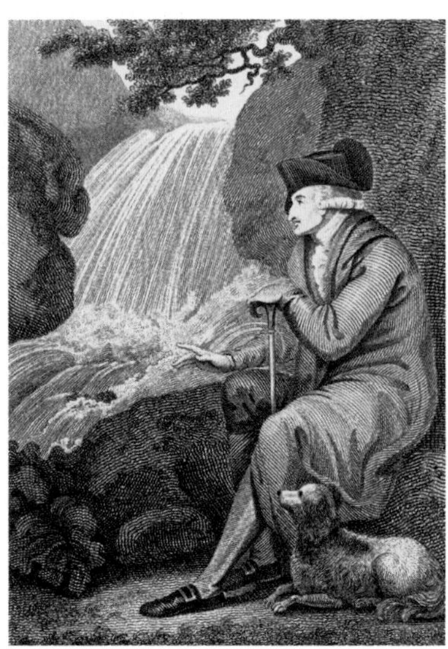

180 'Rousseau contemplating the wild Beauties of Switzerland', from the English edition of Johann Georg Zimmermann's essay *Solitude* (1804).

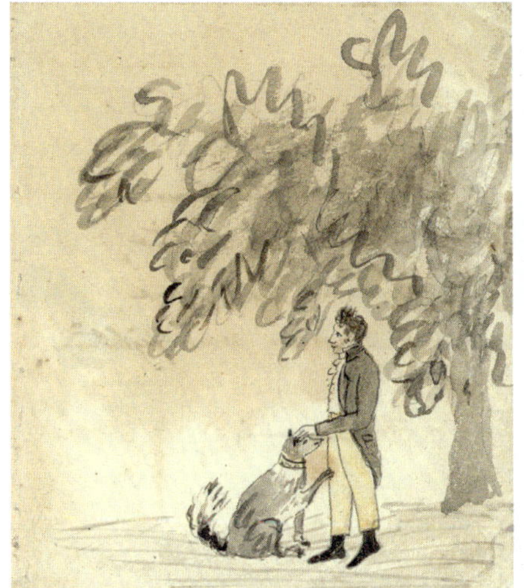

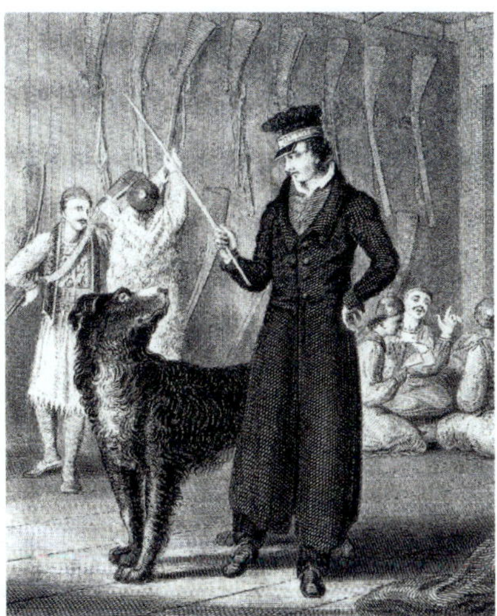

181–182 Byron with Boatswain in watercolour (1807, *left*) and with Lyon in a mass-circulation print (1825, *right*).

There are no such questions about the identity of Byron's dogs, the Newfoundland Boatswain and the wolf-like Lyon, who are joined in text and image with the celebrity poet. Both dogs were widely known to be characters in the very public narrative of his disorderly life. Byron's favourite dog, Boatswain, died of rabies while nestled in his master's arms. The epitaph that the poet wrote for the dog was widely circulated, widely admired, and widely mocked:

> To mark a friend's remains these stones arise;
> I never knew but one – and here he lies.

There is a beautiful portrait by Clifton Towson of Boatswain standing by his master's tomb that still hangs at Byron's Newstead Abbey estate in Nottinghamshire. (Byron is sitting with Boatswain in the statue of him that was installed in Hyde Park in 1882.) Elizabeth Bridget Pigot, the poet's great friend from their teen years and an important source for Byron biographers, produced an entire handmade book about the adventures of the poet and his dog [**181**]. A next-generation Lyon who looked more like a Newfie made his way into a mass-circulation print of the poet in the Greek War of Independence and was known to be his constant companion in the miserable conditions of Missolonghi [**182**]. Dogs of celebrities became celebrities themselves as part of their master's public life.[17]

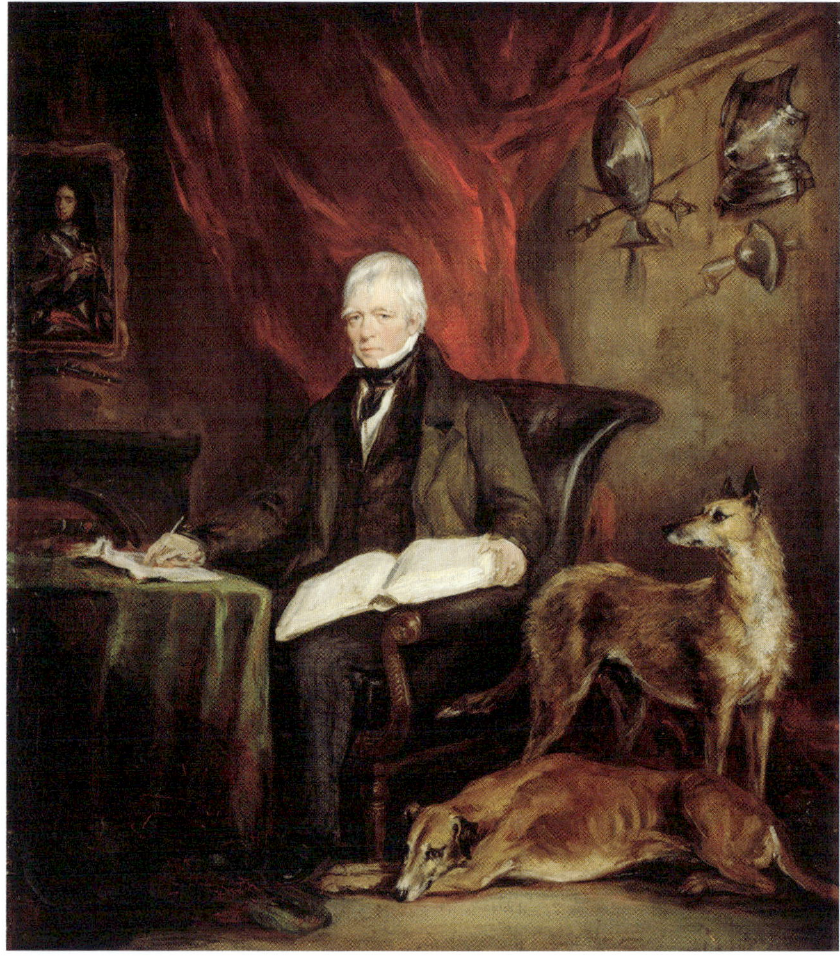

183 Sir Francis Grant's portrait of *Sir Walter Scott* (1831) with Ginger and Maida.

Sir Walter Scott's dogs – Ginger and Maida (his favourite) – took on this part of a celebrity's public image to an extent no canine had ever done before. They are present in formal portraits. They are with him in his study as he reads the newspaper and while he writes [**183**]. And, of course, when he was out for walks on the fells. One of his dogs was imagined to be with him when he famously discovered in his attic – so it was said – the unfinished manuscript of *Waverley*, the first of the series of historical novels that took its name and that he published under the pseudonym 'The author of Waverley'. (Everyone knew he was the author, and he admitted it in 1827.)

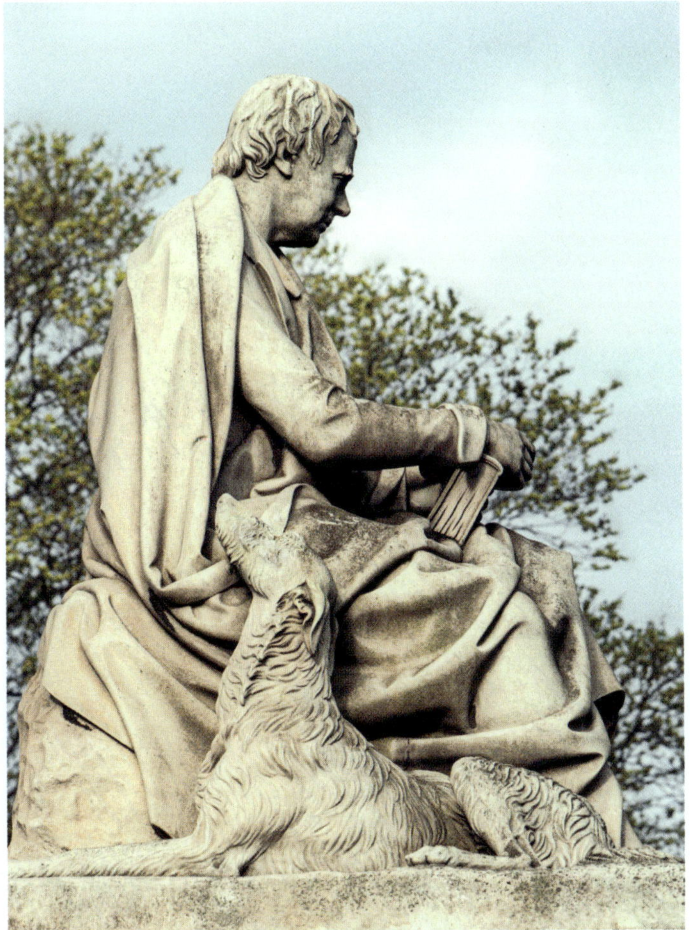

184 Robert Steell's sculpture of Sir Walter Scott with Maida for the Scott Monument (1846), the largest monument to a writer anywhere in the world.

Maida the dog – 'the most perfect creature in the world' – gazes up at him in Sir John Robert Steell's *Scott Monument* in Princes Street Gardens, Edinburgh [**184**], from a bronze version in Central Park in Manhattan, and from a whole bric-à-brac's shop's worth of mugs, porcelain figurines, and lithographs. (Hogarth's statue in Chiswick shows him with his pug Trump.) With Sir Walter Scott, dogs entered the visual vocabulary of how a celebrity's affective and social life was made known to the public; they became part of a brand.

The visually best-documented early twentieth-century version of this story, before the movie-star dogs of the 1920s, is about Colette and her

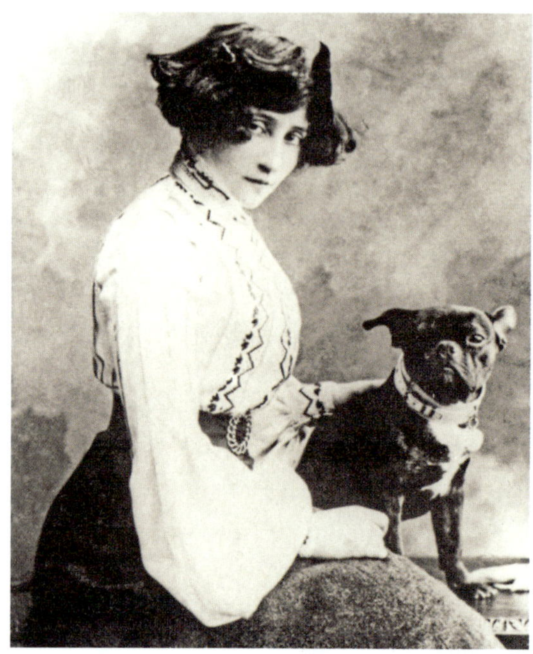

185 Toby Chien was often pictured as Colette's muse and playmate (photograph from *c.* 1895).

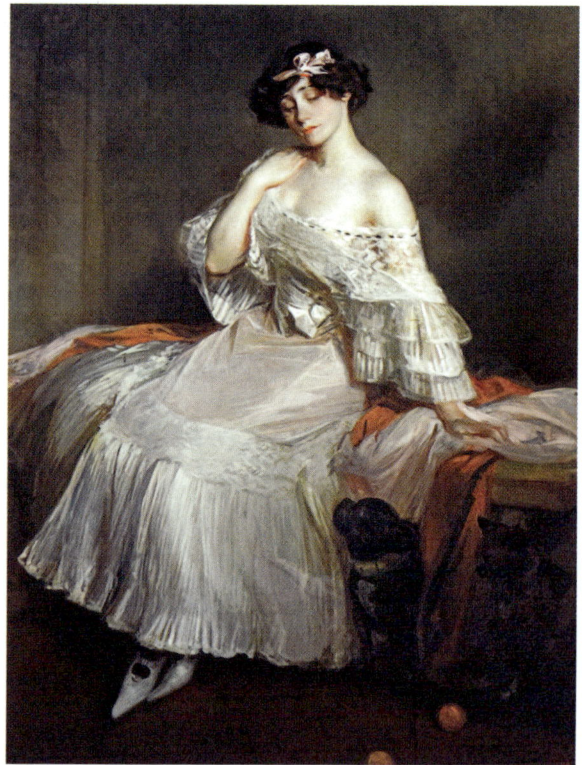

186 Jacques-Émile Blanche's portrait of *Colette* (1905) secured Toby Chien's role as an important part of the author's cult of personality.

French bulldog Toby Chien [**185**]. There are scores of publicity postcards of her and the dog with her soon to be divorced husband 'Willy' (Henry Gauthier-Villars), as well as of her and the dog alone. Willy used these images to promote his purported authorship of his wife's writing. Toby is her muse, her playmate, and a member of her ménage. One could make much of the gender politics of some of these images: why is Willy holding Toby, for example, in one of these photographs? (Neither that image from c. 1896 nor one showing him holding Toby later, as far as I know, was used in the custody battle over the dog when the couple separated. She won.)

Jacques-Émile Blanche's 1905 art nouveau portrait of Colette with Toby Chien depends to a certain extent on these photographs. That she is painted with her dog is not surprising: her relationship with her French bulldog was already part of her public image [**186**]. But the intensity of the relationship that it conveys is a 'communal and affective bond beyond words' between dog and human, as Juliana Schiesari suggests.[18] What we see is a young 'new woman' with short-cropped hair. Her eyes are cast down modestly, a modesty somewhat belied by the luxuriously elaborate white dress falling off her shoulder exposing just a hint of her bosom. Her right hand, touching her other shoulder, may be there to secure the dress. Her lips are an ostentatious red.

The image first appeared as the frontispiece of Colette's *Sept Dialogues des Bêtes* (Société du Mercure de France, Paris) (literally, 'Seven Animal Dialogues' but translated into English in 1913 as *Barks and Purrs*). The painting, from which the frontispiece was derived, subsequently entered the National Museum of Catalonia in 1907. The book was composed of seven stories, purportedly conversations between Toby and Colette's cat Kiki-la-Doucette. The painting could be seen as a classic instance of how the eroticized male gaze is projected onto a female figure, although the actual gazing it represents does not leave much room for a viewer's eroticized gaze.[19] The eros is between celebrity mistress and celebrity dog.

The appearance of the celebrity dog with its celebrity mistress or master represented individualism (indeed heroic individualism) as a new social value in modern art. In twentieth-century mass culture some dogs will become celebrities in their own right – Rin-Tin-Tin, Lassie – their minders relegated to supporting roles.

A Dog in the Family

Dogs in family portraiture appear almost as early as portraiture itself – see for example the fifteenth-century fresco of the Gonzaga family and court with Rubino under the Duke's chair (*see* 19) – but as social beings in their own right, as an important part of the affective bonds of a family, their appearance is more recent. They are there in later Renaissance paintings perhaps to represent faithfulness, or the sort of primordial bonds that were born in the deep time of the dog and have become part of Western consciousness, or as witnesses to family life which is synonymous with patriarchy. Good order more than emotional attachment is the organizing principle in these paintings. The same can be said for much of Dutch Golden Age family portraiture: livelier, more natural, homier, but still emotionally cool.

Le Brun's *The Jabach Family* (1660) is often identified as the first modern family portrait [**187**]. It is by any account a remarkable painting, lost for almost a century, believed destroyed in the Second World War

187 The dog as a family member: *The Jabach Family* (1660) by Charles Le Brun.

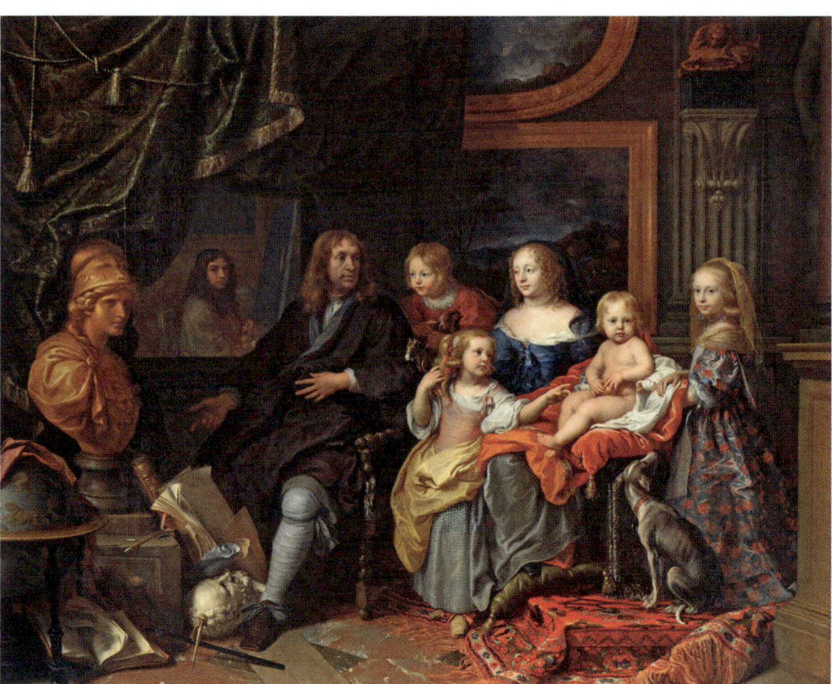

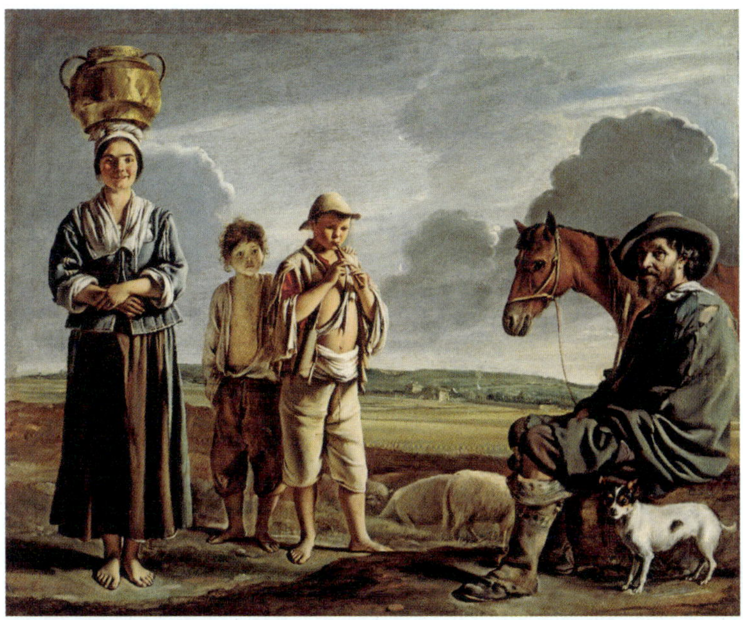

188 Le Nain's *The Resting Horseman* (1640s), one of the earliest French genre paintings.

and subsequently known only from photographs. Before it went underground Goethe saw it in Cologne and admired how it seemed to stop time: the owner and his wife and their children 'all alive, fresh and vivid as if painted yesterday, indeed today, and yet they had all passed away'. (Goethe in this instance, and even more inexplicably in the case of Rembrandt's *Good Samaritan* [*see* 211], did not seem to see the dog.) There is a great deal about this painting that makes it far more than a generic family portrait: the painter's self-portrait reflected in the mirror and also the fact that the interests of the patriarch are almost as much its subject as are his wife and children. Jabach was a great collector and is surrounded by samples of his treasures: a globe, manuscripts, books, and classical sculptures. But the painting is horizontal in the arrangement of the family members; the flesh tones are warm; the intensely engaged whippet is looking lovingly at one of the children: all this gives the painting something of the emotional quality of a modern family portrait. The dog counts as a family member.[20]

It is an idea that artists understood and applied to less exalted families. Le Nain's *The Resting Horseman*, at the very beginning of French genre painting, is an early example [**188**]. It represents a prosperous peasant family – the man's boots and horse speak to his status – on a monumental scale, set in a vast open countryside and backlit by a vast and cloudy sky. The barefoot boy with the pipe may be conventional but because he is standing near sheep it seems more like an allusion to a pastoral trope of a shepherd's pipe. The collarless dog at the very front of the image, its white fur against the horseman's cloak and seat, looks in the same direction as he does. It is plainly not a working breed, that is, not a sheepdog but a kind of terrier that is here because it is, or at least is understood by the artist as being, part of the family.[21]

By the eighteenth century the dog as part of an affectively bound family had become commonplace; dogs and children came to be imagined together across the social spectrum. In Sir Joshua Reynolds' painting *The Family of the Fourth Duke of Marlborough* [189] they are extravagantly

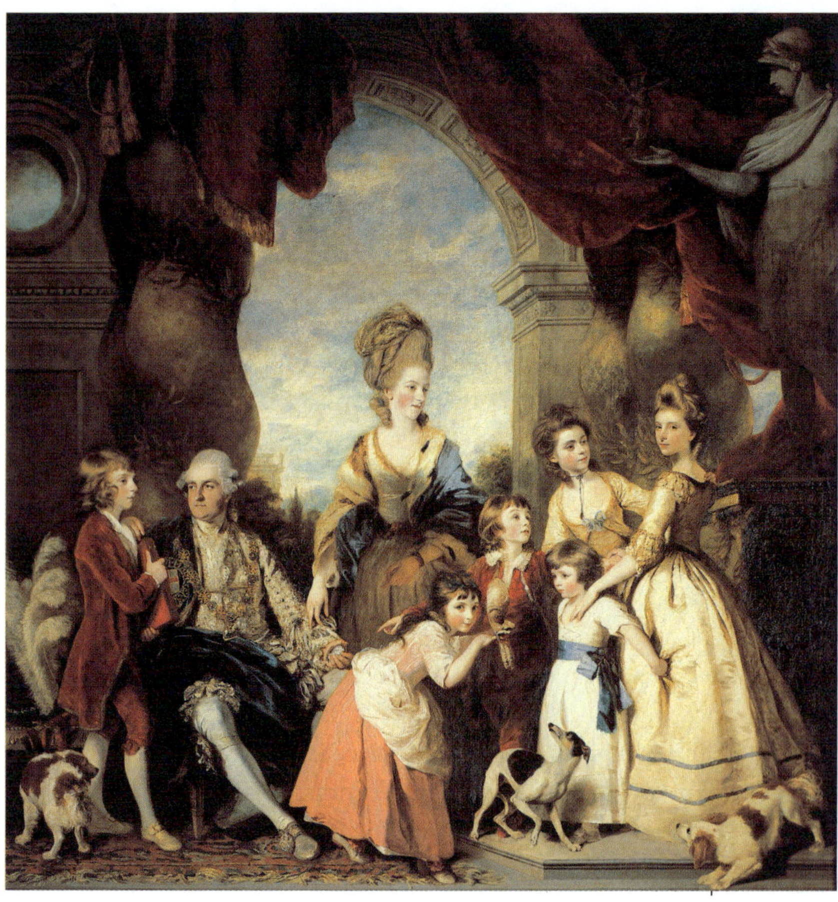

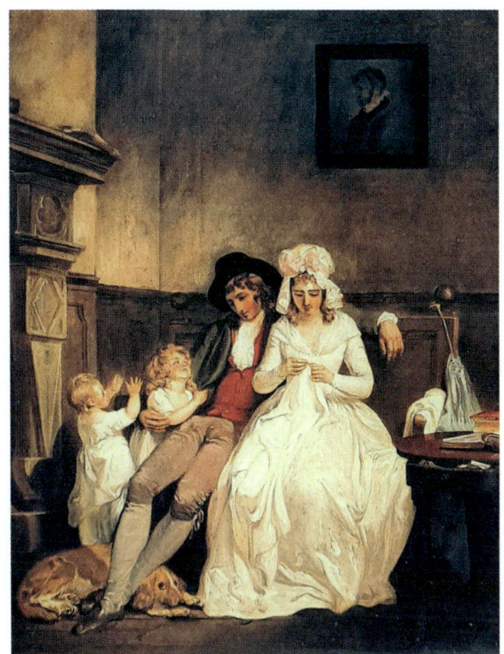

189 (*left*) Sir Joshua Reynolds' *The Family of the Fourth Duke of Marlborough* (1777–9).

190 (*right*) Francis Wheatley's *The Happy Fireside – Married Life* (1791).

present and at work as actors in the family's life and formally in how they structure the image. The spaniel on the left is like a canine follower of Rachel Whiteread, the British artist noted for her casts, bringing to notice the negative space between the calves of George, the future Fifth Duke, and the chair on which his father sits. The curious spaniel helps us focus on the Fourth Duke and his heir, and it reminds me why my daughter named our first family dog Curious because of her interest in looking under furniture. The dog near the middle, highlighted against the white dress of Anne, looks intently at Georgina Charlotte or perhaps curiously at the mask she is holding: a girl and her dog. And the third dog, another spaniel coming into the scene from the right in front of the eldest daughter, Caroline, is looking around her gown at the mini drama of girl and dog at the centre. These are family dogs.

We have little visual evidence for specific family dogs in specific families below the art-commissioning elite. But by the end of the century the family dog had become a commonplace in thinking about and imagining family more generally. In Francis Wheatley's *The Happy Fireside – Married Life* [**190**] the humans form an intimate group, the children looking up at their father and the mother focused on her needlework; in a way an embrace moves from the lower left to the father's arm around his wife. And nestled behind his legs and in front of the girls is a large family dog whose gaze breaks the fourth wall; its eyebrows are raised; its eyes look out. It is a knowing dog.[22]

In 1796 the government of William Pitt the Younger proposed a tax on dogs to help finance the French wars. Proponents cited several good things that would follow in addition to raising revenue: making dogs more expensive would keep irresponsible and dangerous people, namely the poor, from keeping them, thus reducing their numbers, preventing rabies and dog bites, cutting down on poaching, and keeping the improvident poor from wasting food on pets they could not afford. The case against the bill was that these benefits were exaggerated but more importantly that a dog tax was like a tax on children: an assault on the family life of the poor. 'With the poor the affection for a dog was so natural,' argued the Whig statesman William Windham, 'that in poetry and painting it had been constantly recorded, and in any sort of domestic

191 Irresponsible dog-ownership in the eyes of the poor-law authorities: George Morland's *The Miseries of Idleness* (before 1790).

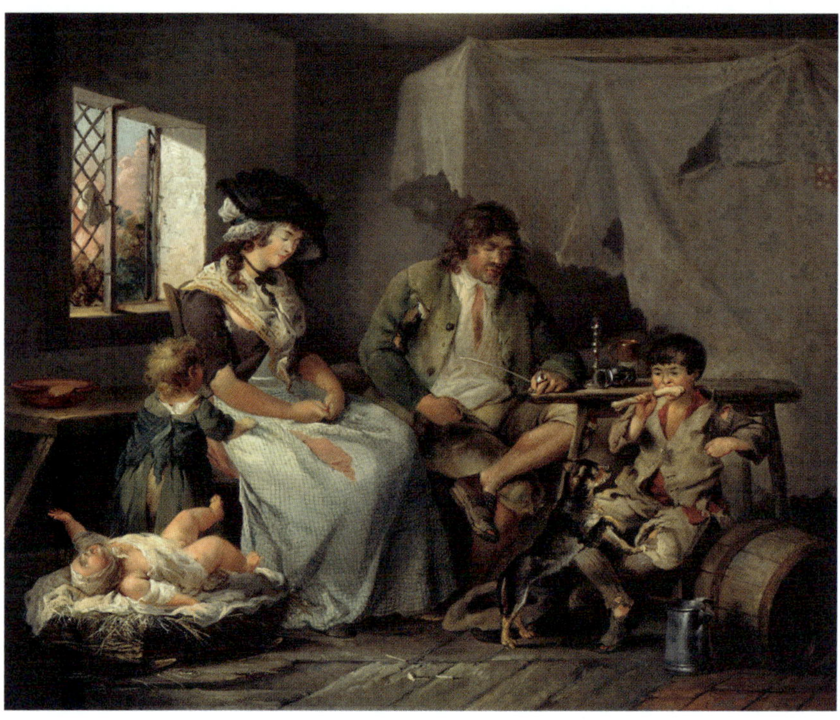

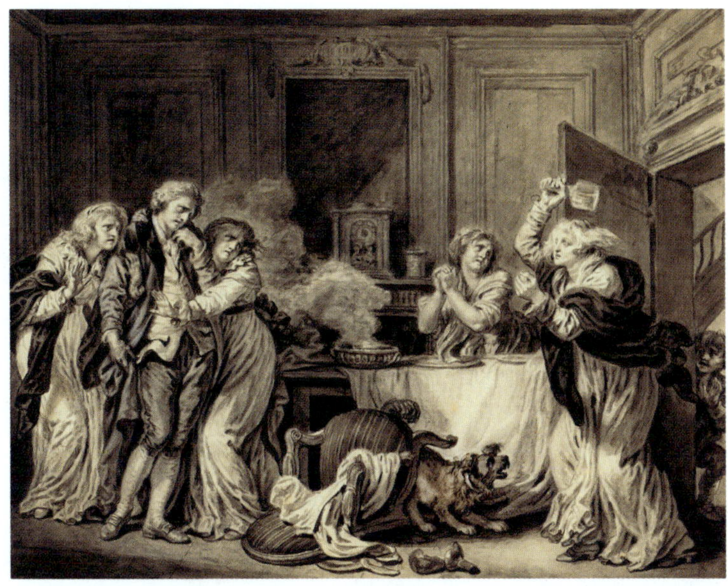

192 Caught in the fracas: Jean-Baptiste Greuze's *The Angry Wife* (c. 1785).

representation, we scarcely see a picture without a memorial of this attachment.'[23] Wheatley's *The Happy Fireside – Married Life* with a dog and children was already a cliché, as was its counter-image of an improvident poor family that also had a dog but, in the view of many poor-law authorities, should not have: George Morland's *The Miseries of Idleness*, for example [**191**]. (A family too poor and improvident to feed itself had no business sharing with a dog.) And there is too the family dog who gets caught up in the fracas of an ill-run household like the one Jean-Baptiste Greuze imagined, based in part on his own acrimonious marriage. A mad woman enters the scene bearing a decanter like a club as the family recoils in horror and the dog makes known that it is alarmed by the collapse of order. The upset chair from which it emerges says it all [**192**].

As the art-commissioning class expanded, so did the art of the family dog. Renoir made his reputation in this new market with *Madame Georges Charpentier and her Children* [**193**]. We know a lot about Porthos, the family dog who anchors the painting and doubles as a stool for the little girl. Named after one of Dumas' Three Musketeers, he was a Landseer Newfoundland, a breed known to be an even-tempered family dog. The breed was named after the artist Landseer because his 1824 portrait of a similar dog named Lion, commissioned by his owner, the writer W. H. de Merle,

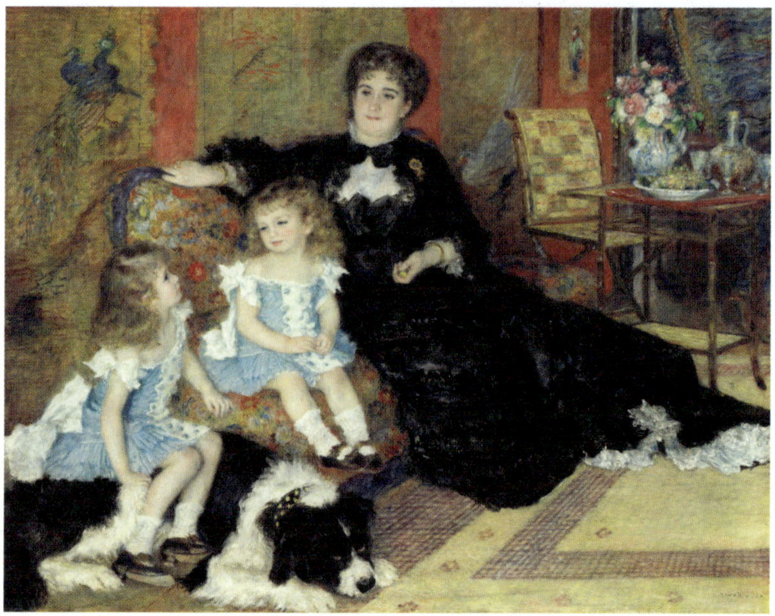

193 The gift of the dog: Renoir's *Madame Georges Charpentier and her Children* (1878).

made the breed famous and desirable. Porthos was given to Georges Charpentier, a publisher, by the niece of one of the writers he published – once again the gift of a dog connects humans. This is a dog with deep cultural roots.

The dog's gaze will not be a surprise by now. The girls look sweetly at each other; Madame Charpentier looks lovingly toward them; and Porthos has a long-suffering look directed out of the painting toward us. Nor will his place in the structure of the painting come as a surprise. Looking from left to right, Porthos is the visual base of the image. One of the family literally sits on him. But the intimacy of the dog with the family is new: the relaxed familiarity in his fashionable surroundings; his palpable patience with the children. Porthos is painted as a member of the family.

One of Thomas Eakins' portraits of family members with their dog has a similar emotional valence in a different genre: realism. 'Harry' – dogs' names had come to be more like that of humans – in Eakins' portrait of Susan Hannah Macdowell, his wife and former student, is a family dog and not, as the Metropolitan Museum label claims, 'his dog' [**194**]. Wife and dog are represented as if at home, although the painting was done in his studio. She looks up from the book she is reading and

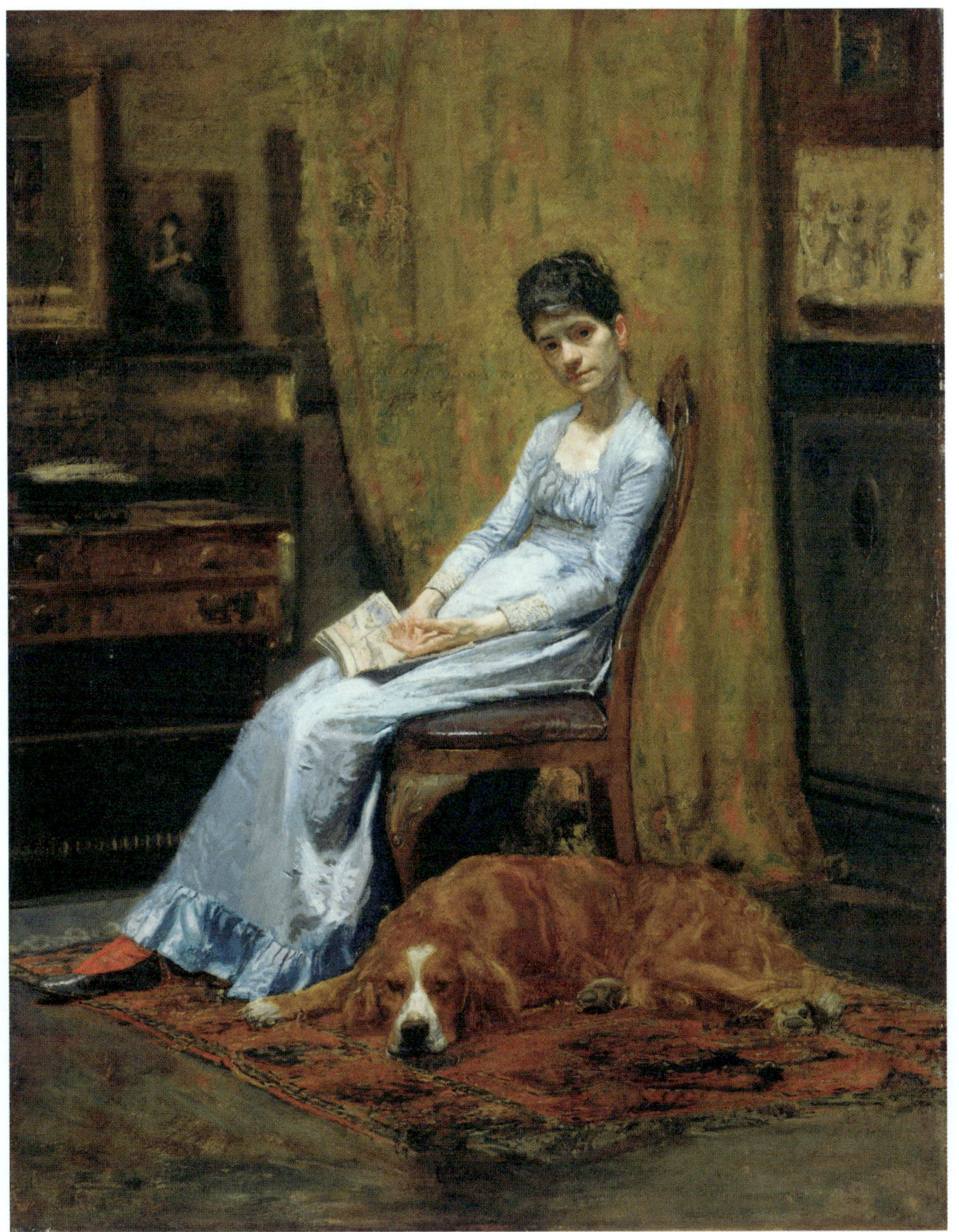

194 Thomas Eakins' wife and their family dog: *The Artist's Wife and his Setter Dog* (1884–9).

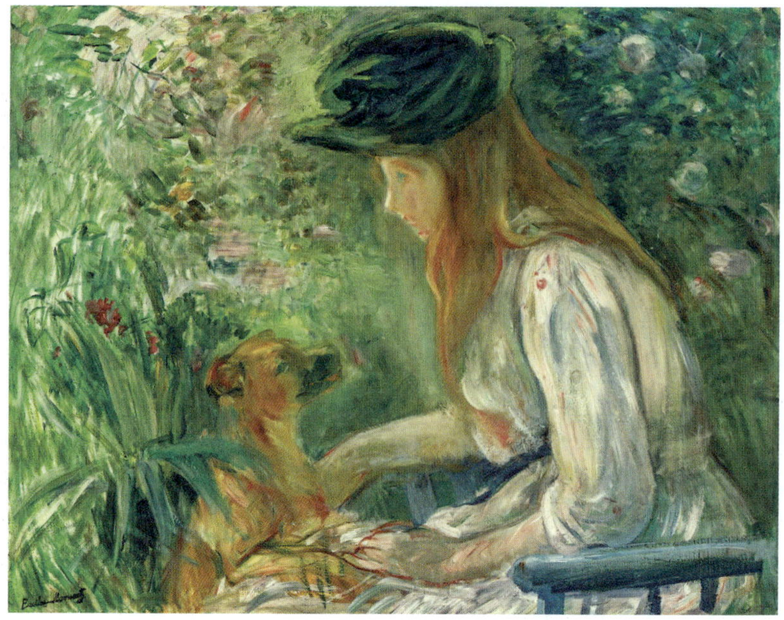

out at the painter; Harry is lying relaxed at her feet looking in the same direction. Not a toy or a lapdog common in many earlier portraits of women, but a family dog. That is why it is there.[24]

What is new about the family portraits of the eighteenth century and onward is not only the social diversity of their subjects, but more importantly, that they are representations of private lives rather than public figures. They idealize domesticity rather than the public authority of the old patriarchal order. They are about couples and mothers and children as much as fathers. Berthe Morisot's *Girl with Dog* [**195**] is in one sense the successor to a long history of paintings of children with dogs but it also exemplifies a new interest in cross-species intimacy and emotional connection. Impressionist art is rich in images like this one. The dog whose domestication represented an epochal change in the history of human communities has become a paradigmatically domestic creature.

This helps us to better appreciate at the same time the appearance of the pornographic dog in art. One of the most striking developments in art that features dogs, and specifically in French art, is the rise of the lapdog as a partner in a game of interspecies frivolity, of a sensuous luxurious world that critics of the *ancien régime* hated, if not of perverse sexuality. (There was a rumour current at the time that when

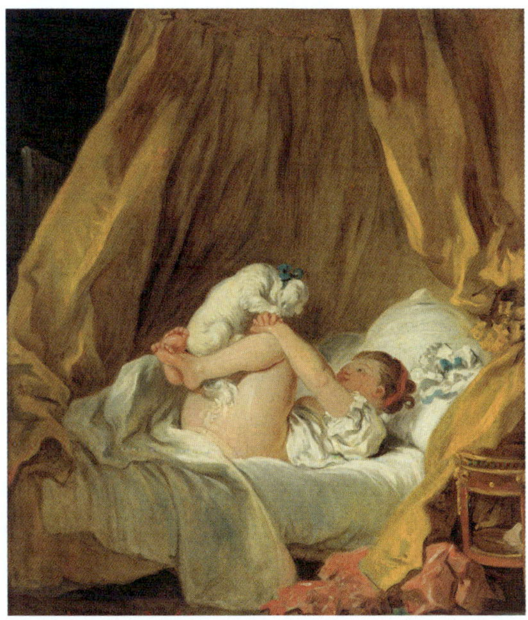

195 (*left*) Berthe Morisot's *Girl with Dog* (1887) pictures the new interest in cross-species emotional connection.

196 (*right*) Fragonard pushes the connection into an erotic realm in *Young Girl Playing with her Dog* (1770).

Marie-Antoinette's little dog Thisbe, who managed to follow her to the guillotine, howled when her head fell, a soldier ran the dog's heart through with a bayonet and proclaimed 'So perish all that mourn an aristocrat.' Another rumour had it that Thisbe drowned when she leapt out of a window of the Tuileries to join her mistress.)[25] The aristocratic lapdog became the visual evil twin of the family dog: the social underbelly of the sentimentalized family portrait. Jean-Honoré Fragonard's *Young Girl Playing with her Dog* is the *locus classicus* for the art of this new form of canine sociality [**196**]. It is a virtuosic painting, an irresistible sketch in colour; it exists in at least four versions by Fragonard himself and in many more engravings that differ in one way or another. And while it is not clear exactly what is happening and who the implied viewer is, the dog is the girl's partner in some sort of auto-erotic fantasy. There is no evidence of this being a post-coital scene. She is engaged in a private, self-absorbed fantasy. A version of this painting – called *Gimlette* (after a type of pastry that she offers) – very quickly made its way into popular prints. Fragonard's painting is a nude version of a larger class of pictures in which dogs are not so much iconographical signs of sexuality like the cat that occasionally appears there but as a participant in the scene itself. In explicit pornography they are active participants.[26]

The Revolutionary Dog

Dogs were transformed by the art of the revolutionary era from the pets of aristocrats into civic heroes and sometimes from agents of oppression to comrades in arms. There are dogs in prints and paintings of the unprecedented political dramas of the age: the revolutions in America, France, Haiti, Greece, and the various national revolutions of 1848. Each of these many images is rooted both in specific socio-political histories and in art-historical traditions.

It is in the American Revolution that the revolutionary dog became iconic. Paul Revere's print of the so-called Boston Massacre on 5 March 1770 became one of the most important pieces of political propaganda in the revolutionary era [**197**]. It was and continues to be widely reproduced; few textbooks of American history are without it.[27]

The image's message is not subtle: the redcoats seem to be enjoying what they are doing – especially the smirking soldier at the end of the line. They are tendentiously depicted as the aggressors whereas in fact the opposite was the case; the Bostonians, mostly labourers, are dressed, improbably, as respectable gentlemen. Blood spurts from one of them; a woman faints in the background but is defended by her compatriots. And square in the middle stands a spotted dog looking out at viewers.[28]

There is an allegorical account of what the dog is doing here: like the colonists, and like the engraver Paul Revere, it is faithful while the British are the revolutionaries who forsake their principles of freedom. There is also the formalist explanation: something needs to be in the space between the two groups to produce the perspective and point of entry for the viewer. Later nineteenth-century versions without the dog make clear the work it does in this version. It stands there patiently – and prominently – demanding that we look at and be part of what is happening. No other animal would do in its place. In either a formalist or an allegorical account there is almost an expectation that a dog would be part of a great event. It is as if the sociability of thousands of years of the dog in art demands its presence here. Faithfulness takes on a new public meaning, a form of civic solidarity in revolution, as elsewhere in public life.

Dogs in visual art of the French Revolutionary period are more difficult to interpret because contemporaries would have seen them in the context of political and philosophical debates about the rights of animals,

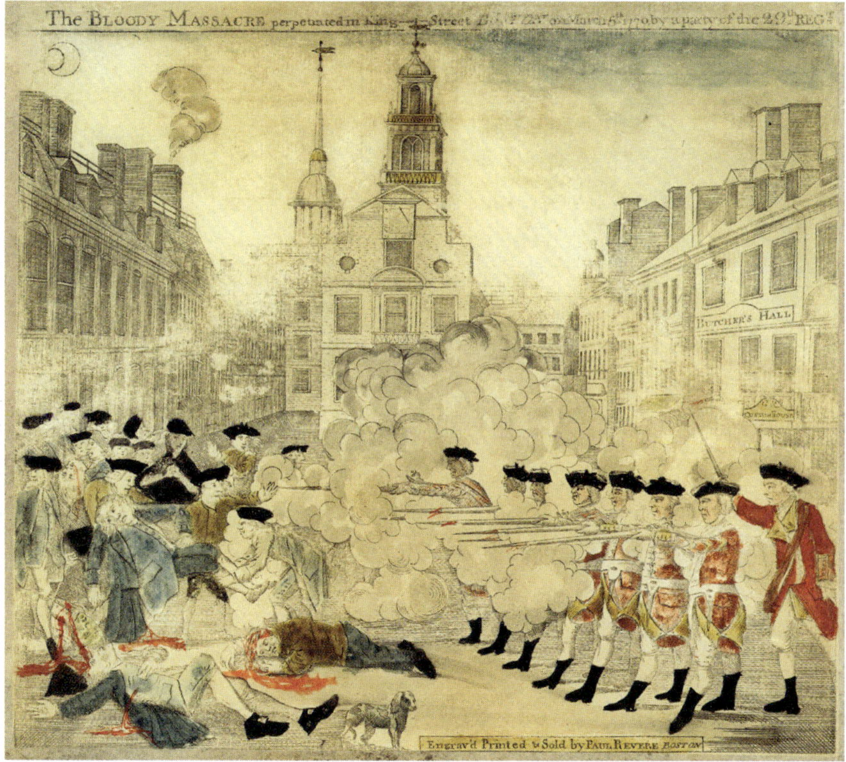

197 Present at history: 'The bloody massacre perpetrated in King Street, Boston' (1770).

the moral meaning of sentiment, and new social policies regarding dogs in particular. The massive dog culls of the *ancien régime* came to an end, for example, as being incompatible with revolutionary values.[29] Dogs were part of this larger story but at the same time were also imagined doing what they supposedly did in life and had done in art in a new social and political setting: old canine behaviours represented in new contexts with new meaning.

The crypto-royalist journalist Louis-Marie Prudhomme writes, for example, about the fate of a dog as a representative of the excesses of the Terror. A judge proposed that the dog belonging to a man who had been guillotined for treason (*lèse-nation*) be tried itself because it attacked Jacobins and went daily to howl at the base of the scaffold where his master had been executed. Apparently, the dog had in fact bitten someone and growled at others but it did not return daily to the site of his master's demise because it was killed a day after he died. The story is new; the

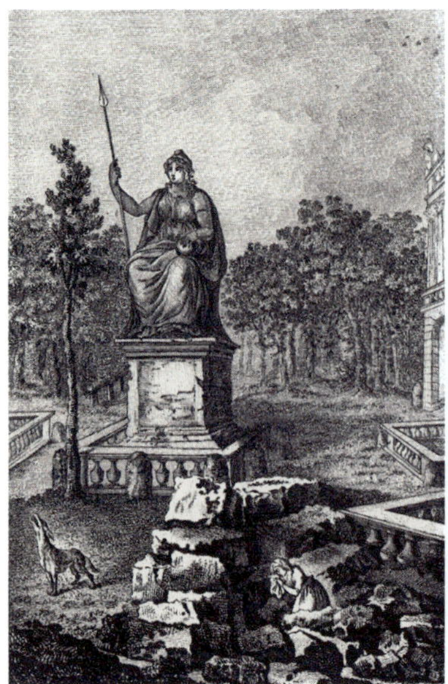
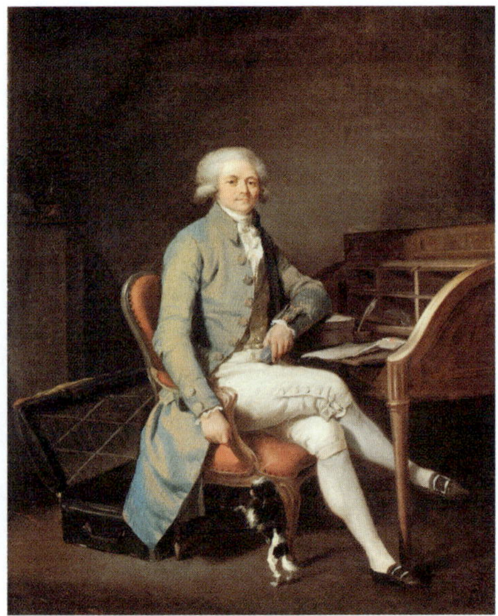

198–199 Crying out: 'Saint-Prix's dog Mourning its Master' (1797, *left*); Louis-Léopold Boilly's portrait of *Maximilien Robespierre* (1783, *right*) with his sweet pre-Revolutionary lapdog.

trope of the mourning dog – in this image a double of the mourning woman – but now it mourns its wrongly executed master [**198**].

A dog is guarding a sleeping *sans-culotte* [**200**], as other dogs guarded St Ursula as she dreamt in Carpaccio's 'Legend of St Ursula' series (*see* 80), for example. The ancient human/canine alliance remains; the meaning of their vigilance has changed.

Robespierre was often seen during the Revolution walking his dog Brount on the Champs-Élysées; a famous portrait of him as a young barrister by Louis-Léopold Boilly shows him working in his office before he became famous. Robespierre as a prominent barrister is looking at his public while the dog is trying to get his master's attention [**199**]. It has become the most widely known portrait of the great 'incorruptible' and one of the architects of the Terror, who in other circumstances was a dog owner at his desk.[30]

The dogs in images of the Haitian Revolution make manifest revolutionary change, as in *The Battle of San Domingo* by January Suchodolski [**201**].[31] Rather than terrorizing slaves (*see* pages 326–35) they have become the allies of slave revolutionaries chasing fleeing whites or standing with the triumphant black leader who holds up the head of an enemy as the Polish troops sent by the French go down to defeat.

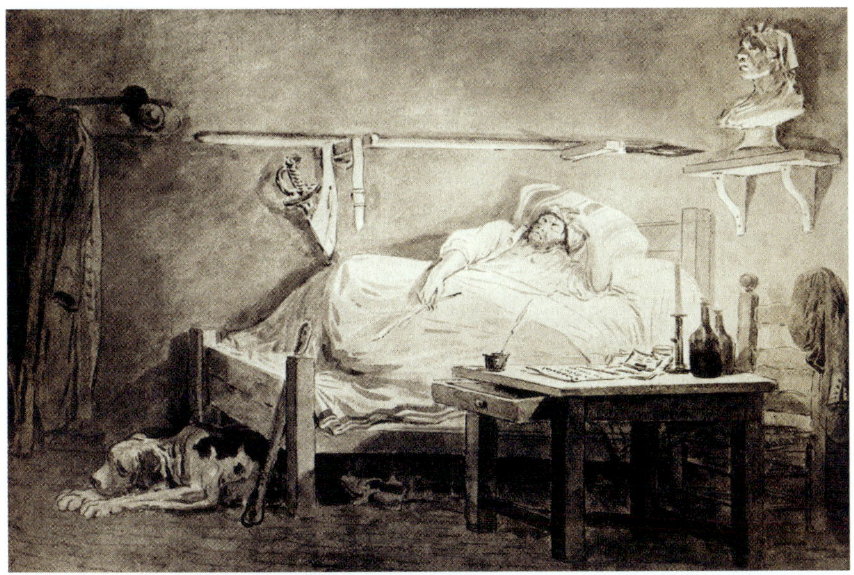

200 Guarding the revolution: Hubert Robert's *The Sleep of Marat* (1793/4).

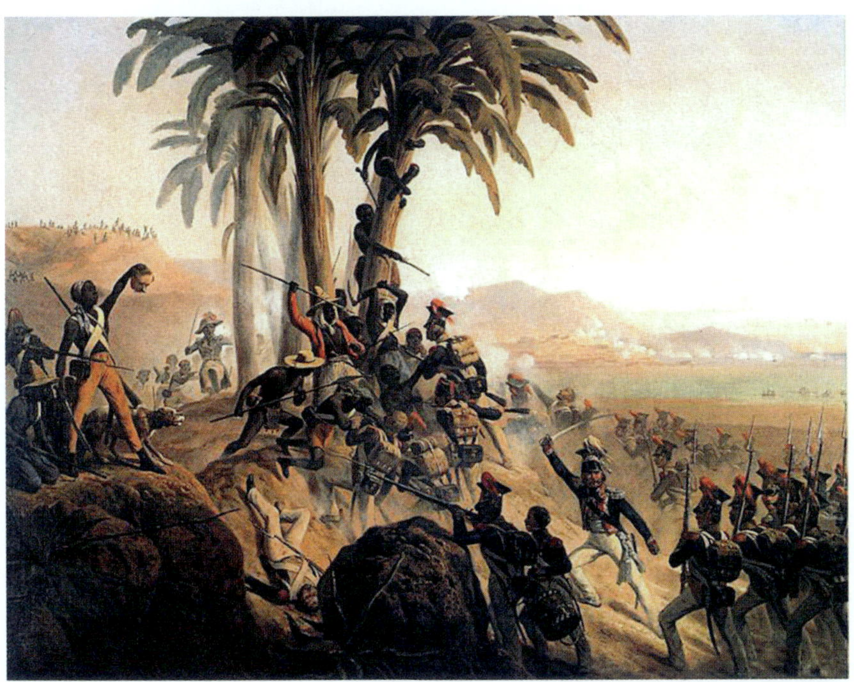

201 Suchodolski imagines dogs as revolutionary allies in *The Battle of San Domingo* (1845).

The Dog Alone

In the late eighteenth century the dog alone in the world became a resonant image in relation to the long tradition of representing its sociability. Loneliness had taken on meaning. Goya's *El Perro* is the first of these mysterious and cosmically unmoored dogs [**202**]. He painted it along with *Saturn Devouring his Children*, *Antropos* (the Fates), *The Two Old Men*, *Witches' Sabbath*, and fourteen other Black Period works on the walls of the house near Madrid where he was living. The paintings, all dealing with mythic, emotionally charged subjects, were transferred to canvas starting in 1874 and given to the Prado in 1881.

This history makes it difficult to describe in a literal sense what we are seeing, much less to interpret the image. When standing before the painting one could almost believe that the dog is looking up at a figure in the sky – or in the void – perhaps a figure of the Virgin. Or maybe we are making too much of shapes that, like clouds, tempt us to read them figuratively. Or maybe we are seeing not the artist's work at all, but the result of the damage done when the painting was transferred, or perhaps the palimpsest of an earlier wall painting. The dog may be drowning in the sea or sinking in quicksand or being overwhelmed by a flood, alone and bereft, or escaping the water. The Prado website identifies the painting as *The Drowning Dog*.

We know that we, and the dog, are looking into an intense field of yellow in various shades that covers most of the canvas above and to the left of a wedge of dark paint along the bottom. The dog's head joins these two fields, these seas of colour. And we know that the eyes of the dog – wide open, beseeching, hollow patches of white with just a hint of its dark iris in a spot of black paint – are looking up into an abyss of brilliant nothingness. *El Perro* – a more agnostic name – now hangs at the far end of a room with Goya's other Black Period pictures. It is where the altar would be if this were a chapel. The painter Joan Miró nearing death asked to be taken to see it for one last time. After half an hour he asked to be taken to see one other painting: *Las Meninas*.[32]

Few paintings have provoked so wide a range of metaphysically charged readings. In some the dog is a doppelgänger once again, but this

202 Goya's cosmically unmoored *El Perro* (c. 1820).

time for bereft humanity. The art historian Lydia Vázquez thinks that 'the dog, humanized and infantilized, displays all the fragility of the child alone in the face of a terrifying reality against which his sole defense is the dream'. Goya's biographer Robert Hughes thought that its 'terrified yearning for safety and its absent master is the misery of man in a comfortless world from which God has withdrawn'. Another critic with a similar sensibility saw it as 'a picture about bare survival in the face of hopeless doom . . . [from which] there is no escape'. Yet another suggested that the ochre sky of the painting represented 'A graveyard of hope, where the canine, drowning in the void, gazes upward not for salvation but in defiance, a stoic rebellion against the cruel silence of fate.'

'A lonesome dog', as Hughes describes it: 'nobody ever saw a lonelier dog – who could be lost in a sandstorm, possibly sinking into quicksand, bewildered by a senseless universe . . . what does it think?' But I also have a sophisticated friend, very knowledgeable about art, who says that she 'always thought the dog is paddling hopefully upwards to safety'. We can conclude little more than what Hughes ends up saying: 'we don't know what it means; but its pathos moves us on a level below narrative.'[33]

El Perro was the first of a line of dogs alone who evoke a sense of the cosmic loneliness of humanity in a godless world or, more prosaically,

203 A lone dog howls in J. M. W. Turner's *Dawn After the Wreck* (*c.* 1841).

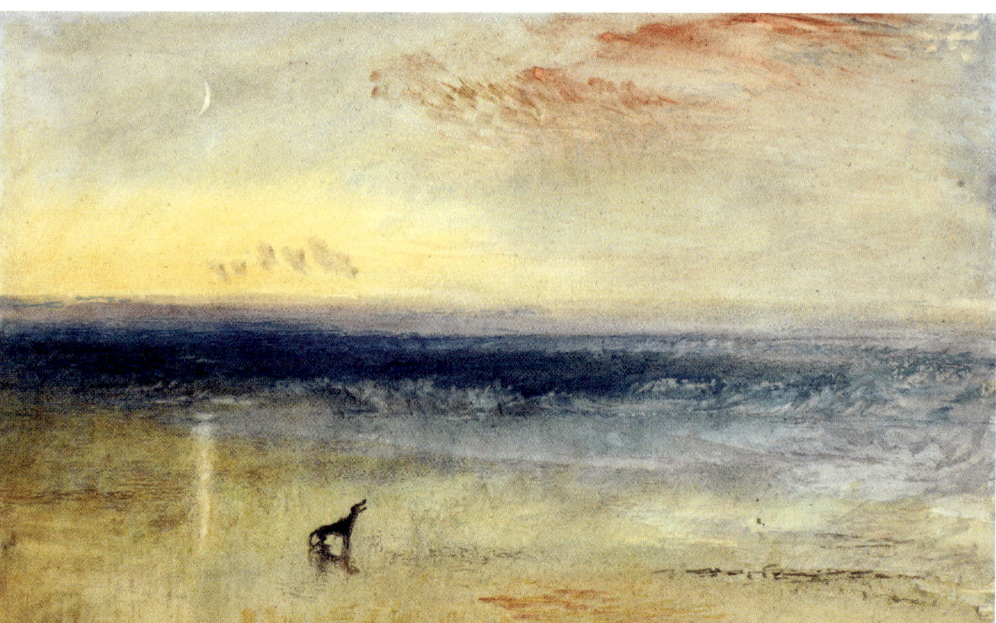

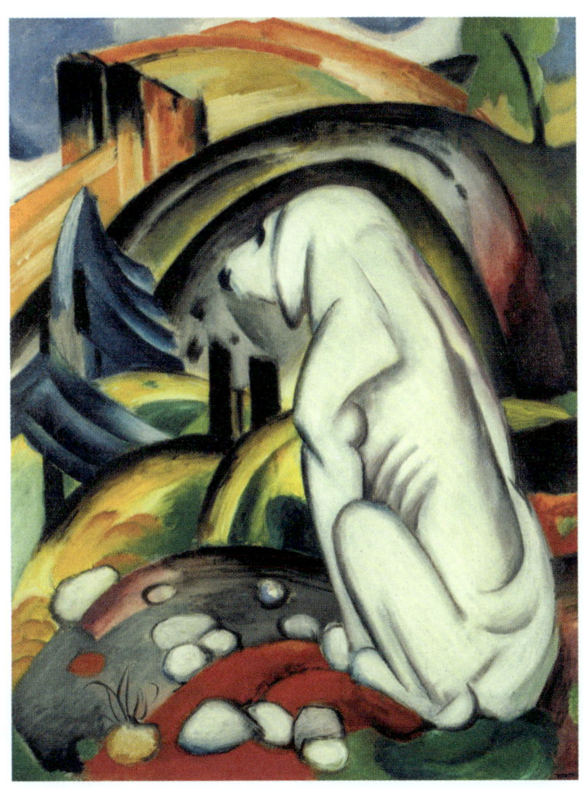

204 Franz Marc's Russian Siberian-shepherd mix models for his *Hund vor der Welt* (1912).

of exclusion from social engagement. There is a thread running from Goya to the present. In Turner's c. 1841 small (25.2 x 36.9 cm) chalk and watercolour *Dawn After the Wreck* a lone dog on an empty stormy beach – 'feeble bloodstain on the sand' as Ruskin thought – howls into an empty and crimson-tinged sky [**203**]. The title is Ruskin's; the shipwreck narrative was invented by him. The melancholy solitude – loneliness might be the better word – of the dog is Turner's invention.

Solitude for humans and for dogs need not, of course, be melancholy or existentially fraught. It can be a condition for being productively with oneself and all creation beyond. That is what distinguishes it from loneliness. The model in Franz Marc's 1912 *Hund vor der Welt* ('The Dog before the World') is exemplary [**204**]. The model is his much-loved Russi, a Russian Siberian-shepherd mix, whom he painted many times in different poses and as an observer in many other paintings – in the Guggenheim's *Yellow Cow* and *In the Rain*, emerging out of a cubist cud of colours in all his whiteness, for example. Russi appears in numerous photographs with

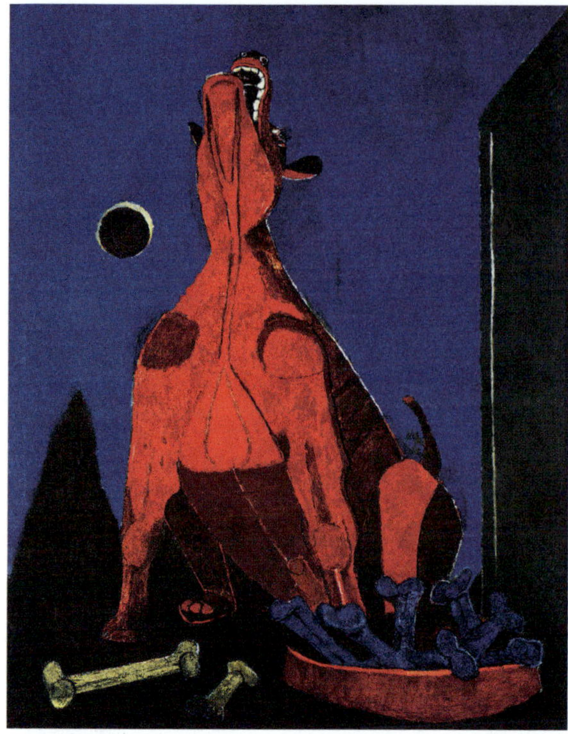

205 (*left*) Rufino Tamayo's *Dog Howling at the Moon* (1942), reflecting pre-Columbian funerary art and Picasso's *Guernica*.

206 (*right*) Paula Rego's *Baying* (1994) from her fearsome 'Dog Woman' series.

Marc and his wife and was also the model for the art of his friends. Marc understood himself, as a painter of animals, to be in search of 'the organic rhythms of all things'. He thought that just as Picasso had discovered how, through cubism, to render the essence of a form, so modern painters ought to be able to capture the essence, '*das sein*', of a dog. Marc was fascinated by thinking about how a dog might think and see its world – 'Ich möchte mal wissen, was jetzt in dem Hund vorgeht.'[34] ('I'd like to know what is going on in a dog's head.')

Hund vor der Welt is an example of Marc's search for a unifying view of the world; an effort to think with animals, and especially with and through his dog Russi, was central. Russi may be looking into an abstract landscape that might suggest a modern German city, but the object of his gaze is less important than its quality and the virtuosity with which he is painted: the knowing head defined by the three black bits of paint that are its nose, eyes, and tips of his ears; the articulation of its haunches that gives it weight; the shadow along the spine. We want to know how this solitary dog sees the world.

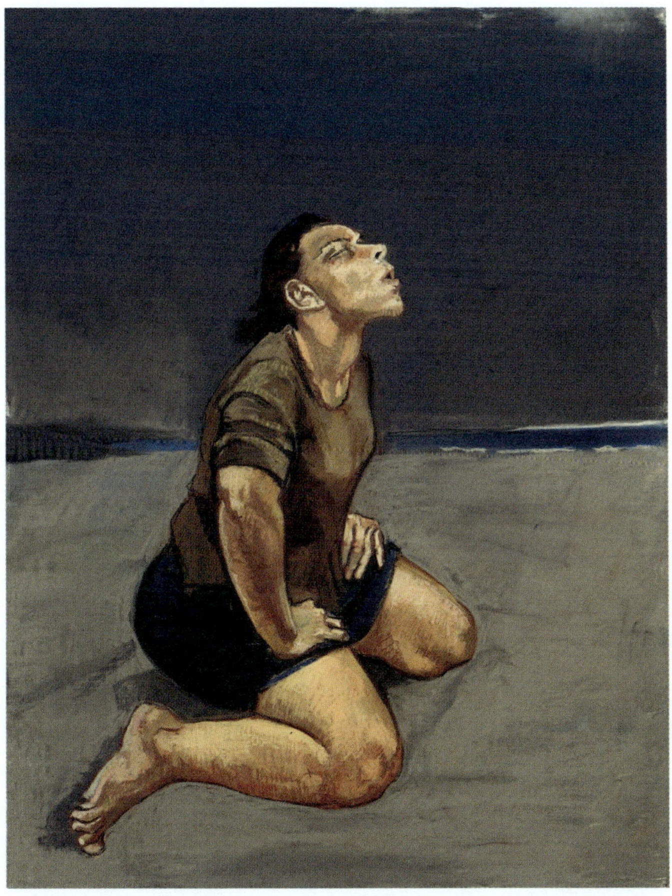

Every painting of a solitary dog asks its own interpretative questions. In *Dog Howling at the Moon* (1942) by the Mexican modernist painter Rufino Tamayo – one of a number he painted, all in one way or another tormented – the dog is desperate, straining, blood red [**205**]. Its veins are bulging. At its feet on the ground and in a bowl are strewn meatless bones: a canine Golgotha. Painted in the shadow of the Second World War and influenced by the agonized horse in Picasso's *Guernica*, which he had studied, as well as by the dogs in pre-Columbian Colima funerary art, this is a dog at the edge of an abyss. Tamayo's dog seems an ancestor of the ferocious, emotionally fraught figure in Paula Rego's *Baying*, one of fourteen paintings from her 'Dog Woman' series in which she imagines herself as a dog in various poses and places, including this one 'howling at the moon' [**206**].[35]

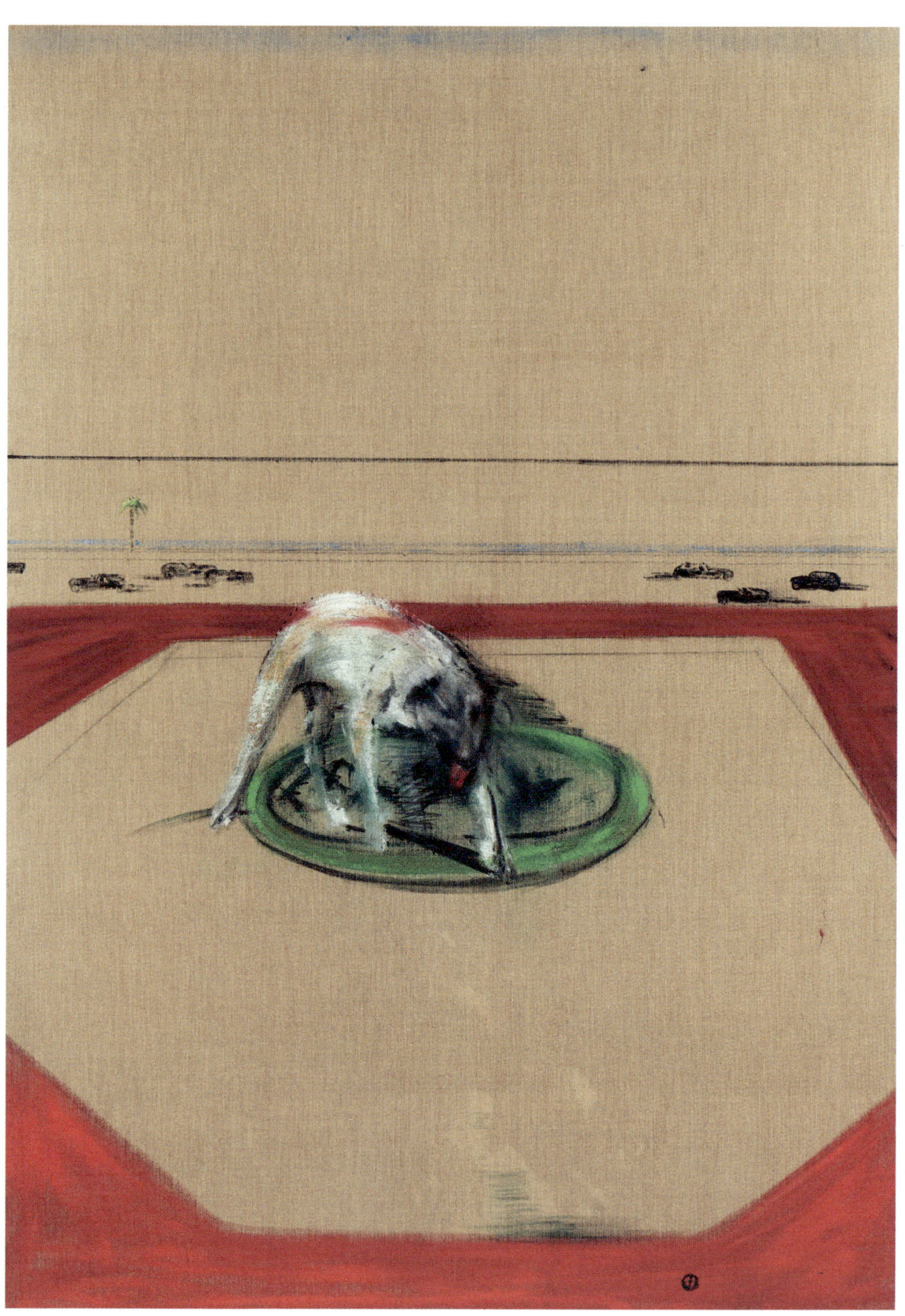

207 A metaphysical loneliness: Francis Bacon's *Dog* (1952).

Francis Bacon's 1952 *Dog* is in many ways a paradigmatic example of how the dog isolated from its social world becomes a synecdoche for the human dilemma in a disenchanted world [**207**]. Frenzied, madly in motion – Bacon studied the work of the photographer Eadweard Muybridge on the question of motion itself – the dog becomes close to the human world without God in which 'we are identical to animals in the inevitability of our mortal plights'. In some of his other dog pictures the dogs are posed alone on streets above sewer grates or cowering in a gutter, in the wind and rain. There is something pure about the artist's identification with the deracinated dog.[36] There are no humans in any of these pictures; the dogs are less commentaries on the social isolation of their species than they are a way of thinking about metaphysical loneliness.

Strays, in the sense of homeless and person-less, living among but not with humans, are another matter: as subjects of art, they are of recent vintage even though the majority of the world's dogs have been and are stray in this sense. They are representative not of existential loneliness but of isolation in an atomized social world. The most famous example is the dog in Georges Seurat's *A Sunday Afternoon on the Island of La Grande Jatte* [**208**]. Seurat spent two years making twenty-eight drawings, twenty panels, and three canvases perfecting the painting's structure and researching pointillist technique. 'I want to make modern people, in their essential traits,' he wrote, 'move about as they do on those friezes, and place them on canvases organized by harmonies of color.'[37] He was referring to the Parthenon. There are three studies of the dog. One seems specifically to be a study of what it is – or in any case what it looks like – to be a dog alone, a dog that does not belong in this human world [**209**].

The whole painting is about the fragmentation of modern urban life, its unknowability. Viewers of the picture might make a story of any one figure or group of figures although that too is not so easy, but there is nothing that binds these groups together other than the fact that each one of them, unknown to one another, is enjoying their leisure on an island in the Seine on a sunny day. The black collarless dog stands out in its isolation. If not quite the axis of the painting it is very close, a dark entry for the eye into the scene, front and almost centre. It stands out also in contrast to the little dog wearing a collar and running happily in its direction, who is not alone but with the woman and

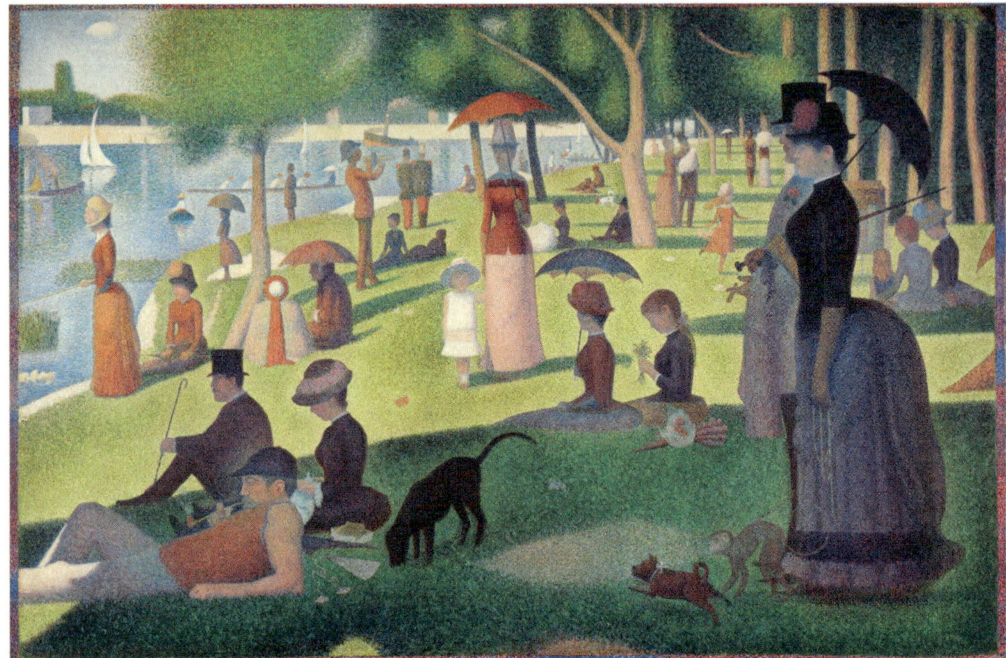

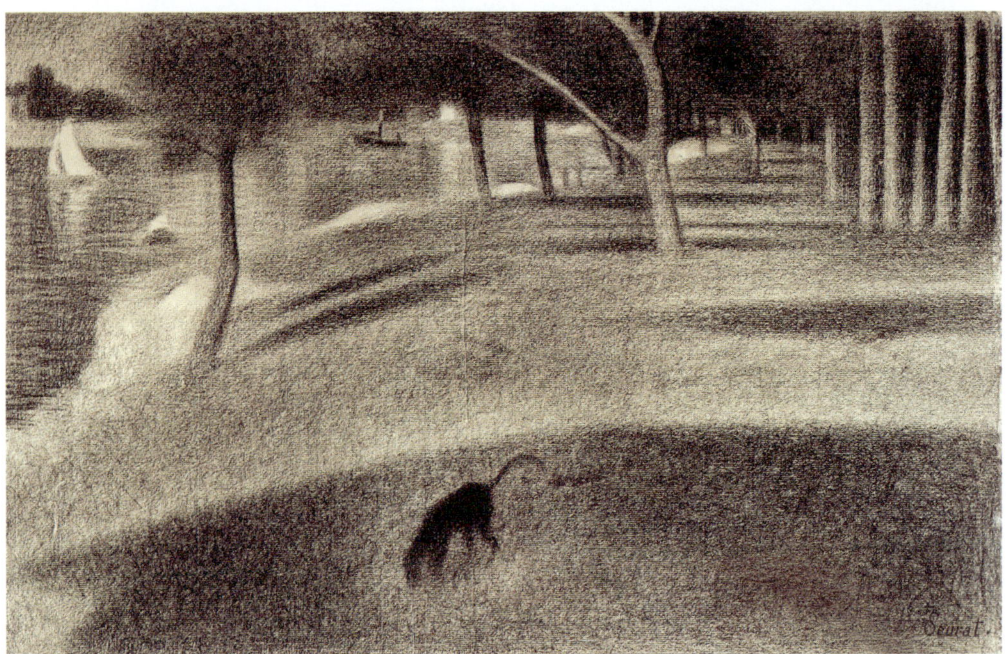

208-209 Georges Seurat's *A Sunday Afternoon on the Island of La Grande Jatte* (1884-6) and a preliminary study of the black dog at the heart of the painting.

her exotic pet. The black dog is alone, perhaps sniffing for food. It is with no one. It is a stark contrast to the brown dog curled up to its owner in Seurat's *Bathers at Asnières* (*Une Baignade, Asnières*) in the National Gallery in London.

The nineteenth-century viewer might well have seen Seurat's dog in the way a twentieth-century critic does: 'the interloper, hooligan and insurgent who upsets conventional social structures', or put differently, 'the vengeful representative of the outcasts and the declasses, a symbol of antagonism, subversion'.[38] But in the context of the tradition of dogs in art since Goya, this one seems less a politically fraught creature than a lonely and isolated one.

Reinventing Tradition

Modernity brought with it a new kind of historical consciousness – not emulation, as with neo-classicism, but rather commentary: the appropriation of tradition for new ends. The Metropolitan Museum's 2014 *Untitled (Studio)* by the African-American artist Kerry James Marshall is grounded in a specific historical past of the dog's gaze and its place in studies and studios, and generally in the dog's ubiquitous thereness in the spaces of humans.[39] It brings the past of canine sociability into the present, minus the iconography: a vernacular successor to Carpaccio's *St Augustine in his Study* (*see* 76), a dog in a scholar's or artist's space, keeping company. And yet it is not without an interpretive twist. The wall label says that the painting recounts an oft-remembered 'episode from [the artist's] childhood in which he . . . visited the studio of his idol [and later teacher] Charles White (1918–1979)', and came to realize that 'making pictures was something that he, too, could do'. It is about 'the discovery of a Black artist's studio' as a 'place of work where an allegorical catalogue of all modes of art making are on display' and as a place rich in the history of painting.[40] It is a specific moment in time, embedded in a particular story.

The label says nothing about the hard-to-miss dog. What is it doing there? It is not an allegorical dog or a dog emblematic of the scores of things dogs have purportedly been emblematic of in the history of art. It is not there because art is imitating nature, at least we have no reason to believe that there was a dog in White's studio, that Marshall was painting an actual studio visit from memory and wanted to get it right. Nor is it a tribute to dogs in White's work. His subjects were 'images of dignity' – lone Black figures – and historical paintings like *Five Great American Negroes* (Howard University Art Gallery, Washington DC). As far as I know, White never painted a dog. And finally, this is not a narrative painting that needs a dog to tell its story.

Formally, the dog is in the painting because it is the base of a triangle of yellows – the dog, the glass, and the sleeve of the man undressing behind the red screen – that, like the head of an arrow, push the picture – and our gaze – up and to the right. It offers instructions about how we should be looking. The dog under the brown table is in a frame within a frame within a frame – the shadows, the table legs, and, of course, the painting's borders. The dog's gaze directs our eyes to the standing woman assistant, who in turn is looking out at where the photographer – or the painter – and we, the viewers, are standing.

It is hard to describe what is happening in the picture: the assistant arranging the model's pose could be looking out at a photographer who is asking for an adjustment of the lighting; or there might be no photographer there at all. The painter – if he is in the studio – is off to the left outside the frame contemplating the portrait of the model – the woman in the chair – who he is painting against a red background. A half-finished portrait sits on the easel. (Or is the woman in the paint-smeared smock the artist?) The man undressing behind the screen whose yellow sleeve has caught our attention could be the man who is modelling by the window to the left. It is a painting that seems easy to read but becomes increasingly puzzling the more one looks at it: a rethinking of Velázquez in his studio painting *Las Meninas* (*see* 92). Marshall's dog, unlike Velázquez's, is not 'dark'; it is bright. It is 'prominent and gives great harmony' to the painting, as Velázquez's first biographer noted of its art-historical ancestor. *Untitled (Studio)* would not be what it is without the dog, and it is a figure as much of the past as the present.

There are lots of historical allusions to the history of art in this painting: portraiture, of course; the dog from *Las Meninas*; the skull and *memento mori* from Holbein's *The Ambassadors* (National Gallery, London); the delicately painted vase with its flowers and the still life from a host of paintings. These and the formal elements create the sense of comfort that fits with the dog in the studio. It is happy under the table watching humans; it gives the scene a settled, grounded quality; its grey shadow is almost like a stone base; like the dogs in Veronese's *Wedding Feast at Cana* (*see* 88), it is weighty. And like the dog in *Las Meninas*, it is accustomed to being with artists. It is patient, even interested and perhaps even empathetic with the struggles of creativity. The yellow dog in Marshall's painting is, finally, also a homage to the long tradition of dogs in studies and studios as discussed in chapter 4.

The makers of art and their subjects – the implied photographer and/or painter in the painting, the woman adjusting the subject's gaze, the man taking off his clothes – are all busy doing what they are doing. The dog seems to be doing little or nothing but is watching, witnessing, keeping people company. Being there. And in doing that it is not only being social but representing 'sociability' in the same way as the dog does in Dürer's *St Eustache* (*see* 98) some four hundred years earlier.

Marshall's dogs do that in some of his other works as well: the dog running beside black children, one riding a bike and another being chased by the dog, in *Our Town*, is an idealized and ironic account of suburban life in which blacks are enjoying what had historically been denied them. But it is also rooted in the art of children at play with dogs that goes back to the eighteenth century, if not earlier: the sociable dog being there at whatever we do. It is an allusion to the history of dogs and humans at play that extends from the Renaissance to the present. And it is an allusion to another past time – the past time of slavery when such dogs were used to capture runaway slaves.[41] Marshall's work constitutes a historically specific, and in some cases ironic, reinvention of a very long and seemingly timeless tradition for new social, political, and aesthetic ends. The timeless has become timely, even contemporary.

CHAPTER 6

Dogs and the Moral Imagination

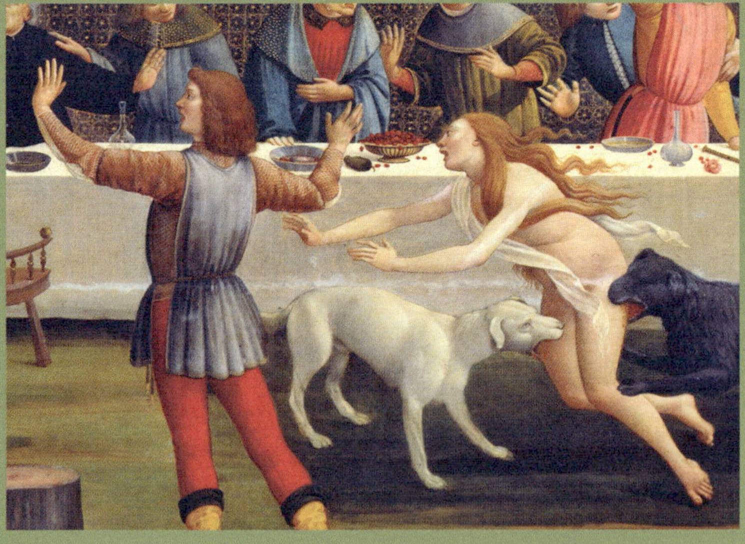

Desperate dogs: Detail from 230, Sandro Botticelli's *The Banquet in a Pine Forest* (1483).

IF A THOUSAND YEARS from now the only record of what humans thought of dogs was based on art, the historians and anthropologists of the future would get a distorted picture. Artists have shown no interest in representing the long history of the cruel treatment that dogs have suffered: no evidence of the great dog mass murders of Enlightenment Paris, where stray dogs were unceremoniously killed, before and after the Revolution, because of their association with disease and the dangerous lower orders; nor of Mexico City, where, between 1770 and 1821, colonial watchmen slaughtered some 25,000 to 30,000 dogs. There are no representations of the so-called Hayirsizida Massacre in 1910 Constantinople, when 80,000 dogs were rounded up and dumped on a bare island where they died a slow and painful death, their cries heard by the city's inhabitants; nor of the Hong Kong dog purge of the 1970s. The visual record says little of the abject dog pounds of the nineteenth and twentieth centuries and the casual cruelties of humans over the millennia.[1]

There are also very few traces in the vast visual archive of a long litany of negative things that have been written about and done to dogs. Already in the age of Homer and Hesiod dogs were described as, on the one hand, near human, but, on the other hand, as humans of the lowest sort: degraded; dirty; aggressive; on the brink of madness and thus the cause of rabies; shameless.[2] Dogs were scavengers, who went so far as to eat their own and others' vomit, excrement, and who knows what else. They have had a reputation for sexual promiscuity that goes back well before cats took that rap; and dogs copulated and defecated and urinated in public. To call someone a dog was an insult, and in parts of the ancient Near East it was polluting to touch one. None of this is represented by visual artists in the Western tradition – and very little in that of other cultures.

But when it is, it's with a moral twist that takes us back to Diogenes the dog philosopher. He embraced his life on the streets, shamelessly eating, sleeping, defecating, and having sex in public – living like a dog – to make the point that we, like them, are material creatures with material needs. He was sceptical of the civilizational boundaries between man and animal. Socrates was condemned to death for impiety and for corrupting the morals of the city's youth. Diogenes went much further in his life and teaching. Plato thought of him as a Socrates figure gone mad; the archetypal counter-cultural figure. It is in this sense, as drawing attention to the human-like qualities of animals, that the shameless dog enters art as a stand-in for the human who is a material creature with bodily needs.

A few moralizing Dutch genre pictures in which copulating dogs prefigure what the humans are about to do are really paintings about humans, announcing and condemning none too subtly that they are like dogs. Rembrandt's version of this theme is different. He was accused by Samuel Dirksz van Hoogstraten, one of his generally admiring pupils, of indecency, indeed of marring a beautiful composition full of expressive human faces, by putting copulating dogs (barely visible in a corner) in his grisaille *St John the Baptist Preaching* (Gemäldegalerie, Berlin). 'One would think,' he charged, 'that it represented the preaching of Diogenes instead of St John.'[3] This is again a charge less against dogs or even humans than against the painter's sense of decorum, a criticism he might well have been courting.

As for dogs defecating, they are doing it on the handles of an ancient Greek kylix while two satyrs masturbate on the front. Low-life stuff with which Diogenes would align himself – he was said to masturbate in public – but rare.

There is the occasional dog defecating in medieval manuscripts, but then little more until the genre art of the Dutch Golden Age when the pooping dog became something of a sub-genre. They are there in paintings mostly for the effect of humorous reality, doing in public what humans often also do publicly. Or the dogs are there for the sheer incongruity of their presence: the dog relieving itself and occupying a bit of empty canvas in Philip Wouwerman's *March of the Armies*. This is the art of ordinary life and would be otherwise unremarkable if it were not for Rembrandt, who added a pooping dog to his modest painting of the *Good Samaritan* in the Wallace Collection, when he reworked it in one of his most important works on paper [**210-211**].

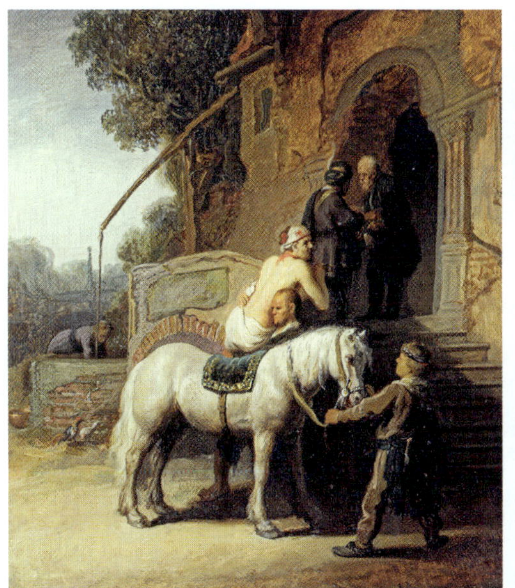
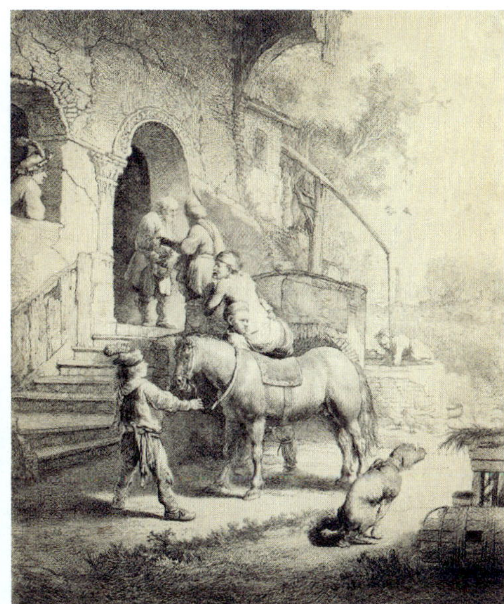

210–211 Rembrandt's *Good Samaritan*: first as an oil painting (1630, *left*) and then as a much more famous work on paper with the addition of a pooping dog (1634, *right*).

The dog is the first thing we see in the etching, right up front in a field of light; we notice it well before we see the hero of the story, the Good Samaritan, whose back is turned to us. We cannot but see the dog, although Goethe managed to write a whole essay about the etching in his *Rembrandt the Thinker* without noticing it. (For him the drama was in the face of the injured man, who thinks he sees his attacker in the inn's window.) As Simon Schama says, the dog has sent scholars 'rushing and blushing for primly learned explanations', which they have not found. Perhaps they are looking for too deep an explanation. In the midst of a morally uplifting scene the dog goes on with its ordinary life in a peasant courtyard. It is there to remind us of its and our materiality, a reminder that the borders of nature and culture can be, and are, breached. That is also what the dogs who attacked their master in accounts of the death of Actaeon remind us of. The dog in Rembrandt is in its own world, dreamily staring off into the distance as it relieves itself. Or rather, it reminds us that there are other worlds.[4]

Dogs represented peeing in public – in churches and town squares – mostly in a few seventeenth-century Dutch genre paintings, seem harmless. Everyone relieved themselves in public in those pre-public

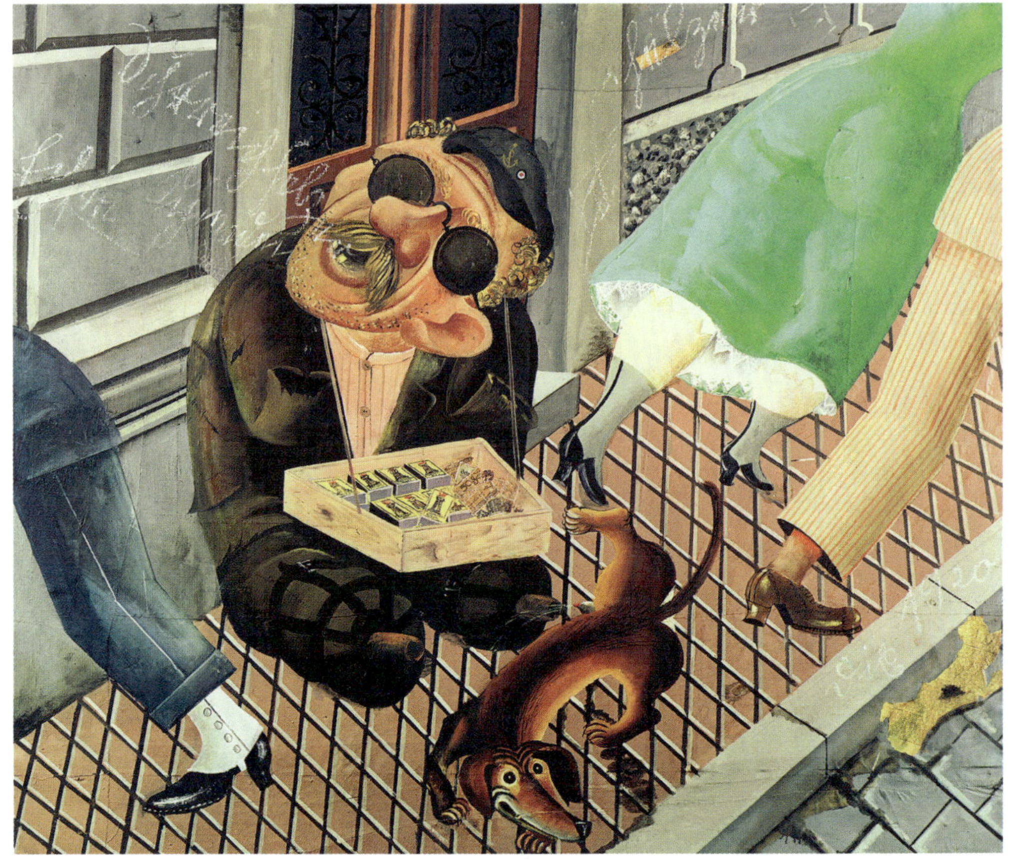

212 Otto Dix's *The Match Seller* (1920). The dachshund peeing on the beggar represents the callous passers-by, *die auf ihm scheissen.*

toilet days; these dogs are in the service of the reality effect. But sometimes they get our attention in ways that suggest a moral judgement: in Otto Dix's painting *The Match Seller* [**212**], for example, in which a dachshund, staring manically out of the frame of the picture, is peeing on a blind, legless veteran of the Great War sitting on the sidewalk. It is a savage indictment not of the dog but of the humans who hurry past – only their legs visible in flight. The dog is at worst clueless; it is the well-dressed and mobile humans who are metaphorically pissing on the beggar – to use the English colloquial expression – who are Dix's real targets. (In German one would say '*auf ihm scheissen*' – to shit on him – which is probably what Dix was saying about them but could not represent visually.)[5]

The Better than Human Dog

Most of the dogs we have seen are good dogs. There is, however, one great dog – an exceptionally good dog – in the Western tradition who is there because it helped a saint – St Roch – after humans abandoned him to his fate: a special case of the friend of last resort. Born to a noble family in fourteenth-century France, Roch renounced inherited wealth, became a pilgrim, and ministered in his travels to those stricken by the plague. He miraculously cured them regardless of their social standing, the poor as well as an English cardinal, until he himself fell victim. The citizens of Piacenza threw him out and left him to die in the surrounding forests.

But God made a spring arise next to his shelter to provide water and sent a better-than-human dog – not Roch's dog but a creature that God chose for the mission – to bring him bread [**213**]. Clearly a special dog who did not eat the food intended for another. In some versions of the story, the dog also licked his wounds until they were healed, an allusion to a long line of thaumaturgic dogs that stretches back to the ancient

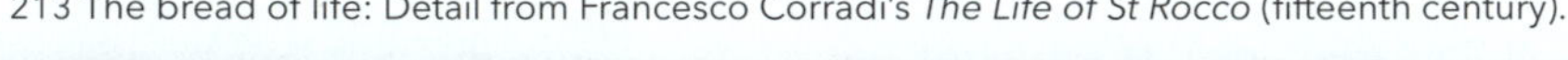

213 The bread of life: Detail from Francesco Corradi's *The Life of St Rocco* (fifteenth century).

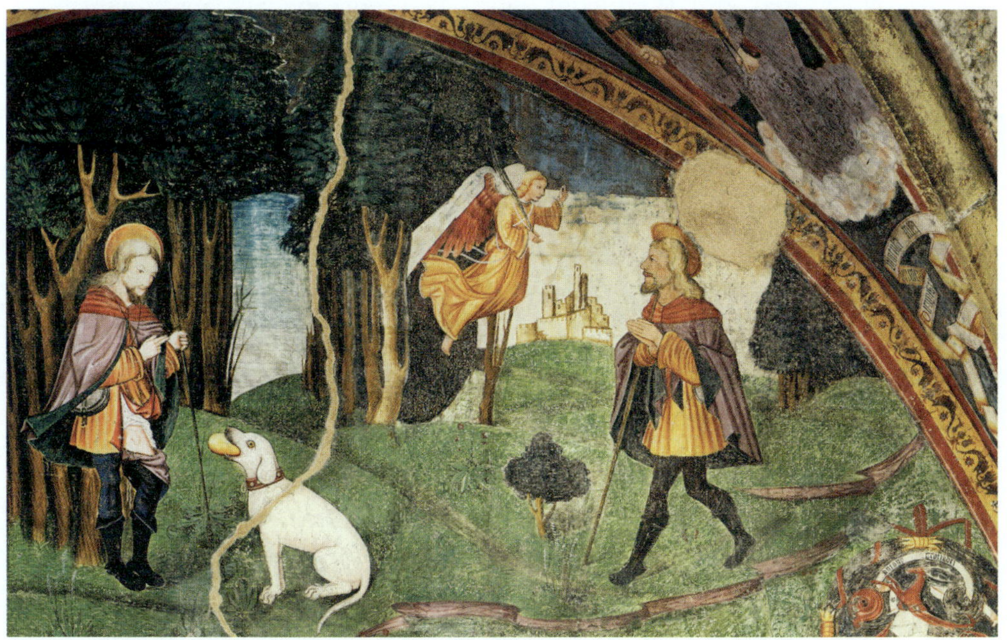

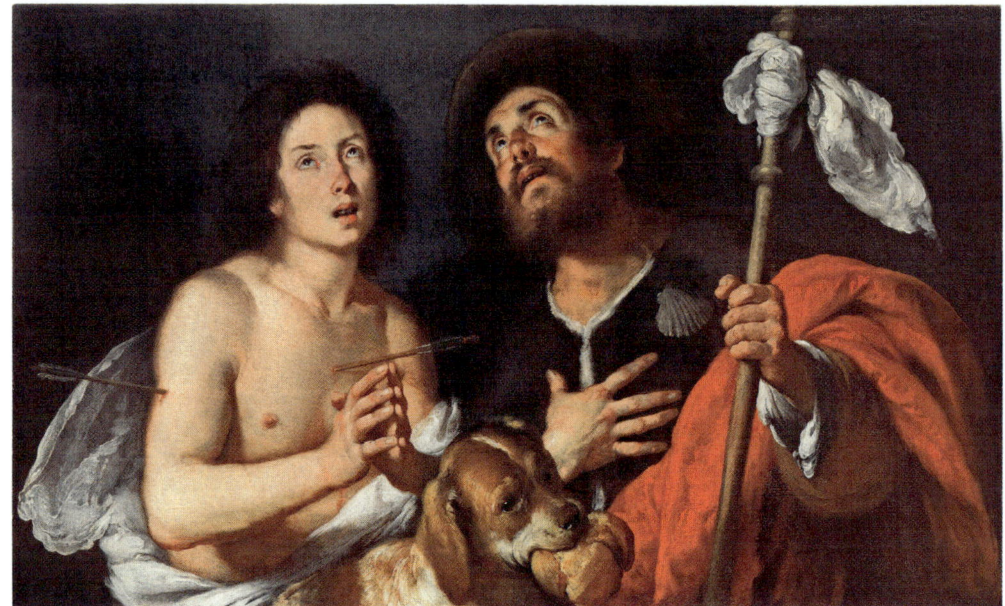

214 *St Sebastian and St Roch* (1635–6) by Bernardo Strozzi, a forerunner of his monumental portrait of the saint in the Scuola Grande di San Rocco.

Near East. The story gave rise to scores of paintings and stained glass as well as mass-produced icons and votives from modest late fifteenth-century Italian frescoes, to an early sixteenth-century French statue in the Cloisters of the New York Metropolitan Museum, to Bernardo Strozzi's painting of the saint as a pilgrim in Venice's monumental Scuola Grande di San Rocco (Confraternity of St Roch) [**214**], to mass-produced votive candles sold at the healing shrine of Lourdes with images of the great dog attending to the saint whom humans had abandoned.

Does it make sense to make these sorts of moral judgements about dogs, good or bad? In all the art in this book the dog is represented as having a mental and emotional life: affections, interests, pleasures, desires, and general social competence. That is why, as we have seen, they can be a second self of artists and viewers and can be so intimately bound to human figures. The dog therefore seems to have agency, which would make it a moral actor. Why then are they so seldom if ever portrayed as being agents of evil?

This was not for artists nor is it for me a jurisprudential or philosophical question. It is about the dog's ability to think and solve problems inside a human-established, and historically grounded, set of rules about sociability and what constitutes acceptable versus unacceptable behaviour. No one these days believes that a dog can make moral judgements about the rules themselves, although miraculous dogs like the one that fed St Roch can and even in secular instances a dog might disobey what we take to be a morally deviant order. Dogs do not have the sort of reason that allows them to have *mens res* – the criminal intent to commit a wrong act like biting someone. Their master might be guilty of using them for an immoral or illegal act, but they are guiltless. Indeed, it is their innocence – their intrinsic guilelessness – that we find morally attractive and that is violated by their ill-use by humans.

Whether we believe they can act morally or not depends on one's view of the foundations of moral action: if it is based on reason, the capacity to know and understand rules and principles, probably not; if we believe ethical behaviour is grounded in emotions and sentiments, as Adam Smith for example argued, because we want to be well regarded by those watching our actions, it seems possible. In that sense dogs might be thought of as moral agents.[6]

But the question of dogs in the moral imagination as represented in art has less to do with these sorts of questions than with how the dog's actions comport with human values, with our actions and values. Chrysippus's dog may or may not have found the rabbit it was chasing by using reason to choose the right path without first smelling it, but it has not decided on the morality of hunting. Dogs have for longer than any other animal shared our social world, and their place in our moral imagination is therefore about how they comport themselves in that world in relation to us, about what we ask of them. They aim to please: do we ask them to do wrong? Do we betray their trust? Three nineteenth-century debates revolve around these issues: about evolution, animal experimentation – vivisection – and slavery. The case of Charles Darwin has produced little art although many pictures of the great man's dogs. But it illustrates how central the question of the place of the dog's moral status was in the intellectual revolution that the theory of evolution had wrought in the nineteenth century.

The Consciousness of Dogs

'Conscience' became for Charles Darwin what 'reason' had been during the long debate about the essential difference between humans and other animals, but with this important difference: his interests were in continuity; there were for him no natural borders to be defended. He spent an enormous amount of intellectual energy thinking about how evolution could account for rational thought and be a guide to 'moral action' and conscience. There was no fixity of species, each created in its distinct niche.[7] Species came into being through natural selection and the subsequent inheritance of variations that suited, and gave advantage to, an organism in a particular environment. This principle operated from the lowest to the highest creature on the phylogenic scale.

In the epochal *On the Origin of Species* (1859), Darwin said little directly about how this might affect how we were to understand ourselves in relation to the rest of animate creation. His task was to adduce as much evidence as possible for his theory without entering into extraneous controversies. In *The Descent of Man, and Selection in Relation to Sex* (1871) he added sexual to natural selection as a motor of evolution but, more importantly, he made explicit the claim that we too descended from pre-existing forms and the claim for monogenesis, that the races of man, different as they might seem, all descended from the same root. More radically still, he also claimed that human psychology, language, religion, and culture more generally – even music whose advantages for survival puzzled him but that he was sure existed – could be understood within an evolutionary framework.

And finally, in the third of the trilogy, *The Expression of the Emotions in Man and Animals* (1872), Darwin made a sustained case, with a great deal of evidence, for the continuity of human and non-human animal psychology. Conscience, the supposedly unique capacity of the human to know right from wrong, became the crux of the argument. It too, he said, was a product of natural causes. Reason did not distinguish humans from the rest of creation and neither did the capacity to act morally.

Darwin's break from earlier thought on the question of animal conscience was precipitous. For many Enlightenment thinkers it had been settled by Descartes in the seventeenth century. Animals were sophisticated machines who, far from having a conscience, did not even feel pain, or suffer, as humans did, because they did not have an immaterial soul. For others, the question had been settled more than two thousand years earlier by Aristotle. Animals had animal souls that accounted for their sense perception and locomotion and the other things they had to do to stay alive. But they did not have the higher, rational soul that accounted for intellect and more generally for what it was to be human – the ability to moderate behaviour in accord with reason.

The existence and extent of an animal conscience became a crux in natural history well before Darwin. The 1749 *Histoire Naturelle* by Georges-Louis Leclerc, Comte de Buffon, was a bestseller in France and abroad. In it he argued that the existence of a conscience marked the indisputable, fundamental difference between humans and other animals. This was not because Buffon believed in the Genesis story of a God-given fixity of species – to the contrary, he thought that nature was constantly in flux. Darwin in fact regarded Buffon as one of his few predecessors.[8]

But on the big question – that of continuity – they differed fundamentally. Buffon thought that non-human animals may seem to be jealous, to show affection, to act out of loyalty. (*Vide* the dog in all the art we have seen.) But behind these appearances, they are 'actuated by appetites alone' while 'man is governed by superior principle'. Any doubts on this point are because we don't know enough yet about how appetites on their own can produce effects in animals and we know too little about how they work in us because of 'the difficulty we have to distinguish what we do in virtue of knowledge, and what we do by the mere force of appetite'.

An animal's consciousness of existence is solely dependent on sensations whereas ours – at least 'ours' when we are being fully human – depends on reason. The soul of man is of a superior sort, a spiritual substance, 'entirely different in its essence and action from the nature of the external senses' which determine animal behaviour. This is, of course, pure metaphysics but Buffon is certain about what is inside – or rather not inside – the black box of the animal mind even if he cannot quite account for why. Darwin rejected his arguments not based on an alternative materialist anti-metaphysics but on what he took to be empirical evidence derived in large measure from his interpretations of how dogs behaved.

By the time of the debate over animal, specifically dog, conscience, everyone involved accepted the general outlines of Darwinian evolution.

At stake was whether it went beyond structure and function – anatomy and physiology – to answer questions about moral capacity. Challenges came from close to home. In September 1868, Darwin received a letter from George Rolleston, Linacre Professor of Physiology at Oxford and a prodigy of T. H. Huxley, his great defender and so-called 'bulldog'. Rolleston was willing to accept that humans and animals were on a continuum of mental traits and that these were a result of evolutionary pressures: 'that a man's ratiocinative powers are qualitatively not dissimilar from those of the lower animals and very largely dependent upon his material organization may be granted'.

But like Buffon a hundred years before, Rolleston drew the line at consciousness of the sort on which conscience depended: 'Here,' he insists, 'the question of the difference of soul or life from spirit comes in.' Descartes is right: lower animals were merely animated machines. Rolleston included with his letter an excerpt from an article by Henry Alford, a Biblical scholar and Dean of Canterbury Cathedral, in the January 1868 issue of the religious magazine *Good Words*, in which Alford says he is comfortable with the basic claims of evolution: continuity of body and intelligence between man and lower animals; there was no special creation species by species. But continuity stops at the chasm of conscience:[9]

> It is the impregnable conviction of our race, unaffected by any adverse theories of philosophers that between the lowest intelligent man and the highest intelligent animal, there is a gulf fixed, impassable by any mere intensification or deprecation of existing faculties.

That gulf is the product of our knowledge of God. We know him, says Alford, because God has endowed us with a conscience that 'no mere animal' has. It might, he admits, seem otherwise. 'An animal can be trained, by reward or punishment, to the *simulate* possession of conscience – to behave *as if* conscious of right and wrong.' An animal may 'by its affections' act '*as if* it were anticipating the feelings and actions of humans or other animals'. But these are only appearances and not evidence of a deeper reality.

Alfred Russel Wallace, who simultaneously developed a theory of evolution by natural selection independently of Darwin, wrote to him in the same spirit. He too had slowly come around to the idea that the emergence of conscience could not be explained by the material forces that drove evolution more generally. Wallace had long had an interest in spiritualism; he did not believe that God had by special creation specifically endowed man with a conscience or consciousness but at the same time thought that it could not have occurred by natural selection either. 'I can quite comprehend your feelings with regard to my "unscientific" opinions as to Man,' he wrote to Darwin. Wallace admits that a few years ago he too would have considered them both wild and unnecessary. But now he thinks that evidence 'demonstrate[s] the existence of forces and influences not yet recognized by science'. Some 'Higher Intelligence' must be guiding organic evolution.[10]

Darwin took on 'the moral sense or conscience' as the test case for the claim that animals differed from humans only in degree and not in kind, and that it could be explained through material forces and did not require metaphysical speculation. Dogs, not human's closest relative on the evolutionary tree, the chimpanzee, provided the solid core of his evidence in part because relatively little was known about the social lives of chimps and because they are notoriously difficult to live with. But more importantly, it was because of Darwin's intimate lifelong knowledge of, and love for, dogs. He grew up with them; he hunted with them, all kinds – sighthounds, scenthounds, terriers, 'mongrels'. He lived with them in his household at Down House in Downe, Kent, from the 1840s until his death in 1882. Polly, a terrier-mix who had belonged to his daughter Henrietta before she married, was 'the love of his life' [**215**]. Darwin's earliest biographer included an illustration of the great man's study with an empty

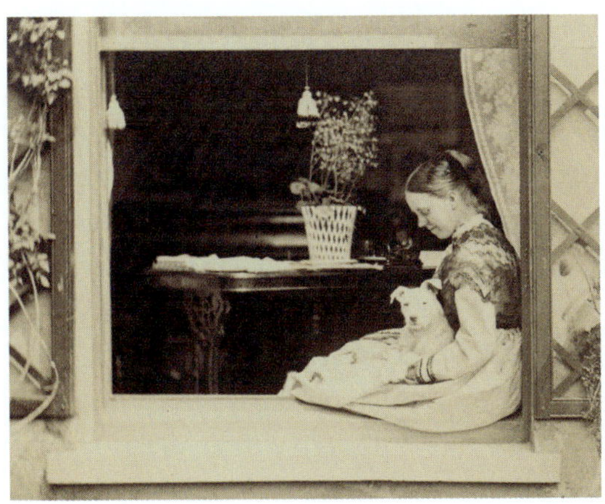

215 Charles Darwin's daughter Henrietta with the beloved terrier Polly (1870s).

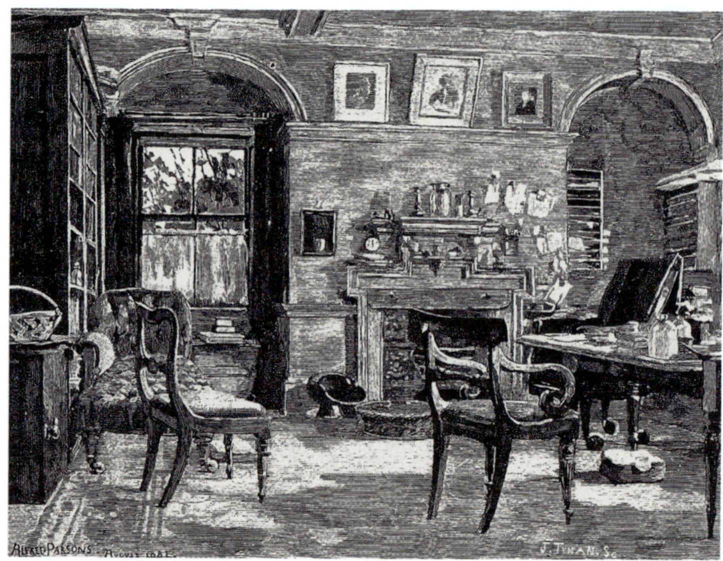

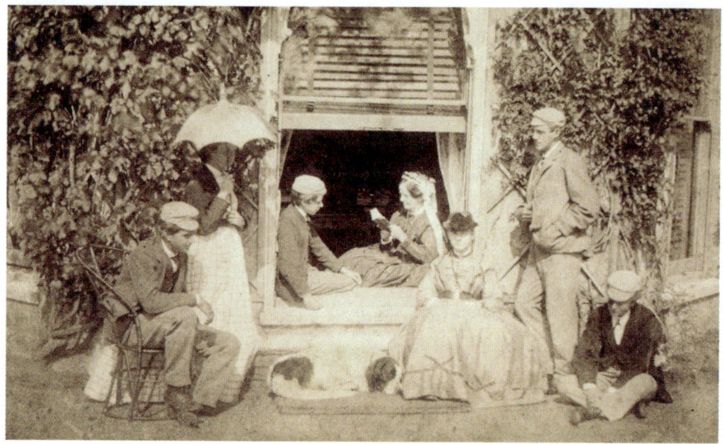

216–217 (*above*) 'Darwin's Study' by Alfred Parsons (1891), with the dog bed waiting for its dog; (*below*) the Darwins at Down House (1870s).

dog bed sitting prominently by [**216**]; family pictures included the dog [**217**]. Admittedly, they were not the only animal he turned to for evidence for his views about animal psychology. The behaviours of crows, elephants, and cats were mobilized as well. But there is no animal whose behaviour he knew better or in more contexts than the dog.[11]

In *The Descent of Man* Darwin discusses the crucial question of whether the origins of religion, the supposed foundation of conscience, could be explained without the intervention of a divine intelligence, and offers the following canine origin story as evidence that it can. On one hot day his 'full-grown and very sensible' setter – a kind of pointer, I think Dash – was lying on the lawn with the family. A slight breeze caused a parasol that was at some distance to flutter. If someone had been near it, the dog would have taken no notice but since there wasn't, it 'growled fiercely and barked'. 'Why?' Darwin asks. Because the dog 'reasoned to himself in a rapid and unconscious manner, that movement without any apparent cause indicated the presence of some strange living agent, and that no stranger had a right to be on his territory'. And from Dash's mistaken assumption that something strange was causing the parasol to flutter, it was not a big leap to the origin of religion – the recognition of spirit.

The dog made the same category of mistake that primitive humans make in attributing a supernatural cause to natural phenomena they don't understand. This is not an original thought on Darwin's part; it was a commonplace of late nineteenth-century anthropological theories of the origins of religion. What Darwin added was the link between his setter's reactions to what he did not understand not only with the origins of religion, but specific superstitions: trial by fire and blood rituals of various sorts, for example. Religion had no adaptive value. The 'indirect consequences of our highest faculties may be compared with the incidental and occasional mistakes of the instincts of the lower animals'. If not Dash then another dog could also be adduced to how a moral sense evolved: 'A pointer . . . would say to himself, I ought . . . to have pointed to that hare and not have yielded to the passing temptation of hunting it.'[12]

Darwin understood that the question of how mind emerged from matter was for the time being intractable: 'only in the distant future' would we come to learn how 'mental powers first developed in the lowest animals'. That future is still not with us; no one has a clue about what consciousness or conscience are, much less how they evolved. But he insists that an animal, endowed with well-marked social instincts, would inevitably acquire a moral sense or conscience, as soon as its intellectual powers had become as well-developed, or nearly as well-developed, as in man. Darwin also says that he feels compelled to take on the question of conscience because no one before has approached it from the perspective of natural history. That is, from a perspective free of metaphysics, of teleology, and of arguments about design. (Darwin's contemporary, the great Russian writer and thinker Alexander Herzen, might say that Darwin's story traces the development of consciousness and conscience through animals to humans and thereby into history.)[13]

Darwin may as a student have encountered the views of David Hume on the relation of animal and human reason, which gave a certain philosophical and methodological warrant to his use of the behaviour of dogs as evidence for thinking about the moral evolution of humans. 'Any theory by which we explain the operations of the understanding or the origin and connection of the passions in man,' Hume argued, 'will acquire additional authority if we find that the same theory is requisite to explain the same phenomena in all other animals.'[14] But given Darwin's deep knowledge of dogs and their place in his psyche going back to childhood, he might not have needed philosophical reinforcement.

Darwin wrote a letter to the important feminist, social reformer, and philosopher Frances Power Cobbe, both complimentary and revelatory, thanking her for sending him her long article on 'The Consciousness of Dogs'.[15] Even though he offered some criticisms he agreed with most of the article and said it was the 'best analysis of the mind of an animal' he had ever read. He thought that it was especially good on the evolution of moral sensibility. Since publishing *The Descent of Man,* he said that he had become more and more convinced that dogs have a conscience and told her a personal story that confirmed his views.

The fact that when 'beloved and beautiful Polly' commits an 'undiscovered offence' she 'is at such times extremely affectionate towards me', recalled youthful memories [**218**]. When as a little boy he had 'committed some minor offence' his conscience would trouble him. When he then met his father, he would lavish 'so much affection on him, that

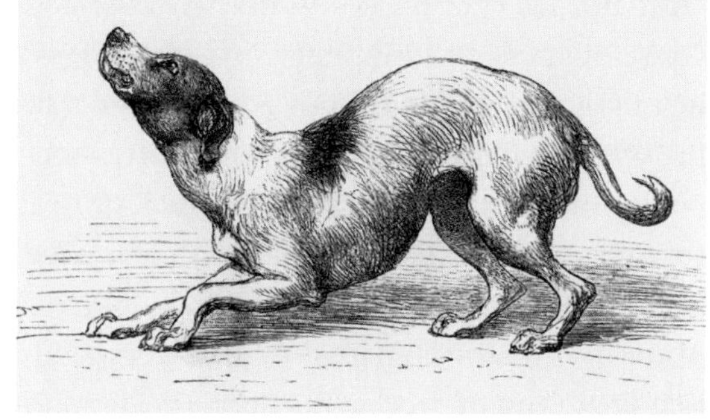

218 Darwin's Polly illustrated by Briton Rivière to demonstrate '[A Dog] in a humble and affectionate frame of mind' in *The Expression of the Emotion in Man and Animals* (1872).

he at once asked me what I had done [and] told me to confess. I was so utterly confounded at his suspecting any thing, [sic] that I remember the scene clearly to the present day.' 'It seems to me,' he concludes, 'that Polly's frame of mind on such occasions is much the same as was mine.' As Polly is in relation to him, so is he in relation to his father, motivated not by fear but by conscience. If, as Rilke said, Cézanne saw like a dog, Darwin imagined himself to be one.[16]

I asked Alexandra Horowitz, the Barnard College, New York, canine ethologist and best-selling author of *Inside of a Dog*, about the conscience of the dog. This was her reply:

> The dog is a social species; they live in social (family) groups; and they are where they are in human society because they are sensitive to the things we care about. There is but no question that a sense of what others expect is a part of being such good social actors. Is this conscience? Well, almost definitely not exactly as we define it (why would it be, outside of language?). But I've seen a dog playing with others who bites too hard, and then rolls on his back as if in apology; I see that dogs are sensitive to human anger toward them almost before we even display it.[17]

I think the problem of imagining the mental world of another human, much less of a different animal, is intractable. We think we can understand how someone else thinks or makes moral decisions or perceives the world, because they are presumably like us. But that comfortable thought very soon runs into serious difficulties. When it comes to other animals the difficulty is even greater. But Horowitz's point is grounded less in the philosophical shoals of the philosophy of mind than in how we manage social interactions. The art of the dog, as we have seen it, is grounded in the view that their gestures are intelligible to us and ours to them whatever the ontological gap that theologians and philosophers might have postulated. Dogs in art are part of our moral universe. In the nineteenth century the dog in evolutionary psychology and in two political movements – anti-vivisection and anti-slavery – also became a way to think about morality, that of animals, of humans, and of the social order more generally. The debates at the level of evolutionary theory and philosophy of mind generated few images. They were central to the work of reform movements.

The Agony

The anti-vivisection movement understood the power of images. The frontispiece to an 1880s anti-vivisection pamphlet[18] exhorts readers:

DO NOT REFUSE TO LOOK AT THESE PICTURES

IF YOU CANNOT BEAR TO LOOK AT THEM, WHAT MUST THE SUFFERING BE TO THE ANIMALS WHO UNDERGO THE CRUELTIES THEY REPRESENT

The images discussed in this section – and in the one that follows as well – are, as they were intended to be, disturbing. They, and many more like them, were published in scores of anti-vivisection tracts. They were drawn from nineteenth-century physiology manuals that taught students in the neutral language of science how to conduct experiments on living animals using specialized instruments. They constitute a widely reproduced library of visual horror [**219**].

Physiological research on live animals goes back to antiquity and dogs had long been the experimental animal of choice because they were plentiful, easy to catch, and trusting. Vivisection became more common during the Scientific Revolution and in the Enlightenment it became, as part of a broader humanitarian movement, morally controversial. But it garnered relatively little attention compared to other animal-rights causes and left a limited visual record until the early nineteenth century. François Magendie's appointment in experimental physiology at the Collège de France in 1831, the culmination of a career already marked by major discoveries, was a turning point in the academic and social history of vivisection. Already in his day he had the reputation of being a brilliant but brutal experimenter indifferent to the suffering of the animals, almost exclusively dogs, that he used. In 1822 he confirmed the earlier discovery by Sir Charles Bell of the different function of the dorsal and ventral spinal nerves, a distinction that is at the foundation of neurology. The two men engaged in a dispute over precedence but in fact Magendie went a step further to show exactly what each spinal nerve did: the dorsal roots allow sensory signals to enter the spinal cord, and the ventral roots allow motor signals to exit.

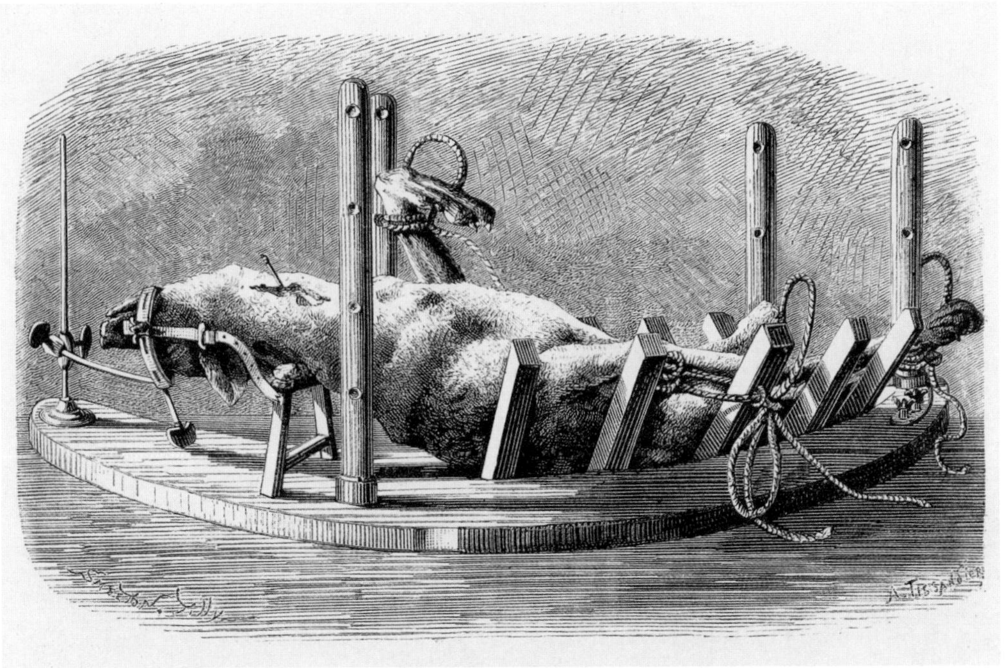

219 'A DOG VIVISECTED – DISSECTED AND TORTURED – NO ANAESTHETIC.' So cries a pamphlet produced by the American anti-vivisection society in 1888. The illustrations were sourced from physiologists' textbooks; this drawing is by Paul Bert.

Bell, in a letter that was printed in an 1842 biography and widely known before, confessed that he had not been able himself to carry out the crucial experiments which Magendie had undertaken on fully awake puppies whose spinal cords had not fully ossified. 'I should be writing a third paper on the nerves,' he confessed:

> . . . but I cannot proceed without making some experiments, which are so unpleasant to make that I defer them . . . I cannot perfectly convince myself that I am authorized in nature, or religion, to do these cruelties – for what? – for anything else than a little egotism or self-aggrandizement.

He ended by noting ruefully that what Magendie was doing was being done daily by others. For nothing, he says, perhaps a bit disingenuously. But he was right about the spread of vivisection.

The Magendie moment in the history of vivisection and its opponents is represented by a strange painting [**220**]. Almost nothing is known about

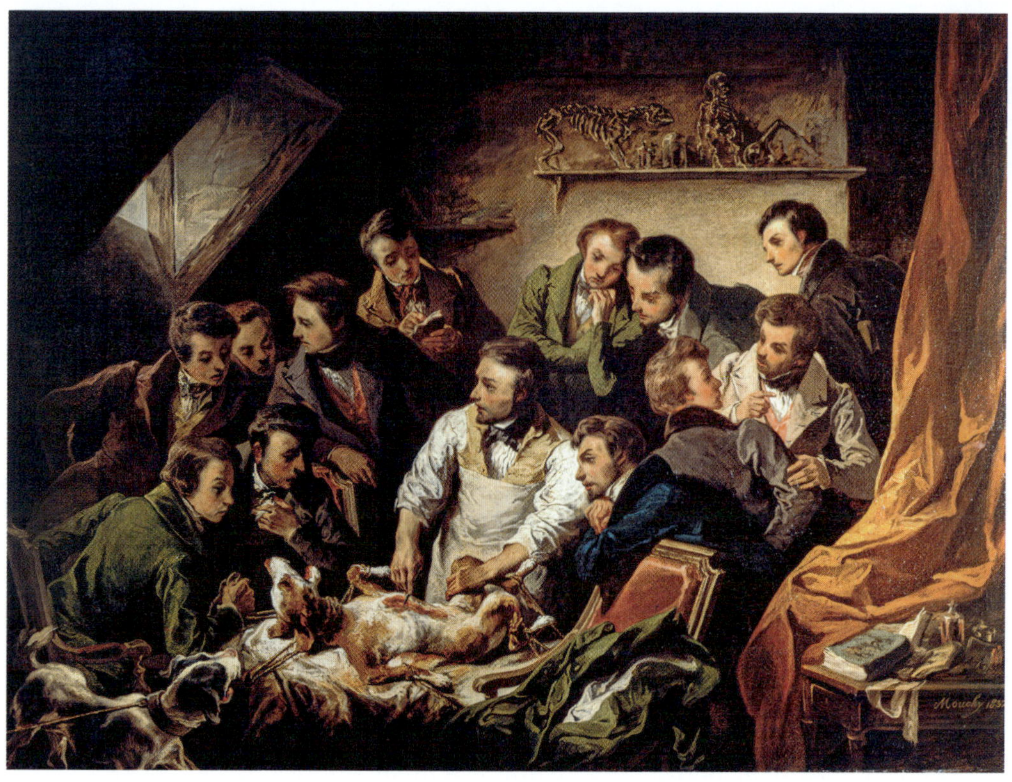

220 Indifferent to pain: The vivisection of a dog painted by Émile-Édouard Mouchy in 1832.

it or the artist who painted it, Émile-Édouard Mouchy. It was shown at the opening exhibition of the Wellcome Historical Medical Museum in London in 1913 and sometime between then and 2023 was relegated to storage, not because it is bad art but because it is morally indecent to contemporary eyes. Its earlier history is murky. We know that a painting of Mouchy's called *Études de chien* (*Studies of the Dog*) was exhibited in the Salon of 1833; presumably it was this one, although that would be a less than descriptive title.[19]

The painting is a group portrait of students watching a vivisection demonstration by someone. It may be Magendie represented at a series of lectures he offered in 1828 in which he laid bare the stomach and intestines of an un-anaesthetized dog kept pinned to a table alive for days. At the centre is the physiologist, scalpel in one hand and the other holding the leg of a dog writhing in pain and trying to escape its bonds. The physiologist is looking over at his students as if to ask whether they are following the demonstration. The centre pair – dog and vivisector – are bathed in bright light. Some of the students are looking intently at what is being demonstrated; others talk to their classmates perhaps to clarify a point or formulate a question. The dog is howling, its mouth, nose, and opened abdomen painted in blood red. One of the students is holding an end of the rope that is around the dog's neck to keep it in place; the other end seems to be tied to the table leg. No one is reacting to its cries or the struggles of the dog right in front of their eyes and ears except the black and white dog, howling, a rope around its neck, coming into the frame of the painting.

We do not know whether Mouchy was familiar with the long tradition of anatomy paintings of which this one is both a successor and a departure. In Rembrandt's *The Anatomy Lesson of Dr Nicolaes Tulp* (Mauritshuis, The Hague), commissioned for the Amsterdam Surgeon's Guild in 1632, the body represented as being dissected is dead; it feels no pain; and it belonged to a criminal, Aris Kindt, hanged for armed robbery. The dog in Mouchy's painting is alive, in great pain, and ipso facto innocent. By the early nineteenth century, anatomized bodies were no longer those of criminals but of men and women who had the misfortune of dying in a hospital or poor house. And anatomical dissection was no longer a matter of controversy or pride; it was also no longer a subject of art. Cutting the living was, and Thomas Eakins' great late nineteenth-century surgery paintings, *The Gross Clinic* and *The Agnew Clinic* (both in the Philadelphia Museum of Art), were in the tradition of anatomy paintings. But the subject on the table in both cases is innocent, sleeping quietly while the doctors explore its body not out of abstract interest but to cure disease. Magendie made no such claims, although later vivisections would justify their practices on utilitarian grounds; claims for scientific medicine based on physiological research were still in the future.

Mouchy's painting was thus near the end of an old tradition and at the beginning of another. Earlier scientific illustrations of vivisection were schematic and morally cool. Mouchy's was the first painting to engage with the practice itself directly. There would be nothing quite like it, in part because it is such a loony, almost surreal painting in which all the men look alike, and in part because it is so horrible in its unashamed representation of violence. But it set the terms of the coming visual debate, which was about the moral status of the enterprise itself and of its animal subject.

By 1860 there were major physiology labs routinely practising vivisection in most major European medical faculties; England was the last with the appointment in 1870 of Michael Foster to a praelectorship in physiology at Cambridge and to a newly created chair in 1883. More alarming to its opponents was the fact that by the 1870s vivisection had become part of university education in medicine and physiology, not just a research tool but part of routine student laboratory experiments. The images of horror that fill anti-vivisection tracts were taken not from scientific articles in small circulation journals but from widely distributed manuals for beginning students.

Organized anti-vivisection movements through which animals entered the nineteenth-century moral imagination began in 1863 with protests against the work of the noted German physiologist Moritz Schiff in Zurich; and with a petition by five hundred British veterinarians against the French practice of requiring veterinary students to perform up to sixty practice operations on live un-anaesthetized horses that were then killed.

The arguments against vivisection had their roots long before that in a wide range of eighteenth-century humanitarian movements. There were the religious arguments: man and brute creation are part of God's Great Design, and that just as he is merciful to us, so we, purportedly at the top of the heap, must be merciful to those below. John Wesley, who throughout his life was interested in the welfare of animals, asked in a sermon that 'If the Creator and Father of every living thing is rich in mercy towards all . . . if he desires even the meanest of them to be happy according to their degree', why is it that 'a complication of evils' oppresses and overwhelms them? Another clergyman made a more universal claim. Just as differences in 'power of mind' or 'complexion' or 'fortune' or size gave 'no man the right to abuse another', likewise 'the difference in shape between a man and a brute cannot give man a natural right to abuse and torment' it. It was also of course an anti-racist, anti-slavery argument. 'Pain is pain . . . and the creature that suffers it, whether man or beast, being sensible of the misery of it whilst it lasts, suffers evil.'[20]

There were secular versions in the mix: Benthamite utilitarianism, for example – 'pain without exception the only evil'. And sentimentalism: Louis-Sébastien Mercier, the French journalist, writes in his 1782 *Tableau de Paris* that 'never a woman will be a Cartesian: never will she agree to believe that her little dog is neither sensitive nor reasonable when he caresses her. She would stare down Descartes in person.' Whether Descartes believed that a dog or any animal was in fact just an elaborate machine that could not suffer is another matter; he had a dog named Monsieur Grat on whom he was said to lavish attention. But his most ardent followers took him at his word. Experimenters at the seventeenth seminary of Port Royal argued that the howling of the dogs they vivisected was nothing but the grinding of gears; they were said to kick dogs on the street to make the point.[21] Nineteenth-century novels in which animals figured as characters and even narrators – Anna Sewell's best-selling *Black Beauty* and the short stories of Turgenev – were also enormously influential in changing how people felt about cruelty toward animals.

There were also arguments based on rights claims that mirrored claims for the rights of man more generally. Olympe des Gouges, author of the *Declaration of the Rights of Woman* (1791), was a well-known proponent of kindness to animals. Pierre Serna in his book on the origins of the rights of animals recounts the story, first told by François-Hilaire Gilbert, co-director of the Republic's new veterinary school, in 1798, of a carter beating three horses harnessed to a stuck cart; one had already collapsed. A market woman rushed over towards him and threatened him with a paving stone: 'Hit him again you dare', 'monstre inhumain'. While the crowd was cheering her on, a learned physician intervened: the carter had every right to beat his horse because it was his. He could do what he wanted with his property including beating it to death.

It was precisely against this claim that in 1796 John Lawrence, an English expert on horses, published the first sustained argument for animals' rights.[22] Ownership did not give unlimited licence to do with living creatures as one wanted, they had rights that arose 'spontaneously, from the conscience or sense of moral obligation in man, who is indisputably bound to bestow them upon animals'. Animals did things for us, and we owed them something in return. And because 'custom, which flatters the indolence of man', keeps us from doing our duty, we need to make laws to translate them into enforceable rights. Laws about cruelty to animals and the fight for anti-vivisection legislation were based on elaborations of Lawrence's work.

And finally, there is the argument that cruelty to animals was not only a sign of an individual's depravity but a symptom of social and political pathology. Turgenev's 1854 short story about a deaf serf – Gerasim – who rescues a drowning female dog whom he names Mumu – makes this sort of claim about the evils of serfdom. Gerasim is passionately attached to

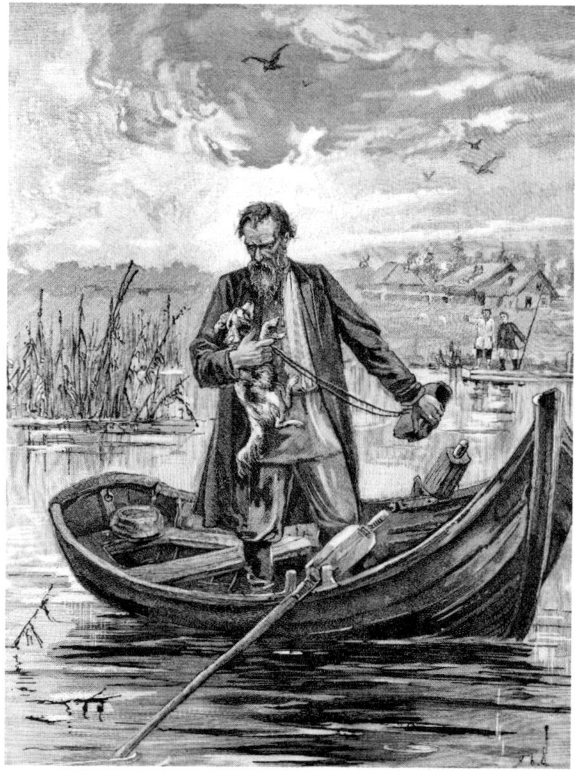

221 A terrible separation: *Gerasim and Mumu* (1893) by Schyubler, after a painting by Vladimir Taburin.

the dog and the dog to him. His hard-hearted, loveless mistress orders the dog to be brought to her; it barks at her and she comes to hate it; she instructs a servant to kidnap and kill it; Gerasim looks for it desperately, finds the dog and hides it. But Mumu makes noises that disturb his owner. It becomes clear that Gerasim's mistress will order the dog to be killed; he decides that if Mumu must die, he will do the deed himself. He takes Mumu for a final treat and then drowns her himself. The story is known to every Russian schoolchild and was a parable for the evils of serfdom in the Soviet period. It produced a rich visual record over the centuries [**221**]. A small statue was erected in St Petersburg in 2004 on Turgenev Square upon the 150th anniversary of the publication of the story: 'In memory of the DOG', the plaque says. For serfdom, the anti-vivisection movement substituted arrogant, heartless – male – science.

In the French doctor Claude Bernard physiology based on vivisection found its hero and its opponents their *bête noir*. Appointed as Magendie's successor at the Collège de France in 1850, he was the greatest physiologist of the century and probably in the history of the biological sciences. He was also the leading advocate for what we would call scientific medicine grounded in laboratory experimentation rather than learned at the bedside. Vivisection was thus claimed to be in the service of mankind. His often reprinted and translated *Introduction to the Study of Experimental Medicine* (1865) remains a major work in the philosophy of science and his *Leçons de Physiologie Opératoire* (1879) was for decades a guide to the use of vivisection in physiology as well as a source of damning quotations and images for his critics.

'Prince among vivisectors', Bernard was an easy target for those who wanted to portray vivisection as the craft of heartless, morally blind men, who worshipped at the shrine of materialist science and would stop at nothing to attain their ends. 'The physiologist is no ordinary man.' He is, Bernard himself writes:

> . . . a learned man, a man possessed and absorbed by a scientific idea. He does not hear the animals' cries of pain. He is blind to the blood that flows. He sees nothing but his idea, and organisms which conceal from him the secrets he is resolved to discover.

His wife, Marie Françoise (née Martin), left him and founded an anti-vivisection society.[23]

Others provided the anti-vivisection movement with more evidence of heartlessness. The Russian physiologist Ilya Faddeyevich Tsion went into exile in Paris, changed his name to Elie de Cyon, and worked closely with Bernard. Cyon proclaimed that 'the true Vivisector must approach a difficult dissection with joyful excitement'. He went on to say that 'the sensation of the physiologist when, from a gruesome wound full of blood and mangled tissue', and in the course of discovering a nerve, had much in common with a sculptor. Set under the picture of a dog strapped to an operating table strewn with knives and subject to a cold male gaze and hand, the Cyon quote made for effective anti-vivisectionist propaganda [**222**].

The portrayal of Bernard and his colleagues by the scientific establishment was largely triumphalist and unapologetic: a proud display of the ascendancy of French physiology and its techniques.

Bernard's students and colleagues look like a homey gathering of men in a Dutch genre painting [**223**]. It is the sort of morally clueless

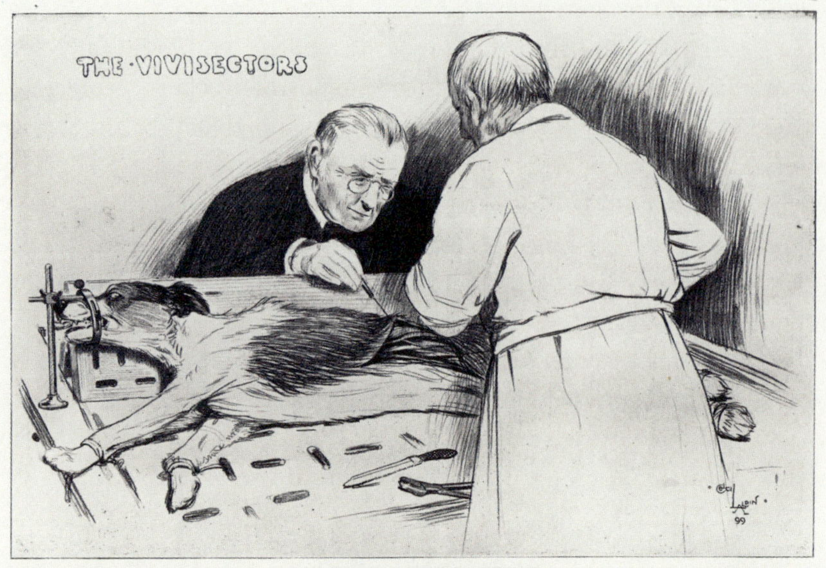

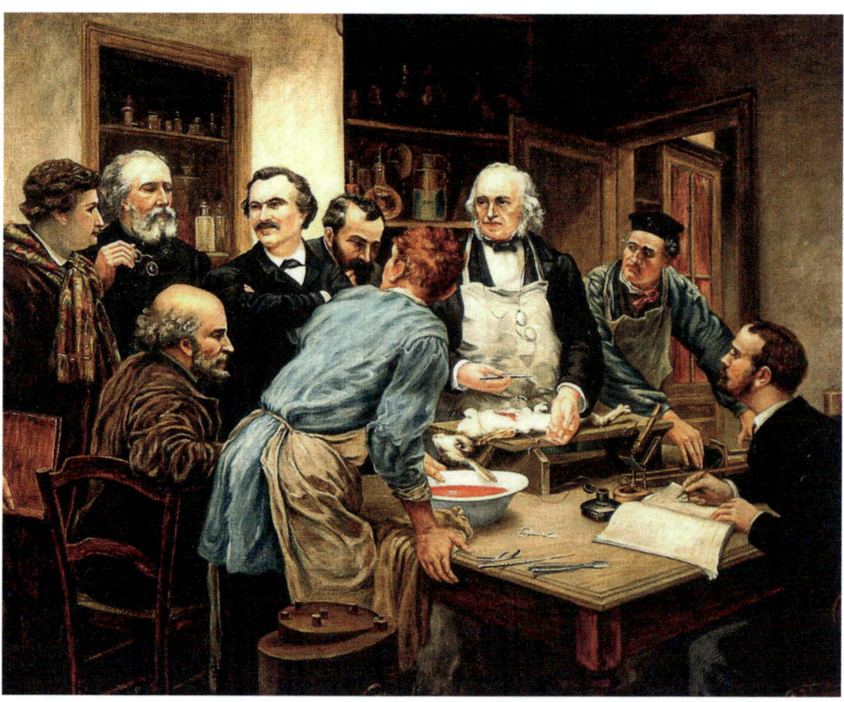

222-223 'Mangling done here': Cecil Aldin's *The Vivisectors* from *The Abolitionist* magazine (15 September 1899, *above*); Léon-Augustin Lhermitte's *Claude Bernard and his Pupils* (c. 1890) is the only extant painting of Bernard, here operating on a rabbit (*below*).

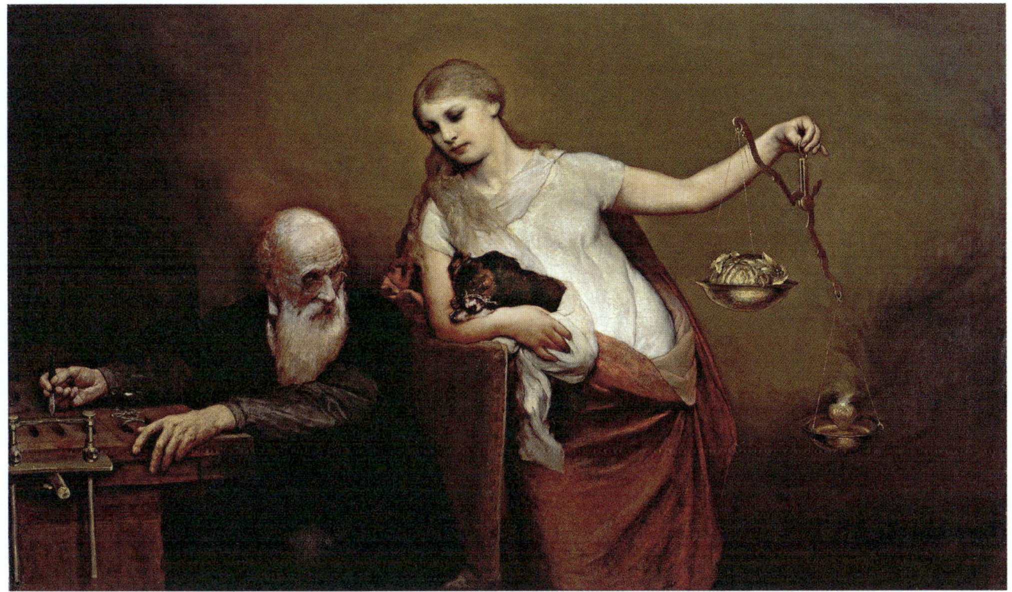

224 A German physiology professor has his conscience pricked in Gabriel Cornelius Ritter von Max's *Der Vivisektor* (1883).

normalization of emotionless cruelty to animals that the anti-vivisectionists used to attack the practice. From the perspectives of Bernard's admirers, he had nothing to hide. In 1886, eight years after his death, a large bronze statue of him was erected in the courtyard of the Collège de France. It was melted down by the German army during the Second World War and was replaced afterward by a stone version.

The anti-vivisection movement reversed the moral perspective of this imagery. The physician in Gabriel Cornelius Ritter von Max's *Der Vivisektor* has second thoughts [**224**]. A stereotypical German professor of physiology sits in his old age at a desk covered by the instruments of his trade: scalpels and restraints of various sorts. He is looking down at the balance held by a female figure representing Virtue and Justice holding her scales. In the balance is a burning heart that easily outweighs a human brain crowned with laurel. A source close to Max at the time he was painting it said the image was inspired by a saying of Kant's that a good heart outweighs a good brain. Enveloped in the folds of Virtue's drape, at the painting's geometric and affective centre, is an injured puppy – innocence itself – whom she has rescued from the vivisector. Its head is nestled in the crook of her arm.[24]

The painting was shown at galleries in Vienna and major German cities. In London it was exhibited under the title *The Genius of Pity staying the Vivisector's Hand*. Photographs of it were sold for the benefit of the Victoria Street Society, the predecessor of the national Anti-Vivisection League. The original oil version was sold at auction in Vienna in 1885 and shown in Berlin in 1889, after which it disappeared from view until 2007 when it was exhibited in Munich. It was thought that the painting might have been bought by partisans of vivisection and destroyed as propaganda, but it survived in lithographs and other media as a mainstay of the anti-vivisection arsenal of images before its re-emergence into a very different world.[25]

The anti-vivisection movement had a wide range of support. Five hundred worthies signed the petition in Zurich against the work of Moritz Schiff; in England, Dickens, Tennyson, Lewis Carroll, Cardinal Newman and many more of the great and good wrote in support. But the movement's most prominent leader was Frances Power Cobbe, activist and moral philosopher, who embodied the connection of the feminist and anti-vivisection causes with a deep distrust of materialism grounded in science. Her 1878 article on 'Wife Torture in England' in the *Contemporary Review*, written in the midst of the fight for parliamentary regulation of vivisection, played a big part in the passage of the Matrimonial Claims Act; she was a leader of the movement to repeal the 1864 Contagious Diseases Act and its successors, which allowed the authorities to force prostitutes to undergo specular examination; she also campaigned against what she took to be the medical abuse of women.

Gynaecological surgery – I think Cobbe had the rage for ovariotomy in mind – she argued, was the human version of vivisection. (This in response to a notorious article by a doctor who claimed that it was 'vivisection of the noblest kind'.)[26] Cobbe travelled in elite literary, social and religious circles. She knew everyone: artists like Rosa Bonheur; the actress Fanny Kemble; Cardinal Newman's younger brother Frank; Cardinal Manning; Elizabeth Barrett Browning and her husband Robert; John Stuart Mill; Harriet Taylor; Harriet Beecher Stowe; the polymath Mary Somerville and fellow feminist activists like Millicent Fawcett and Josephine Butler; Charles Darwin; Gladstone invited her for breakfast. She was probably the most open and widely accepted lesbian of her generation and she shared with her partner a great love for their dog Hajjin.

Cobbe became engaged with the vivisection question in 1863 as part of the protests against Schiff in Zurich and against the practices of French veterinary schools. Her 1855 'Essay on Intuitive Morals' had already touched on the question of our duties to animals; in 'The Rights of Man and Claims of Brutes' (1863) she made a neo-Kantian case that our moral obligations toward animals derived from the duties to ourselves as moral beings. In other contexts she made anti-consequentialist arguments against those who argued for the benefits of vivisection for human well-being: 'few of us would purchase immunity from our own diseases at the cost of the torture of a thousand dogs'. And in any case, consequentialist arguments were weak because the vast numbers of vivisections were done in classrooms to demonstrate well-known facts and not push back the frontiers of knowledge for the benefit of mankind.[27]

But by the 1870s she came to see vivisection as the symptom of a deeper malaise, of a 'rapid deployment of a peculiarly acrimonious disease': godless science, 'the ruling passion of the age'. She focused particularly on evolution, which she claimed grounded 'a moral theory of boundless application – namely that the weak have absolutely no claim at all on the strong'. If they – male scientists with all their social and cultural power – 'can torture a hundred affectionate dogs to settle some curious problem', what would be next? Experimenting on 'idiots in asylums'? Criminals? Infants? Women?

Her moral outrage at evolution theory was not because research in that field demanded vivisection. It didn't. It was because it seemed to her the avatar of a broader cultural materialism that left no room for morality. She was perhaps also bitter that even Darwin, a friend and former summer neighbour who, as she wrote, 'would not allow a fly to bite a pony's neck', did not support the abolition of vivisection and could be seduced or flattered by its supporters into countenancing it. Darwin in fact could scarcely bear the thought of it: 'everyone has heard of the dog suffering under vivisection, who licked the hand of the operator; and this man, unless he had a heart of stone, must have felt remorse to the last hour of his life,' he wrote near the beginning of *The Descent of Man*. Cobbe could not have agreed more. (She would have known this; he had arranged to send her a review copy.) But Darwin could not bring himself to support a complete ban. Vivisection was justifiable for what he called 'real investigations in physiology', but not for 'mere damnable

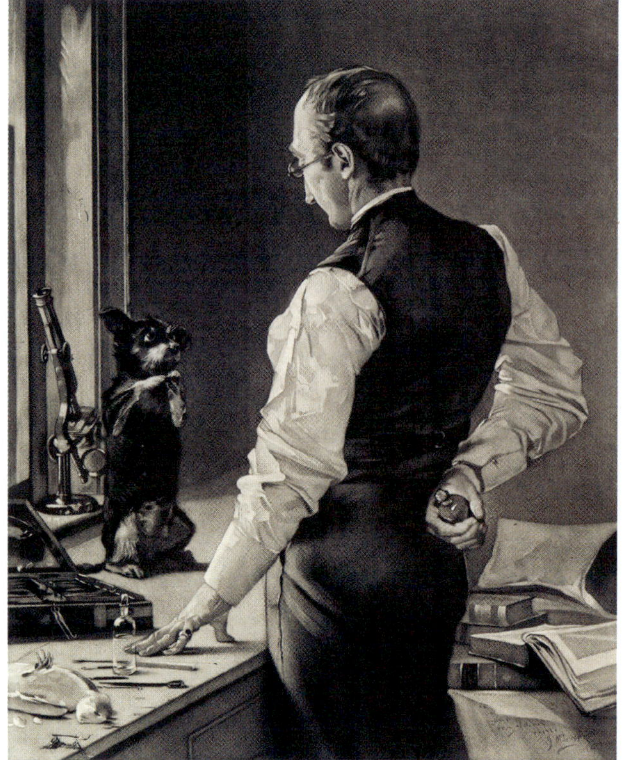

225 No mercy: J. McCLure Hamilton's *Vivisection – the Last Appeal* (1883).

and detestable curiosity', Darwin wrote to the young E. R. (Ray) Linkester, who would become one of Britain's most distinguished zoologists. The subject made him 'sick with horror, so I will not say another word about it, else I shall not sleep to-night'.[28]

The heartless male vivisector became the villain of the anti-vivisection literature. In a much-reproduced mezzotint of a painting by the Anglo-American artist J. McClure Hamilton a small dog is looking with beseeching eyes at a vivisector who is standing between his open books and a table strewn with saws and scalpels [**225**]. He holds a bottle of chloroform behind his back and has no intention of sparing the dog who is begging for his life. In a popular French cartoon version a dog is shown in the first frame happily playing with a young woman; in the second it is lost; and in the third it is tied up saying 'I am afraid . . . help me', while on the table behind him a dog is strapped down on a table; a scientist who looks like Dr Claude Bernard holds a knife over it [**226**].[29]

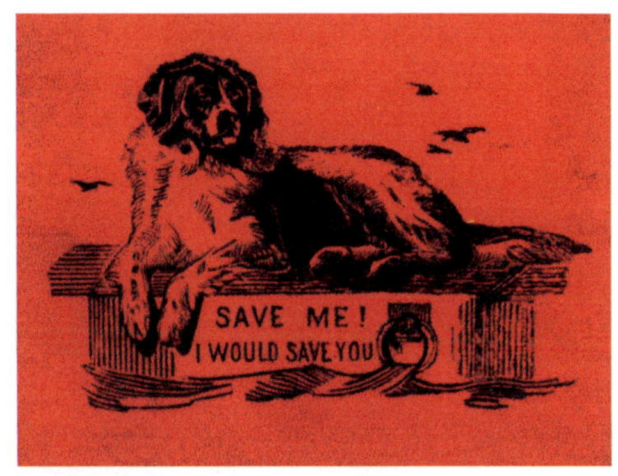

226 (*below*) A French anti-vivisection activist's postcard from the 1890s; 227 (*right*) detail from the front cover of Frances Cobbe's *The Modern Rack* (1889).

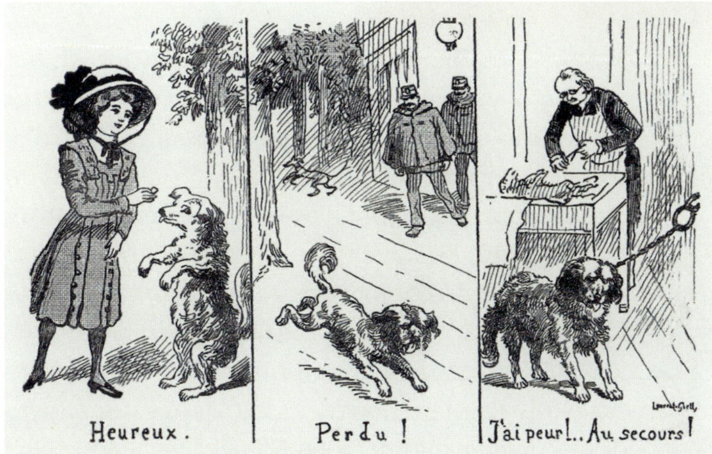

These words find their way onto the cover of one of Cobbe's pamphlet collections, *The Modern Rack* [**227**]. A dog that looks like the Newfoundlands in the popular art of canine maritime rescue rests on a table with a ring attached. Restraints below look broken; vultures circle above: 'SAVE ME! I WOULD SAVE YOU' reads the inscription. The image shares the emotional appeal of the famous anti-slavery slogan 'AM I NOT A MAN AND A BROTHER?'

The women in the anti-vivisection movement recognized an affinity between the status of women and the plight of animals at the mercy of feelingless men. The remarkable Anna Kingsford, a theosophist who often went into trances to communicate with spirits, studied medicine in Paris at the height of Dr Bernard's fame in the 1870s. She told people that she thought she had hastened his death through connections to the spirit world. A woman warrior on a horse – a female St George – is represented killing the dragon 'Vivisection' on the cover of an anti-vivisection pamphlet, and the theme resonates more widely in the fiction of the period.[30] Sarah Grand, among the most prominent 'New Woman' novelists, wrote in her 1897 partially autobiographical *The Beth Book: Being a Study of the Life of Elizabeth Caldwell Maclure, A Woman of Genius* about an intelligent young woman who, to escape a tyrannical father, makes a disastrous marriage to a doctor who works in a Lock hospital, performing examinations on involuntarily incarcerated prostitutes. He is a sadistic unfaithful brute. One day she hears 'horrid cries' coming from a room in her house and finds a 'little black-and-tan terrier' in agony fastened to a frame. She takes something from a shelf and pours a few drops in the poor creature's mouth. His suffering ceased. She forbids her husband to carry on experiments in their house, refuses to have sexual relations, and eventually leaves him just as the author Sarah Grand, like Claude Bernard's wife, left her husband in real life.

Florence Marryat, an enormously popular late nineteenth-century writer who specialized in vampire novels, and sensation novels more generally, also wrote against vivisection but with a twist to the marital plot. The heroine of *Angel of Pity*, Rose Gordon, is herself medically trained. She marries a surgeon and discovers to her horror that he not only experiments on his patients but is also a passionate vivisector. His response to her objections is not to stop doing it but to experiment on her dog. She leaves him but later returns to save him when he injures himself with his knives. He recovers and of course renounces vivisection.[31]

In February 1903 two young Swedish students – Louise Lind-af-Hageby and Leisa K. Schartau – at the London School of Medicine for Women, a vivisection-free college, spied on the laboratory of Ernest Starling and William Bayliss. They discovered that the men had opened the abdomen of a stray brown terrier that someone had found wandering the streets of London. As part of a series of experiments they had ligated the dog's pancreatic duct and closed it up. The procedure was part of a series of experiments that led to the discovery of secretin produced by the intestinal lining to stimulate the pancreatic secretion. It was one of the first hormones to be discovered, chemical messengers as Starling called them. (They had previously cut all the nerves to the pancreas in other animals, demonstrating that the hormone was not secreted in response to nervous stimulation.) After two miserable months in the cage where its howls were

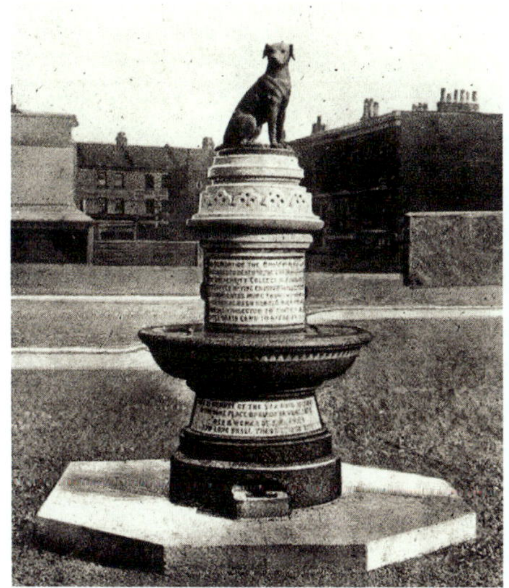

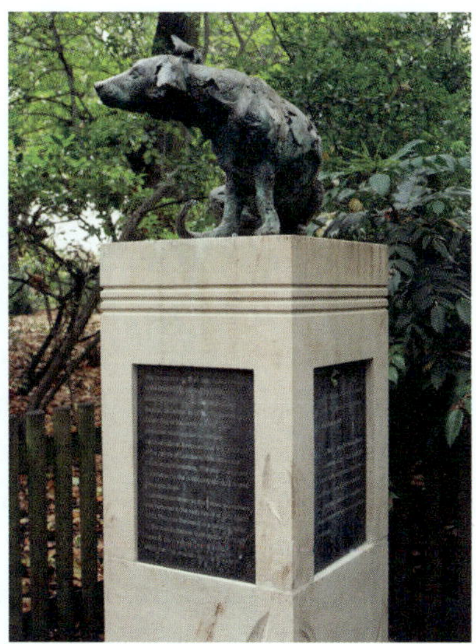

228–229 The original (1906) and the new (1985) *Brown Dog* statues in Battersea Park.

noted by others the little brown dog's abdomen was again opened for another experiment. This one failed. The dog was knifed to death by a young medical student named Henry Dale who, unlike his mentors, would go on in 1936 to win a Nobel Prize in Medicine and Physiology.

In 1906, three years after it was killed, feminist anti-vivisection activists commissioned a statue to honour the little brown terrier. It was put up in Battersea Park [**228**]. In 1907 a series of small riots, led by medical students, attacked it; they became known as the so-called 'Brown Dog riots'. Supporters of the dog marched in a counter-demonstration. For about a year the Battersea Council paid for 24-hour police watch against the 'anti-doggers'. This proved too great a burden on their budget and on the night of 10 March 1910 workmen took the statue down. Three thousand anti-vivisection activists marched to demand its return. It was not until 1985 that a new one was put up in its place [**229**]. It is still there.[32]

'Let slip the dogs'

Evidence for the bad dog that is so abundant elsewhere is rare in art and we need an explanation for why. It is that bad dogs are almost always a proxy for bad humans, for our failings. There is a strange painting by Botticelli illustrating a story from the fifth day of Boccaccio's *Decameron* about a young woman who was indifferent to the suicide of a rejected lover and, when she died, was condemned to be chased by mastiffs, her heart torn out and fed to her canine pursuers [**230**]. This does not reflect badly on the dogs, which are beautifully rendered, and are doing as their master or the gods command them. If they are degraded or uncivilized it is the fault of humans.

This is the premise of the dog in the art of anti-slavery. *The Hunted Slaves* by Richard Ansdell, an English painter of hunting scenes, is set in the Great Dismal Swamp on the border of Virginia and North Carolina [**231**]. The area had a place already in the abolitionist imagination because Henry Wadsworth Longfellow's poem 'The Slave in the Dismal Swamp' and Harriet Beecher Stowe's novel, *Dred: A Tale of the Great Dismal Swamp*, are both set there. On one side of Ansdell's painting is a slave, heavily muscled, unshackled; his wife, her eyes wide and mouth open in terror, hides behind him. They have escaped to a wild wetland. On the other side of the painting are two gigantic, ferocious, larger-than-life dogs,

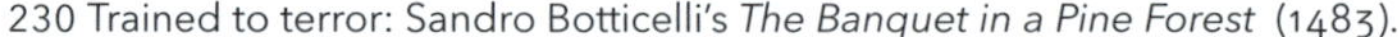

230 Trained to terror: Sandro Botticelli's *The Banquet in a Pine Forest* (1483).

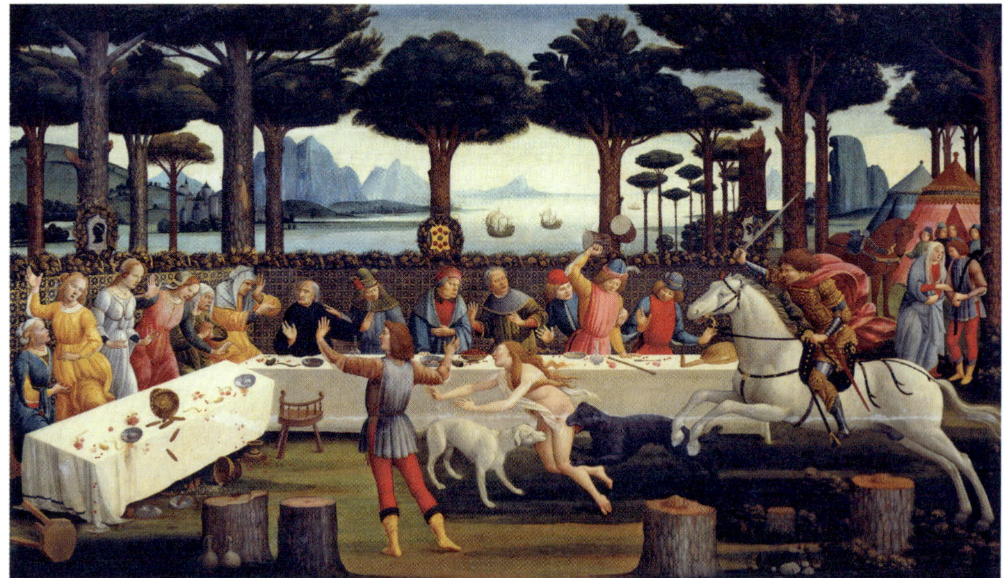

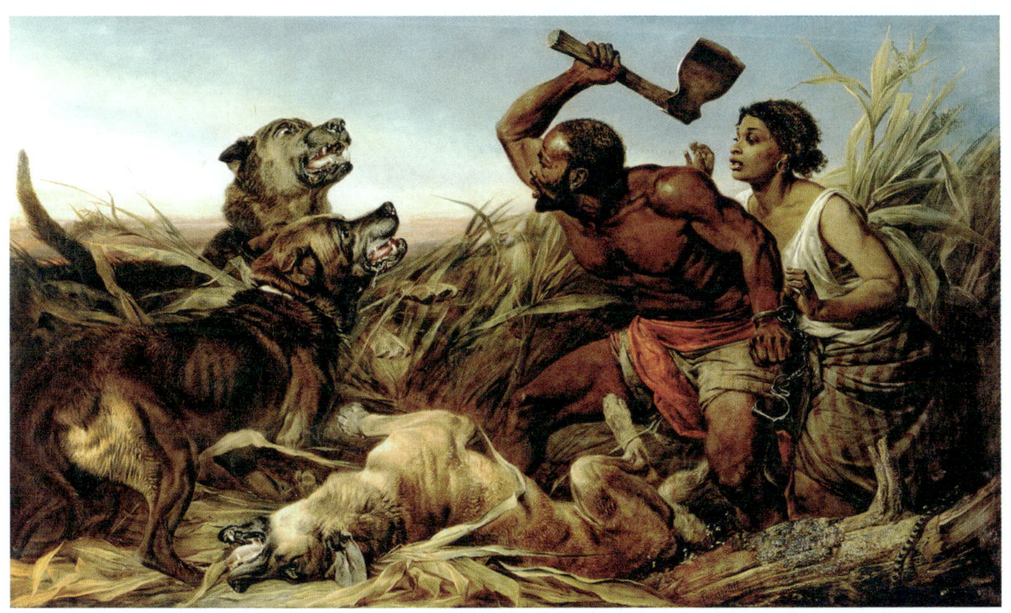

231 Dogs as agents of evil: Richard Ansdell's *The Hunted Slaves* (1861).

crazed, terrified, and terrifying. They are focused not on the man or the woman's eyes but on the axe with which the man is defending himself and his wife. Saliva drips from the open mouth of the dog closest to us, its fearsome teeth rendered in bright detail.

Between them at the base of the composition lies a dead or dying dog on its back, defeated and in the throes of agony; its open jaws and neck are painted in the intense white of the woman's top. These are dogs, a contemporary viewer would have immediately understood, that had been specially trained to track and take down slaves as if they were wild animals rather than human beings to be protected. It is a painting of existential struggle on the one side and the moral inversion and perversion of a hunt scene on the other. Notable by their absence are the dogs' slave-owning masters. The dogs stand in for them. But no one looking at this picture in the nineteenth century would have seen it as being about bad dogs. They have no political or moral agency on their own. Viewers would not have assumed, as one did in the long tradition of the dog's gaze and gesture in art, that their behaviour was intentional. It is about evil humans who have turned the dog's capacity to hunt and guard into police power.

Ansdell was a moderately successful mid-nineteenth-century Liverpool painter of hunting scenes who was often referred to by the critics of his day as a lesser, but still worthy, Landseer. He painted *The Hunted Slaves* in 1861 and exhibited it in the Royal Academy to which he had just been elected as an associate. Critics were generally respectful of his reputation: one commented on the fact that in his work the dog generally forms a 'conspicuous object' and that in this painting their anatomical details were well rendered. The painting's excesses were characteristic of 'the rudely telling force of all he paints' in all his hunting pictures but here were done for a greater good. Overly melodramatic perhaps, wrote another critic, but in the interest of being 'still more heart rending in the horrors of slaves hunted'. The unnaturally large dogs told an impossibly horrible story, 'perhaps too horrible to ensure for any painted version a kind reception for the bulk of sightseers'. It should appeal to 'all people with hearts in them to do all that is in their power to purge civilization of one of its foulest blots'. No one spoke ill of the dogs themselves; like the whip they were the 'instruments' of evil men engaged in an evil system. Images in a humanitarian narrative that demanded sympathy for and action on behalf of its victims.

The painting did its part for abolition in a practical sense. Ansdell donated it as a prize in a lottery to raise money for the relief of Lancashire mill workers who were unemployed because of the 'cotton famine' caused by the American Civil War, and who, despite their own suffering, were on the side of the North. They, as 'wage slaves', identified with 'chattel slaves', and were vocal in support of anti-slavery in the public campaign to keep the government from recognizing the Confederate States. The lottery raised £700. The winner was a local banker named Gilbert Winter Moss, who donated it to the Walker Gallery. It is a small irony that his father and uncles had inherited 1,000 enslaved people and received a huge amount in compensation under the Slavery Abolition Act. No money in Liverpool was clean.

The Hunted Slaves contributed more than money to the cause. It went on tour for abolition to London, Manchester, Bradford, Leeds, and other cities. It was copied in oil – the Smithsonian Museum of African American History and Culture has one – and it was engraved for mass circulation. The Walker Museum has in its files letters that attest to small copies being sold soon after the original was painted, and queries from various people asking if a copy they had might be the original or whether their great-grandfather might have painted it in the first place.

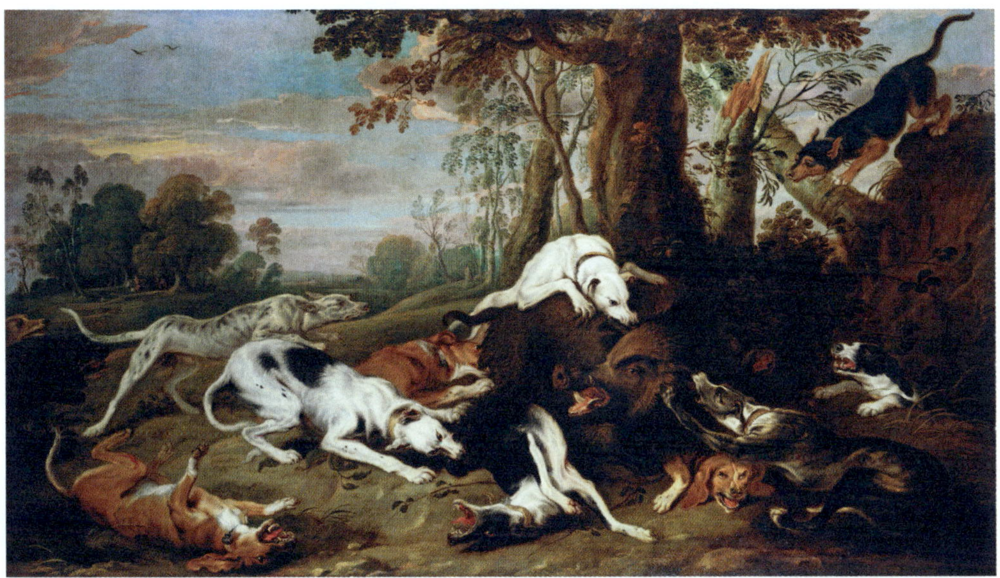

232 Frans Snijders's blood-thirsty *A Boar Hunt* (1653).

Its appeal to the heart was based on two visual traditions. One is the painting of the hunt as it emerged in the late sixteenth and early seventeenth century from the studios of Peter Paul Rubens and his sometime collaborator Frans Snijders, Hondius, Van Dyck, and a host of others. The genre thrived well into the late nineteenth century. Snijders was known to be especially attentive to the dogs themselves, often basing each on individual portraits of specific dogs.

There is something pornographically violent about all of these images and the thousands like them. There is also something unmistakably male; 'man and dog' in the primal hunt. In Frans Snijders's painting, *A Boar Hunt* [**232**], a dying dog lies on its back writhing in pain, its mouth wide open in a howl. It comes at viewers from out of the picture plane; it cannot be ignored. A second wounded dog, also howling, is on the ground, face to face with the boar, on the left; two more enter the fray from the right; a fifth dog is dead in the right foreground; a sixth has its teeth in the boar's back. It is a carnival of canine suffering. The difference in how viewers understood the moral status of *The Hunted Slaves* and *A Boar Hunt* depended not on their formal features but on how – more than two centuries apart – they understood the moral status of the prey and of the hunters, present in *A Boar Hunt* of 1653, implied in *The Hunted Slaves* of 1861.

No one before the rise of the anti-blood sports movement of the late nineteenth and the twentieth centuries said anything about the suffering of the animal prey as represented in hunting pictures. Even Cobbe distinguished the status of the hunted fox and its canine hunters on the one hand and the dog and the scientist in a vivisection experiment on the other. And no one commented either on the suffering of the dogs or on the fact that they were expendable as represented in hunting art. Man and dog, both vulnerable, are engaged together in what had once been a dangerous existential struggle for food and survival and what became a sport that re-enacted its beginnings. Each partner, man and dog, was doing what they were meant to do. If this art touched the moral imagination, it was in its evocation of heroism. Ansdell's *The Hunted Slaves* turns this narrative on its head.

It is also based on a second and more limited visual tradition: the record of the Spanish conquest of the New World. The Dominican Bartolomé de las Casas, who arrived in Hispaniola soon after it was discovered and went on to become Bishop of Chiapas and a defender of the rights of Native Americans, wrote a savage indictment of the cruelties of his countrymen to native people. The dogs of the conquistadors 'hunt after men . . . like deer into the thick of the forests' and feed their bodies to their dogs. (He also includes accounts of the better-than-human dogs who refuse to do as they are told.) His descriptions became the source for the widely circulated engravings by the Protestant Theodore de Bry in various anti-Catholic tracts that became a staple of the Black Legend of Spanish cruelty [**233**]. (The Spanish themselves made little secret of their use of dogs, and their images of their attacks on indigenous peoples differ little from those used by their enemies.)[33]

It was no secret by the early nineteenth century that slave-owners in the United States and the Caribbean bred and trained dogs – the Cuban bloodhound was the generic breed – to terrorize their human property and to hunt those who attempted to escape as they might have pursued deer or other game. Images of the immoral substitution of humans for wild animals in paintings like *The Hunted Slaves* became an important part of the visual rhetoric of abolition: the dehumanization

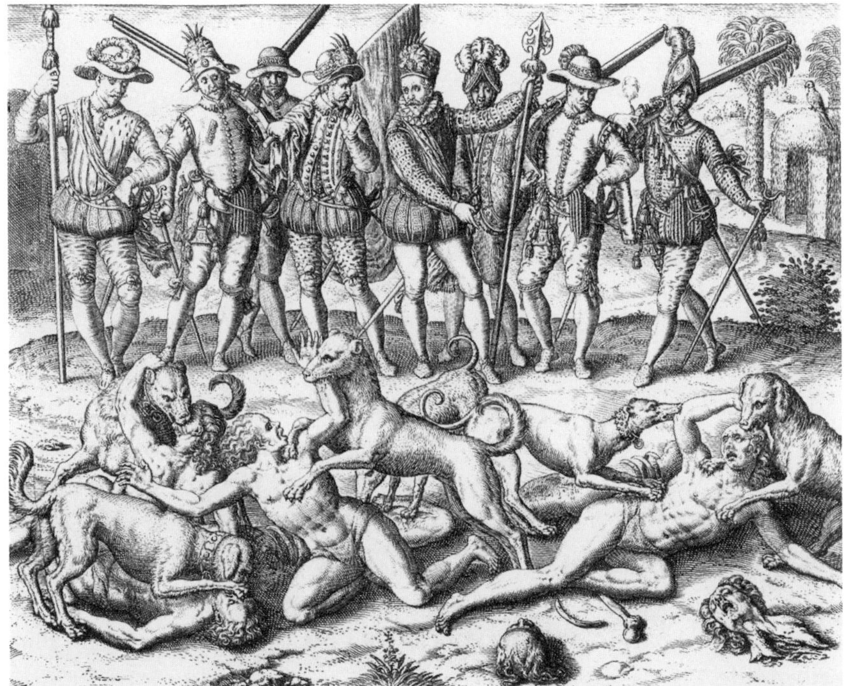

233 Theodore de Bry dramatizes 'The Black Legend' in Bartolomé de las Casas' *A Short Account of the Destruction of the Indies* (written 1542, published 1552).

of slaves; the brutality of slave-holders; the iniquity of the institution of slavery itself.[34]

Early versions of this trope appear in images of the Haitian revolutionary war. The French, like the Spanish before them, had trained dogs to eat the rebellious slaves, alive or dead. (They had been used to control slaves here and in the southern United States earlier.) We are speaking here of primal terror, unbounded violence in excess of any possible instrumental rationale. A strange form of sacrifice; vicarious cannibalism perhaps. Marcus Rainsford in his generally sympathetic account of the Haitian Revolution (1805) writes that 'When taken,' rebellious slaves 'were thrown to these animals, less brutal than their barbarous masters, to be devoured alive!' The masters had 'inspirite[ed] these animals with a ferocity not often known'. He follows this description with an image of giant dogs attacking a black family; the father is not half naked but in a revolutionary uniform identifying him as a member of Toussaint Louverture's

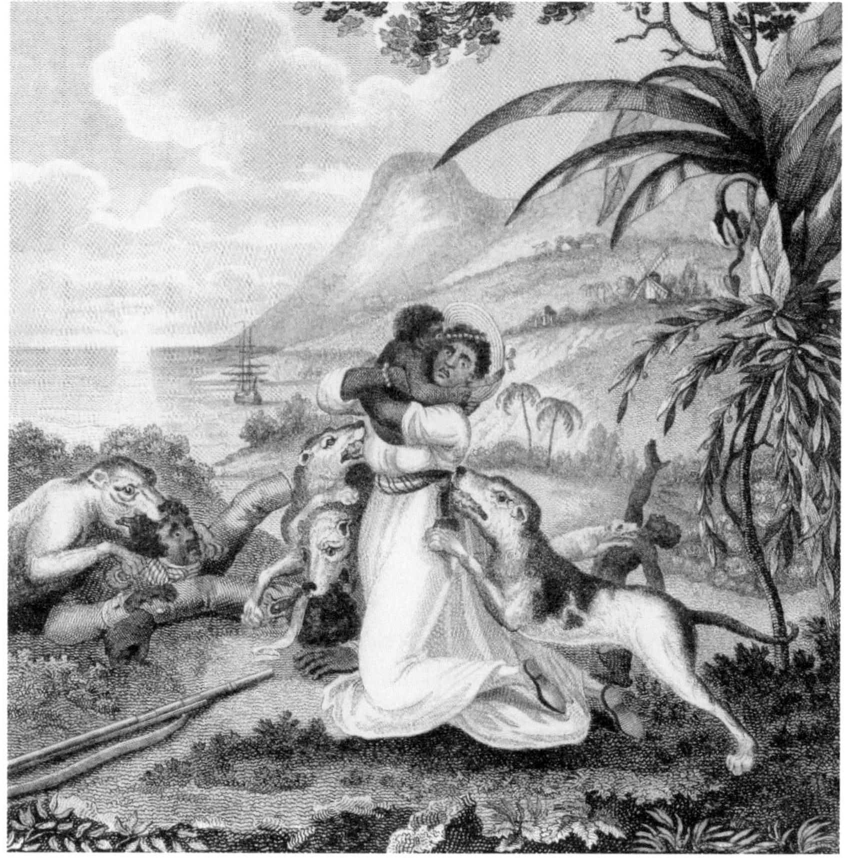

234 'Blood Hounds Attacking a Black Family in the Woods' in Marcus Rainsford's 1805 account of the Haitian Revolution.

army. The terror of the boar or deer in the genre of the hunting picture becomes the terror of family and of a war to free slaves [**234**].[35]

The terror of being hunted by dogs is a theme of anti-slavery literature and art. 'After a while we saw the hounds coming in full speed on our track,' writes Henry Bibb, a black abolitionist and author, who succeeded in escaping after several failed attempts: 'the slave drivers close after them on horseback, yelling like tigers, as they came in sight. The shrill yelling of the savage blood hounds as they drew nigh made the woods echo.' Accompanying the text were a series of widely circulated and often reworked images of the pursuit, all reworkings of the hunting art in which viewers were invited to condemn, rather than identify with, the human pursuers. Slave-holders are reduced to morally subhuman beings, into dogs they made vicious [**235**].[36]

The supposedly bad dog in anti-slavery art and its predecessors is less than an anthropomorphized dog than a canineification of its owners, a representation of the slavers' power. 'He was after her like a hound after a deer,' writes Harriet Beecher Stowe in *Uncle Tom's Cabin* about the trader who is chasing Eliza. The good dog, that is the normal sociable dog, makes its appearance in abolitionist imagery as the harbinger of freedom. Eliza is imagined with such a dog, its head raised as if to speak to Aunt Chloe and Uncle Tom itself, in an illustration to the 1852 edition of Stowe's novel. Eliza goes to their cabin to tell Tom that the dog has been sold and to announce that she was going to escape to keep her son Harry from being sold as well [**236**].

The dogs that pursued Eliza became one of the most common features of the visual history of *Uncle Tom's Cabin*, which itself became an icon of both ante- and postbellum America in all sorts of bizarre ways. Theatrical posters morph into advertisements for minstrel shows that manage to combine a play based on *Uncle Tom's Cabin* with a musical called *The Darkies' Holiday* and a London variety show. Trade cards show dogs

235 'We saw the hounds coming in full speed on our track': A widely circulated etching from an 1864 abolitionist text.

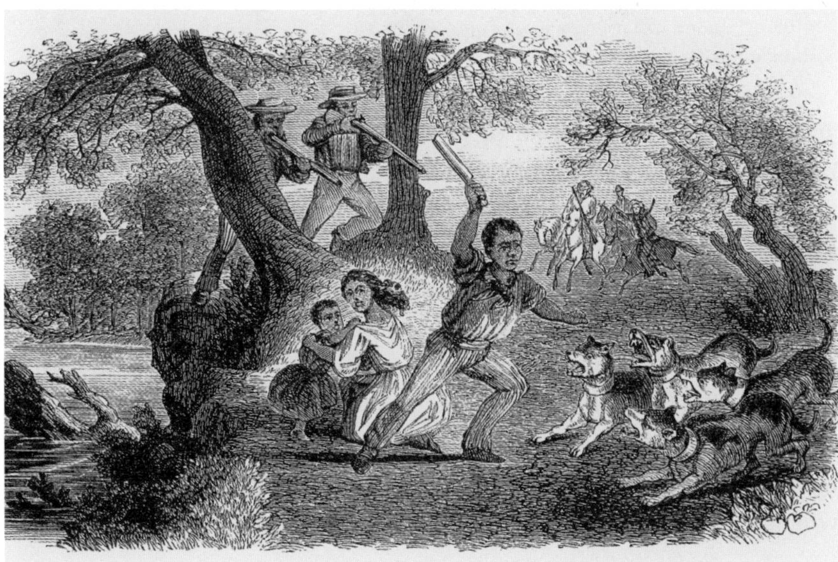

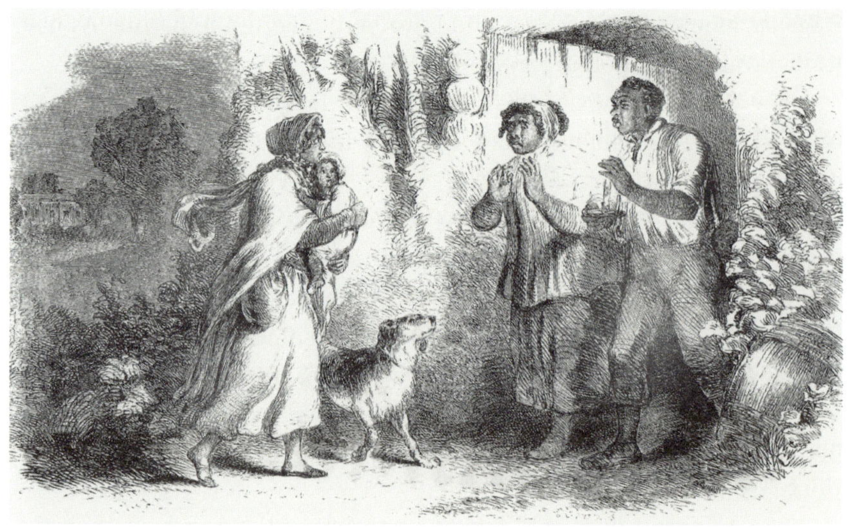

236 The good dog remains: Harriet Beecher Stowe's illustration (1852) in *Uncle Tom's Cabin*.

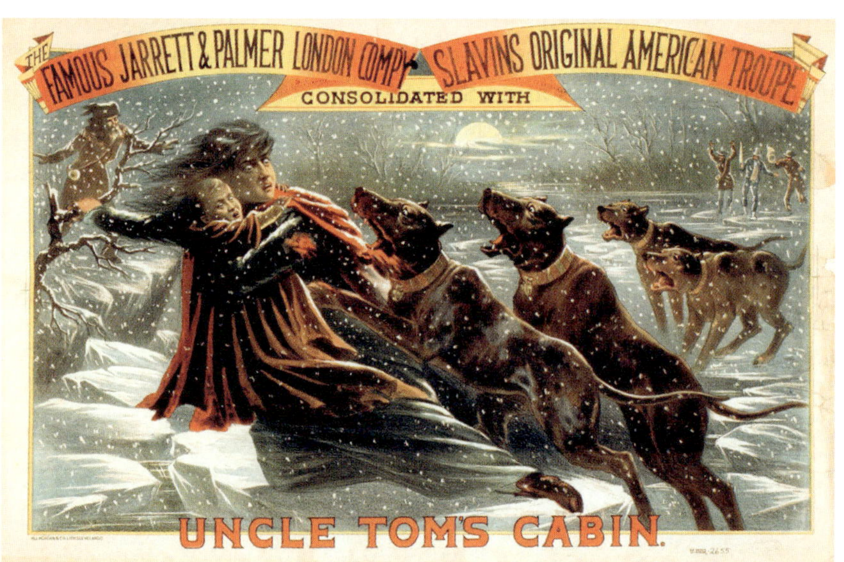

237 Reverting to wolves: Poster for an 1881 theatrical production of *Uncle Tom's Cabin*.

chasing the heroine [**237**]. They have entered melodrama as ciphers for danger; they may as well be wolves, not perhaps as they really subsisted with hunter-gathering cultures but as they came to be understood in the Western history of how the dog became the first domesticated animal.

Dogs became civilized wolves and have here reverted to nature. As have their savage slave-holding owners.

The history of the dog in slavery and in the subsequent enforcement of white supremacy determined in important ways how the descendants of slaves lived with dogs in the world after the abolition of slavery just as, in different ways, the history of the relationship of Jews with dogs in the ghettos of Europe is refracted in their relationship to them in other places and times. Although Israelis own upward of 380,000 dogs – other sources suggest 500,000 – distributed among one-third of its households, the percentage of the population that has dogs is low by international standards, less than 5 per cent compared for example to Germany, tenth in the rankings, at 15 per cent, and Japan at 19 per cent. (Some 36 per cent of families in the UK own dogs.)

Images of dogs attacking black people in the struggles for integration are canonical and news reports of police using dogs in vicious attacks on black suspects well into this decade are notorious. The paintings of Kerry James Marshall are evidence that this long brutal history is being, if not forgotten, then set aside. Still the percentage of black families that have dogs in the United States is just over half of those in white families, 37 per cent compared to 65 per cent for white families and 61 per cent for Hispanic ones.[37]

The visual depiction of dogs as moral subjects leaves open the Darwinian question of canine conscience but leads us to another conclusion: there were no pictures of bad dogs, just of bad and immoral uses of them.

CODA

We Are Not Alone

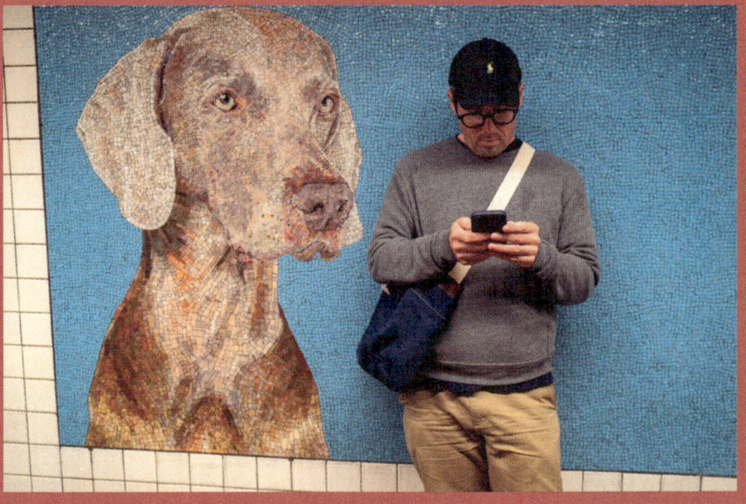

238 Looking together in a New York City subway station. One of William Wegman's eleven *Stationary Figures* murals (2018).

NEW TECHNOLOGIES IN THE last 150 years have opened new possibilities in the art of the dog. Motion pictures appropriated many of the formal and affective qualities of painting to create novelistic narratives about dogs and their humans. Snapshot photography made Everyman an artist of everyday life. Brand logos and mass advertisements made possible by a variety of cheap ways of reproducing images launched the dog's gaze and sociability into wide and rapid commercial circulation. And finally, the rise of conceptual art and of post-modern sensibilities not only inspired more art of the dog but has made us see it in more self-reflexive ways. It is now not only the viewers and creators of high art but all of us who, as John Berger put it, can if we wish feel less alone as a species and more connected to the first non-human animal we came to live with in the Palaeolithic age.

In the very earliest moving pictures, dogs were present in much the same way they had been in paintings of streets and public squares in Italian Renaissance art of the sixteenth century, Dutch cityscapes of the seventeenth century and Impressionist paintings of the nineteenth century as part of daily life. But while painters willed their presence into existence for formal and narrative reasons, dogs made their own way into the first moving pictures. Filmmakers had not yet recognized the distinction between the world on film – what is now called the diegesis – and the world outside. Art and the world were jumbled together as are dogs and humans in life. In the Lumière brothers' *La Sortie de l'Usine Lumière à Lyon* (Workers Leaving the Lumière Factory in Lyon), for example, the first ever for-pay movie, a large mutt bounds onto the screen, barks at some women, and exits quickly to the left. Two years later in the short *False Beggar* a purportedly crippled beggar gets up to pick up a coin that had missed his cup, exposes his ruse, and is chased by a cop. A dog wanders on-stage.

But even before these accidental dogs, the dog-as-uncalled-witness had made its way into moving pictures. In the Thomas Edison company's 45-second 'Athlete with Wand' a man raises and lowers a stick while doing deep knee bends; a dog rests patiently at his side, then raises its head to see what is going on, and lies back down. It is the only gesture in the short clip that suggests that the action is worth anyone's attention. We don't know whether Edison's assistant, William K. L. Dickson, who directed the film, consciously had in his mind's eye the long tradition of dogs watching what we do or simply tapped into some deep collective unconscious that demanded a witness for an action to be real.

By the early twentieth century, dogs entered moving pictures in numbers far exceeding those of any other animal: seven times as many as cats; three times as many as horses.[1] And not just as walk-ons; they became star actors in new interspecies narratives that pick up on older stories. In the 1905 *Rescued by Rover*, for example, a landmark of the British film industry, a collie finds a baby who had been kidnapped by gypsy beggars in retaliation for the nanny's refusal to give them alms. (The dog's real name was Blair and it belonged to the director Cecil Hepworth, but the character's name 'Rover' surged as a popular name for British dogs.)[2] That story of course mobilizes the trope of the dog discovering a lost child in mythologically inspired painting: the whole gallery of painting on the theme of the finding of the infant Cyrus – later Cyrus the Great who had been abandoned into the care of shepherds – or of Moses (*see* 62).

The German shepherd Rin-Tin-Tin became one of the greatest canine film stars – perhaps one of the greatest stars of any species – of the first half of the twentieth century. He had all the trappings of celebrity: a rags-to-riches life story – found starving as a puppy in the trenches of the Great War, rescued by an American soldier who brought him home; a scrappy entrance into the movies – his first film role was as a stand-in for a wolf; and then great success as the lead actor in more than a score of movies. He is buried in a place of honour back in his native France – in the Asnières-sur-Seine Cimetière des Chiens outside Paris. Rin-Tin-Tin made a fortune for his studio, Warner Bros. – indeed he saved it financially – and spawned a century's worth of sequels starring successive generations of

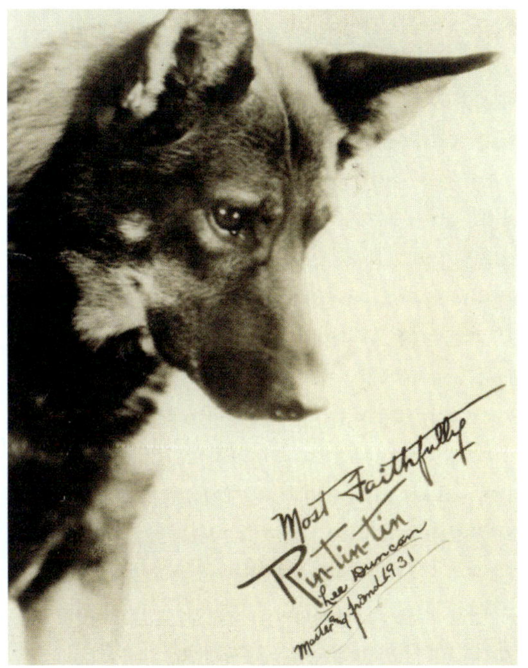

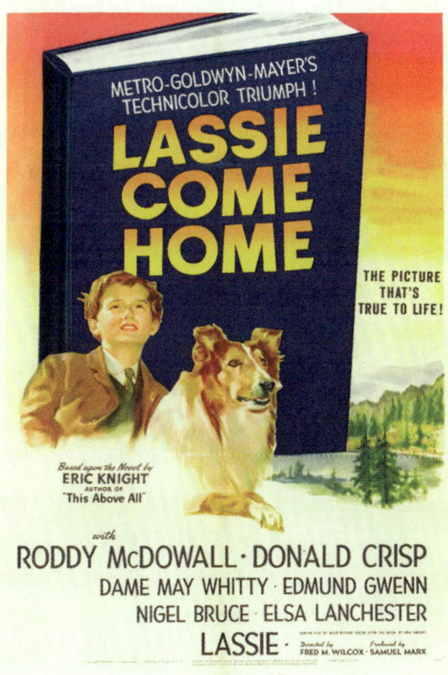

239–240 Two of the great stars of the early twentieth century: a photograph of Rin-Tin-Tin for a fan (1931, *left*); the poster for the film *Lassie Come Home* (1943, *right*).

German shepherds. The implicit narratives of dogs in fixed images – seeing and acting in the world together with humans – could now be represented through the time-expanding form of the motion picture.[3] The still pictures from the movies like Rin-Tin-Tin's autographed portrait [**239**] plays on the long tradition of dogs as both formally and emotionally meaningful. The art of the dog had entered mass culture.

The mirroring of emotions in painting expanded into long-form narratives. MGM's 1943 *Lassie Come Home* is a good example [**240**]. Mr and Mrs Carraclough live on a hardscrabble farm in Yorkshire and have fallen on hard times; they are forced to sell their son Joe's beloved dog – Lassie – to an aristocrat who had long fancied her and who takes her – the movie's hero – to Scotland. Boy and dog are both bereft; after several failed escape attempts Lassie, with the help of the duke's daughter Priscilla, finally succeeds in breaking out and, after overcoming many challenges, makes her way back to Yorkshire. The film is a kind of dual psychological portrait of the boy's longing for his dog on the one hand and the dog Lassie's perseverance against great odds on a long and danger-filled journey home. The poster for the movie mobilizes the double gaze that readers will have seen throughout this book: a static image that the film made dynamic.[4]

Mapping the history of specific social forms of the conjoined gaze and life of dog and human from painting onto film has the same effect. The dog as the poor man's friend of last resort, for example, becomes, in Charlie Chaplin's version, a story about how his famous lonely and rejected, but good-hearted, tramp character rescues his double, a stray dog, in similar circumstances. (He is being attacked by a pack of large dogs.) The movie, called *A Dog's Life*, takes the idea of the dog as the human's second self to a new level. They share their troubles; the dog is Chaplin's surrogate. It finds a wallet that had been stolen from a rich man; robbers steal it back, and after a series of adventures the dog again finds it, allowing the tramp to live happily ever after with a singer from a bar from which he had been ejected earlier. The film's poster is a reprise of some of the images that fill this book and suggests the scale of its success: 'the first million-dollar picture' [**241**].

The better-than-human, heroic dog, like those in paintings of St Roch, patron saint of dogs, and of St Bernards saving travellers in the snow, take on a new life in the movies, and in still photography. They document for a mass audience stories with a long history. The tale of the husky Balto and his mushers is formally indistinguishable from depictions of dogs with St Roch in seventeenth-century paintings. In 1925

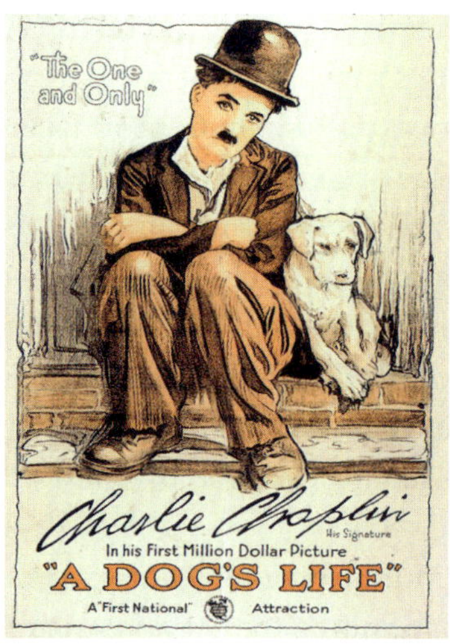

241 A second self: the poster for Charlie Chaplin's film *A Dog's Life* (1918).

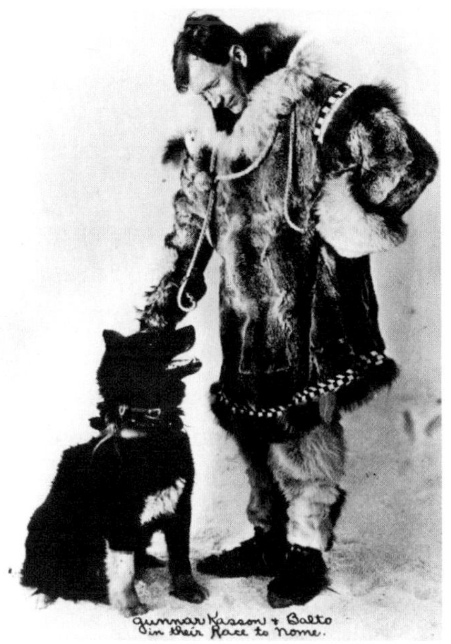

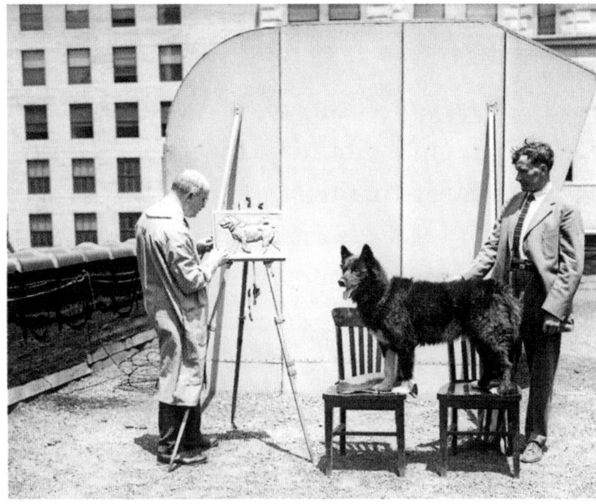

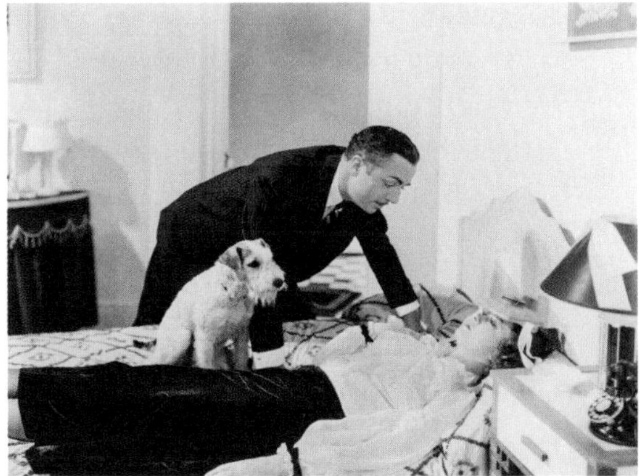

242–244 Heroic dogs in pop culture: Balto and his musher (*top left*); Balto posing for his monument (*top right*); Skippy/Asta on the set of *The Thin Man* (1934; *lower right*).

Balto led a sled team – the human musher was a Norwegian named Gunnar Kasson – through an Alaskan winter blizzard to bring diphtheria antitoxin to the village of Nome. The team's heroics became international news: newsreel recreations of their adventures supplemented widespread press reports.[5] A statue honouring Balto was erected in Central Park, New York, later that year with the canine hero present at the installation. The story, in turn, has spawned a small library of stories and later movies [**242-243**]. In a purely formal sense it is almost as if cinematography framed its shots with an eye to the art history of the dog. The canine star 'Asta' is an avatar of all those dogs we have seen in this book engaging humans with their gaze. In real life she is Skippy, the wire fox-terrier actor who became famous from *The Thin Man* movies of the 1930s based on Dashiell Hammett's novel of that name [**244**].

Intermedia influence has flowed in both directions. Photography from its earliest days influenced paintings including those that engaged with dogs, and of course photographers framed their worlds as they had been taught to see them in earlier visual arts. Indeed, they reproduced them. Among the twenty-three illustrations in Henry Fox Talbot's 1845 *Sun Pictures in Scotland*, the first commercially published photography book, is a calotype picture of the tomb sculpture of Sir Walter Scott's favourite dog: 'O, Maida, you sleep under the stone effigy of Maida' reads part of the Latin inscription.

But the new technology of still photography opened new ways of seeing dogs and humans together, first by the democratization of image-making. There was an enormous expansion of professional photography studios in Europe and the Americas. By the 1860s every city of any size had one or more; Kaiser Wilhelm I designated 150 official 'photographers to the crown', which did not include the hundreds without imperial privileges. Moreover, technical advances vastly increased the numbers of photographs and the reproducibility of images. That fact, and the new cultural significance of pet-keeping as a self-conscious part of life, made the interspecies portrait a commonplace. Dogs could sit still for the five–seven seconds needed to make a daguerreotype and were present from the very beginning of photography in the 1840s. In the *carte-de-visite* craze of the 1860s to 1890s they became ubiquitous, present with humans in their thousands and tens of thousands. *Cartes-de-visite* were calling-card-size photographs – four-to-a-page contact sheets before being cut and mounted on cards – that were the social media of their age, sold usually in batches of twenty to a broad public that traded and collected images of their friends and families in specially designed albums. These in turn were largely replaced by so-called cabinet cards, larger-scale images also on paper that were likewise distributed and collected as postcards.

Carte-de-visite and cabinet-card images of celebrities were reproduced by their copyright holders as well as pirated and sold in tens and occasionally hundreds of thousands of copies. They were the memes of their day. We saw the photograph of Colette with her French bulldog Toby Chien in chapter 5 (*see* 185). The royal photographer William Downing's 1866 portrait of Queen Victoria, still in mourning for Albert (died 1861), with her dog Sharp, gained still wider circulation. It was taken after years during which the queen refused to be photographed and was bought by a public eager to know how she looked. Victoria's hand rests on Sharp's back, his head lowered as if in respectful sadness and gently touching

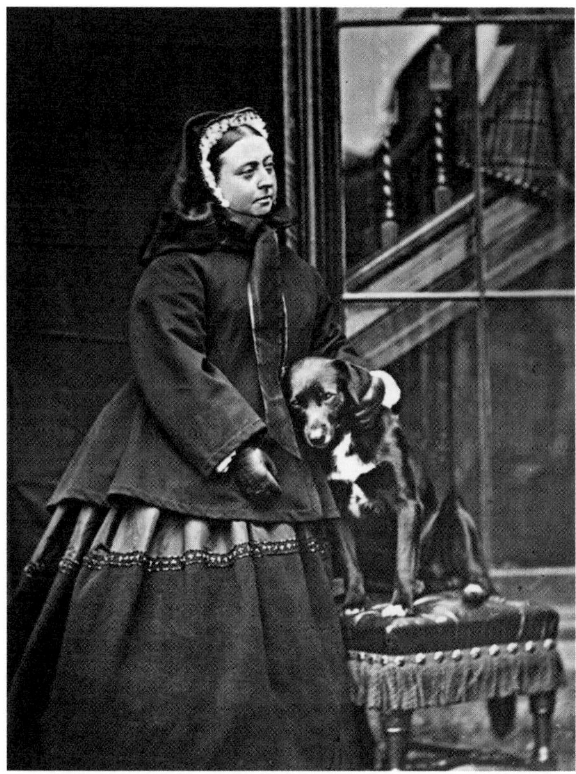

245 Queen Victoria with Sharp in mourning at Balmoral (1866).

her dress [**245**]. The mourning dog joined with the mourning queen became an image seen by hundreds of thousands of her subjects.

The introduction of the Kodak no. 1 in 1888 and Kodak no. 2 a year later, and even more so, the Brownie in 1900, all using paper-mounted rolls of film, took photography out of the studio and the hands of professionals. Image-making became a mass pursuit and dogs entered the visual record of humans in logarithmically greater numbers than all previous ages combined. For the artists in this book a dog in an image was a conscious choice, a question of form or narrative, of the creation of a relationship. This was probably the case for the many amateur photographers trying to take artful and well-composed snapshots. But in the vast archive of amateur still photography the dog is there because it is there, looking with and at humans. These dogs are the successors of the dogs that first became socially competent enough to live with us. The owners of cheap Kodak cameras – and of more expensive ones – unconsciously saw themselves and their world in a frame with dogs just as

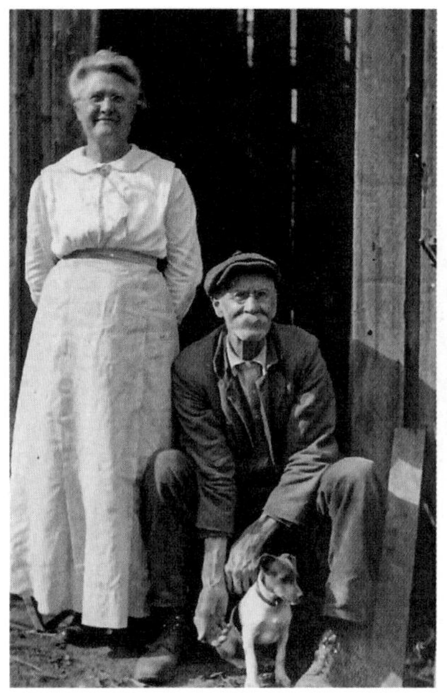

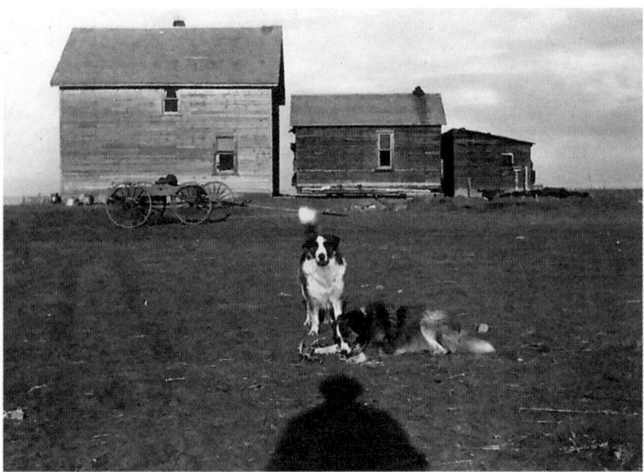

246–247 (*left*) My wife Carla's great-grandparents with Friskie at their orchard in Santa Cruz in 1918; (*above*) Two dogs on the Saskatchewan prairie in 1925.

Western artists had done for thousands of years. The age of mechanical reproduction created the vernacular dog on a whole new scale.

This is quotidian, unremarkable art produced by ordinary people to document their lives. There is a photograph of two dogs alone, lying at right angles, the one looking out at us and at the photographer, the other with a resigned look downward, in front of a failing farm on the Saskatchewan prairie. They are there almost as if they were a natural part of domestic space, a taken-for-granted presence. The shadow of the photographer is just visible at the bottom. The great-grandparents of my wife sit on the porch of a farmhouse of a hardscrabble apple orchard on land in the Santa Cruz mountains that he bought with his Civil War pension, having survived four years of hard fighting. It was a farm with lots of cats and other animals. But it is with their dogs, who appear alone in many other photographs, that they enter family memory. Mass photography has made seeing and being seen by dogs a commonplace of our Western humanity [**246-247**].

The ease of image-making and reproduction also made possible the aggregation in books and exhibitions of great numbers of images that emphasize specific claims about specific human/canine relationships: women and dogs; men and dogs; lesbians and their dogs; gay men and dogs;

families with dogs; black people and dogs; hunters with dogs; movie stars with dogs; children with dogs. Indeed, almost any group and dogs. And each of these connections established through an aggregation of images contains multiple stories as well as claims about multiple identities.

This in turn has made possible the elevation of the dog's gaze and its relation to humans into an extended comment about art, about dogs, about animal aesthetic agency and the role of art-making, and about trans-species bonds. The conceptual artist William Wegman's decade-long studies of his female Weimaraner Man Ray – named after the photographer with his Dada and Surrealist connections – and her successors is the most famous case of the self-conscious exploration of the strangeness of sharing ways of seeing with and being seen together across the species-divide with dogs (*see* 238). The photographs range from the surreal to the parodic and disturbing (the involuntary cross-dressing of dogs in trench coats). In a large body of Wegman's work a dog is dressed as a human and we are forced to think about how fundamentally strange but also magical our relationship is with an animal who has lived among us for at least 20,000 years. Wegman's art is grounded in the dog's gaze. Dogs are not humans in fur, his photography reminds us, but they are an intimate double.

Through various photographic processes – photogravures, half-tone, photolithography, and in the last thirty years various digital processes – and through the mass production of dog memes, the dog and its gaze have entered mass culture and commerce on a vast scale. Hollywood and other filmmaking capitals produced a blizzard of publicity pictures of movie stars with famous dogs, those they act with and those they lived with: Toto with Judy Garland; Bullet with Roy Rogers; the Bogart-Bacall family with assorted dogs. The original of Jeff Koons's 'Balloon' dog is the fourth highest-selling piece of art by a living artist, but knock-offs by the millions go for next to nothing and are known through photographs. And of course, there are the dogs of famous Disney movies – *One Hundred and One Dalmatians, Lady and the Tramp, A Goofy Movie* – and of hundreds of modern films, animated and not.

The news generated still more dog images. Laika, the sad, part-husky, part-terrier stray dog, picked up off the streets of Moscow by Russian space scientists and sent to die as the first living creature to orbit the earth, was the subject of a stream of photographs [**248**]. These in turn have been translated into animated movies; graphic novels (Nick

Abadzis's *Laika* is told in various voices including the dog's); stamps with her image on it; stuffed animals and a whole panoply of trinkets or baubles, plus an opera, poems, and a host of scholarly articles about Laika and about the ethics of animal experimentation, all based on the story her eyes seem to speak. The culture industry loves shaggy-dog stories. A happier version of Laika's is Seaman's, the dog that Captain Meriwether Lewis bought to take along on what is known as the 'Lewis and Clark Expedition'. Seaman survived, lived into old age, and in the last fifty years has been featured in dozens of commemorative sites and children's books, alone and with his master.[6]

Through photography and allied printing technologies the dog was also instrumental in advertising. The most famous image is the iconic 'His Master's Voice' used by RCA, which until recently was the most recognized trademark in the world [**249**]. It is the portrait of a mixed-breed dog named Nipper – mostly Jack Russell terrier – who lived with Mark Russell Barraud, a scenery designer, in the Bristol theatre where he worked. In the painting made by Mark's brother, Francis Barraud, three years after Nipper died in 1895, the dog gazes attentively, his head cocked, into the darkness of the horn of an Edison cylinder phonograph, from which he seems to expect a voice to come. The tilted head, like the raising of a dog's eyebrows, is a

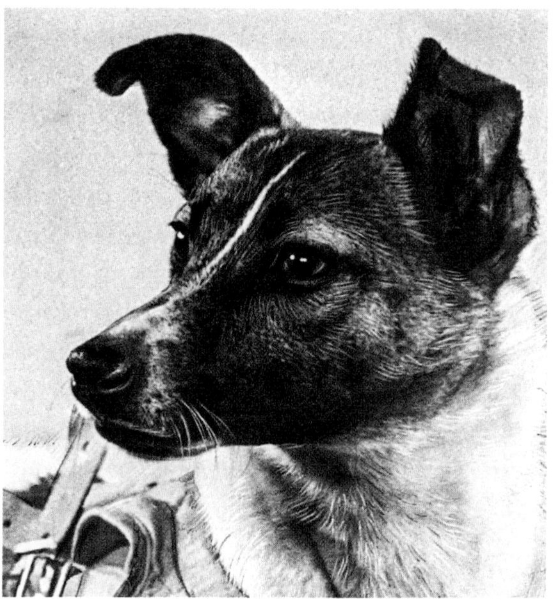

248 Laika, the first living creature to orbit the earth (albeit fatally), in 1957.

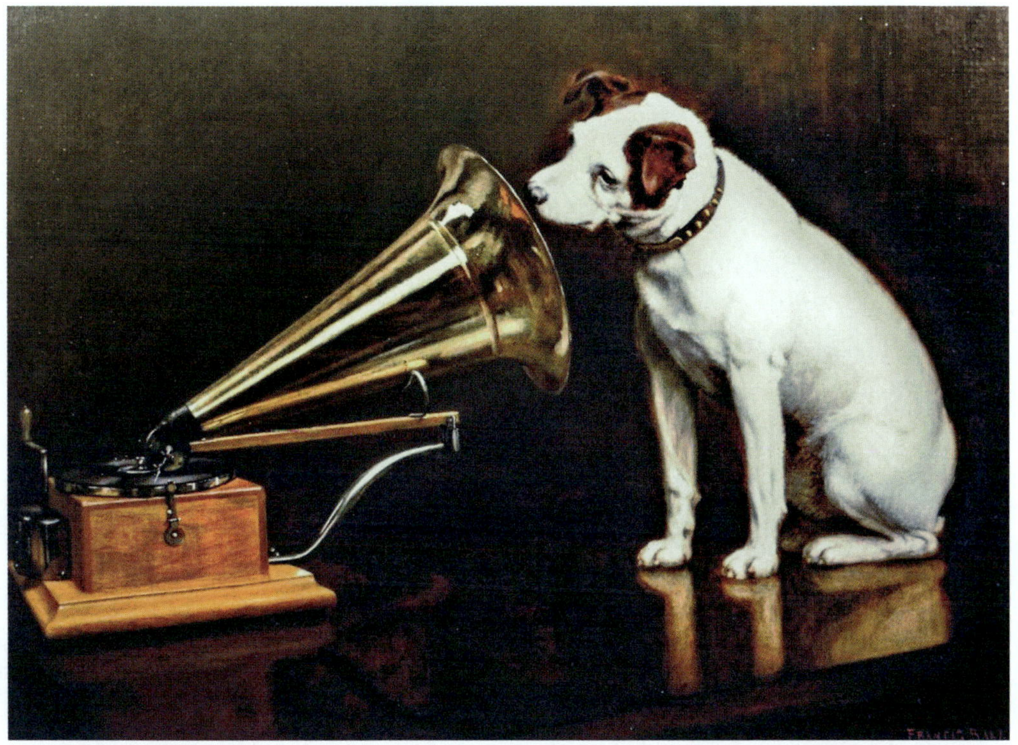

249 One of the most famous images in the history of advertising: *His Master's Voice* (1898) by Francis Barraud.

canine evolutionary adaptation that allows us to interpret its interest as like ours: puzzlement at a voice without an evident human source: Huh? Surprise. It connects the machine and Nipper's living body in a way we think is legible and with which we can identify.

One final twentieth-century image captures the claims of this book about what dogs do in art. A couple are dancing on a rooftop in a city, most likely San Francisco both because we know the artist, Joan Brown, painted many autobiographical images – she is from there – and because a silhouette of the Transamerica Pyramid near the upper right-hand corner gives it away [**250**]. The woman may well be the artist; the man, surreal in his transparent body through which we can see the floor and the city, may be one of her two husbands. We know they liked to dance. Notes float along the base of the image as they emerge behind the dog's body. It comes into the frame – barges in might be a better term – and into the couple's life, its feet as firmly planted as theirs are in motion. We don't

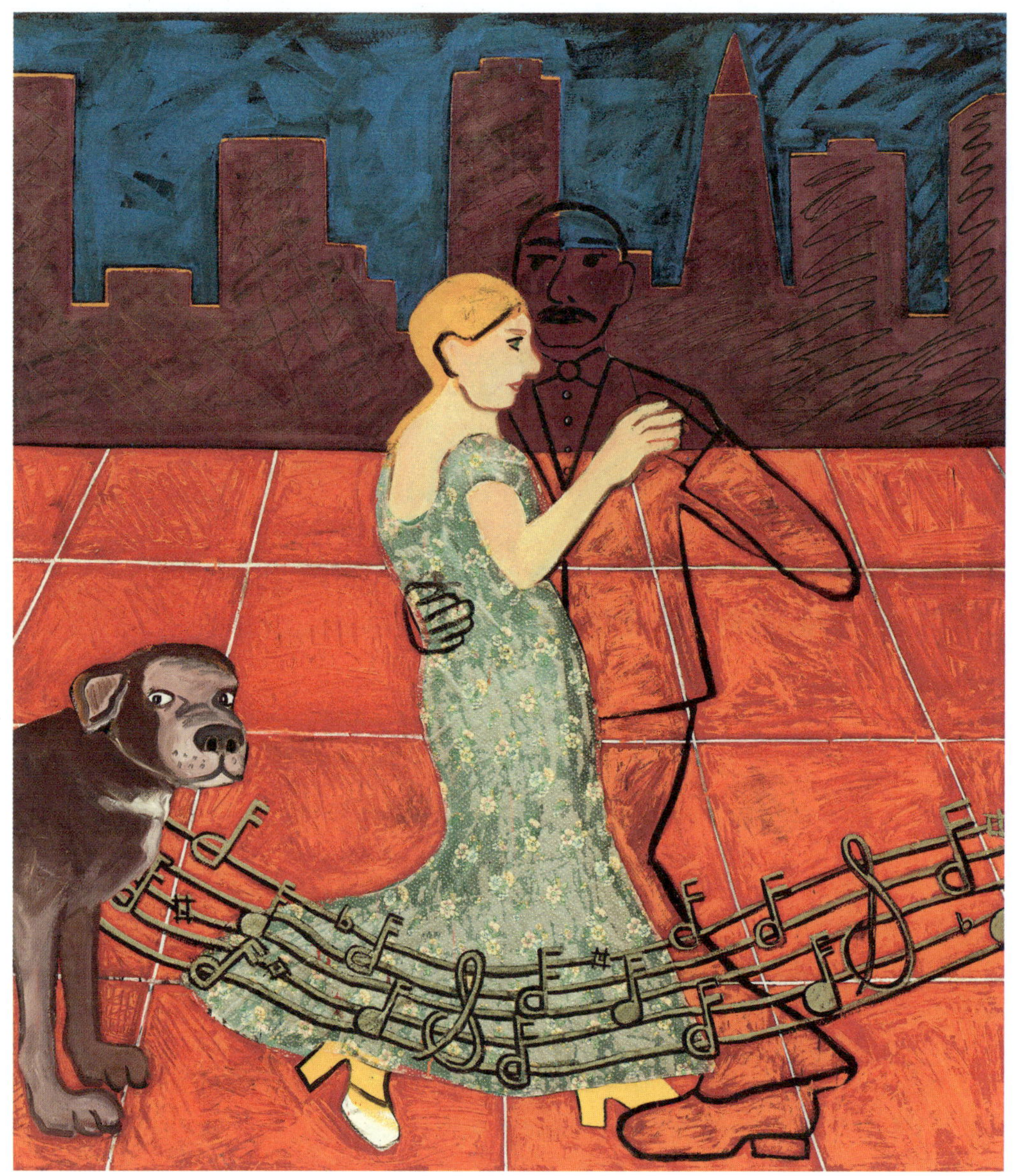

250 The final gaze: Joan Brown's *The Dancers in a City #2* (1972).

know whose dog it is; it doesn't matter except that it has entered the space and social world of the image; a whimsical dog, perhaps unsure what it is doing on the dance floor but certain in how it looks out at us intently from its inside perch as if to insist that we look: the dog's gaze.

The vast visual record of dogs in Western art – indeed in how humans represented their relationship with them since the Palaeolithic era in the Arabian desert – is the foundation of a structure of hundreds of millions of images in the mass culture of the twentieth and twenty-first centuries. Whether we are dog lovers or not, whether we take notice or not, they circulate among us in superabundance. This book has engaged with a small number of these images over the ages: the dog with humans and on its own; the dog seeing and being seen; the dog at the service of artists in the creation of the meaningful configurations that we think of as art. Our cross-species intimacy in daily life and especially in the intimacy of the gaze enfold the dog in the narratives we tell about ourselves. It was the fate of the now extinct grey wolf and its proto-dog successors – or more precisely the cunning of evolution – to evolve into a socially competent creature that shares the world with an art-producing human. In all their ubiquity, dogs are always entering our frame.

Notes

Preface: Dogs and Me

1 Erwin Panofsky, *The Life and Art of Albrecht Dürer* (Princeton, NJ: Princeton University Press, 1955), p. 153; Simona Cohen, 'Animal Imagery in Renaissance Art', *Renaissance Quarterly* 67:2 (Spring 2014), p. 170 and passim; idem, 'Changing Functions of Canine Imagery in Venetian Religious Paintings of the Sixteenth Century', *IKON* 2 (2009).
2 Horapollo Niliacus, *The Hieroglyphics of Horapollo* (Princeton, NJ: Princeton University Press, 1993, 2000), trans. George Boas, with a new introduction by Anthony Grafton, p. 63.
3 Erwin Panofsky, 'Jan van Eyck's Arnolfini Portrait', *Burlington Magazine* 64:372 (March 1934).
4 Edwin Hall, *The Arnolfini Wedding: Medieval Marriage and the Enigma of Van Eyck's Double Portrait* (Berkeley and Los Angeles, CA: University of California Press, 1994), on the hopelessness of item-by-item analysis, pp. 114–15 and ff. Witney Davis's analysis of visuality in the introduction to *A General Theory of Visual Culture* (Princeton, NJ: Princeton University Press, 2019), which suggests ways in which we come to see the elements of a picture as a whole.
5 Michael Baxandall, *Painting and Experience in Fifteenth-Century Italy* (Oxford and New York: Oxford University Press, new edition 1989) pp. 31–5 and 29–108 passim.
6 Sheila Hale, *Titian: His Life* (New York: Harper, 2003), pp. 261–2.
7 See my interpretation of this commitment to being both a Jew and a German in 'My Dead Fathers', *London Review of Books* (7 September 2006).
8 Susan Martha Kahn, ed., *Canine Pioneer: The Extraordinary Life of Rudolphina Menzel* (Waltham, MA: Brandeis University Press, 2023), p. 31 and pp. 3–81 passim.

Chapter 1: The Dog's Gaze

1 This may be just the most extreme version of dogs in paintings of paintings in aristocratic wonder cabinets. There are other examples. Two dogs scamper to the lower left corner of David Teniers the Younger's *Archduke Leopold*

in his Gallery in Brussels, while a dog in Veronese's *Esther before Ahasuerus*, the largest painting within that painting, is looking intently at what is happening. I am not sure if there are dogs within paintings in Hieronymus Francken II's *The Archdukes Albert and Isabella Visiting a Collector's Cabinet: 1623*, but there are five dogs of various sub-species ranging from small to very large and two monkeys. The van Haecht is not a historically accurate representation of the 1615 royal visit. Wildens' *Hunter* was not painted until 1624; Prince Władysław Vasa of Poland in the black hat, lower left, did not visit until that year. There is a fifth dog in this painting of paintings which is helping to herd sheep in Cornelis van Damen's *Rocky Landscape with Nomads* that hangs in the upper centre just below the chandelier.

2 Lawrence Smith, *Bruegel's Dogs*, privately published in *Picture It* (2022).

3 Rinder/Laqueur email (15 October 2024).

4 Edith Wharton, 'Life and I', in Cynthia Wolff, ed., *Edith Wharton: Novellas and Other Writings* (New York: Library of America, 1990).

5 My account of seeing in Dutch painting of this period, here and in the rest of this book, is based on a reading of Svetlana Alpers' influential *The Art of Describing* (Chicago, IL: University of Chicago Press, 1983).

6 Robert Singer and Kawai Masmoto, eds, *The Life of Animals in Japanese Art* (Princeton, NJ: Princeton University Press, 2019), pp. 40–42, 165; see also, for example, Yoshitoshi's 1868 woodcut of Saigo Takamori, 'the last samurai' walking his dog.

7 John Berger, 'Why Look at Animals?', in *About Looking* (New York: Pantheon, 1980), p. 4.

8 See Philippe Fosse et al., 'Les Canidés (Canis, Cuon) de la grotte Chauvet Pont d'Arc: réflexions sur les données paléontologiques et ichnologiques', *Relations Hommes-Canidés, PACEA* (UMR 5199); Institut Ausonius (UMR 5607), Pessac, France (October 2018), pp. 123–40.

9 Marcel Proust, *Within a Budding Grove*, vol. 2 of *In Search of Lost Time*, trans. C. K. Moncrieff and Terence Kilmartin, rev. D. J. Enright (New York: The Modern Library, 1933), pp. 309–10.

10 Adam Smith, *Theory of Moral Sentiments*, eds. D. D. Raphael and A. L. Macfie, Glasgow edition of the *Works and Correspondence of Adam Smith*, I, iii, p. 2.

11 *Nature* 11:576 (December 2019), pp. 442 ff.

12 Jean Clottes, *Chauvet Cave: The Art of Earliest Times* (Salt Lake City, UT: University of Utah Press, 2003).

13 Martin Trautmann et al., 'First Bioanthropological Evidence for Yamnaya Horsemanship', *Science Advances* 9:9 (3 March 2023).

14 Robin Gibson, *The Face in the Corner: Animal Portraits from the Collections of the National Portrait Gallery* (London: National Portrait Gallery Publications, 1998); Colin Eisler, *Dürer's Animals* (Washington DC and London: Smithsonian Institution Press, 1991).

15 James Rubin, *Impressionist Cats and Dogs: Pets and Painting in Modern Life* (New Haven, CT: Yale University Press, 2003), referring to Margaret A. Seibert's

'A Political and a Pictorial Tradition Used in Gustave Courbet's *Real Allegory*', *Art Bulletin*, LXV:2 (1983), pp. 311–16.

16 Here he is quoting with approval François-René, vicomte de Chateaubriand, one of the literary giants of the early nineteenth century.

17 In Veronese's *Venus and Mars with Cupid and Horse*, the horse intruding on his master's love from around a corner is almost a joke. See this painting in the Galleria Sabauda, Turin, at https://www.wga.hu/html_m/v/veronese/10/8venus_m.html.

18 Schmitt cited in Ulrich Raulff, *Farewell to the Horse: A Cultural History*, trans. Ruth Ahmedzai Kemp (New York: Liveright, 2015), p. 231. There is a sense in which the human and animal disciplinary regimes converge in the horse in the late sixteenth century in equitation and in the horse ballet. See, for example, William Cavendish, Duke of Newcastle, *Méthode et Invention Nouvelle de Dresser les Chevaux* (1658), the frontispiece of which shows a circle of horses kneeling down 'paying homage to their master'. The horse ballets of the sixteenth- and seventeenth-century French court mirror the corporeal discipline of human ballet.

19 Titian's portrait is based on a somewhat earlier full-length one by Jakob Seisenegger in which we know that the female dog was painted from life. Charles was dissatisfied with it. The sex of the dog in the Titian is not indicated, although it was clearly the same dog as in the original. See Linda L. Carroll, 'A Newly-Discovered Charles V with Dog', *Ateneo Veneto*, ser. 3.4.2 (2005), pp. 43–77, for an excellent survey of the literature on this early portrait.

20 The Lissipos statue is known through a second-century BCE copy found in Herculaneum. See https://www.getty.edu/publications/artistryinbronze/conservation-and-analysis/44-siano (accessed 26 November 2024).

21 On this see Marcy Norton, *The Tame and the Wild: People and Animals after 1492* (Cambridge, MA: Harvard University Press, 2024).

22 Elisa Tamarkin, *Apropos of Something: A History of Irrelevance and Relevance* (Chicago, IL: University of Chicago Press, 2022), p. 133, and more generally on Homer, pp. 132–70, to which my reading of the painting is indebted. She suggests that Winslow Homer is an artist who 'shows how wonderful a painting can be at seizing something from out of the drift', that is, at making us look at particular features of the image.

23 Nicolai Cikovsky, Jr., 'Winslow Homer's (So-Called) "Morning Bell"', *The American Art Journal* 29:½ (1998), pp. 4–17; Bryan J. Wolf, 'The Labor of Seeing: Pragmatism, Ideology and Gender in Winslow Homer's "The Morning Bell"', *Prospects* 17 (October 1991), pp. 273–318, 282.

24 Jonathan Pageau, 'Understanding the Dog Head Icon of St Christopher', *Orthodox Art Journal* (8 July 2013), https://orthodoxartsjournal.org/the-icon-of-st-christopher (accessed 7 July 2024).

25 St Augustine, *The City of God* XVI, p. 8.

26 Alexandra Horowitz in her best-selling *Inside of a Dog* (2009) makes that clear. I might note that she has also written a book called *On Looking: Eleven Walks with Expert Eyes* (2013).

27 Quoted in Penelope Hunting, *My Dearest Heart: The Artist Mary Beale* (London: Unicorn, 2019), p. 88; the original is in the Bodleian Library, MS Rawlinson, p. 108.
28 'Borrowed Dogs' in Richard Avedon's *Family Portraits*, accessed in 2024 on the Richard Avedon Foundation website, https://www.scribd.com/doc/28808704/Richard-Avedon-Borrowed-Dogs.
29 Homer, *Odyssey*, trans. Daniel Mendelsohn (Chicago, IL: University of Chicago Press, 2025), Bk 17, lines 310 ff.

Chapter 2: The Deep Time of the Dog

1 Maria Leach, *God Had a Dog: Folklore of the Dog* (New Brunswick, NJ: Rutgers University Press, 1961), pp. 5–7 ff; the Tehuelche story is told in Marion Schwartz, *A History of Dogs in the Early Americas* (New Haven, CT: Yale University Press, 1997), pp. 2 and 1–29 passim; Bibek Debroy, *Sarama and Her Children: The Dog in Indian Myth* (Delhi: Penguin India, 2008), tells stories from the subcontinent about the mythic dog of the gods and her progeny. For Iron Age northern Europe see Kate Smith, *Guides, Guards and Gifts to the Gods: Domesticated Dogs in the Art and Archaeology of Iron Age and Roman Britain* (London: BAR Series, 2006), p. 69, for a photograph of a later votive altar from Roman Britain; Miranda Green, *Symbols and Images in Celtic Religious Art* (London: Routledge, 1999).
2 I am grateful to Professor Niek Veldhuis, Department of Middle Eastern Languages and Cultures, University of California, Berkeley, for the translation.
3 Daniel Defoe, *Robinson Crusoe* (Oxford and New York: Oxford University Press, 2007).
4 A. Miklósi and J. Topál, 'What Does it Take to Become "Best Friends"? Evolutionary Changes in Canine Social Competence', *Trends in Cognitive Sciences* 17:6 (June 2013), pp. 287–94. Miklósi develops these ideas in his *The Dog: A Natural History* (Princeton, NJ: Princeton University Press, 2018) and *Dog Behaviour, Evolution, and Cognition*, 2nd ed. (Oxford: Oxford University Press, 2015). He has kindly welcomed me into his Budapest laboratory on a number of occasions. His work is foundational.
5 On the octopus see Sy Montgomery, *Soul of an Octopus* (New York: Atria Books, 2015), and the 2020 documentary, 'Secrets of the Octopus'.
6 The wolves of 30,000, 50,000, 100,000 years ago were genetically closer still to the early dogs of their day.
7 See *Nature* 437 (1 September 2005), pp. 69–87, for the initial sequence of the chimpanzee genome and comparison to the human genome.
8 Elizabeth Abbott, 'Jane Goodall, Rusty, and Me', *Huffington Post* (14 May 2015), www.huffingtonpost.com/elizabeth-abbott/jane-goodall-rusty-and-me_b_7275668.html; Goodall makes roughly the same point in her many interviews; most recently *The New York Times* (27 March 2024).

9 Email from Jasper Rine/author (9 March 2023). He adds that the matter is 'simpler to understand the less data we have, or once we have comprehensive data'.

10 Bridgett M. VonHoldt, 'Structural Variants in Genes Associated with the Human Williams-Beuren Syndrome Underlie Stereotypical Hyper-Sociability in Domestic Dogs', *Science Advances* 3:7 (19 July 2017).

11 Raymond Pierfotti and Brady R. Fogg, *How Wolves and Humans Coevolved* (New Haven, CT: Yale University Press, 2017), p. 15. This is not a controversial claim. I am indebted to this book as the best account of the evolution of the dog from the perspective of specialists in wolf biological and cultural ecology with an interest in the anthropology of the wolf among indigenous people; Christina Hansen Wheat et al., 'Human-Directed Attachment Behavior in Wolves Suggests Standing Ancestral Variation for Human–Dog Attachment Bonds', *Ecology and Evolution* 20 (September 2022), https://doi.org/10.1002/ece3.9299.

12 Belyaev was a careful reader of Darwin's *The Variation of Animals and Plants Under Domestication* (1868). He had a general interest in how only a handful of species came to be domesticated and how the wolf, in particular, became the dog. He reasoned that what might have determined whether a wild animal among humans was kept or killed was its prosocial behaviour, i.e. its ability to live in accord with our norms: to not bite our heads or hands off, for example.

13 L. A. Dugatkin, 'The Silver Fox Domestication Experiment', *Evolution Education Outreach* 11:16 (2018), https://doi.org/10.1186/s12052-018-0090-x; idem, Lee Alen and Lydmila Trut, *How to Tame a Fox (and Build a Dog)* (Chicago, IL: University of Chicago Press, 2017).

14 Wolfgang M. Schleidt and Michael D. Shalter, 'Co-Evolution of Humans and Canids: An Alternative View of Dog Domestication: Homo Homini Lupus?', *Evolution and Cognition* 57 (2003), pp. 9, 1; J. Koster and K. Tankersley, 'Heterogeneity of Hunting Ability and Nutritional Status among Domestic Dogs in Lowland Nicaragua', *Proceedings of the National Academy of Sciences of the U.S.A.* 109 (2012), E463–E470.

15 The 'animal connection' as the anthropologist Pat Lee Shipman calls it. Pat Shipman, *The Animal Connection: A New Perspective on What Makes Us Human* (New York: W. W. Norton, 2011).

16 Michael Tomasello et al., 'Reliance on Head versus Eyes in the Gaze Following of Great Apes and Human Infants: The Cooperative Eye Hypothesis', *Journal of Human Evolution* 52, pp. 314–20; H. Kobayashi and S. Kohshima, 'Unique Morphology of the Human Eye and its Adaptive Meaning: Comparative Studies on External Morphology of the Primate Eye', *Journal of Human Evolution* 40:5 (2001), pp. 419–35; Pat Shipman's general views are in 'The Animal Connection and Human Evolution', *Current Anthropology* 51:4 (August 2010); the claim about Neanderthals is made briefly in idem, 'Do the Eyes Have it?', *American Scientist* 100:2 (May–June 2012), pp. 198 ff, and more fully in idem, *The Invaders: How Humans and their Dogs Drove Neanderthals to Extinction* (Cambridge, MA: Belknap Press, 2015).

17 Mietje Germonpré et al., 'Palaeolithic Dog Skulls at the Gravettian Předmostí Site, the Czech Republic', *Journal of Archaeological Science* 39:1 (January 2012); idem et al., 'Fossil Dogs and Wolves from Palaeolithic Sites in Belgium, the Ukraine and Russia: Osteometry, Ancient DNA and Stable Isotopes', *Journal of Archaeological Science* 36:2 (February 2009), pp. 473–90; Monserrat Hervella et al., 'The Domestic Dog that Lived ~17,000 Years Ago in the Lower Magdalenian of Erralla Site (Basque Country): A Radiometric and Genetic Analysis', *Journal of Archaeological Sciences: Reports* 46 (2022).

18 Luc Janssens et al., 'A New Look at an Old Dog: Bonn-Oberkassel Reconsidered', *Journal of Archaeological Science* (April 2018), pp. 126–38; S. Davis and F. Valla, 'Evidence for Domestication of the Dog 12,000 Years Ago in the Natufian of Israel', *Nature* 276 (1978), pp. 608–10, https://doi.org/10.1038/276608a0; L. G. Koungoulos, J. Balme and S. O'Connor, 'Dingoes, Companions in Life and Death: The Significance of Archaeological Canid Burial Practices in Australia', *PLoS ONE* 18:10 (2023).

19 Angela R. Perri et al., 'Dog Domestication and the Dual Dispersal of People and Dogs into the Americas', *PNAS* 118:6 (25 January 2021).

20 Angi M. Johnson, 'Uncovering the Origins of Dog-Human Eye Contact: Dingoes Establish Eye Contact More Than Wolves, but Less Than Dogs', *Animal Behaviour* 133 (2017), pp. 123–9; Matt A. Field et al., 'The Australian Dingo is an Early Offshoot of Modern Breed Dogs', *Science Advances* 8:16 (2022).

21 Tazeen Ishmann et al., 'Orienting Attention Based on the Gaze of a Dog', *Vision Science* 19:10 (September 2019); Márta Gácsi et al., 'Face Readers of Our Minds? Dogs (Canis Familiaris) Show Situation-Dependent Recognition of Human's Attention', *Animal Cognition* 7 (2004), pp. 144–53.

22 Juliane Kaminski et al., 'Evolution of Facial Muscle Anatomy in Dogs', *PNAS* (17 June 2019), pp. 116, 29.

23 'The Wolf, the Dog and the Collar', *mythfolklore.net* (accessed 25 February 2024); it is no. 346 in the Perry Index of Aesop's fables.

24 Christiana Franco, *Shameless: The Canine and the Feminine in Ancient Greece*, trans. Matthew Fox (Berkeley and Los Angeles, CA: University of California Press, 2014), pp. 43–5. More generally this is the best account I have found of the long history of dogs in Greek prose and poetry.

25 *The Little Flowers of St Francis*, trans. W. Heywood (New York: Barnes and Noble, [1907], 2020), Chapter 21.

26 This trope is still powerful in feminist debates of the nineteenth century.

27 Anne-François-Joachim Fréville, *Histoire des chiens célèbres* (Paris, 1808), p. 9.

28 Pliny the Elder, *Natural History* 8:61; Idan Brier, 'Sumer as the Cradle of History – Canine as Well: The Representation of the Dog in Sumerian Proverbial Literature', *Maarav* 21:1-1 (2014), pp. 83–101.

29 *Totemism*, trans. Rodney Needham (Boston, MA: Beacon Press, 1993), p. 89. Lévi-Strauss was writing about totemism and the many animals that humans used to differentiate themselves through tribes and clans: bears, lions, otters, alligators, ants, antelopes and many more.

30 Kenneth F. Kitchell, 'Seeing the Dog: Naturalistic Canine Representations from Greek Art', *Arts* 9:1 (2020), p. 14; https://doi.org/10.3390/arts9010014. Kitchell makes the case that the careful attention that artists paid to dog gestures is in the context of considerable classical interest in gestures and non-verbal communication more generally. The particular role of dogs' gestures in Greek kraters is explored by Marina Haworth in 'The Wolfish Lover: The Dog as a Comic Metaphor in Homoerotic Symposium Pottery', *Archimède: archéologie et histoire ancienne* 5 (2018), pp. 7–23.

31 Wittgenstein, *Philosophical Investigations*, p. 250 and passim.

32 Luciano Floridi, 'Scepticism and Animal Rationality: The Fortune of Chrysippus' Dog in the History of Western Thought', *Archiv für Geschichte der Philosophie* 79 (1997), pp. 27–57.

33 St Basil the Great, *Homilies on Genesis*.

34 See for this and the following paragraphs, 'Essay for Raymond Sebond', in *The Complete Essays of Montaigne*, trans. Donald M. Frame, Bk 2, ch. 12, pp. 331, 339–40.

35 Nelson Coon, *A Brief History of Dog Guides for the Blind* (Morristown, NJ: The Seeing Eye, Inc., 1959); Coon was the librarian of the Perkins School for the Blind, which has an extensive digitally available collection of images of dogs leading the blind.

36 J. E. B. Mayer, 'King James I on the Reasoning Faculty in Dogs', *Classical Review* 12 (1898), pp. 93–6, gives an account of the disputation from a contemporaneous source: https://penelope.uchicago.edu/Thayer/E/Journals/CR/12/2/King_James_on_Reason_in_Dogs*.html (accessed 25 July 2024).

37 Andrew Aberdein, 'Logic for Dogs', in Steven D. Hales, ed., *What Philosophy Can Tell You About Your Dog* (Chicago, IL: Open Court, 2008), pp. 167–81; David Hume, *A Treatise on Human Reason*, Bk I, Pt II, Sect. XVI.

38 For Kant on animal rationality see Patrick Kain, 'Kant on Animals', in Peter Adamson and G. Fay Edwards, eds, *Animals: A History* (Oxford: Oxford Academic Books, 2018), Chapter 8, pp. 211–38. Accessed online at the UC Berkeley Library.

39 See for example Martin Schongauer, *Altarpiece of the Dominicans* (aka *The Mystic Hunt*), c. 1480. Oil on pine, each panel 116 × 116 cm. Musée d'Unterlinden, Colmar, France. Bottom: Martin Schongauer, *The Mystic Hunt of the Unicorn* (1489), Pushkin Museum of Fine Arts, Moscow.

40 Hume, *Treatise*, Book 2, part 3, section 10.

41 Maria Guagnin, Angela R. Perri, Michael D. Petraglia et al., 'Pre-Neolithic Evidence for Dog-Assisted Hunting Strategies in Arabia', *Journal of Anthropological Archaeology* 4 (2018), pp. 225–36.

42 Frank Hole and Cherra Wyllie, 'The Oldest Depictions of Canines and a Possible Early Breed of Dog in Iran', *Paléorient* 33:1 (2007), pp. 175–85. *JSTOR*, http://www.jstor.org/stable/41496803 (accessed 26 July 2024).

43 Franco Viviani, 'Finding and Losing the World's Oldest Art in Sulawesi'. An anthropologist goes back to see Sulawesi cave paintings he reported in Indonesia decades ago – and mourns their degradation and loss. For references

and details, see https://www.sapiens.org/archaeology/sulawesi-cave-paintings.

44 Martin Trautmann et al., 'First Bioanthropological Evidence for Yamnaya Horsemanship', *Science Advances* 9:9 (3 March 2023); the earliest image seems to be an Egyptian graffito of the goddess Astarte on horseback, Nineteenth Dynasty, Egypt, 1,500 years after humans began riding.

45 Hu Y, Hu S, Wang W, Wu X, F. B. Marshall, Chen X, Hou L, Wang C, 'Earliest Evidence for Commensal Processes of Cat Domestication', *Proceedings of the National Academy of Sciences* 111:1 (7 January 2014), pp. 116–20. The group's work is based on the skeletal evidence of cats found recently in the agricultural village of Quanhucun in Shaanxi, China, which they date to 5560–5280 BCE.

46 Stephanie Lynn Budin, *Artemis* (New York, London: Routledge, 2016), pp. 2–3 and passim.

47 Xenophon, *On Hunting*, trans. E. C. Marchant and Glen Bowersock, in *Xenophon VII*, ed. Jeffrey Henderson (Cambridge, MA: Loeb Classical Library/Harvard University Press, 1968), pp. 365–8.

48 Budin, *Artemis*, pp. 20–24, 111–12.

49 Patricia Zalamea, 'Subject to Diana: Picturing Desire in Renaissance Courtly Aesthetics', PhD thesis, Rutgers University (2007), p. 16, and more generally throughout; Katherine Marsengill, 'Identity Politics in Renaissance France: Cellini's Nymph of Fontainebleau', *Anthanor* XIX (2001), pp. 35–42. See the 'Dish with Diana, the Nymph of Fontainebleau', late sixteenth century, Maiolica plate, Metropolitan Museum of Art, New York, for the same idea in another medium.

50 Ovid, *Metamorphoses*, Book 10.

51 De Kooning talk delivered at Studio 35, 8th Street, New York (Autumn 1949), The Willem de Kooning Foundation website, https://www.dekooning.org/documentation/words/the-renaissance-and-order (accessed 12 July 2023).

52 Carl C. Schlam, 'Diana and Actaeon: Metamorphoses of a Myth', *Classical Antiquity* 3:1 (1984), pp. 82–110; https://doi.org/10.2307/25010808.

53 Pausanias, *A Description of Greece*, trans. W. H. S. Jones (Cambridge, MA: Loeb Classical Library/Harvard University Press, 1926), 4:9, II. 1–4, p. 179.

54 The story is in *Metamorphoses* Book 3, pp. 165–205; Marie-Rose Logan, 'Antique Myth and Modern Mind: Jacque Lacan's Version of Actaeon and the Fictions of Surrealism', *Journal of Modern Literature* 25:3/4 (Summer 2002); 'Global Freud: Psychoanalytic Cultures and Classic Modernism' (Summer 2002), pp. 90–100, https://www.jstor.org/stable/3831856 (accessed 13 June 2023); Leonard Barkan, 'Diana and Actaeon: The Myth as Synthesis', *English Literary Renaissance* 10:3 (Autumn 1980), p. 320, and more generally his *Gods Made Flesh: Metamorphosis and the Pursuit of Paganism* (New Haven, CT: Yale University Press, 1986); for the influence of Ovid in art see C. Allen, 'Ovid and Art', in P. Hardie, ed., *The Cambridge Companion to Ovid* (Cambridge: Cambridge University Press, 2002), pp. 336–67.

55 For Diana's point of view, given the archetypal story of a nymph who lets down her guard while hunting and is assaulted, see John Heath, 'Diana's

Understanding of Ovid's "Metamorphoses"', *The Classical Journal* 86:3 (February–March 1991), pp. 233–43, https://www.jstor.org/stable/3297428 (accessed 13 June 2022).

56 Appolodorus (or Pseudo-Appolodorus), *Bibilotheca (Library)*, trans. James George Franzer (Cambridge, MA: Harvard University Press, 1921, 1956–61), Bk. 3, ch. 4.

57 For a survey of the 'Poésie Series' more generally see Matthias Wivel et al., *Titian: Love, Desire, Death* (New Haven, CT: Yale University Press, 2020), the catalogue of an exhibition of all six paintings at the National Gallery in London and the Isabella Stewart Gardner Museum in Boston where I saw it. The *Venus and Adonis* of the often copied painting – by Titian and others – is the Prado version in the exhibition, the one that was delivered to Philip II. For *The Death of Actaeon*, which did not travel and remained in London where I saw it, see the Cat. 7 essay by Wivel, p. 179 ff.

58 M. Kemp, 'Looking at the Face of the Earth', *Nature* 456:18 (December 2008), p. 876.

59 Naomi M. Maurer, *The Pursuit of Spiritual Wisdom: The Thought and Art of Vincent Van Gogh and Paul Gauguin* (Madison, NJ: Fairleigh Dickinson University Press, 1998), p. 154 and passim; Sue Prideaux, *Wild Thing: A Life of Paul Gauguin* (New York: Faber and Faber, 2024), offers a sympathetic account of Gauguin's search for the primitive and the place of the dog in his imagination.

Chapter 3: The Art of the Dog

1 Whitney Davis's *A General Theory of Visual Culture* makes the point that there is a hermeneutic loop in interpreting any image in which pictoriality (elements in the picture as they come together to constitute a meaningful configuration) cannot be decoupled from 'culturality' (cultural meaning or the world as seen by a community of viewers, including the artist as a privileged viewer). I thank Diliana Angelova for drawing my attention to Davis's work and explaining its importance to me.

2 Svetlana Alpers and Michael Baxandall, *Tiepolo and the Pictorial Intelligence* (New Haven, CT: Yale University Press, 1994), p. 31.

3 Ibid, pp. 30–31.

4 Ibid, p. 31; see also p. 55.

5 *Unrecounted [Unerzählt]*, trans. Michael Hamburger (New York: New Directions, 2003), pp. 56–7.

6 The quote is on the label for this painting in the Musée d'Orsay; https://www.musee-orsay.fr/en/artworks/une-moderne-olympia-1478.

7 See T. J. Clark's account of Cézanne as a phenomenologist in his recent *If These Apples Should Fall: Cézanne and the Present* (London: Thames and Hudson, 2023).

8 Rainer Maria Rilke, *Letters on Cézanne*, trans. Joel Agee (from International Publishing, New York, 1985 [German edition, 1952]) (11 October 1907), p.

46; see also p. vii ff; Filippo Fimiani, 'Portrait of the Artist as an Old Dog: Of Rilke, Cézanne, and the Animalisation of Painting', *Anthropology and Aesthetics* 44 (2003), p. 113 ff; Nina Athanassoglou-Kallmyer, 'Like a Dog, Just Looking: Cézanne, Innocence, and Early Phenomenological Thought in Nineteenth-Century France', in *A Companion to Nineteenth-Century Art*, ed. Michelle Eacos (New York: John Wiley & Sons, Inc., 2019); Helen Bridge, 'Rilke and the Visual Arts', in Karen Leeder and Rober Vilain, *The Cambridge Companion to Rilke* (Cambridge: Cambridge University Press, 2010), pp. 154 and 145–59.

9 Alberti, *On Painting*, ed. J. R. Spencer (New Haven, CT, and London: Yale University Press, 1976), Bk. 2, p. 78.

10 Craig A. Gibson, 'In Praise of Dogs: An Encomium Theme from Classical Greece to Renaissance Italy', in L. Gelfand, ed., *Our Dogs, Our Selves: Dogs in Medieval and Early Modern Art, Literature, and Society* (Brill, 2016), pp. 19–40.

11 See Alexander Samson, 'Between Picaresque and the Picturesque: Bartolomé Esteban Murillo (1617–1682) Visualizing Spain in an Age of Decline', in Stephen M. Hart and Alexander Samson, eds, *Philip IV and the World of Spain's Rey Planeta* (Woodbridge, Suffolk: Tamesis, 2023), pp. 265–95.

12 See Angela Rosenthal, *Angelica Kauffman: Art and Sensibility* (London: Paul Mellon Centre, 2006), Chapter 1, 'Penelope and the Weaving of Narrative', pp. 15–41.

13 John Hayes, *British Paintings of the Sixteenth through Nineteenth Centuries* (National Gallery of Art, Washington DC/Cambridge University Press, 1992), pp. 268–71; see also Anthony Bailey, *Standing in the Sun: A Life of J. M. W. Turner* (London: Sinclair Stevenson, 1997), p. 296. The son of Turner's engraver claimed it was the twenty-five-year-old Edwin Landseer who added the dog. Bailey doubts this and says that perhaps it fell off and Landseer put it back.

14 Bodo Brinkmann, ed., *Cranach: Exhibition Catalogue* (London: Royal Academy of Art, 2007), pp. 202–4. The patron's dog is looking at the painter just as Alfred Bruyas' dog in Courbet's *La Rencontre, ou 'Bonjour, Monsieur Courbet'* (see chapter 5).

15 W. G. Sebald and Jan Peter Tripp, *Unrecounted* (London: Hamish Hamilton, 2004), p. 95.

16 I was led to the Sebald text, 'Like Day and Night', by the wonderful discussion of his comments in Carol Jacob's *Sebald's Vision* (New York: Columbia University Press, 2015), pp. 148–64. She discusses the quotations on pp. 155 and 159. W. G. Sebald, 'Like Day and Night . . . On the Paintings of Jan Peter Tripp', in *A Place in the Country*, trans. Jo Catling (New York: Penguin, 2014), pp. 170–73.

17 T. J. Clark, *Heaven on Earth: Painting and the Life to Come* (London and New York: Thames & Hudson, 2018), p. 48; Giorgio Vasari, *Lives of the Most Eminent Painters, Sculptors and Architects*, trans. with an introduction and notes by Julia Conway Bondanella and Peter Bondanella (Oxford: Oxford University Press, 2008), p. 15; see also pp. 35 and 15–36 passim.

18 See the learned and perceptive article by Jane D. Lang, 'The Commedia of Joachim and Anna at the Scrovegni Chapel', in Laura Gelfand, ed., *Our Dogs, Our Selves: Dogs in Medieval and Early Modern Art, Literature and Society* (London and Leiden: Brill, 2016), pp. 187–218. I base my claims of novelty on her careful documentation.

19 See Emmanuel Levinas, p. xxx; I found the commentary on this essay in Benjamin A. Wurgaft's *Thinking in Public: Strauss, Levinas, Arendt* (Philadelphia, PA: University of Pennsylvania Press, 2019), pp. 89–97, invaluable for thinking about Levinas and dogs. The part of the book from which these pages come is called 'The Dog at the End of the Verse (Exodus 11:17): Emmanuel Levinas Between Ethics and Engagement'.

20 George Orwell in 'A Hanging' writes about a dog like Bobby that burst into a prison yard and 'made a dash for the prisoner, and jumping up tried to lick his face', shocking the warder and interrupting 'the formality of the hanging'. The dog humanizes.

21 I have been much influenced at looking at this cycle, although not at its dogs, by T. J. Clark's *Heaven on Earth*.

22 Orhan Pamuk, *My Name is Red*, trans. Erdağ Göknar (New York: Knopf, 2001), p. 170.

23 Frederick Ilchman, 'Venetian Painting in an Age of Rivals', in idem, *Titian, Tintoretto, Veronese* (Boston: MFA Publications, 2009), pp. 21–41.

24 Jan Morris, *Ciao, Carpaccio! An Infatuation* (London: Pallas Athene, 2014).

25 *Hieronymus, Vita et Transitus* (Venice, 1485), trans. Helen I. Roberts, 'St Augustine in "St Jerome's Study": Carpaccio's Painting and its Legendary Source', *The Art Bulletin* 41:4 (December 1959), pp. 283–97, 292, an important source for the Renaissance cult of St Jerome. It is in turn based on a thirteenth-century source filled with forged letters. I rely on Roberts' interpretation. See also Peter Humfrey, ed., the exhibition catalogue *Vittore Carpaccio: Master Storyteller of Renaissance Venice*, Washington DC, National Gallery of Art, 2023 (New Haven, CT: Yale University Press, 2020), catalogue entry 29, pp. 176–9. On Carpaccio as exemplary of the Venetian narrative tradition I have relied on Patricia Fortini Brown, *Venetian Narrative Painting in the Age of Carpaccio* (New Haven, CT: Yale University Press, 1988). For the full narrative and iconographical context of this particular painting see Brown's learned essay, 'St Augustine in his Study: A Portrait within a Portrait', in Joseph V. Schnaubelt, OSA, and Frederick Van Fleteren, *Augustine in Iconography* (New York: Peter Lang, 1999), pp. 507–49; Panofsky quoted in Roberts, n. 59, p. 293.

26 Meredith J. Gill, in 'Augustine's Dog', *Artibus et Historiae* 87 (2023), pp. 53, 47–61 passim, suggests that members of the Mustela family to which weasels belong were also understood iconographically to be prognosticators and that hence exchanging an ermine for a dog would not have changed the meaning of the painting. In the context of Carpaccio's other uses of the ermine I don't think her interpretation works here.

27 Art historians once thought the knight might be St Eustace because of the deer in the background. (While out hunting this Roman general saw a crucifix in a deer's horns.) But no longer. The ermine, a sign of moral purity, is next to a scroll that reads '*malo mori quam foedari*' ('I prefer to die rather than incur dishonour'). This suggests that the subject might be Ferdinand II of Aragon, who was a Knight of the Order of Ermine. The falcon and heron refer to warfare; the peacock represents immortality or pride; the horse is there as a vehicle for the squire or for imagining the knight when younger if this is a memorial painting. His colours may represent those of the knight's family, but no one knows what family it might be. All the supposed symbols and beautifully painted plants would make one think that the painting must mean something. The online commentary on this painting for the exhibition at the National Gallery of Art, Washington DC, 'Carpaccio: Master Story Teller of Renaissance Venice November 20, 2002–February 12, 2023', suggests that 'looking closely at the animals, plants and other details' offers clues about him and about 'what Carpaccio intended to say about him'. https://www.nga.gov/stories/birds-trees-shining-armor-symbols-objects-carpaccio-young-knight.html (accessed 16 September 2023); Monika Schmitter, 'Describing Giorgione's Tempest: Iconography, Genre, Interpretation', *Studies in Iconography* 43, Article 7, suggests how a similarly mysterious painting might be understood.

28 Peter Humfrey et al., *Vittore Carpaccio: Master Storyteller of Renaissance Venice* (New Haven, CT: Yale University Press, 2022), pp. 224–7.

29 Jean Colombe used the idea almost a hundred years before in his November calendar miniature for the magnificent manuscript *Les Très Riches Heures du duc de Berry*, in this instance for the swineherd's dog following its master into the frame of the image.

30 Humfrey et al., *Vittore Carpaccio*, pp. 136–41.

31 The literature on the unanswered question of what the painting is about is summarized in Ilchman, *Titian*, pp. 237–9, in an essay by Vincent Delieuvin, and in Sheila Hale, *Titian: His Life* (London: HarperCollins, 2012), p. 676.

32 Clark, *Heaven on Earth*, p. 181.

33 Ibid.

34 Philipp Fehl, 'Veronese's Decorum: Notes on the Marriage at Cana', in *Art in the Ape of Nature: Studies in Honor of H. W. Janson*, ed. Barasch Moseed (New York: Harry N. Abrams; Englewood Cliffs, NJ: Prentice-Hall, 1981), thinks it is based on Aretino's *Humanity of Christ* (1535), which describes a scene as lavish and grand as that in the painting.

35 *Luther's Works*, vol. 54, *Table Talk*, ed. Theodore Tappert (Philadelphia, PA: Fortress Press, 1967), pp. 37, 38 (18 May 1532). Luther thought that 'the dog is the most faithful of animals and would be much esteemed were it not so common. Our Lord God has made His greatest gifts the commonest.'

36 For three hundred years the trial transcript had been lost and the painting in question, *Christ in the House of Levi*, was, without question, assumed to be

of that subject. I take my quotations from the translation in H. W. Janson, *History of Art*, 5th ed. (New York: Harry N. Abrams, 1995), p. 625.

37 Dominic's first biographer, Jordon of Saxony, in Francis Lerner, OP, *St Dominic: Biographical Documents* (Washington DC: Thomist Press, 1964), p. 7.

38 See Edward Grasman, 'On Closer Inspection – The Interrogation of Paolo Veronese', *Artibus et Historiae* 59:30 (2009), pp. 125–34, for the context of the trail and for a discussion of the extensive literature about it.

39 Veronese's joust with the Inquisitor inspired the Monty Python version of the conversation. Michelangelo, played by Eric Idle, was called to account by the Pope, played by John Cleese, for painting a Last Supper with three Christs, twenty-eight disciples and one kangaroo:

Pope: Look! . . . A Last Supper I commissioned from you, and a Last Supper I want! With twelve disciples and one Christ!

Michelangelo: One??!!

Pope: Yes one! Now will you please tell me what in God's name possessed you to paint this with three Christs in it?

Michelangelo: It works, mate! [essentially Veronese's answer]

In this Monty Python version, Michelangelo offered to change the name of the painting to 'The Penultimate Supper'. 'Why Didn't Michelangelo Paint the Last Supper?': https://www.facebook.com/BritishComedyClassics/videos/monty-python-why-michelangelo-didnt-paint-the-last-supper/626180224883335.

40 Mengs quoted in Suzanne L. Stratton-Pruitt, ed., *Velázquez's Las Meninas* (Cambridge: Cambridge University Press, 2002), p. 5; Jonathan Brown, *Velázquez: Painter and Courtier* (New Haven, CT: Yale University Press, 1986), p. 253.

41 These paragraphs rely heavily on the articles in Stratton-Pruitt, ed., *Velázquez's Las Meninas*; the Berger quotation is from p. 141. Especially useful was the editor's own essay 'Velázquez's *Las Meninas*: An Interpretive Primer', pp. 124–50; Jonathan Brown, *Velázquez*, and his *Images and Ideas in Seventeenth-Century Spanish Painting* (Princeton, NJ: Princeton University Press, 1978), pp. 87–110.

42 Quoted in Stratton-Pruitt, ed., *Velázquez's Las Meninas*, p. 2.

43 Brown, *Velázquez*, p. 259.

44 *Lives of Velázquez by Francisco Pacheco and Antonio Palomino*, trans. Nina Ayala Mallory (London: Pallas Athene, 2006), p. 143. Palomino was born in 1655, five years before Velázquez's death, and one year before *Las Meninas* was painted in 1656. He was able to interview people who knew everyone in the painting and a great deal about the circumstances of its production.

45 Gertje R. Utley, 'Las Meninas in Twentieth-Century Art', in Stratton-Pruitt, ed., *Velázquez's Las Meninas*, pp. 172 and 172–7, or on this series more

generally, Susan Grace Galassi, *Picasso's Variations on the Masters* (New York: Harry N. Abrams, 1996), pp. 183 and 148–85.

46 The role of Lump in the Picasso household and in this series is told in David Douglas Duncan's lavishly illustrated *Picasso and Lump: A Dachshund's Odyssey* (New York: Bulfinch Press, 2006).

47 Ibid, pp. 82–4.

48 The best modern account of Caillebotte is Kirk Varnedoe, *Gustave Caillebotte* (New Haven, CT: Yale University Press, 1987); see also T. J. Clark, *The Painting of Modern Life* (Princeton, NJ: Princeton University Press, 1999), p. xxx.

Chapter 4: Dogs and the Human Condition

1 Montaigne, 'On Friendship'; Stanley Cavell, *Pursuits of Happiness: The Hollywood Comedy of Remarriage* (Cambridge, MA: Harvard University Press, 1981), p. 88; Alexander Nehamas, *On Friendship* (New York: Basic Books, 2016).

2 Jacobus de Voragine, *The Golden Legend* (1275). In this version of the hagiography his sons are rescued from a lion by dogs during their flight from Rome. Eustacius' hagiography is often confused with that of St Hubertus, a seventh-century French saint, who died peacefully in his bed but who also saw a crucifix in the horns of a deer while out hunting with his dogs. The tiny crucifix is barely visible in his version of the story, but the dogs are looking at the deer along with their master; the horse is paying no attention.

3 From the website of the Staatliche Museen zu Berlin (2006), https://www.smb.museum/en/exhibitions/detail/melancholy, to announce its massive exhibition on the theme of melancholy. Its catalogue is a major source for this section. Jean Clair, ed., *Melancholie: Genie und Wahnsinn in die Kunst (Melancholy: Genius and Madness in Art)* (Ostfildern: Hatje Cantz, 2005).

4 Erwin Panofsky, *The Life and Art of Albrecht Dürer* (Princeton, NJ: Princeton University Press, 1955), pp. 165, 157–71 passim. There is a deep literature rooted in the tradition of Aby Warburg on Saturn, melancholia and creativity, for which see Raymond Klibansky, Erwin Panofsky, and Fritz Saxl, *Saturn and Melancholy: Studies in the History of Natural Philosophy, Religion, and Art* (Montreal: McGill University Press, 2019). On the role of the Florentine Neo-Platonists and Ficino in particular see Klibansky et al., pp. 254–76. These books in the Warburgian tradition inform my discussion.

5 See the catalogue entry 298 in Clair, ed., *Melancholie*, p. 473; Walter Benjamin, *The Origin of German Tragic Drama*, trans. John Osborne (London: Verso, 2009), p. 146 (1,1:34 in the German edition).

6 On this dog's eyes see Colin Eisler, Professor of Fine Arts at NYU, whose chapter 'An Artist's Best Friend' in his book *Dürer's Animals* is by far the best and most thorough study of the artist's extensive engagement with dogs throughout his career.

7 See Bodo Brinkmann, *Cranach* (London: Royal Academy of Art, 2008), Catalogue commentaries 97 and 98, and Klibansky et al., Appendix III, pp. 407–12.

8 https://www.metmuseum.org/art/collection/search/76197.

9 William Feaver, *Lucian Freud* (London: Tate Publishing, 2002), p. 41 and passim; I have also relied on *Lucian Freud: The Studio* (Paris: Editions du Centre Pompidou, 2010), exhibition catalogue.

10 See the catalogue entry 298 in Clair, ed., *Melancholie*, p. 473.

11 Eisner, *Dürer's Animals*, p. 175.

12 Panofsky, *The Life and Art of Albrecht Dürer*, pp. 154–5.

13 Brinkmann, ed., *Cranach*, pp. 252–5, catalogue entries 66 and 67.

14 There is also a portrait of him with his dog in a manuscript as the frontispiece copy of his *De viris illustribus (On Illustrious Men)* in the Hessische Landes- und Hochschul Bibliothek. I learned about the Padua image from Paula Findlen's 'Petrarch's Plague: Love, Death, and Friendship in a Time of Pandemic', in *The Public Domain Review* (11 June 2020), https://publicdomainreview.org/essay/petrarchs-plague (accessed 12 January 2024). For more on the general question of dogs and humanism in art see the extensively illustrated article by Patrik Reutersward, 'The Dog in the Humanist's Study', *Kunsthistorisktidskrift/Journal of Art History* 50:2 (1981), pp. 53–69, and the more focused survey of the subject in Jan Papy, 'Lipsius and His Dogs: Humanist Tradition, Iconography and Rubens' Four Philosophers', *Journal of the Warburg and Courtauld Institutes* 62 (1999), pp. 167–98, for his discussion of Lipsius's 1599 letter to his students on the sagacity of the dog; on Conrad Celtis the so-called 'Ertzhumanist Humanist', 'Archhumanist', in Germany and his dog see Gábor Almási, 'The Humanist Dog', *Renaissance Studies in Honor of Joseph Connors*, ed. Machtelt Israëls and Louis A. Waldman (Florence: Villa i Tatti, 2013), vol. 2, pp. 392–8.

15 In the late sixteenth century, the embalmed body of what was purportedly Petrarch's cat appeared in his house in that city. It is still there, a 400-year-old tourist attraction although clearly a fake, perhaps a joke, whose only possible foundation is an early fifteenth-century manuscript illumination of Petrarch that includes a cat chasing a mouse, a commonplace in such illuminations. We have no evidence that Petrarch had a cat.

16 *Petrarch at Vaucluse: Letters in Verse and Prose*, trans. Ernest Hatch Wilkins (Chicago, IL: University of Chicago Press, 1958), p. 122 (to Francisco Nelli, *Epistolae Familares* XII, 8), p. 187 (to 'Socrates', XVI, 3), pp. 65–6 and 63–8 passim (*Epistola Metrica* III, 5); Juliana Schiesari, 'Portrait of the Poet as a Dog: Petrarch's Epistola Metrica III, 5', *Italica* 84:2/3 (Summer–Autumn), pp. 162–72. She writes of this letter as 'a portrait of a dog as a kind of transitional entity between the human and natural worlds, the urban and rural, the political and poetic'.

17 Reutersward, 'The Dog in the Humanist's Study', p. 56; Almási, 'The Humanist Dog', p. 392; Dickinson to her editor and friend Thomas Higginson. I am indebted for this reference to Maureen B. Adams – personal communication (18 January 2024). I will come back later to her book *Shaggy Muses* about the dogs of the Brontës, Emily Dickinson, Elizabeth Barrett Browning, and Virginia Woolf.

18 Quoted in Papy, 'Lipsius and his Dogs', p. 181, n. 71. The engraving can be seen in context in the 1602 edition of *Astronomiae instauratae mechanica* available on the Hathi Trust website, https://babel.hathitrust.org/cgi/pt?id=gri.ark:/13960/t2z335966&seq=24.

19 Quoted in Papy, 'Lipsius and his Dogs', p. 181, n. 71.

20 For the issue of friendship and the *contubernium* – literally a term for those who share a military tent, but figuratively comrades or, as in Cicero, for the young who accompany a general into battle; for Lipsius's relationship with his students; and for Rubens' investment in neo-stoicism, all of which puts 'Four Philosophers' in context, see Mark Morford, *Stoics and Neo-Stoics: Rubens and the Circle of Lipsius* (Princeton, NJ: Princeton University Press, 1991), pp. 14–17 and 181–210 more generally.

21 The Rubens featured in Johann Zoffany's painting *The Tribuna of Uffizi* (1771) as one of the masterpieces of the Medici collection.

22 Wolfram Prinz, 'The Four Philosophers by Rubens and the Pseudo-Seneca in Seventeenth-Century Painting', *The Art Bulletin* 55:3 (1973), pp. 410–28; the bust is now thought to be probably an imagined likeness of Hesiod or Aristophanes.

23 See Fabio Tutrone, 'Barking at the Threshold: Cicero, Lucretius and the Ambiguous Status of Dogs in Roman Culture', in J. Pahlitzsch and T. Schmidt, eds, *Impious Dogs, Ridiculous Monkeys and Exquisite Fish* (Berlin and Boston, MA: De Gruyter, 2019), pp. 83, 93 and 73–102 passim. Most of this article is about the bad qualities of dogs in Roman thought.

24 Franz Kafka, 'Investigations of a Dog', in *Collected Stories*, ed. and introduction by Gabriel Josipovici (New York: Alfred Knopf, Everyman's Library, 1993), pp. 421, 432; see Stanley Cornland and Benno Wagner, *Franz Kafka: The Ghosts in the Machine* (Evanston, Ill.: Northwestern University Press, 2011); see also Aaron Schuster, *How to Research Like a Dog: Kafka's New Science* (Cambridge, MA: MIT Press, 2024).

25 Jean-Christophe Bailly, *The Animal Side*, trans. Catherine Porter (New York: Fordham University Press, 2011). The writer Ben Hecht's fantasy in his autobiography of trotting along with his dog and sharing his thoughts comes to mind. A scree door bangs, and the dog is off: 'He would be observing life without human confusion and bound to find some wonderful news.' Ben Hecht, *A Child of the Century* (1954).

26 Carlo Ginzburg, *The Souls of Brutes* (Chicago, IL: University of Chicago Press, 2022), ch. 2.

27 Rubin, *Impressionist Cats and Dogs*, p. 26.

28 Ibid, p. XX. Rubin suggests that Manet 'aligned himself with Desboutin [the subject of the painting]'. Dogs, he adds, 'embody ideas about artists'.

29 https://www.guggenheim.org/audio/track/dog-1951-cast-1957-by-alberto-giacometti.

30 See John Golding, *Visions of the Modern* (London: Thames and Hudson, 1994), pp. 191–2 and 185–200 passim, and Jon Wood, 'Brancusi's "white studio"', in Mary Jane Jacobs and Michelle Grabner, eds, *The Studio Reader: On the Space of Artists* (Chicago, IL: School of the Art Institute of Chicago; University of Chicago Press, 2010), pp. 279 and 278–82; Moorhead appears, labelled

'Dundee Artist Suffragist', in a drawing in the March 1912 edition of the *Wizard of the North* magazine with a black scotty at her feet.

31 Miguel Ángel Andrés-Toledo, 'The Dogs of the Zoroastrian Afterlife', *Acta Iranica* 54, ed. Éric Pirart (Leuven: Peeters, 2013), pp. 13–25, for an introduction to the Indo-European and especially Zoroastrian story.

32 See Stith Thompson, *The Motif-Index of Folk Literature* (1930s), B. Animals; B 100–199 and magic animals B 200 ff.

33 Robert J. Losey et al., 'Canids as Persons: Early Neolithic Dog and Wolf Burials, Cis-Baikal, Siberia', *Journal of Archaeological Anthropology* 36:2 (June 2011), pp. 174–89; Darcy F. Morey, 'Burying Key Evidence: The Social Bond between Dogs and People', *Journal of Archaeological Science* 33:2 (February 2006), pp. 158–75.

34 It has also been called 'The Death of Procris [the name of the nymph in one interpretation]' and simply 'Mythological Subject', signs of the fact that no one is sure what the painting is actually about.

35 G. A. Hirschauer and D. Geronimus, eds, *The Art Bulletin* 82:1 (2000), pp. 164–70: 'No Man's Lands: Lucretius and the Primitive Strain in Piero's "Art and Patronage" '.

36 Cephalus at some point set him to hunt the Teumessian fox, who could never be caught, and eventually Zeus, distraught by such an impossible situation, turned the dog into Canis Major – Sirius – the dog star. Or so one version of the story goes.

37 Quoted in Susan Fermor, *Fiction, Invention, and Fantasia* (London: Reaktion Books, 1993), p. 50. See on this painting also pp. 49–54. There is no Cephalus in whose arms Procris dies in Ovid; there is a sad-looking fawn who doesn't appear in the original story at all; and there is no hint of a dog's presence in Ovid. Scholars now think that the painting is based on a version of Ovid's story as retold in a play – *Cefalo* – by Niccolò da Correggio, which was first performed for a princely wedding in 1487. The painting's shape suggests that it might have been a didactic *spalliere* – a panel set into the wall or over furniture – about the importance of trust in a marriage. The sombre, mourning world of Piero di Cosimo's painting comports with the play's story and poetry: 'Weep, mountain glades, rivers and streams / Mourn for her you gods of the woods and hills.'

38 Dennis Geronimus, *Piero di Cosimo: Visions Beautiful and Strange* (New Haven, CT: Yale University Press, 2006), p. 87; Fermor, *Fiction, Invention, and Fantasia*, p. 54.

39 Giorgio Vasari, *Lives of the Painters, Sculptors and Architects*, trans. A. B. Hinds (London: J. M. Dent, 1900), vol. 3, p. 255; Erwin Panofsky discusses Piero in this context in 'The Early History of Man in a Cycle of Paintings by Piero di Cosimo', *Journal of the Warburg Institute* 1:1 (July 1937), pp. 12–30.

40 For the alchemical interpretation of Piero di Cosimo's dog see Rose-Marie and Reiner Hagen, *Masterpieces in Detail* (Cologne: Taschen, 2000), pp. 108–9 and 104–9 more generally in footnotes, p. 495. There is a historically rooted allegorical explanation for these dogs grounded in Piero's interest in alchemy and fire that may account for the otherworldly dreaminess of the picture. It fits into artistic engagement with Horapollo's view of the dog

as a natural sign both of learning and as an embalmer who views the dead. The white dog, on this account, is the 'Armenian hound' of the alchemists and the black one the 'bitch of Coracesium'. And the large brown hunting dog – the double of the dog mourning that is set to intervene in the contest between the two opposites – is Hermes Trismegistus, representing the patron of alchemy (fusion), and also of the god Hermes, an 'intermediary between this world and the next'. Like dogs in the myths of many nations, a guide to the realm of the dead, the Hellenistic magician figure is sometimes portrayed in alchemical texts as having a dog's head. Procris on this account is described as 'wrapped in a red and gold veil, both symbolic colors of the "red-hot" philosopher's stone'.

41 Hagi Kenaan, *Photography and its Shadows* (Stanford, CA: Stanford University Press, 2020).

42 Leonard Barkan, *Transuming Passion: Ganymede and the Erotics of Humanism* (Stanford, CA: Stanford University Press, 1991).

43 In another important emblem book an engraving of the Correggio painting makes it into print in the so-called *Theatrum Pictorum*, a catalogue of 243 paintings owned by Archduke Leopold Wilhelm of Austria. The engraving is by Colin Boel from a copy made by the genre painter David Teniers the Younger, of what the British Museum in its description of Plate 8, A, 8.11 says is an original by Michelangelo. I think this is wrong. The Teniers is a copy of the Correggio that had been owned by Leopold's Hapsburg cousin one generation removed, the Holy Roman Emperor Rudolf II, and somehow stayed in the family. In fact, contrary to what all the museum labels say I suspect most of the emblem book images derive from Correggio. There are 151 symbols in Bocchi's Hermetic emblem book, the *Symbolicarum Quaestionum* of 1574, mostly drawn from Horapollo.

44 Julie-Marie Strange, 'Only a Pauper whom Nobody Owns: Reassessing the Pauper Grave 1880–1914', *Past and Present* 78 (February 2003), pp. 148–75. The title is from a line in Thomas Noel's well-known 1841 poem 'The Pauper's Drive'.

45 John Ruskin, *Modern Painters*, vol. 2 (1851), p. 8; David MacDonald's *The Village Funeral: An Irish Family by a Graveside During the Great Famine*, c. 1850, is another example of the dog at the grave of the poor.

46 Jan Bondeson, *Greyfriars Bobby, the Most Faithful Dog in the World* (Stroud: Amberley Publishing, 2012); Forbes Macgregor, *Greyfriars Bobby: The Real Story at Last* (London: Steve Savage, 2002).

47 Claudette R. Mainzer, 'Who is Buried at Ornans?', in Sarah Faunce and Linda Nochlin, eds., *Courbet Reconsidered* (New York: The Brooklyn Museum, 1988), pp. 80 and 77–81 more generally. For the dog of Ornans see Robert Fernier, *La Vie et L'Oeuvre de Gustave Courbet: Catalogue Raisonné* (Lausanne and Paris: Fondation Wildenstein, 1977–8), pp. 11, 114, entry 184.

48 T. J. Clark, *Image of the People: Gustave Courbet and the 1848 Revolution* (Princeton, NJ: Princeton University Press, 1973, 1982), p. 115. The entire chapter on the subject of this painting, pp. 77–121, has influenced my account.

49 Ibid, p. 83.

50 Nikephoros Basilakes, 'Encomium', in *The Rhetorical Exercises of Nikephoros Basilakes*, ed. and trans. Jeffrey Beneker and Craig A. Gibson (Cambridge, MA: Harvard University Press, 2016), pp. 136–7, cited in Craig A. Gibson, 'In Praise of Dogs: An Encomium Theme from Classical Greece to Renaissance Italy', in *Our Dogs, Our Selves*, ed. Gelfand, pp. 19–40, at p. 28.

51 Thomas Bewick, *History of Quadrupeds* (1807), p. 366.

52 Bruce Weber, 'Al Pacino, Slouching (Again) Toward Shakespeare', *The New York Times* (6 October 1996), section 2, p. 17. Eiser tells a short version of this story, which is where I first encountered it.

53 Dickson Hartwell, *Dogs against Darkness* (New York: Dodd, Mead, & Co, 1968). There is also a short but copiously illustrated book with black and white reproductions of art going back to Pompeii by Nelson Coon, Librarian of the Perkins School and based on its holding, *A Brief History of Guide Dogs for the Blind* (Morristown, NJ: The Seeing Eye, 1968). https://babel.hathitrust.org/cgi/pt?id=coo.31924001179336&seq=1Triust (accessed 23 February 2024). Whether the beggar being led by a dog in Pompeii is blind is unclear because of the deteriorated state of the fresco.

54 Jacopo Bassano's *Lazarus and the Rich Man* (c. 1550) stands near the beginning of a 500-year-old tradition in painting of depicting the kindness of dogs to the poor and outcast. (In sculpture of the capitals of medieval churches the connection between Lazarus and dogs goes much further back.)

55 The medieval images are among those collected by Krista A. Milne at the University of Leiden for 'Guide Dogs in Medieval Art and Literature', https://kristamurchison.com/medieval-guide-dogs. The blind hurdy-gurdy player became something of a meme in seventeenth-century art. There are nineteen known versions by Bruegel's circle. His may not have been the first; some claim he took the image from David Vinckboon's treatment. Kahren Jones Hellerstedt, 'A Traditional Motif in Rembrandt's Etchings: The Hurdy-Gurdy Player', *Oud Holland* 95:1 (1981), pp. 16–30, and also the Rijksmuseum's technical details of the Vinckboon: https://www.rijksmuseum.nl/en/collection/SK-A-2401/catalogue-entry?pdfView=False.

56 Panofsky, *The Life and Art of Albrecht Dürer*, p. 153; Joseph Koerner, *The Moment of Self-Portraiture in German Renaissance Art* (Chicago, IL: University of Chicago Press, 1993), p. 23.

57 Julius S. Held, *Rembrandt and the Book of Tobit* (Northampton, MA: The Gehenna Press, 1964).

58 In his acclaimed biography *Rembrandt: His Life, His Paintings* (1985), Gary Schwartz thinks that the artist's 'first truly accomplished painting' imagines the dog watching anxiously at the feet of the blind Tobit as he falsely accuses his wife Anna of having stolen a goat, and then prays for death in a moment of despair and repentance. Rembrandt, possibly with his apprentice Gerrit Dou, had painted a version of this scene shown in the engraving almost thirty years earlier in which the dog is more actively pushing his master in the right direction and shares the excitement at the return of his son.

59 I was introduced to this image by Ewa Lajer-Burcharth's *The Painter's Touch* (2022), pp. 117 and 115–18 more generally. I do not do justice to her full discussion of blindness as 'a condition of interiority that this painting describes and performs'. In her view the most important difference between Chardin's beggar and the standard iconography is in the treatment of blindness itself: 'His unseeing gaze directed slightly upward . . . the Blind Beggar seems not blind but turned in upon himself . . . visible but un-seeing, the eye appears an instrument of vision directed inward'. It is the dog's eyes that 'in their mute blackness' seem blind like the eyes of the dead rabbit in another of Chardin's paintings. The dog has no interiority – or in its blindness no connection to the world – whereas the main subject, self-reflectively the artist himself, does. For the engraving and the history of the painting see Pierre Rosenberg, 'The Blind Man of the Quinze-Vingts by Chardin', in *Shop Talk* (Cambridge, MA: Harvard University Art Museums, 1995), pp. 211–13.

60 The theme of Tobias's travels was particularly compelling, art historians have argued, to the rich commercial families of Florence because their sons travelled a lot on business, but its popularity was not restricted to these circles.

61 The claim was first made by David Alan Brown in *Leonardo da Vinci: Origins of a Genius* (New Haven, CT: Yale University Press, 1992), pp. 51–2, and has been supported by further evidence based on the naturalistic details of the fish and the dog in relationship to the brocade.

62 There is an extensive survey of minor but telling images and an excellent summary with many footnotes in Alphons Hamer, 'Tobias or not Tobias: A Jesuit Visual Pun', *Simiolus* 39:1 (2017). The quotation from Drost is on p. 95.

Chapter 5: Dogs in the Art of Modern Life

1 More than a century before Fragonard's *Girl in Bed Playing with Her Dog*, Jan Steen was almost as explicit in the scandalously erotic and seductive *A Woman at Her Toilet*. Her small dog is on the pillow looking toward her suggestively crossed bare legs. No amount of symbolic interpretation – the moral probity of the arch, the skull with its warning of mortality, the lute with broken string, i.e. moralizing images from emblem books that was supposed to make this a teaching tool against vice – detracts from the representation of the intimacy of woman and dog, however much the viewer is meant to be instructed by the setting.

2 See Rubens's *The Discovery of Purple by Hercules's Dog* (1636), for example.

3 Ting Chang, '"The Meeting": Gustave Courbet and Alfred Bruyas', *The Burlington Magazine* 138:1122 (September 1996), pp. 586–91.

4 André Dombrowski, 'History, Memory, and Instantaneity in Edgar Degas's "Place de La Concorde"', *The Art Bulletin* 93:2 (2011), pp. 195–219, https://www.jstor.org/stable/23046593; Mari Kálmán Meller, 'Degas's "Place de La

Concorde: Vicomte Lepic and His Daughters" ', *The Burlington Magazine* 145:1201 (2003), pp. 273–81. http://www.jstor.org/stable/3100666.

5 Rubin, *Impressionist Cats and Dogs*, pp. 43–6 and 65–7; the phrase 'psychogeographer' is Julian Barnes' in his review of Bridget Alsdorf's 'Gawkers: Art and Audience in Late Nineteenth-Century France', *The New York Review of Books* (12 May 2022).

6 Jessica Pierce, *The Last Walk: Reflections on Our Pets at the End of Their Lives* (Chicago, IL: University of Chicago Press, 2012), with extensive bibliography, and Louis Hoffman, ed., *Our Last Walk: Using Poetry for Grieving and Remembering Our Pets* (University Professors Press, online, 2016), are but two examples.

7 *Walking the Dog*, photographs by Keith Arnatt, introduction by George Melly (London: Omega Books, 1979), unpaginated; Pierce, *The Last Walk*.

8 Gessner, *History of Animals* (575ᵃ1). The Greek word is 'genos', meaning a general kind of dog defined by where it came from or what it did.

9 Michael Worboys, Julie-Marie Strange, and Neil Pemberton, *The Invention of the Modern Dog: Breed and Blood in Victorian Britain*, 1st ed. (Baltimore, MD: Johns Hopkins University Press, 2018), documents the English case but the story is the same elsewhere.

10 https://www.thefield.co.uk/gundogs/history-of-the-kennel-club-50055.

11 William Secord, *Dog Painting: The European Breeds* (Woodbridge, Suffolk: Antique Collectors' Club, 2002), p. 356. This is the most comprehensive collection of the genre; *Du coq à l'âne: La peinture animalière en Belgique au XIXᵉ siècle* (Brussels: Crédit Communal de Belgique, 1982), offers examples in one national case. It is, as the title suggests, not limited to dogs.

12 Kathleen Kete, *The Beast in the Boudoir: Pet Keeping in Nineteenth-Century Paris* (Berkeley: University of California Press, 1994).

13 The same can be said for the literature of other European countries. See, for example, Albrecht Classen, 'Hunde als Freunde und Begleiter in der deutschen Literatur vom Mittelalter bis zur Gegenwart. Reaktion auf den "Animal Turn" aus motivgeschichtlicher Sicht', *Études Germaniques* 292:4 (2018), pp. 441–66.

14 See Beryl Gray, 'George Eliot, George Henry Lewes, and Dogs', *The George Eliot Review* 434, https://digitalcommons.unl.edu/ger/434 (accessed 26 March 2024), for an excellent survey of dogs in the lives of the protagonists and their relationship with Brown.

15 In its day the earlier one was by far the more often copied version of the painting. It was the one made for Catherine the Great and is now in the Hermitage in St Petersburg. We do not know when the dog was added to the now more famous and often reproduced one in the Musée Carnavalet in Paris. Even the curators of the museum when they argue for the superiority of their version fail to mention the dog. See the *Bulletin du Musée Carnavalet* (November 1960). But the dog version is the one on the cover of the Penguin edition of *Candide*. I am grateful to Gillian Pink of the Oxford Voltaire Foundation for all her help in tracking down the history of this picture.

16 Cited in David Edmunds and John Eidinow, *Rousseau's Dog: A Tale of Two Great Thinkers at War in the Age of Enlightenment* (London: Faber and Faber, 2006), p. 5; see for an imaginary conversation between Rousseau and his dog, D. Boucher, 'The Dangers of Dependence: Sultan's Conversation with His Master Jean-Jacques Rousseau (1712–1778)', in R. N. Lebow, P. Schouten, and H. Suganami, eds, *The Return of the Theorists* (London: Palgrave Macmillan).

17 On the epitaph see Michelle M. Taylor, 'The Curious Case of "Epitaph to a Dog": Byron and *The Scourge*', *Byron Journal* 43:1 (2015). Dogs were always part of the Byron legend, but the illustrations in his friend Elizabeth Bridget Pigot's *The Wonderful History of Lord Byron and His Dog* show him doing all sorts of things with them; the material she supplied to early biographers about the poet's lifelong involvement with dogs very quickly made its way into literary culture. Pigot's handmade book is itself a parody of the eighteenth-century *Old Mother Hubbard and Her Dog*, which was printed and reprinted, sometimes with the same illustrations, sometimes with new ones, and translated into German, French, and Russian. It is still in print, a parody of the idea that it matters not what you do with your friend – or dog – but that what you do you do with your friend – or dog.

18 Juliana Schiesari, *Polymorphous Domesticities: Pets, Bodies, and Desires in Four Modern Writers* (Berkeley and Los Angeles, CA: University of California Press, 2012), p. 43 and more broadly pp. 39–44.

19 My and many other people's attention to the male gaze, and how it represents women for the enjoyment and from the perspective of the heterosexual male viewer, is based on Laura Mulvey's foundational article, 'Visual Pleasure and Narrative Cinema', *Screen* 16:3 (1975), pp. 6–18.

20 Stephan Wolohojian, with Melinda Watt and Michael Gallagher, 'A Grand Tableau: Charles Le Brun's Portrait of the Jabach Family', *The Metropolitan Museum of Art Bulletin* 75:1 (2017), pp. 5–6, 9 and passim.

21 On *The Resting Horseman* see in particular C. D. Dickerson and Esther Bell, *The Brothers Le Nain: Painters of Seventeenth-Century France* (New Haven, CT: Yale University Press, 2016), pp. 302–4. Other paintings that include a terrier are *The Musicians*, p. 212, *The Cart*, p. 294, and *Peasant Interior with Old Flute Player*, pp. 264–8; in this last painting, built around intersecting human gazes, the same dog is looking diagonally from the foreground across the painting at the old woman. It may well have been a studio dog since it appears in a number of Le Nain's – or his brothers' – work including, to take another example, *The Painter's Studio*. I leave the much-vexed question of attribution to the individual Le Nain brothers aside, although there is a lot to be learned from the detailed discussion of individual works in Nicolas Milovanovic and Lue Piralla-Heng Vong, *Le mystère Le Nain* (Paris: Lienart, 2017). See especially pp. 318–19, 279 and 268–9 for discussions of dogs, although they figure more generally. I am grateful to Dorothée Fabre, Librarian of the French Canine-Centrale, and Ciara Farrell, Librarian of the Kennel Club, for help in identifying the proto-breed of these dogs.

22 There is a version, probably also by Wheatley himself, in the Budapest Museum of Fine Arts, in which the dog is lying on the floor to the left of the family group and nearer the hearth, secure of its place in the family.

23 William Windham, *Parliamentary History* (25 April 1796), col. 1003, quoted in Ingrid H. Tague, 'Eighteenth-Century English Debates on a Dog Tax', *The Historical Journal* 51:4 (2008), pp. 917 and 901–20 more generally; http://www.jstor.org/stable/20175208.

24 See also Thomas Eakins, *Elizabeth Crowell* [younger sister of the artist's close friend] *and her Dog*, which is also very much in the tradition of Dutch and later English and French genre painting. The girl and the dog are quiet, at ease, domestically engaged with one another.

25 Donna Haraway, *When Species Meet* (Minneapolis, MN: University of Minnesota Press, 2008), pp. 28–30. (Small dogs and their owners, especially older women and their little house dogs, continue to be treated as silly, abject, or worse in twentieth-century thinking on the subject, argues Haraway in a brilliant attack on Gilles Deleuze and Félix Guattari's *Anti-Oedipus*.) Her work more generally has been formative for me. On the rumours about Marie-Antoinette's dogs see Estelle Ross, *The Book of Noble Dogs* (New York: The Century, 1923), pp. 90–91.

26 See also for more examples Jean-Frédéric Schall's *Avondtoilet* (1752) and his *Young Woman and her Lover* (Rijksmuseum). For the more explicitly auto-erotic version of this story see Thomas Laqueur, *Solitary Sex* (New York: Zone Books, 2003), pp. 341–58.

27 It was copied and modified from one made weeks earlier that the artist and engraver Henry Pelham had lent Paul Revere, who got his version out first, and much to Pelham's irritation, reaped the profits from its commercial success.

28 Eric Hinderaker, *Boston's Massacre* (Cambridge, MA: Harvard University Press, 2017), pp. 227–35, which is based on Clarence S. Brigham, *Paul Revere's Engravings*. I am grateful to Elisa Tamarkin for her interpretations of the dog and the context of Revere's print.

29 These matters have been recently illuminated by Pierre Serna. See his *Comme des bêtes: histoire politique de l'animal en Révolution (1750–1840)* (Paris: Fayard, 2017), and *L'animal en République: 1789–1802, genèse du droit des bêtes* (Toulouse: Anacharsis, 2016).

30 On the controverted history of the understanding of this image see Peter McPhee, *Robespierre: A Revolutionary Life* (New Haven, CT: Yale University Press, 2013). Boilly's many paintings of bourgeois life are full of dogs but in this case the dog is there probably because Robespierre was known to be fond of them.

31 See also *The Battle for Palm Tree Hill, Saint Domingue* by January Suchodolski (1845), in which Jean-Jacques Dessalines, a leader of the Haitian Revolution, is holding up a white man's head as the dog by his side barks. The defeated soldiers are Polish.

32 This story is often recounted. I have it from Arthur Liebow, 'The Secret of the Black Paintings', *The New York Times* (27 July 2003), who heard it from

the Prado's curator of eighteenth-century art Manuela Mena, who had escorted Miró.

33 Lydia Vázquez, 'Goya's Monsters: Grotesque Figurations of a Childlike Imaginary', *Littérateur* 169 (2013), https://www.cairn-int.info/journal-litterature-2013-1-page-102.html (accessed 28 April 2024); Robert Hughes, *Goya* (New York: Alfred Knopf, 2004), p. 382; Tom Lubbock, *The Independent* (11 July 2008); https://www.independent.co.uk/arts-entertainment/art/great-works/goya-francisco-de-the-dog-c1820-864391.html; Evan Connell, *Francisco Goya* (New York: Counterpoint, 2004), p. 207. Regarding the ochre sky, see the artist Sahil Sahu at https://medium.com/@sahilsahu3003/el-perro-the-dog-francisco-y-goya-lucientes-21a75056890b. The friend I mention is Stella Tillyard (2 May 2022), in response to a comment by Simon Schama that the dog was drowning.

34 August Macke and Franz Marc, *August Macke, Franz Marc: Briefwechsel* (Cologne: M. DuMont Schauberg, 1964, 1967), pp. 14–26.

35 See the University of Oregon's website for an account of this painting as part of a larger exhibit of Tamayo's; https://artbridgesfoundation.org/artworks/tamayo-perro-aullando-a-la-luna. A great deal has been written about Rego and a discussion of the 'Dog Woman' series would be another project. But the place to start is a 2011 interview with the artist, https://www.thewhitereview.org/feature/interview-with-paula-rego (accessed 24 April 2024).

36 Rina Arya, *Francis Bacon, Painting in a Godless World* (Farnham, Surrey: Lund Humphries, 2012), p. 133.

37 Robert L. Herbert, *Seurat and the Making of La Grande Jatte* (Chicago, IL: Art Institute of Chicago, 2004), pp. 68–95.

38 Richard Thomson, '"Les Quat' Pattes": The Image of the Dog in Late Nineteenth-Century French Art', *Art History* 5:3 (1982), pp. 334 and 331–4 more generally on this point. The whole article is valuable, pp. 323–37.

39 The David Zwirner Gallery refused permission to reproduce Kerry James Marshall's *Untitled (Studio)* and *Our Town*. The former can be seen on the Metropolitan Museum website https://www.metmuseum.org/art/collection/search/669451; the latter at https://www.metmuseum.org/art/collection/search/668330.

40 It was shown as part of a major retrospective of his work at The Met Breuer in News York in 2016.

41 Helen Molesworth, ed., *Kerry James Marshall: Mastry* (New York: Skira Rizzoli, n.d.), pp. 28–31, 126–7, and the catalogue to her entries 32 and 38.

Chapter 6: Dogs and the Moral Imagination

1 Pierre Serna, 'The Republican Menagerie: Animal Politics in the French Revolution', *French History* xxviii (2014), p. 189; Chris Pearson, 'Stray Dogs and the Making of Modern Paris', *Past & Present* 234 (February, 2017), pp. 137–72;

Arturo Luna Loranca, 'The Dog Remains: Mexico City's Canine Massacres During the Enlightenment, 1770–1821' (PhD, Emory University, 2023), ch. 1.

2 See Cristiana Franco's *Shameless: The Canine and the Feminine in Ancient Greece*, trans. Matthew Fox (Berkeley, CA: University of California Press).

3 Seymour Slive, *Rembrandt and his Critics* (The Hague: Martinus Nijhoff, 1953), p. 99.

4 Susan Donahue Kuretsky, 'Rembrandt's "Good Samaritan": Etching: Reflections on a Disreputable Dog', in Cynthia P. Schneider et al., *Shop Talk: Studies in Honor of Seymour Slive* (Cambridge, MA: Harvard University Art Museum, 1995), pp. 150–55, and Sir Kenneth Clark's far less appreciative '"Rembrandt's "Good Samaritan" in the Wallace Collection', *Burlington Magazine* 118:885 (December 1976), pp. 806–9; Simon Schama, *Rembrandt's Eyes* (London: Penguin, 1999), p. 413; Goethe, *Essays on Art and Literature*, vol. 3, ed. John Gearey, trans. Ellen von Nardroff and Ernest H. von Nardroff (Princeton, NJ: Princeton University Press, 1994), pp. 66–8.

5 In Gainsborough's 'red in tooth and claw' painting, *Two Shepherd Boys with Dogs Fighting* (Kenwood House, London), the boys could easily trade places with the dogs: a bad-boy painting. They should have known better than to find pleasure in the violence; dogs are doing what dogs do.

6 See, for example, Chris Pearson, 'Dogs, History, and Agency', *History and Theory*, Theme issue 52 (December 2013), pp. 128–45.

7 Robert J. Richards, *Darwin and the Emergence of Evolutionary Theories of Mind and Behavior* (Chicago, IL: University of Chicago Press, 1987), pp. 185–243, and especially pp. 206–30, which discuss the criticisms of some of Darwin's closest friends and supporters.

8 George Rolleston/Darwin correspondence (30 September 1868).

9 James Frederick Ferriar had been Professor of Moral Philosophy and Political Economy at St Andrews in Scotland before his death in 1864 and was the author of an article in *Blackwood's Edinburgh Magazine* of 1838. Alford's article is in the religious magazine *Good Words* 9 (January 1868), p. 25 ff.

10 Malcolm Jay Kottler, 'Alfred Russel Wallace, the Origin of Man, and Spiritualism', *Isis* 65:2 (1974), pp. 145–92; http://www.jstor.org/stable/229369.

11 The spectacular Cambridge Correspondence Project and the Cambridge Digital Library of Darwin's manuscripts, in addition to digital access to all his published work, make it easy to search for references to his many dogs and what they contributed to his views. But a fully developed case for their importance in the context of Darwin's life is made in David Feller, *Hunter's Gaze: Charles Darwin and the Role of Dogs and Sport in Nineteenth-Century Natural History*, Cambridge University PhD, 2011. I am grateful to him for allowing me access and sending me a pdf copy. Emma Townshend's *Darwin's Dogs: How Darwin's Pets Helped Form a World-Changing Theory* (London: Frances Lincoln, 2009) makes the same case in a more popular form.

12 On the ways in which Darwin's claim grows out of contemporary anthropological views of the origin of religion see David Chidester, 'Darwin's Dogs: Animals, Animism, and the Problem of Religion', *Soundings: An Interdisciplinary Journal* 92:1/2 (2009), pp. 51–75. Charles Darwin, *The Descent of Man, and*

Selection in Relation to Sex, 2nd ed. (London: John Murray, 1874), p. 95; https://www.jstor.org/stable/41179238.

13 Herzen thought deeply about the ways in which the Darwinian revolution made him think about the philosophy of history. Aileen Kelly, *The Discovery of Chance: The Life and Thought of Alexander Herzen* (Cambridge, MA: Harvard University Press, 2016), pp. 343 ff and 417 ff.

14 David Hume, *An Enquiry concerning Human Understanding*, ed. Stephen Buckle (Cambridge: Cambridge University Press, 2007), ch. 9, 'Of the reason of animals', pp. 92–5 passim.

15 Letter (28 November 1872), *Quarterly Review* 133 (1872), pp. 419–51.

16 Charles Darwin/Cobbe (28 November 1872); *Life of Frances Power Cobbe by Herself* (Boston, MA, and New York: Houghton Mifflin, 1895), pp. 449–50.

17 Horowitz/author email (19 October 2019).

18 *Illustrations of Vivisection or Experiments on Living Animals from the Works of Physiologists* (Philadelphia, PA: American Anti-Vivisection Society, 1888).

19 William Schupbach, 'A Select Iconography of Animal Experiment', in Nicolaas A. Rupke, *Vivisection in Historical Perspective* (London: Croom Helm, 1987), pp. 347–50. There is nothing further to be learned in the archives of the Wellcome Collection. I am grateful to Dr Schupbach for the account of the painting in the collection (Email 24 May 2024). Mouchy exhibited other paintings between 1822 and 1851 but none can now be found. Almost nothing is known about his life. There is no entry for him in the massive 32-volume *Grove Dictionary of Art* and only the barest notice in French sources.

20 John Wesley, Sermon 60, 'the General Deliverance'. Wesley thought that at the end of time animals too would be delivered from the 'bondage of corruption'; Rev. Humphrey Primatt, *A dissertation on the Duty of Mercy and the Sin of Cruelty to brute Animals* (1776), pp. 21–2.

21 Peter Harrison, 'Descartes on Animals', *The Philosophical Quarterly* 42:167 (1992), pp. 219–27; https://doi.org/10.2307/2220217.

22 John Lawrence, *A Philosophical and Practical Treatise on Horses: and on the Moral Duties of Man Towards the Brute Creation* (1796).

23 Deborah Rudacille, *The Scalpel and the Butterfly: The War Between Animal Research and Animal Protection* (New York: Farrar, Straus and Giroux, 2000), p. 19 and passim.

24 For Max, see the *Grove Dictionary of Art*; he was in his day influential and internationally known; on this painting see Schupbach, in Rupke, *Vivisection in Historical Perspective*, pp. 351–3.

25 I am grateful to Cecilia Mackay for this account, which supplements that on the Wellcome site (https://wellcomecollection.org/works/dhae2e4f). 'The painting has been on loan from the Ernst von Siemens Kunststiftung to the Lenbachhaus (Munich). The provenances seem to be intact going back at least twenty years – the painting was first brought into the public eye by Galerie Konrad Bayer. Apparently the art dealer Konrad Bayer was dedicated to bringing von Max's work out of obscurity (Bayer died in 2023 and his gallery is no more), and it was included in a 2010 retrospective at the Lenbachhaus, so it must be authentic. The painting was a highlight at the

Munich Art Fair in 2007, which is when I assume it was acquired by the Ernst von Siemens Kunststiftung.'

26 Dr R. Barnes, 'On the Correlations of the Sexual Functions and Mental Disorders of Women', *British Gynaecology Journal* 6 (1890), pp. 390–413 (392).

27 Samuel Camenzind, 'Kantian Ethics and the Animal Turn: On the Contemporary Defence of Kant's Indirect Duty View', *Animals* (Basle, 2021).

28 Darwin to Linkester (22 March 1871).

29 The original of this image is lost.

30 Traces of Kingsford are everywhere in the anti-vivisection and theosophical literature of her time. There is a biography of her by her companion Edward Maitland – who burnt her papers – that concentrates on her role in various avenues of the occult. I rely on Alan Pert, *Red Cactus: The Life of Anna Kingsford* (Watsons Bay, Australia: Books and Writers, 2006), for the discussion of her anti-vivisection activities.

31 Greta Depledge, 'Experimental Medicine, Marital Harmony and Florence Marryat's *An Angel of Pity* (1898)', *Women's Writing* 20:2 (2013), pp. 219–34; https://doi-org.libproxy.berkeley.edu/10.1080/09699082.2013.773775 (accessed 9 September 2024).

32 Hilda Kean, *Animal Rights: Political and Social Change in Britain since 1800* (Reaktion Books, 2000); Coral Lansbury, *The Old Brown Dog: Women, Workers, and Vivisection in Edwardian England* (Madison, WI: University of Wisconsin Press, 2012).

33 The most extensive account of dogs in the Spanish conquest of the new world is in John Grier Varner and Jeannette Johnson Varner's *Dogs of the Conquest* (Norman, OK: University of Oklahoma Press, 1983), pp. 6 and more generally 3–34; see also John J. Ensminger, 'From Hunters to Hell Hounds: The Dogs of Columbus and Transformations of the Human-Canine Relationship in the Early Spanish Caribbean', *Colonial Latin American Review* 31:3 (2022), pp. 354–80, https://www.tandfonline.com/doi/pdf/10.1080/10609164.2022.2104035 (accessed 16 May 2024), for a more granular account of the dogs themselves.

34 See Marcus Wood, *Blind Memory: Visual Representations of Slavery in England and America, 1780–1865* (Manchester: Manchester University Press, 2000), pp. 78–143, on the iconography of the runaway as a subject that he interprets broadly to include not just images like those of Richard Ansdell (pp. 95–6) but also advertisements and small newspaper icons. For the use of dogs in the policing of slavery see the superb essay by Tyler D. Parry and Charlton W. Yingling, 'Slave Hounds and Abolition in the Americas', *Past & Present* 246:1 (February 2020), pp. 69–108.

35 On dogs and the Haitian story, see Bénédicte Boisseron, *Afro-Dog: Blackness and the Animal Question* (New York: Columbia University Press, 2018); Marcus Rainsford, *An historical account of the black empire of Hayti: comprehending a view of the principal transactions in the revolution of Saint Domingo* (London, 1805), p. 339. Rainsford was a former army officer who was in Haiti during the revolution and was supportive of an independent Haiti, which he thought to be in the interest of Britain.

36 *Narrative of the life and adventures of Henry Bibb, An American Slave, written by himself* (New York: published by the author, 1849), Chapter 11, p. 128, and image, p. 124; see B. L. Smith, '"Open Jaws of this Monster-Tyranny": Abolitionism, Resistance, and Slave-Hunting Canines', *American Nineteenth Century History* 23:1 (2022), pp. 61–92, for many more images and a fuller account of their place in abolitionist literature.

37 See Boisseron, *Afro-Dog*, pp. 37–81 and 121–57; on the Jewish question, see Phillip Ackerman-Lieberman and Rakefet Zalashik, eds, *A Jew's Best Friend? The Image of the Dog throughout Jewish History* (Eastbourne: Sussex Academic Press, 2014); https://www.haaretz.com/israel-news/business/2017-01-06/ty-article/in-israel-mans-best-friend-is-also-his-most-expensive-fr; https://worldostats.com/dog-population-by-country-2024, based on the World Population Review 2024; https://chicagocrusader.com/black-peoples-complicated-history-with-dogs.

Coda: We Are Not Alone

1 Brigitte Vallée, *Les Animaux Acteurs de Cinéma*, École Nationale Vétérinaire D'Alfort, Thèse pour le Doctorat Vétérinaire (Maisons-Alfort, 1979), pp. 38–50, takes the story up to the late twentieth century.

2 See http://www.screenonline.org.uk/film/id/514859/index.html for the history of this remarkable film.

3 See Susan Orlean, *Rin Tin Tin: The Life and Legend of the World's Most Famous Dog* (New York: Simon and Schuster, 2011), for the full story.

4 Whether the story really is 'true to life', as the poster claims, is much debated. Some believe that Eric Knight, who published the novel from which the screenplay was derived, knew about Bobbie the Wonder Dog, a Scotch collie who had run away after being attacked by other dogs while its family was visiting in Indiana, and had then walked 2,551 miles to return home to Oregon in 1924; or about another collie who saved a British seaman whose ship had been torpedoed off the coast of Devon in 1915. Interest in the question attests to the power of the Lassie image in popular culture.

5 I leave aside the controversies that have arisen about whether Balto, with no previous record of working as a lead dog, actually did what he was said to have done. He may have led with another dog called Fox. Togo led a team through the toughest part of the run on the day before the final stage. He sometimes appears with Balto in movies and books.

6 James Holmberg, 'Seaman's Fate', in *We Proceeded On*, the official publication of the Lewis and Clark Trail Heritage Foundation (2000), p. 26. Seaman is a frequent subject in the journal's pages. I am grateful to James Holmberg, the Filson Historical Society curator, for a series of emails (22–23 March 2024) teaching me about the role of the dog in the Lewis and Clark world of today.

List of Illustrations and Photo Credits

Photographs are kindly provided by the artists and galleries listed, unless otherwise stated. Numbers refer to figure numbers in the text.

160 Francis Wheatley, *Man with Dog*, 1775. Tate, London. Photo © Tate.

161 George Romney, *The Evening Walk of Sir Christopher and Lady Sykes*, 1786. Sledmere House, E. Yorks.

162 John Constable, *Weymouth Bay from the Downs above Osmington Mills*, 1816. Museum of Fine Arts, Boston. Bequest of Mr and Mrs William Caleb Loring (30.731). Photo: Bridgeman Images.

163 Gustave Courbet, *Young Ladies of the Village*, 1852. Metropolitan Museum of Art, New York. Gift of Harry Payne Bingham, 1940 (40.175).

164 Gustave Courbet, *La Rencontre* (*Bonjour Monsieur Courbet*), 1854. Musée Fabre, Montpellier. Photo: Historic Images/Alamy.

165 Edgar Degas, *Viscount Lepic and his Daughters Crossing the Place de la Concorde*, 1875. State Hermitage Museum, St Petersburg. Photo: Prisma Archivo/Alamy.

166 Gustave Caillebotte, *Richard Gallo and his Dog Dick at Petit Gennevilliers*, 1884. Private collection. Photo: Incamerastock/Alamy

167 Sketch from Pablo Picasso to Guillaume Apollinaire inscribed *Je ne te vois plus. Tu es mort?* (*I no longer see you. Are you dead?*), 1905. Nationalgalerie, Museum Berggruen (SMB), Berlin. © Succession Picasso/DACS, London 2025. Photo: bpk, Berlin/Scala, Florence.

168 August Sander, *Der Notar* (*The Notary*), 1924. © Die Photographische Sammlung/SK Stiftung Kultur – August Sander Archiv, Cologne/DACS 2025.

169 Vincent Van Gogh, *Woman Walking her Dog*, 1886. Van Gogh Museum, Amsterdam (Vincent van Gogh Foundation).

170 Keith Arnatt, photograph from *Walking the Dog*, 1976–9. © Keith Arnatt Estate. All rights reserved. DACS 2025. Image courtesy Sprüth Magers.

171 'The Terrier', illustration by Sydenham Teak Edwards, from his book *Cynographia Britannica*, 1800, p. 52. Photo: McGill University.

172 Maud Earl, *Portrait of the Black Labrador 'Peter of Faskally' Holding a Cock Pheasant, with his Mate 'Dungavel Jet' in a Landscape*, 1912. Private collection. Photo: Bonham's/Bridgeman Images.

173 The first Westminster Dog Show, illustrated in *Harper's Weekly*, 26 May 1877.

174 Sèvres Manufactory (modeller Henri Robert), after a composition of 1856 by Jean-Baptiste Carpeaux, *Prince Imperial with his dog, Nero*, 1912. Metropolitan Museum of Art, New York. Rogers Fund, 1972 (1972.79). Photo: © The Metropolitan Museum of Art/Art Resource, NY/Scala, Florence.

175 Anon., *Two Sisters and a Collie*, German chromolithograph, *c.* 1900. Private collection.

176 Calendar issued by the First National Bank of Newark featuring a lithograph based on the painting *Keeping Watch* (or *On Guard*) by Arthur J. Elsley, *c.* 1907. Author collection.

177 Engraving by J. Adam after Edwin Douglas, frontispiece to John Brown, *Rab and his Friends*, Edinburgh, 1883. University of California Libraries.

178 William Hogarth, *The Painter and his Pug*, 1745. Tate, London. Photo: © Tate.

179 Jean Huber, *Voltaire Getting Up at Ferney*, after 1759. Musée Carnavalet, Histoire de Paris (P168). Photo: CC0 Paris Musées.

180 Samuel Springsguth after Kirk, 'Jean-Jacques Rousseau contemplating the wild Beauties of Switzerland', illustration from the English edition of Johann Georg Zimmermann, *Über die Einsamkeit* (*Solitude*), London, 1804. British Museum, London. Photo: © Trustees of the British Museum.

181 Elizabeth Pigot, *Lord Byron and his dog, Boatswain*. Watercolour in her book, *The Wonderful History of Lord Byron & His Dog*, 1807. Harry Ransom Center, The University of Texas at Austin. George Gordon Byron Collection (6.8).

182 Engraving after a sketch by William Parry, *Lyon you are no rogue Lyon*, depicting Byron With Lyon II. Frontispiece to William Parry, *The Last Days of Lord Byron*, 1825.

207 Francis Bacon, *Dog*, 1952. Oil and sand on canvas. Tate, London. © The Estate of Francis Bacon. All rights reserved, DACS Images 2025. Photo: Prudence Cuming Associates Ltd.

208 Georges Seurat, *A Sunday Afternoon on the Island of La Grande Jatte*, 1884–6. Art Institute of Chicago. Helen Birch Bartlett Memorial Collection (1926.224).

209 Georges Seurat, study for *A Sunday Afternoon on the Island of La Grande Jatte*, 1884. British Museum, London. Photo: Bridgeman Images.

210 Rembrandt van Rijn, *The Good Samaritan*, 1630. Wallace Collection, London. Bridgeman Images.

211 Rembrandt van Rijn, *The Good Samaritan*, 1634. Wallace Collection, London. Photo: Bridgeman Images.

212 Otto Dix, *The Match Seller*, 1920. Staatsgalerie, Stuttgart. © DACS 2025. Photo: Bridgeman Images.

213 Francesco Corradi, *The Life of St Rocco*, fifteenth century. Detail from a fresco in the Church of San Rocco, Borgo Valsugana, Trentino-Alto Adige. Photo: A. De Gregorio/NPL – DeA Picture Library/Bridgeman Images.

214 Bernardo Strozzi, *San Rocco (St Roch)*, 1635–6. Private collection, Genoa. Photo: Heritage Images/Scala, Florence.

215. Photograph of Charles Darwin's daughter Henrietta with Polly (detail), 1870s. Cambridge University Library, Papers of Lady Nora Barlow (MS Add.8904.4: 1490).

216 Alfred Parsons, 'Darwin's Study', illustration in Charles Frederick Holder, *Charles Darwin: His Life and Work*, 1891. Photo: Bridgeman Images.

217 Photograph of the Darwin family with Bob the dog at Down House, undated. Cambridge University Library, Darwin Archive (DAR 219: 12).

218 '[A Dog] in a humble and affectionate frame of mind'. Illustration by Briton Rivière in Charles Darwin, *The Expression of the Emotion in Man and Animals*, London, 1872, p. 53.

219 Illustration originally from Paul Bert, *La Pression barometrique*, Paris, 1878, re-used in Francis Power Cobbe, *Illustrations of Vivisection; or, Experiments on Living Animals, from the Works of Physiologists*, Philadelphia, 1888, p. 5. Photo: University of Michigan.

220 Émile-Édouard Mouchy, *A Physiological Demonstration with Vivisection of a Dog*, 1832. Wellcome Collection.

221 Engraving by Schyubler after an original by Vladimir Taburin, *Gerasim and Mumu*, 1852. Illustration for Ivan Turgenev, *Mumu*, reprinted in *Niva* magazine, 1893. Photo: Shutterstock.

222 Cecil Aldin, *The Vivisectors*, illustration from *The Abolitionist* magazine, 15 September 1899. Hull History Centre (U DBV2/20–22).

223 Léon-Augustin Lhermitte (copy after), *Claude Bernard and his Pupils*, *c.* 1890. Wellcome Collection.

224 Gabriel von Max, *Der Vivisektor (The Vivisector)*, 1883. On loan from the Ernst von Siemens Kunststiftung to the Städtische Galerie im Lenbachhaus und Kunstbau, Munich.

225 C. J. Tomkins, mezzotint after a painting by J. McClure Hamilton, *Vivisection – the Last Appeal*, 1883. Wellcome Collection.

226 Laurant Lucien-Gsell, *Heureux/Perdu/J'ai peur/Au secours (Happy/Lost/I'm scared/Help)*, postcard issued by the Société Française Contre la Vivisection, *c.* 1890s. Photo: Ernest Bell Online Library.

227 Detail of front-cover binding of Frances Power Cobbe, *The Modern Rack: Papers on Vivisection*, London, 1889.

228 Photograph of the original *Brown Dog* by Joseph Whitehead, prior to being erected in 1906 in the Latchmere Recreation Ground, Battersea, London. Wellcome Collection.

229 Nicola Hicks, *Brown Dog*, 1985. Battersea Park, London. Photo: Ethan Doyle White/ Wikimedia Commons.

Acknowledgements

I can date with some precision when first glimmers of the interests that motivated this book came into consciousness. In the autumn of 1995, James C. Steward, then a curator at the Berkeley Art Museum, now director of the Princeton University Art Gallery, organized an exhibition called 'The New Child: British Art and the Origins of Modern Childhood 1730–1830'. He had invited me to speak at its opening about attitudes toward childhood and, by extension, family and marriage in the eighteenth century, using as evidence the works of artists like Hogarth, Gainsborough, Reynolds, Morland and their contemporaries whose works were in the show. I gave the lecture I had been asked to give. But I began it by saying that I was surprised by how many dogs there were in the art on view – present in over one-third of the works on display – and that, had I been given a more capacious brief, I might also have talked about 'the new dog' in British art of the period. This exhibition was for me a sort of Eureka moment, not of an answer but a question: What were all these dogs doing in eighteenth-century British art and in the art of the child in particular?

I now think there is an answer for the British art of the period. But more than a decade later the question expanded to the more general one that this book addresses: What are so many dogs doing in the visual arts from the Holocene 12,000 years ago to the present? In 2007 I was given the Mellon Foundation Distinguished Achievement Award, which made a significant amount of money available to me for a variety of projects. I thought of sponsoring an exhibition on the dog in art, which might help me find an answer. Nothing came of it, but I am grateful to Patricia Williams for helping me hone proposals written in an effort to interest curators. She is no great lover of dogs, which makes me even more grateful for her consistently good advice. Around the same time, I organized along with Alan Mikhail, then a graduate student, now the Chace Professor of History at Yale, a conference on animals – from bees to elephants in various time periods and places. There I met Ádám Miklósi, Professor and head of the Department of Ethology at Eötvös Loránd University in Budapest, and Alexandra Horowitz, Senior Research Fellow in the Psychology department of Barnard College in New York, both experts on dog cognition, from whom I have learned a great deal and who have generously answered my questions as this project developed. Miklósi also invited me on several occasions to observe experiments in his lab. Mikhail, who himself has written two important books about the social and cultural life of dogs, has continued to provide me with material on dogs in the Islamic world, a misunderstood relationship, but one that I could not follow up.

In the Faculty Research Lecture at Berkeley that I was invited to give in 2015 I made my first foray into a new subject with a talk on 'How Dogs Make Us Human'. It was the real beginning of this project. I am grateful for the invitation. Over the next five or six years I gathered images of the dog in art. Several undergraduate research groups led by Elena Kemph, then a graduate student, now Assistant Professor at MIT, helped organize a database. A. J. Solovy, now an Assistant Professor at Vassar, worked with me to combine these images with thousands of others into a more sophisticated searchable format. One of the members of my undergraduate research group, Samantha Miller, stayed on and mined the catalogues of art museums and resources like the Index of Medieval Art to allow me to make my claim about the overwhelming prevalence of dogs with confidence.

Stuart Proffitt, whom I had known for years, suggested that I write a proposal and get an agent, neither of which I had ever done before. My proposal was taken up and improved by Clare Alexander, the most wonderful agent imaginable as well as a wonderful person. I am grateful to her not only for the work she did on my behalf but for her friendship. Ann Godoff, President and Editor-in-Chief of Penguin Press, acquired the book and has been an encouraging presence throughout its gestation.

Somehow my book came to be edited in England and Stuart became my editor. I had planned to do a survey of the fulsome thanks he had received from authors of other books he had edited, and then try to say something original about him. I failed. All I can say is that he is what others have said of him: a remarkable editor; old fashioned – still on paper; attentive to the small details and to the big questions of structure and argument; substantively knowledgeable; and with near-perfect pitch on all matters editorial. (The few times I did not follow his advice, he proved to be right.) To quote from one of his recent authors, 'I thank him for warm encouragement, expert editing, and constant interest in the enterprise.'

Sam Fulton, commissioning editor at Penguin, along with Stuart Proffit, is responsible for helping me triage the many images I proposed to support the claims of this book and wrestling those that remained into the form that readers see. He did this with great refinement of taste and sensitivity to my arguments combined with a knowledge of what a book can bear. What might have been painful cuts turned into serious discussions of the relationship between word and image. Vartika Rastogi at Penguin helped keep track of the ever-shifting image list and also saved me from some repetitions in the text that others had missed. My picture editor Cecilia Mackay was not only great at finding the best versions of images that I wanted but also on occasion suggesting better alternatives. Her deep knowledge of the long and geographically wide Western visual tradition both greatly improved what readers will see and saved me from errors that I was unknowingly passing on from earlier scholarship. In the last stage Richard Mason expertly and patiently copyedited my text.

All serious books depend on a broad scholarly base and a circle of engaged learned friends. I have tried to acknowledge the former as well as those who helped with specific questions in my endnotes. Roger Grenier's beautiful *The Difficulty of Being a Dog*, translated by Alice Kaplan, is not there, however. Early on in my project it was a model for how to try to think seriously about the relationship of dogs and humans. His book begins with Argos and the tears of Ulysses. There are scholars like Donna Harraway and Sir Keith Thomas whose works are not specifically cited but, as everyone will recognize, inform how I think about the subject of humans and animals.

Various friends have engaged with different versions of this book and generally offered the sort of encouragement and support that makes a life of writing both possible and a pleasure. Seth Koven, Deborah Valenze, Ethan Shagan, Jonathan Sheehan, and Abhishek Kaicker read my woefully inadequate first draft and have been companions throughout all the years of writing. Abhishek sent me many references to dogs in Moghul images and texts that I wish I could have used. My dear friend of more than sixty years, the philosopher Alexander Nehamas, read a second draft, slowly and meticulously the way philosophers read and with the eyes of a man who has written a book about beauty and knows a great deal about art. I have tried to rise to his level. For more than half a century Catherine Gallagher has been a great friend and interlocutor. In the writing of this book as for all my others she helped me clarify arguments and get things right. Martin Jay pushed me to set my claims in a larger framework of intellectual history. Diliana Angelova read a later draft with an art historian's eye; she saved me from errors and in many other ways made this a better book. The Princeton art historian Patricia Fortini Brown, an expert on Renaissance Venetian art, read and commented on chapter 3.

Our Weimaraner Rudi, who died just as this book was finished, kept me company in my study as had the dogs of everyone from Petrarch to Thomas Mann (see page 177 for Rudi's picture).

Finally, I thank my wife the historian Carla Hesse for being unstintingly generous with her time, her analytic intelligence, and her creative imagination. She made me understand what my editors and other critics were asking of me and repeated back to me with her characteristic crisp logic the muddled arguments that I had presented to her. Her sense of the structure informs this book at every level. But for her, the book would not be what it is. She is of course absolved from its deficiencies. I dedicate it to her with gratitude and respect.

Index

Figures in **bold** refer to illustrations.